HISTORICAL DICTIONARY
OF OCEANIA _____

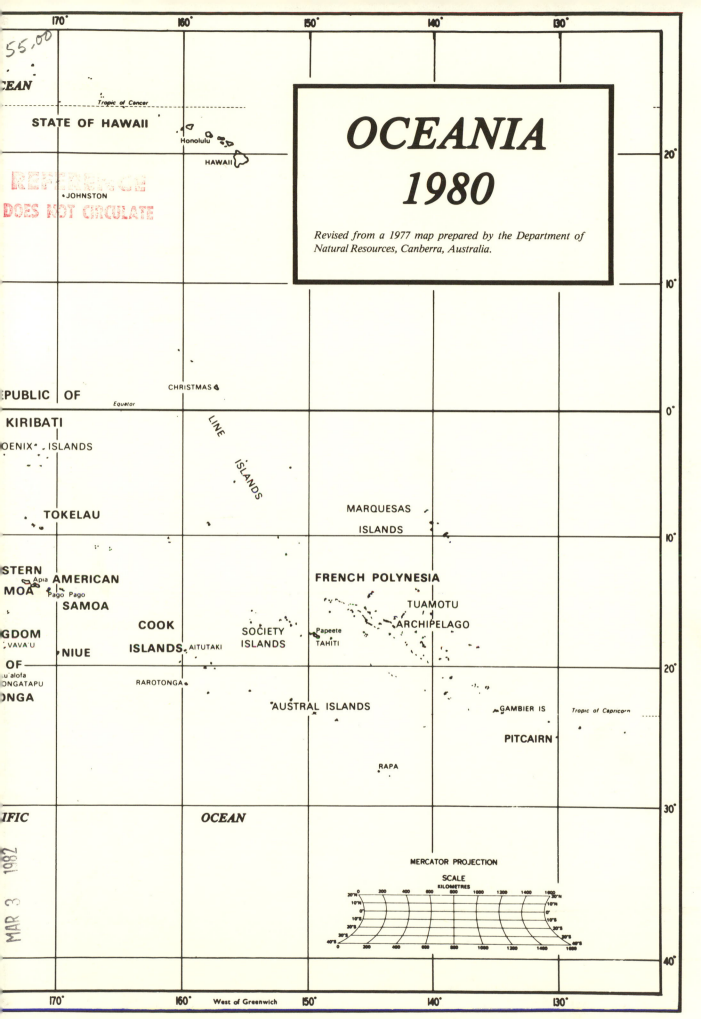

OCEANIA 1980

Revised from a 1977 map prepared by the Department of Natural Resources, Canberra, Australia.

170° 160° 150° 140° 130°

Tropic of Cancer

STATE OF HAWAII

Honolulu

HAWAII

20°

•JOHNSTON

10°

CHRISTMAS

Equator 0°

EPUBLIC OF

KIRIBATI

OENIX ISLANDS

LINE

ISLANDS

MARQUESAS

ISLANDS

TOKELAU

10°

STERN   AMERICAN   FRENCH POLYNESIA

Apia

MOA   Pago Pago

SAMOA   TUAMOTU

GDOM   COOK   SOCIETY   ARCHIPELAGO

VAVA'U   Papeete

OF   NIUE   ISLANDS AITUTAKI ISLANDS TAHITI

20°

u'alofa

NGATAPU   RAROTONGA

NGA   GAMBIER IS   Tropic of Capricorn

AUSTRAL ISLANDS

PITCAIRN

RAPA

30°

IFIC   OCEAN

MERCATOR PROJECTION

SCALE
KILOMETRES

20°N 0   200   400   600   800   1000 1200 1400 1600 20°N
10°N   10°N
0°   0°
10°S   10°S
20°S   20°S
30°S   30°S
40°S 0   200   400   600   800   1000 1200 1400 1600 40°S

40°

170°   160°   West of Greenwich   150°   140°   130°

"The New Pacific" (prepared by the State of Hawaii's Department of Planning & Economic Development, and permission to copy can be obtained if map is useful.)

HISTORICAL DICTIONARY OF OCEANIA

Edited by Robert D. Craig and Frank P. King

GREENWOOD PRESS
WESTPORT, CONNECTICUT • LONDON, ENGLAND

Library of Congress Cataloging in Publication Data

Main entry under title:

Historical dictionary of Oceania.

    Bibliography: p.
    Includes Index. Bibliography: p.
    1. Oceania—History—Dictionaries. I. Craig,
Robert D., 1934-   II. King, F. P.
DU10.H57   990'.03'21   80-24779
ISBN 0-313-21060-8 (lib. bdg.)

Library of Congress Catalog Card Number: 80-24779
ISBN: 0-313-21060-8

First published in 1981

Greenwood Press
A division of Congressional Information Service, Inc.
88 Post Road West, Westport, Connecticut 06881

Printed in the United States of America

10 9 8 7 6 5 4 3 2 1

Contents

Maps

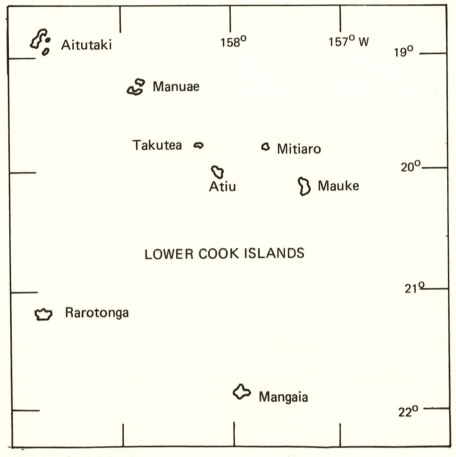

Aitutaki   158°   157° W   19°

Manuae

Takutea   Mitiaro   20°

Atiu   Mauke

LOWER COOK ISLANDS

21°

Rarotonga

Mangaia   22°

Map 1. Cook Islands

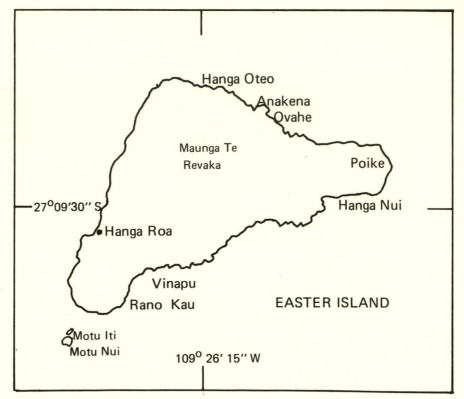

Hanga Oteo

Anakena

Ovahe

Maunga Te
Revaka

Poike

27°09'30" S

Hanga Nui

● Hanga Roa

Vinapu

Rano Kau

EASTER ISLAND

Motu Iti
Motu Nui

109° 26' 15" W

Map 2.   Easter Island

THE FIJI ISLANDS

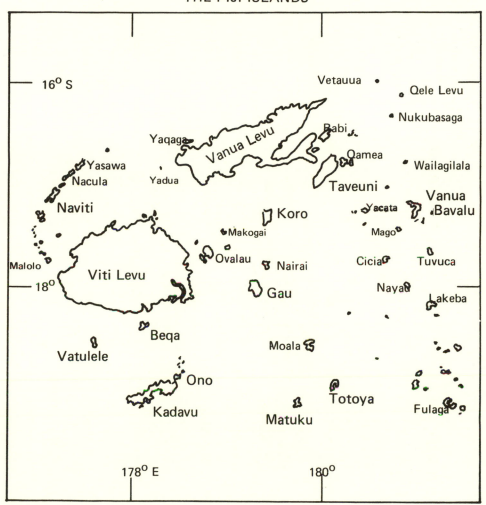

Map 3. Fiji Islands

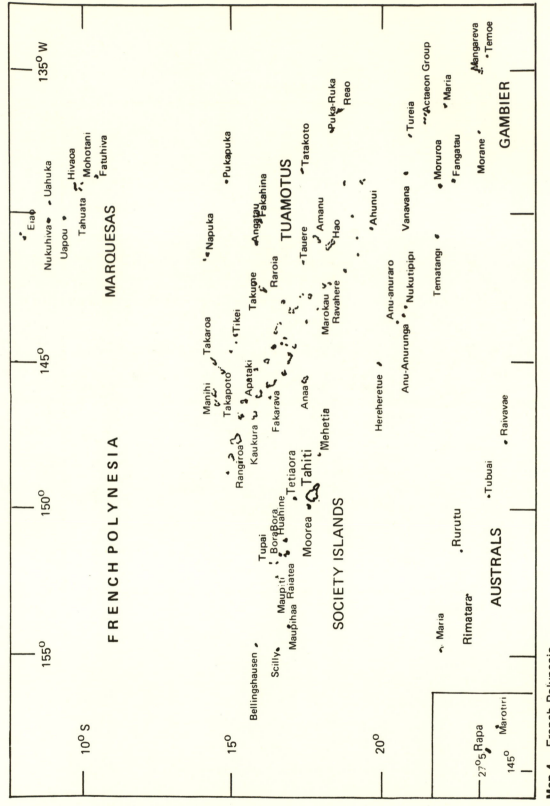

Map 4. French Polynesia

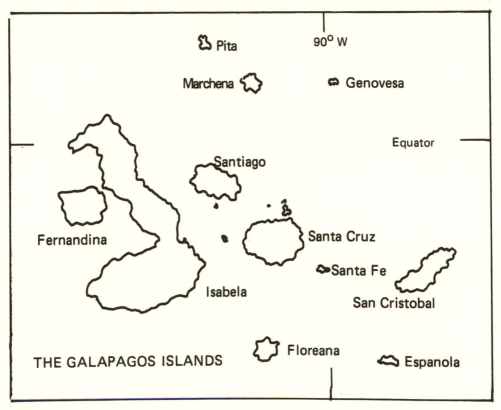

Map 5. Galapagos Islands

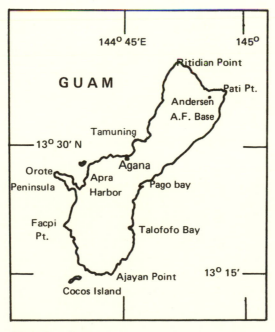

Map 6. Guam

GUAM AND THE MARIANAS

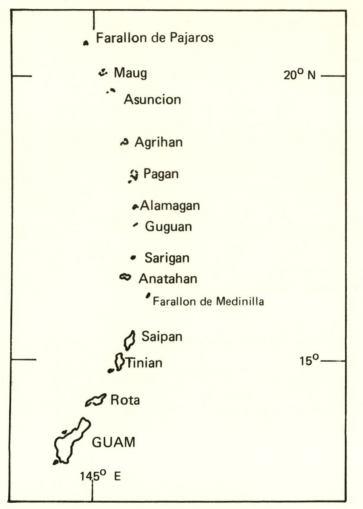

Map 7. Guam and the Mariana Islands

THE HAWAIIAN ISLANDS

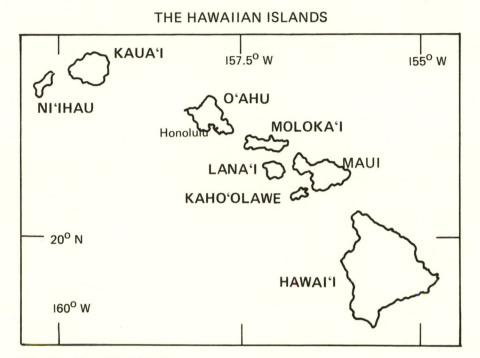

Map 8. Hawaiian Islands

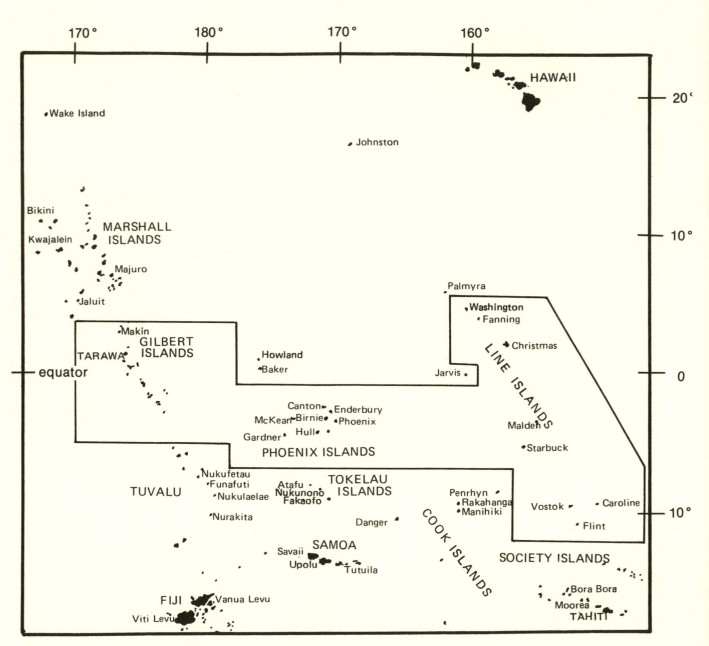

Map 9. Kiribati, Republic of

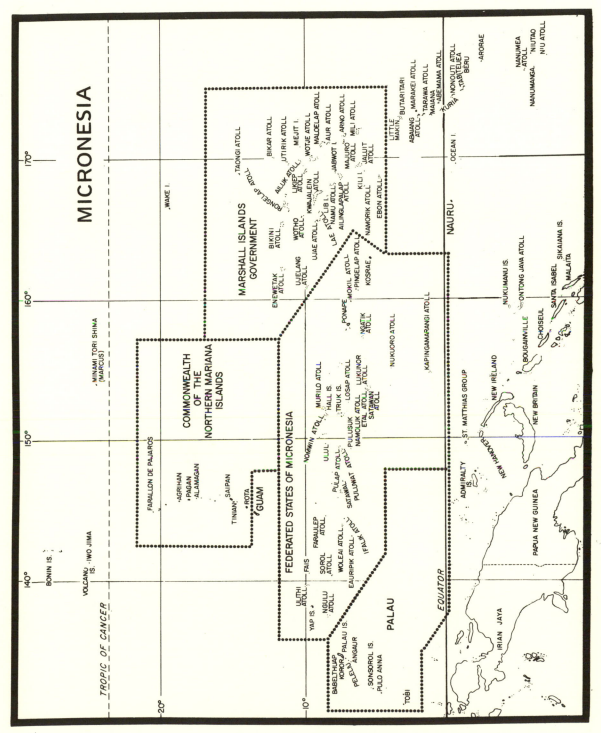

Map 10. Micronesia (former Trust Territory of the Pacific Islands): includes island groups of Commonwealth of the Northern Mariana Islands, Marshall Islands Government, Federated States of Micronesia, and Palau.

THE MARQUESAS ISLANDS

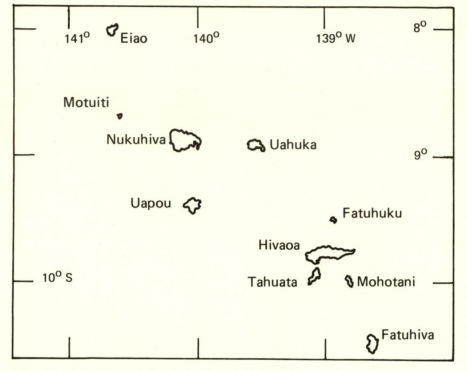

Map 11. Marquesas Islands in French Polynesia

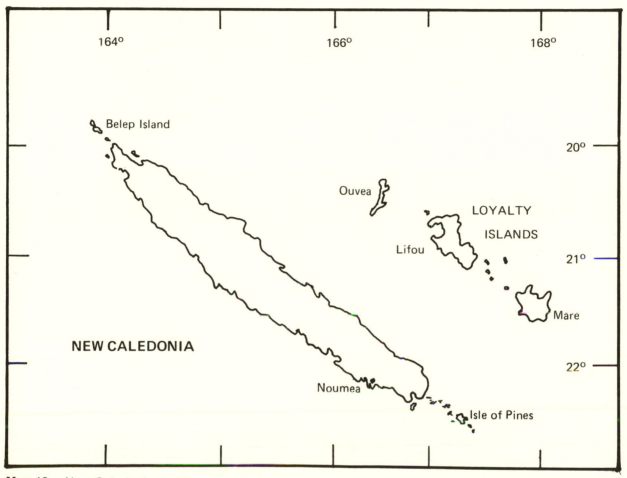

164°   166°   168°

Belep Island

Ouvea

LOYALTY

ISLANDS

Lifou

20°

21°

Mare

NEW CALEDONIA

22°

Noumea

Isle of Pines

Map 12. New Caledonia and Loyalty Islands

PAPUA NEW GUINEA

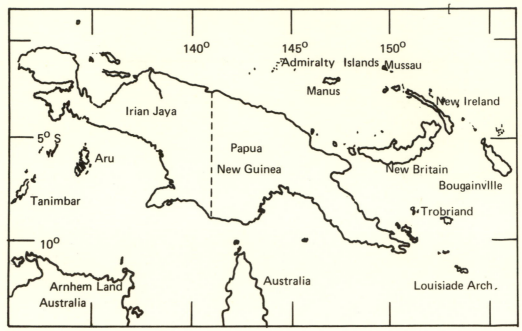

Map 13. Papua New Guinea

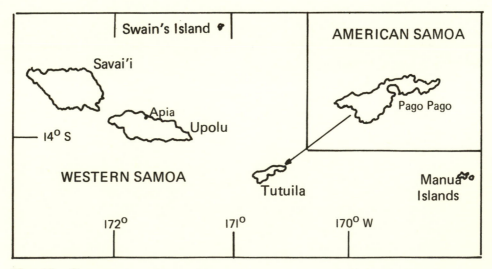

Map 14. Samoa

THE SOCIETY ISLANDS

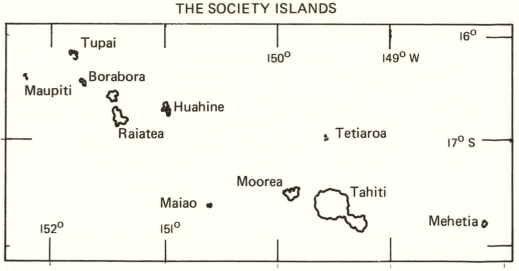

Map 15. Society Islands in French Polynesia

THE SOLOMON ISLANDS

Map 16. Solomon Islands

THE TONGAN ISLANDS

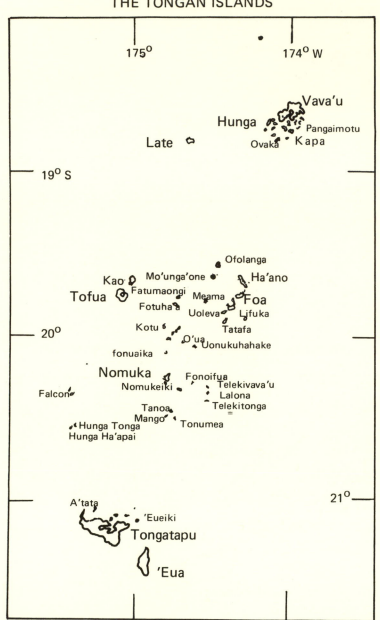

Map 17. Tonga

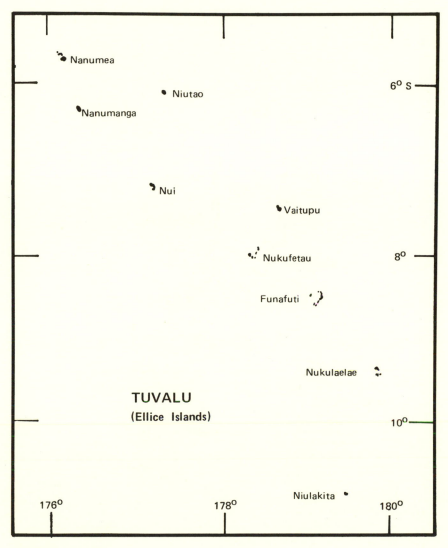

Map 18. Tuvalu

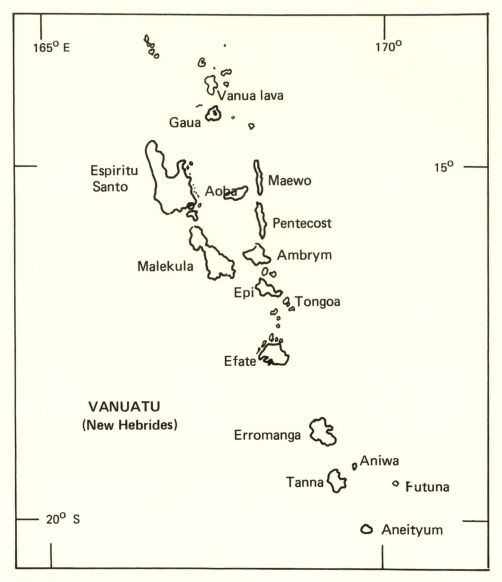

Map 19. Vanuatu (New Hebrides)

Acknowledgments

The contributors would like to express their sincere appreciation to all librarians and archivists who have helped compile this reference book by making public and printed materials available for research. The editors would also like to acknowledge the contributions made by Dr. Jerry Loveland for his special expertise of the Pacific and to his staff at the Institute for Polynesian Studies.

Introduction by C. Harley Grattan

There are many ways of looking at the Pacific islands but no easy way to get a comprehensive view of them. They can be viewed geologically, geographically, anthropologically, historically, as locales for exotic adventure, seats of sublime indolence, or simply as tourist attractions, to name a few of the possible approaches. Even when an approach is selected, it is difficult to get in hand data that are comparable over all the many groups, for the islands have been very unevenly studied. Some groups have been expertly examined from many possible angles, but others have scarcely been studied at all. Moreover, the islands have been seen very differently, not only by the specialists differently oriented but by successive generations of students following, necessarily, the changes of emphases and conception within their disciplines. No single approach has remained constant over the decades. Thus, this book's valiant effort to "cover" the Pacific islands as comprehensively as seems wise today is bound to be "uneven" (a cant word of reviewers) and sure to be convicted of factual errors which the editors will see as nit-picking and the critics as demonstrations of their own superior expertise. But, with all the risks, the job was worth attempting, for somebody, somewhere, will be stimulated to correct the errors and fill the gaps.

For how many centuries the Pacific islands have been known to man, we do not know. The common presumption is that they were occupied by man as a consequence of the migrations of early men in Asia. This explanation assumes that some people were pushed off the continent into the islands, but whether before or after men had moved from Asia into North and South America is speculative. The observed differences between the indigenes of the islands, noted first by the Europeans, and the names first used by a Frenchman—Polynesians, Melanesians, Micronesians—led to the assumption of successive migrations into the islands; but there is the likelihood, ratified by archaeological techniques, that even these had predecessors. The different types of islanders were found on islands scattered over thousands of miles of ocean, notably the Polynesians, thus implying a considerable skill in navigation in the pioneers or a wonderfully extensive operation of chance. The scatter of the islands also allowed over the centuries after the original dispersion a noticeable measure of cultural differentiation within the inclusive differentiation, so that there were, for example, obvious differences between the Polynesians of the Hawaiian chain, the Society Islands (Tahiti), and the Maori of New Zealand. And this was not all, for the island peoples were commonly organized tribally and usually hierarchically, and therefore on all but the very smallest islands the indigenous population was not to be seen as a single collectivity but as one fragmented into often small, hostile groups. This, then, was what the extra-island intruders found when they got among the islands, whether in the far north toward the Arctic or in the far south toward Antarctica or in between. And the original contacts were made long before anthropology became a recognized "science."

The "discovery" of the Pacific islands by Europeans was a protracted process extending over centuries, by no means systematic, beginning, one supposes, with the accidental landfalls of the peoples of the Asiatic littoral areas and continued by Europeans after they discovered the Pacific Ocean from the east and west, involving among the latter nationals of Portugal, Spain, Britain, France, Holland, Russia, Germany, and the United States. The task involved not only formal, organized, exploring expeditions of which the most famous—indeed the most exemplary —were the three British efforts led by Captain James Cook but also discoveries incidental to voyages towards a known destination that traversed little-traveled seas in behalf of legitimate commercial enterprises: sealing, whaling, trading. Since many of what were later perceived as, or assessed to be, *groups* were first discovered as single islands, multiple dates for the discovery of groups are to be expected.

Since rather early the Europeans developed established points of reference in the islands—Hawai‘i in the north, Tahiti in the south—something like a pattern of understanding of relations early emerged. This led to a differentiation of *value* of the many islands and groups on various bases: their use to navigators; their relation to the exploitable resources of the islands themselves or of the environing sea; their strategic value in relation to larger and more important concentrations of economic, political, and cultural values within the island world (for example, New Zealand) or contiguous to it (for example, Australia); their relation to the intention of a European intruder contending with a rival, on or near actual or projected routes of communication with Asia, America, or Europe. Naturally the assessed importance of the groups, or single islands, changed over time and perhaps only since the early twentieth century has the assessment of the worth or value or significance become reasonably fixed, though it is fairly certain that the defensive value of the islands has been reduced, or radically redefined, by the changes in weapons technology since the end of World War II. (Both the Americans and the French have tested atomic weapons in the islands in recent years.)

It is the story of the penetration of the islands by Europeans, including the Americans among them, that chiefly engages our attention, though students of Asian history are, of course, interested in Asian activities in some of them long before the Europeans arrived. The Europocentric bias has insured that much that passes today for island history is really an account of the impact of the Europeans on the islands, correctly called in some instances a "fatal impact." Only in recent years has a major effort been made to put the island indigenes more centrally into the stories, this often giving the studies a significant anthropological component. In any event, the island response to change is different in each case. There is no universally valid pattern, but then neither is any case *sui generis*, viewed historically and comparatively.

In reading an account of a particular island, or group, the reader may profitably keep in mind the following points or observations:

a. The general anthropological background.

b. The probable state of the pristine culture at the time of European discovery.

c. The earliest contacts: for instance, explorers and crews, the first beachcombers or castaways, when trading began, and whatever casts light upon when the pristine culture began to be modified by external influences and examples.

d. The arrival of missionaries and the profound cultural changes they initiated and encouraged, ranging from religious and moral ideas, to trade, production of goods for sale, and styles of living.

e. The slow buildup, usually near some useful harbor, of a "permanently" resident European population, leading to the creation of a town oriented to servicing in various ways, including the immoral, to visiting European ships and crews and also to serving

as the focal point at which the outside influences are strongest and from which they are dispersed with diminishing impact throughout the group. Classic examples are Honolulu in the Hawaiian group, Pape-'ete in Tahiti, Kororareka in New Zealand, and Levuka in Fiji.

f. After the initial, principal, economic reliance of the Europeans on "gathering" the indigenous resources of the island or its environing ocean, a turn was made by the Europeans to systematic production for sale, involving the establishment of plantations. In many islands, "gathering" never ceased to be the principal economic reliance, though the methods were somewhat sophisticated, for example, gathering coconuts for copra, and in most groups it has always remained of considerable importance. On the other hand, plantation agriculture often had a checkered history, as in Tahiti, as to success or failure of product, and sometimes it became basic to the economy, as in Fiji and Hawai'i. What economic structure a group developed turned upon location, land resources, and other related factors. As a rule, the products profitably produced were agricultural—plant or tree culture—in nature, but sometimes a variation proved possible, such as minerals, notably in New Caledonia and Nauru, but also supplementally in Fiji and New Guinea. It should be kept in mind that the Europeans tended to dominate the profitable economic activity —and indeed the profitability was in the last analysis determined in European markets—while the indigenes were ordinarily reduced to a peripheral participation. In specific cases, moreover, the islanders were further disadvantaged economically by the deliberate introduction among them of indigenes of other islands as more tractable or coercible labor, and even by the introduction of workers from Asia, notably Indians, Chinese, Indo-Chinese, Indonesians, and Japanese. In Fiji the introduced Indians eventually became more numerous than the indigenous Fijians. It should be kept in mind that the indigenes have been increasing in numbers since about 1910 after having experienced a sharp decline after "discovery." It should also be kept in mind that no single, economically valuable island product has for long ever been dominant in the world market for that product, though it might have enjoyed a regional advantage.

g. Politically the succession was from an unstructured free-for-all, to the tacit recognition of a local "chief" as paramount, to a formally but loosely structured government headed by a chief who had achieved his position by his own efforts, including violence, and who was supported by the missionaries and other "responsible" resident Europeans. Further recognition came to these leaders when European governments felt that their own "interest" was sufficient to warrant appointing commercial agents or "residents" or consuls and backing them up by visits of national warships. To this point, the intruders were more or less serious about "native sovereignty"; but from about 1840 the culmination of the process was, with remarkably few exceptions, the subversion of native sovereignty and the setting up of a colonial government, thus insuring the domination of the local scene by agents (of various titles and grades) finally answerable to the metropolitan authorities, though heavily under the local influence of the resident white entrepreneurs. In each case, the form and consequences of colonial government were different. Accurate understanding involves examining each case as though it was unique.

h. The problem of the indigenes in dealing with the dominating intruders would have been difficult enough if the intruders had been of a single nationality, but they were not. Reading from north to south, they were from Russia, Britain, Spain, the United States, France, Germany, Peru, Chile, Australia, and New Zealand. Without specifying the nationality of those who participated in economic exploitation, the indigenes often had overtime experience of government by more than one nationality: Russian and American, Spanish, German, Japanese and American, German and Australian, German and New Zealanders (preceded by joint rule by Germans, British, and Americans), British and French, French and British, and even joint rule by the latter two. But, taking the islands as a whole, the British were the predominant colonial power. This calls attention to the fact that from around 1840 to World War II most of the islands were parts of empires, including the unacknowledged American empire. They were not, however, important parts of any empire. Just what role they played in the imperial drama must be ascertained in each case, but the point is that the consequences of their presence in an empire must always be explained by reference to considerations considered compelling at the capital of empire, as often as by local or regional considerations. In sum, the islands historically viewed can only rarely be said to have autonomously determined their destiny, especially after intruders got among them, particularly the Europeans.

i. Inevitably, then, the islands have consistently been involved in the wars of their masters, for example, (to cite only those wars in which the United States has been involved as a principal participant): the War of 1812, the Civil War, the Spanish-American War, World War I and, truly climactically, World War II. All of these wars included passages at arms in the Pacific of greater or lesser magnitude, especially

World War II, and it is profitable for students of island affairs to know about them and assess their significance to the islands. The wars also provoked diplomacy during their course, fierce discussion at the succeeding negotiations of peace, and what was decided affected subsequent developments in the islands. Thus, at Paris in 1918, the decisions were taken that led to the elimination of Germany from control of Pacific lands, introduced the Japanese to control, brought in Australia and New Zealand as mandatories in succession to the Germans, and thus began the erosion of the principle of sovereignty. The obvious instability of the Pacific after World War I provoked a fascinating contretemps at the highest level of the British Empire which led to the famous Washington Disarmament Conference of 1921-1922 at which was devised a paper equilibrium, expressed in treaties, that insufficiently took into account the forces of change obviously at work, particularly north of the equator. Within a few years, it was fairly plain that the documents embodying the treaties were indeed pieces of paper, though for another decade or so the signatories tried to pretend utter collapse was avoidable by fancy diplomatic footwork. A devastating collapse finally came in 1941. World War II transformed the power relations of the nations in the Pacific, shrinking Japanese and British power, increasing American and Soviet power, leaving the Chinese in a position as ambiguous as long before. The shrinkage of British power east of Suez, in process since around 1900, proceeded in fairly stately fashion to its effective end, but the logic of the dominion relation left behind a small and a middle power, New Zealand and Australia, and the logic of the mandate principle (now renamed the trusteeship principle) led on to decolonization, effectively a return to native sovereignty.

As the American historian Charles Beard was fond of saying, "History is irreversible." Sovereign or not, no island people can return to their condition at "discovery." All are what they are today because of what they have been through, and the end result is in each case sufficiently unique to warrant the careful attention of the observer. Now that the islands are recovering autonomy—though often in qualified fashion—only one group, the Hawaiian, has, contrarily, been fully absorbed into the polity of its erstwhile imperial master. As for the others, it is up to us not only to gain a sense of how they got the way they are but also to form sensible views of their probable, or desirable, futures and of our best role in their futures. This book will assist us to do so with, one sincerely hopes, enhanced understanding.

C. HARTLEY GRATTAN

HISTORICAL DICTIONARY
OF OCEANIA ⸻

A

THE ADMIRALTY ISLANDS. Located in the Bismarck Archipelago, the islands are among the most northerly outliers of Melanesia. Politically they are part of Papua New Guinea. The forty or so islands have a landmass of approximately 2,072 km² (800 mi²). They lie scattered over an area six times that size whose center is 402 km (250 mi) north of the Huon Peninsula of New Guinea. While most of the smaller islands are coral flats, the larger ones—Manus, Lou, and Rambutyo—are volcanic projections, often densely vegetated. Manus, by far the largest of the islands in this group, is about 80 km (50 mi) long and 27 km (17 mi) wide; its central range reaches 718 m (2,356 ft) in height. On average, these islands receive about 381 cm (150 in) of rain a year. The population exceeds 23,000 persons.

The inhabitants of the Admiralties traditionally formed themselves into three groups—Manus, Matankor, and Usiai—which were ecological types rather than political, cultural, or linguistic associations. Communities within each group occupied clearly defined resource areas and generally specialized in the production of particular commodities. These were then exchanged for different ones by means of a sophisticated trading network dominated by the seafaring Manus.

The Manus people lived mainly in villages of stilt houses dotted among the islands and reefs off the south coast of Manus Island. They attracted the attention of early European visitors to the Admiralties who noted particularly their expert seamanship, their trading acumen, their thieving ability, and their hostility towards strangers. The visitors also frequently commented on the seemingly incessant warfare waged between islanders, their murderous obsidian-tipped spears, and the delicacy of their wood carving.

Spaniards, commanded by Alvaro de Saavedra, probably chanced on the Admiralties in 1528. The Dutch navigator William Schouten visited Manus in 1616. In 1767 the islands were given their European name by Philip Carteret. Organized ethnographical investigation of the islanders began during 1875 with the brief visit of H.M.S. *Challenger.* The islands were annexed by Germany in 1884, but it was not until about 1908 that the influence of European cultural practices began to erode irrevocably the traditional ways of island life.

Of crucial importance in this respect was the recruitment of islanders for indentured labor. Between 1905 and 1913, 2,321 male islanders—about one in three—worked in increasing numbers for European commercial enterprises, generally outside the Admiralties. Children from the islands were among the first to be admitted to the Namanula school at Rabaul, New Britain, in 1913; others were to follow in succeeding years. After the expulsion of the Germans from the islands in October 1914, Australians imposed a quasi-colonial administration on the islanders until they in turn were expelled by the Japanese in April 1942. From the late 1920s onwards, Catholic, Lutheran, and Seventh-Day Adventist missionaries were active in the Admiralties. By the outbreak of World War II, most of the islanders had been proselytized.

Following the occupation of the islands by American troops in March 1944, the islanders had an unprecedented opportunity to observe Western material culture at first hand. From this and from the concurrent revival and expansion of prewar groups which had sought to modernize the islanders' way of life sprang the Paliau Movement. Supporters of Paliau wanted to transform their culture to a totally Western one. The movement, which incorporated cargo cultism, died out during 1954.

As Manus Province, the Admiralty Islands are now part of Papua New Guinea. That they are so appears primarily the consequence of decisions taken during the nineteenth century by the architects of European imperialism. That the Admiralties have been generally neglected by Western nations would seem to indicate that the islands did not possess sufficient economic, political, or strategic advantages to sustain colonial ambitions.

RELATED ENTRIES: Cargo Cults; German Colonial Empire; Mead, Margaret; Melanesians and Colonial Servitude; Papua New Guinea; Schouten, William; South Pacific Commission.

SOURCES AND READINGS: Theodore Schwartz, "The Paliau Movement in the Admiralty Islands, 1946-54," *Anthropological Papers of the American Museum of Natural History* 49, no. 2 (1962): 211-421.

Wil King

ALCOHOL IN THE PACIFIC.

The people of Oceania did not make or consume alcoholic beverages of any sort prior to European contact. Despite this, foreigners who came among them wasted little time in introducing the islanders to "Demon Rum." Following an initial rejection of liquor, many islanders heartily embraced this new substance, an embrace which led to a host of new problems in social control. While beachcombers, whalers, and traders were teaching Pacific islanders how to manufacture homemade liquors and were selling them cheap commercial whiskey, missionaries were working just as hard to wean their converts away from the "sinful excesses" of drunkenness. In much of Oceania, abstinence from beverage alcohol became an important badge of Christian identity.

As colonial empires expanded into the Pacific, new laws were enacted to control alcohol manufacture and consumption. In a few places, such as Abemama in the Gilberts, locally imposed prohibitions on alcohol use were enforced by traditional chiefs, but attempts at prohibition from within were a rarity. By and large, none of these efforts at prohibition, colonial or otherwise, proved successful for very long. In this respect the experience of Pacific islanders echoes that of persons elsewhere in the world where official efforts to stamp out alcohol use have been made and failed. Sporadic attempts at total prohibition continue to be made in parts of Oceania but their likelihood of success is dim.

Scholarly research on alcohol use and abuse in Oceania has been limited in spite of the fact that alcoholism and drunkenness are widely remarked to be major problems. Studies completed by 1973 have been summarized and reviewed and two bibliographies of publications on alcohol and kava use in the islands also are available. Only one full-scale ethnography of drinking behavior and drunken comportment in a Pacific society exists.

During the century or two that most Pacific islanders have had access to commercially produced alcoholic beverages or the knowledge of how to make their own, most alcohol consumed has been produced abroad and imported to the islands. Increasingly, however, commercial alcoholic beverage manufacture has become a part of island life. For example, local beers are brewed in Fiji, Western Samoa, French Polynesia, and Papua New Guinea, and both *sake* and pineapple wine (*Maui Blanc*) are made in Hawai'i.

While social disruption is associated with alcohol use in much of Oceania, many islanders have learned to drink in moderation and to temper the behavioral excesses of an ealier age. Edwin Lemert (1964) attributes this to the development of island values that integrate drinking into the local life-style and the evolution of Tahitian drinking customs is cited as a case in point. However, an investigation of Trukese beliefs and behaviors surrounding alcohol use (M. Marshall 1979) shows that alcoholic beverages can be integrated into a culture while still resulting in social disruption.

Pacific islanders have turned to or from beverage alcohol for a host of reasons, only some of which are well understood. A great deal of fascinating information remains to be learned about alcohol use and abuse in Polynesia, Micronesia, Melanesia, and Papua New Guinea.

RELATED ENTRIES: Betel Nut Chewing; Kava and Betel; Tuba.

SOURCES AND READINGS: Paul Freund and Mac Marshall, "Research Bibliography of Alcohol and Kava Studies in Oceania: Update and Additional Items," *Micronesica* 13 (1977): 313-17; Edwin M. Lemert, "Forms and Pathology of Drinking in Three Polynesian Societies," *American Anthropologist* 66 (1964): 361-74; Mac Marshall, "Research Bibliography of Alcohol and Kava Studies in Oceania," *Micronesica* 10 (1974): 299-306; "A Review and Appraisal of Alcohol and Kava Studies in Oceania" in Michael W. Everett, Jack O. Waddell, and Dwight B. Heath, eds., *Cross-Cultural Approaches to the Study of Alcohol: An Interdisciplinary Perspective* (The Hague: Mouton, 1976), pp. 103-18; and Mac Marshall, *Weekend Warriors: Alcohol in a Micronesian Culture* (Palo Alto: Mayfield Publishing Co., 1979).

Mac Marshall

AMERICAN BOARD OF COMMISSIONERS FOR FOREIGN MISSIONS (ABCFM) (1810-1961).

Resulting from requests by Congregationalists at Williams College in 1806 for support by Congregational churches in Massachusetts of missionary activities, the American Board of Commissioners for Foreign Missions (ABCFM) was active in Oceania and elsewhere. Between 1820 and 1855 more than 150 Congregational ministers, farmers, printers, business persons, doctors, and teachers worked in Hawai'i and Micronesia for this first American missionary society. In the latter area the ABCFM during the 1850s established mission stations in Kosrae (Kusaie), Ponape, and Ebon and in the 1870s in the Mortlock Islands and in Truk. By the 1880s the board had established, at the least, fifty churches in the Marshall and Caroline Islands.

The ABCFM was patterned after other Christian groups such as the London, Baptist, and Netherlands Missionary Societies. The ABCFM's activities ended when the Congregational Christian Church and the Evangelical and Reformed Church merged into the United Church of Christ but continued to function as the United Church of Christ, Board of World Ministries.

RELATED ENTRIES: Anglican Missions; Catholic Church in the Pacific; Doane, Edwart T.; Hawai'i, Religions of; Logan, Robert W.; London Missionary Society; Micronesia; *Southern Cross*.

SOURCES AND READINGS: John A. Andrew, *Rebuilding the Christian Commonwealth: New England Congregationalists & Foreign Missions, 1800-1830* (Lexington, University Press of Kentucky, 1976.) The ABCFM archival material is located at Houghton Library, Harvard University.   *Frank P. King*

AMERICAN SAMOA. This unincorporated territory of the United States of America is an archipelago that stretches 467 km (290 mi) from approximately 169° to 171° west longitude, lies approximately 14° south latitude, and consists of six islands: Tutuila, Ta'u, Olosega, Ofu, Aunu'u, and Rose. A coral atoll, Swain's Island, 338 km (210 mi) northwest of Tutuila and geographically not a part of the archipelago, was made part of American Samoa in 1925. The total population of 32,500 (1980 estimates) consists primarily of Polynesian extraction (over 90 percent) and most of the population live on Tutuila where Pago Pago is the chief administrative center. American Samoans are nationals, not citizens, of the United States, who may freely enter the United States at any time and who may become citizens. Large communities of Samoans live in Hawai'i and California.

Climate, Land, Natural Resources. The climate of these tropical islands is moist and wet. The average sea level temperature is 26.3° C (79.4° F), and rainfall on mount Pioa averages 500 cm (200 in) a year, one of the rainiest areas in the world. The southwest trade winds prevail but vary during the rainy season from November to March. The islands are volcanic rock and the highest peak is Matafao, 702 m (2,303 ft) high. The islands are ringed with coral reefs and shallow lagoons, and the rich volcanic soil supports a lush natural vegetation of taro, coconut, and breadfruit on the coast and a rain forest farther inland.

Animal life consists mainly of birds (fifty-three species) and a few mammals and reptiles.

History. See the entry on Western Samoa.

U.S. Involvement in Samoa. The first active European country in Samoan affairs was Great Britain in her support of the London Missionary Society (LMS) Christian missionaries in the Pacific. In 1836 formal evangelization of American Samoa was begun. The Reverend Archibald W. Murray landed on Tutuila and within a year most of the inhabitants were converted. High Chief Mauga and his son Pomare were active in the proselyting work.

Word of the magnificent harbor at Pago Pago spread among sailors, and whaling ships of many countries began making it a frequent port of call. During the 1830s U.S. interest in the Pacific was aroused as a result of earlier exploration voyages and as complaints from shipowners and whalers from the Pacific became louder. In 1836 the U.S. Congress authorized the president to send out a surveying and experimental expedition to the Pacific Ocean and to the South Seas. Command of the expedition was given to Lieutenant Charles Wilkes. The expedition left Virginia on 8 August 1838, and in 1839 its ships sailed into Samoan waters. Wilkes made his survey and appointed a provisional American consul before his departure. For the next forty years, internal struggles in Samoa for political titles broke out in open warfare while the major Western countries, especially Great Britain, Germany, and the United States, competed for control of its economy and strategic geographical location. As American trade with Asia increased after the completion of the first transcontinental railroad in 1869 and the extension of a steamship line from San Francisco to New Zealand, certain U.S. business groups regarded Samoa with new interest, and the navy eyed the harbor at Pago Pago on Tutuila. Instructed by the American minister at Honolulu to promote U.S. interests and enterprises by all legal and proper means, Commander Richard W. Meade of the U.S.S. *Narragansett* arrived in Pago Pago on 4 February 1872. Three days later, he drew up an agreement with High Chief Mauga promising American protection for his people in return for the exclusive privilege of establishing a naval station in Pago Pago harbor. Although the U.S. Senate, preoccupied by the problems of Reconstruction, shelved the agreement, its existence helped discourage claims by the British and Germans in the area.

William H. Webb, a prominent New Yorker with Pacific shipping interests, persuaded President Ulysses S. Grant to appoint a mutual friend, Colonel Albert B. Steinberger, as special agent of the State Department to assess conditions in the islands and return, it was hoped, with a report which would prompt the U.S. Senate Foreign Relations Committee to act favorably on Commander Meade's agreement. Arriving in August 1873, Steinberger was asked by the war-weary chiefs who were fearful of losing their lands to Europeans if the U.S. would extend its protection over them. In October some of them wrote to the president endorsing the concept of union between Samoa and the United States.

After an unsuccessful effort to get the treaty passed in Congress, Steinberger returned to Samoa in April 1875 with a vague response from President Grant expressing the hope that Samoan unity and independence would remain inviolable. Clearly exceeding his instructions, Colonel Steinberger soon established a new Samoan government in which he occupied the key position of prime minister. Within a year, his power so antagonized the British and American consuls that, with the assistance of British naval officers, they arrested and deported him.

For the next ten years, the three powers scrambled and intrigued for dominance in Samoa, playing off one ruler against another and coming dangerously close to war. In an effort to restore peace, the consuls of the U.S., Great Britain, and Germany signed a convention on 2 September 1879. It did limit violence in Apia, but rivalry among the three powers continued. The Germans became particularly aggressive in pursuit of their ambitions after Bismarck adopted an imperialistic policy in 1884. American policy opposed the annexation of Samoa by any power. The British were ambivalent, torn between the desire to get along with Germany, whose help might be needed should Russia threaten India, and the firm opposition of Australia and New Zealand to any expansion of German influence in the South Pacific.

At American initiative, a tripartite conference opened in Washington on 25 June 1887 to try to resolve differences over Samoa. It failed a month later when the United States rejected British and German demands that the latter be awarded temporary control over all the islands. In subsequent months, the combat between rival Samoan claimants for authority became more violent. As they had on previous occasions, the three powers dispatched warships to Apia (Western Samoa) to protect their nationals. The crew of these vessels occasionally participated in the military operations ashore. On 14-15 March, a violent hurricane struck. Six of the seven warships foundered or went ashore. One hundred fifty naval personnel were lost. The three governments pondered the cost of their South Pacific rivalry.

The Berlin conference convened on 29 April 1889. The result was a de facto condominium in which the three foreign states shared authority and designated a king whom the absent Samoans were expected to accept and a foreign chief justice with more authority than the Samoan king. Within months of their adoption, several of the provisions of the Berlin treaty had become inoperative, and violence again promoted the dispatch of warships. By the end of the decade, American and British marines, with their governments now acting in concert, had disembarked to take the field against the Samoan faction backed by Germany, and a joint Anglo-American bombardment had damaged the German consulate.

German ambitions in the Pacific revived when Bismarck retired in 1890 and von Bülow took responsibility of foreign affairs. The Caroline and Mariana groups were purchased from Spain. In 1898 the British were asked by Berlin if they would agree to a division of Samoa between the U.S. and Germany in return for American and German acquiesence to Britain's annexation of the Tongan Islands. In July 1899 a German special envoy proposed to Secretary of State John Hay that the islands be divided among the powers. America was in the grip of its brief imperial phase, and President McKinley's response was positive. The Germans then negotiated an arrangement with the British by which the latter renounced all their claims in Samoa in return for the award of all German rights in Tonga, all German islands in the Solomons to the east and south of Bougainville, several concessions in German territories in West Africa, and German renunciation of extraterritorial rights in Zanzibar. On 2 December 1899 the tripartite convention was signed. By its terms, all claims to the islands were renounced except those of the United States east of 170° longitude and Germany's west of the same line. Germany received Upolu and Savai'i and seven much smaller islands while the islands east fell to the United States.

Without any reference to the Samoans, President McKinley signed an executive order on 19 February 1900 instructing the navy to take the steps necessary to establish U.S. authority in the eastern islands and give protection to their inhabitants. The navy complied and on 17 April 1900 the chiefs signed a deed ceding their island to the United States. In July 1904 a separate deed of cession was concluded with the Manu'a group (Ta'u, Olosega, and Ofu). (Swain's Island, a privately owned coral atoll, became part of American Samoa by a joint resolution of Congress on 4 March 1925.) Although the Samoan deed of cession was not to be ratified by Congress until 1929, President Theodore Roosevelt nevertheless recognized the cession of 1904 by executive decree and awarded medals and inscribed silver watches to the chiefs.

The navy, with funds only for the operation of a

coaling station, largely left the governance of the islands it administered to the chiefs. They continued to be guided by Samoan custom (*fa'aSamoa*). The navy prohibited alienation of Samoan land, provided some medical care, while education was generally the responsibility of the missionaries. The navy's efforts to secure funds to improve Samoan living conditions were rebuffed by the Treasury Department.

World War I brought a change in the administration of Western Samoa when New Zealand troops overwhelmed the small German militia in a bloodless invasion. After the war, New Zealand was awarded the islands as a League of Nations mandate which became a United Nations trusteeship after World War II.

After congressional acceptance of the cession of the islands in 1929, a commission visited American Samoa in 1930 to investigate *inter alia* the demands for civilian government being made by the *Mau* movement—a political force which was to have much greater influence in the political evolution of Western Samoa. Most of those who testified before the commission, however, requested the continuation of naval administration, and the *Mau* movement lost its modest force once it appeared likely there would be an organic act for American Samoa. However, subsequent efforts to obtain passage of such legislation failed in the House of Representatives in 1933 and in the Senate four years later. Indeed, Congress never has passed further legislation regarding governance of the islands. In 1951, when the naval station was closed, President Truman transferred governing authority to the Department of the Interior which continues to exercise this responsibility.

Indirect rule, benign neglect, and the prohibition of the sale of land to non-Samoans helped preserve Polynesian culture in American Samoa during the navy's administration. That culture was remarkably adaptive. For example, it had accepted Christianity quickly and without disruption, the Samoan pastors being accorded the status of honorary chiefs. A bill of rights was enacted, but most authority remained securely in the hands of the chiefs.

World War II was a major shock. Population doubled as marines and soldiers arrived to defend Tutuila, to train in its jungles, and to use it as a base for strikes against Japanese forces to the west. Tutuila's physical infrastructure was greatly improved, and hundreds of Samoans went overseas as volunteers in the U.S. military services. American mores intruded more forcefully on *fa'aSamoa* than ever in the past.

Closure of the navy station in 1951 was a body blow to the economy. Approximately two thousand Samoans left for Hawai'i with the navy or during the following year as the economy contracted. Expenditures remained very modest under the Department of the Interior's administration. In 1956 a Samoan employed by that department, Peter Tali Coleman, became the first Samoan to be appointed governor. A tight budget limited his ability to improve living standards.

The 1960s brought criticisim of the U.S. administration of Samoa in the United Nations and in the American media. A congressional committee composed of Senators Long of Hawai'i and Gruening of Alaska, each of whom had served as territorial governor of his respective state, visited Samoa. They reported the dilapidated conditions, both of the physical plant and of the government and of the economy itself. The two senators cited an urgent need for additional federal funds in public works, health, and education. They also called for assistance to agriculture and for the extension to American Samoa of federal legislation providing the states with assistance in numerous sectors.

The stage was set for initiatives which were to have profound influence on *fa'aSamoa*. Congress increased appropriations for American Samoa from $1.3 million in 1959 to $13 million by 1963. Under the energetic direction of a vigorous young governor, H. Rex Lee, a capital investment program was implemented. Roads were improved and a jet airport and a first-class hotel were constructed to attract tourists. The world's first large-scale educational television system (ETV) was introduced and new schools were constructed throughout the territory. ETV and the new schools were an ambitious effort to leapfrog the educational barriers created by the marginal English and rudimentary formal education of Samoan teachers.

Greater federal spending and the payrolls of the fish canneries further transformed Samoan life. Television soon was bringing American values and problems into the Samoan home. The thatch-roofed, open-sided *fale* in which Samoans had resided for two thousand years frequently was replaced by homes of concrete or wood. Bonds of the *'aiga* or extended family began to loosen as younger Samoans, better educated than their elders, resented the authority of the *matai*, the *'aiga* heads who comprise Samoa's aristocracy. To escape the levies of the *matai* and the demands of unemployed *'aiga* members, many Samoans left for Honolulu or West Coast U.S. cities. Others joined the military service. Samoans traveled more frequently and returned home with more interests and tastes.

Samoan society gradually became more democratic. In 1948 a bicameral legislature replaced the advisory body formed early in the naval administration.

Also called the *fono* (or meeting), its membership included in the upper chamber the twelve high chiefs with whom the naval governor had consulted. A house of representatives to be elected from among lower-ranking *matai* was also instituted. Four years later, the secret ballot was adopted for election to the house, a non-*matai* became eligible for election, and suffrage was extended to all adults including those without title.

The *fono* mandated a constitutional committee in 1954. Six years later, American Samoa had its first constitution. Revised in 1966, it incorporates the civil rights guarantees of earlier legislation and sanctions the existing tripartite form of government. Although the *fono* had responsibility for allocation of locally generated revenue and eventually was to participate in reparation of the entire budget for the territory, there was little delegation of real authority. The governor retained a veto which he exercised frequently. Although the *fono* could appeal to the secretary of the interior to override the governor's veto, the secretary was unlikely to question the governor's decisions.

American Samoa's political status appeared anachronistic when compared in the late sixties with the movements toward self-government elsewhere in Polynesia: Tonga, Western Samoa, Nauru, Fiji, the Cook Islands, among others. In 1969 the *fono* created a Future Political Status Study Commission and after much study, the commission recommended that there be no change in the relationship between American Samoa and the United States. It ruled out independence, reunification with Western Samoa, statehood, commonwealth status, passage of an organic act, and inclusion in Hawai'i. The commission did propose popular election of senators, representation in the U.S. Congress by a delegate-at-large, and the popular election of Samoa's governor. In three successive annual plebiscites beginning in 1972, however, Samoan voters rejected the proposal that they elect their own governor. The hesitance to elect their governor had origins both in the depths of *fa'aSamoa* and in much more recent influences. Family ties being as strong as they are in Samoa, many feared a Samoan governor would favor his *'aiga*. Many traditional chiefs who could influence the votes of their subordinates were reluctant to see any Samoan elected governor because this position could be interpreted as equivalent to that of a paramount chief (*fa'aSamoa* recognizes five supreme titles and attempts by individual high chiefs to obtain all five had been among the causes of the incessant wars of the nineteenth century). Suspecting there must be some unforeseen danger, many were confused and their apprehension prompted negative votes. Finally in August 1976,

however, the vote swung in favor of this step toward self-government. There was a variety of reasons why it succeeded that year. The most broadspread appears to have been dissatisfaction with Governor Ruth. Drought and a series of accidents forced the closure of the canneries in 1974, causing a serious shortfall in anticipated local revenue, and there was also a sharp curtailment of the programs administered by the Government of American Samoa (GAS). Many Samoans, including numerous influential chiefs, became convinced that their self-respect and the territory's economy probably would be safeguarded better by a Samoan governor than by future political appointees.

The yes vote of some Samoans was influenced by knowledge that Peter Tali Coleman probably would stand for election. The only Samoan to serve as an appointed governor, Coleman was deputy high commissioner for the Trust Territory of the Pacific Islands in 1976. He visited American Samoa during the period prior to the plebiscite and discussed his possible candidacy. Coleman had avoided favoritism while in the governor's office, had twenty-five years experience in administration of dependent areas, and, perhaps more importantly, he was believed to know his way around Washington well enough to assure continuation of the U.S. subsidy.

The 1976 referendum was conducted more carefully than the previous three. To encourage voters to express their own preferences rather than those of their *matai*, all of the ballots collected throughout the territory were dumped together prior to counting, which took place before television cameras. The results were clear: the local election of a governor was approved by almost 70 percent of the voters. Elections for the governor were held on 8 and 22 November 1977 and Peter Tali Coleman became American Samoa's first elected governor, receiving 56 percent of the 5,948 votes cast. Coleman's main emphasis since taking office has been to bring more private economic development into American Samoa and to make better use of federal programs. His government has restricted foreign immigration and at the same time hopes to encourage some of the 45,000 Samoans living in Hawai'i and California to come back to Samoa to work. Coleman has actively participated in the meetings of the Pacific Islands Development Commission to discuss barriers to interisland trade among the South Pacific countries and to try to reduce overlapping, duplicatory services. Naturally, fish-cannery operations remain a major concern as Pacific nations begin to enforce the 200-mile limitations on fishing rights, an entangling problem where the limitations of island groups overlap one another.

RELATED ENTRIES: Anglo-German Agreement of 1899; Berlin Act of 1889; Bingham, Hiram; Bismarck Agreement; Central Polynesian Land and Commercial Company; Coleman, Peter; Diaper, William; Erskine, John E.; Foreign Residents' Society; German Colonial Empire; Judd, Lawrence M.; Krämer, Augustin; Lackawanna Agreement; London Missionary Society; Malietoa; Mead, Margaret; Polynesia, Settlement of; Polynesian Culture (Ancient); Poppe, Alfred; H. M. Ruge & Co.; Selwyn, George; South Pacific Commission; Steinberger, Albert B.; Stevens, Charles E.; Tui Manu'a; Tupu'o Samoa; United States and Pacific Island Bases; United States in the Pacific; Unshelm, August; Vaitupu Company; Webb, William H.; Weber, Theodor; Western Samoa; Williams, John.

SOURCES AND READINGS: J. A. C. Gray, *Amerika Samoa* (Annapolis, Md.: U.S. Naval Institute, 1960); James Bishop, "American Samoa: Which Road Ahead?" *Pacific Studies* 1 (1977): 47-53.

James Bishop and Robert D. Craig

AMERICAN SAMOAN COMMISSION. President Herbert Hoover appointed the American Samoan Commission (ASC) in 1930 to confirm the cession of the eastern Samoan Islands to the United States and to propose a form of civil government for the islands which had been governed by the United States Navy since 1900. Senator Hiram Bingham was chairman of the commission which also included Senator Joseph Robinson, Congressmen Carrol Breedy and Guinn Williams, and Samoans Mauga, Tufele, and Magalei.

The ASC held hearings for three days in Honolulu (18-20 September) and for eleven days in Samoa (27 September-5 October). Three different positions emerged from the Honolulu testimony. Expatriate Samoans strongly opposed the U.S. naval government; Hawaiian business interests called for extensive land reform in Samoa and the destruction of communal family law; staff members of the Bishop Museum in Honolulu suggested that whites be excluded from the islands to preserve Samoan culture.

The Samoan hearings were held at Pago Pago, Leone, Ta'u Island, and Nu'uuli. Resident white merchants testified that the naval government had been detrimental to business. Samoans proposed that a civil government be established in which Samoan chieftains played an active role. United States citizenship was requested.

The commission recommended granting the Samoans citizenship and the right to appeal legal cases to the U.S. District Court in Honolulu. The commission also recommended the formation of a civil government comprising an American governor and the

fono, a chieftain organization. If necessary, the *fono* could override a governor's veto and appeal to the president of the United States. A modified bill of rights was suggested; no change of Samoan land laws was proposed. The U.S. Senate passed the recommended legislation but the House of Representatives balked at granting citizenship and rejected the bill in February 1933. The United States Navy continued to govern American Samoa until 1 July 1951.

RELATED ENTRIES: American Samoa; Bingham, Hiram (1875-1956).

SOURCES AND READINGS: *Congressional Record*, 1930-1933; Reuel S. Moore and Joseph R. Farrington, *The American Samoan Commission's Visit to Samoa* (Washington, D.C.: United States Printing Office, 1931).   *Frank L. Miller*

ANGLICAN MISSIONS. The Anglican Church in the Pacific islands had its origins in the Established Church of England. The distinctive character and structure of the church in each region has been largely molded by the circumstances of its foundation and by the policies of its successive bishops.

The first Anglican services in the Pacific, outside Australia and New Zealand, were held on board British and American warships and exploration vessels, but there was no organized Anglican missionary activity until the mid-nineteenth century. This was initiated by George A. Selwyn, first bishop of New Zealand, who believed that the Anglican branch of Christianity should have a major place in the South Pacific mission field, alongside the English Protestant and French Roman Catholic missions. To this end, in 1849, he founded the Melanesian mission which he hoped would extend, through Melanesian evangelists, to every island between New Caledonia and New Guinea. Selwyn's plan for an island missionary diocese linked with the Anglican Church in New Zealand was fulfilled in 1861 when his principal assistant, John C. Patteson, was consecrated first bishop of Melanesia. In 1867 the mission's headquarters and training school were moved from New Zealand to Norfolk Island where they remained until transferred to the Solomon Islands in 1920.

The Melanesian mission did not achieve the rapid success that had been anticipated. From the 1860s, its field of work was confined to the northern New Hebrides and Solomon Islands, where its scattered village schools were visited regularly by the mission ship *Southern Cross*. A period of rapid expansion began around the turn of the twentieth century when the mission benefited from the pacification which followed the establishment of a British colonial administration in the Solomon Islands and from the return to their homes of a large number of Melanesian laborers who had been Christianized while working on plantations in Queensland and Fiji. By this time, however, other missionary bodies were beginning work on islands where the Melanesian mission had previously enjoyed a religious monopoly. Nevertheless, the Anglican Church has remained the largest religious denomination in the Solomon Islands, claiming the adherence of about one-third of the population.

The second Anglican missionary bishopric in the Pacific was founded in Hawai'i. This originated in a request from King Kamehameha IV and Queen Emma who were anxious to strengthen the Hawaiian monarchy through closer ties with England and the support of the Episcopal church. The first bishop, Thomas N. Staley, began work at Honolulu in 1862, assisted by a small party of English clergymen and later by a community of English nuns. The patronage bestowed on Staley's ''Reformed Catholic Church'' by the royal family and government officials, and the rigid attitudes of the English clergy, aroused strong opposition from the American Protestant missionaries of the American Board of Commissioners for Foreign Missions who were already at work in the group, and for many years the Anglican mission made little headway. In 1902, following the incorporation of Hawai'i into the United States, the diocese of Hawai'i was transferred from the oversight of the archbishop of Canterbury to the jurisdiction of the Protestant Episcopal Church in the United States of America. Since then, the Episcopal Church in Hawai'i has developed a regular school system and has undertaken missionary work among Asian Americans.

The Anglican mission in New Guinea was commenced as a result of a decision of the general synod of the Australian church in 1886. As British rule had recently been extended over southeast New Guinea, it was claimed that the Church of England had an obligation to undertake work there. The first missionary party, led by Albert Maclaren and Copland King, arrived in British New Guinea in 1891 and established a headquarters at Dogura on the northeast coast of Papua. The first bishop, M. J. Stone-Wigg, was appointed in 1898.

Although seriously hampered by a constant shortage of funds, the New Guinea mission gradually established a chain of mission stations and village schools along 500 km of coast. After World War II (in which ten European missionaries lost their lives), work was begun in the New Guinea highlands and a struggling mission on New Britain was taken over from the Melanesian mission. Increased overseas support in the postwar period was partly prompted by popular accounts of the rescue work among Allied servicemen performed by Papuan stretcher-bearers (''Fuzzy Wuzzy Angels''), some of whom came from Anglican mission areas in northeast Papua.

The fourth center of Anglican missionary activity in the Pacific was Fiji where, in 1870, William Floyd began a long ministry in the port town of Levuka. Because the Methodist mission had already evangelized most of the Fijian population, the few Anglican clergymen in Fiji concentrated their efforts on the English settlers (many of whom were members of the Church of England), Melanesian plantation laborers, Indian indentured laborers, and Suva's Chinese community. In 1901 Bishop Alfred Willis, formerly of Hawai'i, began an independent Anglican mission in Tonga at the invitation of a small group of ex-Methodists, who had originally been led by the former prime minister of Tonga, Shirley Baker. This action embarrassed and angered many Anglican leaders in New Zealand and England. To regularize Anglican work in the region (and to bypass Willis), a diocese of Polynesia was therefore founded in 1908. In 1923 it became a missionary diocese of the Anglican church in New Zealand. It comprised a network of small congregations in which Europeans initially predominated but which since the 1960s has become fully multiracial in both composition and leadership.

Anglican missions in the South Pacific islands have displayed many common characteristics. In British colonial territories they gained considerable prestige from their association with the rulers of the British Empire. In their teaching they are Anglo-Catholic, emphasizing the dogmatic and sacramental aspects of Christianity. Until the 1930s a majority of missionary clergy were recruited from England, and a relatively high proportion were university educated. In their approach to indigenous cultures the Anglicans tended to be tolerant and believed that Christianity should conserve as much as possible of the traditional religious and social order. Several missionaries, notably Robert H. Codrington and W. G. Ivens of the Melanesian mission, made significant contributions to Pacific anthropology. As an essential step towards the goal of an autonomous church, most bishops encouraged the development of an indigenous ministry. In Melanesia the first locally born priest was ordained in 1873; the first Papuan priest was ordained in 1917. After World War II the process of indigenization was hastened and a village-based priesthood became firmly established.

Since 1963 the Anglican churches in the South Pacific have been linked together by the South Pacific Anglican Council. Autonomous provinces within the Anglican Communion were formed in Melanesia in 1975 (the Church of Melanesia: four dioceses) and in New Guinea in 1977 (the Anglican Province of Papua New Guinea: five dioceses). Pacific islanders were first appointed to the leadership of the dioceses of Hawai'i in 1970 and Polynesia in 1975.

RELATED ENTRIES: Baker, Shirley; Codrington, Robert H.; Micronesian Mission; *Morning Star*; Patteson, John C.; *Southern Cross*; Staley, Thomas N.

SOURCES AND READINGS: David Hilliard, *God's Gentlemen: A History of the Melanesian Mission, 1849-1942* (St. Lucia, Queensland: University of Queensland Press, 1978); W. P. Morrell, *The Anglican Church in New Zealand: A History* (Dunedin: John McIndoe, 1973); Henry Bond Restarick, *Hawaii, 1778-1920: From the Viewpoint of a Bishop* (Honolulu: Paradise of the Pacific, 1924); David Wetherell, *Reluctant Mission: The Anglican Church in Papua New Guinea, 1891-1942* (St. Lucia, Queensland: University of Queensland Press, 1977).

David L. Hilliard

ANGLO-GERMAN AGREEMENT OF 1899. As a settlement between Britain and Germany of their rival colonial claims in the Pacific, the Anglo-German agreement provided for Britain's renunciation of its interests in Samoa and led in the following year to the partitioning of the islands between Germany and the United States. The local context of the agreement was the breakdown of the tripartite British-German-American condominium in Samoa with death of King Malietoa Laupepa in 1898 and the renewal of civil strife the following year. The British and American consuls on the one hand and the German consul on the other threw their support behind rival native factions, and a full-scale war threatened to develop. At that point the three powers dispatched a commission to Samoa to restore peace, form a temporary government, and reach a final settlement of their own conflicting interests.

The international background to the agreement of 1899 was the growing imperialist rivalry between Britain and Germany, Britain's diplomatic isolation and conflict with the Boers in South Africa, and rising German militarism. Both the British colonial secretary, Chamberlain, and the German foreign ministry were eager to come to a quick resolution of the Samoan problem and thereby reduce tensions between their countries. Negotiations were carried out

between September and November 1899 involving principally Chamberlain and the German ambassador, Hatzfeldt. Largely for reasons of sentiment neither power was willing to relinquish claims to Samoa, particularly to the key island of Upolu. A breakthrough came only when a British Admiralty report noted the limited strategic value of the islands. Only then did Britain propose to yield its Samoan interests in return for a strengthening of its position in more valuable Tonga and some territorial gains in the Solomon Islands. The German negotiators, anxious to reach a settlement before the kaiser's planned visit to England in November, wanting to forestall the need for closer ties with Russia, and hoping to silence extreme nationalist groups at home, willingly accepted the British plan. The agreement was officially signed on 14 November.

A tripartite convention the following month recognized German control over the western islands of Upolu and Savai'i and American primacy in the eastern islands of Tutuila and Manu'a. The following year witnessed the annexation by the two powers of their respective Samoan holdings. Although the Anglo-German Agreement of 1899 ended nominal Samoan sovereignty in the islands, it did lead to the establishment of relative peace, stability, and renewed economic prosperity in Samoa.

RELATED ENTRIES: American Samoa; German Colonial Empire; Western Samoa.

SOURCES AND READINGS: Paul M. Kennedy, *The Samoan Tangle* (Dublin: Irish University Press, 1974); Robert M. Watson, *History of Samoa* (Wellington: Whitcombe & Tombs, 1918).   *Ralph C. Canevali*

ANZAC (AUSTRALIAN — NEW ZEALAND AGREEMENT, 1944). Australian fears of the consequences of Japanese victory in the Pacific had waned by the end of 1942. They were soon succeeded by fears of the consequences of United States victory. Both the *Chicago Tribune* and the *Chicago Daily News*, owned by Secretary of the Navy Frank Knox, published leading articles early in 1943 discussing the need for the United States to retain bases in former British and French colonies in the South Pacific after the war. President Franklin D. Roosevelt referred, in the Pacific War Council in August 1943, to the need to establish new bases in the islands, to be developed for all nations and not by any single nation.

This directly challenged the view of Australian Prime Minister John Curtin (Labour party) and his attorney-general, Herbert V. Evatt, that Australia should itself assume primary responsibility for the preservation of British colonialism south of the equator. Evatt insisted that the Australian effort against Japan had been sustained not merely by a resolution to defend Australia and its territories, but also by "a determination to maintain the prestige of the British Commonwealth in areas where Japanese military occupation and political infiltration have subjected the United Nations to tremendous risks." (*Parliamentary Debate*, 14 October 1943). On 20 October 1943 he invited the New Zealand government to attend a conference in Canberra to consider the postwar situation in the Pacific as a whole, including the proposition "whether it would be wise for Great Britain to transfer all British colonies in these areas to Australia and New Zealand" (Kay, pp. 47-48).

The conference was scheduled for 17 January 1944. Early in December, Curtin and Evatt learned from press reports that Churchill, Roosevelt, and Chiang Kai-shek had resolved in Cairo on 1 December that Japan should be stripped of all the islands in the Pacific acquired since 1895. This seemed to them to indicate the need for summary action in case other colonial possessions might be treated the same way. Evatt abruptly asked a New Zealand delegate in the corridor, "Why don't we make a treaty?" Nobody could say why not, so the two Dominions entered into the first treaty ever contracted between two members of the British Commonwealth.

The agreement was quite unambiguously directed against United States pretensions in the Pacific at the expense of colonial empires other than the Japanese. It sustained the Commonwealth preferential-trading system to which the United States had always been totally opposed; rejected any idea of a condominium with the United States in the Solomons, New Caledonia, or the New Hebrides; insisted that no change in the sovereignty or system of control of any of the islands of the Pacific should be effected except as a result of an agreement to which both the Australian and New Zealand governments were parties and in the terms of which they had both concurred; and proposed that "it would be proper for Australia and New Zealand to assume full responsibility for policing or sharing in policing such areas in the South West and South Pacific as may from time to time be agreed upon" (Kay, pp. 47-48). Canberra and Wellington had declared a Monroe Doctrine for the South Pacific.

The main results were undoubtedly negative. Secretary of State Cordell Hull compared the Australians unfavorably with the Russians in terms of abrasiveness and intransigence. The New Zealanders agreed. Department of State officials tended to regard the agreement as final confirmation of a growing conviction that Evatt was impossible to work with. They accordingly fended off repeated attempts by Evatt after the war to attract the United States into a security relationship with Australia. By 1949 American diplomats were eagerly awaiting the defeat of the Australian Labour Government at the polls, simply so that they might be relieved from the task of dealing with the architect of the Australian-New Zealand agreement.

RELATED ENTRIES: Defense Planning for Oceania between the Wars; Oceania, Strategic Importance of since 1945; War in the Pacific Islands, 1914-1945.

SOURCES AND READINGS: Australia, *Parliamentary Debates*, House of Representatives, 14 October 1943, 7 Geo. VI, 176, 572; Robin L. Kay, ed., *The Australian-New Zealand Agreement 1944* (Wellington: Historical Publications Branch, Department of Internal Affairs, 1972); Carolyn A. O'Brien, "Australia's Achievement in Regional Defence Planning 1919-44." (Ph.D. diss., University of Queensland, 1978).

Glen St. J. Barclay

ANZUS. When Australian Ambassador to the United States Sir Percy C. Spender called down the blessing of Almighty God upon the United States-Australia-New Zealand Tripartite Security Pact on 1 September 1951, he was assisting at possibly the greatest personal achievement of any Australian diplomat. Australians had sought assiduously after the defeat of Japan to commit the United States to underwriting their country's security in the Pacific for the future. The Americans were no more willing to accept a commitment so far from their shores in that region than they were initially willing to involve themselves in a European defense system. The decision to enter the North Atlantic Treaty Organization (NATO) in 1949, in fact, made the prospect of an additional involvement in the Pacific even less attractive for Washington.

This unresponsive attitude was more difficult to maintain after the outbreak of war in Korea in June 1950. Spender, then Australian minister for external affairs, seized every opportunity to demonstrate Australian support for the United States as conspicuously as possible. Australian ships and aircraft were the first United Nations forces actually to serve with the United States in Korea. Spender made no secret of the fact that his intention was to recreate the old wartime alliance against Japan on a permanent basis. The continued opposition of President Harry S. Truman and his secretary of state, Dean G. Acheson, was finally overcome by their anxiety to conclude a peace treaty with Japan, which the Australians refused to contemplate without the assurance of a formal American alliance. Effective also to some extent was the support of John Foster Dulles for a Pacific pact linking the United States with Australia and New Zealand. The outcome was the Tripartite Security Pact, ever since known as ANZUS, under which "each Party recognizes that an armed attack in the Pacific area on any of the Parties would be dangerous to its own peace and safety and declares that it would act to meet the common danger in accordance with its constitutional processes" (Article IV).

ANZUS has remained the cornerstone of Australian defense and foreign policy, endorsed without reservation by successive governments in Canberra. It has nonetheless never entirely fulfilled Spender's hopes. The United States has never felt required under the pact to consult with Australia or New Zealand on the actual formulation of policy, although it has provided a convenient mechanism through which to obtain approval of decisions already taken in Washington. There is also reason to believe that changes in the Pacific since 1951 have rendered the terms of the treaty so anachronistic as significantly to impair its legal validity. ANZUS was conceived at a time when the United States and the British Dominions in the Pacific perceived a common threat from the Soviet Union and Communist China and when Australia and New Zealand had both undertaken defense commitments beyond their own shores in respect to other Commonwealth countries. The People's Republic of China has now emerged as the most dedicated opponent of Russian expansionism in the region, and the notion of a Commonwealth defense system has long since evaporated. The United States for its part has given every indication of having abandoned the strategy of involvement, of which the various mutual security pacts were manifestations. The ANZUS treaty would need to be substantially reworded and updated to represent accurately the nature of the existing security relationship among its members.

RELATED ENTRIES: Defense Planning for Oceania between the Wars; Oceania, Strategic Importance of since 1945; War in the Pacific Islands, 1914-1945.

SOURCES AND READINGS: Dean G. Acheson, *Present at the Creation* (New York: Signet, 1970); Glen St. J. Barclay, "The Future of Australian-American Relations," *Australian Outlook* 30 (1976); Glen St. J. Barclay and Joseph M. Siracusa, eds., *Australian-American Relations since 1945* (Sydney: Holt-Saunders, 1976).   *Glen St. J. Barclay*

ARI'I TA'IMA'I, PRINCESS (1821-1897). Ari'i Ta'ima'i was a high-ranking chiefess on the island of Tahiti, French Polynesia, when the American historian Henry Adams visited there in 1891. His many hours of conversation with the princess resulted in a publication entitled *Memoirs of Arii Taimai.* His historical record reveals the dislike this high-ranking family held for the ruling Pomare family who Ari'i Ta'ima'i claimed usurped royal power when the Europeans arrived in Tahiti. Her daughter Marau married heir-apparent Teri'i Tari'a (1839-1880). When his mother Queen Pomare IV died in 1877, there was a move by Marau's supporters to have her crowned queen to rule rather than her husband. The French squelched the move and Teri'i Tari'a was crowned King Pomare V. France annexed the islands in 1880 and ended the monarchy. Ari'i Ta'ima'i continued to live in Pape'ete until her death on 24 June 1897.

RELATED ENTRIES: French Polynesia; Pomare Family.

SOURCES AND READINGS: Henry B. Adams, *Tahiti: Memoirs of Arii Taimai* (1901; reprint ed., Ridgewood, N.J.: Gregg Press, 1968); Patrick O'Reilly, *Tahitiens* (Paris: Musée de l'Homme, 1962).

Robert D. Craig

ARMSTRONG, RICHARD (1805-1860). A political and religious leader in Hawai'i, Armstrong was born in McEvensville, Pennsylvania, 13 April 1805. He graduated from Princeton Seminary and served as pastor of the Kawaiaha'o church in Honolulu. While the head of the English schools in Hawai'i, he recommended that greater attention be paid to the proper education of Hawaiian girls. In 1854 he proposed the reduction in size of Hawaiian schools and the elimination of controversial religious instruction in the "mixed" schools. In 1848 he succeeded William Richards as minister of public instruction. Fear of the growing American community in the islands caused the Hawaiians to oppose the views held by Armstrong and Dr. Gerrit P. Judd (a medical missionary) concerning Americans moving to the islands. When a devastating epidemic of smallpox broke out in 1853, Armstrong was blamed for the spread of the disease and was dismissed from the ministry by the king. However, his duties were later restored, and he continued to work and serve as a missionary until his death in Honolulu on 23 September 1860.

RELATED ENTRIES: Hawai'i; Judd, Gerrit P.; Richards, William.

SOURCES AND READINGS: Ralph S. Kuykendall,

Hawaii: A History (Englewood Cliffs, N.J.: Prentice-Hall, 1948); Ralph S. Kuykendall, *A History of Hawaii* (New York: Macmillan Co., 1933).

Brenna J. Rash

'ATENISI INSTITUTE AND UNIVERSITY. 'Atenisi Institute was founded in 1966 by Professor 'I. Futa Helu, now chairman of the university's governing committee. Initially, it was a night school in Nuku'alofa, the capital of Tonga. It now occupies extensive grounds some way out of the city. The high school division has over eight hundred students. 'Atenisi is unique in Tonga in that it is completely independent of state and church and is entirely self-supporting. The university division opened officially in August 1975 with a total of eight students and four full- or part-time staff. Courses at degree level had been offered by the institute since 1971, but until 1975 no degree programs had been offered. The university's first full academic year began in February 1976.

The institute as a whole, and the university division in particular, is committed to the ideal of education as an end in itself. The institute aims at being a center of academic excellence and not simply a means of fulfilling current social needs. Being without government subsidy, 'Atenisi is free to pursue this policy.

The university division offers two degrees, the associate of arts and the associate of science. These degrees are gained by completion of twenty-four courses, each consisting of at least four hours per week, which takes a minimum of two years. Each degree requires study in three groups of subjects: arts, social sciences, mathematics and natural sciences. Several courses are specified as degree requirements. At present there are forty students in a degree program, six full-time and four part-time faculty members, and a library staff of three.

The university has no full-time administration at present. It is run by its governing committee which meets several times each term. Routine administration is handled by the secretary of the committee. The committee is responsible to the institute's executive committee and to the board of trustees, the institute's supreme governing board. The university uses the quarterly system with three teaching terms in late February to November and a vacation. The academic year ends in late November. The university has a small but growing library and laboratories which have been greatly expanded due to a generous gift from the government of New Zealand. New classrooms have been opened and housing is provided for staff, rent-free. There is a small staff refectory. Further information can be obtained from: The University Division, 'Atenisi Institute, P.O. Box 220, Nuku-'alofa, Tonga.

RELATED ENTRIES: Education in the Pacific, Higher; Tonga.

Etta Harris

AUSTRAL ISLANDS. Sometimes called Tubuai after one of the islands in the chain, the Austral Islands represent one of the five major groups belonging to French Polynesia and consist of five inhabited islands and several rocks or smaller uninhabited islands lying due southwest and southeast of Tahiti. The highest peak is Mount Hiro (Raivavae), 437 m (1,433 ft) high. Many of the islands are fertile and grow tropical coconuts, breadfruit, oranges, bananas, taro, coffee, and vanilla which make their way to the markets in Pape'ete, Tahiti. Rapa, the southernmost island, cannot grow some of the more tender plants which can be cultivated in the warmer climates to its north.

Modern archaeological expeditions have disclosed that before European "discovery" the islands were heavily populated. Internal wars between 1818 and 1828 killed up to two-thirds of the population, and Western diseases reduced it even further. The most recent census (1977) placed the total population at 5,199 with an average annual increase of approximately 0.4 percent.

Two of the islands, Tubuai and Raivavae, were ceded to Pomare II of Tahiti in 1819, declared a French protectorate at the same time as Tahiti in 1842, and then annexed by France in 1880. The other islands came under the French protectorate and then were annexed: Rurutu in 1889 and 1900; Rimatara in 1889 and 1900; Rapa in 1867 and 1900; and Maria, annexed in 1901. Today, the Australs combine with western Tahiti and the Leeward Society Islands to send one deputy to the French National Assembly in Paris. They also send two deputies to represent them in the new autonomous Territorial Assembly in Pape'ete.

RELATED ENTRIES: France in the Pacific; French Polynesia; Pomare Family.

SOURCES AND READINGS: F. Allan Hanson, *Rapan Lifeways* (Boston: Little, Brown & Co., 1970); Donald S. Marshall, *Island of Passion (Raivavae)* (London: G. Allen & Unwin, 1962).

Robert D. Craig

AUSTRALIA AND THE SOUTHWEST PACIFIC. Since the European settlement of Australia in 1788, varied contacts have linked Australia and the neighboring southwest Pacific islands, first as separate colonies and later as a single nation. The French territories of eastern Polynesia, the former German and Japanese League of Nations mandates, and the U.S. Trust Territory of the Pacific Islands have historically been beyond the sphere of Australian interests. Papua New Guinea has assumed a special relationship because of the colonial and trusteeship status which existed prior to Papua New Guinea's independence in 1975 and which in different forms continues today.

When the establishment of a penal colony in Australia was first considered, discussion took place in London on the use of the settlement as a base to extend British influence into the southwest Pacific region. The evidence suggests that regional, commercial, and strategic considerations were determining factors in the final decision to establish the settlement. At the time the decision was made, the Pacific was mostly uncharted and unclaimed by European powers. However, knowledge of its peoples, waters, and the produce it might provide for world markets was known through naval logs, official reports, and published accounts of voyages and meetings of mariners in the ports of the world.

Sydney quickly became the base for trading voyages seeking pork in Tahiti, *bêche-de-mer* and sandalwood in Fiji, flax and timber on Norfolk Island, and coconut oil in the Gilbert Islands (Kiribati). Whalers and sealers were provisioned in Sydney for voyages along the line or south into the feeding and mating grounds. Initial contacts were irregular, brief, and generally friendly. Both islanders and visitors were keen to acquire what they needed: for the Sydney trader, island produce to trade in the China market; for the islander, iron, cloth, and tobacco. Individuals and companies soon established trading stations on the most favored islands and then usually abandoned them when resources became depleted. Rather than diverting trade and shipping from Sydney, these beach communities and embryonic port towns strengthened Sydney's position as a base on the perimeter of and a link to the wider world. Throughout the nineteenth century, Sydney maintained this role as the trading, shipping, and communication center for the southwest Pacific, though not without challenge from Auckland, New Zealand.

Prior to 1850 Australian, or more correctly, colonial involvement had taken three forms. The initial contacts arose out of the penal colony's struggle to remain self-sufficient from supplies from Europe. Then, after the official prohibition on free-enterprise ventures in the China trade was removed and the East India Company's monopoly on regional shipping was rescinded, private trade between Sydney, the is-

lands, and China increased. The third link was activity centered on the whaling and sealing industries. These three types of involvement, all related to trade, gave the colony a stable base for growth. After 1850 colonial involvement took on an added dimension: the evangelical movement. Although controlled from Europe by churches and mission societies, the missionaries in the islands were given colonial support through fund raising, provisioning, and mainland theological training centers. In the latter half of the nineteenth century, Australian churches assumed responsibility for furthering conversion and maintaining the religious and secular welfare of islanders. Public interest in the islands was aroused on several occasions by the combined influence of pulpit and newspaper. Mass meetings followed the murder of Bishop Patteson, petitions and lobbying were employed to counter French moves in the New Hebrides, and similar campaigns were mounted against the evils of the Pacific island labor trade.

On occasions, the colonial press popularized Australia's destiny in the islands, but ulterior motives usually linked those calling for expansion and those promoting investment and land schemes. New Guinea, Fiji, and the New Hebrides were offered as promising fields for immigration and profitable investment, and there was a small but significant movement of colonists to the islands seeking fortunes as planters. Expansionist calls also arose from fears of Russian, Prussian, or French attack. The danger of foreign bases in the nearby Pacific was voiced regularly in colonial parliaments, and the annexation of islands was an oft-repeated byline for editorials. These fears led to the formulation of a defense policy relying on the twin planks of a colonial militia and coastal fortifications with limited local naval forces, and secondly, *Pax Britannia* manifested in the presence of a British squadron in Australian waters. Calls for expansion whether stemming from economic, missionary, or strategic considerations were destined to be fruitless as Great Britain was unwilling to grant colonial parliaments any scope to claim the Pacific as a sphere of interest and was herself unwilling to become involved in expensive flag-planting adventures.

When the Commonwealth of Australia was proclaimed in January 1901, it carried with it a legacy of varied relationships going back to 1788. These contacts began to lose their importance as Australia, as a nation, looked to strengthening political, economic, and social ties with Britain and other major world powers. The granting of a new imperial status in 1901 did not change Britain's attitude towards Australian interference in the islands. In addition, the flags of Germany, France, Britain, and the United States of

America hung firmly over their respective island empires. Australia remained a small, not yet fully unified, former colony on the fringe of an ocean ruled from Europe.

In the early decades of the twentieth century, involvement followed the pattern that had been evolving since the mid-nineteenth century. Some colonial opinions were formalized into Commonwealth policy after 1901, but generally Australian involvement in the labor trade, defense, missionary work, mining, and trade remained much as it had been. Of the changes caused by World War I, the capture and subsequent trusteeship of former German possessions was the most important.

Not until the outbreak of World War II did a distinct, though limited, forward-looking policy towards the islands emerge in Australia. During the last years of the war, Australia asserted her interests in the neighboring Pacific region by assuming varying degrees of colonial responsibility for Papua New Guinea, Nauru, and Norfolk Island, and through the Canberra Agreement (1947) by taking the lead in drawing the islands together under a regional banner. The results were the South Pacific Commission and several postwar technical, educational, and development programs bearing the trademark of Australia's new-found responsibility.

A concurrent emphasis on developing links with Asia, increased emphasis on international and Third World affairs, a revision of links with Europe, and a courting of the United States all far outweighed the attention paid to the islands. Australia's contribution to the islands was initially small in comparison to the dollars and aid directed to Asia, Europe, and even Africa; but by the 1970s, on a per capita basis, the Pacific was a major recipient of Australian aid. The new links which developed highlighted the importance of aid to the struggling pocketbook economies of the Pacific microstates. Australian aid became a major source of island revenue and one of the key factors in the establishment of long-term stability. Australia's contribution includes the official assistance offered to all Third World countries. Education, training schemes, and scholarships bring islanders to Australia, and a substantial grant is set aside to help foster and preserve island cultures. Running costs of the University of the South Pacific, the South Pacific Games, and the South Pacific Festival of the Arts are provided, as are other types of special aid projects, supplement aid grants, and official financial assistance.

Another link is formed by the presence in Australia of Australian-born descendants of the sixty thousand islanders brought to the colonies during the years of the labor trade. The descendants of the sixteen hundred who remained legally after the Pacific Island Labour Act of 1901 ended the recruiting system and those who went into the bush until deportations ceased now number around ten thousand. These Melanesian-Australians have begun to revive an interest in their culture and traditions and to reestablish contacts with their homelands in the Solomons and New Hebrides.

In the postwar period, Australian involvement and policy formulation has occurred on two levels, nation-to-nation and nation-to-region. Links between Australia and the region function through regional bodies such as the South Pacific Commission, the South Pacific Forum, and the South Pacific Bureau for Economic Development. Australia is also linked to the region through international agencies such as the United Nations, World Health Organization, Red Cross, Asian Development Bank, and the World Bank. At the nation-to-nation level, Australia does not have regular relations with any Pacific nation, excluding Papua New Guinea. The responsibilities of the diplomatic representative on Nauru, for example, also include Kiribati and the Trust Territory of the Pacific Islands, while the high commission in Fiji is also responsible for Tuvalu and Tonga and, until recently, Western Samoa.

Charitable, volunteer, and missionary work have continued in the postwar period, but these activities have altered as island churches and institutions gained autonomy. Australian church and mission societies still share the task of achieving religious and secular goals determined in the main by the island churches.

Tourism has been a recent and highly significant factor in the relationship between Australia and the islands. Airline promotions, package deals, and Pacific cruises have promoted an idyllic South Seas image and have led Australians to the islands in ever-increasing numbers. In Fiji, for example, 45 percent of tourists are Australians. In economic terms this means Australians are contributing a major share of the tourist revenue earned each year in Fiji.

Investment, trading, and commercial companies and banks have maintained and often expanded their island interests. Recent developments include oil exploration and mining. Import-export figures show marked increases but the balance of trade is heavily in Australia's favor.

Australia's presence in the region was also felt when Australia took France to the International Court of Justice over nuclear testing on Moruroa Atoll and when a Labour and Employment Ministers Conference was organized in 1973 to discuss common problems in the maritime industries, labor-training, and employment. Australian advisors continue to assist island nations with law-of-the-sea agreements and the formulation of legislation for a 320 km exclusive economic zone.

Australia's involvement, however, is not without its critics. As independent and soon-to-be independent nations assert their national consciousness, they are critical of Australia in several ways: for not allowing short-term work permits to islanders; for allowing investment and commercial interests to exploit island economies; for not opening Australian markets to island produce; and for failing to establish a clear policy on Australian-Pacific relations for future decades. Partly in response to these changes in 1978 an Australian parliamentary inquiry into Australia's relations with the South Pacific concluded that Australia needed to forge a new identity and widen its scope of involvement. Dollars and material aid are one aspect of this involvement. What the other links are to be will emerge as the island and Australian governments agree on relevant and feasible projects and policies.

Extending over the period since 1788, the islands have at times been influential in the policies and directions taken as Australia changed from penal settlement to self-governing colonies, to Commonwealth status, and finally to regional giant. In the 1970s, this played an ever-increasing and influential role in affairs and developments in the region. The major change in the relationship, however, has been that the islands of the southwest Pacific have demanded more than a benign and occasionally paternal concern from their neighboring giant.

RELATED ENTRIES: Anglican Missions; ANZAC; ANZUS; Australian Perceptions of the Russian Threat in the Nineteenth Century; Australian Projects for Annexation in the Pacific Islands in the Nineteenth Century; Fiji; German Colonial Empire; Labor Trade; Melanesian Recruitment to Queensland, Patterns of; Melanesians and Colonial Servitude; Papua New Guinea; Patteson, John C.; Solomon Islands; South Pacific Forum; Vanuatu (New Hebrides); Western Pacific High Commission.

Alan Maxwell Quanchi

AUSTRALIAN PERCEPTIONS OF THE RUSSIAN THREAT IN THE NINETEENTH CENTURY. Russian traders had been active in the Pacific since the latter half of the eighteenth century. Their only territorial interest was Hawai'i, as a potential base for the Alaskan fur trade. A Russian expedition also arrived in Japan on 21 August 1853 just six weeks after Commander Matthew G. Perry, USN. Australian consciousness of the Russian presence in the Pacific was, however, first awakened by the outbreak of war in the Crimea in October 1853. The New South Wales Legislative Council promptly introduced a bill to provide for the formation of a volunteer and yeomanry corps and to build the colony's first warship in case the winds of war should sweep into the South Pacific. They did not. But the colonials found cause for alarm in the visit of the powerful Russian frigate *Svetlana* to Melbourne in 1862, particularly when it found that the batteries at Port Phillip Bay were unable to acknowledge the Russians' salute for lack of ammunition. They were even more concerned when the even more powerful corvette *Bogatyr* arrived in Australian waters the following year, at a time when it was feared that the Polish insurrection might lead to renewed hostilities between Russia and the British Empire.

The Russians themselves seem genuinely to have had no plans other than to enjoy the facilities of Melbourne and the company of its women. The Victorian government, nonetheless, urgently requested London to provide them with some naval defense capacity. The British responded by passing the Colonial Naval Defense Act that authorized the colonies to raise and maintain their own naval forces. It was the beginning of the Royal Australian Navy.

The outbreak of the Russo-Turkish War in 1877 coincided with the report of the governor of South Australia that local defenses developed so far would be totally useless against any serious attack. The colonies renewed their efforts to build up a more formidable militia. Then, in 1883, the commandant of the Queensland defense forces reported that the Russians had acquired a powerful Asiatic squadron and were visiting Yokohama and San Francisco with the idea of using Japanese and American ports as bases from which to attack Australia. Their naval officers were even marrying British and American ladies in order to improve their English so they could become more familiar with the state of Australia's defenses.

These arguments did not impress the British who pointed out that Vladivostok was five thousand miles away from Australia and closed by ice three months of the year. In any case, fear of Russia was shortly displaced by more urgent fear of Japan. The outbreak of the Russo-Japanese war in 1904 caused the menace of the nineteenth century to be hailed as the potential savior of the twentieth. "Hold them, IVAN!" intoned popular versifier Henry Lawson in 1904:

Hold them, IVAN! staggering bravely beneath your gloomy sky;

Hold them, IVAN! we shall want you pretty
   badly bye-and-bye!
It means all to young Australia—it means life
   or death to us;
For the vanguard of the White Man is the
   vanguard of the Russ.

RELATED ENTRIES: Oceania, Strategic Importance of since 1945.

SOURCES AND READINGS: Glen St. J. Barclay, *A History of the Pacific* (London: Sidgwick and Jackson, 1978); Thomas B. Millar, "In Case They Were Needed: The Story of the Victorian Colonial Defences from 1836 to 1900" (Ph.D. diss., University of Melbourne, 1952); C. Roderick, ed., *Henry Lawson, Collected Verse, 1901-1909* (Sydney: University Press, 1961).   *Glen St. J. Barclay*

AUSTRALIAN PROJECTS FOR ANNEXATION IN THE PACIFIC ISLANDS IN THE NINETEENTH CENTURY.

Australian interest in New Guinea was first aroused by the Russian naval visits of 1862 and 1863. Private citizens appealed to the British government to annex the island before any foreign power could use it as a base from which to harass the Australian colonies. More tangible arguments were provided by the report of Captain John Moresby in 1874 that gold-bearing quartz had been discovered in the highlands. Moresby also reported the presence of Russian, French, and Italian explorers. Accordingly, Secretary of State for the Colonies Lord Carnavon canvassed the views of the governors of the Australian colonies. All were in favor of annexing New Guinea to the British Crown, but none was prepared to contribute to the cost of the enterprise. The British let the matter drop. However, the government of Queensland established an agent in New Guinea in the form of a failed sugar planter, William B. Ingham. He reported in October 1878 that gold had actually been discovered in the mountains fifty miles behind Port Moresby.

Queensland Premier Sir Thomas McIlwraith was looking for some means of retrieving his sagging political fortunes. He informed the governor of the colony in February 1883 that New Guinea was in danger of being annexed by Germany. His solution was that it should be annexed by Queensland. McIlwraith did not wait for the British government to express an opinion. He sent the stipendiary magistrate on Thursday Island in the Queensland government's police cutter on 19 March 1883 to take possession of eastern New Guinea in the queen's name. His vigor was applauded by Victorian Premier James Service. The governments of New South Wales and South Australia approved the idea of New Guinea

being annexed by the British Crown though not necessarily of its being annexed by Queensland. The British, however, disallowed the project in July. The Queenslanders were again being vague over the question of who was actually supposed to bear the cost of governing New Guinea. London also had misgivings about allowing additional indigenous peoples to fall under the control of a colonial government which had perhaps the worst reputation in the world for the mistreatment of subject peoples. The Australians were, however, not prepared to give up so easily. The agents-general of New South Wales, Victoria, Queensland, and New Zealand all pressed in November for the British government to declare a protectorate over eastern New Guinea if the colonies were prepared to contribute financially. The New Zealanders were also demanding the annexation of the New Hebrides as well before the French could establish themselves there too firmly.

The British government had already reached an understanding with the French over the New Hebrides. Each agreed to leave the group alone, so as to be free of the fear of the other's moving in. However, the British decided to extend a vague protectorate over the southern littoral of eastern New Guinea. This was done on 28 August 1884. Four months later, the German government declared a protectorate over the northern part of the territory. A great foreign power had established itself in New Guinea after all, to the consternation of the Australians.

This left the New Hebrides. British Prime Minister Lord Salisbury warned the Australians that the French were perfectly ready to defend their interests by force, and that they should be content with an undertaking from Paris not to send any more convicts to the group. Victorian Premier Alfred Deakin prepared to emulate McIlwraith by sending a detachment of the Victorian defense forces to the New Hebrides in a fast steamer with orders to hoist the British flag there and keep it flying until told by London to haul it down. The project was abandoned at the last moment only when assurances were received from the British that the French genuinely had no plans for annexation. The Australians had their desire for island colonies satisfied eventually but not until after World War I.

RELATED ENTRIES: British New Guinea; German Colonial Empire; Labor Trade; Papua New Guinea; Port Moresby; Vanuatu (New Hebrides).

SOURCES AND READINGS: Glen St. J. Barclay, *The Empire is Marching* (London: Weidenfeld and Nicolson, 1976); Kay E. Saunders, Raymond L. Evans, and Kathryn Cronin, *Exclusion, Exploitation and Extermination: Race Relations in Colonial Queens-*

land (Sydney: Australia and New Zealand Book Co., 1975).   *Glen St. J. Barclay*

AUSTRONESIAN LANGUAGES. The Austronesian language family is the most numerous and (after Indo-European) the most widely dispersed of the world's great language families. It contains more than eight hundred languages, spread around two-thirds of the earth's circumference. Upwards of four hundred Austronesian languages are spoken in Melanesia, from New Guinea to Fiji, and some forty are dispersed across the archipelagos of Micronesia and the Polynesian triangle. About a third of the languages are found in Indonesia, Malaysia, and the Philippines. Smaller numbers are present in Madagascar and parts of Formosa, Vietnam, and Cambodia.

The most important members of the family are Bahasa Indonesia (spoken as a first or second language by over 100 million Indonesians with a variant, "Malay," used in Malaysia), Javanese (about sixty million speakers), Sundanese (about fifteen million), Malagasy (the official language of the Malagasy Republic), and several languages of the Philippines, including Filipino (the national language, based on Tagalog, and known as a first or second language by some forty million), Cebuano (ten million), and Ilokano (six million). In Oceania, Austronesian languages are spoken by much smaller communities. The largest are standard Fijian (about 250,000), Samoan (200,000), New Zealand Maori (100,000), and Kuanua or Tolai of New Britian (80,000).

In spite of the distances separating them, the genetic relationship of the most far-flung Austronesian languages is easily established by the Comparative Method of linguistics. The existence of the family was first adumbrated in 1706 when a Dutch scholar, Hadrian Reland, observed fundamental similarities between vocabularies brought to Europe from Madagascar, Indonesia, and Polynesia. During the second half of the nineteenth century it was realized that the languages of Micronesia and much of Melanesia are also Austronesian. The following comparisons illustrate the resemblances between Tagalog (Philippines), Indonesian, Standard Fijian (Melanesia), Woleai (Micronesia), and Samoan (Polynesia). The reconstructed forms in the common ancestral language, Proto-Austronesian (PAN), are added. (The asterisk marks a reconstructed, hypothetical form.)

The extreme fragmentation of the Austronesian family can be attributed largely to the geography of the Pacific Ocean and to the culture of the early Austronesian peoples. The early Austronesians were perhaps the world's first accomplished seafaring people. Possessing the outrigger canoe and sail, they were able to settle not only the whole of the Philippine and Indonesian archipelagos, and those of western Melanesia, but also to reach the remote islands of eastern Melanesia, Micronesia, and Polynesia, which previously had lain beyond the reach of man. A knowledge of agriculture (taro, yams, and other root crops), horticulture (breadfruit, banana, coconut, and other tree crops), and diverse fishing techniques enabled Austronesian speakers to survive permanently on small islands. Archaeological research indicates that the Austronesians began to disperse not later than 4,000 to 3,000 B.C., and had attained substantially their present distribution, except for the settlement of

TABLE 1   COMPARISON OF SOME AUSTRONESIAN LANGUAGES ILLUSTRATING THE RESEMBLANCES

English	Tagalog	Indonesian	Fijian	Woleai	Samoan	PAN
mosquito	namok	namuk	namu	lamw	namu	*namuk
coconut	niyog	niur	niu	liu	niu	*niuR
fish	ikan	isda	ika	igal	l'a	*ikan
eye	mata	mata	mata	mat	mata	*mata
ear	telinga	tainga	ndalinga	taling	talinga	*tali
cry	umiyak	tangis	tangi	tang	tangi	*ta is
new	bago	baru	vou	feo	fou	*baqeRu

* a reconstructed, hypothetical form

Madagascar, eastern Polynesia, and New Zealand, by 1,000 B.C. But once the population had become widely dispersed in any region each island or island group developed a separate language, for the lack of a centralized political system and regular communications to maintain unity.

The reconstruction of Proto-Austronesian in a systematic way was begun by the German scholar Dempwolff in the 1920s. In his major work (1934-1938), Dempwolff reconstructed the PAN sound system and some 2,200 roots. Later scholars have slightly modified his PAN sound system and have greatly expanded the reconstructed vocabulary. Comparative study of morphology and syntax has begun.

From agreements across the family, it is evident that most roots or word bases in Proto-Austronesian contained two syllables, and had the structure CV(C) CVC (where C = consonant, V = vowel). Consonant clusters occurred only in the middle of a base and were highly restricted in type (usually comprising a nasal plus an obstruent, for example, *mp, nt, ŋk*). Sentences without verbs were common. The predicate preceded the subject. There is some dispute about the structure of transitive verbal sentences, the majority view being that word order and case marking were of the general type exhibited by Philippine languages. In this type, the word order is either Verb-Patient-Agent, or Verb-Agent-Patient, except when the Agent is a pronoun when Agent immediately follows the verb, for instance, Tagalog *s-in-untok niya ako* (hit-past he me) "he hit me." There are several different types of "passive" construction where the subject may be, variously, the Patient or Goal, the Location, the Beneficiary, or the Instrument. In a passive construction the semantic role of the subject is marked by an affix on the verb (in PAN, *-en for Goal subject, *-an for Location subject, *i- for Instrument subject). The case marker for Agent of a passive is characteristically the same as for Possessor; the agentive and possessive pronouns are often the same or similar in Austronesian languages while different from the nominative pronouns. A "genitive" marker *ni linking head and possessor noun and a "ligative" *na linking numeral or adjectival attribute and head are widely reflected among contemporary Austronesian languages.

During the twentieth century the term *Malayo-Polynesian*, once in general use as a name for the family, has been gradually supplanted by *Austronesian*. Malayo-Polynesian is sometimes used for a large subgroup, consisting of most or all of the Austronesian languages exclusive of those spoken in Formosa. A number of scholars have advanced evidence

indicating the primary division within Austronesian is between a branch or branches comprising the Formosan languages and a branch containing all other members of the family (for example, Dahl 1973). In general, however, it has proved hard to establish high-order subgroupings within Austronesian. Until the last twenty years or so, many students simply resorted to a four-way division (Indonesian, Melanesian, Micronesian, Polynesian) based on geographic lines and having no solid linguistic basis.

Above all, it was the relationships of the Melanesian languages which puzzled early scholars. *Melanesian* was the label given to any Austronesian (or Austronesianlike) language, other than Polynesian, spoken in the area from New Guinea and the Bismarck Archipelago through the Solomon Islands south to New Caledonia and east to the New Hebrides, Fiji, and Rotuma. One source of puzzlement was the physical appearance of Melanesians. Whereas most Austronesian speakers have straight or wavy hair and light-brown skin color, Melanesians typically have frizzy hair and a darker skin. Equally perplexing was the heterogeneity of the Melanesian languages, about four hundred distinct languages concentrated within a fairly small geographic region, nearly all spoken by communities of fewer than ten thousand people. During the hundred years 1860 to 1960, the most widely accepted theory explained Melanesian languages as hybrids: a mixture of Austronesian and non-Austronesian (or Papuan) elements. It was suggested that in Melanesia different groups of Indonesian traders or colonists had over the centuries come into contact with diverse non-Austronesian aboriginal populations; in many cases the latter adopted a pidginized form of the Austronesian colonists' language, while retaining a Papuan substratum. An alternative interpretation of Melanesian diversity was offered by Dyen (1965). Dyen took the small common vocabulary of the Melanesian languages to indicate a great time-depth of Austronesian occupation. Indeed, he proposed Melanesia as the likely dispersal center of Proto-Austronesian.

In the 1920s and 1930s, a historical treatment of Melanesian strikingly different from these theories emerged from the work of Dempwolff. Dempwolff traced the development of PAN roots in a number of Oceanic (Melanesian, Polynesian, and Micronesian) languages. He found that the Oceanic languages agree in unifying PAN *b and *p; in merging the entire palatal series *s, *z, *c, *j, and *Z into a single sound; in merging *e with *aw (generally as *o*); and in sharing a few other common alterations of the PAN sound system as he had reconstructed it. No western Austronesian (non-Oceanic) language shows the same set of innovations. On this basis, Dempwolff posited an Oceanic subgroup, concluding that the Melanesian, Polynesian, and Micronesian languages underwent a period of continued common development after their separation from western Austronesian languages. But although Dempwolff's reconstructions of PAN became the foundation for all subsequent reconstructive work, his Oceanic hypothesis was not accepted, at first, by most scholars.

After World War II increasing numbers of trained linguists began to work in the Austronesian field. The volume and quality of descriptive and historical research rose sharply, and by the 1970s the main lines of the development of most of the Melanesian languages were fairly well understood. Their apparent genetic diversity has turned out to be largely fictitious —a reflection of poor descriptions and the lack of systematic application of the Comparative Method. On reexamination, Dempwolff's Oceanic subgrouping hypothesis has been pronounced sound. Comparative lexical and grammatical studies have, indeed, revealed many additional innovations common to the Oceanic group, for example: PAN *aku (first person singular) is reflected as Proto-Oceanic (POC) *au, with irregular loss of *k; PAN *limaw (citrus) is reflected as *moli instead of the expected *limo; *maRi (come) is reflected as *mai. In the marking of possessive relations Proto-Oceanic showed a three-way contrast where PAN had only one way of marking possession: a relation controlled by the possessor was marked by *na- plus person-marker before the possessed noun; one not controlled was marked by *ka-; while inalienable relationships (kin terms and body parts) were marked by directly suffixing the person-marker to the possessed noun. Modern standard Fijian preserves the essential contrast, as in ke-mu itukutuku "your story (told about you)," ulu-mu "your head (part of you)," no-mu ulu "your head (property, for example a fishhead)." In Proto-Oceanic *ka- was also used to mark possession of edibles and drinkables, for example, Fijian ke-mu ulu "your head (for eating)." In some Oceanic languages (chiefly those of Fiji, the northern New Hebrides and Micronesia) the POC system was elaborated by adding a distinction between edible and drinkable possession. In the Polynesian group, this possessive system was simplified to a two-way contrast between controlled and noncontrolled possession (marked by a and o, respectively) with only vestiges of the earlier drinkable category and with direct suffixation-marking preserved in petrified suffixes in a few kin terms, for instance, Maori tupu-na "ancestor," tuaka-na "older sibling of same sex."

In verbal constructions the Oceanic languages share several features which set them off from languages of the Philippine type. For example, in many languages the verb takes an affix marking the semantic role, not of the subject, but of the direct object. A wide range of nominal roles could appear as direct object in Proto-Oceanic, with *-i marking Patient or Location role and *-akin marking Cause, Instrument, Comitative, or Beneficiary. These last features are shared with many languages of Indonesia, though the latter generally make a three-way distinction between Patient (unmarked), Location (*-i), and Cause, etc. (*-aken). Many eastern Indonesian and Oceanic languages show a similar system of pronominal determiners or concord markers, in which all human (or animate) nouns require an accompanying person marker to specify its person and number, for example, "the men saw the children of the woman" is expressed roughly as "they-the-men saw them-the-child of she-the-woman."

Certain Austronesian languages have changed the PAN syllable and word structure canons. Such restructurings have sometimes led to far-reaching sound shifts and morphological changes, as in some Micronesian languages and Rotuman. But a high proportion of Austronesian languages have kept close to the PAN pattern and in these languages many words are retained from PAN almost without change, showing a conservatism which by Indo-European standards is astonishing.

SOURCES AND READINGS: Otto Christian Dahl, Proto-Austronesian. Scandinavian Institute of Asian Studies, Monograph no. 15, (Lund, Sweden, 1973); Otto Dempwolff, Vergleichende Lautlehre des austronesichen Wortschatzes, 3 vols. (Berlin: Dietrich Reimer, 1934-38); T. E. Sebeok, ed., Current Trends in Linguistics, vol. 8. Linguistics in Oceania (The Hague: Mouton, 1971); Isidore Dyen, A Lexicostatistical Classification of the Austronesian Languages (Baltimore: Waverly Press, 1965). Dempwolff is the foundation work in comparative Austronesian linguistics. Dahl is the most comprehensive comparative work in English by a single author, but Sebeok is the best introduction, containing survey articles on many different regions written by a number of specialists.

Andrew Pawley

BAKER, SHIRLEY WALDEMAR (1836-1903).
A Methodist missionary to Tonga and later prime minister to George Tupou I, King of Tonga, Shirley Baker was born and died in obscurity, and his professional life was marked by conflict and turmoil. Working in a pivotal period in Tonga's history, he generated intense loyalties and hatreds. By turns missionary and statesman, he was always the politician, yet he was largely responsible for the Free Church of Tonga and for Tonga's constitution. He was ambitious, not overly nice in his methods nor averse to a profit, and somewhat vindictive. In spite of this, through his years of cooperation with Tonga's King George he did more than any other European to insure that Tonga would enter the twentieth century as an independent nation. Born in London in 1836, Baker traveled to Australia in 1850 where he embraced Methodism and declared himself ready to go on a mission "to the heathen." Accordingly, he was sent to Tonga, arriving 14 August 1860. He formed a friendship with King George Tupou I and in 1862 formulated a comprehensive set of laws for Tonga. In 1863, again at the king's request, he designed a flag. In 1866 he left Tonga because of his family's health, but when he returned in 1869 he did so as the chairman of the Friendly Islands district of the Wesleyan mission. Between 1869 and 1875 Baker advanced the causes of an independent Tonga and a Wesleyan church free of foreign domination. In so doing he made enemies among both Tongans and Europeans. In 1875 Baker wrote a constitution for Tonga, paving the way for that country to be recognized by other powers as a civilized nation and weakening Britain's claims to the island kingdom. Reaction from Britain and Australia was negative, and Baker was charged with a variety of wrongdoings. Though cleared of these charges, he was relieved of his chairmanship and ordered back to Australia. He sailed to Tonga again in 1880, ostensibly on a visit, but while there was offered and accepted the office of prime minister to the king. He resigned his office of missionary (it would probably have been taken from him anyway), and began his career as a statesman.

From 1880-1885 he worked hard at his task, reforming the government and balancing the budget, but making enemies all the while. In 1885, he created the Free Church of Tonga, partly to free Methodism from outside influence and partly to get revenge on his old companions. King Tupou forced his citizenry to adopt this new church, using methods sometimes harsh and sometimes outright bloody. After 1885 Baker's fortunes declined. His enemies hounded him, his investments were going bad, and he was blamed for the violence which accompanied the birth of the Free Church. Finally, in 1890, he was dismissed by an aging Tupou, who was under pressure, and was deported. In 1898 Baker returned to Tonga, to Ha-'apai. He had been reduced to relative poverty by business setbacks, but he was still planning, still plotting. He started a mission of the Church of England in Tonga and gained a number of converts, but the mother church denied any affiliation and this enterprise too failed. Crushed in spirit and body, Baker died of a heart attack in November 1903.

RELATED ENTRIES: Tonga; Tongan Constitution 1875.

SOURCES AND READINGS: Lillian Baker and Beatrice Shirley Baker, *Memoirs of the Reverend Dr. Shirley Waldemar Baker, D.M. LL.D., Missionary and Prime Minister* (Dunedin: Coulls Somerville Wilkie, 1927); Sione Lātūkefu, *Church and State in Tonga* (Canberra: Australian National University Press, 1974); Noel Rutherford, *Shirley Baker and the King of Tonga* (Melbourne: Oxford University Press, 1971); Basil Thomson, *The Diversions of a Prime Minister* (London: Dawsons of Pall Mall, 1968).

Ronald Shook

BARET, JEANNE. The first woman to circumnavigate the world (1767-1773), Jeanne Baret hired on as a "male valet" to botanist Philibert Commerson and sailed from France aboard the ship commanded by the famous navigator Bougainville. After eighteen months of disguising her "secret," her sex was immediately detected by the Tahitians when the French landed on their island in 1768. Commerson and Baret were both asked to disembark at Mauritius in November of 1768. They traveled on to Madagascar where Commerson continued his botanical work, assisted by Baret whose name is immortalized in several botanical names beginning with *Baretia*. She soon returned to France where she married and lead a more tranquil life.

RELATED ENTRIES: Bougainville, Louis A. de; French Polynesia.

SOURCES AND READINGS: Louis de Bougainville, *A Voyage Round the World*, trans. John Reinhold Forster (London: J. Nourse, 1772); Jean Dorsenne, *La Vie de Bougainville* (Paris: Gallimard, 1930).
Robert D. Craig

BARTON, FRANCIS RICKMAN (1865-1947). An administrator and soldier, Francis Barton was born at Fundenhall, Norfolk, England. After graduating from the Royal Military Academy at Sandhurst, he was posted to the West India Regiment as second lieutenant on 16 March 1889 and, after routine promotion to captain, arrived in British New Guinea in 1899 as private secretary to Lieutenant Governor George Le Hunte. After serving as a magistrate, he was appointed acting administrator after the suicide of C. S. Robinson. A Royal Commission, appointed from Australia later in 1906 to investigate the near collapse of his administration, found him guilty of favoritism, though zealous in protecting the rights of the indigenous peoples. He later served as first minister of Zanzibar before retiring in 1913.

RELATED ENTRIES: Papua New Guinea.

SOURCES AND READINGS: C. A. W. Monckton, *Some Experiences of a New Guinea Resident Magistrate* (London: Lane, 1921).   *H. J. Gibbney*

BATAILLON, PIERRE-MARIE (1810-1877). Bataillon, the first Catholic vicar apostolic of central Oceania, was born 6 January 1810 at Saint-Cyr-les-Vignes (Loire), France. Bataillon joined the new Marist missionaries (Society of Mary) who had been given responsibility for the conversion of the peoples in the western Pacific. In December 1836 the group under the direction of Bishop Pompallier left France. Bataillon and Brother Joseph Luzy were landed on Wallis Island (1 November 1837) and Pierre Chanel and Brother Nizier on neighboring Futuna. Fierce civil war between island chiefs and the general opposition to religion in general made initial conversion difficult. Chief Tungahala became an ally and intermediary between them and King Lavelua. Through their diligent and endless work, they were finally able

to convert the king. By 1842 the entire population of Wallis followed his example. When Bishop Pompallier's vicariate apostolic of western Oceania was divided in 1842, Bataillon was appointed Bishop of Central Oceania (New Caledonia, New Hebrides, Fiji, Tonga, Samoa, Tokelaus, Wallis and Futuna). Mission work was stepped up by missionaries being sent to Tonga (1842), Samoa (1845), and Fiji (1844). In 1847 Bataillon opened the first seminary in Oceania to train a native clergy. Just before his death his see was divided and his vicariate was restricted to Wallis, Futuna, and Tonga (becoming a separate vicariate in 1937). Bishop Bataillon died on Wallis Island 10 April 1877.

RELATED ENTRIES: Catholic Church in the Pacific; Chanel, Pierre; Pompallier, Jean-Baptiste; Wallis and Futuna.

SOURCES AND READINGS: A. M. Mangeret, *Mgr. Bataillon et les missions de l'Océanie Centrale*, 2 vols. (Paris: Lecoffre, 1884); Nicholas A. Weber, *Brief Biographical Dictionary of the Marist Hierarchy* (Washington, D.C.: Catholic Education Press, 1953).
Robert D. Craig

BAU. This small but important island is within wading distance of the eastern coast of Viti Levu in Fiji. For about two generations before continuous European contact began in the 1920s Bau had been the seat of chiefs who established dominance over the greater part of coastal Fiji. These chiefs became dominant apparently through marriage alliances and the consequent command of widespread resources, though the origins of Bau power are as yet to be defined fully. From Bau came the *Tui Viti* ("king of Fiji"), Ratu Apenisa Seru Cakobau, Vunivalu of Bau, who was actually installed as *Tui Viti* in November 1873 though the title was of course not traditional; from him descends the current governor-general of Fiji, Ratu Sir George Cakobau. Bau's power was so widely established at the time of British annexation in 1874 that the Bauan dialect became virtually the official version of the Fijian language. Some specifically Bauan institutions, it is arguable, have been seen as applying to the whole group, while individual Bauans have held high rank under the colonial administration, certainly out of proportion to their numbers. The Bauans at large lost ground under colonial rule, however. Before 1874 they had been great chiefs and overlords, not actual occupants of land. When the colonial government registered land to occupants, no provision was generally made for overlords' rights. A grant of land on Koro Island to Bau chiefs in the 1920s hardly made up for this deprivation; and so, for the free-ranging, heavy-handed chiefs of Bau, colonial rule was not generally advantageous.

RELATED ENTRIES: Fiji.

SOURCES AND READINGS: R. A. Derrick, *The Fiji Islands: A Geographical Handbook* (Suva: Government Press, 1965) and *A History of Fiji* (Suva: Government Press, 1957).   *Deryck Scarr*

BEACHCOMBERS. The word "beachcomber" has a mildly pejorative flavor, as if a beachcomber was a Pacific island version of a vagrant or tramp. Among historians it means a person of non-Oceanian origin who lived with Pacific islanders and became an assimilated member of an island society in the era before intensive European settlement and official colonization. Beachcombers were thus present in only small numbers in any one place or time. They had their counterparts in areas where the cultural frontier was continental: Australia, Africa, and the Americas. Historically, there have always been such people where cultural groups abut and mingle.

Beachcombers were present in all parts of the Pacific but their distribution was not homogeneous. Polynesia was the principal beachcombing zone for a number of reasons. First, it was the area most frequented by European shipping in the early decades of foreign penetration. Second, Melanesians were believed to be more ferocious and less hospitable. Third, the conditions which favored beachcombing quickly changed: the presence of missionaries, resident traders, and colonial officials was hostile to beachcombing and inhibited its development in the west at the same time as it was becoming less acceptable in the east. Beachcombing was therefore a phenomenon mainly of the late eighteenth and early nineteenth centuries.

Most beachcombers were deserters from whaling vessels, some deserted from other commercial shipping, and a minority were shipwrecked. A few, including some of the most famous, for example, William Mariner and John Young, were captured by their island hosts and held involuntarily. Enchantment with the islands as an earthly paradise was very rarely a motive for beachcombing; most were driven by dissatisfaction with shipboard conditions and expected, or hoped to have, only a short stay ashore before shipping aboard another vessel to resume the normal pattern of their lives. Most lifetime beachcombers thus became so through having their plans miscarry.

The cultural contact process in which beachcombers found themselves was often violent and increased the frequency and dangers of war in island societies.

Beachcombers were necessarily involved in these events, and their lives were often both tempestuous and short. The uncertainty of life induced an insouciance manifested as a casual attitude towards life and death, a capacity to live for the moment, a willingness to take chances and to change their circumstances on a whim. Their indifference towards time and the future and their carelessness of the opinions of other Europeans was frequently remarked by observers. Generally, they preferred to live apart from others of their race; and when a group of beachcombers did come together, their relationships were marked by distrust and violence more often than by friendship and mutual support.

Survival and happiness in island society, therefore, did not depend upon beachcomber solidarity. It depended more on individualism: steadiness of mind, quickness of wit, and strength of limb were more likely to ensure survival or longevity than were companions. Marriage or adoption was usually necessary to provide a beachcomber with a local identity and to ease the pain, often deeply felt, of alienation and marginality; it also helped in the necessary task of acquiring the local language.

A hospitable reception by the islanders could not be taken for granted. Melanesians were traditionally hostile to strangers but would welcome foreign residents when self-interest seemed to be so served. Similarly, the traditionally hospitable Polynesians and Micronesians accepted only as many as they were willing to adopt or felt would advance their interests. Total submission to indigenous authority and surrender of all possessions was the course of action most likely to promote survival, at least initially. The islanders themselves soon came to prefer men with useful manual skills, especially in working wood and metal.

Accordingly, after the initial, short-lived novelty of having a resident white man had passed, the status of beachcombers in island society depended on their utility. Useful men were sometimes rewarded with high personal prestige and wives of high birth; formal high rank was rarely bestowed. Most enjoyed privileges but did not become celebrities.

Notwithstanding this emphasis on utility, the beachcombers' contribution to change was circumscribed. Their resources were meagre, their ability to communicate usually poor, and their freedom of action was restricted by the demands and expectations of their hosts. Their own interests were perhaps best served by not promoting change, nor was change an inadvertent corollary of their presence. Similarly, the role they played in island societies was minor: initiative lay with traditional authority figures and structures, and beachcombers were thereby precluded from becoming powerful political figures in their own right. Nor did they contribute appreciably to political change through advice, planning, or military prowess. They were foreign and few in number, and at the time they flourished islanders remained in control of their own affairs.

The historical significance of beachcombers is that they provide a window on island societies before Western-induced change became profound; their fascination lies in their appeal to Western romanticism with its enduring nostalgia for escapism, the exotic, and the primitive.

RELATED ENTRIES: Campbell, Archibald; Davis, Isaac; Diaper, William; Hagerstein, Peter; Mariner, William; Robarts, Edward; Savage, Charles; Vason, George; Whippy, David; Young, John.

SOURCES AND READINGS: Francis X. Hezel, "The Role of the Beachcomber in the Carolines" in Niel Gunson, ed., *The Changing Pacific: Essays in Honour of H. E. Maude* (Melbourne: Oxford University Press, 1978); H. E. Maude, *Of Islands and Men* (Melbourne: Oxford University Press, 1968); Caroline Ralston, *Grass Huts and Warehouses* (Canberra: Australian National University Press, 1977).

Ian C. Campbell

BEAGLEHOLE, JOHN CAWTE (1901-1971). The world's leading authority on the voyages of Captain James Cook, Beaglehole was born 13 June 1901 in Wellington, New Zealand. Beaglehole studied at Victoria University College and at the University of London where he received his Ph.D. in 1929. Returning home, he spent most of his life in his native country researching, teaching at Victoria University College, and writing not only on history but on painting and architecture, music and literature. In the early 1930s Beaglehole became interested in the life of Cook when writing *The Exploration of the Pacific*. For the next forty years he meticulously edited Cook's vast journals in three large volumes and wrote the definitive *Life of Captain James Cook* which was published posthumously. Many of his students remember him as "the most influential teacher I ever had." He received honorary degrees from Oxford (1966) and Wellington (1968) and awards for his various contributions to scholarly research. When the International Bicentennial Conference on Captain James Cook and His Times was held in Vancouver in April 1978, there was little doubt but that it would not have been possible had there not been a Beaglehole. He died 10 October 1971 at his home in Wellington.

RELATED ENTRIES: Cook, (Captain) James.

SOURCES AND READINGS: John C. Beaglehole, ed., *The Journals of Captain James Cook*, 3 vols. (Cambridge: Hakluyt Society, 1955-67) and *Life of Captain James Cook* (London: A. & C. Black, 1974); J. W. Davidson, "The New Zealand Scholar," *Journal of Pacific History* 7 (1972):151-54. Papers at the Vancouver conference appeared in Robin Fisher and Hugh Johnston, eds., *Captain James Cook and His Times* (Seattle: University of Washington Press, 1979) and in *Pacific Studies* 1, no. 2 (Spring 1978).

Robert D. Craig

BELAU, REPUBLIC OF. *See* Palau.

BERLIN ACT OF 1889. Formally known as the "Final Act of the Conference on the Affairs of Samoa," the Berlin agreement was signed 14 June 1889 by the United States, Great Britain, and Germany. The agreement reached in the discussions preceding the Berlin act was designed to settle the conflicts between the contending parties in Samoa at that time. There were several Samoan factions in the traditional system. The three Great Powers were drawn into these disputes at the time they were also attempting to extend their influence in the country and to establish economic advantages for themselves. A conference of the three powers had been held in Washington, D.C., in 1887 but had failed to produce an agreement. In March of 1889 these three nations had warships anchored in the harbor at Apia, protecting the interests and property of their nations. A hurricane descended upon the harbor and destroyed six of the seven warships with a large loss of life. This event and the civil war determined the three Western countries to return to their deliberations and the conference on Samoan affairs was convened shortly thereafter in Berlin.

The stated primary objectives of the conference were to protect the interests of the Great Powers and to provide a workable government for Samoa. It is obvious that the primary purpose of the conference, however, was to secure the property and commercial privileges of Europeans in the country. There was no Samoan representation at the conference.

The nine-page act provided for the establishment of a supreme court presided over by a single judge, the chief justice of Samoa. He was to be named by the three powers with the Samoan government being given ostensible authority to ratify the appointment. The Apia municipality was reestablished. Provisions were made for the reorganization of public finance. The importation of arms and ammunition was prohibited. Alcoholic beverages were not to be sold or given to any Samoan or other islander.

The most useful provision of the act concerned itself with land claims. For a number of years various parties had claimed to have purchased land or to have other claims upon it which amounted to about twice the total land area of Samoa. A land commission was established to investigate these claims. Eventually it confirmed the foreign ownership of about 20 percent of the total land area of Samoa. The act also imposed strict provisions and regulations upon the further alienation of Samoan land. The effect of this provision was to diminish the political importance of land questions.

The real effect of the Berlin act was to establish a three-power condominium in Samoa, with Britain, Germany, and the United States governing through their consuls in Apia and the chief justice. This governing arrangement was obviously cumbersome, a factor which led to its short life. The act also failed to end traditional rivalries, and in 1893 the supporters of *Malietoa* Laupepa and *Mata'afa* Iosefa again went to war in a contest over ceremonial and political supremacy in Samoa. The inability of the new system to resolve these fundamental, traditional, political controversies ultimately wrecked the system established by the Berlin act. The consequence was the division of Samoa between Germany and the United States in 1901.

RELATED ENTRIES: American Samoa; Anglo-German Agreement of 1899; German Colonial Empire; United States in the Pacific; Western Samoa.

SOURCES AND READINGS: J. W. Davidson, *Samoa Mo Samoa: The Emergence of the Independent State of Western Samoa* (New York: Oxford University Press, 1967); R. P. Gilson, *Samoa 1830 to 1900: The Politics of a Multi-Cultural Community* (New York: Oxford University Press, 1970).   *Jerry K. Loveland*

BERNART, LUELEN (1866-1946). The first Micronesian to write a history of a Micronesian island, Luelen Bernart was born of noble blood in the Kitti kingdom of Ponape Island. He attended the American Protestant mission school at Oa in Madolenihmw where he studied English, mathematics, geography, the Bible, and world history. Bernart's ability to read and write distinguished him from most Ponapeans of his day. Plans to attend a religious seminary in Hawai'i were dropped at the insistence of his parents. Luelen then spent a good part of his life as a teacher in the mission schools and as an advisor and confidante to Henry Nanpei, the most prosperous Micronesian businessman of the late nineteenth and early

twentieth centuries. Luelen journeyed with Nanpei to Hong Kong and other Asian ports in 1896, a singular feat for Ponapeans in those days. During the Japanese administration of the island, Luelen served with distinction as a village chief. At the time of his death, he held the title of *Nansaurirrin*, the third highest in the Naniken's or prime minister's line. *The Book of Luelen* was written over a twelve-year period from 1934 to 1946 in several school notebooks. The last nineteen chapters of the manuscript were dictated by a weakened Luelen to his daughter Sarihna. The book contains many of the legends, myths, chants, and magical spells which form the basis for Ponapean culture and tradition. Reflecting Luelen's early religious training, the book follows an orderly sequence of events which, like the Bible, are divided into chapters and verses. The book offers a rough chronology of Ponapean times from the prehistoric migration of Pacific peoples to the German period (1900-1914). *The Book of Luelen* was discovered in 1947 by Saul Riesenberg, a former trust territory anthropologist and later senior ethnographer of the Smithsonian Institution. It was not until 1963, however, that Riesenberg was able to secure a copy. Fellow anthropologists John L. Fischer and Marjorie G. Whiting assisted in the translation and editing of the manuscript.

RELATED ENTRIES: Micronesia; Nanpei, Henry.

SOURCES AND READINGS: Luelen Bernart, *The Book of Luelen*, eds. Saul H. Riesenberg, John L. Fischer, and Marjorie G. Whiting (Honolulu: University Press of Hawaii, 1977); Kenji Imanishii, *The Island of Ponape: An Ecological Study* (Tokyo, 1944).
David L. Hanlon

BETEL NUT CHEWING. The practice of chewing betel nuts is characteristic of the Micronesian area but is most widely observed in Yap and Palau. The betel nut is picked rather green throughout the year. Small nuts are split open, some of the juicy center pulp removed with a knife or fingernail, and a pinch of lime (the caustic chemical) is added to the middle, after which the nut is wrapped in a piece of *kebui* leaf. Only one-half or one-third of the larger nuts are used at a time. Due to the scarcity of *kebui*, only a small portion is placed atop the lime part of the nut. Sometimes a piece of twist tobacco or cigarette is added. The combination is placed between the back molars and chewed.

The lime is white, the *kebui* green, and the betel nut is green-husked with a yellow or pinkish-yellow inside, but the juice one spits out when chewing the combination is a bright red. Evidently there is a factor in the betel nut-lime-*kebui* combination that acts as an indicator for alkali. The juice, when drooled on one's clothes, results in a stubborn stain which can be effaced by rubbing it immediately with lime (the fruit) juice, vinegar, or bleach.

Micronesians obtain lime by burning staghorn coral with hardwood. The calcium carbonate of the coral is converted to calcium hydroxide or quicklime. Too much lime in a chew can burn the mouth. *Kebui*, related to the pepper plant, is a creeping vine which grows around the trunks of tall, straight trees. When *kebui* is scarce, some villages require all persons who go about at night to identify themselves to a patrol whose members know where all *kebui* vines grow in the village and inspect them periodically. Rules apply to all persons within the village, and fines and punishments are levied on violators.

Claims that betel nuts have narcotic properties are groundless. Frequent chewing of betel nuts causes the teeth to become red. After many years of chewing, if a person has been negligent in cleaning his teeth, they will become quite black. There is no evidence that betel nut chewing causes or enhances tooth decay. It may even be beneficial in that the frequent presence of alkali in the mouth may neutralize the acids produced by oral bacteria which are responsible for tooth decay. Very old people who have lost most of their teeth carry a mortar and pestle with which they pulverize the ingredients of a chew before putting it in their mouths.

Some college parasitology texts state that the incidence of certain intestinal parasites among betel nut chewers is less than among nonchewers. This may be in part due to the possible effectiveness of the swallowed juice as a vermifuge and also to the fact that the constant spitting of chewers helps rid their throats of larval worms which otherwise would be swallowed.

Altogether, betel nut chewing in Micronesia is considered to be a healthful and pleasurable activity.

RELATED ENTRIES: Alcohol in the Pacific; Kava and Betel; Micronesia.

SOURCES AND READINGS: Dirk A. Ballendorf and Douglas Watts, "Betel-Nut Mania," *Micronesian Reporter* 16 (1968):30-31.

Dirk A. Ballendorf

BINGHAM, HIRAM (1789-1869). A pioneer missionary to Hawai'i, Bingham was born 30 October 1789 to Calvin and Lydia Bingham in Bennington, Vermont. Hiram graduated from Middlebury College in 1816 and attended Andover Theological School (1816-1819) to further his professional train-

ing. The American Board of Commissioners for Foreign Missions appointed Bingham and Asa Thurston to lead a mission to Hawai'i and there to construct a Christian commonwealth. Bingham married Sybil Moseley three weeks before the mission company sailed from Boston on 23 October 1819. To construct a Christian commonwealth, Bingham and his colleagues developed a written Hawaiian language and sought to influence the Hawaiian nobility. In 1822 the first Hawaiian grammar was published and Bingham began to preach in the vernacular. Attendance at the mission's schools and churches increased. Bingham's attempts to secure the nobility's favor were successful: when Ka'ahumanu and her husband, Kalanimoku, became regents in 1824 they proclaimed the establishment of moral law: the Sabbath was sacred and school attendance was encouraged. This mission victory did not go uncontested: throughout the 1820s, sailors and foreign residents bitterly opposed the mission's principles. Bingham's staunch defense earned the Hawaiians' favor and his colleagues' gratitude; by the end of the 1820s, his position was paramount. Bingham's stature within the mission began to deteriorate in the 1830s. This decline was in part a result of his dogmatic personality and in part due to factors beyond his control. The mission's successes brought it continual reinforcement by younger missionaries who were profoundly influenced by the American evangelical and temperance movements. Since their concerns differed from Bingham's, conflicts arose. When a Catholic mission was established in Honolulu (1837) the vision of a solely Protestant Hawai'i proved untenable. These changes shook Bingham's self-image and, when Sybil Bingham became ill in 1839, the family sailed to America. In retirement, Bingham published his autobiography *A Residence of Twenty-One Years in the Sandwich Islands* (1847) and eked out a penurious existence until his death on 11 November 1869.

RELATED ENTRIES: American Board of Commissioners for Foreign Missions; Hawai'i; Hawai'i, Religions of.

SOURCES AND READINGS: Gavan Daws, *A Shoal of Time: A History of the Hawaiian Islands* (New York: Macmillan Co., 1968); Frank L. Miller, "Fathers and Sons: The Binghams and American Reform, 1790-1970" (Ph.D. diss., Johns Hopkins University).

Frank L. Miller

BINGHAM, HIRAM (1875-1956). The third Hiram Bingham was born 19 November 1875 to the missionaries Clarissa and Hiram Bingham, Jr., in Honolulu,

Hawai'i. He attended Punahou School and graduated from Yale University (1899). Subsequently, he was superintendent of the Palama Chapel Mission, Honolulu. He left missionary service to study South American history at the University of California and Harvard (Ph.D., 1905). As director of the Yale Peruvian expedition (1911-1915), Bingham made the first ascent of Mount Corpuna and discovered the ruins of Machu Picchu and Vitcos, the last Inca capital. A Republican, Bingham's public career began when he was elected lieutenant governor of Connecticut in 1922. Two years later he became governor but only served two days: he resigned to fill the vacancy in the U.S. Senate left by Senator Bandagee's death in 1924. Bingham was elected to a full term in 1926. Because of his birthplace and his tenure as chairman of the U.S. Senate Territories and Insular Affairs Committee, Bingham was known as "Hawai'i's Senator." He sponsored legislation to aid his native state: he introduced bills to restructure Hawai'i's public debt, modernize leprosy treatment, introduce electricity to Moloka'i, and initiate a Pan-Pacific Conference. He also chaired the American Samoan Commission. Bingham lost his bid for reelection in 1932 due to his antiprohibition sentiments, his censure by the Senate for immoral and unethical conduct (1929), and a Democratic party electoral sweep. He later served as chairman of the Civil Service Loyalty Review Board (1951-1953). Bingham died in Washington, D.C., 6 June 1956.

RELATED ENTRIES: American Samoan Commission; Hawai'i; Hawai'i, Religions of.

SOURCES AND READINGS: Anna Roth, ed., *Current Biography 1951* (New York: H. W. Wilson & Co., 1951); *Congressional Record*, 1924-1933.

Frank L. Miller

BINGHAM, HIRAM, JR. (1831-1908). Born in Honolulu 16 August 1831 to missionary parents, Hiram and Sybil Bingham, Hiram Bingham, Jr. was educated at Yale and entered Andover Theological School in 1855. Although ill health forced him to leave school after eighteen months, the American Board of Commissioners for Foreign Missions selected him to lead a mission to the Gilbert Islands. He and his wife, Clarissa Brewster, sailed from Boston on the brig *Morning Star* in December 1856. The Binghams labored on Abaiang and neighboring islands for seven years. His efforts to introduce Christianity went largely unrewarded: the number of converts fluctuated yearly. He was strongly opposed to commerce but had little success in convincing his charges to shun worldly pursuits. His poor health

and Abaiang's negligible food supply interfered with his capacity to work. In 1864 the Binghams left the Gilberts for Hawai'i, where Hiram worked as corresponding secretary for the Hawaiian Evangelical Association and for the Hawaiian government as protector of South Seas immigrants. Bingham's most significant accomplishments were his translations of the New Testament (1873) and the complete Bible (1890) into Gilbertese. Among his many other accomplishments were a *Gilbert Island Bible Dictionary* (1895) and a Gilbertese dictionary (1908). After 1864 Bingham made infrequent visits to the Gilbert Islands from his Honolulu base. He captained the *Morning Star* on two voyages (1867 and 1868) but nearly died on one extended visit (1873-1874) and thereafter remained in Hawai'i. He died in Baltimore, Maryland, 25 October 1908 while attending to the publication of his Gilbertese dictionary.

RELATED ENTRIES: American Board of Commissioners for Foreign Missions; Hawai'i; Hawai'i, Religions of; Kiribati; *Morning Star*.

SOURCES AND READINGS: Bingham Family Papers, Yale University Library, New Haven, Conn.; Frank L. Miller, "Fathers and Sons: The Binghams and American Reform, 1790-1970" (Ph.D. diss., Johns Hopkins University).   *Frank L. Miller*

BISHOP, CHARLES REED (1822-1915). Educator, banker, philanthropist in Hawai'i, Charles Reed Bishop was born 25 January 1822 in Glen Falls, New York, to Samuel and Maria (Reed) Bishop. In February 1846 he left on a 231-day voyage to Oregon from Newburyport, Massachusetts, by way of Hawai'i. Arriving in Honolulu in October, he decided to stay. He married Bernice Pauahi, the daughter of Konia and Paki Pauahi. Working his way up from janitor, he eventually became owner and manager of the Bishop National Bank. He distributed much of his wealth to various schools, girls' and boys' homes, and churches. In 1873 he was on the Lunalilo board of education, became president, and held the position until he resigned in 1894. Bishop supervised and paid for the construction of a major portion of the Kamehameha schools. He was the trustee of the O'ahu College from 1867-1891. He started the Honolulu Library and the Hawaiian Historical Society, and in 1889 he established the Bernice P. Bishop Museum as a memorial to his wife, to which he donated all their personal artifact collections. His other activities involved him in the sugar industry, the Hawaiian Immigration Society, the O'ahu Railway and Land Company, the Pacific Cable, and the

YMCA. In 1894 he moved to California where he died at the age of ninety-three on 7 June 1915.

RELATED ENTRIES: Bishop Museum, Bernice P.; Hawai'i.

SOURCES AND READINGS: Harold Winfield Kent, *Charles Reed Bishop, Man of Hawaii* (Palo Alto, Calif.: Pacific Books, 1965).　　*Brenna J. Rash*

BISHOP MUSEUM, BERNICE P. The museum will be "... a scientific institution for collecting, preserving, storing and exhibiting specimens of Polynesian and kindred antiquities, ethnology, and natural history ... and the publication ... of the results. ..." (From the 1896 *Deed of Trust*, Bishop Museum)

The Bishop Museum celebrated its ninetieth anniversary in 1979. When Charles Reed Bishop considered a museum as a memorial to his wife, it was with a more restricted purpose than that expressed above. Chiefess Bernice Pauahi Bishop, last survivor of the founding dynasty of the Hawaiian monarchy, left her important ethnographic and historical items to her husband, one of Hawai'i's most successful businessmen and a leading philanthropist. These were soon augmented by similar materials left by Queen Emma (wife of Kamehameha IV) and the holdings of the inactive (Hawai'i) National Museum.

William Tufts Brigham, first curator and then (1898-1918) the first director, had a large role in extending the museum's mandate to include emphasis on natural history as well as cultural materials, to cover the Pacific area broadly, and to stress research and publication. Charles R. Bishop responded to Brigham's ideas; but Bishop did more, for his informed interest in the sciences directly influenced the museum's broad mandate. The museum has had only five directors after Brigham, each of whom significantly influenced its progress: Herbert E. Gregory (1919-1938), Peter H. Buck (1938-1951), Alexander Spoehr (1952-1961), Roland W. Force (1962-1976), and Edward C. Creutz (1977-).

Some biological materials also were acquired by Bishop even before the founding of the museum; exchanges with other institutions were begun as early as 1893, and a collector was sent to the south and west Pacific beginning in 1900. However, it was not until the 1920s and 1930s that the museum sponsored a number of large-scale expeditions to other parts of the Pacific. As one example, the Bayard Dominick Expedition (1920-1922) to Tonga, the Marquesas, and the Austral islands was planned in consultation with four American universities and museums and with leading anthropologists. The approach reflected the philosophy of Director Gregory who saw inter-institutional cooperation as essential in carrying out scientific exploration in the vast and changing Pacific. Gregory convened the First Pan-Pacific Scientific Conference in Hawai'i in 1920, which was the beginning of the Pacific Science Association and Congresses and of a continuingly active role of the museum in their proceedings.

The museum has continued to seek cooperation in Pacific research. For example, a program administered by the museum, the University of Hawai'i, and Yale University was funded in 1953 by the Carnegie Corporation and for eleven years supported work on cultural growth and social change. In 1961 a permanent New Guinea Field Station was established by the museum's Dr. J. Linsley Gressitt. In 1971 this was incorporated in Papua New Guinea as Wau Ecology Institute, with the museum as founding sponsor and Gressitt as director.

The museum is located on ten acres a few miles west of the center of Honolulu. The first building, which continues as the public entrance, was started in 1888 and was constructed of cut lava stone with beautifully carved koa wood interiors. Other buildings are Bishop Hall and Polynesian Hall (1894), Hawaiian Hall (1903), Paki Hall (1911), Konia Hall (1926), Planetarium and Science Center (1961), Pauahi Hall (1964), Hawai'i Immigrant Heritage Preservation Center (1977), and Atherton Halau (1980). Further construction is planned and is necessary to provide adequate space for collections, research, exhibits, and other needs and to bring the buildings into a fully integrated relationship.

Off-campus facilities include a museum ship, the *Falls of Clyde* (world's last surviving full-rigged, four-masted sailing ship), and a small branch in Waikiki. Since 1972 these have been made accessible through the museum's London, double-decker buses.

Through most of its history, the museum had largely overlapping trusteeship with the Bishop estate (the Kamehameha schools), despite the two being financially separate. In 1975 the Bishop Museum became a private charitable corporation with trustees representative of the community.

Collections and research are organized in five departments: anthropology, botany, entomology, history, and zoology. Zoology is subdivided into the divisions of malacology, invertebrate zoology, ichthyology, and vertebrate zoology. The library has the leading Pacific research collection in the Western Hemisphere.

The Bishop Museum Press has brought out 236 bulletins, 24 volumes of occasional papers, and 66 special publications, plus various miscellaneous publications and reports. Also issued through the press but edited within the departments are two publication series in anthropology and five in entomology.

The Bishop Museum is one of the leading American institutions maintaining collections and conducting research in natural and cultural history. The central Pacific location has contributed to this status and provides exceptional potential for development. In most cases, the collections are of the first order not only for Hawai'i but for the Pacific as a whole. Anthropological-historical artifacts number over 150,000 and biological specimens exceed 19,000,000. It is the quality, documentation, and use of these materials in research and education, including exhibits, that make the Bishop Museum an outstanding institution and the paramount museum of the Pacific.

RELATED ENTRIES: Bishop, Charles Reed; Buck, Peter Henry; Hawai'i.

SOURCES AND READINGS: Association of Systematics Collections *Newsletter* 7, no. 5 (October 1979): 40-47.
Frank J. Radovsky

BISMARCK AGREEMENT OF 1879. The Bismarck settlement was engineered in 1879 by the consuls of the Great Powers in Samoa and the commander of the German warship *Bismarck* then in port in Apia. Contending Samoan factions were threatening war with each other, and such a conflict was considered by the Western powers to be a threat to their interests. The agreement aimed at ending the civil war and establishing a more viable governmental order, one that could effectively rule in Samoa and guarantee the interests of the European residents. An agreement on 15 December ended hostilities between the two contending parties, and another on 23 December attempted to restructure the Samoan government. A shaky government had been established earlier at Mulinu'u but defectors from that government had instituted periodic warfare against it.

Under the terms of the constitutional portion of the agreement, Malietoa Talavou was to become the king or *Tupu*. Malietoa Laupepa was to serve as regent. An attempt was made to strengthen the Samoan parliament, (*Ta'imua* and *Faipule*). This group, consisting of representatives from the traditional districts in Samoa, was empowered under the terms of the agreement to enact laws which were to be binding upon all Samoa. Each district was to elect its own governor. The king or the regent was to have an absolute veto over legislation enacted by the *Ta'imua* and *Faipule*. A council consisting of members of the *Ta'imua* and *Faipule* was to be created to assist the king and the regent in enforcing the laws.

The new constitutional order never developed as the Great Powers had hoped it would. They had attempted to put the burden of governing Samoa upon the Samoans themselves, but the Samoans' internecine conflicts would not permit the establishment of a stable government. The agreement failed to resolve the fundamental disputes within the Samoan traditional system and before August 1880 a new war had erupted.

The foreign consuls had promised to protect the new government, but they insisted that the successor to the ailing Talavou should be acceptable to them. They also insisted that the king was to have an executive council of three Europeans who would conduct most of the important governmental functions of the government. These ministers were to be nominated and dismissed at the will of the consul of the minister's nationality. British and American objections to this system helped lead to the demise of the Bismarck Agreement.

RELATED ENTRIES: Anglo-German Agreement of 1899; Western Samoa.

SOURCES AND READINGS: J. W. Davidson, *Samoa Mo Samoa: The Emergence of the Independent State of Western Samoa* (New York: Oxford University Press, 1967); R. P. Gilson, *Samoa 1830 to 1900: The Politics of a Multi-Cultural Community* (New York: Oxford University Press, 1970). *Jerry K. Loveland*

BISMARCK ARCHIPELAGO. Encompassing more than 300 islands, the archipelago lies northeast of Papua New Guinea, just south of the equator. The islands include the Admiralty, Duke of York, Lavongai, and Mussau groups. The two largest are New Britain (land area 36,500 km²) and New Ireland (area 8,651 km²). The total land area is 48,640 km² (18,780 mi²), and the total population exceeds 220,000 Melanesians. The larger islands have forested mountains rising to 2,290 m (7,500 ft); New Britain has active volcanoes. Tropical agriculture is the chief source of income. Germany first claimed the islands in the archipelago in 1884. Australian troops captured them after the outbreak of World War I in 1914. In 1920 the League of Nations awarded the islands as a mandate to Australia. After World War II the islands were administered as part of the United Nations Trust Territory of New Guinea which in turn became in 1973 part of the self-governing Australian territory of Papua New Guinea which then became the independent country of Papua New Guinea in 1975.

RELATED ENTRY: Papua New Guinea.

SOURCES AND READINGS: R. Parkinson, *Im Bismarck-Archipel. Erlebnisse und Beoachtungen auf der Insel Neu-Pommern* (Leipzig: F. A. Brockhaus, 1887); Richard Salisbury, *Vunamami, Economical Transformation in a Traditional Society* (Berkeley: University of California Press, 1970).   *Frank P. King*

BLACKBIRDING. *See* Labor Trade; Melanesian Recruitment to Queensland, Patterns of; Melanesians and Colonial Servitude.

BLIGH, WILLIAM (1754-1817). An English admiral, born of a Cornish family, Bligh accompanied Captain Cook on his second expedition (1772-1774) as sailing master of the *Resolution*. During the voyage, breadfruit was found at Tahiti. Bligh saw service under Lord Howe and was later sent to the Pacific as commander of H.M.S. *Bounty*. Nicknamed "Breadfruit Bligh," he spent six months in Tahiti. He then sailed for the West Indies to introduce breadfruit there, but near Tonga a mutiny broke out on board the *Bounty* (28 April 1789), headed by the master's mate, Fletcher Christian. Bligh and eighteen loyal crewmen were set adrift in the ship's launch. Bligh and his companions suffered severely from hunger, thirst, and bad weather but survived a 5,820 km journey to Timor in the East Indies in the open boat. Bligh returned to England in 1790. Court-martial proceedings against Bligh ended in his being exonerated. He was later reassigned to the *Providence* in which he introduced the breadfruit into the West Indian islands. In 1797 he commanded the *Director* at the mutiny of the Nore, a sandbank at the mouth of the river Thames. Several ships of the British fleet were involved, and Bligh's ship was strikebound by mutineers. Afterwards, Bligh spoke up for and gained the release of nineteen of his crew. He was also involved in the battle of Camperdown, where the Dutch were defeated by Admiral Duncan. In 1801 he commanded the *Glatton* in the battle of Copenhagen, winning the personal commendation of Admiral Nelson. In 1805 Bligh was court-martialed for oppression and for the use of abusive language towards one of his junior lieutenants. He was reprimanded, although the case revealed that he demanded high standards and was harsh only on those he felt were shirking their duties. In 1806 he was appointed governor of New South Wales but was deposed in 1808 and held prisoner until 1810 by the mutineers who rebelled at his harsh exercise of authority. He returned to England in 1811 where he was promoted to rear admiral and in 1814 earned promotion again to vice admiral. An active, persevering, and courageous officer, Bligh died in London in 1817.

RELATED ENTRIES: *Bounty* Mutiny; Cook, (Captain) James; French Polynesia; Pitcairn Island.

SOURCES AND READINGS: Gavin Kennedy, *Bligh* (London: Duckworth, 1978); Geoffrey Rawson, *Bligh of the Bounty* (London: Philip Allen and Co., 1930).   *Vernice W. Pere*

BONIN ISLANDS. *See* Ogasawara Islands.

BOO, LEE (?-1784). Lee Boo was a personable Palauan youth who became well known throughout Europe in the late eighteenth century as a result of the publication of *An Account of the Pelew Islands* by George Keate. Lee Boo was born to a woman from Peleliu Island in southern Palau and subsequently adopted into the household of Ibedul, highest-ranking chief of Koror Island, Palau (Pelew).

Early on 10 August 1783 the English packet *Antelope*, commanded by Captain Henry Wilson, wrecked on reefs lying just southwest of Palau near Koror. Captain Wilson, his crew of thirty-two, and the sixteen Chinese passengers were helped by the people of Koror to build another vessel in which to sail to China. On 12 November 1783 the English departed Palau, taking Lee Boo with them. After visiting Macao and Canton, Lee Boo traveled with Wilson to England aboard the *Morse*, arriving at Portsmouth on 14 July 1784. Captain Wilson took him into his household at Rotherhithe for his entire stay in England. Shortly after Lee Boo's arrival, George Keate met him and was impressed by his lively countenance and instinctive good manners. Lee Boo studied reading and writing at an academy in Rotherhithe and was making good progress when his studies were interrupted by illness. He contracted smallpox in the middle of December and died on 27 December 1784. Keate's description of Lee Boo's life in England and his early death have inspired a number of authors from the late eighteenth century down to the present.

RELATED ENTRIES: Micronesia.

SOURCES AND READINGS: John Hockin, *A Supplement to the Account of the Pelew Islands* (London: G. Nichol, 1803); George Keate, *An Account of the Pelew Islands* (London, 1788).   *Mark L. Berg*

BORA BORA. *See* French Polynesia.

BORA BORA, U.S. MILITARY LIFE DURING WORLD WAR II. Many of the emotions men experience in war are as timeless and unchanging as war itself. Fear, courage, fatigue, boredom, and loneliness are encountered in some form in all wars. These conditions touched the lives of U.S. servicemen in the South Pacific during World War II but were influenced by many factors peculiar to that area of the globe.

U.S. military forces first came to Bora Bora in the early months of 1942. In the wake of the Pearl Harbor disaster and the Japanese advance into the South Pacific, this island in the Society group, midway between Australia and the Panama Canal, suddenly became essential to U.S. plans. American naval construction and defense troops were hastily dispatched to Bora Bora, code named "Bobcat," to establish a fueling depot needed to support the vital supply line to Australia and New Zealand.

On 17 February 1942 a 4,500-man U.S. occupation force arrived at Bora Bora and began base development operations that would be repeated on numerous other South Pacific islands. The army contingent, whose main units were the Second Battalion, 102d Infantry (Connecticut National Guard) and the 198th Coast Artillery Battalion, was charged with defending this outpost. More than 250 of the 500 navy personnel comprised elements of the First Naval Mobile Construction Battalion, the soon-to-be-famous Seabees. This unit was assigned the task of constructing the fuel depot, a seaplane base, and other necessary shore facilities.

Fully expecting a Japanese landing, the green soldiers spent tense, sleepless nights scanning the horizon for the as-yet-unbeaten enemy. The men, however, had little time to dwell on possible Japanese actions. During the day, work parties aided the navy in building gun emplacements and hauling eight 7-inch coastal guns 1,000 to 2,000 feet up forty-five-degree slopes to prepared positions. In addition, all hands were required to unload the six cargo ships of the Bobcat force, improve the island's one road, build dams to store scarce water, and construct supply shelters. As always in a military operation, field expediency was required to compensate for lapses in planning, faulty equipment, and inexperienced personnel. The difficulty of these tasks was increased immeasurably by the tropical climate of steamy heat and torrential downpours. The mud resulting from these rains often brought work to a standstill. A host of debilitating equatorial diseases such as malaria, elephantiasis, yaws, and dysentery also plagued the troops on Bora Bora. The final misery was provided by the ubiquitous mosquito. Under these conditions, apprehension about enemy action soon gave way to a concern for minimal comfort and a numbing fatigue.

By mid-1942 the frenetic activity of the first half of the year had subsided. Emergency measures were eventually superseded by the planned construction of the logistic complex. In June the fuel depot began pumping to waiting ships offshore and work on a seaplane ramp was started. At the end of September construction of defensive installations, fuel storage tanks, and other structures had been nearly completed. By the end of the year Bobcat was fully operating as the filling station of a growing armada of U.S. ships enroute to the South Pacific war. Bora Bora fueled many of the ships that took part in the battles in the Coral Sea and in the Solomon Islands.

As the war moved farther and farther from Bora Bora and the functioning of the logistic base became routine, the men of the army defense force and the naval facilities faced other problems common to war: loneliness and boredom. Isolated thousands of miles from home and family, the American serviceman on the island was restricted in contact with his known world. Unsurprisingly, mail call was the high point of his day. To compensate for the separation and prolonged absence from loved ones, many developed close, lifelong friendships with the other men of their units.

The problem of boredom was especially pronounced in the South Pacific environment. Confined to small islands in a vast ocean, the U.S. serviceman was unable to vary his existence significantly. On Bora Bora this was partially offset by the unadorned beauty of the setting. The verdant island rose sharply from the surrounding lagoon to the summit of 2,379-foot-high Mount Temanu. The island command also encouraged sports competitions, sponsored musical entertainment, and promoted other social activities. And those so inclined could swim and fish in Fanui Bay, play baseball, or join the ever-popular poker game. But even these distractions became routine. Bora Bora was typical of islands of the region in that it lacked most of the amenities found in the other theaters of the world. Shops, restaurants, and places of historic or cultural interest were simply nonexistent. Contact with the civilian population was limited because the Polynesians there were few in number and possessed a culture too dissimilar to that of the average American serviceman. It was not uncommon for soldiers or sailors to request reassignment to the forward area, as much to escape the ennui of island life as to fight the Japanese. Most men, however, endured this trial as their contribution to the common cause.

The army-navy advance-base-force command on Bora Bora continued to carry out its critical mission. After the construction in early 1943 of an airfield and assembly facilities for army fighter-aircraft staging to the forward area, the importance of the base gradually diminished. The army troops deployed westward in increments and the Seabees moved on to other building tasks. In the spring of 1944, with battles now raging far from the Society Islands, the Bora Bora base was placed in a reduced operating status. For over two years the men of the Bobcat force had provided the logistic support so essential to the U.S. victory over Japan in the broad expanse of the Pacific.

RELATED ENTRIES: French Polynesia; War in the Pacific Islands, 1914-1945.

SOURCES AND READINGS: Duncan S. Ballantine, *U.S. Naval Logistics in the Second World War* (Princeton: Princeton University Press, 1949); Richard M. Leighton and Robert W. Coakley, *Global Logistics and Strategy, 1940-1943* in *The War Department of United States Army in World War II* (Washington, D.C.: Office of the Chief of Military History, Department of the Army, 1955); Edward D. Marolda, Pvt., Co. E, Second Battalion, 102d Regiment, Connecticut National Guard, interview with author, Winsted, Conn., 29 January 1979; James A. Michener, "History of United States Naval Station Bora Bora, Society Islands of French Oceania," 9 July 1945, World War II Command File, Office of the Chief of Naval Operations, Operational Archives, Naval History Division, Washington, D.C.; U.S. Bureau of Yards and Docks, *Building the Navy's Bases in World War II: History of the Bureau of Yards and Docks and the Civil Engineering Corps, 1940-1946*, vol. 2 (Washington, D.C.: Government Printing Office, 1947).   *Edward J. Marolda*

BOUARATE (ca. 1815-1873). Bouarate, a great chief of the Hienghène tribe in New Caledonia at the time of European possession was known as Basset to the English. This well-known chief was active in early English trading and French colonization in New Caledonia. The Hienghène tribe was one of the largest (6,000-8,000 members) and most influential. From 1843 when the first Sydney-based English sandalwood traders anchored in Hienghène Bay until his death thirty years later, Bouarate was probably more important to Europeans than any other New Caledonian. Early English traders established good relations with Bouarate. He was the first New Caledonian to use a rifle, reportedly practicing his skill upon lowly members of his tribe. Bouarate traveled to Australia and New Zealand aboard English ships. Beginning in the early 1850s, he was hostile to French Marist missionaries and French sovereignty. In 1858 after several clashes, Bouarate was exiled to Tahiti until 1863. Upon his return, he became a close and loyal ally of the Guillain administration in New Caledonia until 1870.

RELATED ENTRIES: New Caledonia.

SOURCES AND READINGS: Bronwen Douglas, "Bouarate of Hienghène: Great Chief in New Caledonia" in Deryck Scarr, ed., *More Pacific Islands Portraits* (Canberra: Australian National University Press, 1979); Patrick O'Reilly, *Calédoniens* (Paris: Musée de l'Homme, 1953).   *Russell T. Clement*

BOUGAINVILLE, LOUIS ANTOINE DE (1729-1811). The French navigator Bougainville was born in Paris on 11 November 1729. Educated to be a lawyer, he became a soldier and then secretary to the ambassador to London where in 1756 he published his *Traité du calcul intégral* and was accepted as a member of the Royal Academy. He served with Montcalm in the French and Indian War where he was promoted to colonel. After the war, Bougainville was commissioned to conduct France's first around-the-world sea voyage. Leaving Brest, France, 5 December 1766 on the *Boudeuse*, he stopped at Rio de Janeiro, then rounded the Strait of Magellan into the Pacific. Here he discovered several Tuamotuan islands and on 2 April 1768 anchored on the eastern side of the island of Tahiti. Not knowing Samuel Wallis had just been there, Bougainville claimed the island for France. His description of this *Nouvelle Cythère* in his journal did more than any other single work to inflame European writers with the concept of the "noble savage." The Tahitian myth, the mirage of the South Seas, began to exercise its charm. After visiting several other Pacific islands, he returned home. Afterwards, he took part in the American Revolution under the command of the Count de Grasse. He returned to France to continue his scientific studies for which he was named a member of the institute (1795). Napoleon named him senator and then count. An island in the Solomons and the beautiful flowering vine *Boungainvillaea* have been named for him. He died in Paris on 31 August 1811.

RELATED ENTRIES: France in the Pacific; French Polynesia.

SOURCES AND READINGS: Charles la Concière, *A la gloire de Bougainville* (Paris: Nouvelle Revue Critique, 1942).   *Robert D. Craig*

BOUGAINVILLE (NORTH SOLOMONS) SECESSIONISM. The copper-rich island of Bougainville (renamed North Solomons) has sought self-determination from Papua New Guinea. On 1 September

1975, less than three weeks before Papua New Guinea itself was scheduled for independence from Australia, Bougainville leaders Leo Hannett and John Momis unilaterally declared the island's independence, which precipitated a major crisis that nearly led to civil war. This crisis had fundamental economic implications for Papua New Guinea. The copper mine on the island is one of the largest in the world. Conzinc Rio Tinto of Australia has invested over $500 million (Australian) to construct the open-cut facilities. When the world price for copper is moderate to high, as it was in 1974 and 1975, the mine can yield between $30-90 million (Australian) in revenues to the central government which depends on Australian foreign aid to meet about 40 percent of the Papua New Guinea annual budget. To lose the revenues from Bougainville would deepen Papua New Guinea's dependency on foreign aid for its survival. However, revenues apart, an independent Bougainville would encourage similar regional movements to challenge the authority of the central government, inevitably leading to the balkanization of the new nation. Intense negotiations between leaders on both sides of the conflict prevented impending warfare from erupting, but not before maximum internal autonomy was conceded to the separatists to run their own affairs.

Bougainville's disenchantment with the central government is attributable to several factors. First, the island is geographically and culturally part of the Solomon Islands archipelago. Bougainville was formally separated from the rest of the Solomons in territorial exchanges to settle a dispute between Germany and Britain in 1899. Bougainville then became a part of German New Guinea which in turn was taken by the Australians in 1914 during World War I. When decolonization of the colonial territory occurred in 1975, Bougainville was not returned to the Solomon Islands but was integrated into Papua New Guinea. The secessionists accuse the imperial powers of imposing "false unity" with a group of people different from them. Second, the separatists complain of the many years of isolation and neglect that their island suffered until copper was discovered in the mid-1960s. Third, they point to the discriminatory treatment their people experience from other Papua New Guineans. The Bougainvilleans are a jet-black people; they are disparagingly called "black bastards." They, in turn, refer to all non-Bougainvilleans as "red skins." Because they are a small minority of only 85,000 people in relation to Papua New Guinea's total population of some 2,990,757, they would be permanently disadvantaged in trying to protect their interests against superior numbers in the parliament. Thus, they could fall prey to the prejudices of an intolerant majority via internal colonialism. Finally, Bougainville's leaders point to the lack of consultation in the construction of the mine. A large number of people were virtually evicted from their traditional land, and the activities of the mine have led to increased crime, juvenile delinquency, and social disruption generally. In addition, large numbers of unemployed "red skins" have entered their small island (155 km²), squatted on traditional land, and allegedly undermined law and order. The physical operations of the mine have also caused massive ecological damage and dislocations. The secessionists feel that since they and their people are directly affected by the disruptive aspects of the mine, then they must be allocated a large share of the benefits in jobs, royalties, and other revenues. It was the latter issue that triggered the open conflict between Bougainville and the central government in 1975.

Sustained and organized activities for Bougainville secession were initiated in 1968 by Leo Hannett and other Bougainville students attending the University of Papua New Guinea. Much of the impetus that supported the claims for self-determination has come from educated Bougainvilleans. The people of Bougainville, themselves, have rallied with virtually complete solidarity behind their leaders. The objective complaints have been temporarily appeased, but they may change and become more intractable over time. The threat of secession to compel the central government to make concessions is Bougainville's best bargaining weapon. In this respect, Bougainville (North Solomons) will continue to be a difficult problem for future governments of Papua New Guinea.

RELATED ENTRIES: British New Guinea; Papua Besena; Papua New Guinea; Papua New Guinea, Decentralization and Provincial Government; Papua New Guinea, Government and Political System; Papua New Guinea, Mixed-Race People in.

SOURCES AND READINGS: Leo Hannett, "The Case for Bougainville Secession," *Meanjin Quarterly*, Spring, 1975 pp. 285-95; Ralph R. Premdas, "Ethnonationalism, Copper, and Secession in Bougainville," *Canadian Review of Studies in Nationalism*, Spring, 1977 pp. 247-65.   *Ralph R. Premdas*

BOUNTY **MUTINY.** In 1787 the British Admiralty commissioned Lt. William Bligh (1754-1817) to sail the *Bounty* to Tahiti to secure cuttings of the tropical breadfruit tree and to transport them to the West

Indies where they were to become a staple food for the black slaves. Of the forty-five seamen aboard, only fourteen were experienced sailors; the *Bounty* was extremely small, and there were no marine troops assigned to help maintain order as usually was the case. Attempts to round the stormy Cape Horn (South America) failed, and the *Bounty* was forced eastward via South Africa. The storms, gales, cold, snow, and lack of experienced hands added to Bligh's short temper. Although his men complained of bad food and stern discipline, Bligh's conduct was no harsher than the average commander of his time. Arriving in Tahiti (October 1788), he and his crew gathered approximately one thousand thriving shoots of the breadfruit plant. Spending five months in the leisurely, free life of Polynesia, his men became disgruntled at the naval discipline reestablished once they set sail. On the morning of 28 April 1789, Fletcher Christian, master's mate, convinced seventeen crewmen to mutiny against the "tyranny" of Bligh's command. Bligh and eighteen "loyalists" were forced into a small launch on the open seas. After stopping in Tahiti for supplies and women, Fletcher and crew chose to settle on the island of Tubuai. The Tubaians, however, proved hostile and after another stop in Tahiti (where several mutineers and other loyalists disembarked), they sailed on to Pitcairn Island where they finally burned the *Bounty* and hoped to lead a peaceful Polynesian life-style. Arguments over the lack of women broke out between the Polynesians and the crew. All of the men except one, Alexander Smith, were murdered. When the survivors were "discovered" in 1808, there were thirty-five people on the island: Smith, eight women, and twenty-six children, all descendants of the *Bounty* mutineers. Captain Bligh along with his men made a harrowing and unbelievable 5,820 km journey in the small boat to the East Indies where they gained passage to England. In a court-martial hearing, Bligh was exonerated and promoted to captain. In March 1791, the mutineers on Tahiti were captured by Captain Edwards of the *Pandora*. A trial in London found six of them guilty (two finally were pardoned, one freed, and three hanged). Public opinion against Bligh was expressed in a series of popular pamphlets although the court never found him guilty of any flagrant abuses. Bligh continued a tumultuous career. He served with Nelson in 1801, was reprimanded in a second court martial in 1804, and then appointed governor of New South Wales (Australia) in 1806. He finally returned to England where he died in 1817. Bligh successfully carried out a second mission to Tahiti to gather breadfruit starts (1791-1793), but the irony of the whole affair is that the slaves in the West Indies did not like the breadfruit and refused to eat it.

RELATED ENTRIES: Bligh, William; French Polynesia; Pitcairn Island.

SOURCES AND READINGS: Bent Danielsson, *What Happened on the Bounty* (London: G. Allen & Unwin, 1962); George Mackaness, *The Life of Vice-Admiral William Bligh* (Sydney: Angus & Robertson, 1931).
Robert D. Craig

BOVIS, EDMOND DE (1818-1870). A French naval officer, Bovis' research and writings on ancient Tahitian life became an invaluable source for later historians and ethnographers. Bovis was born in southern France on 15 July 1818. He entered naval school and became a sailor. In 1843 he left on the ship *Phaeton* for the South Pacific where he spent five years making hydrographic studies. He returned to France between 1848 and 1859 and then returned to Tahiti for another six years. In September 1853 Bovis was an important member of the French command that sailed to New Caledonia and took possession of the island for the French government. He returned to France in 1854. The following year his writings concerning his research into ancient Tahitian life appeared: "L'état de la Société Tahitienne à l'arrivée des Européens," *Revue Coloniale*, Paris. His essay appeared frequently in the *Annuaire de Tahiti* until published in a single volume in 1909. Bovis' work is indispensable in studying ancient Tahitian society.

RELATED ENTRIES: French Polynesia; Henry, Teuira; New Caledonia.

SOURCES AND READINGS: Robert D. Craig, ed. and trans., *Tahitian Society before the Arrival of the Europeans by Edmond de Bovis*, 2d ed. (Laie, Hawaii: Institute for Polynesian Studies, 1980); Patrick O'Reilly, *Tahitiens* (Paris: Musée de l'Homme, 1962).
Robert D. Craig

BRIGHAM YOUNG UNIVERSITY—HAWAI'I CAMPUS. Formerly called the Church College of Hawai'i, BYU—Hawai'i Campus is an accredited four-year, coeducational institution sponsored by the Church of Jesus Christ of Latter-day Saints (Mormons). It was established in 1955 in the town of La'ie on the windward shore of O'ahu, thirty-eight miles from Honolulu.

The main purpose of BYU—Hawai'i Campus is to help students develop academic excellence, professional/vocational competence, and Christlike character. With its central location in the Pacific Basin, the university assumes a special responsibility to prepare qualified men and women who can live, serve, and contribute in Hawai'i, the South Pacific, and East Asia. To this end, the university uses both campus and off-campus location as appropriate in providing learning experiences.

On 21 July 1954, David O. McKay, the president of the church, announced the intent of the church to establish a college in Hawai'i. Following a survey with recommendations concerning the location and nature of the institution, groundbreaking services for the new campus were held on 12 February 1955. In September 1955, 153 students enrolled in the first academic school year as a junior college. Temporary facilities were used until permanent buildings could be constructed. The new facilities were completed and dedicated in December 1959. In July 1959 the third and fourth years were added to make it a four-year, degree-granting college. On 1 July 1974, by decision of the board of trustees, the Church College of Hawai'i was renamed the Brigham Young University—Hawai'i Campus and became administratively associated with Brigham Young University in Provo, Utah.

The following individuals have served as presidents of the Church College of Hawai'i and Brigham Young University—Hawai'i Campus for the periods designated: Reuben D. Law, 1955-1958; Richard T. Wootton, 1958-1964; Owen J. Cook, 1964-1971; Stephen L. Brower, 1971-1974; Dan W. Andersen, 1974-1980; and J. Elliot Cameron, 1980-.

The student body has increased from its original 153 students in 1955 to 1800 students in 1980. Thirty-two different countries are represented at BYU—Hawai'i Campus. Thirty percent of its students come from Hawai'i; 25 percent from the various South Pacific island groups (notably Fiji, Tonga, Tahiti, New Zealand, American Samoa, and Western Samoa); 15 percent from the Asian Rim (notably Japan, Korea, Hong Kong, Taiwan, Philippines, Thailand, and Singapore); and the remaining 30 percent from the United States mainland, Canada, and other countries throughout the world. Ninety-five percent of the students are members of the Church of Jesus Christ of Latter-Day Saints. The majority of the students are from nonaffluent backgrounds and as a consequence about 80 percent hold part-time jobs while they are in school.

Because of its geographical location in the Pacific Basin, the school from its outset has assumed a special responsibility to present programs aimed at the specific needs of students from Hawai'i, the South Pacific, and the Asian Rim. A two-year associate program is available with eleven subject areas offered, including travel and tourism management, industrial

studies, and agriculture. At the bachelor's level, B.A. and B.S. majors are offered in twenty-two subject areas in the following six academic divisions: behavioral and social science; business; communications and language arts; education; fine arts; mathematics, natural science, and technology. In addition to the above-mentioned, the BYU—Hawai'i Campus makes available its resources on a statewide and international basis through its Continuing Educational Division. There are now ninety-five full-time and part-time faculty members at BYU—Hawai'i Campus. Forty-eight percent of the full-time faculty hold doctor's degrees. The staff is composed of 164 members who are employed in twenty-four divisions and departments. The campus occupies 218 acres. Student residence halls provide housing for 1,150 single students and 202 family units for married students and their families. At the center of the campus academic activity is the new two-story Joseph F. Smith library and media center. An integral part of the agricultural program of the Hawai'i Campus is a 150-acre tropical agricultural farm with a large variety of tropical fruits and vegetables cultivated by students in the program.

Adjacent to the campus is the Polynesian Cultural Center, constructed in 1963 for the dual purpose of helping to preserve and display the various Polynesian cultures and providing jobs for approximately 800 students at the university. The BYU—Hawai'i Campus and the Polynesian Cultural Center jointly sponsor the Institute for Polynesian Studies. The primary work of the institute is the sponsoring of scholarly research into Polynesian cultures which has resulted in the publishing of a journal called *Pacific Studies* as well as other scholarly works.

RELATED ENTRIES: Education in the Pacific, Higher; Polynesian Studies, Institute for; Polynesian Cultural Center.

SOURCES AND READINGS: *Brigham Young University —Hawai'i Campus General Catalog, 1980-1981* (Laie, Hawaii, Brigham Young University—Hawaii Campus, 1980).   *Dan W. Andersen*

BRITAIN IN THE PACIFIC. The growth of the British Empire in the Pacific displayed the same basic characteristics as in North America, earlier, and in Africa, later. It combined the maximum of acquisition with the minimum of enthusiasm. Initial forays were disarmingly casual. Manila was seized in 1762 in the course of a war with Spain but was handed back at the end of hostilities. Samuel Wallis annexed Tahiti for George III on 17 June 1767. It was reannexed by Louis Bougainville for France nine months later, by

Gayangos for Spain in 1774, and by James Cook again for England in 1777. It was the French annexation that stuck. But Cook had in the meantime, on 22 August 1770, claimed for King George a continent, Australia, almost as large as the United States and inhabited by a conveniently small, scattered, and effectively defenseless indigenous population. With Australia in their hands, the British could hardly help becoming eventually the dominant power in the Pacific Ocean.

It was, nonetheless, a surprisingly long time before they decided actually to do something with their vast new acquisition. The loss of the American colonies in 1783 finally inspired the British government, on 13 May 1787, to ship out to Australia convicts for whom the Carolinas in America were no longer available as depositories. The need to provide food and other basic requirements for the rapidly growing number of jailbirds and their guards led to the development of trading links with Tahiti. By the dawn of the nineteenth century, New South Wales had become the epicenter of Western influence in the region. Economic domination did not, however, lead to the extension of British political control. Captain George Vancouver was under the impression that Kamehameha I of Hawai'i had accepted British sovereignty on 25 February 1794. Kamehameha I himself had other ideas, and the government in London was not prepared to argue the point.

It was indeed not until seventy years after Cook annexed Australia that the British formally took possession of more territory in the Pacific. Their choice this time was in fact the next largest island group in the region, marginally more extensive than the entire United Kingdom and at least as suitable for European colonization. Captain William Hobson secured the signatures of the Maori chiefs of the North Island of New Zealand in February 1840 to a treaty accepting Queen Victoria as their sovereign and himself as their governor, and proclaimed British authority over the whole group, without further formality. The move was inspired partly by the urgent demands of the missionary societies to have New Zealand reserved for their own activities before France and the Roman Catholic Church could establish a claim and partly by the fear that the Australian colonies were not going to prove economically viable.

This was more than enough, as far as London was concerned. Having made sure of the vast landmasses of the region, it was content to leave the rest to the French and to anybody else who might be interested. This was not the attitude of the colonists themselves. The New Zealanders clamored for Fiji, Tonga, and Samoa. The Australians wanted Samoa and the New

Hebrides and New Caledonia before the French could take them. The British government did indeed accept reluctantly the cession of Fiji from the engagingly incompetent tyrant Cakobau and his Tongan mayor of the palace, Ma'afu, on 10 October 1874, after the endemic anarchy of the group had reached a point at which Western intervention had become unavoidable. They continued, however, to resist Australasian demands for the New Hebrides, and they annexed the south coast of eastern New Guinea in 1884 only after the Germans had seized the north, following an attempt by the Queensland colonial government to take over the whole territory. New Zealand was allowed to acquire tiny Rarotonga in 1891 because nobody else wanted it and because the Rarotongans were ethnically linked with the New Zealand Maoris. New Zealand and Australia then renewed their demands for the New Hebrides, and the colonial government of Victoria hatched a plot to seize the group with their own defense forces. London and Paris solved the immediate problem in 1906 by agreeing on a Franco-British condominium. The system erected looked as if it had been deliberately designed not to work. Each of the two administering powers appointed its own high commissioner, its own resident commissioner, and its own police force. No indigene was allowed to have either British or French nationality. A joint court was established to deal with cases involving both the administering powers. It had a Spanish judge and Dutch officials to ensure impartiality, but its proceedings had to be conducted in either French or English, or both. It would have been difficult to conceive a more effective deterrent to litigation.

World War I resulted in the acquisition of German New Guinea by the Australians and of Samoa by the New Zealanders. The change was immediately disastrous for the Samoans at least, who lost a quarter of their population from pulmonary influenza, largely because of the total failure of the New Zealand authorities to cope effectively with the epidemic.

During the interwar period, the former imperial territories gradually exchanged the United States for Britain as guarantor of their security and as the acknowledged leader in the Pacific region. At issue was the specter of Japanese expansion in the Pacific. The British recognized that the tensions between their commitments and their capabilities in Europe and the Pacific had never been so great. Australia and New Zealand redoubled their efforts to obtain a specific British guarantee as a basis for Pacific security. The British refused until March 1939 to examine critically this vital aspect of imperial strategy. By this time, the opportunity for reflective analysis had passed and suspicions had become rooted. The era of Britain as the guarantor of security for her Pacific dominions was ended.

The new imperialists had gained considerably in maturity by the end of World War II. The Labour governments in Australia and New Zealand resolutely claimed a role as protecting powers and indeed as the heirs of British colonialism in the South Pacific because of the demonstrated incapacity of the British and other European colonial powers to protect their island possessions against the Japanese thrust. The major administrative consequence of this assertion of responsibility by Canberra and Wellington was the creation of the South Pacific Commission, to be financed 30 percent by Australia, 15 percent each by New Zealand, the United Kingdom, and the Netherlands, and 12.5 percent each by the United States and France.

There is no doubt that the Australians and New Zealanders displayed a far more responsible approach to the dismantling of their authority over the island peoples than they ever had to its extension. Having largely bailed the Samoans out of their immediate economic problems, the New Zealand government told them in 1959 that they could have full independence whenever they wanted it. Samoa in fact became fully independent in 1962. Its first action as a free state was to contract a treaty of friendship with New Zealand, under which their former rulers effectively agreed to perform free of charge any service which the Samoans required of them in the conduct of their international relations. The Cook Islands acquired self-government in 1965, with the blessings of common citizenship with New Zealand and an annual subsidy of $1.5 million. Australia, which had taken over Nauru from the British in 1947, granted full independence and a guarantee of financial assistance in 1968. Papua New Guinea became formally independent on 16 September 1975 with the assurance that it would continue to receive the lion's share of Australia's foreign aid program. One might well have anticipated the dimmest of political futures for a territory the majority of whose inhabitants are still literally living in the Stone Age, and who had experienced sixty-nine years of colonial rule by a people whose traditional attitude towards indigenes has been reasonably described as one of exclusion, exploitation, and extermination. Papua New Guinea has, however, remained impressively stable since independence and has even achieved an orderly and nonviolent change of government, something beyond the capacity of many older nations, more readily identifiable with the twentieth century.

London had meanwhile negotiated the tricky process of granting independence to Fiji in 1970. The Solomon Islands achieved independence on 7 July 1978 and were rewarded by the Australian government with the gift of a patrol boat a year later. Not surprisingly, the one area where the course of British withdrawal encountered a real snag was the New Hebrides, where the condominium maintained its track record of engineered chaos until the end. Independence was granted by London and Paris on 30 July 1980. An insurrection, armed mainly with sticks and umbrellas, occurred, however, on the island of Espiritu Santo on 29 May 1980 apparently directed against the governing party of the Reverend Walter Lini. The French sent in *Gardes Mobiles*. The British sent in the Royal Marines. The French then protested the presence of the marines and withdrew the *Gardes Mobiles*. Later, shortly before independence was in fact granted, the *Gardes* returned, but not before the British were involved in complicated negotiations with all sides.

The United Kingdom has now for practical purposes left the Pacific. Its withdrawal was infinitely more orderly and conciliatory than that of the Dutch or the Portuguese. The British presence, as inherited by Australia and to a far lesser extent New Zealand, is, moreover, more dominant than ever. The former Australasian colonies are still overwhelmingly the centers of population and production in Oceania. Australia's growing acceptance of its role as protecting power has also led to the establishment of low-key but extensive defense links with Tonga, the Solomons, and Fiji, as well as with Papua New Guinea. The British may have been unenthusiastic about going to the Pacific. Their impact on its destiny has, however, been far greater than that of any other intruders, including for practical purposes even that of the original Polynesian adventurers themselves.

RELATED ENTRIES: American Samoa; Fiji; French Polynesia; Nauru; Papua New Guinea; Solomon Islands; South Pacific Commission; South Pacific Forum; Tonga; Vanuatu (New Hebrides); Western Pacific High Commission; Western Samoa.

SOURCES AND READINGS: Glen St. J. Barclay, *The Empire Is Marching* (London: Weidenfeld and Nicolson, 1976); John C. Beaglehole, *The Exploration of the Pacific* (London: Black, 1966); Carolyn A. O'Brien, "Australia's Achievement in Regional Defense Planning 1919-44" (Ph.D. diss., University of Queensland, 1978); Angus Ross, *New Zealand Aspirations in the Pacific in the Nineteenth Century* (London: Oxford University Press, 1964); Christopher Thorne, *The Limits of Foreign Policy: The West, the League and the Far Eastern Crisis of 1933-1937* (London: Macmillan & Co., 1972); John M. Young ed., *Australia's Pacific Frontier* (Melbourne: Cassell, 1967).

Glen St. J. Barclay
Carolyn A. O'Brien

BRITISH NEW GUINEA (1884-1906). In 1884 the British government acceded to Australian demands and declared a protectorate over the south coast of eastern New Guinea. Financed by colonial contributions, it was administered by a special commissioner under the authority of the Western Pacific Order in Council. Before his death Sir Peter Scratchley, the first commissioner, established an administrative center at Port Moresby. His successor, John Douglas, created a rudimentary administration and began some exploration.

In 1887 Britain annexed the territory as the Crown Colony of British New Guinea. Dr. William Mac-Gregor of Fiji became its administrator, working under loose supervision by the governor of Queensland. He reached Port Moresby in September 1888, rapidly reorganized the administration, and began the primary tasks of exploration and pacification. By demonic energy and almost constant movement in the government steamer *Merrie England*, he completed much of this work but was unable to do much more because of financial limitations. Knighted in 1889 and promoted to lieutenant governor in 1895, he was succeeded in 1898 by George Le Hunte.

Soon after Australia federated, administration of New Guinea was transferred to Australia by letters patent which gave the governor-general the supervisory role carried out hitherto by the governor of Queensland until the Australian government provided a constitutional act. A bill introduced on 15 July 1903 was opposed by enthusiastic reformers and, because of unstable governments, was not passed for another two years. After two unwise temporary appointments as administrator, the territorial administration almost disintegrated. Eventually, administrator Francis R. Barton asked for a Royal commission.

The commissioners arrived late in 1906 and, in a series of public hearings, found that the administration was riven by bitter personal feuds. The incumbent, Francis R. Barton, believed in British ideals of managing the country for the benefit of the inhabitants but was an incompetent administrator guilty of blatant favoritism. John H. P. Murray urged Australian ideas of economic development, using force without hesitation where necessary. Partly because of Murray's strong personality and forensic skill, the commissioners accepted his point of view. Barton and a number of his friends were retired, and Murray became acting administrator of British New Guinea under its new name, the Australian Territory of Papua. Government of the territory was formally accepted by Australia on 1 September 1906.

RELATED ENTRIES: Barton, Francis R.; MacGregor, William; Monckton, Charles A. W.; Murray, John H. P.; Papua New Guinea; Port Moresby; Scratchley, Peter H.

SOURCES AND READINGS: R. B. Joyce, *Sir William MacGregor* (Melbourne: Oxford University Press, 1971); J. A. La Nauze, *Alfred Deakin: A Biography* (Melbourne: Melbourne University Press, 1965); F. West, *Hubert Murray: The Australian Pro-consul* (Melbourne: Melbourne University Press, 1968).

H. J. Gibbney

BROMILOW, WILLIAM EDWARD (1857-1929). A Methodist missionary in British New Guinea (1891-1908), Bromilow was born at Geelong, Australia, on 15 January 1857. After an education at a private school and at Melbourne University, he taught in a primary school at Queenscliff in Victoria. He became a probationer in the Methodist church at the age of twenty-one and a year later volunteered for the Methodist mission field. In 1879, after marrying Harriet Lilly Thomson, the daughter of American settlers in Australia, he left Sydney aboard the mission brig *John Wesley* for the Fiji Islands where he worked as a circuit minister until 1889.

Bromilow's experience in Fiji was of considerable value in preparing him for the oversight of a large mission. After a short term in Victoria, he was chosen in 1890 to lead the Australasian Wesleyan Methodist Missionary Society's mission to the newly annexed colony of British New Guinea. He left Sydney on 27 May 1891 in a chartered labor vessel, the *Lord of the Isles*, with a party for New Guinea and New Britain numbering about seventy people, including twenty-two teachers, twelve wives, and seven children from Fiji, Samoa, and Tonga.

Because of its strategic position, as well as the desire of the administrator, William MacGregor, to put down raiding and fighting, the island of Dobu in the D'Entrecasteaux group was selected as the center of missionary operations. The teachers were soon dispersed to East Cape, Fergusson Island, and the Engineer group, and strongholds of mission influence were later established in Kiriwina, Woodlark (Murua), Misima, and other islands. For fifteen years Bromilow directed the expansion of the Methodist mission from Dobu until shortage of land on Dobu made necessary the removal of the head station to Ubuia at the southwestern end of Normandy Island.

In 1908 Bromilow and his wife retired from the mission and accepted a circuit in New South Wales. The difficulties of the Methodist church in Papua during the ensuing period were attributable partly to Bromilow's withdrawal. In 1920 after holding various appointments in Sydney, Bromilow and his wife once again volunteered for the Papua mission. After serving a second term as chairman of the district and continuing his scriptural translations, he left Papua finally in 1924. The Reverend M. K. Gilmour succeeded Bromilow as chairman at the end of each of his terms.

Bromilow died in Sydney on 24 June 1929. His main achievements were the organization of large mission circuits in Fiji and British New Guinea. His interest in Melanesian languages bore fruit in his Dobuan grammar, catechism, and the Dobuan Bible, which had been compiled in collaboration with a Papuan student, Eliesa Duigu. In his theological position, Bromilow was liberal by nineteenth-century Methodist standards, but in moral questions he was uncompromising. In spite of his published ethnological studies of Papuan life, he tended to sympathize with less experienced missionaries who disapproved strongly of many features of Papuan culture, and his influence led to the discouragement of those social practices which appeared to conflict with the moral teachings of contemporary Methodism. However, at a personal level Bromilow's relations with the Dobuans appear to have been benign. He was accepted into a Dobuan clan and was member of the *kula* exchange circle. Known to the Dobuans as *Saragigi* ("he who twists out his teeth"), he was believed to be the embodiment of supernatural prowess and is commonly held to have been responsible for the cessation of tribal fighting in Methodist mission areas. The survival in legends of Bromilow's achievements bears testimony to his impact on the folk memories of the people of the D'Entrecasteaux.

RELATED ENTRIES: British New Guinea; MacGregor, William; Papua New Guinea.

SOURCES AND READINGS: British New Guinea, *Annual Report 1889-90 to 1905-06*; William E. Bromilow, *Iesu Keriso* (Sydney, 1894); *Buki Tapuaroro* (Geelong, 1898); *Vocabulary of English Words, with Equivalents in Dobuan (British New Guinea), Fijian, and Samoan, with a Short Dobuan Grammar* (Geelong, n.d.); "Some Manners and Customs of the Dobuans of Southeastern Papua" in *Report of the Twelfth Meeting of the Australasian Association for the Advancement of Science, 1909* (Sydney, 1909); "New Guinea," in J. Colwell, ed., *A Century in the Pacific* (Sydney, 1914); *Twenty Years among Primi-*

tive Papuans (London, 1929); Methodist Church of Australasia, *Overseas Missions Papers* (Mitchell Library); Michael W. Young, "Doctor Bromilow and the Bwaidoka Wars," *Journal of Pacific History* 12 (1977):130-53.

David Wetherell

BROOKE, JOHN MERCER (1826-1906). John Brooke was an officer in the United States Navy, a senior astronomer and hydrographer with the United States North Pacific-Bering Straits-China Seas Expedition (1852-1855), and commander of an expedition to explore and survey a steamship route from San Francisco to China, passing through the region of Oceania. Born in Tampa, Florida, on 18 December 1826, Brooke was descended from a family established in Maryland as early as 1650. His father was a brevet major-general in the U.S. Army who had served with distinction in the War of 1812. In 1841 Brooke entered the navy as a midshipman. After four years of service he entered the newly established naval academy at Annapolis, graduating in 1847. His naval experience included service with the African, Brazilian, Mediterranean, and Pacific squadrons, as well as with the coast survey. He was the inventor of an innovative deep-sea sounding device known as the Brooke lead for which he received a scientific gold medal from the Berlin Academy in 1860. While on duty at the Naval Observatory in Washington, D.C., he was ordered to join the United States North Pacific-Bering Straits-China Seas expedition. Upon the return of this expedition to the United States in 1855, he went to Washington, D.C., to prepare scientific data for publication and in 1858 received orders to take command of the U.S.S. *Fenimore Cooper* for the purpose of charting a steamship route between San Francisco and China.

On 26 September 1858 the *Fenimore Cooper* sailed from San Francisco with a crew of twenty men. By 9 November 1858 Brooke had reached Honolulu, surveying and charting on the way. On 29 December 1858 Brooke started to survey the area to the northwest of Honolulu and took possession for the United States of the islet called French Frigate Shoals. Other islands visited were Johnson Island, Gaspar Rico or Smyth's Island, and Cabras Island in the outer reaches of San Luis d'Apra on Guam in the Marianas. Deep-sea soundings were made off Luzon, one to a depth of 3,300 fathoms. On the return voyage Brooke stopped at Kanagawa Bay near Yokohama. While there, a typhoon hit the area and the *Fenimore Cooper* was beached to prevent her sinking. Salvage operations proved unsuccessful and Brooke returned to the United States as a passenger in the Japanese war steamer *Kanrin Maru*, arriving at San Francisco on 17 March 1860. When the Civil War broke out he joined the Confederacy and his name was stricken by the president from the rolls of the United States Navy. During the Civil War Brooke served with distinction in the Confederate Navy. From 1865 to 1899 he held an appointment as professor of physics and astronomy at the Virginia Military Institute. He died at Lexington, Virginia, on 14 December 1906.

RELATED ENTRIES: United States in the Pacific.

SOURCES AND READINGS: "Annual Report of the Secretary of the Navy, 2 December 1859," *Congressional Globe*, 36th Cong., 1st sess., 1859 app.: 16-17. George Mercer Brooke, Jr., "John Mercer Brooke, Naval Scientist" (Ph.D. diss., University of North Carolina, 1955).   *Vincent Ponko, Jr.*

BRUAT, ARMAND JOSEPH (1796-1855). The first governor of French Oceania, Bruat was born in Colmar (Alsace), France. He entered the French Naval College in 1811, served as an officer on several vessels, and distinguished himself at the Battle of Navarino in 1827 and at the conquest of Algeria by the French in 1830. Appointed French Commissary to Queen Pomare IV of the Society Islands in 1843, he became the first governor of the French Establishments of Oceania. A difficult situation awaited him there on account of the rivalry between the English and French interests in the area, remembered as "The Pritchard Affair." Bruat had George Pritchard, the English consul, expelled from Tahiti in 1844. With skill and determination, he suppressed a Tahitian uprising encouraged by Queen Pomare IV who had fled to the island of Ra'iatea. After the return of peace in 1846 and at the queen's request, he brought her back to Tahiti and restored her as a ruler under French protectorate in 1847. He left shortly thereafter. Bruat was made a Great Officer in the Legion of Honor and continued serving his country in various capacities. During the Crimean War, he was made an admiral. He died at sea, but was buried in France. Auguste Bartholdi, his fellow townsman and creator of the Statue of Liberty, designed a monument to him in Colmar. One of Pape'ete's main streets is now Avenue Bruat.

RELATED ENTRIES: French Polynesia; Pomare Family; Pritchard, George.

SOURCES AND READINGS: Georges Benoit-Buyod, *Bruat, amiral de France* (Paris: A. Bonne, 1960); Antoine Bourbon, "Le Colmarien Bruat, Gouverneur des Iles," *Dernières Nouvelles d'Alsace*, 12, 19, and 25 January 1976; Patrick O'Reilly, *Tahiti au Temps de la Reine Pomaré* (Paris: Société des Océanistes,

1975); L. Sittler, *Admiral Bruat, 1796-1855*, trans. M. Kieffer (New York: L'Union Alsacienne, 1956).
André Gschaedler

BUCK, PETER HENRY ("TE RANGI HIROA") (1880-1951). Born at Urenui, Taranaki, New Zealand on 15 August 1880, of an Irish father and a Maori mother, Peter Buck attended Te Aute College, graduating in 1898, and received a medical degree in 1910 from New Zealand University. He worked as Maori health officer from 1905-1909, and as member of Parliament from 1909-1914. He was the second-in-command and medical officer of the Maori battalion in World War I, serving in Egypt, Gallipoli, France, and Belgium. On his return to New Zealand he became Director of Maori Hygiene from 1919-1927. Leaving New Zealand, he became an ethnologist at the Bishop Museum in Honolulu, Hawai'i, from 1927-1936. In 1936 he was made the director of the Bishop Museum. He also served as president of the board of trustees of the museum, and as a full professor of anthropology at Yale University. He died on 1 December 1951 while still director of the museum. An active participant in Maori affairs and in New Zealand affairs generally, Sir Peter's lifetime love was the study of ethnology. He earned many awards including a knighthood but always felt that his most satisfying work was in the field of anthropology among the people of Polynesia. His painstaking research produced many publications on the history, traditions, customs, culture, and social organizations of Polynesia. He considered the Polynesian ancestors as bold, intrepid mariners who conquered the Pacific with Stone Age vessels and gave to present-day Polynesia a rich cultural heritage.

RELATED ENTRIES: Polynesian Culture (Ancient).

SOURCES AND READINGS: Peter Henry Buck, *Arts and Crafts of Hawaii* (Honolulu: Bishop Museum Press, 1957); Peter Henry Buck, *The Coming of the Maori* (Wellington: Maori Purposes Fund Board; distributed by Whitcombe & Tombs, 1949); Peter Henry Buck, *Vikings of the Sunrise* (New York: Frederick A. Stokes Co., 1938).   *Vernice W. Pere*

BULU, JOEL (ca. 1810-1870). An early Tongan Wesleyan missionary to Fiji, born in Vava'u, Tonga, Bulu was "a big lad" when Christianity was introduced into the islands. He was impressed with the teachings of the Wesleyan missionaries and was converted in 1834. Concerned over the plight of the missionaries in Fiji, Bulu volunteered to go to their aid. The Reverend John Thomas sent him to Fiji where William Cross and David Cargill in 1835 had established the first Christian station on the Tongan-influenced island of Lakemba. There, he learned the language and helped the Reverend James Calvert in the printing of the first books in the Fijian language. From Lakemba he was sent to various new areas to prepare the way for the English ministers. Conversion to Christianity in Fiji succeeded primarily as a result of these indigenous teachers like Bulu making the initial contacts with the Fijian people. After some foothold had been secured (and many hardships encountered), the Wesleyan ministers moved in and supervised the work. For many years Bulu was directly responsible for the mission on Ono Island, a period of time in which he was the happiest. His compassion and devotion to Christian principles endeared him to Fijians and Englishmen alike. In his later years, he was called upon frequently for advice and to act as intermediary between British consuls and the Fijian chiefs. Upon his death in 1870, the missionaries compiled an ''autobiography'' which was published by the Wesleyan mission house in 1871. It stands as a memorial to all the Tongan and Fijian missionaries who helped pave the way for the other Wesleyan ministers to Fiji.

RELATED ENTRIES: Calvert, John; Fiji; Hunt, John; Lyth, Richard B.

SOURCES AND READINGS: Joel Bulu, *The Autobiography of a Native Minister in the South Seas* (London: Wesleyan Mission House, 1871); George G. Findlay and W. W. Holdsworth, *The History of the Wesleyan Methodist Missionary Society*, vol. 3 (London: Epworth Press, 1921).   *Robert D. Craig*

BYRON, JOHN (1723-1786). English naval officer. John Byron's voyage circumnavigating the globe began a series of expeditions leading to eventual British domination in the southwest Pacific. Byron was born in Newstead, England, 8 November 1723, and his first experience in the Pacific came as a midship-

man of seventeen on Lord Anson's well-known raid against the Spanish in 1741. Unfortunately for the young officer, his vessel, the *Wager*, was wrecked on the Chilean coast, but, upon his return to England in 1745, he wrote an account of the adventure which later influenced his grandson, George Gordon Byron, to write the famous poem, *Don Juan*.

In spite of this limited experience in Pacific waters, Byron was selected by the Admiralty, in 1764, to command a mission whose purpose was ostensibly scientific exploration. Actually, there were also important strategic considerations involving the Atlantic phase of the voyage in which the commodore surveyed and took possession of the Falkland Islands for the Crown. Although the claim was disrupted by the Spanish, these islands would provide an important base for British penetration into the Pacific. From the Falklands, Byron sailed through the Strait of Magellan and proceeded across the Pacific. Ignoring his instructions to search for a northwest passage, he set out to find the Solomon Islands reported by Mendaña. The search proved fruitless, but the expedition did visit numerous islands, including several in the Tuamotu Archipelago and the Gilberts. Byron rounded the Cape of Good Hope and returned to England in May of 1766. He ultimately reached the rank of vice-admiral before his death in 1786.

RELATED ENTRIES: Britain in the Pacific.

SOURCES AND READINGS: J. C. Beaglehole, *The Exploration of the Pacific*, 3d ed. (Stanford: Stanford University Press, 1966); Robert E. Gallagher, ed., *Byron's Journal of his Circumnavigation, 1764-66* (Cambridge: At the University Press, 1964); John Hawkesworth, *An Account of the Voyages. . . . by Commodore Byron, Captain Wallis, Captain Carteret and Captain Cook*, 3 vols. (London: W. Strahan and T. Cadell, 1773); Andrew Sharp, *The Discovery of the Pacific Islands* (Oxford: Clarendon Press, 1960).   *David Warren Bowen*

CAKOBAU. *See* Bau; Fiji.

CALVERT, JOHN (1813-1892). Calvert was an early Wesleyan missionary to Fiji. Born in Pickering, York, 1813, he received an early training as a printer and bookseller. At seventeen, he underwent a religious experience and turned to preaching. He became interested in the South Seas' work and especially in the success of Peter Turner in Samoa. In 1838 he was chosen along with John Hunt and Thomas Jaggar to travel to Fiji to bolster the work already begun by William Cross and David Cargill three years earlier. Clavert's wife Mary accompanied him and she herself ranks among the heroines of Wesleyan Christian missions. Arriving in Fiji, Calvert worked in Lakemba where he helped in the translation and printing of Fijian texts and where he acted as director of the station while John Hunt and Richard Lyth worked elsewhere. Calvert's continuous administration sustained the work of the missionary society in Fiji that soon became the center of a mission that included over twenty islands in his circuit. Not of peculiarly intellectual force, Calvert's commanding personality, warmth, and good humor were remembered by his follow missionaries. With the death of Hunt in 1848, Calvert inherited the task of completing the translation of the Bible into Fijian, a task he continued for over forty years. He returned to England in 1844. He made two subsequent trips to Fiji, one in 1860-1864, and then again in 1886 in an attempt to heal the schism between the Tongan Free Church and the parent mission. Calvert died 8 March 1892 and is buried in the Calvert Memorial Chapel in Hastings.

RELATED ENTRIES: Fiji; Hunt, John; Lyth, Richard B.

SOURCES AND READINGS: George G. Findlay, *The History of the Wesleyan Methodist Missionary Society*, vol. 3 (London: Epworth Press, 1921).

Robert D. Craig

CALVO, PAUL McDONALD (1934-). Calvo, the third elected governor of Guam, was born 25 July 1935 in the capital city of Agana. He attended George Washington High School in Guam, Peacock Military Academy in San Antonio, Texas, and the University of Santa Clara, California, where he received a bachelor of science degree in commerce in 1958. Calvo then entered the business world as a partner in a firm formed by his father and two brothers. In 1960 he joined Calvo's Insurance Company, now one of the major insurance organizations on Guam. In 1965 he was elected to the office of senator for the eighth Guam legislature. During his term he served as chairman of the Committee on Finance and Taxation and was also a member of the Committees on Rules and on Governmental Operations. Calvo also served in the eleventh and twelfth Guam legislatures in 1970 and 1972 as Republican minority leader for both terms. He was elected governor in 1978.

RELATED ENTRIES: Guam.

SOURCES AND READINGS: Robert D. Craig and Russell T. Clement, *Who's Who in Oceania* (Laie, Hawaii: Institute for Polynesian Studies, 1981), p. 24.

Ruth Limtiaco

CAMPBELL, ARCHIBALD (1787- ?). A beachcomber on O'ahu, Hawai'i (1809-1810). Campbell's book is one of the principal historical sources for Hawai'i at that time. Campbell, a native of Paisley, Scotland, was one of the few beachcombers to have a definite goal to live in the Pacific region. Having lost both feet and some fingers as a result of frostbite and inexpert surgery in the Russian Aleutian settlements, Campbell arrived in Hawai'i where King Kamehameha I provided him with a means whereby he could make a living. His case illustrates both Kamehameha's compassion and the opportunities for a foreigner of talent and sobriety, even though crippled, to prosper by serving the interests of his island hosts. Campbell left Hawai'i to return to his native Scotland after only ten months residence, homesick and needing medical attention. After his book was published in 1816, he emigrated to the United States, and although he aspired to return to Hawai'i, he never did.

RELATED ENTRIES: Beachcombers; Hawai'i; Kamehameha I.

SOURCES AND READINGS: Archibald Campbell, *A Voyage Round the World from 1806 to 1812* (Honolulu: University of Hawaii Press, 1967), a facsimile reproduction of the third American edition, 1822.

Ian C. Campbell

CANNON, GEORGE Q., (1827-1901).

One of the first Mormon missionaries to come to Hawai'i, Cannon was born 1 January 1827 in Liverpool, England. He was the youngest of ten missionaries representing the Church of Jesus Christ of Latter-day Saints (Mormons) who set sail for Honolulu in November 1850 on the ship *Imauma of Muscat* to establish a mission in the Sandwich Islands. After a four-week journey, the ship reached the island of O'ahu where the missionaries were assigned companions and islands on which to work. Cannon and his companion were sent to Maui where he first preached among the white settlement while he learned the Hawaiian language. After successfully mastering the language, he was invited to preach and teach in the home of Jonathon H. Napela, a man of chiefly rank. Because of local persecution, Cannon moved to Kula, Maui, where a thatched-roof "church" provided shelter for his first sermon on 21 May 1851 in the Hawaiian language. In January 1851, with the support of Napela, he began to translate the *Book of Mormon* into Hawaiian. It was completed three years later on 31 January 1854. Cannon spent his four-year mission traveling to the various Hawaiian islands preaching and organizing the church. Completing a successful mission, Cannon set sail from Honolulu to San Francisco. He died 12 April 1901 in Monterey, California.

RELATED ENTRIES: Hawai'i; Mormons in the Pacific.

SOURCES AND READINGS: George Q. Cannon, *My First Mission* (Salt Lake City: Juvenile Instructor Office, 1882); Joseph H. Spurrier, *Great Are the Promises unto the Isles of the Sea* (Salt Lake City: Hawkes Publishing, 1978).   *Brenna J. Rash*

CANTON ISLAND QUESTION (1936-1939).

The American occupation in early 1935 of Howland, Baker, and Jarvis, three islands lying near the equator, and Pan American Airways' effort to establish an air route to New Zealand focused Britain's attention on these South Pacific islands. England planned an around-the-world airmail service but could not fly the Pacific without entry rights at Hawai'i. England attempted to use the Pan American request for a permit to force open Hawai'i, but the U.S. rejected the bid. To strengthen its position, England, through New Zealand, began to search for South Pacific islands with aeronautical possibilities. Early in May 1936 American newspapers reported that the British intended to investigate various equatorial islands in connection with possible Pacific air routes. The islands occupied by the U.S., which are now under the Department of the Interior, were then uninhabited. An emergency expedition rushed new colonists to the islands that June before the arrival of the British.

Warships of the New Zealand Naval Division conducted the island search which resulted in the claiming of the eight islands of the Phoenix group. The search information was studied at the air conference held at Wellington in September by England, New Zealand, and Australia. A decision was reached to set up a Commonwealth air route and to gain entry into Hawai'i. Pan American was allowed to keep her New Zealand permit but the reciprocity provision was made even stronger.

In March 1937 England issued an Order in Council officially claiming the Phoenix Islands as part of the Gilbert and Ellice Islands colony. The National Geographic Society asked the navy to transport a scientific expedition to Canton Island in the Phoenix group to observe a total eclipse of the sun that June. The navy requested the State Department to give the usual notice to England regarding the projected visit. Reviewing the status of Canton, the State Department concluded that no notice was necessary because the U.S. also had a claim to the island. When the State Department learned of the Order in Council, it was too late to notify England. The expedition was at Canton only a few days when a New Zealand scientific party arrived. No friction arose but the Americans left behind a cement plinth with a stainless steel American flag on it and the British requested that it be removed.

While the scientific party had been on Canton, an aeronautical survey had been carried out by the navy showing that Canton had great potential. At the cabinet meeting in late July, the Department of the Navy asked permission to land colonists on Canton. The inadequacies of Howland during the search for Amelia Earhart in early July had caused Navy to turn to Canton as its desired base. President Roosevelt at first supported Navy but State appealed to him on the grounds it would cause friction with England. State suggested negotiations with a view to gaining joint use of the island as a minimum objective. Roosevelt agreed on condition that there be a standstill by both sides until a settlement was made. State so notified Britain that August and was promised a prompt reply. But weeks passed with no reply and information was received that the British were not honoring the standstill. On 20 October 1937 they indicated their willingness to discuss the sovereignty of the Pacific islands but not the sovereignty of the Phoenix group which was definitely claimed by England.

State now suggested landing colonists but Roosevelt decided on another effort at negotiations.

In December, Pan American flew its first commercial flight to New Zealand. On the second trip, the clipper airship blew up and the route had to be temporarily abandoned until new equipment was available. Their two stopovers, Kingman Reef and Pago Pago, had proved unsuitable and Pan American requested a permit from State to use Canton. Finally, in February 1938, Roosevelt approved the landing of colonists on Canton and Enderbury during the next equatorial cruise. The colonists were landed in March, and the British were informed that the U.S. had acted to put itself on an equal footing with Britain.

With the news of the colonization, Pan American asked for and received a permit from the Department of the Interior to use the island. Outraged, the British claimed the permit gave exclusive use of the island to Pan American. State maintained that the island was open to a British airline. The British countered with an offer of joint use of the island on condition that there be complete reciprocity in the Pacific, meaning Hawai'i, and that colonists might be sent from other British islands to relieve overcrowding. The British hinted that the Pan American permit might be cancelled. State rejected the British conditions, basically because the question of Hawai'i was a military one, not a commercial one. State would only discuss the island question. In August England agreed to a joint use of the island on condition that the Pan American permit be replaced by one indicating the joint control. Even here Britain tried to slow things down. But when Pan American obtained the right to use Nouméa, New Caledonia, from the French and Interior indicated it would allow Pan American to operate under the original permit, Britain agreed to issue the new permit in April 1939. The following August Pan American ran its survey flight from Hawai'i to Auckland via Canton using a new Boeing 314. The company still had some worrisome months as the British pushed to set up their own route. But with the outbreak of World War II in Europe, the pressure on Britain and its Commonwealth members increased. In July 1940 Pan American put the route into commercial operation with New Zealand's approval and with an airmail contract from the U.S.

RELATED ENTRIES: Equatorial Islands.

SOURCES AND READINGS: Francis X. Holbrook, "Aeronautical Reciprocity and the Anglo-American Islands Race, 1936-37," *Journal of the Royal Australian Historical Society* 57 (1971): 321-35; and "The Canton Island Controversy," *Journal of the Royal Australian Historical Society* 59 (1973): 128-47.

Francis X. Holbrook

CARET, FRANÇOIS (1802-1844). A French Roman Catholic priest who brought Christianity to the islands of Gambier, Marquesas, and Tahiti, Caret was accompanied by Fathers Laval and Murphy. Caret preached successfully in the islands of Mangareva (largest of the Gambier Islands), Akamaru, Taravai, and Aukena from 1834 to 1835. Maputéoa, king of the Gambier islands, was an early convert. In 1836 Caret and Laval attempted to found a Catholic mission in Tahiti but were rejected by Queen Pomare IV upon advice from George Pritchard. Father Caret returned to France one year later, solicited support throughout the country, and returned in 1838 with over two thousand sets of European clothing for the Gambier islanders. He labored with Etienne Rouchouze in the Marquesas until French relations improved in Tahiti. In 1841 his dream for a Catholic mission in Pape'ete was realized. Opposed by the British consul, George Pritchard, and the English Protestants, the mission began slowly. Father Caret was visited in Tahiti by Herman Melville in 1842. Persecutions continued, and in June 1844 his house and small chapel were burned. His manuscripts on Tahitian and Marquesan languages (including a Tahitian dictionary nearing completion) and his many translations were destroyed. Caret, suffering from lung complications, barely survived the fire and died at Rikitea in 1844.

RELATED ENTRIES: French Polynesia; Laval, Louis; Pritchard, George.

SOURCES AND READINGS: Patrick O'Reilly, *Tahitiens* (Paris: Musée de l'Homme, 1962).

Russell T. Clement

CARGO CULT. When a given group of people are thrown into contact with another better able to manipulate the physical environment, a pattern of ideas, activities, and practices arises among them to which Weston Le Barre has assigned the term *crisis cult*. Such a serious disruption of the normal way of life creates problems and hazards for which traditional responses are totally inadequate. It calls for new modes of thought and action which are often millenarian and grandiose in character, that is, a time will come, it is prophesied, when a supernatural event will transform the lives of the people, so that it is most important to prepare for the anticipated changes right here and now. Movements of this kind have a widespread distribution both geographically and historically and are by no means rare in modern times, technological cultures not excluded. Common to them all are consciously perceived inequalities of status as compared with the conspicuously different persons of the alien culture in contact with them.

There is a marked feeling of inferiority, with its associated conflict and anxiety, and an attempt is made restore the original self-image with differing degrees of success. Underlying much of this nonlogical, magico-religious endeavor, to which Vilfredo Pareto has referred, is a strong desire for a better way of life through the resolution of economic and political problems. The specifically Melanesian subvariety is known as *cargo cult*. In addition to the features mentioned above, this form is often characterized by the presence of visual and auditory hallucinations that are said to be uncommon in those movements not of the cargo cult kind; by an intense individualism and customary display of locally defined wealth and status; by the customary methods of achieving prestige through the number of pigs or wives one has, or the size of one's yams; and by the unusual language picture in the country with its more than seven hundred discrete cultural-linguistic groups. In Papua New Guinea the cults arise within the language group and do not usually spread beyond its border, but may do so when communication is by means of a *lingua franca* such as pidgin English, *Hiri Motu*, and *Bahasa Indonesia*.

Although cargo thinking is endemic in the Melanesia region there is much divergence in the mode of expression of individual cults. There is, nevertheless, a basic nucleus common to most of them. Looking at it as a descriptive amalgam, cargo thinking is an anxiety-reducing device which meets psychological needs. The style of cult development may take many forms depending upon the varying emphases of the different factors impinging upon it. Such thinking may occur in an isolated person as is often shown in the symptomatology of mentally sick individuals, or more usually, in group situations. Among other things, there is a marked desire for material goods to be obtained by rapid magico-religious methods. A prophet, leader, or messiah emerges. His cardinal manifestation is status anxiety. Contrary to what one might expect, he is often a mediocrity as defined by other cultural standards and sometimes by his own people as well. He may use sorcery in bringing nonbelievers into line. He may, or may not, be suffering from mental disorder, defined as such not only by the alien medical system but also by his own kinsmen. He sometimes suffers from a physical disability which when present aggravates feelings of inferiority. He has a fantasy-based solution to offer his followers initiated by a dream, or a visual or auditory hallucination, all three of which are powerful agents in the recruitment of followers. He announces a great future event or millennium and may even supply the date for its appearance. Preparations are made to cope with the expected changes. New moral and legal codes are introduced, and the important ego-strengthening device of new and elaborate clothing may be adopted. Jetties, helicopter pads, airstrips, or roads are built in preparation for the arrival of ancestral spirits who are to bring in the much desired cargo. Traditional agriculture is abandoned, pigs and chickens killed, and money burnt on the theory that they will no longer be necessary. The cult subsides with the nonappearance of cargo but may reappear again in response to some new stimulus.

It is highly likely that cargo cults have existed for a very long time, and the first written reports began to appear in the late nineteenth century, although they did not then receive that designation. Samarai magistrate R. J. Kennedy in 1893 described a young man named Tokerua who was in communication with a spirit residing in a traditionally sacred tree and who prophesied a catastrophe in which the whole coast would be submerged in a tidal wave. Believers would be saved, he said, if the people heeded his message. They did no work, ate their pigs, and consumed the remaining food in their gardens. With Tokerua in charge, these items were considered no longer necessary. The next report was from Chinnery and Haddon who studied the German Wislin movement of 1913 on the island of Saibai in the Torres Strait. The first systematic account of a cargo cult was F. E. Williams' study of the Vailala Madness in 1923. He is one of the very few students of the subject who endeavors to see and evaluate the operation of psychological factors in the motives and ideals of the people. Subsequent studies in limited geographical areas by cultural anthropologists have concentrated on the Tangu of the Bogia region, on the Tommy Kabu movement in the Purari delta, on the Paliau movement in Manus province, on the Yali of the Rai Coast, and on the Yangoru cargo cult. At least eighty instances have been referred to in the literature. These are a fraction of the totality, for many are not divulged to Europeans, and others are noted only by missionaries, traders, and raconteurs. Explanations of cargo cult are varied and include relative economic deprivation, magico-religious frustration, stress, envy, and irrational fantasy theories. No explanation is completely satisfactory by itself. Irrationalistic theories of the group aspects of cargo movements and cargo analogue, for example, are of limited social utility in the present period of rapid change in the area. But this should not blind us to the fact that some of the individual leaders have suffered from serious mental disorder which has its bearing on the character, duration, and outcome of the cult. What can be said concerning the future of cargo cult behavior? Economic growth, educational opportunities, and the influence of European values in relation to material appurtenances are bound to have their effect. But some cultural elements are more refractory to change than others. Cargo cults are unlikely to disappear suddenly, but they will certainly undergo kaleidoscopic modifications.

RELATED ENTRIES: Cargo Cult, John Frum; Papua New Guinea.

SOURCES AND READINGS: P. Christiansen, *The Melanesian Cargo Cult* (Copenhagen: Akademisk Forlag, 1969); Weston La Barre, *The Ghost Dance* (London: G. Allen & Unwin, 1972); Vilfredo Pareto, *The Mind and Society* (New York: Harcourt, Brace & Co., 1935). *Burton G. Burton-Bradley*

CARGO CULT, JOHN FRUM. A cultural revitalization movement, the John Frum cargo cult emerged on the island of Tanna, Vanuatu (New Hebrides), in 1941. The cult prophet, the mysterious John Frum, ordered the revival of abandoned traditions of kava drinking and dance. Virtually the entire population left the Christian churches and joined the movement. Cult leaders were arrested and deported a number of times until the New Hebrides Condominium government, in 1956, recognized the cult as a religion. The arrival of American forces in the New Hebrides during World War II, an arrival claimed to be predicted by John Frum, lent certain symbols to the cult. The U.S. flag, military uniforms, and army marching drill continue to be used in the cult ceremony. The John Frum ideology has evolved from cultural revitalization, to predictions of the coming of American cargo, to one increasingly concerned with local politics. The movement ran candidates in the 1975, 1977, and 1979 elections to the National Assembly.

RELATED ENTRIES: Cargo Cult; Kava; Nambas; Tanna; Vanuatu (New Hebrides).

SOURCES AND READINGS: Jean Guiart, *Un Siècle et Demi de Contacts Culturels à Tanna* (Paris: Musée de l'Homme, 1956). *Lamont C. Lindstrom*

CAROLINE ISLANDS. The largest archipelago in Micronesia stretches over three thousand miles beginning with Tobi Island at 131° east latitude and 4° north longitude and runs eastward to Kosrae Island (Kusaie) at 162° east latitude and 5° north longitude. There are some 952 islands containing about 1170 km² (452 mi²) of land area. The 1980 estimated population was 91,942, less than 1 percent of which was foreign.

The Carolines are high and low volcanic and coral islands and atolls. Within the Carolines, there are five administrative districts of the Trust Territory of the Pacific Islands. Geographically the group is divided into the eastern Carolines, which comprise the districts of Truk, Ponape, and Kosrae, and the western Carolines, which comprise the districts of Yap and Palau (Belau).

The people are Carolinians, but they are specifically referred to by island and linguistic groupings such as Yapese, Trukese, Palauans, Ponapeans, and Kosraeans. The chief cities, or administrative centers, are Koror in Palau, Colonia in Yap, Moen in Truk, Kolonia in Ponape, and Lelu in Kosrae.

Physically, Carolinians are characterized by medium stature, brown skin, straight to wavy black hair, relatively little facial and body hair, and high cheek bones. People of the eastern Carolines tend to have stronger Malaysian characteristics than those in the eastern islands of the Pacific.

Vegetation varies from high islands to low atolls, though coconut and breadfruit are common to both. Coral atolls abound in pandanus and shore plants. On high islands there are mangrove swamps on the tidal flats, coconut palms on the slopes, and mixed forest growth on the uplands.

Hogs, dogs, and one species of rat were introduced by migrations prior to Western and Oriental contact. Domestic and farm animals are present. There are many marine and shore birds. Two species of saltwater crocodiles are found in Palau, as are monkeys introduced by the Japanese.

With the exception of about one thousand Polynesian inhabitants of Kapingamarangi and Nukuoro atolls in the Ponape district, Carolinians are Micronesians. Anthropological evidence and studies indicate that these Carolinians probably originated in Southeast Asia and Malaysia. All Carolinian island societies are similar in cultural characteristics such as adjustment to life on small islands, highly specialized stone and shell technology, the use of fibers and local materials, complex clan distinctions, narrow political loyalties, close kinship ties, the cult worship of ancestors, and leadership by chiefs. Differing degrees of this acculturation can be seen today.

The Carolines were visited by the Portuguese and Spanish in the sixteenth century. In 1513 Vasco de Balboa claimed for Spain the Pacific Ocean and all the lands it touched. Gomez de Sequeira visited Yap or Palau in 1526. Alvaro Saavedra landed at Ulithi in 1528 and at Truk and Kosrae in 1530. In 1595 Pedro Fernándes de Quirós landed at Ponape. The Spanish claims were challenged by the Germans in 1885 at which time the dispute was mediated by the Roman Catholic pope who determined the validity of the Spanish claim but upheld the trading and supply station rights of the Germans in the Carolines. After the Spanish-American War in 1898 the Spanish sold the Carolines to Germany for $4.5 million. In October 1914, after the outbreak of World War I, Japan seized all the Carolines from the Germans, and subsequently they were awarded these islands under a League of Nations mandate. In 1933 Japan withdrew from the league and prepared for war. After a series of battles, especially at Truk, Peleliu, and Anguar (Palau), the United States wrested the Carolines from Japan in 1944. Following the war, a United Nations strategic trusteeship was established with the United States as the administering power. In October 1969, the Carolinian people, along with other Micronesians began political status negotiations with the U.S. In 1978, the Hilo Accord (Statement of Agreed Principles for Free Association) was reached and signed by the negotiators and the U.S. In January 1980, the Marshallese indicated their acceptance and willingness to work out the fine details in their relation with the U.S. The Caroline districts of Truk, Ponape, Kosrae, and Yap formed a new government, the Federated States of Micronesia, before the November 1980 U.S. elections, and some major issues are still unresolved. Wary of committing any portion of their land to foreign use, the Palauans became the Republic of Belau only on New Year's Day 1981, and it is still negotiating the final agreement of its compact with the U.S.

RELATED ENTRIES: Micronesia; War in the Pacific Islands.

SOURCES AND READINGS: Dirk A. Ballendorf and Frank P. King, eds., *Towards New Directions and Political Self-Actualization* (Mangilao, Guam: Micronesian Area Research Center, 1980); F. W. Christian, *The Caroline Islands* (London: Cass, 1967); Donald M. Topping, "Micronesia: The Long, Long Haul to Ending the U.S. Trusteeship," *Pacific Islands Monthly* (January 1981), pp. 13-18.

Dirk Anthony Ballendorf

CARTER, GEORGE ROBERT (1866-1933). Hawai'i's second governor (1903-1907) and a distinguished statesman and territorial diplomat, George Carter was born 28 December 1866. He began his public service when he was elected to the Hawaiian Senate in 1901. Before his election to the Senate, Carter had graduated from Yale University in 1888 and had served in positions with the Seattle National

Bank, the Hawaiian Trust Company, the Hawaiian Fertilizer Company, and the Bank of Hawai'i. It was during the administration of Governor Carter that counties were created in Hawai'i. An act providing for county governments was passed in 1905 and at the beginning of the following year five counties came into existence—O'ahu, Hawai'i, Maui, Kaua'i, and Kaho'olawe. Governor Carter, through careful legislative means, rescued the sinking territorial treasury of Hawai'i, and within a few months after his inauguration, he helped place the financial affairs of Hawai'i on a more satisfactory base. After his retirement and until his death on 11 February 1933, he maintained an active interest in the affairs of the community.

RELATED ENTRIES: Hawai'i.

SOURCES AND READINGS: A. Grove Day, *Hawaii and its People* (New York: Meredith Press, 1968); Edward Joesting, *Hawaii* (New York: W. W. Norton & Co., 1972); Ralph S. Kuykendall and A. Grove Day, *Hawaii: A History* (Englewood Cliffs N.J.: Prentice-Hall, 1961).

Ned B. Williams

CATHOLIC CHURCH IN THE PACIFIC. Catholics were the first Christian missionaries in the Pacific islands, although it took them over two hundred years to reach all the major groups. In intention, if not in effect, their work may be said to have begun in the sixteenth century. One of the objectives of the Spanish navigators Medaña and Quirós in searching for the mythical southern continent (in three voyages between 1567 and 1606) was to discover people who could be converted to Christianity. But practical evangelization began later and in the north Pacific, an area which had become familiar to the Spaniards through the voyages of the Manila galleons, trading vessels that sailed regularly between the Philippines and the Americas from 1565 to 1815.

The first missionaries, Spanish Jesuits led by Diego Luis de Sanvitores, landed at Guam in the Marianas in 1668. They met stern resistance. By 1685 twelve Jesuits had been killed by their prospective converts. But from that time, with the islanders dominated by Spanish soldiers and ravaged by introduced disease, conversion proceded steadily. All were Catholics by 1710 when (of a population of about 100,000 in 1668) only 3,678 of the native Chamorro people survived.

Fortunately for the people of the neighboring Marshall and Caroline groups, the Spanish made no serious efforts to extend their influence beyond the Marianas until the late nineteenth century. Attempts to establish missions in the western Carolines failed when missionaries were killed at Sonsoral in 1710 and Ulithi in 1731.

The next phase in the Catholic penetration of Oceania contrasts with the beginnings of Micronesia. It focused on Polynesia, where Protestants were already established, and was undertaken by French missionaries whose work was not part of a joint church-state enterprise. The missionaries were supplied by new religious orders founded in the religious revival which followed the French Revolution. Leading the advance were three priests and three brothers of the Congregation of the Sacred Hearts of Jesus and Mary (or Picpus Fathers) who landed in Hawai'i in 1826.

Meanwhile another French priest, Henri de Solages, encouraged by a former Pacific trader, Peter Dillon, was urging the Vatican to set up a new ecclesiastical jurisdiction covering the rest of Polynesia. This was done in 1830 when the Prefecture Apostolic of the South Sea Islands was created. De Solages was put in charge in this domain but died before he reached the Pacific. In 1833 the prefecture was divided along a line running from Hawai'i to the Cook Islands and the Picpus Fathers were given responsibility for a vicariate embracing the Polynesian islands to the east of it. Accordingly, they landed missionaries at the Gambiers in 1834, at Tahiti in 1836, at the Marquesas in 1839, at the Tuamotus in 1849, at Easter Island in 1864, and at the Cooks in 1894.

Western Polynesia, together with all of Melanesia, and Micronesia except for the Marianas, was incorporated in the Vicariate Apostolic of Western Oceania which was created in 1836. This vast area was entrusted to the Society of Mary (or Marist Fathers). Led by Bishop Jean-Baptiste-François Pompallier, the Marists entered the Pacific in 1837. After leaving men at Wallis (or Uvea) and Futuna, Pompallier established his headquarters in New Zealand, and had little more to do with the northern islands. Wallis was converted by Pierre Bataillon in 1840 and the Futunans turned to Catholicism after Pierre Chanel was killed by order of chief Niuliki in 1841. Chanel was declared a saint in 1954.

Since it was impossible for one person to direct operations over such large areas, the original vicariates were progressively divided into smaller administrative units. That of central Oceania, extending from Samoa to New Caledonia, was created in 1842. New Caledonia, where Marists landed in 1843, became a separate vicariate which in 1847 included the New Hebrides. Meanwhile, Wallis and Futuna, under the direction of Bataillon, who was made bishop in 1843, became the center of Catholic expansion in western Polynesia. Marist missionaries went to Tonga in 1842, Fiji in 1844, Samoa in 1845, and Rotuma in 1846.

Since Protestant missionaries had preceded them to these islands, the coming of the Catholics, in most other parts of Polynesia, often led to bitter sectarian disputes. The Protestants resented competition for the religious allegiance of the few remaining heathens. Consequently, in some places, it was only through the support of French naval commanders, who forced treaties of friendship on island rulers, that Catholics were able to gain a secure foothold. This occurred at Tahiti in 1838, Hawai'i in 1839, Tonga in 1855, and Fiji in 1858. The passions of the early years gradually subsided and of these incidents only that at Tahiti has had lasting significance. Naval intervention on behalf of the missionaries provided the occasion for France to take Tahiti in 1842.

Having arrived too late to become predominant in Polynesia, Catholic missionaries hoped for greater success by arriving early in the less hospitable islands of Melanesia. There Protestants preceded them only in the southern New Hebrides. In 1844 Pompallier's vicariate of western Oceania was further subdivided with the creation of two new ones, those of Melanesia (New Guinea and the Solomons) and Micronesia. Marists began work in the Solomons in 1845 but malaria and the hostility of the people forced them out in 1847. Proceeding nearer New Guinea, to the islands of Murua and Umboi, they encountered similar difficulties. In 1852 they were replaced by members of the Milan Foreign Missions Society. These, in turn, were forced to withdraw in 1855. It had been a costly venture for both orders. Five missionaries had been killed and four others died of sickness.

Nor was the going much easier in the southern islands of Melanesia. In 1846 the Marists fled from New Caledonia, where one missionary was killed by the islanders, and although they maintained a post on the Isle of Pines from 1848, they did not return to the mainland until 1851. Their security was not finally assured there until France annexed the island in 1853. Other Marists settled in the New Hebrides in 1848 but left on account of sickness in 1850. And three who were attempting to settle on Tikopia vanished mysteriously in 1852.

The difficulties of the Catholics in establishing themselves in Melanesia clearly indicate that faith and courage were not sufficient to guarantee security, let alone evangelical success. For that, it was also necessary for conditions of life there to change. This occurred as a result of the steadily increasing activity of European gunboats and administrators and traders in Melanesia in the latter part of the century. The islanders were gradually discouraged from acts of violence and their interest was aroused in European goods and ideas. Besides finding the indigenes more receptive, the missionaries were also less cut off from European support. From the 1880s, therefore, their progress was steady.

In 1881 the vacant vicariates of Melanesia were handed over to the Missionaries of the Sacred Heart (MSC). They began work near Rabaul, the commercial center of the New Guinea area, in 1882. Following the division of eastern New Guinea between England and Germany in 1885, Melanesia was divided in 1889 into two new vicariates coterminous with the new political jurisdictions. After further subdivisions, missionaries of the Society of the Divine Work (SVD) landed in the northeast of German New Guinea in 1896 while in 1898 the Marists returned to the Solomons. In 1887 they had also returned to the New Hebrides where the number of French settlers was increasing rapidly.

Meanwhile, the vicariate of Micronesia was waiting but not for long. MSCs were sent in 1888 to the Gilberts, which became a vicariate in 1897, and in 1892 to the Marshalls which became one in 1905. The Carolines, where Spanish Capuchins had been working since 1886, also became a vicariate in 1905.

Only then, with each major island group constituting a distinct ecclesiastical unit was the introduction of Catholicism to the Pacific formally complete. Even so, the main part of the missionaries' work was everywhere far from complete and the process by which this completion was achieved was as uneven and spasmodic as that by which "the Word" was carried around the Pacific. The evangelization of Polynesia was complete by 1900, yet most Melanesians had still to see their first missionary. By the 1970s, however, discrepancies of development were becoming less conspicuous as local churches emerged, that is, as indigenous bishops and clergy everywhere took over the running of religious affairs in their dioceses from expatriate missionaries.

(Note: the territorial divisions of the Catholic Church subject to the Congregation for the Evangelization of Peoples are ranked as follows in order of increasingly independent jurisdiction: prefecture apostolic, vicariate apostolic, diocese. The head of a vicariate or diocese is usually a bishop and that of a prefecture usually a priest with quasi-episcopal powers. Prefectures are now rare, as are vicariates. The Pacific vicariates were raised to the status of diocese in 1967.)

RELATED ENTRIES: Bataillon, Pierre; Caret, François; Chanel, Pierre; Dillon, Peter; Pompallier, Jean-Baptiste.

SOURCES AND READINGS: Hugh Laracy, *Marists and Melanesians: A History of Catholic Missions in the*

Solomon Islands (Canberra: Australian National University Press, 1976; Hugh Laracy, "Roman Catholic 'Martyrs' in the South Pacific, 1841-55," *Journal of Religious History* 9 (1976): 189-202; Hugh Laracy, "The Catholic Mission," in Noel Rutherford, ed., *Friendly Islands: A History of Tonga* (Melbourne: Oxford University Press, 1977), pp. 136-58; R. Wiltgen, *The Founding of the Roman Catholic Church in Oceania, 1825-1850* (Canberra: Australian National University Press, 1979).   *Hugh Laracy*

CENTRAL PACIFIC AIR ROUTE (1934-1936). In 1934 the South Seas Commercial Company (Donald Douglas, president; Harold Gatty, vice-president) was formed to build both land and seaplane facilities on selected Pacific islands to create a route from the United States to the Philippines through Hawai'i, Midway, Wake, and Guam, and a southwestern route from Hawai'i to American Samoa. The company would rent the facilities to any airline which wanted to use them.

Harold Gatty had spent the summer of 1934 in Washington, D.C., studying charts of various Pacific islands and the status of their ownership. With Elliott Roosevelt's encouragement, Gatty applied to the navy on 22 September for long-term leases on Midway, Wake, Guam, Johnston, Jarvis, Howland, Baker, and American Samoa. The navy was enthusiastic because it would establish aeronautical facilities in an area covered by the Naval Limitation Treaty of 1922. Already, the navy had sent a cruiser to investigate the aeronautical potential of Howland and Baker islands.

On 3 October the navy received a request from Pan American Airways for leases on Wake, Guam, and possibly Midway to create a route to the Philippines for flying boats. The company had learned of the existence of the South Seas Commercial Company and was trying to block them to prevent any competition on the route. Only an airmail contract made a route profitable and it could not be shared.

Early in 1935 the navy decided to give the central Pacific leases to Pan American while encouraging the South Seas Commercial Company to create the southwestern route. Pan American was believed to be better equipped to set up the island bases and to run the route than a new, untested company. During the spring of 1935 Pan American set up its bases at Midway, Wake, and Guam and prepared a modified Martin M-130 for the longer Pacific flight. On 22 November 1936 Captain Edward Musick, Pan American's chief pilot, took off from Alameda and six days later landed at Manila. Later Pan American extended its terminal first to Portuguese Macao, then to British Hong Kong and finally to Singapore.

Pan American's appearance in the Pacific upset Japan. To reassure the Japanese, the U.S. State Department suggested to Pan American in March 1935 that the Japanese be given the privilege of connecting with the company at Wake. Pan American agreed but suggested that Guam be the terminal. The navy supported this idea providing Japan was not given the right of entry into the Philippines. But several members of the new Interdepartmental Committee on Civil Aviation opposed the idea and the State Department dropped the plan. The idea of Guam as a Union Station was raised again in March 1937 but before a final decision could be made Japan invaded China in July. The State Department decided to drop the idea rather than seem to condone Japan's actions by making such an offer.

RELATED ENTRIES: Canton Island Question; Gatty, Harold.

SOURCES AND READINGS: Correspondence of Harold Gatty, Library of Congress, Washington, D.C.; Francis X. Holbrook, "Commercial Aviation and the Colonization of the Equatorial Islands, 1934-36," *Aerospace Historian* 17 (1970): 144-49; Henry Ladd Smith, *Airways Abroad* (Madison: University of Wisconsin Press, 1950).   *Francis X. Holbrook*

CENTRAL POLYNESIAN LAND AND COMMERCIAL COMPANY (1871-1895).

A land speculation scheme in Samoa was devised by San Francisco stockbrokers in 1871. They formed the Central Polynesian Land and Commercial Company which claimed more than 200,000 acres in the Samoan Islands. Company agents acquired land cheaply during the island civil wars of 1869-1973 by courting warring parties and lodging large, often exaggerated, titles. The company was linked to another San Francisco scheme, a transpacific steamer service, which the promoters hoped would attract attention to the speculative and investment prospects of the newly opened island civil wars of 1869-1873 by courting warring struggles and, although no settlers took up land in the company's name, the impact of the Central Polynesian Land and Commercial Company, which claimed more than 200,000 acres in the Samoan Islands. Company agents acquired land cheaply during the island civil wars of 1869-1873 by courting warring inquiry lasted until the late 1890s. All land claims in its name were rejected by a land claims commission in 1891-1894, and the company was liquidated the following year.

RELATED ENTRIES: American Samoa; Western Samoa; Woods, George A.

SOURCES AND READINGS: J. W. Davidson, *Samoa Mo Samoa* (Melbourne: Oxford University Press, 1967); R. P. Gilson, *Samoa: 1830-1900: The Politics of a Multicultural Community* (Melbourne: Oxford University Press, 1970).   *Alan Maxwell Quanchi*

CHAMORROS (ANCIENT).

The precontact inhabitants of the Mariana Islands were the ancient Chamorros. These pre-Spanish, proto-Malayan people had settled the Mariana Islands between 3000 B.C. and 2000 B.C. While their point of origin is obscure, linguistic and archaeological evidence points to the central Philippines as the most probable point of origin. There is also some evidence that the Marianas were invaded around 800 B.C. by a warrior group of canoe people who may have brought rice culture and the latte stone technology to the islands. Latte stones were huge stone pillars apparently used as supports for buildings.

The Chamorros possessed a high stage of neolithic culture. They were organized into matrilineal clans and lineages. Marriage was monogamous with divorce permitted. The children became members of the mother's clan and had little or no contact with the paternal side of their family.

In addition the society was organized into a two-tiered caste system. The upper caste consisted of two groups, the *Matua* and the *Atchaot*. The *Matua* possessed most of the privileges and wealth within the society. They controlled land usage and monopolized the high-status occupations such as navigation, canoe building, deep-water fishing, trade, and war. They had high status and had to be shown respect by the *Atchaot* and the lower caste.

The *Atchaot* were members of the families or near relatives of the *Matua*. They had similar privileges and assisted the *Matua* in the honorable professions. *Matua* could be demoted to *Atchaot* status for life or for a specified number of years for breaking customary law.

Members of the lower caste were known as the *Manachang*. According to Spanish accounts, they lived like slaves and were set apart from the rest of society. Their lives were completely governed by restrictions and taboos. They were forbidden to work in the honorable professions, could only eat certain types of foods, and had to show respect to the upper caste.

The clans in the Mariana Islands were grouped into villages, the majority of which were located on the beaches and consisted of from fifty to one hundred fifty huts. Modern estimates of the population of the islands at the time of contact range from fifty to one hundred thousand people. The villages in turn were grouped into districts. The districts were governed by a council or assembly of nobles in which the eldest male and his sister held the highest authority.

Between districts and villages there existed a perpetual state of warfare. The Chamorros made war easily and apparently for almost any reason. They used slings and spears and had no official war leaders. Similarly, they made peace easily. They usually fought until two or three men were killed. At that time, the side that had sustained the greatest losses surrendered and returned home. The victors then held a feast during which they ridiculed the losers.

The economic system resembled that of the other Pacific islanders. It centered on three major types of activities: gardening in jungle clearings, gathering in the jungle and on the reef, and fishing. Unlike the other peoples of Micronesia, the Chamorros also cultivated rice as a ceremonial food.

The Chamorros were skilled craftsmen. They produced a variety of articles in stone, shell, bone, wood, clay, and the other raw materials found on the island. Of the various artifacts that they produced, the most impressive were the latte stones which supported houses, canoe sheds, and the homes of the high caste. Trade was carried out throughout the island chain utilizing shell money as a medium of exchange.

Economic relations within the society were characterized by reciprocity and conspicuous display. Those tasks that were too large for one extended family to accomplish by itself were carried out by the clan as a whole. Everyone within the clan was expected to help, and strict records were kept of each family's contribution. The families that worked on a given task expected repayment at some future time in kind or in an equal commodity.

The principle of conspicuous display tied an individual's or a family's status within the society to what they could afford to share or lose. An individual or family with high status was expected to share their wealth with other individuals or families and, to a large extent, the maintenance of their position depended upon their willingness to do so. The most honored and influential members of the society were those who could afford to be the most generous.

The religious beliefs of the Chamorros are also somewhat obscure. From the extant evidence, they apparently venerated the spirits of the dead, the *Aniti*. The *Aniti*, while no longer a part of the Chamorro's physical environment, were still present and had the power to help or hinder the clan, family, or the individual.

The Chamorros had no organized priesthood, but they did have three types of shamans or sorcerors.

The most powerful of the three was the *makahna*. The *makahna* could communicate with the *Aniti* and invoke them by the use of skulls. They could cause sickness or death, produce rain, and bring good luck in fishing. While the *makahna* specialized in dealing with the *Aniti*, they did not have a monopoly. Any individual could summon an individual *Aniti*, especially if the spirit was a member of his clan or family.

Less powerful than the *makahna* were the *kakahnas*. These men had the power to cause or cure sickness by supernatural means but apparently were not able to control the *Aniti* to the same extent that the *makahnas* could. Finally, there was a group of herb doctors known by the Spanish terms, *suruhano* and *suruhana*. While this group may have used some magic or ritual in their activities, they specialized in curing sickness by physical means.

RELATED ENTRIES: Chamorros Peoples, Origin of; Commonwealth of the Northern Mariana Islands; Guam.

SOURCES AND READINGS: Paul Carano and Pedro Sanchez, *A Complete History of Guam* (Tokyo: Charles E. Tuttle Co., 1964); Laura Thompson, *The Native Culture of the Marianas Islands* (Honolulu: Bernice P. Bishop Museum Bulletin, 1945).

George J. Boughton

CHAMORRO PEOPLES, ORIGIN OF. It was accepted until recently that characteristics shared by the Chamorro and the Philippine languages were of enough significance to indicate that those languages had undergone a common development; and, therefore, that the people of the Mariana Islands had emigrated from the Philippine archipelago. Yet the latest research in linguistics shows that Chamorro does not share the innovations unique to the Philippine languages which resulted in a merged Proto-Philippine 'd.' Such a sound change if found in Chamorro would have indicated that it had developed from a Philippine speech, while the absence of that change suggests that the Chamorro and the Philippine languages are not so closely related as once believed. Thus, places other than the Philippines, especially in Southeast Asia, must be considered as the possible homeland of the Chamorro people.

Historical, cultural, and archaeological research also shows connections between the Marianas and the Philippines. Some of those connections, such as pottery styles and defensive structures, predate the Spanish administration of both areas, an era which lasted from 1565 to 1898 and which resulted in similarities in the cultures and the languages of the two island groups. Today scholars also believe that the rice found growing in the Marianas in the sixteenth century was introduced from the Philippines before European contact. In the seventeenth century, a time of continuing voyages between the two archipelagos, the earliest Christian missionary in the Marianas saw enough similarities between the Chamorro people and those of the Philippines to suggest that they shared common origins. Nevertheless, as with the linguistic data, none of this other evidence is of enough significance to prove that the Chamorros emigrated from the Philippines.

If the similarities between the Chamorro and the Philippine languages and cultures do not indicate a path of migration, they do suggest shared origins and a common development that may have occurred in an area other than the Philippines and from which both groups would have left to settle, directly or indirectly, the Philippines and the Marianas. Those migrations probably would have occurred at different times.

Other scholars have recently suggested that the original Chamorros set out from either Palau, Truk, Ponape, the Celebes, or Japan, to people the Marianas; yet the evidence linking the Chamorro population to those places is not substantial.

Scholars cannot turn to the Chamorros' own beliefs as to their origins, since those beliefs have been lost or altered with time. Further archaeological research has shown that the Marianas were settled by 1527 B.C., and more linguistic comparisons may, in time, give added clues to the origins of the Chamorro people.

Like other Pacific islanders, the people of the Marianas originated somewhere in Southeast Asia, but it remains unknown both where in that area they came from and the route of their migration to the Mariana Islands.

RELATED ENTRIES: Austronesian Languages; Commonwealth of the Northern Mariana Islands; Guam.

SOURCES AND READINGS: J. Gibson, D. Koch, C. Latta, "Chamorro in the Austronesian Language Family," mimeographed (Honolulu: University of Hawaii, 1977); Robert Graham, "The Origins of the Chamorro People," *Micronesian Reporter* 3 (1978): 11-15; Donald M. Topping, *Chamorro Reference Grammar* (Honolulu: University of Hawaii Press, 1973).   *Robert Graham*

CHANDERNAGOR (1879-1882). A three-masted schooner, the *Chandernagor* took the first contingent of colonists to Nouvelle France. Before her departure from Holland in September 1879 the ship was the object of a collusive sale to an American to evade French control and left with neither the mandatory health papers nor a determined flag. The ship carried on board the first appointed governor of the colony with the grand title of Baron Titeu de la Croix de Villebranche. The ship was captained by an American who had never been at sea, but in practice the *Chandernagor* was operated by a Belgian. The passengers were a motley group of eighty-five Germans, Italians, Swiss, Belgians, and French, who were looking for a new home in Nouvelle France. By the time the ship arrived at her destination, in January 1880, a rift had already developed and shortly after landing, de la Croix and the officers of the ship abandoned most of the crew to their fate. While sickness rapidly wreaked havoc and a number of the men died in most distressing circumstances, *Chandernagor* sailed back to Europe via Sydney. When the ship reappeared in the region in September 1882, she was carrying the missionaries of the Order of the Sacred Heart whom the Marquis Charles de Rays had been largely instrumental in having sent to the newly formed diocese of Melanesia and Micronesia. They established themselves on New Britain where to this day the mission is a prosperous center of stability. After her two brief passages in the Pacific, *Chandernagor* was sold by auction in Hong Kong.

RELATED ENTRIES: Catholic Church in the Pacific; *Genil*; *Nouvelle-Bretagne*; Nouvelle France; Rays, Charles (Marquis) de.

SOURCES AND READINGS: G. Brown, *An Autobiography* (London: Hodder and Stoughton, 1908); Public Records Office: General Correspondence: France, FO 27; Pacific Islands, FO58; *Sydney Morning Herald*, 1880.   *Anne-Gabrielle Thompson*

CHANEL, PIERRE (1803-1841). The first canonized Roman Catholic martyr of the Pacific, Pierre Chanel was born in Cuet (Ain), France, 12 July 1803. In 1819 he entered the seminary and was ordained a priest 15 July 1827. In 1831 he became one of the initial priests to join the Marists (Society of Mary), a new missionary order whose *regula* was approved by Pope Gregory XVI in 1836. Chanel, along with a group of other missionaries under the direction of Bishop Pompallier, sailed from Europe and arrived in the Pacific in September of 1837. After visiting Tahiti, the Marists continued on to Wallis Island where they landed Fathers Bataillon and Luzy. On 8 November Fathers Chanel and Delorme arrived on Futuna where they alone began the conversion of the islanders. Bishop Pompallier continued to New Zealand where he established the headquarters of his new see. Continuous warfare among the chiefs on Futuna as well as the frequent arrival of whalers, traders, and beachcombers created a difficult situation in which to teach the Catholic faith. Just when progress was being made both on Wallis and Futuna, disagreement broke out; and on 28 April 1841 chief Musumusu surrounded Chanel's lodgings, entered, and clubbed him to death. Hearing the news in New Zealand, Bishop Pompallier returned to Futuna in May of 1842 to investigate the matter and landed two new missionaries. By 1843 the whole island had become Catholic and has remained so. Pierre Chanel was beatified 17 November 1889, canonized 12 June 1954, and his relics were returned from Paris to Futuna in 1976.

RELATED ENTRIES: Catholic Church in the Pacific; Pompallier, Jean-Baptiste François; Wallis and Futuna.

SOURCES AND READINGS: Florence Gilmore, *The Martyr of Futuna* (New York: Catholic Foreign Mission Society of America, 1914); Claude Rozier, *Ecrits de S. Pierre Chanel* (Paris: Musée de l'Homme, 1960).   *Robert D. Craig*

CHEVRON, (FATHER) JOSEPH (1808-1884).
Father Chevron was an early Catholic missionary in the South Pacific and the first priest to conduct a Catholic mass on Tongan soil. Catholicism reached Tonga on 22 October 1837 when the first group of French Marists (Society of Mary) reached Vava'u. The group was headed by Bishop J. B. Pompallier whose plan was to spread Catholicism to all the Pacific islands. King George I of Tonga agreed to receive only two missionaries if his Wesleyan advisors agreed. The Wesleyan missionaries disliked the idea and opposed the move. The bishop and his party left Vava'u and headed for Wallis Island. No more attempt at Catholic conversion on Tonga was made until 1842 when on 30 June Father Chevron and Brother Attale arrived at Pangaimotu, an island near Nuku'alofa harbor. On this island Father Chevron conducted the first mass on Tongan soil. Paying their respects to chief Aleamotu'a, they were received politely but were told to approach Moeaki, chief of the Ha'a Havea stronghold of Pea. Here they were accepted for the first time. Opposition to the Catholic religion, especially by the followers of King George after 1845, led to open war between 1852 and 1855. The intervention of French war ships brought about a forced toleration of the Catholic faith. Conversion was slow, but by 1892 about one-eighth of the population was Catholic, a growth brought about primarily by natural increase. The first Catholic church was build at Mu'a in 1847 by Father Chevron, and a

school was established in 1855. After forty-two years of Tongan missionary work, Father Chevron died 6 October 1884.

RELATED ENTRIES: Catholic Church in the Pacific; Pompallier, Jean-Baptiste François; Tonga.

SOURCES AND READINGS: A. Monfat, *Les Tonga; ou, Archipel des Amis et le R. P. Joseph Chevron de la Société Marie* (Lyon: E Vitte, 1893); Noel Rutherford, ed., *Friendly Islands: A History of Tonga* (Melbourne: Oxford University Press, 1977).
                      Robert D. Craig

CHIN FOO (1879-1958).
Chin Foo, a banker and industrialist in Tahiti, was born 11 April 1879 in China. He arrived in Tahiti in 1896 where he began a successful career in business: vanilla, copra, and banking. Well respected by his colleagues, Chin Foo was elected president of the Sin Ni Tong Society (building organization). He helped in the establishment of an old-people's home, aided the Red Cross and other health organizations, and greatly expanded the Chinese cemetery outside of Pape'ete. He was the founder and first president of the Chinese Philanthropic Association, and he helped establish one of the three Chinese schools in Pape'ete. He died 26 September 1958 leaving seven children many of whom own successful business there today.

RELATED ENTRIES: French Polynesia.

SOURCES AND READINGS: Gérald Coppenrath, *Les Chinois de Tahiti* (Paris: Musée de l'Homme, 1967); Christian Gleizal, *Histoire et Portrait de la Communauté Chinoise de Tahiti* (Pape'ete: Hibiscus Editions, 1979); Patrick O'Reilly, *Tahitiens* (Paris: Musée de l'Homme, 1962).   *Robert D. Craig*

CIMA (1947-1949).
The Coordinated Investigation of Micronesian Anthropology (CIMA) was a large-scale social science research project coordinated by the Pacific Science Board of the National Academy of Sciences and funded by the U.S. Navy. Forty-two investigators were sent to study various aspects of traditional and contemporary Micronesian cultures in the Marshall, Caroline, and Mariana islands. The project was designed to provide the navy with information that would facilitate the effective and humane administration of the islands, formerly governed by Japan under a League of Nations mandate which had become part of the U.S. Trust Territory of the Pacific Islands. The investigators were free, however, to research subjects of interest. The completed reports covered such diverse topics as material culture, language, geographical knowledge, traditional poli-

tics, and rehabilitation problems. CIMA provided a great deal of information on Micronesian cultures. Some of the investigators remained in the trust territory as anthropological advisors to the naval administration.

RELATED ENTRIES: Micronesia.

SOURCES AND READINGS: H. G. Barnett, *Anthropology in Administration* (New York: Row Peterson, 1956).   *Craig Severance*

CODRINGTON, ROBERT HENRY (1830-1922). Anglican missionary and anthropologist, Robert Codrington was born at Wroughton, Wiltshire, England and educated at Charterhouse and Wadham College at Oxford University. He was ordained in 1855 and elected to a fellowship of his college. In 1867 he joined Bishop John C. Patteson in the Melanesian mission and became headmaster of its training school, newly established at Norfolk Island. A scholar of wide learning, he undertook on the basis of information supplied by his Melanesian pupils a systematic study of the languages and cultures of the northern New Hebrides and Solomon Islands. His books, *The Melanesian Languages* (1885) and *The Melanesians* (1891) are important pioneer works in Pacific linguistics and anthropology. He retired from the mission in 1887 and until his death held various church appointments in the diocese of Chichester, England.

RELATED ENTRIES: Anglican Missions; Patteson, John C.

SOURCES AND READINGS: David Hilliard, *God's Gentlemen: A History of the Melanesian Mission, 1849-1942* (St. Lucia, Queensland: University of Queensland Press, 1978).   *David L. Hilliard*

COMMERCIAL/ECONOMIC IMPORTANCE OF THE PACIFIC ISLANDS. The islands of the Pacific have had a far greater significance in world commerce than figures on production and consumption suggest. As way stations in transpacific trade, as bases for supply and refreshment for fur traders, whalers, and others, as entrepôts to the supposedly limitless markets of Asia, as naval outposts for the defense or harassment of trade, and as tempting tropical paradises that seemed to hold out to the industrious the promise of high productivity, the Pacific islands have had a major impact on decision-makers in the world's diplomatic and commercial centers.

The islands nearer to Asia, especially those of Indonesia, have held an important place in the commerce of the globe since the Age of Discovery. They have yielded spices, rubber, oil, and much more in large quantities. But most Pacific islands have supplied little. Their small total land mass, limited population, and general paucity of resources have kept the productive capacity of Polynesia, Micronesia, and Melanesia low. Isolation has increased production and transportation costs, undermining the competitive position of island products. Still, over the years investors, traders, and other architects of commercial empire have arrived in large numbers, ever hopeful.

Germany's Pacific possessions illustrate the point. Germans worked assiduously from 1856 to 1914 to build a firm economic position in the islands. Yet by 1909 Oceania still represented less than 1/7 of 1 percent of Germany's foreign trade. Copra was the main product of the German-held islands, but under 8.5 percent of the country's copra imports came from there. Phosphates, the second leading export, provided only 5 percent of Germany's needs; Nauru and Angaur loomed large in the Pacific context but supplied a mere 3 percent of the world's phosphate—in contrast to France's North African colonies, which produced 46 percent. Clearly, Germany's quest for colonies in Oceania must be explained in terms other than the productive capacity of the islands, either existing or potential. The same could be said of the commercial activities in the Pacific of most other nations during the nineteenth and twentieth centuries.

It had not always been so. The East Indies were a vital element in the trading empire built by Portugal in the sixteenth century and in the commercial revolution of which Portuguese trade was a part. The East Indies were equally important to the Dutch who supplanted the Portuguese there. The trade of both depended, as did much of the early English commerce in the area, upon Western-controlled ports through which hinterlands and outlying islands could be tapped. Beyond these ports, local control continued largely undisturbed.

Such early Western commercial activities intruded into only one corner of the Pacific. Similarly, traders from China, Korea, Japan, the Ryukyus, and Southeast Asia confined themselves to commerce along the ocean's Asian perimeter. Only Spain did otherwise. From the early seventeenth to the early nineteenth century, Spanish galleons made annual voyages between Manila and Acapulco with mid-ocean stops in Guam, carrying Chinese goods eastward in exchange for Mexican silver. Important though this trade was in securing the Spanish foothold in the Philippines, it was but a small chapter in the larger story of Spanish, to say nothing of world, trade. Not until the nineteenth century did new conditions and technology combine to bring Oceania proper into the world's commerce in an important way.

The United States, once independent, found itself in desperate need of new sources of trade to replace those barred to its citizens by Britain's mercantilistic trading regulations. Americans plunged into the China trade, open to them now that they no longer had to respect the monopoly granted the East India Company by the British Crown. But while there were profits in carrying tea, silk, and other Oriental products from Canton to the West, the United States could not long afford the drain of hard currency of such a one-way trade. Casting about for things to sell in China, Americans found a number of items, including the pelts of sea otters and fur seals, sandalwood, *bêche-de-mer*, shark fins, trochus shell, and ginseng. All came from the Pacific save ginseng which was collected in the forests of the eastern United States. Taken alone, only the fur trade was significant, but collectively the others had importance too. The quest for these luxury items carried Americans into every corner of the Pacific. Goods obtained there made possible a level of trade with China that was important in keeping the American economy afloat until it could build a viable domestic base with the wealth of natural resources within its own boundaries. Moreover, the quest for goods to sell in China did much to increase American activity in Hawai'i and the Pacific Northwest and thus helped pave the way for eventual American hegemony in both.

In later years the dream of wealth through the China trade drew American attention to the West Coast of North America and beyond to the islands, but it was a chimera. Trade with China never again assumed the importance it had during the early years of the Republic, although the shift of whaling from Atlantic to Pacific waters insured a continuation of American vessels calling at Pacific islands.

As Western settlement expanded into the Pacific Basin during the mid-nineteenth century, China and the islands assumed a different role. New settlements on the West Coast of the United States, in Australia, and in New Zealand—separated from the societies that had given them birth by great distances and high transportation costs—turned to lands in and around the Pacific for many of the supplies they needed as well as outlets for a significant portion of their products. Lumber, coal, and foodstuffs went forth in quantity; sugar and other tropical products came back. Hawai'i became tied economically to California, Oregon, and Washington; Fiji and Tahiti to Australasia. The pattern of trade had numerous variations. Coal and lumber went to China; rice, tea, and other Chinese goods were carried either on the return voyage or to third ports in a triangular trade. As important as its volume was the complementary nature of the trade; it supplied an outlet for types and grades of goods not in demand in other available markets. Laborers also became a major traffic. Chinese were carried to Hawai'i and the west coasts of North and South America, Indians to Fiji, and islanders—in that infamous commerce known as blackbirding—to Peru, Queensland, Fiji, and Samoa. In short, the lands in and around the Pacific became entwined in an economic network that supported the development of these isolated lands so far removed from the world's main trade routes and commercial centers. The volume of trade was small compared to that of the great commercial emporiums of the globe; but until better, cheaper means of transportation tied the region more closely to the metropolitan economy near the beginning of the twentieth century, this trade remained vital for the economic prosperity and growth of the Pacific Basin. The area's resulting development was to have world, not merely local, repercussions.

As supply and rest stops for whalers and fur traders and as places to be plundered by sandalwood gatherers and their like, the islands had been but loosely tied to the dominant economies of the world. Plantation agriculture introduced a new order during the late nineteenth century. Henceforth, the world and the islands were closely linked through a resident managerial class. Sugar plantations wrought sweeping changes in Hawai'i, Fiji, and the Marianas. Copra plantations changed less, but affected more places. Pineapple, cotton, coffee, tea, and rubber plantations all had their time and place. For all of these, the metropolitan economy was the main market, the source of expertise and capital, and the vital, shaping force.

The pattern for mining was similar to that for plantation agriculture. Guano extraction on minor islands near the equator came first, but the subsequent development of phosphate mines on Nauru, Angaur, Ocean, and Makatea was more important. So, too, were gold production in Fiji and New Guinea and chromite and nickel production in New Caledonia, once the world's leading producer of these two minerals. Beyond Oceania proper, Indonesia has over the years been a leading producer of oil and has exported much tin as well.

In spite of their geographical propinquity to the islands, neither China nor Japan had significant economic activity there during the nineteenth century. Through much of the period the governments of both discouraged their citizens from going abroad. Licensed traders carried out a "country trade" between

China and the islands off Southeast Asia, and a few Chinese merchants opened small trading operations and stores on various islands farther out into the Pacific, but the overall impact both on China and on the islands was limited. Japanese activity was at first even more restricted, but Japan's conquest of Micronesia during World War I led to a sharp increase thereafter.

But if Asian interest was limited, that of the United States was not. Buoyed by the wave of new Western activity in the area, many Americans around the turn of the century looked to the Pacific as an emerging "New Mediterranean," a center of commerce and civilization where East and West would be tied together by the ocean they shared and the commerce it supported. A new center of world power would emerge dominated by Asia and the United States. Europe and the Atlantic, which had supplanted the old Mediterranean world as the vital center, would themselves soon be supplanted. The writings of American naval strategist Alfred Thayer Mahan, the annexation of Hawai'i and the Philippines, and the belated growth of industry and railroads in China and Japan all conspired to turn the attention of Americans to the Pacific giving credence to the idea of a New Mediterranean. The number of Americans engaged in business on the China coast rose appreciably; attention to Samoa, Hawai'i, and Manila as bases for the protection and support of trade grew; new transpacific steamship lines appeared; and port cities on the Pacific shore looked forward confidently to a period of vibrant growth. The high hopes were soon dashed. The distances involved, the poverty of much of the Pacific Basin's population, and the continuing dominance of the eastern United States and Europe in political and economic matters insured that dreams of Pacific ascendancy were but a will-o'-the-wisp. Neither optimism nor local or national pride could surmount geopolitical realities.

As hopes dimmed, more realistic expectations came to the fore. The Pacific islands lost their anticipated place as vital stepping-stones in a world-dominating New Mediterranean to become economic adjuncts of neighboring powers and minor contributors to the general economic welfare of the globe. Hawai'i was tied ever more closely to the mainland, and to California in particular; the islands of the southwest Pacific to Australasia; and Micronesia to Japan. When Pacific islands once again assumed a major place in the thoughts of world leaders during the period leading up to and during World War II, it was because of their strategic location rather than their economic value. As in the earliest days of European trade in the Pacific, insofar as there was a real economic lure in the islands, it was in those off Southeast Asia, not in those of Oceania.

For all the changes being wrought by tourism, tuna fishing in the central and south Pacific, independence of former colonial lands, the prospect of deep-ocean mining, and other recent developments, there is no reason to assume that the picture will change in any basic way in the years ahead. Indeed, with technological advances in transportation and warfare, some of the importance possessed by Pacific islands earlier in the century has been lost. What economic significance Oceania is to have in the future will primarily result, as it has in the past, from indirect rather than direct sources; production and consumption will remain a tiny part of the global whole. The Pacific islands will remain subservient to economic forces shaped in other quarters.

RELATED ENTRIES: Britain in the Pacific; France in the Pacific; German Colonial Empire; Spain in the Pacific; United States in the Pacific.

SOURCES AND READINGS: Foster Rhea Dulles, *The Old China Trade* (Boston: Houghton Mifflin Co., 1930); Frederick V. Field, ed., *Economic Handbook of the Pacific Area* (New York: Doubleday & Co., 1934); Douglas L. Oliver, *The Pacific Islands*, rev. ed. (Garden City, N.Y.: Doubleday & Co., 1961); John Kearsley Thomson, "Economic Development in the South Pacific: Some Problems and Prospects" in Frank P. King, ed., *Oceania and Beyond: Essays on the Pacific since 1945* (Westport, Conn.: Greenwood Press, 1976).   *Thomas R. Cox*

COMMONWEALTH OF THE NORTHERN MARIANA ISLANDS. The northern Mariana Islands consist of a chain of high volcanic, coral, and limestone outcroppings in the western central Pacific, stretching north to south between Guam and Japan on the eastern border of the Philippine Sea. They are populated primarily by peoples of the Chamorro and Carolinian ethnic groups.

In 1980 the total population was 16,758, centered primarily on the islands of Saipan (13,000), Rota (1,200), and Tinian (750). The islands of Pagan, Agrihan, and Anatahan, to the north of Saipan, are sparsely inhabited; Farallon de Medinilla, Farallon de Pájaros, Las Urracas (Maug), Asunción (Asomsom), Alamagan, Guguan, and Sarigan are unpopulated. About 2,000 alien laborers and residents (primarily Filipino and Korean construction workers) and several hundred American citizens were on Saipan and the other major islands. Until the establishment of the Federated States of Micronesia in 1979, about eight hundred citizens of other trust territory districts were also resident employees of the trust territory government headquartered on Saipan.

Since Spanish explorations beginning with Magellan in 1521 and the first Spanish settlement on Guam in the 1560s, the original Chamorros have been successively colonized by large groups of Spanish, German, Japanese, and presently American citizens.

The island of Guam, ethnically and geographically one of the Marianas, became an American territory in 1898 following the end of the Spanish-American War.

From 1922 to 1945 the Commonwealth of the Northern Marianas was a part of Japan's League of Nations mandate over territories captured from the Germans in World War I and was heavily populated by Japanese nationals. Following the end of World War II, the United States assumed control of the islands as a part of what would become, in 1947, the Trust Territory of the Pacific Islands under the aegis of the United Nations.

In addition to the Japanese influence, the predominantly Chamorro population throughout the northern Marianas has had considerable exposure since 1898 to the American presence on Guam through family and clan relationships which have transcended national and island boundaries.

Economically, the northern Marianas were used by the Japanese as an agricultural area specializing in the production of fruit, sugarcane, and commercial fisheries. Under the American administration, the economic base has been primarily government employment with some semicommercial agriculture and tourism. During the years between 1952 and 1962, Saipan was a major military training area for anticommunist Nationalist Chinese sponsored by the Central Intelligence Agency (CIA) and the United States Navy.

With the presence of the American military on Saipan during the 1950s, considerable development took place on the islands which was not present in the other districts of the trust territory (Micronesia), Truk, the Marshalls, Palau, Yap, and Ponape. When the CIA left in 1962 and the trust territory headquarters was moved into the facilities on Saipan from Guam, that development accelerated. The trust territory government provided employment for over one thousand Micronesians on Saipan during peak years. The net result was a relatively rapid growth in standards of living which outpaced that of the other districts and created a position of advantage for the northern Marianas.

These and other factors (the ethnic rivalries among the Micronesian groups themselves, for example) combined when the United States offered a common-

wealth status to the whole trust territory in 1969. All of the other districts, through the Congress of Micronesia, rejected the offer. The northern Marianas, through their Congressional delegation and district legislature, accepted it. In that same year, the voters of Guam rejected a proposal of unification with the northern Marianas in a referendum, although many citizens of the northern Marianas favored union with Guam.

Efforts of the Congress of Micronesia and the pro-unity forces in the trust territory delayed separation for several years. At that time, the United States favored a unified Micronesia encompassing all of the trust territory, but this position was reversed in 1973 when it accepted separate negotiations with the Northern Marianas Political Status Commission, created by the legislature, which lasted until 1975. The United Nations ineffectively pressed for maintaining a union in the trust territory.

The negotiations with the United States were carried out simultaneously with those of the Congress of Micronesia which were directed towards a status of free association with the United States. The northern Marianas group participated in both sets of negotiations on the principle that the United States might reject the covenant to establish a commonwealth or that the people of the northern Marianas might reject it in favor of union with the rest of Micronesia.

In 1975, negotiations were completed on the covenant to establish the commonwealth "in Permanent Union with the United States." A plebescite, observed by representatives of the United Nations Trusteeship Council, was held on 17 June 1975: 78.8 percent of the nearly 95 percent of the registered voters turned out to vote for the commonwealth covenant.

As a result of the plebescite, administrative separation of the northern Mariana Islands from the rest of the trust territory under a resident commissioner took place on 1 April 1976, following approval of the covenant by the United States Congress.

In December 1976 a Marianas constitutional convention completed its work and drafted a commonwealth constitution which was approved by the voters in a referendum in March 1977. The constitution was further approved by President Gerald Ford who found that it "was not in conflict" with the covenant; elections were held on 10 December 1977 for the first elected governor and legislature of the northern Marianas under the constitution. This government took office on 9 January 1978 with Carlos Camacho, a medical officer, as the first governor.

The constitution and the covenant do not become fully effective until the trusteeship is terminated for all of the trust territory, probably in 1981. Until that time, the citizens of the northern Marianas will still be trust territory citizens, although they are classed as "interim U.S. citizens" with special privileges within the United States. Full American citizenship will occur upon termination of the trusteeship.

RELATED ENTRIES: Guam; Micronesia; Micronesia, Constitution of the Federated States of; Solomon Report.

SOURCES AND READINGS: Paul Carano and Pedro C. Sanchez, *A Complete History of Guam* (Rutland, Vt.: Charles E. Tuttle, 1964); Frank P. King, ed., *Oceania and Beyond: Essays on the Pacific since 1945* (Westport, Conn.: Greenwood Press, 1976); Donald F. McHenry, *Micronesia: Trust Betrayed* (Washington, D.C.: Carnegie Endowment for International Peace, 1975); James H. Webb, *Micronesia and U.S. Pacific Strategy* (New York: Frederick A. Praeger, 1974).   *Sam McPhetres*

CONTEMPORARY STRESS SYNDROMES. One characteristic of Pacific history has been rapid social change following contact between European and Oceanian cultures. Often this contact was abrupt, sometimes harsh. In the past few decades especially, exchange between traditionally distinct societies has increased dramatically, and characteristics of life in the later twentieth century have jointly influenced patterns of human behavior with regard to health. Nowhere is this more apparent than in societies of relatively recent exposure to the modern world, and it is not likely that the sequence can be reversed. This acculturation or mixing of cultures resulted in new roles and life-styles which were not part of earlier Melanesian, Micronesian, and Polynesian patterns. Such changes for traditional authorities, families, and individuals have resulted in new stress patterns, or syndromes, for contemporary Oceania.

Recent developments increasingly view health as not only the ability to rally from disease and injury but also the ability to learn and grow. Thus, stress-related syndromes involve cultural, economic, ecological, psychological, physiological, and social factors linked together and affecting health at the individual level. Changes of life-style from rural subsistence to town and city living, the money economy, modern technology and work, and different consumption patterns further promote the appearance of new stress-related patterns of behavior. These can be exacerbated by diet deficiencies such as undernutrition, protein-calorie malnutrition, and high intake of refined starches, sugars, and salt. Such syndromes, also, are expressed as psychosomatic maladies, for example, obesity, diabetes, hypertension, and heart

disease. Significant, also, are increased mental health problems, especially among urban residents, abuse of alcohol, the use of drugs, and automobile accidents. In Papua New Guinea, for example, the motor vehicle accident rate is twice that of Australia.

These stress-related behavior patterns or syndromes are part of the changing Pacific world and call for broad and practical attention. Yet, stress is a necessary part of life and can be productive if it leads to learning and growth. Thus, the continuation of traditional patterns of achievement, such as the "Big Man" complex in Melanesia, reflects an evolutionary selection producing newer generations linked to both past and present. The challenge is how to manage these new stress-related problems, and Pacific governments are increasingly aware of this need for their citizens.

RELATED ENTRIES: Cargo Cults; Micronesia; Papua New Guinea; Papua New Guinea, Mental Health Services in; Squatter Settlements.

SOURCES AND READINGS: T. Bayless-Smith and R. Reachem, eds., *Subsistence and Survival—Rural Ecology in the Pacific* (London: Academic Press, 1977); B. G. Burton-Bradley, *Stone Age Crisis, a Psychiatric Appraisal* (Nashville: Vanderbilt University Press, 1975); H. Selye, *The Stress of Life* (New York: McGraw-Hill, 1956).

Kerry J. Pataki-Schweizer

COOK ISLANDS. The Cook Islands are an internally self-governing state in free association with New Zealand. The archipelago consists of fifteen islands located between the Samoan and Society islands (between 156° to 167° west longitude and between 8° to 23° south latitude). The total land area is 240 km² (95 mi²). The largest volcanic islands are Rarotonga (65 km²) and Mangaia (51 km²) in the southern group while the islands in the northern group are submerged volcanic peaks covered with coral which form small atolls. The total population consists of approximately 19,000 most all of whom are Polynesian by extract and nearly one-half live on Rarotonga where Avarua is the chief administrative center.

Climate, Flora, and Fauna. The climate of the Cook Islands varies, but generally it is moderate tropical with an average mean temperature of 23.6° C (74.5° F). Average rainfalls measures 2,030 mm (80 inches). The islands produce coconuts, breadfruit, bananas, mangoes, sweet potatoes, pandanus, taro, and yams. Citrus fruit, pineapples, cotton, and coffee have all been introduced. Land shortage prevents any great agriculture or animal husbandry. Fish are limited.

Pre-European History. Tradition tells us that the ancestors of the Cook Islanders came from Tahiti and Samoa sometime in the thirteenth century; but upon landing, they found that the islands had already been peopled by immigrants from the Marquesas. The culture of each of the fifteen islands, therefore, developed separately; and it was not until 1901 that they were brought into a single governing unit. The traditional invaders from Tahiti and Samoa (Tangia and Kariha) divided the land into *tapere* (districts) which were governed by subchieftains whose positions were passed down generally through the senior male line (although land and other rights could be inherited through a mother's line). Extended family units lived in close proximity of one another. Chiefs (*ariki*) were required to provide leadership during war, to settle district disputes, to allocate land, and to represent their people in the religious ceremonies in the *marae* (temples) in return for respect as well as goods and services. Tradition indicates a hierarchy of titles and social positions (especially on Rarotonga, probably the most stratified of any in the Cook Islands). Conflicts between chiefs were frequent, and their reasons were many: wife and food stealing, ambition, and disputes over titles, lands, and crops.

European Intrusion. The first European to sight any of the Cook Islands was Alvaro de Mendaña in 1595; Quirós landed on Rakahanga in 1606; and James Cook (after whom the islands were named) located five in the southern group in the 1770s. Captain Bligh and his mutineers visited Aitutaki, Rarotonga (1789), and Muretu.

The Missionary Period 1821-1888. In 1821 John Williams, a member of the London Missionary Society on his way from Tahiti to Sydney, landed two Tahitian missionaries, Papehia and Vahapata, on Aitutaki. Two years later in 1823 Williams returned to the islands and Papehia volunteered to proselyte the island of Rarotonga. With only one companion from the island of Ra'iatea, Papehia successfully introduced Christianity among the Rarotongans using the age-old technique of first converting the chiefs who set the example for their followers. Papehia married a daughter of Chief Tinomana and took a chiefly title. Williams returned again in 1827, learned the language, and devised an alphabet and a written vocabulary. Other English missionaries arrived; and in 1834 Williams left for Samoa. Villages developed as the missionaries encouraged the people to gather together in several centers where they imitated European ways: built single-family dwellings, clothed themselves in cotton garments, met together for daily prayers, and worked in their gardens in the new order.

Christian legal codes were adopted (using the Ra-'iatean code as a base) as high offices in the church were filled by chiefs and their favorites, and it is not surprising that a theocratic system developed here as it had in Geneva and Zurich under Calvin and Zwingli. Heavy fines were levied against dancing, kava drinking, wearing of flowers, using coconut oil on the body, and countless other acts to "supress pagan ideas and barbarous revivals." Thus, the abolition of violence led to a more stable political situation in the islands. Schools were established and by the mid-1850s most Rarotongans could read the religious literature available to them. Many old beliefs, of course, remained in their early Christian history. The power of the chiefs (*ariki*) continued to dominate both church and state. As a result, no one individual ever became "king" over the group. Women's positions in society were enhanced; and in 1845 the Mahea (*ariki*) title was inherited by a woman. Crafts were taught, and surplus goods and crops were traded to outsiders, a situation that by 1870 had brought in the "undesirable" influences that profoundly affected the islands' history. By 1860 Europeans in fairly large numbers could be found on the islands. French expansion into the Pacific and New Zealand's merchants' plot to annex Rarotonga alarmed the *ariki* who petitioned for British protection. No annexation occurred; but by the end of the 1860s, New Zealand continued to be the trading center for Cook Islands' produce.

Throughout the 1870s, the islanders prospered while their economic and social ties with New Zealand became even closer. The attempt of the Reverend James Chalmers to create a centralized government failed to materialize as the *ariki* council maintained its authority, although Mahea ("Queen") Takau dominated affairs in and around Avarua, the growing political and economic center of the islands. Leaders of the islands more and more began to imitate Western ways—often not the ways of the London Missionary Society members. As a result, mission influence in the islands waned while the authority and power of the local *ariki* increased.

French expansion in the Pacific again convinced the British Foreign Office in 1881 to appoint trader C. E. Goodman as British consul for the islands.

British Protectorate 1888-1901. Pressure from the New Zealand government and especially those who wished to see a "British Pacific Ocean" (Sir George Gray, for example) lead to the eventual establishment of a British protectorate over the islands. In 1885 the New Zealand legislature proposed that the islands between New Zealand and the Panama Canal should be brought under British control. When Mahea visited

Auckland and suggested such an eventuality, the British Foreign Office on 27 September 1888 declared a protectorate over Rarotonga and neighboring islands. In October 1890 Frederick Moss, former member of the New Zealand House of Representatives, became the British resident, appointed and paid by the New Zealand government. Bitter disputes and factions within the Cook Islands society awaited Moss' arrival.

Moss encouraged the chiefs to establish a more centralized or federal-type government with a general council. Laws passed by the council also required the approval of the British resident and Mahea was chosen head of the government.

In 1893 another reorganization of the government included the establishment of an elected lower house —House of the People—where laws were to originate (although the House of *Ariki* held a veto over any laws passed). Public-works projects were initiated, taxes levied, liquor traffic controlled, primary schools taught in English established, health services made available, a first census taken (1895 with a total population of nearly twenty-five hundred). Moss' suggested change in land tenure, however, fell on deaf ears; and his efforts at financial and tax reforms were premature.

After some serious dispute between Moss, Parliament, and the West Pacific high commissioner, the Colonial Office felt that Moss should be recalled and that the islands should be annexed and taken over by New Zealand. Backed up by a show of naval strength and with great ceremonial pomp, Lt. Col. W. E. Gudgeon landed on Rarotonga. He set about reorganizing the local court system and placed it under the Resident's authority as chief justice of the high court, abolished lower district councils, restricted Oriental immigration, established stricter liquor laws, repealed many of the "blue laws," and provided for the deportation of "undesirables."

By 1900 the Cook Islands had apparently in the eyes of the British been readied for a different status than just a protectorate. In 1896 the Colonial Office had agreed to eventual incorporation of the islands within the boundaries of New Zealand. When the premier promised loans to purchase an island schooner, reciprocal trade agreements, restriction of the number of Oriental immigrants, stronger liquor laws, and higher educational standards, the *ariki* agreed to annexation. The bill was passed on 26 September 1900 by the New Zealand legislature and signed by the *ariki* on 8 October 1900.

Changes 1901-1935. Gudgeon's administration (1901-1909) departed significantly from that of the protectorate. As resident commissioner and with little or no supervision from Wellington, Gudgeon carried out a series of reforms that essentially made him the sole executive power in the islands. District governments as well as *ariki* courts were abolished, islanders lost control of finances and of appointment of officials, and the native land court was headed by a European judge.

In 1908 the *ariki* expressed their dissatisfaction with the way in which the government was being handled from New Zealand. As a result, the Cook Islands Ministry was placed under the Minister for Native Affairs whose ministers (James Carroll 1909-1912, Sir Maui Pomare 1913-1918, and Sir Apirani Ngata 1928-1934) were members of the Young Maori Party who adopted a policy of gradual (*Taihoa*) Europeanization for the Cook Islanders. Although the Cook Island Act was passed in 1915 (containing over 660 sections which codified most of the islands' laws), fewer and fewer Cook Islanders were involved in administrative decisions.

During World War I, many islanders served in military service for Britain; as they returned, they became restless with the state of affairs in their country. In 1920 a New Zealand investigating team visited Rarotonga and heard their complaints. Subsequent parliamentary action provided for European representation in the courts (they had had no representation up to this time) and the prohibition of alcoholic beverages. (Europeans had also been generally "outside" the previous laws passed regarding alcohol.)

The 1920s generally brought prosperity to the islands while an effort was made to improve educational and medical services and to increase exports. Health and sanitation conditions were improved by women's committees to inspect houses and plantations. The *ariki* grew less and less important, and their functions became more and more advisory in character. Little political development toward any local self-government was emphasized by the New Zealand government.

The Labor Government in Power 1935-1949. When the New Zealand government had annexed the islands, it had done so primarily because of commercial interests. The Taihoa ministry emphasized the improvement of medical and educational facilities. When the New Zealand Labour Party came to power between 1935 and 1949, again the emphasis was economic. An investigating team from New Zealand made several recommendations to improve the orange exporting business: a citrus expert was appointed to aid growers, fertilizers were required to be used, pruning and replanting were to be carried out, and land was to be partitioned into individually owned units. The citrus industry began recovery from the world depression just as World War II broke out. Storms in 1940, 1943, and 1944, however, did havoc to the industry. Making up for it, however, was the growth and development of trade in island curios sold to Americans stationed in the Pacific, especially in New Zealand.

Although Cook Islanders were not recruited for the war effort, many young men traveled to New Zealand where they enlisted. Other Cook Islanders moved to New Zealand as well as Makatea where they found well-paying jobs. Women were in demand as domestic servants and unskilled workers in shops and factories. It is estimated that approximately three hundred to four hundred Cook Islanders under the age of thirty emigrated to New Zealand during the war. Islanders who returned came back with accounts of the better conditions in New Zealand. To make it even more pointed, the American military on Aitutaki hired islanders at relatively high wages while at the same time they criticized the New Zealand government for neglecting the islands.

Grievances mounted, and the agitators met and formed the Cook Islands Progressive Association (CIPA) units which sprang up on Aitutaki, Rarotonga, and then among Cook Islanders in Auckland where, in 1945, Auckland became the headquarters of the movement. Albert R. Henry, secretary of the Auckland branch and son of an Aitutakian chief, compiled lists of demands which included higher wages, improved shipping, Cook Islands representation in the New Zealand parliament, and other requirements. In January 1946 the large number of CIPA members in Avarua held a successful strike against the Union Company. Meanwhile the government organized a Cook Islands Industrial Union of Workers (CIIUW) primarily from anti-CIPA members in the islands. Another successful mass demonstration against the New Zealand administration in December of 1947 enhanced the position of the CIPA in the eyes of the people.

The resident commissioner appealed to Wellington for armed assistance. On 4 March 1948 twelve police flew to Rarotonga where a few days later they were able to disperse the CIPA pickets led by Albert Henry. This affair was settled when the CIPA renounced any connections with the Communist party and agreed not to involve themselves in Cook Islands unions.

Road to Independence. As a result of the United Nations concern over non-self-governing territories and the recent events in the Cook Islands, the New Zealand government stated in 1946 that they would be happy to create a closer association with the islands. An appellate court was created and provision was made for the formation of a Cook Islands legis-

lative council with members from each of the islands whose powers generally controlled some internal affairs. The island councils were reconstituted. Since council meetings were held only one or two weeks out of the year and council members were elected yearly, little "education" could be gained by this short term of office.

The legislative council, however, was reorganized in 1957 into the legislative assembly with twenty-two elected and five official members, having increased local power. An executive committee was established replacing the financial committee to advise the government and generally to supervise appropriations of funds, even those granted from New Zealand. With continual pressures from the United Nations to grant independence to colonial countries and peoples, New Zealand announced in 1962 that the Cook Islands would have internal self-government within three years. After discussion in the legislative assembly and the New Zealand parliament, the main principles of a Cook Islands constitution were worked out. On 17 November 1964 the Cook Islands Constitutional Act was passed by the New Zealand parilament to be effective following island elections in 1965.

CIP and Sir Albert Henry 1965-1978. The New Cook Islands Party (CIP) headed by Albert Henry swept the elections, winning fourteen of the twenty-two seats. Henry's party was successful primarily because it was the only organized party with a dynamic leader, a cause, and a constitution. Henry had been active in the labor organizations in New Zealand where he had been living. On 28 July Albert Henry was appointed premier and on 4 August 1965 the Cook Islands became a self-governing state in free association with New Zealand who retained responsibility for external affairs and defense.

At the same time, the constitution was amended to allow Henry to run for a government position (he had been out of the country) and to establish the House of Ariki as an advisory or consultative body in matters relating to land and local custom. Henry's thirteen-year administration (1965-1978) has been so criticized that it may be sometime before an accurate accounting can be made of his contributions to the islands. In March 1978 he called a general election. Fear that his opposition, led by Dr. Tom Davis (Democratic Party), might gain seats in the assembly, Henry and colleagues chartered Ansett Airlines to fly his "selected supporters" from New Zealand to Rarotonga for a "weekend free trip," and, of course, to vote for him in the elections. Henry and his CIP party won. Davis and other influential leaders filed charges in the Cook Islands court accusing Henry of conspiracy and misappropriation of public funds. On 24 July 1979 Chief Justice Gaven Donne found

Henry and colleagues guilty. A fine was levied and Henry was forbidden to engage in any Cook Islands politics for three years. Other charges of overt nepotism, bribery, corruption, misuse of public funds, disregarding the democratic process, and many others were publically leveled at his past government by citizens and leaders of the opposition. Having been knighted in 1974 by Queen Elizabeth II, Henry was stripped of those honors in 1980 by the same powers. Upon his unexpected death on 1 January 1981, his cousin Geoffrey Arama Henry became the new head of the Cook Islands Party.

RELATED ENTRIES: Cook, (Captain) James; London Missionary Society; Mangaia, Cook's Visit to; Mangaian Chiefs and Colonial Authorities; Mangaia's New Order; Moss, Frederick J.; Polynesia, Settlement of; Polynesian Culture (Ancient); South Pacific Commission; South Pacific Forum; Williams, John.

SOURCES AND READINGS: William Coppell and Bess Flores, *Cook Islands Bibliography* (Laie, Hawaii: Institute for Polynesian Studies, forthcoming); Tom Davis, Ron Crocombe, et al. *Cook Islands Politics: The Inside Story* (Auckland: Polynesian Press, 1979); Richard Gilson, *The Cook Islands 1820-1950*, ed. Ron Crocombe (Wellington: Victoria University Press, 1980).   *Robert D. Craig*

COOK, (CAPTAIN) JAMES (1728-1779). Considered the greatest of all Pacific explorers and navigators, James Cook was born in Yorkshire, England, 27 October 1728. At the age of seventeen he was apprenticed to a shipowner in Whitby. In 1752 he joined the British navy and saw military action in 1756 in Newfoundland against the French. Between 1763 and 1767 he surveyed and mapped the Newfoundland coast, a work that gained for him a reputation as a scholar as well as a first-rate seaman.

First Voyage 1768-1771. In 1768 the Royal Society commissioned Cook to sail to Tahiti to observe the passage of the planet Venus before the sun and to try to find the unknown southern continent, the *Terra Australis*. Accompanying Cook was a scientific crew headed by Joseph Banks. Everywhere that Cook's ship landed, samples of flora were collected while Cook charted and mapped everything he could. His stay in Tahiti (and other islands) allowed him to log ethnographic data concerning these newly discovered Pacific peoples. After leaving Tahiti, Cook sailed to New Zealand where he charted the 3,540 km coast. No *Terra Australis* was located. Finally, after a journey of almost three years, he returned home.

Second Voyage 1772-1775. Cook was quickly promoted to commander and commissioned once again

to sail to the Pacific to try to locate the illusive southern continent. For months, Cook's ships, the *Resolution* and the *Adventurer*, sailed into the Antarctic regions of the South Atlantic and the South Pacific without finding the continent. After stopping in Tahiti to refurbish the ships and to rest his men, they were off once again and for the next year Cook sailed the Pacific trying to locate islands that had been previously "discovered" by other Europeans whose faulty equipment had led to erroneous locations being given. The scientific and cartographic results achieved by Cook were outstanding, and when Cook arrived back in England in July of 1775, he was hailed a national hero.

Third Voyage 1776-1779. Once again the Royal Society asked Cook to command yet another expedition to the Pacific to find the fabled Northwest Passage that might connect the North Atlantic with the North Pacific. After visiting the Society Islands, Cook and his crew were ready for the journey northward. In January 1778 Cook discovered the Hawaiian Islands, naming them the Sandwich Islands after his friend and patron, the Earl of Sandwich. After failing to find the Northwest Passage, Cook returned to the warm Hawaiian waters. On 14 February 1779, in a scuffle with the Hawaiians, Cook was killed. His second-in-command, Captain James Clerke, continued the expedition, but he was no more successful than Cook in the attempt to find the Northwest Passage.

Cook's Achievements. Cook's achievements were unparalleled. He discovered or rediscovered Hawai'i, Christmas Island, New Caledonia, Cook Islands, Gilbert Islands, Fiji, Tonga, Solomons, Easter, part of the Tuamotus, and the Antarctic. He proved the nonexistence of the great unknown southern continent as well as the fabled Northwest Passage to the Atlantic. He proved that New Guinea, New Zealand, and Australia were not part of the same landmass. During his many voyages, Cook never lost one man due to the killer disease of the time—scurvy. His strict dietetic laws helped prove that proper diet could prevent this common disease at sea. Navigators, scholars, and laymen today still testify to his greatness. He is regarded as the most moderate, humane, gentle circumnavigator who ever went upon discoveries . . . the ablest and most renowned navigator that any country has produced.

RELATED ENTRIES: Britain in the Pacific.

SOURCES AND READINGS: J. C. Beaglehole, *The Life of Captain James Cook* (Stanford: Stanford University Press, 1974); Robert D. Craig, *Captain Cook in the Pacific* (La'ie, Hawai'i: Brigham Young University, Hawai'i Campus Press, 1978); Alan Villiers,

"The Man who Mapped the Pacific" *National Geographic* 149 (1971): 299-349.   *Robert D. Craig*

COPRA TRADE. No other Western economic activity has touched the lives of so many Pacific islanders as has the copra trade. Coconut palms grow on all but the most forbidding atolls. Drying the meat of coconuts to make copra is a process simple enough for even the most technologically unsophisticated. Production requires but little investment capital. Moreover, copra has drawn outsiders—traders, planters, and their governments—to places where few would have otherwise gone. From its rise to importance in the late nineteenth century, copra has provided the main export for much of the Pacific world. The Philippines, Indonesia, Ceylon, and Malaysia have been the largest producers, but in Oceania copra's impact has been greater—and more readily apparent. Life in many areas has been, and continues to be, dominated by copra.

European demand created the trade. By the 1860s supplies of animal fats were insufficient to meet rising needs. Lacking America's ready source of cottonseed oil, Europeans turned to tropical vegetable oils. Many proved cheaper than animal fats even with the added cost of transportation. Of them, coconut oil was easily the most important. It went into soaps, margarine, explosives, and other products. By 1910 coconut oil, although still largely unknown in the United States, was widely used in Europe despite the opposition of the dairy and cattle industries.

Germans pioneered the copra trade. The firm of J. C. Godeffroy and Son of Hamburg established a factory at Apia in 1856. At first the firm exported coconut oil in casks, but it soon discovered the advantages of shipping unpressed copra. Pressing in Europe yielded a purer oil that was not rancid on arrival, and the residue could be profitably sold for cattle feed. Beginning in 1865 Godeffroy and Son acquired extensive acreage in Samoa for coconut plantations. Others followed suit, and plantation-raised coconuts soon furnished most copra. Tonga, more politically stable than Samoa, soon became the company's main supplier. In 1869 Godeffroy entered into an agreement with the Wesleyan mission which gave the German firm a virtual monopoly of Tonga's export trade. By the 1870s Godeffroy's agents were scattered across the Pacific from Tahiti to the Marianas. Godeffroy and Son collapsed in 1879 due to unsuccessful mining speculations and the effects of the French blockade during the Franco-Prussian War. Its role as dominant force in the commerce of the southwestern Pacific was assumed by *Deutsche Handels-und Plantagen-Gesellschaft der Südsee-Inseln zu Hamburg* (DHPG) which took over key Godeffroy holdings.

The development of coconut plantations drew Westerners ever more deeply into island politics, especially in Samoa. But their impact was felt in other ways too. Local populations were unable or unwilling to meet the demand for plantation labor. DHPG's plantations came to rely on New Britain and New Ireland for most of their laborers and in the process unleashed powerful forces for acculturation and social disruption. The trade, coupled with the contact Melanesians had with the outside world while working on plantations, helped to generate demand for Western goods. One observer noted that when Germans first arrived in the Bismarck Archipelago "business was restricted to barter trade of the humblest kind; the people had no needs. . . ." (Oliver, p. 91). Gradually demand developed not only for iron and cotton goods, but for beer, ship's biscuit, canned goods (especially corned beef), sewing machines, and much more. Yet for all the changes it unleashed, the copra trade was, in Douglas Oliver's words, "a stabilizing influence, with slow evolutionary effects on native life." Other forms of Western incursion into Oceania have generally been more destructive.

Price fluctuations have plagued coconut planters. After the expulsion of Germans as a result of World War I, many British, Australian, and New Zealand small landholders moved in. Underfinanced and inexperienced, most failed. By 1939 the small planter was almost gone. Large firms, including Lever Brothers Pacific Plantations and Burns Philp (South Seas) dominated production. But some output remained in the hands of islanders, stemming in large part from the successful development of cooperatives in the Gilbert and Ellice islands. The adoption of the inexpensive and efficient Ceylon dryer, which yielded a better product than smoke drying, also proved a boon to production by islanders in areas where sun drying was impractical.

World War II had disastrous effects on the trade. Prices were high, but shipping unavailable. Disease and insects, such as the rhinoceros beetle, wreaked further havoc. Recovery was slow in the Philippines and Indonesia, opening the way for a larger share of the trade for Oceania, but detergents, which replaced soap, and awareness of the dangers to health from saturated fats such as coconut oil subsequently dampened demand. On Guam the continuing military presence has pushed wages and expectations upwards and opened new economic opportunities, and as a result, coconuts are now left to rot on the ground. Meanwhile, in an effort to provide jobs and keep profits in the area, plants have been established at

Suva and Rabaul to press copra once more in the Pacific. The great days of the copra trade may be over, but on islands where tourism, military posts, and other alternative sources of income are not available, copra will surely remain the backbone of the economy for years to come.

RELATED ENTRIES: Commercial/Economic Importance of the Pacific Islands.

SOURCES AND READINGS: Stewart G. Firth, "German Firms in the Pacific Islands, 1857-1914," *Journal of Pacific History* 8 (1973):10-28; E. J. E. Lefort, *Economic Aspects of the Coconut Industry in the South Pacific* (Noumea: South Pacific Commission, 1956); Douglas Oliver, *The Pacific Islands*, rev. ed. (Garden City, N.Y.: Doubleday & Co., 1961). *Thomas Cox*

CORAL SEA ISLANDS TERRITORY. Located 77° 30' south latitude and 151° 00' east longitude, the Coral Sea Islands since 1969 have been Australia's newest external territory (the others being the Australian Antarctic Territory, Ashmore and Cartier, Christmas, Cocos [Keeling], Heard and McDonald, and Norfolk Islands). The territory lies east of Queensland outside the Great Barrier Reef and is comprised in part of Herald Beacon Islet, Bird Islet, Bougainville Reef, Cato, Chilcott Islet, Frederick Reef, Lihou Reef islands, Mellish Reef, Pocklington Reef, West Islet, Wreck Reef, and the Willis group. The islands are uninhabited but are used as weather stations and lighthouse sites. This territory was acquired from Britain and was originally surveyed by His Majesty's ships *Cato* (1803), *Frederick* (1812), and *Herald* (1854-60).

RELATED ENTRY: Norfolk Island.

Frank P. King

CREAGH, STEPHEN MARK (1826-1902). A missionary and printer of the London Missionary Society, Stephen Creagh arrived in the Loyalty Islands with John Jones in 1854. The missionaries began a successful Protestant mission in the Si Gwahma region of Maré Island. Supported by the Naisiline chiefs, the mission soon numbered three thousand followers. The mission stations were very prosperous centers boasting large houses, workshops, and printing presses. Creagh's wife died on Maré in 1855. The same year he voyaged to Samoa to print the Gospel of Saint Luke in the Maré language. From Samoa he journeyed to Sydney where he remarried. Returning to Maré in 1858 Creagh worked on additional translations and organized a school for children. In 1864 he printed the entire New Testament. Difficulties

with the French administration in New Caledonia and the growing Catholic missions made his later years in the Loyalty Islands troublesome. He left for England in 1876 where he published more translations. Creagh returned to Lifou two years later and labored there until 1886. After settling in Sydney he made frequent trips to the Loyalty Islands, the last in 1893.

RELATED ENTRIES: Jones, John; Loyalty Islands.

SOURCES AND READINGS: K. R. Howe, *The Loyalty Islands: A History of Culture Contacts 1840-1900* (Honolulu: University Press of Hawai'i: 1977); Patrick O'Reilly, *Calédoniens* (Paris: Musée de l'Homme, 1953). *Russell T. Clement*

CROCKER, (CAPTAIN) W. (d. 1840). Noted for his heroic attempt to arbitrate a peace settlement between Tongan King George I and his enemies, Captain Crocker of the H.M.S. *Favourite* arrived in Nuku'alofa on 21 June 1840 in the midst of a war between King George and those rebelling against his rule. On 22 June the king sent a petition for help to Crocker and on 24 June with about half of his men, Crocker set out for Pea, the enemy's fort. At about one hundred yards from the fort, Crocker approached with a flag of truce. The terms of peace he suggested were that all fortifications of both parties be torn down and everyone return to his own village. He gave the chiefs only a half hour to consider the terms. After the specified time, Crocker attempted to intervene once again. The insurgents refused, commenced firing, and Crocker was killed in the melee.

RELATED ENTRIES: Britain in the Pacific; Tonga.

SOURCES AND READINGS: W. P. Morrell, *Britain in the Pacific Islands* (Oxford: Clarendon Press, 1960); Noel Rutherford, ed., *Friendly Islands: A History of Tonga* (Melbourne: Oxford University Press, 1977); A. H. Wood, *History and Geography of Tonga* (Victoria: Border Morning Mail, 1972). *Etta Harris*

CROOK, WILLIAM P. (1775-1846). A missionary of the London Missionary Society, William Crook sailed on the *Duff* to the South Pacific in 1796. His first mission was in the Marquesas (1797-1798) where he met with no success. He returned to England and then went back to Australia in 1804 where he founded the first school for girls and the First Congregational Church in Sydney. In 1816 he left for Tahiti where he aided the missionaries in the conversion of the Tahitians. He helped the Reverend Henry Nott in the translation of the Scriptures and the Reverend William Ellis in the printing of the first books in the

Polynesian languages. He revisited the Marquesas in 1825 but again without success. He returned to Australia in 1830 where he died 14 June 1846.

RELATED ENTRIES: Ellis, William; French Polynesia; London Missionary Society; Marquesas; Nott, Henry; Thomson, Robert.

SOURCES AND READINGS: Patrick O'Reilly, *Tahitiens* (Paris: Musée de l'Homme, 1962); James Sibree, ed., *Register of the Missionaries of the London Missionary Society* (London: LMS, 1923); Crook's journal is being edited by Neil Gunson and will be published by the Australian National University Press.

Robert D. Craig

D

D'ALBERTIS, LUIGI MARIA (1841-1901). An Italian naturalist and explorer, d'Albertis was born at Voltri, near Genoa, on 21 November 1841 and died at Sassari, on Sardinia, on 2 September 1901. He fought for Giuseppe Garibaldi in 1860 and then traveled widely in Europe before scientific curiosity and the desire for adventure led him to New Guinea. He spent most of 1872 in Irian Jaya with his countryman, the botanist Odoardo Beccari. In 1875 he explored the Papuan coast and the lower Fly River. He returned to the Fly in 1876 and 1877.

During his most famous exploit, the 1876 expedition, he named the Victor Emmanuel Range. But his chief importance lies in the scientific value of his collections of animals, plants, and artifacts which are now housed in various institutions in Europe and Australia. His book, *New Guinea: What I Did and What I Saw*, was published in English and Italian in 1880. It is a valuable historical source on account of its wide-ranging descriptions though it also shows him to be a ruffian. The cause of science, he wrote, could not allow the "slightest repentance" for robbing villages, and for security it was necessary to inspire the islanders "with a wholesome dread of approaching you."

Like those of the Marquis de Rays, d'Albertis' activities are also significant in that they contributed to the fear of the Australian colonists that a non-European power might establish itself in Australia's near north. This fear led to the declaration of a British protectorate in southeastern New Guinea in 1884.

RELATED ENTRIES: British New Guinea; Papua New Guinea.

SOURCES AND READINGS: Eugénie and Hugh Laracy, *The Italians in New Zealand and other Studies* (Auckland: Società Dante Alighieri, 1973); Gavin Souter, *New Guinea: The Last Unknown* (Sydney: Angus and Robertson, 1963). *Hugh Laracy*

DAMIEN, (FATHER) JOSEPH (1840-1889). Priest and missionary to the leper colony on Moloka'i, Hawai'i, Joseph Damien des Veuster was born at Treme-

lo, Belgium, 3 January 1840. He was professed into the Congregation of the Sacred Hearts of Jesus and Mary (Picpus Fathers) at Louvain, Belgium. He arrived in Honolulu, Hawai'i, in March 1864 and was ordained on 21 May. Damien served for eight years as a missionary on the island of Hawai'i before volunteering to serve the lepers at Kalaupapa on the island of Moloka'i in 1873—eight hundred lepers neglected except for clothing and food. Officially, Damien was the pastor of the Catholic colony, but he served as the lepers' physician, counselor, house builder, sheriff, and undertaker. For ten of his sixteen years, he was without the companionship of other priests. He founded two orphanages at the colony and effectively fought the immorality, drunkeness, and lawlessness that he found among the lepers. In 1884, he discovered that he had contracted leprosy, but he continued his labors with the aid of two priests, two brothers, and a group of Franciscan sisters. He continued the work untiringly until a month before his death. His last years were also plagued by the misunderstanding between him, his superiors, and fellow priests. One attack upon Damien's reputation by a Protestant clergyman was answered by the famous writer, Robert Louis Stevenson, in his *Open Letter to Dr. Hyde* (Boston, 1900).

RELATED ENTRIES: Catholic Church in the Pacific; Hawai'i.

SOURCES AND READINGS: Gavan Daws, *Holy Man: Father Damien of Molokai* (New York: Harper & Row, 1973); John Forow, *Damien: The Leper* (New York: Sheed and Ward, 1937); May Quinlan, *Damien of Molokai* (London: MacDonald and Evans, 1909). *Michael P. Singh*

DAMPIER, WILLIAM (1652-1715). English explorer, navigator, hydrographer, buccaneer, and author, William Dampier was born in East Coker, Somersetshire.The son of a tenant farmer, Dampier was orphaned at an early age. As a young man he fought as an able seaman in the Dutch War of 1673, later briefly managed a plantation in Jamaica, became a logwood cutter in Honduras, and actively participated in various buccaneering expeditions against Spanish settlements in the New World.

In 1683 he sailed on a buccaneering enterprise from Virginia, crossed the Atlantic to West Africa, rounded Cape Horn, and entered the Pacific to attack Spanish towns on the western coast of South America. Eventually Dampier joined a group led by Captain Swan to the Ladrones (Mariana Islands) and then the southern Philippines. After several months the crew, including Dampier, abandoned Captain Swan and several others on the island of Mindanao and proceeded eastward. Following a series of curious adventures and unexpected misfortunes, including being marooned on the Nicobar Islands, Dampier finally returned to England in September 1691. Several years later he published an account of his adventures in his book *A New Voyage Round the World* (1697) and a supplemental volume, *Voyages and Descriptions*, which included his *Discourses of Trade Winds*, an important treatise on hydrography.

Through the help of influential friends, Dampier became a naval officer and received an appointment to command the *Roebuck*, an old vessel of approximately 292 tons and loaded with twelve guns. The Admiralty commissioned him to undertake a voyage to New Holland (Australia), and in formal instructions reminded the newly appointed officer that the expedition would be an expensive one and that he must use his best efforts to make some discovery of value. Thus the expedition of 1699-1701, with a small crew commanded by Dampier, using the route via the Cape of Good Hope, sailed to New Holland, New Guinea, and New Britain. His ship, the *Roebuck*, foundered off Ascension Island in February 1701, but all his men were rescued by a homeward-bound convoy of ships of war and East Indiamen.

Between 1703 and 1707 Dampier commanded a fruitless privateering expedition in the Pacific. On his last voyage, he served as chief pilot to Captain Woodes Rogers whose ship sailed around Cape Horn. This voyage turned out to be a financial success, and the backers realized an enormous profit from their investment. Dampier, however, did not live to receive his share, for he died in March 1715 in St. Stephen parish, London.

RELATED ENTRIES: Britain in the Pacific; Mariana Islands.

SOURCES AND READINGS: Willard H. Bonner, *Captain William Dampier, Buccaneer-Author* (Stanford: Stanford University Press, 1934); William Dampier, *Dampier's Voyages . . .*, ed. John Masefield, 2 vols. (New York: E. P. Dutton, 1906); William Dampier, *A New Voyage Round the World*, ed. Sir Albert Gray (London: Argonaut Press, 1927); Charles C. Lloyd, *William Dampier* (London: Faber, 1966); Clennell Wilkinson, *William Dampier* (London: J. Lane, 1929).

Bernerd C. Weber

DANGEROUS ISLANDS. *See* Tuamotu-Gambiers.

DARLING, ERNEST WILLING (1871-1918). A well-known American nudist and a proponent of natural foods, Ernest Darling practiced his life-style in Tahiti and Fiji from 1903 to 1918. He contracted tuberculosis at Stanford University and reportedly regained his health by living close to nature, eating uncooked food, and practicing nudism. Darling preached his life-style in California, Arizona, Oregon, and Washington. He was arrested numerous times and finally, in search of a tropical climate, he stowed away on a ship bound for Hawai'i. Expelled from Hawai'i, Darling journeyed to Tahiti in 1903 where he began a nudist colony and plantation on an eighty-acre plot in the mountains behind Pape'ete. Known as Tahiti's "Nature Man," he was visited in 1907 by Jack London who wrote about him in *The Cruise of the Snark* (New York: Macmillan Co., 1911). Many South Pacific adventurers (George Calderon, Frederick O'Brien, and others) also recounted meeting him. Darling also advocated socialism and phonetic spelling. He returned to the United States in 1913-1914, then spent his last years in Suva, Fiji, where he died on 9 December 1918.

RELATED ENTRIES: French Polynesia.

SOURCES AND READINGS: George Calderon, *Tahiti* (London: Richards, 1921); Robert Langdon, "Tahiti's 'Nature Man'—Symbol of a Revolution," *Pacific Islands Monthly*, September 1970, pp. 73-79; Patrick O'Reilly, *Tahitiens* (Paris: Musée de l'Homme, 1962).

Russell T. Clement

DARWIN, CHARLES (1809-1882). The English naturalist Charles Darwin set out aboard the H.M.S. *Beagle* in 1831. His five-year voyage led Darwin to the development of his theory of organic evolution and its operating principle, natural selection, which revolutionized human knowledge. Although Darwin visited much of the Pacific (Tahiti, New Zealand, Australia, Tasmania, the Keeling Islands, Mauritius), his ideas about evolution developed largely from his four-week stay on the Galapagos Islands, 965 km west of the coast of Ecuador. Upon his return to England in 1836, Darwin classified and labeled his collection of animals and retired to forty years of writing, some of which altered and expanded scientific thought about the origins of life. In 1842 his *Structure and Distribution of Coral Reefs*, based upon his observations of the Keeling Islands, established him as one of the foremost scientists of his time. His seminal work, *Origin of Species* (1859), refined and developed his theories founded in the Pacific and gave him world acclaim long after his death in 1882.

RELATED ENTRIES: Galapagos Islands.

SOURCES AND READINGS: Samuel Anthony Barnett, ed., *A Century of Darwin* (New York: Books for Libraries Press, 1969); Sir Gavin Rylands DeBeer, *Charles Darwin: Evolution by Natural Selection* (Garden City, N.Y.: Doubleday & Co., 1964); William Irvine, *Apes, Angels and Victorians* (New York: McGraw-Hill, 1955); Alan Moorhead, *Darwin and the Beagle* (New York, Evanston: Harper & Row, 1969); Leslie Stephen and Sidney Lee, eds., *Dictionary of National Biographies* (New York: Macmillan Co., 1908).   *Jeffrey Butler*

DAVIDSON, JAMES WIGHTMAN (1916-1973).
Davidson, a political adviser, has sometimes been referred to as the "Father of Pacific History." Born 1 October 1915 and educated in Wellington, New Zealand, he received his Ph.D. from Cambridge (1942) for a dissertation on "European Penetration of the South Pacific, 1779-1842." While spending four years in British naval intelligence, he helped complete a four-volume geographical handbook on the Pacific islands for the British armed services. After the war, he lectured at Cambridge and then, in 1947, was asked by the New Zealand government to assist in its program to prepare independence for the state of Western Samoa. During 1949-1950 he served as a member of the Samoan public service and the legislative assembly. From 1959 to 1961 he was constitutional adviser to the government of Western Samoa. He continued to consult the new government after it gained independence in 1962. He assisted in drafting the constitutions of the Cook Islands and Nauru, acted as adviser to the Congress of Micronesia, and at his death 8 April 1975 was a consultant to the constitutional planning committee in Papua New Guinea. He had also been professor of Pacific history at the Australian National University for twenty-three years. One of his books, *Samoa Mo Samoa: The Emergence of the Independent State of Western Samoa*, details his personal involvement in the independence of that state. He authored or edited other books and articles dealing with the Pacific. In 1966 he was one of the founders of the *Journal of Pacific History* and remained one of the editors until his death.

RELATED ENTRIES: Western Samoa.

SOURCES AND READINGS: James W. Davidson, *Samoa Mo Samoa: The Emergence of the Independent State of Western Samoa* (New York: Oxford University Press, 1967); *Pacific Islands Monthly*, May 1973, p. 127.   *Robert D. Craig*

DAVIS, ISAAC (ca. 1757-1810). Hawaiian beachcomber, close friend, and aide of King Kamehameha I, Isaac Davis, an Englishman, arrived in Hawai'i in 1790, the only survivor of the massacre of the crew of the *Fair American*. He became the intimate friend of John Young, and together they were known as "Kamehameha's white men." Only the barest fragments of Davis' life are known, but it seems that he was closer to Kamehameha than even was Young. He married twice but left only three children at the time of his death. It was said that he was assassinated, by poisoning, in 1810 by personal enemies for his role in effecting a reconciliation between Kamehameha and his rival Kaumuali'i, paramount chief of Kaua'i. Both Young and Davis were almost invariably held in high esteem by foreign visitors for their probity, integrity, and good influence with the Hawaiian chiefs at a time when beachcombers generally had an evil reputation.

RELATED ENTRIES: Beachcombers; Hawai'i; Kamehameha I; Young, John.

SOURCES AND READINGS: R. S. Kuykendall, *The Hawaiian Kingdom, 1778-1854: Foundation and Transformation* (Honolulu: University of Hawaii Press, 1938).   *Ian C. Campbell*

DEFENSE PLANNING FOR OCEANIA BETWEEN THE WARS (1919-1939). The subordinate position occupied by the Pacific islands as either mandates or overseas possessions of European powers precluded any initiation of defense policy on their part. However, Australia and New Zealand, due to their increasing fear of Japan during the interwar period, offered the islands a positive, albeit limited role, in the security arrangements of the region. This, unfortunately, did nothing to alleviate their fundamentally dependent role.

As early as the Washington conference in 1921, Australian representative Senator George Pearce had expressed great anxiety over the right to construct fortified bases in the Pacific islands. The head of the British delegation dismissed the problem as coming under Australian local defense. But Pearce forcefully argued that New Guinea was not only important to Australian forward-defense planning but also deserved consideration as part of imperial-regional security in the Pacific. The Australian government had also shown interest in other islands in the region, specifically the Netherlands East Indies and Portuguese Timor. They demanded detailed and continuous information from the British Foreign Office and the British minister in The Hague. The disinclination of the British to concern themselves in either area appeared ominous for the security of the region. Nor was American participation viewed with any more optimism, given the distance over which the United States fleet would have to operate from its nearest bases.

Attention, nevertheless, became more sharply focused on the region, as the Singapore base project became increasingly suspect. Australia assumed the role of entrepreneur in promoting joint cooperation in the region. Direct control was proposed over certain islands in the western Pacific, with the pious rider that there should be a union of all island groups in this region under the Pacific Flag. The French interest was also reluctantly emphasized. The islands indeed continued as mere pawns in any defense arrangements. Careful analysis was nevertheless made of their use in definite defense projects, such as the construction of communications, the establishment of stores and depots for military purposes in time of war, and the development of seaplane and submarine bases. The island peoples themselves were never actually consulted in Australia's attempts to form a loose multilateral alliance system with Britian, the United States, the Netherlands, France, and Portugal. However, they were viewed as essential to the overall Australian strategy of coordinating forward-defense planning in the Pacific area with general regional security perspectives.

The linkage between forward-defense planning and regional needs concerned the Netherlands East Indies and New Zealand as well as Australia. The possibilities of an air route from Singapore to Timor, and thence to northwest Australia or Port Darwin were examined by the several governments. They carefully left open the question whether there could be a dual usage for both civil and military purposes. However, the persistent British disinterest proved constantly worrying. Australia "reminded" the British that it was anxious to have any information concerning the position of Portuguese Timor: especially its possible sale to an undesirable purchaser, namely Japan. It was unfortunately obvious that Britian did not share Australian, New Zealand, or Dutch concern. The British defense advisers indeed refused to see the Netherlands East Indies either as vital to the

security of the Dominions or as a partner in regional defense.

The Australian and New Zealand governments continued to stress their "special responsibility" in the Pacific area. Both, in particular, emphasized the close relationship of Dutch defense problems to their own defense planning. The Dutch themselves had cautiously approached London in July 1936 for informal talks about the mutual defense of their colonial empires. Although conceding that the Netherlands East Indies were of vital concern, the British advised the Dutch merely to improve their own defenses. It was hardly an encouraging step in the promotion of any regional security arrangement, especially considering that Australia was at this time beginning to canvass a Pacific pact for the area.

The French had suffered a similar fate over their attempts to discuss European security problems with the British. Naturally they did not consider the time propitious to enter into lengthy negotiations concerning their Pacific possessions. The only faint ray of hope came from the British Air Ministry, which in 1937 took up the Australian initiative for a regional security pact. It recommended that effective defense could be achieved only through a coordinated security system covering European interests from the South China Sea to the western Pacific. The plan would call for close cooperation among British, French, Dutch, and Dominion forces. But nothing occurred. Indeed such a scheme, while emphasizing the regional significance of the Pacific islands, still distinguished sharply between their strategic and their political importance.

Australia and New Zealand, nevertheless, continued to protest the British disregard of the region. The Australian government continuously requested throughout the 1930s British dispatches relevant to both the Netherlands East Indies and Portuguese Timor. The air routes clearly provided a means of linking political and security requirements and strengthening regional relationships. But the Netherlands East Indies continued to be overlooked in British strategic thinking despite the fact that the air connection between Australia and Singapore was impossible, except via the Dutch islands. The British chiefs of staff were apprehensive lest conversations with the Dutch might involve them in some specific commitment.

As the credibility of the Singapore strategy declined, the security of Australia and New Zealand was increasingly seen by the governments of both countries as the central pivot of the imperial security system. For Australia, interest was mainly concentrated on the defense of Papua New Guinea. Port Moresby was proposed as a base for aircraft and for the anchorage and fuelling of cruisers. The air route to Dili on Portuguese Timor was also regarded as being of primary importance. New Zealand viewed the defense of Fiji and Tonga as having similar priority and also emphasized the use of the air connection. This concern culminated in New Zealand's invitation to Australia in 1939 to participate in a conference on the strategic value of the Pacific islands with particular reference to the development of air facilities. The islands were to be divided between Australian and New Zealand areas of responsibility. Australia assumed the direction of planning for New Guinea, the Solomon Islands, and New Caledonia; and New Zealand was to look after the New Hebrides, Fiji, and Tonga.

Australia and New Zealand had thus achieved a measure of regional cooperation. Despite the new prominence of the Pacific islands in defense plans, their dependent status persisted. Indeed, it seemed that they had merely exchanged a subordinate role to a distant power for a similar fate with a nearer one. Given Australia's and New Zealand's growing conception of their own primacy in the region, the Pacific islands could look forward to a new role as a counterpoise to the overwhelming predominance of the major European powers south of the equator.

RELATED ENTRIES: Fiji; New Caledonia; Oceania, Strategic Importance of since 1945; Papua New Guinea; Port Moresby; Tonga; Vanuatu (New Hebrides); War in the Pacific Islands 1914-1945.

SOURCES AND READINGS: Australian Commonwealth Archives, Canberra: A816, item 14/301/113, Australian-New Zealand Conference, 1939; A816, item 19/301/587, Portuguese Timor, 1935; A1608, item no. B. 45/1/3, Port Moresby, 1938; A816, item 11/301/6, Imperial Conference, 1937; CRS. AA1971/216, Council of Defense Meeting, 1935; A981, item Imperial 126, 1930; A981, item Pacific 13, 1927; PREM 1/310, 1938; CAB 2/7, 1938; CAB 63/66, 1934; 948/P/31, 1938.   *Carolyn O'Brien*

D'ENTRECASTEAUX, ANTOINE DE BRUNI (1737-1793). D'Entrecasteaux was the French navigator who led an expedition for the missing Lapérouse from 1791 to 1793. A member of the professional middle class, d'Entrecasteaux gained naval experience in Corsica and the Far East. He was appointed by the revolutionary French government to leave in September 1791 on the *Recherche* and the *Espérance*, the latter commanded by Huon de Kermadec. Lapérouse

was not found but the geography and natural history of southwestern Oceania benefitted greatly through the detailed work of botanist La Billardière, hydrographer Beautemps-Beaupré, and officer Rossel. D'Entrecasteaux sailed around the Cape of Good Hope, investigated the western coast of New Caledonia, explored the Solomon and Admiralty islands, and New Guinea, circumnavigated Australia, visited Tasmania, and reached the Santa Cruz Islands. The expedition "discovered" the Kermadec group, Beautemps-Beaupré atoll, numerous small islands in the Louisiade archipelago, and D'Entrecasteaux, Trobriand, and other islands near New Guinea. By the beginning of 1793 dysentery and scurvy had thwarted the exploration. Kermadec was buried at New Caledonia and d'Entrecasteaux died at sea on 20 July 1793. The expedition disbanded at the Dutch East Indies settlement of Surabaja in October 1793.

RELATED ENTRIES: New Caledonia.

SOURCES AND READINGS: J. C. Beaglehole, *The Exploration of the Pacific*, 3d ed. (Stanford: Stanford University Press, 1966); John Dunmore, *French Explorers in the Pacific*, vol. 1 (Oxford: Clarendon Press, 1965); Andrew Sharp, *The Discovery of the Pacific Islands* (Oxford: Clarendon Press, 1960).
                                        Russell T. Clement

DIAPER, WILLIAM (1820-1891). One of the most celebrated of all beachcombers, William Diaper was born at Ardleigh, Essex, England, the son of a well-to-do yeoman farmer. Diaper, who used the aliases John Jackson and "Cannibal Jack," exemplifies perhaps more than any other the "typical" beachcomber: a wanderer, adept at many trades, living sometimes with islanders, at other times with traders, missionaries, or other beachcombers. His versatility, arrogant individualism, quick intelligence, racial tolerance, and undoubted charm, together with his literary flair preserve for him an identity lacking for almost all other beachcombers. He lived at various times in most island groups of the southwest Pacific: Samoa, Tonga, Fiji, New Caledonia, New Hebrides, Solomon Islands, and perhaps New Guinea. His surviving autobiographical writings are classics of nineteenth-century, Pacific-islands literature. A man who loved life and tackled all things with enthusiasm, he was, at the last known count, the father of thirty-eight children and the grandfather of ninety-nine.

RELATED ENTRIES: Beachcombers.

SOURCES AND READINGS: William Diapea [sic], *Can-*

nibal Jack: The True Autobiography of a White Man in the South Seas (London: Faber and Gwyer, 1928); John Jackson, "Narrative by John Jackson of his Residence in the Feejees," in J. E. Erskine, ed., *Journal of a Cruise Among the Islands of the Western Pacific* (London: John Murray, 1853); Christopher Legge, "William Diaper: A Biographical Sketch," *Journal of Pacific History* 1 (1966): 79-90.

Ian C. Campbell

DILLON, PETER (1788-1847). Pacific navigator and author, Dillon was born 15 February 1788 in Martinique of aristocratic Irish-Catholic parents. After serving in the Royal Navy for several years, he set sail for the Pacific. He arrived in Fiji in 1809 where he served as seaman, mate, and later master and became active in the sandalwood trade. In 1810 he sailed to the Society Islands, fought in their wars there, and won command of the *Hunter*. By 1816 he owned his own ship, and for six years he traded throughout the Pacific islands. One of his writings was a personal interview with Jenny of Pitcairn Island, an account of the *Bounty* from her departure from Tahiti. He traveled to Vanuatu (New Hebrides) where he found the people more "uncivilized" than any other islanders. His writings of their culture, religious manners, and cannibal practices were read throughout Europe. While in the New Hebrides he discovered a bay on Eromanga now known as Dillon Bay. An important contribution was his discovery of the wreck of the French explorer Lapérouse's ship. Dillon found the ship washed ashore on Vanikoro, after which he wrote his two volume *Narrative and Successful Result of a Voyage in the South Seas . . . to ascertain the Actual Fate of Lapérouse's Expedition . . .* In appreciation of his accomplishments, Charles X awarded him the title *Chevalier*. But his funds soon ran out, and by 1840 he regretted much of what he had done. He died in Paris 9 February 1847.

RELATED ENTRIES: Fiji; French Polynesia; Vanuatu (New Hebrides).

SOURCES AND READINGS: J. Davidson and D. Scarr, *Pacific Islands Portraits* (Wellington: A. H. and A. W. Reed, 1973).   *Joseph A. Montoya*

DOANE, EDWARD T. (1820-1890). A prominent Protestant missionary in Ponape, Caroline Islands, Doane had joined the American Board of Commissioners for Foreign Missions (ABCFM) mission there in 1855, three years after it had been established. In 1857 he and his wife were posted to teach at Ebon, Marshall Islands. They returned to the U.S. twice for medical reasons and were released from service in 1887. As a widower, Doane returned to the Ponape station in 1885 and became the senior member. In 1887 Doane became a cause célèbre in American newspapers because of a diplomatic dispute involving American Protestant and Spanish Catholic rivalry and the mission's land rights. Pope Leo XIII had arbitrated the dispute between Germany and Spain over rights to the Caroline Islands by giving Spain sovereignty and Germany freedom of trade. Spain had also assured the U.S. that ABCFM mission efforts would be allowed to continue. In 1887 Posadillo, the newly appointed Spanish governor, arrived to establish a station on land at Kenan (Jamestown Harbor, now Kolonia). This area had been deeded to the mission by Ponapean chiefs, but Doane had agreed to make a portion of it available to the Spanish. Shortly thereafter Doane formally protested Spanish encroachment on other parts of the mission land and was arrested on 13 April 1887 for disrespectful behavior. He was deported on other charges, but on arrival in Manila was freed by the governor-general of the Philippines and repatriated to Ponape. On his return in September, he and the Spanish ship captain were surprised to learn of the rebellion in July which had resulted in the death of Posadillo and a number of soldiers. Conditions were temporarily stable, but Doane left Ponape for health reasons in 1889. ABCFM claims for damages to property at Doane's station and the station at Oa that was destroyed in the 1890 naval bombardments of Ponapean rebels continued to be a subject of U.S. diplomatic negotiations with Spain in the 1890s.

RELATED ENTRIES: American Board of Commissioners for Foreign Missions; Spain in the Pacific.

SOURCES AND READINGS: J. L. Fischer and A. Fischer, *The Eastern Carolines* (New Haven: Human Relations Area Files Press, 1957).   *Craig Severance*

DOLE, SANFORD BALLARD (1840-1926). Leader of the revolutionary movement which ended the Hawaiian monarchy in 1893 and of the negotiations which resulted in Hawai'i becoming a territory of the United States, Dole was the first and only president of the Republic of Hawai'i (1893-1894) and the first governor of the territory (1894-1903). Equally noted in history as a diplomat, statesman, and jurist, Dole possessed the unique distinction of being the only American who has ever been the chief executive of an independent foreign nation. Dole was born in Honolulu 23 April 1844. His parents came to Hawai'i from Maine in 1840, the elder Dole taking charge of Punahou College. After his return from the United States in 1867 where he had graduated from law school,

Sanford Dole engaged in private practice and at the same time took an active part in politics. In 1886 he was appointed to the Supreme Court bench as an associate justice, remaining there for six years. In 1893 when Queen Lili'uokalani lost her throne, Dole was elected president of the Republic of Hawai'i. In the interest of annexation, Dole went to Washington in 1898 to confer with President McKinley. When annexation became a fact, he was made governor of the Territory of Hawai'i, retiring from that office on 1 November 1903. Appointed U.S. district judge that same year, he remained on the bench until 1916 when he retired to private practice. He died 9 June 1926.

RELATED ENTRIES: Hawai'i; Hawaiian Annexation Treaty; Lili'uokalani.

SOURCES AND REFERENCES: A. Grove Day, *Hawaii and Its People* (New York: Meredith Press, 1968); Edward Joesting, *Hawaii* (New York: W. W. Norton & Co., 1972); Ralph S. Kuykendall and A. Grove Day, *Hawaii: A History* (Englewood Cliffs, N.J.: Prentice-Hall, 1961).   *Ned B. Williams*

DOUARRE, GUILLAUME (1810-1853). Douarre was a Marist (French Roman Catholic) missionary who founded the Catholic mission in New Caledonia. After brief visits to the Marquesas and Wallis Islands, Monsignor Douarre landed with four other priests at Balade, New Caledonia, in December 1843. From the outset their efforts were thwarted by unfriendly islanders. In 1846 hostile Melanesians drove them off the island by burning the mission and killing one priest. Douarre returned to France and the mission closed. In 1849 he went back to New Caledonia but was again rejected. He retreated to nearby Isle of Pines where a successful mission was founded. In 1851 he made two attempts to reestablish Catholicism on New Caledonia but again failed. At his death on 27 April 1853 the area had three missions, twelve priests, and two hundred members.

RELATED ENTRIES: New Caledonia.

SOURCES AND READINGS: Jean Le Borgne, *Géographie de la Nouvelle-Calédonie et des Iles Loyauté* (Nouméa: Ministère de l'Education, 1964); Patrick O'Reilly, *Calédoniens* (Paris: Musée de l'Homme, 1953).
                            Russell T. Clement

DRAKE, (SIR) FRANCIS (ca. 1540-1596). An English admiral, explorer, and Elizabethan seaman, Drake was born near Tavistock. He participated as a young man in voyages to the west coast of Africa and to the West Indies. In 1567-1568 he commanded the *Judith* (of fifty tons) in the third slaving expedition of his kinsman, Sir John Hawkins.

Drake became one of the most famous English privateers who raided settlements on the Spanish Main. In 1572 he made a surprise attack on the Caribbean port of Nombre de Dios, burned Porto Bello, and captured some coastal vessels. He crossed the Isthmus of Panama during that same year and obtained his first glimpse of the Pacific. Between 1577 and 1580 Drake became the first Englishman in command of a ship to circumnavigate the globe. He had charge of the *Pelican* (later renamed the *Golden Hind*) and four other vessels carrying in all about 160 men. Crossing the Atlantic in a slow passage, he sailed down the eastern coast of South America and reached Port Saint Julian in June 1578 where he quickly crushed an incipient mutiny. Sailing through the Strait of Magellan with a fleet then consisting of three vessels, Drake reached the Pacific on 6 September. A tremendous gale drove him southward, resulting in the discovery of some islands below Tierra del Fuego. One ship foundered with the loss of its crew, another became separated from Drake's ship and subsequently returned to England. After the storm had finally subsided, Drake in the *Golden Hind* proceeded northward, plundering Spanish settlements along the coasts of Chile and Peru. He obtained a particularly rich prize in the seizure of *Nuestra Señora de la Concepción* (also called the *Cacafuego*), a great treasure ship laden with Peruvian silver headed for Panama.

How far north Drake sailed is a matter of dispute, for no log of this voyage now exists. Possibly he reached somewhere in the latitude of Vancouver, where he searched in vain for the supposed Strait of Anian. Bad weather forced a return southward and somewhat north of modern San Francisco he found suitable anchorage, named the land New Albion, and claimed the territory for the queen of England. From the California coast, Drake sailed in July 1579 across the Pacific to the Philippines and then to the Moluccas where he made arrangements with the sultan of Ternate for a rich cargo of spices. Then he returned to England after crossing the Indian Ocean, rounding the Cape of Good Hope, and sailing up the west African coast. He arrived at Plymouth on 26 September 1580 completing a lengthy voyage which brought enormous profits for its promoters.

In 1585 Drake commanded an amphibious expedition to the West Indies, where he seized the Spanish towns of Santo Domingo, Cartagena, and Saint Augustine. He also rescued members of Raleigh's colony at Roanoke. Two years later he attacked the Spanish port of Cadiz on the Atlantic coast, a daring exploit described by Geoffrey Parker of as "singeing of the King of Spain's beard" (p. 152). In 1588, the year of the Spanish Armada, Drake served as vice admiral under Lord Admiral Howard Effingham and carried out various tactical operations which helped to defeat the Spaniards. The following year Drake and Sir John Norris jointly commanded an expedition to Portugal to destroy the remnants of the Spanish Armada, but this venture ended disastrously. In 1585 Drake participated in his last voyage to the New World. He sailed with Sir John Hawkins to the West Indies. Spanish defenses, however, proved too strong for English operations to be effective. Hawkins died at sea in November 1595, and slightly over two months later Drake succumbed to fever and dysentery off Porto Bello. He was solemnly buried at sea on 28 January 1596.

RELATED ENTRIES: Britain in the Pacific.

SOURCES AND READING: Kenneth R. Andrews, "The Aims of Drake's Expedition of 1577-1580," *American Historical Review* 73 (1968): 724-41, and *Drake's Voyages: A Re-Assessment of Their Place in Elizabethan Maritime Expansion* (London: Weidenfeld and Nicolson, 1967); Sir Julian Stafford Corbett, *Drake and the Tudor Navy: With a History of the Rise of England as a Maritime Power*, 2 vols. (New York: Burt Franklin, 1965); John Hampden, ed., *Francis Drake, Privateer: Contemporary Narratives and Documents* (Tuscaloosa, Ala.: University of Alabama Press, 1972); Geoffrey Parker, *Philip II* (Boston: Little, Brown, 1978); George M. Thomson, *Sir Francis Drake* (London: Secker and Warburg, 1972); Henry R. Wagner, *Sir Francis Drake's Voyage around the World: Its Aims and Achievements* (San Francisco: J. Howell, 1926); James A. Williamson, *The Age of Drake*, 4th ed. (London: Adam and Charles Black, 1960); Derek A. Wilson, *The World Encompassed: Francis Drake and His Great Voyage* (New York: Harper & Row, 1977).

Bernerd C. Weber

DUMONT D'URVILLE, JULES-SÉBASTIEN-CÉSAR (1790-1842). One of the greatest of all French Pacific explorers, Dumont d'Urville was born 23 May 1790 in Condé-sur-Noireau, France. His first voyage to the Pacific was with his colleage Louis-Isidore Duperrey (1822-1825). Dumont d'Urville's next two voyages were conceived, planned, and conducted by himself. His first voyage (1826-1829) continued Duperrey's work in exploring the western Pacific while at the same time he tried to find the remains of Lapérouse's lost ships. He visited Australia, New Zealand, Fiji, the Loyalty Islands, and New Guinea. Everywhere he charted new coastlines and collected scientific data. Having found some evidence concerning Lapérouse's whereabouts, he concluded that Lapérouse must have been shipwrecked on Vanikoro, a fact confirmed later by the work of Peter Dillon. In 1834 the twenty-four octavo volumes of his work appeared in print. His second voyage (1837-1840) is considered the last of the great French voyages of discovery that had begun in the 1760s. Its purpose was to explore the southern polar regions of the Pacific. Leaving France in September 1837 he pushed southward in the Pacific but was stopped by ice caps in front of the Antarctic continent. Crossing the Pacific, he stopped in the Gambiers, Marquesas, Society Islands, Samoa, Fiji, Solomons, Carolines, Marianas, went back to the coast of the Antarctic and then north to New Zealand and home. After his return, he edited his massive material into a publication of ten large tomes. He was promoted to rear admiral on 31 December 1840. He died in a railroad accident on 8 May 1842.

RELATED ENTRIES: Dillon, Peter; Lapérouse, Jean-François.

SOURCES AND READINGS: Camille Vergniol, *Dumont d'Urville* (Paris: Renaissance de Livre, 1920); Jean-Paul Faivre, *L'Expansion Française dans le Pacifique 1800-1842* (Paris: Nouvelles Editions Latines, 1953).

Robert D. Craig

DUPETIT-THOUARS, ABEL AUBERT (1793-1864). Dupetit-Thouars was the French admiral responsible for carrying out the French policy of gaining control of the Marquesas and the Society Islands (1838-1844). Born 7 August 1793 at Turquart, Dupetit-Thouars began his sea career as a ship's boy at the age of eleven. He quickly rose to command position and directed the French round-the-world voyage on the *Venus* between 1836 and 1839. He rounded Cape Horn and stopped in Hawai'i to protest the expulsion of two Catholic priests. Hawai'i law prevailed, however, and the priests had to leave. After a lengthy exploration journey in the Pacific, including the Galapagos and Easter islands, Dupetit-Thouars turned southward and rested his men at Valparaiso, Chile. There he learned of the unsuccessful attempt by two French Catholic priests to proselyte in Tahiti. He set out via the Marquesas where he landed two other Catholic priests and arrived in Tahiti 29 August 1838. He extracted a statement of redress from Queen Pomare IV, demanded an indemnity of two thousand piastres, and a twenty-one-gun salute to the French flag. After some little embarrassment on the part of the Tahitian government, all requirements were met, including a statement allowing freedom of religion among the queen's subjects. After Dupetit-Thouars returned to France and gave his report of the international political situation in the Pacific, Minister Guizot ordered him to return and take possession of the Marquesas for a French naval station. During April and May 1842, he sailed among the Marquesas Islands and took possession of them. Arriving in Tahiti, he intervened in its political affairs, declared a French protectorate, and left. Returning 1 November 1843 and finding deteriorating conditions between the English Protestant missionaries (especially George Pritchard) and the new French governmental officials, he declared an outright French annexation of Tahiti. Armand Joseph Bruat, another French admiral in port, was appointed governor and Dupetit-Thouars left. He was promoted to vice admiral in 1843, elected deputy from Maine-et-Loire in 1849, and died in Paris in 1864.

RELATED ENTRIES: Bruat, Armand; French Polynesia; Marquesas Islands; Moerenhout, Jacques; Pritchard, George.

SOURCES AND READINGS: Auguste Caillot, *Les Polynésiens orientaux au contact de la civilisation* (Paris: Ernest Leroux, 1909); Abel A. Dupetit-Thouars, *Voyage autour du monde sur la frégate la* Venus *pendant les années 1836-39*, 4 vols. (Paris: Gide, 1840-

64); Patrick O'Reilly, *Tahitiens* (Paris: Musée de l'Homme, 1962).   *Robert D. Craig*

DUTROU-BORNIER, J. P. (?-1877). A French entrepreneur who settled on Easter Island, Dutrou-Bornier bought large areas of land from the islands in 1866 in exchange for pieces of cloth. In 1870 he imported sheep and laid the foundations for a prosperous agricultural undertaking at Mataveri. He persuaded Torometi to be his bodyguard and was successful in forming a small army for his protection. With Dutrou-Bornier's support, Torometi had visions of becoming a powerful chief with the people of Hangaroa and Vinapu as his slaves. Raids were made in villages and huts were burned resulting in the murder of many Hangaroa villagers. In 1871 an evacuation was ordered by the bishop of Tahiti. All the missionaries and most of the islanders left. Dutrou-Bornier forced ill islanders to stay with him as servants. Acts of violence and rape of island women resulted in his murder in 1877. Dutrou-Bornier's Tahiti-based partner, John Brander, took over the sheep farm and imported many Tahitian workers.

RELATED ENTRIES: Easter Island.

SOURCES AND READINGS: Alfred Métraux, *Easter Island: A Stone Age Civilization of the Pacific* (London: Oxford University Press, 1957).   *David Welch*

EARHART, AMELIA (1898-1937). The first woman pilot to attempt to fly around the world, Amelia Earhart was lost over the South Pacific on her unsuccessful flight in July 1937. In September 1936 Earhart announced plans to fly around the world using an equatorial route. The key was Howland Island in the South Pacific where runways were to be prepared by the U.S. government. With help from the army and the WPA, the runways were finished in March 1937, but Earhart crashed on take-off in Honolulu. In June she renewed her flight with the route reversed to avoid the Asian monsoon season. Starting from Miami, Earhart hopped through the Caribbean to Brazil and then across the Atlantic to Dakar. Africa was crossed in easy stages, followed by a long jump to Karachi. A series of short flights brought her down to the Netherlands East Indies where she stopped over, due to mechanical trouble. She reached Lae, Papua New Guinea, after a brief medical hold-up at Darwin, Australia, where the plane was overhauled for the 3,800 km flight to Howland Island. Earhart left Lae on 2 July and was heard by Lae radio and Nauru Island radio over the next twelve hours. Two hours later, she was first heard by the Coast Guard at Howland who continued to hear her until her last transmission, some twenty hours into the flight. At no time did she acknowledge receiving messages. She failed to reach Howland. A massive search was mounted, starting with a lone Coast Guard cutter, then the battleship *Colorado*, and finally the aircraft carrier *Lexington*, whose planes conducted a search, but nothing was found.

SOURCES AND READINGS: Amelia Earhart, *Last Flight* (New York: Harcourt, Brace & Co., 1937); Francis X. Holbrook, "Amelia Earhart's Final Flight," *U.S. Naval Institute Proceedings*, February 1971.

Francis X. Holbrook

EASTER ISLAND. Also known as Rapa Nui and Te Pito te Henua ("The Navel of the World"), Easter Island is the most isolated island in Polynesia. It is located at 27° 9′ south latitude and 109°26′ west longitude, about 3,200 km (2,000 mi) west of the South American continent and 2,000 km (1,130 mi) southeast of Pitcairn Island. Easter Island is a composite of three major volcanic centers which coalesced to form a roughly triangular landmass, 22.5 km by 11.3 km (14 mi × 7 mi), with an area of about 156 km² (60 mi²) and a maximum elevation of 510 m (1,673 ft) above sea level. There are no permanent streams on the island, but good sources of fresh water exist in three crater lakes. The founding Polynesian population is believed to have come from the Marquesas around A.D. 400.

Climate, Fauna, and Flora. The climate of Easter Island is subtropical with an average annual temperature of about 22°C (72°F). Rainfall is moderate, averaging between 1,250 mm and 1,500 mm (50-60 in) per annum, but can vary considerably from the norm. Southeast trade winds blow fairly constantly from October to April. The extreme geographical isolation of Easter Island is reflected in a markedly impoverished biota. The island has been sparsely vegetated for a period of at least 250 years, but some evidence exists to suggest the presence of forests and a generally more diversified flora farther in the past.

Pre-European Culture. The prehistoric culture of Easter Island developed one of the most highly evolved technologies in the world at a Neolithic level. An unusual preoccupation with religion, and ancestor worship in particular, was productive of some of the most stylized and technologically advanced forms of megalithic art and architecture in Polynesia. A building and carving compulsion for religious purposes is manifested in a variety of structures called *ahu* and in monolithic stone statues (*moai*), representing deceased ancestors of high rank, that were placed in an upright position on the central platforms of many *ahu*. There are an estimated thousand stone statues or images and three hundred *ahu* on the island, most appearing to have been made in the first millennium of local prehistory. Easter Island culture appears also to have developed a highly sophisticated system of solar observation, which may have been employed in the construction of some *ahu*. The development of a unique bird cult, involving an annual competition to find the first egg of the migratory sooty tern, is another element in the pattern of religious efflorescence that characterizes the pre-European culture of Easter Island. The climactic symbol of a remarkably ingenious population was the invention of a written hieroglyphic script on wooden tablets, collectively known as *kohau rongorongo*. Most scholars regard the tablets as a mnemonic device to aid in the chanting of royal genealogies and oral traditions. The last several hundred years of prehistory were a period of general cultural decadence characterized by widespread civil wars between kin groups. Feuding resulted in the toppling of *ahu* images, famine, and the emergence of cannibalism.

Early European Contacts. The European "discovery" of Easter Island was made by the Dutch explorer Jacob Roggeveen on Easter Day in 1722 whereby the island obtained its modern name. Nearly half a century passed before a Spanish expedition under the command of Captain Felipe Gonzalez y Haedo reached the island in 1770. A much celebrated ceremony of annexation took place that made the island for a time the property of Spain. Four years later, in 1774, Captain James Cook and his scientific party landed. The French navigator Lapérouse made a landfall in 1786 but, like his predecessors, spent only a short time there due to the lack of safe anchorages and a scarcity of fresh foodstuffs to reprovision depleted supplies. Lapérouse left some livestock and seeds for planting, but there is no indication that either was successfully propagated.

Modern History. In 1862-1863 an estimated 1,000 to 1,500 islanders were taken prisoner by Peruvian entrepreneurs to work as slaves in the mining of guano deposits on the Chincha Islands. Many died and the few returning survivors introduced smallpox, which nearly decimated an already dwindling populace. Catholic missionaries arrived in the early 1860s and quickly converted the small population to Christianity. A Tahitian-English trading firm (John Brander) established itself on the island in 1868 and the following year entered into a contractual agreement with the Catholic mission and the firm's agent to develop a sheep ranch operation. Relations between the agent and the mission quickly deteriorated, causing islanders to take opposing sides. In 1871 many islanders left for Mangareva with a Catholic priest, while others went to Tahiti to work on the plantations of the Brander company and the Catholic mission. A census taken in 1877 revealed a native population of only 110 individuals. The island was annexed by Chile in 1888 and has continued to be administered by the government of that country.

Economics, Population, and Culture Change. The introduction of a wage-labor economy has had a profound effect on the modern Easter Island life-style as demonstrated by, for example, an increasing reliance on imported goods and desire for modern material conveniences. In response to the uncertainties of shipping schedules, agricultural and fishing cooperatives have developed to provide for a rapidly growing population, which now numbers about two thousand on the island, with many hundreds more islanders residing on the Chilean continent and elsewhere. The problem at this time is not a lack of agriculturally productive land, but of people to farm it, since a higher proportion of the population now works for the government or in tourism, which has grown considerably since the completion of an airstrip in 1967. Tourism is an essential necessity for this small, isolated island, incapable of marketing export goods except for a limited number of handcrafts. Large numbers of islanders have moved to the continent, particularly younger people who, like many Pacific islanders today, feel bored in their island home. In spite of these new attitudes, Easter Islanders remain proud of their cultural heritage and are now actively contributing to its preservation.

RELATED ENTRIES: Cook, (Captain) James; Dutrou-Bornier, J. P.; Englert, Sebastian; Eyraud, Eugene; Lapérouse, Jean-François; Métraux, Alfred; Polynesia, Settlement of; Polynesian Culture (Ancient); Routledge, Katherine; South Pacific Commission.

SOURCES AND READINGS: P. S. Englert, *Island at the Center of the World: New Light on Easter Island* (New York: Charles Scribner's Sons, 1970); Thor Heyerdahl and Edwin Ferdon, Jr., eds., *Reports on the Norwegian Archaeological Expedition to Easter Island and the East Pacific* (Santa Fe: School of American Research, 1961); Patrick McCoy, *Easter Island Settlement Patterns in the Late Prehistoric and Protohistoric Periods* (New York: International Fund for Monuments, 1976); Patrick McCoy, "Easter Island," in Jesse D. Jennings, ed., *The Prehistory of Polynesia* (Cambridge: Harvard University Press, 1979); Alfred Métraux, *Ethnology of Easter Island* (Honolulu: Bishop Museum Press, 1940).

Patrick C. McCoy

EDUCATION IN THE PACIFIC, HIGHER. Today in Oceania (outside of Hawai'i) there are five major institutions of higher education together with a number of postsecondary affiliates in technical, vocational, and occupational areas. The five major ones are the University of the South Pacific in Fiji, the University of Papua New Guinea in Port Moresby, the College of Micronesia in the Trust Territory of the Pacific Islands, the University of Guam, and the Community College of American Samoa at Pago Pago. Together these institutions serve a population of several hundred thousand people in some thirty-nine Pacific island countries and groups with a combined enrollment of well over 15,000 students of all ages and stages of educational development. At least that many more are participating in various subsidiary programs and workshops across the Pacific.

It has been only during the decade of the 1970s that these institutions of higher learning have come into their own. The College of Micronesia is the newest addition having been founded by an Act of the Congress of Micronesia in March 1977. In the future there will be considerable expansion and change among these institutions as the Pacific population grows. Major research facilities and scholarly research capacities in both the physical and social sciences can be found at Guam, Fiji, and Papua New Guinea. Well-developed instructional programs can be found in all the institutions.

These colleges and universities train and educate the future professionals, technicians, artisans, and politicians of the area. They conduct research and give their collective energies in helping solve the pressing social and physical problems of the area. They also are developing at a time of retrenchment of and keen competition for scarce resources. Since they are all public in nature, they must vie for funding together with many other agencies.

Although widely scattered over the vast Pacific Ocean, these institutions form a rather close-knit intellectual community because in their ocean environment they share many of the same problems: clients spread over wide distances who are coming from a variety of language groups; difficulties in scheduling classes, quarters, and semesters. With many decades' experience and growth behind them, the Pacific area colleges and universities are ripe to plan their own futures in specialized areas where interinstitutional cooperation is timely. Areas of high priority include: accreditation of multi-institutional and nontraditional programs; off-campus and continuing education; nursing, mental, and health fields; arts and higher education; cooperative education; regionalization; and public/private cooperation.

RELATED ENTRIES: American Samoa; Fiji; Guam; Micronesia; Papua New Guinea; University of Guam; University of the South Pacific. *See also* Brigham Young University—Hawai'i Campus; Hawai'i.

Dirk Ballendorf

ELLIS, EARL HANCOCK ("PETE") (1880-1923).
A military strategist, planner, tactician, and the first American undercover agent to penetrate Micronesia during the Japanese administration, Ellis was commissioned in the U.S. Marine Corps in 1901. His first duty was in the Pacific. From 1911 to 1913, he served at the Naval War College, first as a student, then as an instructor. He wrote several papers on advance base forces and on the defense of several Pacific islands including Guam, Peleliu, and Samoa.

After making reconnaissance of Culebra and Vieques islands near Puerto Rico for the 1914 marine advance-base exercise, the secretary of the navy sent him to Guam with a joint army-navy board to prepare a defense plan of the island. Ellis remained on Guam for a year and continued his development of advance-base tactics. In 1915 he demonstrated for the first time that artillery could be landed from boats when he and a small group of men took a three-inch gun across the reef at Orote Point. For service in France during World War I, he received the Croix de Guerre and Palm, the Legion of Honor, the grade of Chevalier, and the Navy Cross.

In 1920 Colonel Ellis went to marine headquarters in Washington to work on war plans. There he completed "Operations Plan 712-H: Advance Base Operations in Micronesia," the military report for which he is best known. Working in the realm of pure theory, he pointed out step-by-step what island bases would have to be seized to carry U.S. sea power within striking distance of Japan. Ellis had such a complete grasp of the many elements involved that twenty-three years later the navy's drive across the Pacific followed every essential of Ellis' plan. Ellis was able to see that Japanese control of Micronesia would so strengthen her strategic position as to make war in the Pacific inevitable.

In 1921 Ellis came to the Pacific to investigate specific sites for American advance bases and to determine if the Japanese were fortifying the islands. Well supplied with maps, charts, navigational books, and confidential codes, Ellis set out on his mission under the guise of a commercial traveler. He visited Australia, Samoa, Fiji, the Philippines, and then went on to Japan. There he became ill. At the U.S. Naval Hospital in Yokohama he was ordered home, but instead he left immediately for Micronesia. Ellis traveled by steamer through the Marianas, Carolines, and the Marshalls where he stopped at Jaluit to be hospitalized again. He made extensive notes of his observations, recuperated, and pushed on to Kosrae, Ponape, and Palau where he again became ill and after a few weeks died on 12 May 1923. Investigations made after his death concluded that there had been no foul play surrounding his death.

RELATED ENTRIES: Defense Planning for Oceania between the Wars; Guam; Micronesia; Oceania, Strategic Importance of since 1945; War in the Pacific Islands.

SOURCES AND READINGS: Dirk A. Ballendorf, "The Micronesian Ellis Mystery," *Guam Recorder* 4, no. 4 (1975); Dirk A. Ballendorf, ed., "A Report of the Military Reconnaissance of the Island of Guam by Earl H. Ellis," *Guam Recorder* 3, no. 3 (1973); Frank O. Hough, *The Island War: The United States Marine Corps in the Pacific* (Philadelphia: J. B. Lippincott Co., 1947); E. B. Potter and Chester W. Nimitz, eds., *Sea Power* (Englewood Cliffs, N.J.: Prentice-Hall, 1960); John J. Reber, "Pete Ellis: Amphibious Warfare Prophet," *US Naval Institute Proceedings*, November 1977.   *Dirk Ballendorf*

ELLIS, WILLIAM (1794-1872). Born 29 August 1794 in London, Ellis became an ordained missionary for the London Missionary Society in the Pacific. He left England in 1816 for the Society Islands where he was to serve for six years. While there he learned Tahitian, introduced the first printing press to the South Pacific, gained the trust of the islanders, and taught them to raise many fruits and plants which later proved a source of material wealth to them.

During a visit to O'ahu in 1822 Ellis so impressed American missionaries serving in Hawai'i with his understanding of Polynesian culture that they requested his help on a trip they planned for the big island of Hawai'i. The next year Ellis and three American missionaries became the first white men to circle the island and to visit the volcano Kilauea. Returning to England in 1824, Ellis enlarged his journal of the exploration by adding many observations to it and by inserting comparisons of life and customs as he had seen them on the Hawaiian and Society islands. Published in 1825 under the title *A Tour Through Hawaii* this account made Ellis famous in England. The book went through five editions by 1828. Later, in 1842, Ellis published this information in connection with material about other South Pacific islands (Tahiti, Huahine, New Zealand, and dozens of other small island groups within the Polynesian triangle) under the title *Polynesian Researches*. These four volumes constitute one of the finest historical records of its kind, accurately describing through word and drawings Polynesian culture, social organization, and religious beliefs of that period.

Appointed secretary of the London Missionary Society, Ellis was requested by the directors of the society to prepare a history of Madagascar whose queen, Ranavolona, had gained British attention through her persecution of Christian converts on the island. Published as two volumes in 1838, Ellis' *History of Madagascar* established him as England's expert on island affairs. Consequently, when persecutions in Madagascar increased by 1852, Ellis was sent to the island to improve the conditions of Christians there. Unsuccessful in three visits to gain a meaningful audience with the queen, Ellis returned to England. However, in 1861 he set out on his fourth and most successful trip to Madagascar which by then had acquired a Christian queen. During his four-year stay on the island, Ellis' influence on this queen was profound and led to an increase of Christian converts. Further, his advice helped stabilize the new government, helping it to deal effectively with French attempts to cause political disruption. Partially as a result of Ellis' input, state matters were settled on a basis which provided for autonomous government, constitutional liberty, and freedom of religion.

Returning to England with much recognition in 1865, Ellis went on to write three books about his Madagascar experiences by 1870. Two years after the publication of his last work Ellis died at Hoddesdon, Hertsfordshire, on 9 June 1872.

RELATED ENTRIES: French Polynesia; Hawai'i; London Missionary Society; Polynesian Culture (Ancient).

SOURCES AND READINGS: Austin S. Allibone, *Allibone's Dictionary of English Literature and British and American Authors* (Philadelphia: J. B. Lippincott Co., 1963); John Eimeo Ellis, *The Life of William Ellis, Missionary to the South Seas and to Madagascar* (London: H. Allen, 1873); William Ellis, *Journal of William Ellis* (Rutland, Vt.: Charles E. Tuttle Co., 1979); Leslie Stephen and Sidney Lee, eds., *Dictionary of National Biographies* (New York: Macmillan Co., 1908).   *Jeffrey Butler*

ENCYCLOPEDIAS OF OCEANIA. Encyclopedias of the region of Oceania fall rather naturally into two groups, each typified by period of publication, format, and intended readership. Those appearing before World War I were single editions aimed at small local markets and had a large biographical and historical content in classified arrangement. They lacked the authority of an objective factual compilation. Later publications have had wider appeal and are usually in the modern alphabetical arrangement. If publication is so recent that there is not yet a record of successive revisions and expansions, the stature of the publishers or sponsors gives some guarantee of continuation.

Following the *Cyclopaedia of Australasia* (1881), Australian publishing produced a rash of encyclopedias around the first decade of this century. The Cyclopaedia Company, and related houses, introduced a volume for each state of Australia (Queensland excepted), several volumes concerning various Pacific islands, and the *Cyclopaedia of New Zealand* (1897-1908). The latter, although of six volumes, cannot be construed as an attempt at a national encyclopedia. Rather, it was six works treating each province separately, and as such it was more akin to the works on the Australian states.

None of these was an encyclopedia as defined by the *Encyclopaedia Britannica* (1968, vol. 8, pp. 365-66) but more closely resembled a yearbook or gazette. Beginning with general outlines of the geographical, naturalistic, biographical, and historical aspects of the place, these encyclopedias proceeded to demographic and commercial statistics and thence to a description of the government and bureaucracy, characterizing their structures and portraying the personalities in control. Advertisements comprised a significant portion and were an important part of the structure of these volumes. They were patently one-time publications, catering for specific parochial audiences.

The *Cyclopaedia of Fiji* and the *Cyclopaedia of Samoa, Tonga, Tahiti, and the Cook Islands*, both published in 1907, each followed this pattern, although, aiming as they did at a smaller group of readers, they exuded rather more of an inbred, late-nineteenth-century flavor. Of more interest than the merit or accuracy of the intriguing information these volumes contain is whether they grant some insight into prevailing attitudes towards the Pacific islands held by nations bordering the Pacific. Unfortunately, this does not appear to be the case. The tone of these encyclopedias was of that from within the island community, or if there was some reflection of the sentiments held toward the region, it could only be that of a romantic but uninfluential minority. For example, in the section on Samoa, the partition by Germany and the United States was lauded for its settled government and pacification. The Germans were praised for their able colonial development, albeit this success was attributed to their copying British methods. These sentiments sat oddly with Australian fears of a German presence and persistent efforts to persuade Britain to annex Samoa in the 1890s.

Perhaps the best indication of Australian attitudes is to be found in the advertisements section. Trade dangled before the readers consisted mainly of consumer goods, at mainland prices with free delivery and guaranteed durability in tropical climes. There were Henderson's Honey Kisses ("Poems for the Palate"), numerous ads for the ubiquitous Australian piano, and other luxury items. New Zealanders, doubtless regarding trade links in a more sober light, offered dairy products, education, cement, and tombstones.

Overall, the encyclopedias were directed at readers living in the islands, and the information they proffered seemed to be what the colonists either thought they already knew, would want to know, or be convinced of. There was little information of real value, and one is largely left in the dark concerning the relationships within and between the islands, and with their larger neighbors.

The second phase may be seen to begin with the *Encyclopedia of Australia* (1925-1926), which has since passed through two revised and expanded editions, the most recent in 1977. Next was *The Pacific Islands Yearbook* (1932) which, despite its compactness, concessions to advertising, and mild recognition of tourism, is more substantial than the title might suggest. A triennial publication until 1977, when the twelfth edition appeared, it now appears annually, with a new format, and required two printings to satisfy demand for the 1978 edition. Since 1978 an annual, scholarly feature article of general Pacific islands interest has been included. The various sections, for all their conciseness, contain a great deal of information and analysis.

Following a 1959 cabinet decision, the New Zealand government sponsored, funded, and ultimately printed and published *An Encyclopedia of New Zealand* (1966). With support from Australian firms and the government, the University of Papua New Guinea produced the *Encyclopedia of Papua and New Guinea* (1972) shortly before that nation's independence.

A number of works have appeared in other languages. *L'Encyclopédie Coloniale et Maritime* appeared throughout the 1950s and includes the volume *Océanie Française* on French possessions in the Pacific. There are also the various *Publications de la Société des Océanistes* which cover a wide range of Oceaniana. Included is the dictionary of biography for the New Hebrides, *Hébridais* (1957), edited by Patrick O'Reilly, and *l'Homme dans le Pacifique Sud* (1966). This last, although encyclopedic in length and scope, is not quite an encyclopedia. Also of this type is the Dutch-language, two-volume *Nieuw Guinea* sponsored by the Netherlands government in 1953.

SOURCES AND READINGS: Robert Collison, *Encyclopaedias: Their History Throughout the Ages* (New York: Horner, 1966); Neville Meany, *The Search for Security in the Pacific 1901-14* (Sydney: Sydney University Press, 1976); *Pacific Islands Yearbook* (Sydney and New York: Pacific Publications, annual).

Phil Diamond

ENGLERT, SEBASTIAN (1888-1969). An Easter Island anthropologist-missionary, Englert was born near Augsberg, Germany, 17 November 1888 where his father was professor at the Museum of Ancient

Languages. Like his father, Englert excelled in linguistics. In 1912 he became a Capuchin monk and nine years later left for Chile to study Amapuchie, a Chilean Indian tongue, which he learned fluently. In 1935 Englert went to Easter Island to study that language, but by then the language had become so mixed with Tahitian and other languages that Englert determined to discover the ancient one by searching out the legends of the island. He traveled the entire land by horseback, living on what food he could find. He visited every statue and painted a large white number on each to aid in description and identification. Originally planning to spend only six months on the island, he decided to settle there in 1936. His stay on Easter Island gave him the opportunity to become fluent in the native tongue and acquainted in native folklore. He wrote several books among which was a dictionary and a grammar text. His influence on the islanders has been greater than any other Westerner who has visited the island.

RELATED ENTRIES: Easter Island.

SOURCES AND READINGS: Sebastian Englert, *La Teirra de Hotu Matu'a*, ed. and trans. William Mulloy (Santiago, Chile: Padre las Casas, 1948) and *Island at the Center of the World: New Light on Easter Island* (New York: Charles Scribner's Sons, 1970).   *David Welch*

EQUATORIAL ISLANDS, U.S. AERONAUTICS IN. The equatorial islands, Howland, Baker, and Jarvis, were first examined for aeronautical potential in 1924 and the U.S. Navy urged the federal government to advance U.S. claims to their sovereignty. Nothing was done and the islands remained vacant for ten years. In 1934 Harold Gatty of the South Seas Commercial Company, interested in establishing an air route from Hawai'i to American Samoa, pinpointed the islands as possible airports to land planes. There was a problem, however, over their sovereignty. In January 1935, at President Roosevelt's suggestion, representatives of the U.S. State Department, the Department of the Navy, and the Department of Commerce met and decided to colonize the islands. The Department of Commerce was put in charge so that Japan would not be perturbed by the American appearance close to their islands. After a period of occupation, the Department of State was to bring up the question of sovereignty with England.

In March the first equatorial cruise took place. Besides colonizing the three islands, the expedition examined Palmyra Island, Swain's Island, and Pago Pago for their aviation potential. That June, Pan American Airways informed the Department of State

that Oceanic Nitrates Corporation was considering occupying the islands to mine guano and would request leases from the Department of the Interior. In June Oceanic sent a party to inspect the islands for guano. Harold Gatty, now with Pan American which had absorbed South Seas Commercial Company, was with the expedition and he studied Palmyra, Kingman Reef, and Pago Pago as possible stopovers for flying boats. Several men were landed on the equatorial islands to claim exclusive rights. Pan American hoped to prevent competition from land planes on the route by gaining exclusive control through a guano lease. The application was rejected by Interior.

In March 1936 Interior was given control of the three islands and Commerce withdrew its colonists. A report circulated in May that England was investigating the South Pacific islands including the equatorial ones. Roosevelt ordered an emergency reoccupation of the islands that June. Foreign countries were interested in the islands. Japan, England, and France all checked them out during this period. The Department of the Navy took an active interest in Howland that November and attempted to install deep-sea moorings for patrol planes. It proved possible to establish only one and on the leeward side of the island.

Amelia Earhart planned a world flight using an equatorial route which depended on landing at Howland. With help from the WPA and the army, runways were prepared on Howland but Earhart crashed in taking-off from Honolulu. On her second attempt, she flew from Lae, New Guinea toward Howland but never arrived. A vast, fruitless search ensued.

This search caused the downgrading of Howland. Its inadequate facilities for handling patrol planes; the inability of land planes to use it; and the difficulty of landing supplies there caused the U.S. to look to Canton in the Phoenix group as the needed island. On 7 December 1941 the islands held only colonists. Howland and Baker were shelled and bombed by Japanese forces and two men were killed on Hangaroa beach, and orange, fig, and mulberry evacuate the colonists and colonization was ended. During the war Jarvis became a radio station facility. Howland was turned into an emergency airfield. Baker became an operational airfield from which advanced Japanese positions could be attacked. With the end of the war, the islands returned to their pre-1934 state—unoccupied and ignored.

RELATED ENTRIES: Canton Island Question; Central Pacific Air Route; Earhart, Amelia; Gatty, Harold; Oceanic Nitrates Corporation; South Seas Commercial Company.

SOURCES AND READINGS: Francis X. Holbrook, "Commercial Aviation and the Colonization of the Equatorial Islands, 1934-1936," *Aerospace Historian* 17 (1970): 144-49 and "Aeronautical Reciprocity and the Anglo-American Island Race, 1936-1937," *Journal of the Royal Australian Historical Society* 57 (1971): 321-35. *Francis X. Holbrook*

ERSKINE, JOHN ELPHINSTONE (1805-1887). John Erskine, a British naval officer, was born 13 July 1805, in Cardross, Scotland. He entered the navy in 1819, was commissioned in 1826, and assumed his first command of the gunboat *Arache* in 1829. After service in the Mediterranean, he was promoted to captain on 28 June 1839. In February 1848 he was appointed to H.M.S. *Havannah* as senior officer on the Australian Station. Soon after his arrival, Erskine made a short trip on the *Havannah* through Samoa, Tonga, Fiji, the New Hebrides, the Loyalty Islands, and New Caledonia. While in Samoa he visited the three main islands of Manu'a, Tutuila, and Upolu. On the island of Manu'a he met its high chief. His next call was Apia where he met American consul John Williams who informed Erskine of the bitter wars between the people of A'ana and Malo. In Apia he also met British consul George Pritchard. They tried to mediate between the people of A'ana and Malo but the proud and self-assured chief of Malo would not yield. As a demonstration of British might, Erskine ordered his crew ashore and demonstrated the destructive ability of the British rifles and gun powder. Erskine, having received a complaint about Malo's brutality toward the people, warned him to reconcile with A'ana. Erskine finally left Samoa in July 1849. He returned to England in 1853. His account of the first cruise was published in 1853 as *Journal of a Cruise among the Islands of the Western Pacific*. In 1857 he was promoted to rear admiral and in 1865 was elected member of Parliament for Stirlingshire. He became a parliamentary leader of the influential lobby working for the Pacific Islands Protection Act of 1872. He retired from the navy in 1872 and lived in London till his death in June 1887.

RELATED ENTRIES: American Samoa; Pritchard, George; Western Samoa; Williams, John.

SOURCES AND READINGS: Peter H. Buck, *Explorers of the Pacific* (Honolulu: Honolulu Star Bulletin, 1953); John Elphinstone Erskine, *Journal of a Cruise among the Islands of the Western Pacific* (London: Dowsons of Pall Mall, 1967); Douglas Pike, *Australian Dictionary of Biography* (Melbourne: Melbourne University Press, 1966).
Michael P. Singh

ESPIRITU SANTO. *See* Britain in the Pacific; Vanuatu.

'EUA ISLAND (TONGA). The island of 'Eua, with an area of 87 km² (34.8 mi²) lies about 19 km (12 mi) south and east of Tongatapu ("Sacred Tonga") island. Tasman visited it in 1643 and called it Middleburgh. Captain James Cook landed there in 1773 and 1777 and recognized it to be Tasman's Middleburgh. He held a high opinion of its fertility and beauty.

The Tongan creation myth indicated that 'Eua was the very first island in the Tongan group to be formed by Tangaloa, the god of the heavens, from wood-carving chips thrown down from the sky into the sea. Early explorers as well as scientists, however, have described 'Eua as an elevated, coralline, atoll-crowned island. W. M Davis in 1928 wrote that 'Eua was already one of the most interesting reef-bearing islands in the Pacific coral seas. Darwin colored 'Eua red on his chart to indicate that it had been fringed with a sea-level reef after its elevation from the ocean. The Tonga islands have no distinct mountains, except 'Eua which rises to a height of 324 meters.

'Eua, geologically the best known of the Tongan islands, is composed of a nucleus of bedded, volcanic material on which has been deposited a coating of limestone. The oldest rocks discovered on 'Eua are volcanic tuffs, breccias, ash beds, and various pyroclastics. Much of the material is heavily stained with iron oxides and hydroxides. 'Eua is the only island of the Tongan group where plutonic rocks, in this case boulders of norite, have been found.

The people of 'Eua are Polynesians and the census of 1976 revealed a population of 4,486. George Forster, an assistant scientist to his father, J. R. Forster in the Captain Cook 1777 expedition, gave a detailed early description of the 'Euans as usually from 1.60 to 1.78 meters tall; more muscular than the Tahitians; and with faces more oblong than round, sharper noses and thinner lips.

It appears safe to assume that the population of 'Eua prior to and after Cook's visits in 1773 and 1777 was not much different from the 200 figure of the 1840 census. It was not until 1860 that the population doubled. That year King George Tupou I ordered 200 inhabitants of 'Ata Island, located 85 miles south-southwest of Tongatapu and named Pylstaart by Tasman in 1643, be removed to 'Eua because the islanders were being taken away by South American kidnapping ships to work in the mines of either Chile or Peru.

In 1946 the population of 'Eua quadrupled when 1,300 inhabitants of Niuafo'ou ("Tin Can Island"), which is on the outskirts of the Tonga group and nearly 640 kilometers from Tongatapu, were removed and eventually resettled at 'Eua Island. This resettlement took place following a violent volcanic eruption in September 1946, which wiped out practically the whole of the government headquarters and the villagers' homes and property. Thus, the peopling of 'Eua was accomplished by three groups: the early pre-Cook settlers, the migrant people of 'Ata Island, and the refugees of Niuafo'ou Island.

The internal marketing of 'Eua's subsistence crops and vegetables is carried out to a certain extent in 'Eua, but most goods find their way to the Talamahu market in Nuku'alofa on Tongatapu island, shipped there in local interisland freight-passenger vessels. In external marketing, 'Eua has been exporting some of her commodities, mainly bananas, watermelons, taro, and yams to the New Zealand markets.

Natural supplies of fresh water are scarce in Tonga. 'Eua, however, is the only Tongan island with several nontransient creeks which provide sufficient supply of water for the villages. But the normal way of obtaining water elsewhere in Tonga is to dig wells and collect rain water. With good soil and climate the vegetation in 'Eua is fairly luxuriant. Wild vegetation still occupies a relatively large proportion of the total land area, mostly confined to the mountainous regions. 'Eua is the only island where rain forests occur. Several sawmills, including one owned and operated by the government, provide lumber locally from the easily accessible timber reserves now being utilized. Forestry planting and a development program have been put into effect to replenish the fast-diminishing supply of lumber trees. This renewed interest has permanently established the headquarters of the Tonga Forestry Division of the Ministry of Agriculture at 'Eua.

'Eua has a limited but interesting variety of land birds like doves, rails, starlings, kingfishers, owls, cuckoos, shrikes, bulbuls, whistlers, honey eaters, purple swamp hens, and swiftlets. Additionally, on 'Eua are two of the most beautiful birds in the Pacific, the redbreasted musk parrot (*platycercus tabuensis*) called *kakā*, and the blue-crowned lory. The red-tailed and white-tailed tropic birds make their home in the cliffs.

'Eua has its seaport at 'Ohonua, its chief village which is situated on the northwest side of the island. Only small internal ships may berth; they operate daily services from Nuku'alofa to 'Eua and back. 'Eua also has an airfield with a 689-meter grass runway. Daily flights to and from 'Eua are operated by the Tonga Air.

The government operates four primary schools in 'Eua. The private sector, namely the Catholic, Mormon, and Wesleyan churches, provide education in two primary schools, one middle school, and one secondary school. Hango Agricultural School is the only postsecondary institution. It is sponsored and operated through a combined effort of the Methodist churches.

Like many other Tonga islands, 'Eua faces problems of unsealed secondary coral or earth roads, inadequate seaport facilities, and no electrical system, to name a few. However, its fertile soil and good vegetation, its natural beauty and tranquil rural environment, and its proximity to Tongatapu, the center for all significant social and economic activities in Tonga, give 'Eua further opportunities to grow and to contribute to the future development and general welfare of the Kingdom of Tonga.

RELATED ENTRIES: Tonga.

SOURCES AND READINGS: E. W. Gifford, *Tongan Society* (Honolulu: Bernice P. Bishop Museum, 1929); Edward Hoffmeister, *Geology of 'Eua, Tonga* (Honolulu: Bernice P. Bishop Museum, 1932); Noel Rutherford, ed., *Friendly Islands: A History of Tonga* (Melbourne: Oxford University Press, 1977).

'Inoke F. Funaki

EYRAUD, EUGENE (?-1868). A Roman Catholic missionary to Easter Island, Eugene Eyraud was born in Belgium. He emigrated first to Argentina and then to Chile were he worked to pay for his brother's religious education. Although a mechanic by trade, he worked at many different jobs. After his brother completed his education he became a missionary in China and his work inspired Eyraud to join him in his labors. He became a novice with the Fathers of the Holy Spirit and left Chile in 1862 with other missionaries for Easter Island. The others quickly became discouraged and Eyraud alone landed at Hangaroa, Easter Island, on 4 January 1864 where he was looked upon as a curiosity by the islanders. He tried to teach Christianity, but at first the islanders mistook his prayers as ritual chants and spells. Some quickly learned that they might become powerful through this new magic and listened to him. In June 1864 he returned to Chile only to come back to Easter Island in December 1865 with two other missionaries. Through Eyraud's efforts, timber houses were built on Hangaroa beach, and orange, fig, and mulberry trees were planted in the mission gardens. Before his death on 14 August 1868 he had succeeded in teaching and baptizing every person on the island.

RELATED ENTRIES: Easter Island.

SOURCES AND READINGS: Alfred Métraux, *Easter Island: A Stone Age Civilization of the Pacific* (London: Oxford University Press, 1957).

David Welch

F

FARRINGTON, WALLACE RIDER (1871-1933).
A former president and publisher of the *Honolulu Star-Bulletin*, Wallace Farrington served as the sixth governor of Hawai'i from 1921-1929. Perhaps no other public official during the first half of the century in Hawai'i made a greater contribution to the prosperity and welfare of the citizens of Hawai'i than Governor Farrington. Born in Orono, Maine, 3 May 1871, Farrington was educated in his home state, earning a bachelor of science degree from the University of Maine in 1891. Three years later Farrington arrived in Honolulu where he worked as a newspaper editor. As governor, Farrington promoted social, political, economic, and educational rights for the people of Hawai'i. He is credited with the establishment of the College of Hawai'i (later, the University of Hawai'i), the implementation of the Hawaiian Rehabilitation Act, and the application of the Bill of Rights Act, which provided federal money for various development projects in Hawai'i. Upon his retirement as governor in 1929, Farrington returned to the newspaper business, which work he was engaged in when he died on 6 October 1933.

RELATED ENTRIES: Hawai'i.

SOURCES AND READINGS: A Grove Day, *Hawaii and Its People* (New York: Meredith Press, 1968); Edward Joesting, *Hawaii* (New York: W. W. Norton & Co., 1972); Ralph S. Kuykendall and A. Grove Day, *Hawaii: A History* (Englewood Cliffs, N.J.: Prentice-Hall, 1961).   *Ned B. Williams*

FAUTUA ("ADVISER"). A Western Samoan position, that of *fautua* ("adviser"), was created in 1912 by the German governor Wilhelm Solf in an effort to prevent continual rivalry between the major chiefly families (*tama'āiga*) for the position of *tafa'ifā* (paramount chief). In June 1913 Tupua Tamasese Lealofi and Malietoa Tanumafili I were sworn in as the first *fautua*. During New Zealand's administration (1914-1962), those holding these positions constituted advisers who maintained contact with the people of the villages through an advisory council,

the *fono* of Faipule. The position became increasingly important as Western Samoa was being prepared for independence. Two *fautua* became joint chairmen of the steering committee of the constitutional convention (1954). When independence was declared on 1 January 1962 the two *fautua*, Tanumafili Malietoa II and Tupua Tamasese Mea'ole (d. 1963), were named joint heads of state, thereby extinguishing the title.

RELATED ENTRIES: Malietoa, Tanumafili II; Western Samoa.

SOURCES AND READINGS: J. W. Davidson, *Samoa Mo Samoa: The Emergence of the Independent State of Western Samoa* (New York: Oxford University Press, 1967).   *Robert D. Craig*

FEILLET, PAUL (1857-1903). The first civilian governor of New Caledonia (1894-1902), Paul Feillet was instrumental in transforming the island from a penal colony to a permanent French settlement. He mounted a successful campaign against the flow of convicts and persuaded 525 French families to emigrate between 1895 and 1902. Three hundred stayed to farm and provide the basis for New Caledonia's European population. During his administration the first Asians arrived as indentured mining workers. A lawyer by training, Feillet promoted rural government at the expense of Nouméa's municipal council. In 1900 he completed the policy of settling the indigenous Melanesians on reservations. He was controversial, authoritarian, yet far-sighted. He returned to France in October 1902 and died in Montpellier on 2 September 1903.

RELATED ENTRIES: New Caledonia.

SOURCES AND READINGS: Patrick O'Reilly, *Calédoniens* (Paris: Musée de l'Homme, 1953).
                    Russell T. Clement

FIJI. A British colony from 1874 to 1970, Fiji became an independent Dominion within the British Commonwealth on 10 October 1970. The Fiji group consists of over 300 islands lying in the southwest Pacific between longitude 175° east and 176° west and between latitude 15° and 22° south. Included also is the small Polynesian dependency of Rotuma to the north. The two main islands, Viti Levu and Vanua Levu, contain 87 percent of the total land area of 18,272 km² (6,148 mi²). Only two of the eighty-nine other inhabited islands exceed 100 square miles. Of the total population of approximately 632,000, 44 percent are indigenous Fijian, 50 percent of Indian descent, 2.6 percent full or part-European, another 2.6 percent Rotuman, Pacific islander, or other ancestry, and 0.8 percent Chinese. The chief administrative center is Suva, located at the southeast end of Viti Levu, the side of the island opposite that of the international airport at Nadi.

Climate. The group has wide regional and local variations in the physical environment and the generally tropical climate, with an average annual rainfall on the windward wide of the main islands of about 120 inches. Temperatures usually stay between 21-32° C (70-90° F). The average mean temperature is 25° C (77° F) falling 6° C (10° F) at night. High humidity levels are usually offset by steady sea breezes. Long spells of hot, dry weather are frequent in the leeward sugar-growing regions.

Flora and Fauna. About half the larger islands are covered with forest, including some fine stands of hardwoods. Tropical rain forests with areas of intermediate forest dominate the windward slopes, while mangrove flats are an important coastal resource. The drier regions are covered with tall reeds (*gasau*). Indigenous fauna is limited to species of flying foxes, bats, a few snakes, with the Polynesian rat, pigs, and dogs introduced at an early period. Fiji is noted for over a hundred species of birds, some exceedingly beautiful and rare.

Pre-European History. The group was discovered and colonized in the second millenium B.C. by Austronesian-speaking peoples moving out of Melanesia, crossing the formidable 400-mile wide Melanesian trench to do so. Almost certainly these were the same people who later developed the proto-Polynesian culture farther east, not impossibly in the Lau group, though Tonga or Samoa are more likely. The first settlers may have been joined later by another related population, perhaps from New Caledonia. These dual origins are reflected primarily in an irreducible division between eastern and western Fijian dialects and a different style among the pottery fragments used by archaeologists to help identify the major waves of immigrants. A third wave, possibly from the central New Hebrides, seems to have been present from the twelfth century of the modern era. For the next seven centuries there is abundant material and oral evidence of intensified warfare and a general state of ferment lasting through the first seventy years of European contact in the nineteenth century.

The flow of genes back and forth from Melanesia and Polynesia over these three millennia of ancient history produced a distinctive people and culture, the exact nature of whose intermediate status between the two cultural areas it is difficult if not pointless to determine. Ancient Fijian societies still await the labors of an ethnohistorian. Unquestionably cultural, social, and political life was rich, sophisticated, and exuberant. The relatively affluent subsistence economy could provide on call a surplus of perishable root crops and fruit. Fine handicrafts, notably hand-beaten paperbark cloth (*masi*) and superbly carved wooden weapons and utensils, were important items of regional specialization and trade. Fiji's great double-hulled canoes (much sought after by the lumberless Tongans), splendid domestic architecture, and ingenious ring-ditch or hilltop fortifications testified to their specialized skills and flair for communal enterprise. Communities could rely on a variety of socioeconomic and political "paths of the land" to facilitate the exchange of complementary manpower, or natural resources such as salt, seafood delicacies, fine mats, and canoe timbers. Especially in the resource-poor outer islands these linkages enabled communities to recover speedily from natural disaster, principally hurricanes and droughts. Competitive festivals of property exchange (*solevu*) brought hundreds and even thousands of people together, often coinciding with the great occasions of chiefly installations, funerals, and alliances.

Most Fijians, it seems, participated in a cycle of production, labor services, offerings, and exchange which revolved around the installed chief at each level of a hierarchy of social groups. The most stable of these was a small federation of related communities usually called the *vanua* (literally "land" or "state"). The ancestral guardians came forth from the chief to ensure the fertility of the land and the people's prosperity. To the chief, then, more especially in the eastern parts, belonged the style and dignity of a supernaturally sanctioned office: his person was hedged with elaborate taboos and etiquette. He (very rarely she) represented the honor of the group in its dealings with other groups, and to a remarkable extent this principle survived the whole colonial period. To insult a chief was to insult his people.

The eyewitness accounts of early European observers and Fijian oral traditions reveal that Fijian political life had its full quota of intrigue, treachery, humiliation, and bloody revenge. War was an integral part of Fijian life. As the principal avenue to personal glory, it shaped the ambitions of the young and left the old defended by few conventions of restraint. Through armed superiority and diplomacy certain chiefly houses were able to obtain the cooperation of far-flung social groups transcending a great variety of local linguistic and cultural differences. The advent of muskets and cannon obtained by trade in the early nineteenth century and a monopoly of the services of the beachcombers accelerated the rise to power of the chiefs of Bau (a small islet just off the mouth of the Rewa river north of Suva). The Bauans enlarged their ambitions later in the century to oust their Tongan rival, Ma'afu, from his eastern Fijian dominions and create a national kingdom. Already there was perhaps by mid-century a sense of shared origins and cultural distinctiveness as a result of centuries of interaction throughout the group, trading networks, kinship connections, migrations, and common problems with Tongan imperialism. Colonial rule would bring to fruition these seeds of Fijian national identity.

European Penetration. The Dutch navigator Abel Tasman careered through reefs to the northeast in 1643 and counted eighteen or twenty islands in latitude 17½° south without attempting a landing. Leaving Tonga in 1774 in search of ''Quiros' Isles'' on his second voyage, Captain James Cook touched at the southern outlier, Vatoa. On his third voyage he learned more about the group from the Tongans and met Fijians on Tongatapu, but uncharacteristically chose not to follow up these leads. William Bligh, abandoned in 1789 by the mutineers of the *Bounty*, sailed his open boat through the main islands, egged on at one point by a canoe of warriors giving chase from one of the Yasawas. In 1792 Bligh was able to examine some of the islands more comfortably on H.M.S. *Providence*, but the group was not adequately charted until the voyages of Bellinghausen (1820), d'Urville (1827-1828), and Wilkes (1840).

Meanwhile fine stands of sandalwood had been discovered by a shipwrecked sailor at the beginning of the century, and his rescue led to an extensive trade, much of it conducted on Fijian terms, until the trees were cut out by 1814. *Bêche-de-mer* traders, in search of the same holothurians for the same Chinese luxury market that had long sent fleets from Macassar to Australia's northern shores, found good Fijian supplies in the 1820s. As this trade also required shore establishments and extensive Fijian cooperation, traders indulged Fijian tastes, patronized chiefs, and even helped them in their wars. The famous captain Peter Dillon found among Fijians the very best

of men and urged French Roman Catholic priests to claim them for Rome.

However, the Wesleyan missionaries William Cross and David Cargill (preceded by two Tahitian London Missionary Society teachers on Oneata) established their first base on Lakeba in 1835. In the following years missionaries were stationed at Rewa, Somosomo, and Viwa. Lacking substantial material incentives to offer Fijians, they made little headway for the first fifteen years until the conversion of the Tu'i Nayau, paramount chief of Lau in 1849 (and other chiefs thereafter), ushered in mass conversions. With the vigorous and not always apolitical assistance of Tongan ministers, Ma'afu championed the Wesleyan cause in eastern Fiji. The mission made remarkable progress during the 1860s in all but interior Viti Levu. Catholic Marist priests, present in the group from 1844, were never serious contenders with the Wesleyan hegemony except in parts of Bau and Cakaudrove. Wesleyan church structures were admirably congruent with Fijian districts, while the wide range of church offices open to Fijians, Wesleyan deference to chiefly authority, and their dedication to Fijian literacy ensured that the church became rapidly integrated with the very fabric of Fijian life. By the 1870s, Fijian missionaries were being sent to evangelize Melanesia, and much of the younger population was literate in the Bauan dialect of the Fijian Bible.

Hundreds of European settlers, the majority by way of Australia and New Zealand, were attracted to Fiji by the prospects of cotton growing during the boom caused by the American Civil War. Large areas of prime arable land including most of Taveuni and entire small islands were alienated during the 1860s. The copra techniques and successful marketing of the product in Europe (pioneered by German trading firms) enabled planters to switch to coconuts when cotton became unprofitable, and the port of Levuka flourished as an increasingly self-aware advance post for the relentless march of Anglo-Saxon civilization in the South Seas.

In the late 1860s Fijian chiefs and some of the European settlers participated in a few short-lived attempts to form Western-style governments. In 1871 a national monarchy was established under Cakobau, high chief of Bau. Beset with virulent opposition from those hoping to see Fiji become a proper British colony run in the interests of Englishmen and Empire, John B. Thurston led the king's ministry from 1872 and championed Fijian local autonomy even as he guided the chiefs through the years of intermittent negotiations that led finally to the loss of Fijian independence in 1874.

Cession to Independence. The deed of cession that was formally signed at Levuka on 10 October 1874 was an unconditional transfer of sovereignty to Queen Victoria, but the signatory chiefs were given the strongest verbal assurance that their rights and privileges and the welfare of their people would always be Britain's first priority. Remarkably enough, the first governor, Sir Arthur Hamilton Gordon, was of a mind to take these conventional pieties as his charter to make Fiji a significant exception to the dismal history of British expansionism in Australasia. He gave the European settlers no political representation at all; nor were they given seats in the legislature for forty years. Gordon, with Thurston his closest adviser, devised a complete system of all-Fijian administration and law to guarantee Fijians a separate area of autonomy and dignity in the colony's affairs. A hierarchy of government-subsidized chiefs, councils, and courts, with taxes paid in kind for the first four decades, gave Fijians a real sense of participation in government. The "communal system," as it was often called, freed them from dependence on the plantation economy, but it rested on a good deal of conscripted labor for village and other public projects. Land alienation was halted, while existing customary land rights were eventually codified and registered to communal descent groups. In general—and where the Fijian administration was offensive to liberal thought and resistant to the structures of capitalism—absolute priority was given to community needs above the personal rights of individuals. The system sustained some powerful chiefly leaders, notably Ratu Sir Josef Lalabalavu Sukuna (1888-1958) and his cousin, Ratu Sir Kamisese Mara, who led the nation through independence in 1970.

The European sector of the colonial economy was salvaged by the momentous decision of Gordon to import and exploit identured Indian laborers. Between 1879 and 1916 the arrival of 60,553 Indians led to the growth of a substantial sugar industry dominated almost from its inception, and until 1973, by the exceptionally hard-nosed Australian corporation, the Colonial Sugar Refining Company (CSR). Indian farmers and laborers, under indenture until 1920 and thereafter as subtenants of CSR holdings of freehold or leased Fijian land, largely sustained a commercial economy directed from abroad in close cooperation with colonial authorities.

Fijians withdrew from the sugar industry at the century's turn and then made a small reentry as growers in the 1930s. From the 1920s they were quite willing, however, to be indentured for short periods as laborers, often living in the old Indian lines. The most substantial Fijian contribution to the economy was for several decades that of more than half the exports of copra and most of the bananas, both products grown on communal land. The collapse of the original taxation scheme by 1910 removed the government marketing organization and left Fijians at the mercy of small traders. Almost immediately, and until World War II, there was a ground swell of support for a powerful illegal movement called the Viti Company whose charismatic leader, Apolosi R. Nawai, articulated the frustrations of the ordinary villagers with their inability to find an easy road to education and control over their own resources and labor. Indians meanwhile were beginning a long political struggle of their own, never fully achieved, to win the place of dignity and equality due to them as British citizens.

World War II evoked a remarkable mobilization of Fijian manpower for the war effort, including over two thousand infantrymen who served with distinction in the Solomons and Bougainville in 1943 and 1944. Several thousand more manned labor battalions to handle the huge American traffic through the Suva and Lautoka ports.

Ratu Sukuna was rewarded for his recruiting efforts by promotion to the top of the Fijian administration. He worked with Governor Sir Phillip Mitchell to reorganize its structures closer to the original design of Gordon and Thurston. Postwar Fijian policy was firmly committed to integral community development, with the village as the heart of the neotraditional way of life Ratu Sukuna was determined to protect as long as possible from "the omnipotence of the great octopus of the modern world."

Communal development schemes and continued dependence on indirect political representation through traditional leaders seemed anachronistic in the 1960s, and in the last years of colonial rule drastic reforms reasserted the ideals of individualism and democracy. The main effects of these, added to an urban drift, were to deprive villages of strong local leadership and to undermine their own systems of social security: they entered into an accelerated physical and social decline.

Economic Resources. National development plans following independence tried to address the problems of villages in terms of rural self-help projects and the like, often boosted by small aid projects, and a few major new economic schemes such as cattle raising and cultivating pine forests. Tourism, sugar, coconut oil, timber, and a dwindling amount of gold, with some promise of a new copper mine, constitute Fiji's footnote to the world economy. In the 1970s a small start was made on urgently needed import-substitution industries. Two Australian groups continued to dominate the importing, wholesaling, and major urban retailing sectors, leaving smaller retailing activities to Indian and Chinese merchants or Fijian cooperatives. The economy is heavily dependent on foreign investment, most visibly in the tourist industry, with minimal restraints on the expatriation of profits. Agriculture, fishing, and forestry employ less than half the work force.

National Goverment. The constitution adopted upon independence (10 October 1970) provides for a Westminster-style parliament consisting of the British sovereign as head of state represented by a governor-general and a bicameral legislature. The executive government is formed by a cabinet of ministers chosen by the prime minister from the elected members of the House of Representatives or the nominated senators. The House of Representatives has fifty-two members elected according to a complex cross-voting arrangement whereby an equal number of seats (twenty-two) are reserved for Fijian and Indian electoral rolls and eight for other races on a separate roll. A crucial feature of the composition of the Senate is that eight of its twenty-two members are appointed by the Great Council of Chiefs and the consent of six of them is necessary to enact any legislation affecting certain entrenched measures concerning Fijian land or customary rights. The constitution, then, gives ironclad security, short of revolution, to the paramountcy of Fijian interests maintained during the colonial period; it defines the parameters for the working compromises, the balance of imbalances, achieved by the Fijian and Indian communities through the first decade of independence. These years were notable for the willingness of ascendant Fijian leaders to foster multiracial participation in selected areas of national life, while accepting sharp racial boundaries as a fact of ordinary community life.

Fiji moved very comfortably into the international arena, enjoying an enviable reputation for stability despite local pessimism. The purchase of CSR's Fijian operations and establishment of the Fiji Sugar Corporation was a major demonstration of the government's capacity to safeguard vital national interests. At the same time the prime minister, Ratu Sir Kamisese Mara, worked to strengthen regional cooperation in the South Pacific, searching for a "Pacific Way" to preserve humane values in national and international life.

RELATED ENTRIES: Anglican Missions; Bau; Bromilow, William E.; Bulu, Joel; Calvert, John; Cook, (Captain) James; Defense Planning for Oceania between the Wars; Diaper, William; Dillon, Peter; Gatty, Harold; Gordon, Arthur; Hunt, John; Island Confederation Movements; Joske, Adolph; Lapita Culture; Latianara; Levuka; Lockerby, William; London Missionary Society; Lyth, Richard; Moss, Frederick J.; Navosavakadua; Nawai, Apolosi; Patel, Ambalal D.; Polynesia Company; Polynesia, Settlement of; Polynesian Culture (Ancient); Pritchard, William; Rotuma; St. Julian, Charles; Sandalwood Trade; Savage, Charles; South Pacific Commission; South Pacific Forum; Sukuna, Josef Lalabalavu; Swanston, Robert S.; Thompson, William K.; Thomson, Basil H.; Thurston, John B.; University of the South Pacific; Western Pacific High Commission; Whippy, David; Wilkinson, David; Williams, John Brown; Woods, George A.

SOURCES AND READINGS: Peter France, *The Charter of the Land: Custom and Colonization in Fiji* (Melbourne: Oxford University Press, 1969); K. L. Gillion, *Fiji's Indian Migrants: A History to the End of Indenture in 1920* (Melbourne: Oxford University Press, 1962); K. L. Gillion, *The Fiji Indians Challenge to European Dominance, 1920-1946* (Canberra: Australian National University Press, 1977); R. R. Nayacakalou, *Leadership in Fiji* (Melbourne: Oxford University Press, 1975); Deryck Scarr, *Ratu Sukuna: Soldier, Statesman, Man of Two Worlds* (London: Macmillan, 1980).   *Timothy J. Macnaught*

FIJI BANKING AND COMMERCIAL COMPANY (1873-1876). During the cotton boom and the "Fiji rush" (1860s), a bank became necessary to stabilize monetary exchange and commerce, to finance plantation developments, and to provide a safe repository for land titles. After proposals by a consortium of Levuka merchants, a land company in Melbourne, and banking promoters in both Melbourne and Auckland, the Cakobau government granted a charter, signed by Ratu Seru Cakobau to a group of Auckland investors. This first bank in Fiji, the Fiji Banking and Commercial Company, began business in December 1873 with a staff appointed from Auckland. The Crown Colony administration was the main customer, but the company became involved in commercial transactions, produce marketing, and, through mortgages and liens, in land alienation. After cession, the company's charter, commercial activities, and land holdings were declared invalid; it was allowed to continue only its fiscal operations. In 1876 the promoters, who were closely linked to the Auckland-based Bank of New Zealand, arranged a takeover. In 1876 the Fiji Banking and Commercial Company was liquidated, and the Bank of New Zealand assumed all assets and liabilities. Negotiations and settlements between the two banks and the British government over Crown Colony administration overdrafts, land titles, and banking operations were not settled until the late 1880s. The bank of New Zealand has continued in Fiji to the present.

RELATED ENTRIES: Fiji; Fiji Planting and Trading Company.

SOURCES AND READINGS: R. A. Derrick, *History of Fiji* (Suva: Government Printer, 1946, 1968); R. H. Griffin, *Bank of New Zealand: A Century in Fiji, 1876-1976* (Auckland: Bank of New Zealand, 1976).
Alan Maxwell Quanchi

FIJI, FEDERAL MOVEMENT IN. In a series of attempts European settlers in Fiji tried to unite Fiji with an outside power. The rapid increase in European population during the "Fiji rush" (1860s) and the failure of indigenous political systems to maintain order led to campaigns for the annexation of Fiji by Great Britain, Germany, the United States of America, and the Australasian colonies of New South Wales, Victoria, and New Zealand.

British annexation in 1874 was regarded by the European community as a chance to finally profit by the financial commitments they had made in Fiji. However, the first governor, Sir Arthur Gordon (1829-1912), and subsequent governors were more sympathetic to Fijian interests than to planter and settler profits. Antigovernment opinion culminated in campaigns for union with the colony of New Zealand (1882-1885), for inclusion in a proposed Australasian federation (1883), and for inclusion within the colony of Victoria (1887). Although there was support in Fiji and in the colonies, British colonial practice would not accommodate the type of union being sought. Influential banking, investment, and commercial circles in the colonies were also loath to risk money in Fiji as a result of losses during the cotton boom and collapse. Successive governors in Fiji censured moves by the European community and maintained Gordon's policy of the paramountcy of Fijian interests. The movement lost momentum in the early 1890s. A Fiji-New Zealand scheme was well supported in 1900-1902, and Fiji-Australia plans were revived briefly in 1912 and 1921. The federal movement sought to improve the internal economic conditions of the settler and planter community by changing the mode of government. These various movements for political union did not succeed. Fiji remained a separate British colony that gained independence in 1970.

RELATED ENTRIES: Central Polynesian Land and Commercial Company; Fiji; Fiji Planting and Trading Company; Fiji Trading Company; Gordon, Arthur.

SOURCES AND READINGS: A. Ali, "The Federal Movement in Fiji, 1880-1902: Causes and Course" (Master's thesis, University of Auckland, 1969); R. A. Derrick, "The Federal Movement in Fiji," *Transactions and Proceedings of the Fiji Society* (Suva: By the Society, 1958); A. M. Quanchi, "Fiji Star in the Australasian Federation," *Pacific Islands Monthly*, August 1976, pp. 37-38.   *Alan Maxwell Quanchi*

FIJI PLANTING AND TRADING COMPANY (1868-1875). A short-lived planting enterprise typical of companies formed during the "Fiji rush" of the late 1860s, the Fiji Planting and Trading Company was incorporated in the large Australian gold-mining town of Ballart. Organized at the height of the Fiji cotton boom, it quickly attracted investors. Surveyors, suppliers, and a plantation manager were sent to Suva promontory to begin operations. The company held 466 acres behind Nabukulo Creek and another 1,500 unspecified acres on the promontory. Several hundred Tokelauns, Solomon islanders, and Fijians cleared and cultivated the land. When the cotton market plummeted and sugarcane experiments failed, the company collapsed. The plantation manager, C. D. Cuthbert remained on the land, served in the legislative council and various government posts, and then as secretary to the Suva Planters Association. The company was liquidated in 1875.

RELATED ENTRIES: Central Polynesian Land and Commercial Company; Fiji.

SOURCES AND READINGS: Commissioners' Reports No. 443 and 444, Land Claims Commission Records, National Archives of Fiji, Suva, Fiji; Defunct Company File No. 191, State Archives of Victoria, Melbourne, Australia; *Leader* (Melbourne) 6 August 1870.   *Alan Maxwell Quanchi*

FIJI, RACE RELATIONS IN. Relations between the indigenous Fijians and the immigrant Indians have been remarkably harmonious despite profound religious, linguistic, and social differences, economic inequalities, and the rarity of intermarriage. Fijian dominance of government and the army since independence in 1970 has not produced markedly chauvinistic policies. Conflict has been controlled by features of the political structure and the economy discussed below.

The colonial government indentured laborers from India to work the sugarcane plantations owned by white settlers. Movement of Fijians from traditional villages into wage employment was thereby restricted, and the authority of their hereditary chiefs maintained. A degree of segregation continues to limit interracial contacts and rivalry. The majority of each group lives in separate though sometimes neighboring rural communities. Most Indian farmers depend on leases of Fijian land, and their access to land has been facilitated by the fact that few Fijians have themselves taken up cane farming. The Fijians' principal commercial crop is copra, grown mainly where there are few Indians. Fijians are represented in the urban middle class as teachers, bureaucrats, and other white-collar workers. The Indians' demand for salaried careers has been offset by their successes in commerce and industry and in the legal and medical professions, though competition for government jobs is growing. The degree of racial separation in the economy has, by limiting occasions for rivalry, favored collaboration in trade unions and political parties, and sociability in urban clubs and associations.

Indians and Fijians have on occasion been united by common resentment of the wealth and privileges enjoyed by the white minority. But the lesser extent to which Fijians have depended on regular money incomes has limited their animosity toward the whites. Indians, depending wholly on cash incomes as laborers or tenant farmers, were more disposed to challenge the colonial status quo, particularly when inspired by leaders who brought to Fiji their experience in Mahatma Gandhi's movement. These radicals sometimes sought Fijian support but usually aroused their hostility and apprehension, especially after the Indians had outnumbered them. European politicians representing commercial interests feared the British government might accede to Indian demands for political equality and so cultivated ties with Fijian chiefs in parliament, urging them to be vigilant against the common threat.

This opposition to Indians was mitigated, however, by the concern of the whites in both business and official circles to advance the sugar industry by securing Fijian leases for Indians to farm. The objective of maintaining racial complementarity in the economy played an important part in patterning administrative and political institutions: Fiji's prosperity, it was said, depended on the collaboration of Fijian land, European capital, and Indian labor. The colonial government, through the principal chiefs, persuaded Fijians to lease out some of their land.

While relations of land inevitably became the most contentious political issue there were some mitigating circumstances. Few owners became wealthier than their tenants—inequalities in rent income associated with differences in customary rank have been greater. Furthermore, government control over leasing arrangements and rent collection restrained the devel-

opment of personal animosities at the local level—both owners and their tenants became the subordinates of the Native Lands Trust Board managed by the governor in association with leading chiefs. This political control facilitated interracial negotiation and compromise over land.

The role of interracial mediator has been assumed by the principal Fijian chiefs, typically senior administrators who became representatives of the Fijians in parliament. Collectively they symbolize the Fijians' identity and prerogative as a racial group with a distinctive culture, but at the same time encourage them to make concessions to Indians in matters of land—by agreeing to periodical reform of the conditions of leasing. Indeed the chiefs' very success in securing racial identity and solidarity has allowed this margin for compromise.

The chiefs' own unity and influence, on which compromise has depended, were strengthened by their joint authority in the Fijian administration. This institution helped to maintain racial group complementarity in the economy by extolling the virtues of village life and restricting the extent to which Fijians could compete with Indians in commercial farming and wage employment. While many Fijians resented the restraints on their personal freedom, most of them jealously defended the administration and the chiefs as the central supports of a social system that gave them identity, land, and a consciousness of their special worth beside the other groups in the wider society. Preservation of the "Fijian way of life" was made a hallowed enterprise securing Fijian prerogative and solidarity in the face of the numerical and economic advances of the Indians and the continuing power of expatriate whites. This objective in fact strengthened the position of the whites and the chiefs by discouraging radical political unity among Fijians and Indians: Fijians were urged to cooperate with Indians for the sake of the sugar industry, but were dissuaded from joining them to challenge the ruling elites.

Official institutions, including the Native Lands Trust Board and the Fijian administration, structured the opposition between Fijians and Indians as a system of accommodation. The Fijians who dominated the first government of independent Fiji achieved their influence within this system, sustaining the racial division by rallying Fijian solidarity in opposition to Indians, but also providing a bridge in dealing with Indian political leaders over the negotiable issues of land.

Indian leaders have been less united than their Fijian counterparts: cultural group antagonisms and factional rivalries have subverted attempts to maintain solidarity. Yet the rival Indian groups tend to compete with each other to succeed as negotiators with Fijian leaders rather than as challengers of Fijian prerogatives.

The potential for rivalry among Fijians is a more serious threat to interracial cooperation. One body, the Fijian National Party, accused the ruling Alliance Party of neglecting Fijians in order to woo Indian voters. It appealed to Fijians discontented with the administration of the land and resentful of Indian successes in commerce and even proposed that the Indians be repatriated. This kind of movement may become more popular as population pressures on land increase, as consequent urban migration intensifies competition for jobs and housing, and as this rivalry in turn makes Fijians even more reluctant to share their land.

RELATED ENTRIES: Fiji.

SOURCES AND READINGS: K. Gillion, *The Fiji Indians* (Canberra: Australian National University Press, 1977); A. Mamak, *Colour, Culture, and Conflict: A Study of Pluralism in Fiji* (Sydney: Pergamon Press, 1978); A. C. Mayer, *Peasants in the Pacific*, 2d ed. (New York: Routledge & Kagan, 1973); R. Norton, *Race and Politics in Fiji* (New York: St. Martin's Press, 1978).   *Robert Norton*

FIJI, TONGAN IMPERIALISM IN. The first Tongan venture in territorial expansion was their occupation of Samoa from sometime in the thirteenth century to sometime early in the seventeenth century, A.D. Nothing, unfortunately, is known of the nature of their rule or the circumstances of its abandonment. Their next bid for conquest came two hundred years later. Tongan nobles had been visiting Fiji and establishing residences there since the fourth or fifth century, A.D. The size of the expatriate Tongan community increased substantially during the "time of troubles" in Tonga itself between 1799 and 1833. The able and shrewd Taufa'ahau united most of the group under his rule as King George Tupou I in 1833, safeguarding his position by sending Prince Ma'afu, whose claim to the throne was at least as valid as his own, to rule over the Tongan community in Fiji.

Ma'afu began to extend his control along the coast, accepting the allegiance of Fijians opposed to their local tyrant, Cakobau of Bau. King George Tupou, however, offered Cakobau Tongan assistance to suppress opposition to his tyranny. Tupou and Ma'afu then combined forces to crush resistance to the Bauan imperium. Ma'afu carried matters farther by waging war in Vanua Balavu, allegedly in defense of Christianity, known in Fiji as "the religion of Cakobau." The tyrant of Bau sought to escape Tongan domination by ceding Fiji to the British Crown. He was successful to the extent that the British appointed a consul, who managed to deter a Tongan assault on Bau itself in 1857. However, Tupou demanded in 1861 that Cakobau pay him $60,000 for Tongan military aid and despatched commissioners to enquire into Tongan claims to land in Fiji. The commissioners reported back that these comprised all the peripheral islands of the Fijian group, the western coast of Viti Levu, and the eastern coast of Vanua Levu.

Fiji was preserved from complete Tongan domination only by the anxiety of Tupou and Ma'afu not to provoke European intervention. It was agreed as a compromise that the various Tongan dominions and satellites should be amalgamated into the Lau confederacy, governed by Ma'afu on behalf of King George Tupou. Cakobau was then crowned puppet king of the rest of the group which became effectively a white settler dominion. Tupou then discreetly ceded all Tongan claims in Fiji to Ma'afu, who was commanded not to involve Tonga in Fijian affairs any more. Another era of Tongan imperialism had come painlessly to an end.

RELATED ENTRIES: Fiji; Tonga; Whippy, David.

SOURCES AND READINGS: Glen St. J. Barclay, *A History of the Pacific* (London: Sidgwick and Jackson, 1978); R. A. Derrick, *A History of Fiji* (Suva: Government Printer, 1946); Sir Basil Thomson, *Diversions of a Prime Minister* (Edinburgh: Blackwood, 1894).   *Glen St. J. Barclay*

FIJI TRADING COMPANY (1875-1892). A merchant, shipping, and trading enterprise in Fiji arose in 1871 when the trading and plantation partnership of Brewer and Joske established trade stores, timber mills, plantations, and shipping services on Suva promontory. In 1875 the partnership was dissolved and William K. Thompson, the managing director of James McEwan and Company of Melbourne, assumed all assets. The old store "Brewer and Joskes" continued as the Fiji Trading Company, though it was better known as "Thompson and Renwicks," the names of the Australian directors of the company. Activities included postal services, pilotage, engineering works, and freight and steamship services to Australia in addition to the commercial operations begun during the original partnership. In 1892 the commercial business passed to Marks Brothers and later to Morris Hedstrom. New Zealand and Fiji interests took over the other operations. Morris Hedstrom continued to trade in Fiji. The original title used since 1871 has now disappeared.

RELATED ENTRIES: Fiji; Joske, Adolph B.; Thompson, William K.

SOURCES AND READINGS: P. S. Allen, ed., *Cyclopaedia of Fiji* (Sydney: Cyclopaedia Company, 1907).   *Alan Maxwell Quanchi*

FIJIAN LAND TENURE. Land tenure has long been recognized as one of Fiji's major problems. Since 1875 the alienation of native land has been prohibited, with the result today that almost 84 percent of the total land area remains in the hands of the indigenous Fijians. Within traditional Fijian social structure, the *tokatoka* or family groups are the basic land-working unit. These are subdivisions of the *mataqali*, the basic landholding unit. Land rights are safeguarded today by legislation affecting Fijian land requiring the consent of a majority of the eight senators appointed by the Great Council of Chiefs.

Indians first arrived in Fiji as indentured laborers in 1879. This system was halted in 1916 at which time some 40,000 Indians elected to remain in Fiji as free settlers. Because of Fiji's legislation protecting Fijian ownership of the land, Indians were required to lease the lands they farmed. European settlers had gained title to a good proportion of cultivable land prior to cession of Fiji to Britain in 1874. Other land was alienated in the early 1900s, but since 1909 there has been no further alienation. Today, Indians make up about 50 percent of the population and much conflict is engendered by the fact that they can only lease the lands which they have continued to farm for many years.

Fiji's agricultural crops are sugar, coconuts, and root vegetables. The sugar industry became a permanent part of Fijian economics with the establishment of the Colonial Sugar Refining Company, an Australian corporation, which built its first sugar mill at Nausori, about 22 km from Suva, in 1882. The company further established mills at Rarawi, Labasa, and Lautoka. The sugar was then grown on large estates and indentured Indian laborers were brought in to work the cane fields. After 1916 when this system ceased, the sugar estates were divided and farmed almost wholly by Indian tenant farmers working small holdings.

In 1940 the Native Land Trust Board was established by law to administer the land in the owners' interests. As the agency for every landowning unit, it handles all business related to leases. Comprised of the governor as president, the minister for Fijian affairs as chairman, five Fijian members appointed by the Great Council of Chiefs, three Fijian members appointed by the Fijian Affairs Board, and two members of any race appointed by the governor, the board may lease any land not in a reserve area to anyone and without the consent of the owners. Reserve land can only be leased to Fijians and only on written consent of the owners. Twenty-five percent of all income generated by leasing of the land is retained by the board. Some dissatisfaction has always existed over this administration of private land by a public agency. Some owners today remain apprehensive about the intent of the board, seeing it as an agency which caters to the demands of the Indian tenants rather than the Fijian owners.

Disputes over lease boundaries, correct ownership, and length of time assigned to leases have always existed in Fiji. In the past, Fijian owners who chose not to renew leases but to work the land themselves often did not produce as much from the land as the Indian tenant farmer was able to. Moreover, they sometimes found that the sugar mills refused to process their cane. More recently, an agricultural tribunal set up by the Agricultural Landlord and Tenant Ordinance (ALTO) decided on several rulings which could be made in claims of hardship affecting the status of land. This meant that a landlord had to prove greater hardship than a tenant if an extension of a lease was to be turned down. This proved very difficult to do, because the tribunal further decided that if owners were not fully using all of their lands, they could not suffer hardship by the renewal of a lease to part of them. The tribunal arrived at these decisions by assessing the *mataqali* as a whole rather than individuals within the unit. For the Indian lessee, hardship was often easier to prove because his whole subsistence was involved in the piece of land he rented. Consequently, when a lessee died leaving a family, the Fijian owner could rarely prove hardship greater than the children of the dead farmer.

Discontent over land tenure continues to shape legislation in Fiji and reflects continuing rivalry between the islands' two main cultural groups.

RELATED ENTRIES: Fiji; Fiji, Race Relations in; Western Samoa, Land and Titles Court.

SOURCES AND READINGS: Ron Crocombe, ed., *Land Tenure in the Pacific* (Melbourne: Oxford University Press, 1971); Michael Moynagh, "Land Tenure in Fiji's Sugar Cane Districts Since the 1920s," *Journal of Pacific History* 13 (1978): 53-73; O. H. K. Spate, *The Fijian People: Economic Problems and Prospects* (Suva: Legislative Council of Fiji, Council Paper no. 13, 1959).   *Vernice W. Pere*

FOREIGN RESIDENTS' SOCIETY. In the early 1850s the European settlers in Samoa organized themselves into the Foreign Residents' Society. Largely confined to the Apia area, it nonetheless claimed jurisdiction over all settlers. All foreigners were entitled to membership in the society. About half of them gave it some loyalty. It functioned as a sort of town meeting type of government with the entire group serving as a legislature. It elected a chairman, councillors, and judges, all of whom were unpaid. The society presumed to lay down rules for the maintenance of community order and for the conduct of trade. Its influence among the Samoan community was negligible. The officers of the society conducted investigations into various complaints and imposed fines. These were the sole revenues of the society which were used for small public-works projects. The society was tolerated by the chiefs, but it had no real legal status. It was heavily dependent upon the resident counsuls for any real authority. In 1864 it was replaced by the Association for the Mutual Protection of Life and Property.

RELATED ENTRIES: American Samoa; Western Samoa.

SOURCES AND READINGS: J. W. Davidson, *Samoa Mo Samoa: The Emergence of the Independent State of Western Samoa* (New York: Oxford University Press, 1967); R. P. Gilson, *Samoa 1830 to 1900: The Politics of a Multi-Cultural Community* (New York: Oxford University Press, 1970).   *Jerry K. Loveland*

FORSTER, JOHANN REINHOLD (1729-1798) AND FORSTER, JOHANN GEORGE ADAM (1754-1794). The two Forsters were German explorers and scientists who participated in Cook's second voyage in the Pacific (1772-1775). The elder Forster was born in Dirschau and trained as a Calvinist clergyman, although his real interest always lay in natural history. After a time in Russia, Forster moved with his family to England in 1766 where he eked out a meager existence through teaching until, together with his son George, he was invited to serve as naturalist aboard Cook's second world voyage. This expedition traversed the icy waters near Antarctica and visited Tahiti, New Zealand, New Caledonia, and other South Pacific islands before returning to England. Before embarking on this cruise, Johann Reinhold had entered into an agreement with the British Admiralty allowing him to publish an official narrative account of the voyage. Relations between Forster and Cook, however, were not amicable, and after the conclusion of his travels Forster was denied such publication rights. Nevertheless, Johann Reinhold did achieve modest fame as a result of his travels and

eventually published a scientific account of the Cook voyage. His *Observations Made During a Voyage Round the World* (1778), later translated by George into German, dealt with a wide range of topics from geology to ethnology. His son George, born in 1754 near Danzig and who had followed his father on all of his travels, did not feel constrained by the Admiralty's restrictions and proceeded to write a narrative of Cook's voyage. His *A Voyage Round the World* was published in two volumes in 1777 and a German translation appeared the year after. Though never a scientist of his father's calibre, George as a political and philosophical writer far surpassed him in historical significance. At the time of the Cook voyage George's ideas were still conservative and reflected his religious upbringing, but his early travels and views of "primitive" societies contributed to a broadening of his intellectual horizons that would ultimately lead him to become a freethinker and political radical. Although George's work could not compete with Cook's own official treatment of the voyage, it did win for him great renown in Germany. George accepted a teaching position in Kassel, and in 1780 his influence enabled him to win for his father a university post at Halle. The elder Forster remained at Halle until his death in 1798, publishing scientific travel literature. George moved on to various jobs, eventually becoming university librarian at Mainz. There he became immersed in the radical politics of the time and soon was the leading spirit of the city's Jacobin club. George cooperated with the French during their occupation of the Rhineland and died in Paris in 1794. George's writings set standards for German travel and scientific literature and influenced his contemporaries such as Humboldt, Herder, and Goethe.

RELATED ENTRIES: Cook, (Captain) James.

SOURCES AND READINGS: *Neue Deutsche Biographie*, vol. 5 (Berlin: Duncker & Humblot, 1961); Thomas P. Saine, *Georg Forster* (New York: Twayne, 1972); Ralph-Rainer Wuthenow, *Vernunft und Republik* (Bad Homburg, Berlin, Zürich: Verlag Gehlen, 1970).   *Ralph C. Canevali*

FRANCE IN THE PACIFIC. Compared to the other European countries who played major roles in the history of the Pacific island states, France entered the Pacific scene late and still maintains a strong presence. Although official French support of overseas navigation came only after the Seven Years War (1756-1763), there were at least a hundred Frenchmen who had already circumnavigated the world. In 1764 the French government seriously began to sponsor overseas expeditions aimed primarily to gain prestige, to aid science, and to obtain whatever land masses they happened to find.

Louis Antoine de Bougainville set out first in 1764 to surrender Falkland Island to Spain and then again in 1766 to circumnavigate the Pacific. He successfully visited and took possession of Tahiti, Samoa, New Hebrides (Vanuatu), then sailed through the Great Barrier Reef, through the Louisiade archipelago, past Choiseul, Bougainville, and New Ireland before returning home. Jean de Surville and Nicholas de Fresnes both lost their lives in their Pacific ventures, Surville by drowning (1769) and Fresnes by being slain by New Zealand Maoris (1771). France's second most important exploration of the Pacific in the eighteenth century was by Jean-François de Lapérouse (1785-1787) whose valuable contributions to Pacific geography are prodigious. His journal was fortunately sent to France via Kamchatka before he and his crew mysteriously disappeared.

Despite her revolution and subsequent international wars, France commissioned two navigators, Étienne Marchand and Antoine d'Entrecasteaux, to make voyages before the close of the eighteenth century. Marchand's voyage (1790-1792) added new lands and new commercial outposts for France. D'Entrecasteaux's voyage (1791-1793) failed to find Lapérouse's ships and crew although naturalist Julien de Labillardière's description of Tongan customs remains a major contribution of that voyage. By the end of the eighteenth century, almost all of the Pacific islands had been "discovered" by European powers and then, during the first half of the nineteenth century, they were to become pawns in an international rivalry that culminated in outright annexation of all of them.

The Napoleonic Wars, especially between France and Great Britain, gave some respite to the Pacific; but after France's humiliating defeat at Waterloo she turned her attention once more to a vigorous competition against her old rival—England. France's principle goal was to frustrate England by surpassing her in the Pacific in commerce, in science, in navigation, and in religious proselytizing. French whaling ships rivaled but never surpassed her American and British competitors. Her scientific voyages were resumed by Louis C. D. de Freycinet who continued to collect scientific data between 1817 and 1820. Louis I. Duperrey's voyage (1822-1825) obtained substantial information on terrestrial magnetism and magnetic variation while Dumont d'Urville's several voyages (1820-1829, 1837-1840) produced twenty-three volumes of new scientific data on Oceania.

Although Roman Catholicism had been introduced early in the Pacific, it was not until the French Restoration (1815) that there was a rebirth of this effort. Naturally, the English Protestants who had already established themselves in the islands opposed such French action. In 1827 the French landed a band of Catholics in Hawai'i, but they were expelled. It was not until French naval officers actually seized the Hawaiian government in 1842 that they were allowed entrance into the islands. A similar experience in Tahiti ended in outright annexation of the islands as a protectorate by France in 1842. Afterwards, Tahiti became the center from which Catholicism and French domination spread thoughout eastern Polynesia.

By the end of the nineteenth century, France had annexed the Society Islands, the Tuamotus, the Marquesas, the Australs, the Gambiers, and New Caledonia, and had entered into a condominium agreement with Great Britain over the control of the New Hebrides (Vanuatu). By World War I international competition had led the major world powers to gain control of every island group in the Pacific.

During World War I the French Pacific possessions, called *Etablissements Français de l'Océanie* (EFO), rallied willingly behind their metropolitan government while at the same time they suffered heavy casualties at Verdun, Champagne, and on the Somme.

The government of the EFO generally reflected the unconcerned sentiment of metropolitan France. Inept and inexperienced governors who had little concern for Pacific peoples were dispatched to Oceania. During fifty-eight years (1881-1939) forty-four governors were sent to Polynesia (an average of fourteen months per governor), and New Caledonia was no different. Although a consultative council was appointed in Pape'ete in 1903, the governor had virtually absolute authority over the islands. Agitation in Tahiti in the 1920s resulted in the establishment of a new council in 1933 but still with only consultative powers. Internal political problems over fascism in France during the 1930s left little time to hear the complaints from her small dependencies so far removed from Paris. When World War II broke out in 1939 each of France's colonies rallied again to her side; but when the war ended, each was not content to remain the passive colony it once had been. Within two decades almost all had severed their ties completely, but France was most reluctant to consider total independence for her Pacific possessions. In 1958 President Charles de Gaulle allowed the colonies a choice between voting yes to remain in the French community, or voting no for immediate severance (and an end to all French monetary aid). In French Polynesia the vote was 64 percent yes and 36 percent no compared to an almost unanimous yes (96 percent) in New Caledonia where the electorate was overwhelmingly made up of expatriate Frenchmen. Compared to New Caledonia, French Polynesia was still primarily Polynesian—there had been little colonization.

This changed drastically, however, when France announced in 1963 that her African Sahara atomic tests were being transferred to the Pacific. Overnight, Tahiti and Pape'ete especially enjoyed a new prosperity paid for by metropolitan taxpayers. Tahitians no longer were content to cultivate land and fish, but they became wage laborers for the burgeoning atomic industry. This military-urban complex became the largest single employer for the Tahitians. Although the Nationalist Party commands a majority of French Polynesian voters, it has never gone as far as to suggest absolute, total independence from France. When French Guinea voted no in 1958 France pulled out, taking with her their normal budgetary funds. This example is always used by the Gaullists when discussing the consequences of severing their ties with France. Demonstrations and radical protests for more internal control (especially in 1976) forced France to promulgate a new statute which appeared to give the Polynesians more internal autonomy. The governor was replaced by a high commissioner, and a local assembly with a vice-president (similar to a prime minister) was organized.

An extremely tenuous situation prevails today while Polynesia attempts to gain further control over its affairs without causing the metropolitan government to decide to pull out of Pape'ete. Tahitian nationalists generally prefer the self-government model of the Cook Islands where they are generally independent while at the same time citizens who can travel freely to and from New Zealand. France, however, is reluctant to be so generous. Although small, radical groups demonstrate for absolute autonomy, the majority of the electorate is tied to the dependency state created by the French atomic tests. It seems unlikely that France's role in the Pacific will diminish in the next few decades.

RELATED ENTRIES: Bougainville, Louis Antoine de; Dumont d'Urville, Jules; French Polynesia; Lapérouce, Jean-François de; Marchand, Étienne; New Caledonia; Vanuatu (New Hebrides).

SOURCES AND READINGS: L. and F. Chabonis, *Petite histoire naturelle des établissements français de l'Océanie*, 2 vols. (Paris: St. Amand-Montrond, 1954); Herman R. Friis, *The Pacific Basin: A History of its Geographical Exploration* (New York: American Geographical Society, 1967); Philippe Mazellier, ed., *Le Mémorial Polynésien*, 6 vols. (Pape'ete: Hibiscus Editions, 1977-80).   *Robert D. Craig*

FREAR, WALTER FRANCIS (1863-1948). The only man to serve in Hawai'i as governor (1907-1913) and as chief justice of the supreme court, Walter Frear was born 29 October 1863. Governor Frear graduated from O'ahu College (Punahou Academy) in 1881 and received his A.B. degree at Yale University in 1885. Five years later he received his law degree from the same university. Returning to Hawai'i after graduate work at Yale, he began to practice law and was appointed judge of the first circuit court by Queen Lili'uokalani in 1893. Mr. Frear was appointed chief justice of the supreme court of the territory of Hawai'i, 1900-1907, during which time he revised and annotated all the laws of Hawai'i. President Theodore Roosevelt appointed Frear governor of Hawai'i in 1907, who remained in office until 1913. Noted for his efficiency and progressive drive, Frear helped stabilize Hawai'i's judiciary system and promoted the territorial affairs of the islands. After his retirement from his law practice in 1934 Governor Frear became director of the Bishop Trust Company until his death on 22 January 1948.

RELATED ENTRIES: Hawai'i.

SOURCES AND READINGS: A. Grove Day, *Hawaii and Its People* (New York: Meredith Press, 1968); Edward Joesting, *Hawaii* (New York: W. W. Norton & Co., 1972); Ralph S. Kuykendall and A. Grove Day, *Hawaii: A History* (Englewood Cliffs N.J.: Prentice-Hall, 1961).   *Ned B. Williams*

FRENCH POLYNESIA. An overseas territory of France, French Polynesia consists of approximately 130 islands divided into five island groups located in the southeastern corner of the Pacific: the Society Islands, Tubuai (or Australs), Marquesas, Tuamotus, and Gambiers. The total land area is 4,014 km² (1,544 mi²). All of the island groups are high volcanic islands except the Tuamotus which are primarily atolls. The total population of approximately 140,000 consists of 77 percent Polynesians, 14 percent Europeans, and 9 percent Chinese-Asians. Approximately one-half of the population lives on the island of Tahiti where Pape'ete is the chief administrative center for French Polynesia.

Climate. The climate of French Polynesia varies. Generally it is tropical, hot, and humid, but cooled by the trade winds. Temperatures between 35° and 16° C (95° and 61° F) have been recorded. The average mean temperature is 26° C (80° F). There are two seasons: one mainly dry and cool (March to November) and one hot and humid (November to March). Rainfall averages about 165 cm (65 in) a year.

Flora and Fauna. The subtropical flora is dense along the coast and in the valleys but is less so on the mountains. Plants consist of the coconut, mango, breadfruit, bougainvillea, frangipani, and many others. Land fauna is rather poor. However, sea life is extremely rich where over three hundred species of fish live in the lagoons and open sea. Tides are the most regular of any in the world. High tide occurs at noon and midnight, low tide at six in the morning and evening.

Pre-European History. The Polynesians who first settled these eastern islands apparently came from the west—Samoa and Tonga. The Marquesas were first settled about the second century B.C. From here groups settled the Society Islands, the northern Tuamotus, Hawai'i, Mangareva, and then Easter Island by 500 A.D. From the Society Islands, groups sailed to the Cooks, to New Zealand (1200 A.D.), to the southern Tuamotus, to Hawai'i, to the Australs, and to the island of Rapa. The culture of all these eastern Polynesian groups presents a close similarity in contrast to their western neighbors.

This ancient society appears to have been highly stratified and complex. The ruling class, the *ari'i*, were treated with great respect by the lower classes: the *ra'atira* (subchieftains) and the *manahune* (commoners and servants). Their oral legends, myths, genealogies, and history tell of their many gods who were endowed with great powers and who required homage, obedience, and constant offerings. The observance of rituals was exacting and had to be done with extreme care. Their religious ceremonies were observed in sacred stone enclosures called *marae*. The most sacred *marae* in all of eastern Polynesia was Taputapuatea on the island of Ra'iatea. Royal families throughout Polynesia sought marriage alliances with the high chiefs and priests of Ra'iatea. Warfare was common between districts on the same island and between neighboring islands. Jealousy, self-aggrandizement, rebellion against an oppressive leader, or a woman's love usually formed the reasons for their warfare.

Throughout their long history, there never existed a single ruler who dominated any of the major groups. When the Europeans arrived, they found each island divided into numerous districts each ruled over by an independent chief. This system had probably never changed in the many hundreds of years of their history. It was only after the arrival of the Europeans that a concept of monarchy was introduced into the islands. There were certain families, however, that claimed high social and religious titles through genealogical connections, but that did not necessarily give them political control over one another. During the early European period (about 1767-1800), at least two families on the island of Tahiti claimed equal authority and, as a result, war broke out frequently between them. It was only because of European support that one contender, Pomare I, was finally able to gain political control over his rivals.

European "Discovery." Magellan discovered Pukapuka, an island in the northeast corner of the Tuamotus in 1521. The Marquesas were discovered by the Spanish explorer Mendaña in 1595. The Australs were gradually discovered first by Cook in 1768, then by Guyangos, Varela, and Vancouver. Tahiti and the Society Islands were discovered by Wallis in 1767, then visited by Bougainville in 1768, Cook in 1769, and Bligh in 1788. These early navigators arrived at a crucial time. Rivalry on Tahiti between the Pomares in the north and the Papara family in the south broke out in war. Both claimed high religious and social titles, but neither politically controlled or dominated all of Tahiti.

The arrival of navigators and of members of the London Missionary Society (LMS) in 1797 enhanced the power of the Pomare family. Civil war forced most of the missionaries away in 1799 and in 1809; by 1815, however, Pomare II gained supremacy and most of his followers accepted Christianity. Shortly, all of the other islands followed Tahiti's example. Between 1815 and 1837 the missionaries and especially George Pritchard exerted great political control over the affairs of the kingdom. In 1836 Fathers Caret and Laval attempted to land and introduce Catholicism into the islands. They were forced to leave. There followed six years of intrigue that left the islands under a French protectorate (the "Pritchard Affair"). Almost immediately civil war broke out between the Tahitian-English party and the French that lasted until 1847. (Treaty of Jarnac, 1847.)

The Protectorate, 1847-1880. Under the protectorate, Queen Pomare IV (1827-1877) ruled jointly with a French military commander. A legislative assembly was created, but by 1880 neither the monarch nor the assembly exercised any great authority in the islands. When the queen died in 1877, her son Pomare V came to power. In 1880 he was persuaded to cede his kingdom, the windward Society Islands, to France. (Annexation of 1880.) France annexed the Marquesas in 1880, the Gambiers in 1881, the Australs in 1900, and Rapa in 1901. These formed the *Établissements Français de l'Océanie* (EFO) under a French governor appointed from Paris to Pape'ete, the recognized capital of the EFO.

World War I to 1939. Tahitian life generally remained passive until after World War I. During the war, Pape'ete was heavily damaged by the German ships *Scharnhorst* and *Geisenau* commanded by Admiral von Spee. Over a thousand Tahitian volunteers served both in the Balkans and in France where they received the highest commendation for bravery in the war. Two hundred lost their lives before the war was over.

After the war the veterans returned home where they found that the influenza epidemic of 1918 had killed over three thousand citizens in the islands. A depression in the early 1920s helped to inflame a growing animosity against the outdated governmental structure. When the governor attempted to raise taxes in 1922 a popular demonstration forced him to rescind the bill. Through the ballot box in 1932 the Tahitians ousted a government-sponsored candidate (Gratien Candace) as their representative to the Colonial Ministry in Paris. Opposition continued to mount and the governor was forced to reestablish an old advisory council consisting of thirteen members, seven of which were elected. These few demonstrations showed that reform could be forced upon the government. In the 1930s, the Kong Ah bankruptcy and the Rougier affair created local scandals. The Chinese, first brought to Tahiti in the 1860s to work on the Stewart plantation at Atimanoo (Papara), had now gained fairly wide control of the local economy. The Chinese-controlled Kong Ah Society declared bankruptcy in 1933 and the government appointed an interim committee to run the company to pay off its debts. For eighteen months the committee members pocketed much of the profits while they liquidated most of the assets to their own advantage. The affair became public, several were arrested, and Governor Montagné was recalled.

During the 1930s, worldwide interest in Tahiti resulted from various movies produced there (*Taboo* in 1928 and *Mutiny on the Bounty* in 1934), from Tahitian participation in the World's Fair in 1922, and from the French Colonial exhibit in 1931. In January 1934 the first boatload of American tourists arrived in Pape'ete from California.

World War II to the Present. When France fell to the Germans in June 1940 Tahiti voted (5,564 to 18) to join Charles de Gaulle's Free French movement under its new governor Emile de Curton. Tahitian soldiers volunteered willingly as they had in World War I. Over three hundred sailed from Pape'ete in April of 1941 to fight in Libya, Italy, and France. Bora Bora became a naval air base for some five thousand American troops whose money and ideas were to have far-reaching influence after the war.

By 1947 Tahitian nationalism spurred the organization of the party *Comité Pouvanaa*, headed by Marcel Pouvana'a a Oopa. His newspaper, *Te Ara-'Tai*, pressed for more political, economic, administrative, and cultural freedom, less French authority, and more Tahitianization. A massive demonstration by the *Comité* on 22 June 1947 prevented French of-

ficials aboard the *Ville d'Amiens* from landing in Pape'ete. Pouvana'a and several of his men were imprisoned for five months during which time their popularity increased substantially. In 1949 Pouvana'a was elected as French Oceania's representative to the French parliament, a seat he gained again in 1952 and 1956.

On 10 August 1957 Tahiti's territorial assembly gained considerable local power as the EFO was reorganized and the eastern EFO became French Polynesia. Pouvana'a became vice-president of the new territorial assembly. His pressure for independence continued. When his unpopular income tax increase created strikes and demonstrations in April 1958, Pouvana'a abrogated the new law. In the October elections his campaign "Tahiti for Tahitians" received only 30 percent of the total vote. A few days later Pouvana'a and his followers were arrested, charged, and convicted of attempting murder, arson, and illegal possession of firearms. Tahitian politics quieted down as the executive power was once again in French hands.

In October 1960 a new jet airport opened at Fa'a'a. As a result, tourism drastically increased, while Hollywood's movie producer, MGM, poured large sums of money into the economy with a new filming of *Mutiny on the Bounty*, starring Marlon Brando. In 1963 the French began nuclear tests on the Moruroa atoll while enlarging Pape'ete harbor to handle the large numbers of incoming French personnel. Fresh opposition to France's domination of the islands began anew under the leadership of Francis Sanford who had been the government's liason officer assigned to the American military on Bora Bora during World War II.

On 22 July 1977 the French national assembly voted to grant a new status of autonomy to French Polynesia. The vice-president of the territorial assembly (Francis Sanford, in effect, the prime minister) was granted considerable prerogatives over local and budgetary affairs.

Present Administration. The inhabitants of French Polynesia are French citizens in every respect. They have the right to vote, the right to representation in the French parliament, and the right to run for elected office. They elect one senator to the French Senate, two deputies to the National Assembly and they also send a representative to the economic and social council (all in Paris). The local government is comprised of: (1) the Territorial Assembly (thirty members elected every five years) which handles its own financial matters, and has jurisdiction over all local aspects of law, the budget of the territory, bills ratifying international conventions, and other such matters; (2) the Council of Government (seven members chosen by the Territorial Assembly) which is presided over by the high commissioner from Paris and which debates proposed changes and recommendations in internal affairs; (3) the economic and social committee which is a consultative body composed of representatives of various professional groups and trade associations. Representation is directly proportional to the number of inhabitants employed in each occupational sector and its relative importance to the territory's economy. The territorial budget is funded primarily through indirect taxes (56 percent), contributions from the French government (10 percent), and from loans (34 percent). Seventy-five percent of the local tax revenue comes from sales tax and import and export duties.

Economy. The coconut remains the mainstay of Polynesian agriculture; it provides the people with food, housing, fuel, and medicine. Two by-products, copra and coconut oil, are the chief exports of the territory. The production of copra has been decreasing largely due to the fluctuating market as well as the age of the coconut palm groves. Vanilla was introduced into the territory in 1846, and although still among the principal crops, its exports have dropped considerably. Cultivation of other vegetables and fruits is limited mainly to local consumption. Although the French government has tried to institute the legal registration and delimitation of private property, this Western concept conflicts with the Polynesian tradition of collective landownership; 85 percent of the land still remains in Polynesian hands. Pape'ete and its suburbs are among the relatively few areas which have taken to the Western system because of the high monetary value of land. Fish remains a staple element in the diet and tuna fishing is being developed commercially. In 1977 exports totaled 12,000 metric tons, most going to the cannery in American Samoa. Local crafts provide employment and although fractured into small units such as home workshops and craft stores, they nevertheless provide an important source of revenue for the territory. This includes the manufacture of tapa cloth, carved wood objects, shell jewelry, and engraved mother-of-pearl objects. There exists also a substantial mother-of-pearl and cultured black pearl production, a large amount now going to Japan. In 1977, 28,000 round pearls were harvested while the figure for 1978 was estimated to be 50,000.

Tourism. Although French Polynesia has long been renowned for its beauty, its tourist industry did not really begin to develop until the airport at Fa'a'a was opened in 1960. Today, thanks to regular flights, it is easy to visit not only Tahiti but most of the other large islands as well. Many hotels have been built in the islands. In 1979 a total of 101,194 tourists spent vacations there, while the 1980 rate was approximately 12 percent lower because of the depressed world economy. The Tahiti Tourist Development Board promotes the industry.

Nuclear Test Center. The construction of the CEP (Pacific Nuclear Test Center) in 1966 provided the single largest impetus in transforming French Polynesia into an international marketplace. The evolution of the work force from the agricultural to the service sector is a striking example. Over a nine-year period, the agricultural sector decreased by 57 percent while services grew by 34 percent. From 1960 to 1970, the gross domestic product rose by 406 percent, while salaries skyrocketed by 1,222 percent during the same period of time. The nuclear test site on Moruroa is 1,197 km (744 mi) from Tahiti. The nearest inhabited island is Tureia (Gambier group) eighty miles north-northeast of the firing site.

Scientific Research. ORSTOM (Office for Overseas Scientific and Technical Research) has been conducting research in tropical and subtropical areas for over thirty years in the study of the earth, human, and life sciences. There is a seismological laboratory on the island of Tahiti to measure and record information on earthquake activity in the area, and an agricultural research center on Mo'orea that is concentrating on developing hybrid plants for cultivation in the tropical climate. CNEXO (National Center for the Exploitation of the Oceans) is experimenting with the breeding of shrimp and the cultivation of oysters.

Education. Education is compulsory and free in government schools. There are 148 public and 16 private primary schools and 10 public and 7 private secondary schools. Seven public and 3 private schools offer technical instruction. There is an agriculture school on the island of Mo'orea which has its own model farm. The most advanced farming methods are taught here in view of the importance of agriculture to the economy. Students wishing education beyond the secondary school level usually enroll in the universities in France. A hotel training school was founded in Tahiti in 1962. It trains young people in the various aspects of hotel management. The Chamber of Commerce of Tahiti also offers a number of adult education courses in business English, shorthand, typing, etc.

Press and Telecommunications. There are three daily papers: *La Dépêche de Tahiti*, *Le Journal de Tahiti*, and *Nouvelles de Tahiti*. In addition, the Oceanic Studies Center publishes its own quarterly bulletin. French Polynesia has an extensive radio network. There is a central station in Pape'ete and an additional thirty-seven primary and secondary stations throughout the islands. A daily radio program informs inhabitants of outlying islands of mail deliveries which are often quite difficult to make due to the remoteness of certain areas. There is a new space telecommunications station at Papeno'o on the island of Tahiti. It is the first French station equipped with a special automatic tracking system by which the antenna rotates in calibrated positions and stops once the signal received is at its maximum. This station is able to receive television broadcasts transmitted via satellite from France.

RELATED ENTRIES: Ari'i Ta'ima'i; Austral Islands; Baret, Jeanne; Bataillon, Pierre-Marie; Bligh, William; Bora Bora, U.S. Military Life; Bougainville, Louis Antoine de; *Bounty* Mutiny; Bovis, Edmond de; Bruat, Armand; Caret, François; Chanel, Pierre; Chin Foo; Cook, (Captain) James; Crook, William P.; Darling, Ernest; Dillon, Peter; Dumont d'Urville, Jules; Dupetit-Thouars, Abel; Ellis, William; France in the Pacific; French Polynesia, Formal Education in; Gauguin, Paul; Gerbault, Alain; Hagerstein, Peter; Hall, James; Henry, Teuira; Henry, William; Jarnac, Convention of; Kong Ah Bankruptcy; Krusenstern, Adam; Laval, Louis; London Missionary Society; Loti, Pierre; Marau, Joanna; Marchand, Étienne; Marquesas Islands; Marsden, Samuel; Melville, Herman; Moerenhout, Jacques; Moruroa Atoll; Nordhoff, Charles B.; Nott, Henry; Omai; Orsmond, John; Polynesia, Settlement of; Polynesian Culture (Ancient); Pomare Family; Pomare Law Code; Pouvana'a a Oopa; Pratt, Addison; Pritchard, George; Robarts, Edward; Ropiteau, André; Salmon, Alexander; Sandalwood Trade; Sanford, Francis; South Pacific Commission; Stewart, William; Tahitian Annexation; Tati; Te Moana, Charles; Teraupo'o, War of; Teri'iereo'o a Teri'iero'oterai; Thomson, Robert; Tuamotu-Gambier; Tupaia; Vahekehu, Elisabeth; Vernier, Frédéric; Wallis and Futuna; Williams, John.

SOURCES AND READINGS: A. C. Eugene Caillot, *Histoire de la Polynésie Orientale* (Paris: Ernest Leroux, 1910); Robert Langdon, *Island of Love*, 4th ed. (Sydney: Pacific Publications, 1972); Philippe Mazellier, ed., *Le Mémorial Polynésien*, 6 vols. (Pape'ete: Hibiscus Publications, 1978-80).   *Robert D. Craig*

FRENCH POLYNESIA, FORMAL EDUCATION IN. French Polynesia, composed of 130 islands spread over five archipelagos (Society, Marquesas, Tuamotu, Gambier and Austral or Tubuai), is situated in the center of the South Pacific, some 8,000 km from Latin America and 6,000 km from the Australian continent. Politically, it is controlled by France as a French Overseas Territory. From the onset of Western contact with these islands, (Wallis, 1767; Bougainville, 1768; and Cook, 1769), they became an object of rivalry between the French and the English, with educational matters being a point in case. Even though the inhabitants of these islands had their own means of transmitting knowledge, values, skills, and attitudes from one generation to the next, formal compulsory education, as defined from a Western point of view, commenced with the arrival of the Europeans.

The first attempts to organize formal educational programs in French Polynesia were made by the ministers and missionaries of the London Missionary Society in the early 1800s. Their initial effort was through the use of the vernacular; first by establishing a standardized, written Tahitian, and then by printing the Bible and other limited works in Tahitian. A Bible school existed in Mo'orea in 1813, and with the encouragement and protection of King Pomare II, who himself knew how to read and write as early as 1807, several other schools were soon opened throughout the islands, using both English and Tahitian. In 1824, a more advanced institution, the Academy of the South Seas, was organized using English as the principal language of instruction. At this time, the Academy, as well as most of the other Protestant schools, essentially served to provide education for the children of the Protestant missionaries and settlers, although a growing number of Polynesians attended, with limited use of Tahitian. By 1842, when French Polynesia became a Protectorate of France, the Protestant missionaries had turned over much of the teaching responsibilities to young Tahitians who taught in the vernacular.

It was not until 1854 that the French Catholic missionaries, who had been present in the islands since 1836, attempted to establish a French school in Pape'ete. The experiment lasted only three years because of a lack of Tahitian Catholics in Pape'ete and a fierce objection to the French language, since English had been the accepted foreign language for nearly half a century. The Dames de Cluny opened the first public school using French in Pape'ete in 1857, and a French Sergeant Scintenac had eleven students in his Pape'ete school established in the late 1850s, including children of royal families. However, the first substantial success of education in French was instigated by a Catholic religious order of educators, the Congregation of the Brothers of Ploërmel, who arrived in Tahiti in 1860 with the express goal of establishing schools. Within a month, their school boasted sixty students and over the following years continued to make progress, marking the beginning of mass education in French Polynesia. Although initially encouraged and supported by the French government, which officially annexed the territory in 1880, political leaders as well as Protestant leaders feared an eventual Catholic monopoly of education in French Polynesia, and pressure was applied to secularize education. In 1882 three teachers were sent from France to establish public secular education.

From this point onward, the public school system expanded throughout the islands, and relations between the public, Catholic, and Protestant school systems became highly competitive, often with little or no cooperation. Other private schools followed in the coming decades, including two schools serving the Chinese community, which used the Hakkah dialect as the language of instruction, and schools established by three other principal religions of the Territory (Mormon, Reorganite, and Adventist). It was not until the late 1960s that, because of laws reforming and standardizing private and public education, a new spirit of stability and cooperation developed that has led to equal educational opportunities and possibilities of progress for the entire community. Today in French Polynesia, the public school system is far more important than the private school system in terms of actual numbers of students enrolled, especially at the primary school level. For the 1980-1981 school year, of 38,908 students at the nursery and primary levels, 30,996 were in the public school system, while of the total 13,306 students

matriculated in post-primary schools, 9,183 attended public institutions. Table 2 summarizes the total student enrollment throughout the territory. One contributing factor in the rapid development of the public school system was the almost total lack of established private schools outside of Tahiti and the other Society Islands, (with the exception of a strong Catholic influence in the Marquesas) although some do exist presently. The public school system opened up most of the outer islands and has retained its stronghold. The past decade has seen an especially successful effort in the promulgation of the public system, with many new nursery, primary, vocational, and secondary schools built throughout the islands, the training and recycling of a growing number of local educators and the development of adult and community educational programs.

Today in French Polynesia formal education is compulsory from the ages of six to fourteen. The public school system is free, while private schools generally charge a minimal tuition fee. However, but for one exception (the Mormon Primary School) all the so-called private institutions receive significant financial aid from the government, with the minimum cooperative contract (between the government and the institution) providing the teaching staff salaries and the maximum aid including funds for staff salaries, facilities maintenance, and purchase of teaching materials and equipment. The remaining funds needed for the private schools come from their sponsoring churches and private sources. Funds for

TABLE 2
STUDENT ENROLLMENT IN FRENCH POLYNESIA SCHOOLYEAR 1979–1980

Island Groups	Number of Nursery + Primary Schools		Enrollment in Nursery + Primary Schools		Number Post Primary Schools		Enrollment in Post Primary Schools		Total Enrolled	
	Public	Private	Public	Private	Public	Private	Public	Private	Public	Private
Society:										
Windward (Tahiti/Mo'orea)	82	13	2108	7008	13	6	7184	3705	28292	10713
Leeward	38	2	4804	429	5	2	1340	265	6144	694
Austral (Tabuai)	15	—	1670	—	1	—	410	—	2080	—
Marquesas	25	2	1348	475	2	1	249	153	1597	628
Tuamotu and Gambier	39	—	2066	—	—	—	—	—	2066	—
TOTAL	199	17	30996	7912	21	9	9183	4123	40179	12035

SOURCES: Department of Education and Vice-Rectorate of French Polynesia.

the support of public schools and semi-support of private schools, although channeled through various agencies, city and community budgets, originate entirely from France, as there is no income or property taxation in French Polynesia. The financial statistics for the 1977-1978 school year indicate the sum of $70 million spent on territorial education, excluding funds from private sources, or a per annum cost of $1,500 per child. It is interesting to note that in spite of earlier competition and lack of cooperation, the government presently keeps private institutions functioning by heavy subsidization with the accurate understanding that a heavier financial burden would result from the collapse of the private sector in the territory's educational structure. This approach has done much to bring about a new era of cooperation and mutual understanding between the two sectors.

As presently organized, two administrative structures control the educational system of French Polynesia: the Department of Education (Service de l'Education), which oversees the public nursery and primary schools as well as certain vocational programs, and the Vice-Rectorate, which supervises private institutions and all post-primary educational matters. While the Department of Education has been granted a limited amount of autonomy from the central structure in France (allowing some curriculum adaptation and local hiring policies), the Vice-Rectorate is but a local branch of the highly centralized French educational system. Consequently, secondary school requirements, curriculum, testing, and scoring are not adapted to local conditions but governed by existing policies and conditions in France. Furthermore, except in some cases in the private sector, nearly all teaching and administrative personnel in the secondary schools are from France, generally hired on a three-year overseas contract. The Vice-Rectorate also ensures that the private institutions comply with established curriculum and policy requirements. All testing required for placement, advancement, or graduation for students of both public and private institutions is standardized and centralized.

Even though French Polynesia is located in the southern hemisphere, to avoid administrative difficulties with France, the school year runs from September to June. With slight variations, the weekly schedule is as follows: 7:30 a.m. to 3:30 p.m. on Monday, Tuesday and Thursday and 7:30 a.m. to 11:30 a.m. on Wednesday and Friday. The curriculum, as in France, remains highly academic both in primary and secondary schools with no local history, language, or geography taught except on a limited scale in primary school. Secondary school requirements include one foreign language in the first cycle (B.E.P.C.) and two in the second cycle (*Baccalauréat*). Tahitian is not an acceptable possibility. A child who enters the first year of primary school at age six becomes eligible for secondary school admittance at age eleven after the fifth year. A commission of teachers from various institutions determines admissions according to each individual student's academic records and age. Any student over thirteen years of age becomes automatically ineligible and remains in a primary terminal class at least until the age of fourteen. The minimum requirement needed to enter a vocational school is the Primary School Certificate that necessitates passing an exam administered to the students in the terminal classes at the end of each school year. For the 1980-1981 school year, 2,872 students were enrolled in the primary terminal class. Those students who enter secondary school are eligible to sit for the first cycle exam, the *Brevet Elémentaire du Premier Cycle* (B.E.P.C.), after four years of study at a college or *lycée*, and sit for the *Baccalauréat*, the highest French secondary school degree, after three additional years at a *lycée*, three of which exist in the territory. In French Polynesia, statistics show that approximately 60 percent of all the students enrolled in primary school enter secondary school, of which only half will complete the first four years and be eligible for the B.E.P.C. examination. Sixty percent of those students sitting for the B.E.P.C. in 1979-1980 passed. One third of those students with the B.E.P.C. completed the following three years, and of those sitting for the *Baccalauréat* in 1979-1980, 56 percent passed. Thus presently only about 3.4 percent of the students starting primary school will complete the pre-university cycle. Furthermore, it must be noted that only about 10 percent of those receiving the *Bacallauréat* are ethnically considered as Polynesian, the rest being of Caucasian, Chinese, or mixed ethnicity. As there exist no institutions of higher learning in French Polynesia, those students desiring to pursue advanced studies must leave the territory. Most, of course, go to France, where a *Baccalauréat* is required for university admittance. Generally, these students (if they are bona fide residents of the territory), are awarded government scholarships covering travel expenses (round trip), tuition, fees, and housing. In the past three years about fifty students per year have received such aid. There are also a few students who have partial scholarships for studies in France, and a handful who go to Hawai'i, the U.S. mainland, or New Zealand where the *Baccalauréat* is not a prerequisite, but where the language barrier, college entrance testing, and financial requirements prove prohibitive.

A discussion of the educational system of French Polynesia, however brief, is not complete without an objective consideration of the special educational problems and difficulties faced by the territory. It must be recognized that a factor motivating parental support of compulsory education has been the necessity of parents procuring enrollment certificates for their school-age children in order to receive government family allocation payments. However, although absenteeism, a vital problem since the onset of formal education in French Polynesia, has abated in recent years, there nevertheless remains an intrinsic lack of parental involvement in their children's educational experiences. Certainly most parents now understand the importance of modern education (largely in terms of future employment opportunities), but little concrete aid or support is given at home and few parents interact with school personnel. Furthermore, this particular attitude is magnified in the less modernized outer islands, where the traditional Tahitian life-style and values have yet to be totally modified by European concepts and culture. These communities face an additional language handicap, for most families not only use Tahitian in the home but have a limited understanding of French. Consequently, children entering nursery and primary school are faced with an educational structure using a foreign language. Though the problem is less severe in Tahiti, it is nonetheless still existent. Furthermore, the more qualified teachers are often reluctant to accept teaching positions outside of Tahiti or the Society Island group, which contributes to the significantly lower achievement level in the four other archipelagos. Secondary education is available on only a limited scale in the outer islands, which results in the displacement of students desiring to continue their education either to inter-island boarding schools (Colleges d'Enseignement Secondaire) with B.E.P.C. levels or to one of the three lycées of the Society Islands for the Baccalauréat. Another challenge faced by the territorial school system because of the centralized system is the obtaining and redistributing of books, examinations, and other educational materials sent from France. This becomes a significant problem in many outer islands that rely on irregular sea transport.

Statistics cannot belie the fact that the French educational system as applied in Polynesia favors an elite minority, with less than 4 percent able to take advantage of the complete cycle. Although those students who receive the B.E.P.C. or Baccalauréat can be proud of the fact that their achievements are in no way inferior to the degrees awarded in France, in most cases the system produces failure and dropouts. Already by the age of eight years, eleven students out of a hundred are two years behind. By age ten, 35 percent are two or more years behind and by thirteen years of age, 75 percent are two or more years behind. Every year nearly 2,000 fourteen-year-olds leave the educational system facing idleness, delinquence, or early menial labor experiences. The future is increasingly bleak for those youngsters who, because of poor scholastic performance, are excluded from secondary school and even vocational schooling at such a young age, as well as for those who are enrolled in post-primary education but who are unable to keep up with the scholastic pace. Thus, in spite of the millions of dollars expended annually and the undeniable amount of human dedication directed toward education in the territory, the question must be raised as to whether an unadapted structure has been the best answer to meet the educational needs in French Polynesia, for contrary to prevalent belief, an adapted program does not mean an inferior program, but a different program.

RELATED ENTRIES: French Polynesia.

SOURCES AND READINGS: Comité Territorial d'Action Laïque, L'École en Polynésie (Pape'ete: Comité Territorial d'Action Laïque, 1973); Fédération des Oeuvres Laïques, L'Échec Scolaire en Polynésie (Pape'ete: Fédération des Oeuvres Laïques, 1976); Frères de l'Instruction Chrétienne en Polynésie Française, Cent Ans au Service de la Jeunesse Tahitienne (Pape'ete: École des Frères, 1960); Service de l'Education, Population Scolaire (Pape'ete: Service de l' Education, 1980); Vice Rectorat de Polynésie Française, Données Essentielles Pour Connaître Mieux l'Enseignement en Polynésie Française (Pape'ete: Vice Rectorat de Polynésie Française, 1980).

Yves R. Perrin

FRIENDLY ISLANDS. See Tonga.

FUTUNA. See Wallis and Futuna.

GALAPAGOS ISLANDS. The Galapagos Islands are situated near the equator in the Pacific, approximately 965 km (600 mi) west of Ecuador. The group consists of thirteen large islands, six smaller ones, and numerous associated islets and rocks. Because of their history, most islands have both an English and a Spanish name. Administered as a province of Ecuador, the islands have a population near 4,000 and a land area of 7,000 km² (2,692 mi²).

Climate. Although located near the equator, the Galapagos Islands have a climate low in rainfall, humidity, and in air and water temperatures. This peculiarity is partially caused by the Humboldt Current, a cold water current which flows by the islands to the south. With the current come cool and dry southeast winds which often result in drought conditions on the lower portions of the islands. In the higher areas of greater rainfall, found particularly in several of the larger islands, vegetation is dense. Nevertheless, fresh water is rare throughout the Galapagos chain, and less than 4 percent of the land area is fit for agriculture.

Flora and Fauna. Animal life on the islands is famous throughout the world, largely due to the reports made by Charles Darwin after his visit to the islands aboard the H.M.S. *Beagle* in 1835. Then, as now, the islands had a large number of endemic forms of reptiles (iguanas, lava lizards, and giant tortoises) and birds (finches, flamingos, pelicans, penguins, and albatrosses). Many of these species have developed subspecies on various islands throughout the chain, and some of these subspecies have adapted physically to meet the needs of differing food supplies. This is particularly striking among Darwin's finches, which differ mainly in beak size and shape.

Forty percent of the higher plants on these islands are also unique to this area, although some subspecies show resemblance to others in South and Central America. Cactus forests, guava trees, ferns, and grasses can be found differentiated throughout the four primary vegetation zones of the islands.

Pre-European History. According to oral history, the first non-Polynesians to set foot on this chain of islands were Incas, who evidently arrived in the latter half of the fifteenth century, led by a Cuzco prince, Tupac Inca Yupanqui, who later became a famous Inca king.

History since European Discovery. The first recorded discovery of the Galapagos archipelago was in 1535 by Tomas de Berlanga, third bishop of Panama. His ship arrived in the Galapagos after being swept 800 km off course by high winds and the south equatorial current during a trip from Panama to Peru. His writings tell of iguanas, giant tortoises, and the remarkable tameness of most forms of animal life on the islands at that time. Little more is recorded about the islands until the latter half of the seventeenth century when British buccaneers used the archipelago as a base of attack against gold-bearing Spanish galleons doing commerce on the west coast of South America. It was during this period that the English names for these islands were adopted.

From the late eighteenth century until the 1860s, waters near the islands were a favorite hunting area for sperm whalers. Relying largely upon the giant Galapagos turtles as a major source of food, whaling ships frequently visited the islands, killing thousands of tortoises and fur seals for the sustenance of their crews.

Aboard the H.M.S. *Blonde* the English man of letters, Lord Byron, visited the archipelago in 1825. At the time of his visit he was on his way to Hawai'i with the bodies of King Kamehameha and his queen, both of whom had died of measles during a short visit to England.

In 1832 the chain was annexed by newly independent Ecuador and given the official name of Galapagos Islands. Further, each island was given a Spanish name, although earlier English names are still commonly used for purposes of continuity by historians and scientists. These anglicized names were also used by the English naturalist Charles Darwin who visited the islands for five weeks in 1835. Darwin's subsequent development of the theory of evolution, along with its crowning principle, natural selection, is rooted in his observations of the many endemic species of bird and animal life he found on the islands.

Attempts at colonization on the Galapagos chain were difficult, largely due to a lack of fresh water and a reduction of the tortoise population as a food source. Within five years of the founding of the first colony of 250 people on Charles Island in 1832 the attempt had to be abandoned due to a lack of food and water. In 1869, however, Chatham Island was successfully colonized with slave labor, and the village of Progreso remains as a small agricultural settlement even today.

Involvement of the Galapagos chain in World War I was limited to a few visits by Germans who, following tradition, found fresh meat for their Asiatic fleet. During World War II, however, the Galapagos were considered strategic enough for the United States to build a base on Baltra Island to patrol the Panama Canal. Fresh water for this base had to be brought in from nearby Indefatigable Island because Baltra had none of its own.

In 1959, a century after the publication of *Origin of Species*, the Charles Darwin Research Station was founded at Academy Bay, Indefatigable Island. Dedicated in January 1964 the station, operated by the Charles Darwin Foundation, provides facilities for visiting scientists, promotes conservation and study of the Galapagos flora and fauna, and operates weather and oceanographic equipment.

By 1968 the government of Ecuador had proclaimed the whole archipelago a national park and passed legislation protecting its flora and fauna. Success of the Darwin Research Station as a center of study has led the foundation to enlarge its concerns to include marine life in addition to its earlier responsibility for flora and fauna. Consequently, in conjunction with the research station, the foundation will shortly dedicate a marine science center at Academy Bay. These conservation and research measures have been taken to protect the unique animal, plant, and marine life of the islands, many of which have been seriously threatened with extinction by plant and animal life introduced since the seventeenth century.

Present Status. Protected by legislation as a national park, the Galapagos Islands are currently divided into three cantons and are under the supervision of an Ecuadorian naval governor. Aside from limited agriculture, residents of the islands depend on tourism for the majority of their jobs.

RELATED ENTRIES: Darwin, Charles.

SOURCES AND READINGS: Robert I. Bowman, ed., *The Galapagos Proceedings of the Symposium of the Galapagos International Scientific Project* (Los Angeles: University of California Press, 1926); Irenaus Eibl-Eibesfeld, *Survey on the Galapagos Islands* (Paris: UNESCO, 1959); Ian Thornton, *Darwin's Islands* (Garden City, N.Y.: Natural History Press, 1971); *Report of a Biological Reconnaissance of the Galapagos Islands during 1957* (Paris: UNESCO, 1960).   *Jeffrey J. Butler*

GATTY, HAROLD CHARLES (1903-1957). A pioneer in trans-Pacific air routes, Harold Gatty was born 5 January 1903 in Tasmania. He graduated from the Australian Naval College in 1920, served in the merchant marine until 1928 when he joined the U.S. merchant marine briefly, and set up an aerial navigation school in Los Angeles in 1928. Recognized as an expert navigator, Gatty participated in several unsuccessful attempts to fly the Pacific in 1930 and, the following year, in Wiley Post's record-setting circling of the world. Employed by the Army Air Corps as a navigation instructor in 1932, he taught Anne Lindbergh aerial navigation so she could navigate on her husband's survey flights. He was instrumental in 1933-1934 in the creation, with Donald Douglas, of the South Seas Commercial Company which was involved in setting up trans-Pacific air routes. When that company was taken over by Pan American Airways, he became their agent in New Zealand and Australia until 1941. During the war he served as a group captain in the Royal Australian Air Force for whom he prepared navigational and survival manuals. After the war he moved to Suva, Fiji, where he set up the Fiji Airways. He died in Suva 30 August 1957.

RELATED ENTRIES: Central Pacific Air Route; South Seas Commercial Company.

SOURCES AND READINGS: *New York Times* (obituary), 31 August 1957; Papers of Harold Gatty, Library of Congress, Washington, D.C.   *Francis X. Holbrook*

GAUGUIN, PAUL (1848-1903). A French painter, Paul Gauguin appreciated the merits of using Polynesian art forms in his works. Born in Paris on 7 June 1848, Gauguin spent some of his early childhood in Peru where he no doubt received his first appreciation of "primitive" art. He took up painting (1875-1880) and then abandoned everything to sail to Tahiti where he hoped to find a pure, unadulterated civilization from which he could gain inspiration for his paintings. He arrived in Pape'ete, Tahiti, in June 1891 and then immediately left for the southernmost tip of the island. The simple Polynesian way of life allowed him the free time he most desired. He returned to Paris with his paintings in 1893. His planned exhibition flopped, his health was impaired, his wife left him, and after two years he returned to Tahiti where he hoped he could pick up the pieces of that idyllic life he had left. Money and mental problems became insurmountable. Finally at the age of fifty-three he decided to leave for the Marquesas. He was disappointed in his search. Both the Marquesans and their primitive art forms had almost vanished. His worries and mental sufferings added to his deteriorating physical condition and on 7 May 1903 he died. His paintings were sold for a few francs and were scattered throughout the world. It was not until well into the twentieth century that the world began to appreciate this new art form that he had helped to develop. A small museum is dedicated to him at Papeari on the island of Tahiti.

RELATED ENTRIES: French Polynesia; Marquesas Islands.

SOURCES AND READINGS: Bengt Danielsson, *Gauguin in the South Seas*, trans. Reginald Spink (London: G. Allen & Unwin, 1965); Paul Gauguin, *Writings of a Savage*, ed. Daniel Guerin (New York: Viking Press, 1974); Patrick O'Reilly, *Tahitiens* (Paris: Musée de l'Homme, 1962). *Robert D. Craig*

GENIL. The 350-ton steamer *Genil* was sent by Marquis Charles de Rays to provide military support to his colony of Nouvelle France. She carried on board large quantities of ammunition and a number of Spanish soldiers, most of whom defected en route. Yet *Genil* was the only one of de Rays' ships to remain in the colony for any length of time and was actively involved in the survival of every subsequent expedition to the "Phantom Paradise."

She arrived in New Ireland in September 1880 just as the twenty-odd survivors from *Chandernagor* were about to abandon the settlement. Faced with a non-existent colony to defend, *Genil* cruised around the island until the arrival of the *India* in October 1880. As provisions rapidly dwindled and death was taking its toll among the three-hundred-odd Italians whom de Rays had sent to build his Nouvelle France, the ship left for Sydney to fetch supplies. Various difficulties delayed the return of the party: the colonists lost heart and abandoned the settlement in February 1881.

Following his return to the deserted colony in March 1881, the captain of the *Genil* once more took his ship around the islands. It was then that he found in the Solomons the sole survivor from a group of men from *Chandernagor* who had taken to sea shortly after the sudden departure of their ship. By the time the *Nouvelle-Bretagne* arrived in July 1881 the *Genil* was involved in small-scale slave trafficking.

Nouvelle France was finally abandoned in February 1882 and *Genil* took the survivors to Australia, despite the unexplained sudden death of the captain during a brief stopover at the Duke of York Islands.

After her short but eventful participation in the history of the southwest Pacific, *Genil* was sold at auction in Sydney in mid-1882.

RELATED ENTRIES: *Chandernagor*; *Nouvelle-Bretagne*; Nouvelle France; Rays, (Marquis) Charles de.

SOURCES AND READINGS: J. Poulain, *Le Rocher de Port Breton: Journal d'un voyage en Océanie* (Nantes: Paul Pledran, Imprimeur éditeur, 1883); Public Records Office: Admiralty, Records of the Australian Station, 100; Queensland, *Maryborough Chronicle*, 1881-1882. *Anne-Gabrielle Thompson*

GERBAULT, ALAIN (1893-1941). A French writer and solo adventurer who navigated the world's oceans. Gerbault was born 17 November 1893. After completing studies in engineering, he served in World War I as an aviator. His fame began in 1923 when he became the first person to cross the North Atlantic alone on a small cutter named the *Firecrest*. From 1925 to 1929 he completed a solo voyage round the world, again aboard the *Firecrest*. It was during this journey that he became enraptured with Oceania. Gerbault returned to France and built a new sailboat, the *Alain Gerbault*, which he sailed to French Polynesia in 1932. He avoided civilization, preferring remote areas and tribes and was particularly fascinated with the Marquesas and Gambier islands, Tahiti, and Bora Bora. In 1940 he was summoned by French authorities in Tahiti to enlist for World War II. Gerbault refused and vigorously protested France's induction of Polynesians and its colonial administration. Harassed by local authorities, he sailed westward to American Samoa and Tonga, finally arriving feverish and emaciated at Dili, Timor Island. He died there on 16 December 1941. A student of French Polynesia's indigenous cultures, he collected ancient legends and genealogies, most of which were lost at his death. The accounts of his voyages reflect his disillusionment with modern society and serve as indictments against its encroachment upon Polynesia.

RELATED ENTRIES: French Polynesia.

SOURCES AND READINGS: P. Albaran, *Alain Gerbault mon ami* (Paris: Fayard, 1952); Patrick O'Reilly, *Tahitiens* (Paris: Musée de l'Homme, 1962). *Russell T. Clement*

GERMAN COLONIAL EMPIRE. The Germans came late to the Pacific and, initially, without any territorial ambitions. The worldwide trading firm of J. C. Godeffroy und Sohn, was the first to establish a regular German presence in Oceania, to carry emigrants to the Australian gold fields, and to trade around the rim of the Pacific with agencies in Chile, North America, Cochin China, and Australia. That was in the 1850s and Godeffroys came flying the flag, not of imperial Germany—for a German nation-state did not exist until 1870—but of the rich and ancient Hansa city of Hamburg. In 1857 Godeffroys established an agency on Upolu in the Samoan group in order to capture a share in the coconut oil trade. German penetration of the Pacific grew out of this small beginning.

From Samoa, Godeffroys expanded in all directions: south to Tonga, north to the Marshall and Caroline islands of Micronesia, and finally in 1874 to New Britain in the New Guinea islands. Other companies, like that of Eduard Hernsheim based in Micronesia, joined Godeffroys so that by 1879, according to a government memorandum, German firms were exporting from the Pacific over four million deutsche marks worth of copra annually, a million deutsche marks worth of cotton, and half a million deutsche marks of pearl shell.

This growing sphere of commercial influence contributed to the pressure on the German chancellor, Otto von Bismarck, to change his hard-line "no colonies" policy. When Bismarck embarked on colonial annexations in 1884, German firms in the Pacific were among the first to have their reward. The annexation of Samoa was as yet out of the question because of diplomatic difficulties with England and America, but New Guinea interests were well catered for. In November 1884 a German cruiser hoisted the imperial flag over most of the large archipelagic islands and the coast of mainland New Guinea north of the Huon Gulf. On 17 May 1885 the New Guinea Company, founded by Berlin bankers to exploit the area as an immigrant colony, was awarded a far-reaching charter to administer the new protectorate while carrying out its development plans.

This was the beginning of a gigantic failure in Germany's first Pacific colony. The company was never able to entice settlers to colonize the forbidding, malarial coasts of New Guinea. Neither was it able to resolve the conflict between its commercial aspirations and the administrative obligations accepted under the charter. No efficiently functioning administration was set up, no real police force or security system. Relations with the New Guineans went from bad to worse over problems of land alienation, the maltreatment of labor, and the company's punitive methods of regulation. After a decade of futile struggle, the New Guinea Company finally surrendered its charter to the Reich in 1898.

With an imperial administration after 1900 a more systematic attempt was made to develop the protectorate, area by area, starting with the Gazelle Peninsula and northern New Ireland and gradually encompassing the mainland coast and the other islands. By 1914 32,000 hectares of land were under cultivation by Europeans with copra supplying the major export product (some 17,300 tons). About fifteen hundred Europeans of every nation, plus Chinese and Japanese artisans, lived throughout the protectorate. There was also more systematic attention paid to the indigenous population. A head tax was progressively imposed on local groups that brought in nearly half a million deutsche marks by 1914. Land reserves were set up to ensure an economic existence to groups in the vicinity of European plantations; labor recruitment was regulated under government supervision. The treatment of New Guineans was not thereby automatically improved. Abuses during labor recruiting went on; land reserves came slowly or not at all because of the conflicting interests of large firms; many New Guineans had to suffer severe disciplinary measures on plantations—flogging, confinement, and reduction of rations—over which there was only nominal administrative control. Conflict between black and white was taken for granted in German New Guinea, at least by the whites; and, as a result, the German colonial period was punctuated with acts of violence: a string of early murders; major wars in the Gazelle in 1890, 1893, and 1902; revolts in Madang in 1904 and 1912, and in southern New Ireland in 1913; and a continuing tradition of punitive reprisals against resisting New Guineans on the part of the German administration.

North of New Guinea the far-flung islands of Micronesia, with the exception of the Marshalls which were annexed in October 1885, did not join the German empire until 1899, though German traders had been active there since the 1860s. The Germans, in fact, dominated the copra trade of the area by the mid-1880s but when Bismarck tried to annex the Carolines and Palau groups in 1885 Spain claimed the islands and the Marianas as part of her old seaborne empire. The Spanish interlude did not destroy Germany's trade dominance; and when the Micronesian islands were sold to Germany in the wake of the Spanish-American war, this tiny island sphere was in quite a prosperous position. It continued to float along as a reasonably productive appendage of German New Guinea to which it was linked administratively, occasionally devastated by typhoons or disrupted by strikes in the Marshalls or by the major revolt in Ponape in 1910 which was only put down by the application of overwhelming German might and severity.

The real pearl of the Pacific empire was Samoa. For the average German at home, Samoa symbolized the whole colonial endeavor of Germany: The compact and prosperous plantation empire of Godeffroys and its successor after it went bankrupt in Europe, the D.H.P.G. (*Deutsche Handels-und Plantagen-Gesellschaft der Südsee Inseln zu Hamburg*), had been built upon private initiative and an intimate participation by Germans in the violent history of Samoa in those years. The final acquisition of the western islands of Samoa for Germany in 1899 cost a great deal of German sweat and blood—according to Bismarck, a cost which the islands were never worth. Much of the struggle and violence was due to a fierce triangular competition between Germany, the United States, and Britain, at a time when imperialist rivalries were at their height in Africa and a parade of self-willed, energetic consuls in Samoa was determined to secure the limelight for their countries.

Germany enjoyed the greatest commercial weight in the islands, with 98 percent of the export trade in her hands in the mid-1880s and the largest land claims of any nation (some 31,000 hectares). This preponderance finally tipped the scales in her favor when a final, ferocious civil war in 1898-1899 persuaded the powers to end their rivalry. Samoa was partitioned: Germany acquired the western islands of Savai'i and Upolu; America gained Tutuila with its majestic harbor of Pago Pago. The Samoans murmured at this effrontery but accepted the solution.

Considering all that had gone before, the fourteen years left to Germany in Samoa were unusually quiet. According to the ledger books, Samoa was almost the model colony that achieved a favorable balance of trade in 1906 and required no more imperial subsidies after 1908. By 1914 thirty-five plantation companies were active in Samoa, and the total value of exports topped five million deutsche marks, mostly from copra. The governor, Wilhelm Solf, also managed, unlike his consular predecessors, to establish good relations with the Samoan people. He successfully disarmed the population within two years, organized a workable system of village administration run by the Samoans themselves, and set up a national assembly of chiefs (*Fono o Faipule*) whose powers were carefully controlled. There were shadows of course, among them labor problems for the plantations, company rivalries, and a small group of highly chauvinistic German settlers bent on creating a fortress colony and a servile native population. Neither were all Samoans entirely happy with Solf's regime. While the people in the villages acquiesced readily enough, old chiefs and speakers whose powers were curtailed worried away at the roots of the German administration. The Germans experienced two main threats to their rule: one an attempt by chiefs in 1904 to regain their influence through a copra-producing cooperative for Samoans, and the other a daring putsch against Solf by the leading orator chief of Savai'i. Neither erupted into full-scale violence.

German colonial rule in the Pacific, and in Africa, suffered from propaganda manufactured by Britain during World War I which accused Germany of militarizing her colonies, of commercial rape and pillage, and of indescribable brutality against her colonial peoples. Much of this was pure invention. The island colonies were far from militarized. Samoa got by with fifty Samoan policemen who doubled as messengers, boat crew, and plantation supervisors. In Micronesia the situation was similar. Only New Guinea had a substantial police force, nearly one thousand New Guineans by 1914, but they in no way constituted a standing army. Where the treatment of the indigenous inhabitants was concerned, though the worst abuses were over by 1914 in the Pacific and Africa, maltreatment of islanders at least remained a feature of the German colonial ethos throughout the period. Public and private floggings of men and women, forced labor, unjust alienation of land, and racial discrimination were part and parcel of everyday life, especially in New Guinea. There was a constant tug-of-war between humane administrators and colonial law on the one hand and, on the other, the demands of white settlers who were convinced of their racial superiority and who were bent on commercial development. When war intervened in 1914, a humane policy was by no means a foregone conclusion in Germany's Pacific empire.

The colonies were taken over within weeks of the declaration of war in August 1914; Samoa by a New Zealand expeditionary force, Micronesia by the Japanese, and New Guinea by Australian troops after a token encounter. The empire had lasted a mere thirty years; and by the end of the war, much of its assets were stripped and its large companies expropriated. In the scales of Germany's history, the Pacific empire, and indeed the African also, weigh very little. But, the impact on the Pacific islands was substantial. Many islanders were introduced to the cash economy by the Germans, experienced the first modernization and urbanization of their societies, and enjoyed a new freedom of movement and security in their land. Others were dispossessed, driven off their lands and onto plantations, while losing in the process their ties with their village societies and traditional religions. The social effect for all was immense, for the Germans laid the basis for much of the modern development of the Pacific islands.

RELATED ENTRIES: German South Seas Expedition; Jaluit Company; Micronesia; Papua New Guinea; Ruge and Company, H. M.; Tonga.

SOURCES AND READINGS: Peter J. Hempenstall, *Pacific Islanders under German Rule: A Study in the Meaning of Colonial Resistance* (Canberra: Australian National University Press, 1978); Paul M. Kennedy, *The Samoan Tangle: A Study in Anglo-German-American Relations 1878-1900* (New York: Harper & Row, 1974); Reichskolonialamt: Südsee Akten, Zentrales Staatsarchiv [Central State Archives], Potsdam, German Democratic Republic; H. Schnee, *Deutsches Kolonial-Lexikon*, 3 vols. (Leipzig: Quelle & Meyer, 1920).   *Peter J. Hempenstall*

GERMAN SOUTH SEAS EXPEDITION (1908-1910). A two-year survey of the cultures of islanders in German Pacific colonies the South Seas expedition was funded by the *Hamburgische Wissenschaftliche Stiftung* (Hamburg Science Foundation). Approval for the expedition was given by the foundation on 20 December 1907 and the party left on 15 May 1908. Dr. Georg Thilenius of the *Hamburgisches Museum für Völkerkunde* (Hamburg Museum of Ethnology) directed the expedition and the publication of its results. The staff for the first year included Friedrich Fülleborn, the leader of the group and its doctor, Otto Reche, Wilhelm Müller, Franz Hellwig, and Hans Vogel. The captain of the *Peiho* during both years was R. Vahsel. Rabaul (Papua New Guinea) was chosen for the base of the operations.

Five trips were made from August 1908 until June 1909 to the Admiralty and Hermit Islands, New Britain, along the northeastern coast of New Guinea, then to Yap and Hong Kong. A different staff left Hong Kong in July 1909 bound for Germany's Micronesian colonies (except for the northern Marianas, which were passed over because of the extensive Spanish and Philippine influence on the Chamorros). Augustin Krämer led the expedition accompanied by his wife Elisabeth, Paul Hambruch, Ernst Starfert, Wilhelm Müller and Franz Hellwig. The expedition that lasted from 31 July 1909 to 12 March 1910 visited a large number of the islands and atolls in the Caroline and Marshall islands. By 16 April 1910 the Germans were on their way back to Hong Kong and Hamburg where a reception was held 24 March 1911 in honor of all who took part in the two-year undertaking.

The findings of the researchers were published in separate volumes in a series entitled *Ergebnisse der Südsee-Expedition, 1908-1910*. The first volume to be published was Reche's work on the peoples along the Sepik River (1913); the last volumes in the series were issued in 1938. The series consists of twenty-nine volumes broken down into three categories: Part I, an introductory volume explaining the plan of the expedition (written by Thilenius) with notes on nautical matters, weather, geology, and terminology; Part II A, three volumes on the ethnography of Melanesian peoples along the Sepik River and in the Admiralty and Hermit islands; Part II B, twenty-five volumes on the ethnography of Micronesian peoples in the Carolines (twenty volumes), in the Marshalls (one volume), on Nauru (two volumes), and on Luangiua and Nukumanu in the Solomons (two volumes).

Although certain members of the expedition seemed to want to restrict the Pacific peoples they studied to ways of life as free as possible from European influence, the expedition as a whole accomplished its purpose: to record in as much detail as possible the cultures of Pacific peoples under German control before both death and rapidly mounting cultural change had forever washed away many intrinsically interesting and worthwhile indigenous practices.

RELATED ENTRIES: Admiralty Islands; Kubary, Johann; Micronesia; Nauru; Papua New Guinea; Semper, Carl; Sepik River; Solomon Islands.

SOURCES AND READINGS: Georg Thilenius, "Allgemeines" in G. Thilenius, ed., *Ergebnisse der Südsee-Expedition, 1908-1910*, vol. 1 (Hamburg: Friederichsen, de Gruyter and Co., 1926).   *Mark L. Berg*

GIBBON, JAMES (?-1904). James Gibbon was a half-caste West Indian who became the interpreter to high chief Ibedul of Palau and thereby greatly influenced the direction of foreign contact in Palau. Jumping ship in Palau in the 1860s, Gibbon (or Gibbons) was valued for his grasp of English and was speedily adopted into the household of Ibedul, the top-ranking chief of Koror, whom he served until his death. In this position, he handled relations between Ibedul and visiting captains. When H.M.S. *Espiegle* came to Palau in August 1883 to intervene in the long-standing dispute between Koror and Melekeok, Gibbon translated the treaty that was drawn up by the British into Palauan. During the Spanish administration of Palau (1885-1899), Gibbon appears to have held no official position. When the Germans took control of Palau (1899), Gibbon was made station supervisor and given a lifetime use of a house and land on Malakal Island which served as the harbor of Koror. He was also made chief of the police force that consisted of several Palauans and some Melanesians. As supervisor, it was his duty to call the high chiefs into session once a month, especially to promote the cultivation of the coconut palm. After nearly completing three years of service, Gibbon died 8 February 1904 and was replaced by a German official. One of his sons, William, served as a policeman during German rule and later became one of the ten top chiefs of Koror. Charlie Gibbons, William's son, is a well-known artist.

RELATED ENTRIES: Beachcombers; Micronesia.

SOURCES AND READINGS: Augustin Krämer, "Palau," in G. Thilenius, ed., *Ergebnisse der Südsee-Expedition, 1908-1910*, vol. 1 (Hamburg: L. Friederichsen, 1917).   *Mark L. Berg*

GIBSON, WALTER MURRAY (1822-1887). A worldwide adventurer, Mormon colonizer in Hawai'i, and premier of the kingdom of Hawai'i during the reign of King Kalakaua, Walter Gibson as a young man sought fortune and power in the California gold fields, Mexico, Central America, South America, the South Atlantic, and the Dutch East Indies. In the late 1850s, he took an interest in the plight of the Utah Mormons who were under occupation by U.S. Army forces. Gibson proposed to President Buchanan and to Utah religious and political leaders that the solution to the "Mormon Rebellion" was a resettlement of the Mormons on an island of central Oceania—probably New Guinea. While both President Buchanan and Mormon President Brigham Young refused the proposal, it launched a friendship between Gibson and Young and a Pacific adventure for Gibson.

Gibson presented himself to Young as a fellow visionary, called by God to play a major role in the establishment of His kingdom. Reportedly a voice had spoken to him in a jail in Java telling him that he would show the way to a people, who would build up a kingdom in the isles that would influence the whole earth. Shortly after baptism and a brief missionary apprenticeship in the eastern United States, Gibson left Utah charged by Brigham Young to bring the gospel to all of Asia and the Pacific, carrying letters of introduction to the kings and rulers of Japan and Asia.

This extensive mission was cut short at its first step when Gibson stopped in Hawai'i to check into the affairs of the Hawaiian "Saints" (Mormons). Gibson fell in love with the Pulawai Mormon colony on the island of Lana'i and decided that this was the place to fulfill his dreams. The church was in general disarray since the withdrawal of missionaries at the time of political difficulties with the U.S. government. Gibson found the people to be primitive but degraded, an evaluation that fit into his Southerner's understanding (he was raised in South Carolina) of the relationship between the races.

Gibson's dream held strong for about three years as he ruled princely and fatherly. He was a stern leader, preaching charismatically in his white temple robes. During this time he built up a considerable fortune by extracting large contributions from new members and selling church positions. At the request of concerned members, an apostolic delegation from Utah arrived on Lana'i and confronted Gibson. When Gibson refused to transfer title to lands and property, he was excommunicated and the colony was disbanded.

Gibson developed both friends and enemies in the Hawaiian government during his Mormon period. After leaving Lana'i, Gibson gained Hawaiian citizenship and was appointed to travel to the Pacific islands and Malaya to find workers for the sugar plantations. Instead, he went to the U.S. east coast where he lobbied for a trade treaty with Hawai'i and recruited workers for his own land on Lana'i. Upon his return, he focused his attention on Hawaiian politics. He became close friends with King Kalakaua with whom he shared visions of repopulation of the disease-ridden islands and worldwide influence. After election to the legislature, Gibson was considered for a cabinet post. To the white, Protestant, business establishment, this was unthinkable. Research was done on Gibson's checkered past in Lana'i and even the Dutch East Indies. Gibson weathered the ensuing storm of pamphlets by appealing to racial fears and was eventually reelected by a large majority. During a legislative crisis, Kalakaua asked him to assume both the premiership and the foreign ministry. Five years later, after depleting the public coffers to maintain the monarch's rapidly expanding ego and engaging in abortive expansionist policies that embarrased the Hawaiians and placed them in peril of the wrath of Bismarck's Germany, Gibson was forced out by a group of white reformers. He left Hawai'i a short while later after escaping a lynching attempt and an embezzlement charge. He died in San Francisco in 1887.

RELATED ENTRIES: Hawai'i; Kalakaua, Prince David; Mormons in the Pacific.

SOURCES AND READINGS: Jacob Adler and Gwynn Barrett, *The Diaries of Walter Murray Gibson 1886-1887* (Honolulu: University of Hawaii Press, 1973); Gwynn Barrett, "Walter Murray Gibson: The Shepherd Saint Revisited," *Utah Historical Quarterly* 40

(1972); Gaven Daws, *A Dream of Islands* (New York: W. W. Norton & Co., 1980).

Dale B. Robertson

GILBERT ISLANDS. *See* Kiribati.

GODEFFROY AND SON. *See* Copra Trade; German Colonial Empire; Jaluit Company; Ruge and Company, H. M.

GORDON, ARTHUR CHARLES HAMILTON (1829-1912). Son of Lord Aberdeen, the British prime minister, Arthur Gordon became one of the most distinguished administrators of British colonies during the latter half of the nineteenth century. Following service as lieutenant governor of New Brunswick and governor of both Trinidad and Mauritius, he became Fiji's first governor after it entered the British Empire in 1874. During his five years in this colony, Gordon balanced the Fijian budget, attracted capital for colony development, protected Fijians from kidnapping and enslavement by enforcing the Pacific Islanders Protection Act, settled numerous pre-cession land claims, and provided other essential government services. Further, he set the tone for twentieth-century British policy in colonies with large indigenous populations by emphasizing development of native capacities for self-government. Believing that native institutions would eventually crumble before the assault of Occidental civilization, Gordon wished the change to take place slowly to reduce the shock and keep friction between government and governed at a minimum. Appointed as high commissioner and consul-general of the western Pacific high commission, established in 1878, he negotiated most-favored-nation treaties with Samoa and Tonga in 1878-1879. After acting for a year-and-a-half as governor of New Zealand, Gordon closed his foreign career by serving in that same position in Ceylon 1883-1890. Retiring to London where he was appointed to the House of Lords as Lord (Baron) Stanmore in 1893, he wrote and lectured until his death in 1912.

RELATED ENTRIES: Fiji.

SOURCES AND READINGS: J. K. Chapman, *The Career of Arthur Hamilton Gordon: First Lord Stanmore 1829-1912* (Toronto: University of Toronto Press, 1964); James Wightman Davidson, *Samoa Mo Samoa* (Melbourne: Oxford University Press, 1967); "Lord Stanmore Dies," *New York Times*, 31 January 1912, p. 11, col. 5.   *Jeffrey J. Butler*

GREY, (SIR) GEORGE (1812-1898). A statesman and scholar, George Grey was born in Lisbon, Portugal, on 14 April 1812. He entered Sandhurst Royal Military College and was assigned to the 83d Foot Regiment in 1829. He attained a captaincy in the regiment. On 20 June 1837 he sailed on the *Beagle* as leader of a government expedition to explore northwest Australia. He was named governor of South Australia in 1841 at the age of twenty-nine. He governed until 1845 when he was then appointed governor of New Zealand in the midst of the first Land War between the Maoris and white settlers. He established peace and governed until 1854. In 1855 he published the first compilation of *Polynesian Mythology* in Maori and English. His book aroused romantic interest in the Pacific and attracted the many Pacific scholars who were to follow him. Refusing to proclaim the constitution for New Zealand which was sent from the British Parliament, Sir George was given the authority to draw up another. He was named the first governor of Cape Colony in 1854 and served there until 1859 during a period of much unrest. He was recalled home in 1859 because of his efforts to federate South Africa, a move disapproved by the British government. He was later reinstated and returned to Cape Town with orders to drop his federation plans. He remained there until 1861 when he was named to his second governorship in New Zealand, 1861-1867. During this period the second Land War involved much of his time. From 1868 to 1870 he was involved in English public life and from 1870 to 1894 in Australasian affairs. He was made premier of New Zealand, 1877-1879. He died in London on 19 September 1898 and was buried in Saint Paul's Cathedral. An honest administrator, Sir George was respected by all who had dealings with him, as he always treated men fairly regardless of their circumstances of race or birth.

RELATED ENTRIES: Polynesian Culture (Ancient).

SOURCES AND READINGS: James Milne, *The Romance of a Pro-consul* (London: Thomas Nelson and Sons, 1911); W. P. Morrell, *British Colonial Policy in the Age of Peel and Russell* (London: Frank Cass and Co., 1966).   *Vernice W. Pere*

GRIMSHAW, BEATRICE ETHEL (1870-1953). Beatrice Grimshaw, a Pacific writer, was born in County Antrim, Ireland, and worked as a journalist in Dublin and London before visiting New Zealand in 1904. From there she visited the Cook Islands, Samoa, Tonga, and Niue, gathering material for tourist advertisements she was commissioned to write for the Union Steam Ship Company. In 1905 she visited Fiji and the New Hebrides to assess the prospects for European settlement and investment there and in 1907 she visited Papua. Intending at first to stay only a few months, she made it her home for the next twenty-seven years. One reason for her decision was her admiration of the policies of the governor, Hubert Murray, and her desire to help him attract settlers and capital. For a while she even became a planter herself, but writing remained her main occupation. As the need for her promotional talents declined she turned from nonfiction to fiction. Of all the writers associated with the Pacific, she was one of the most prolific. As well as numerous articles and pamphlets, she produced four books describing her experiences and forty romantic novels, nearly all with a Pacific setting. One of them, *Conn of the Coral Seas* (1922), became a Hollywood film, "Adorable Outcast." Apart from some literary merit, Beatrice Grimshaw's writing, especially her fiction, is valuable as a historical source. It reflects with unequalled volume and consistency some of the basic values and concerns of the European settlers in Papua under colonial rule. She left Papua in 1934 and died at Bathurst, Australia, on 30 June 1953.

RELATED ENTRIES: Murray, John H. P.; Papua New Guinea.

SOURCES AND READINGS: Susan Gardiner, "For Love and Money: Early Writings of Beatrice Grimshaw, Colonial Papua's Woman of Letters," *New Literature Review* (1977): 10-21; Eugénie and Hugh Laracy, "Beatrice Grimshaw: Pride and Prejudice in Papua," *Journal of Pacific History* 12 (1974): 154-75.

Eugénie and Hugh Laracy

GUAM. The southernmost island in the Marianas chain, Guam lies approximately 144° east latitude and 13° north longitude or 1,500 miles (2,414 km) east of Manila. The island is within the typhoon belt and is struck by a major storm on the average of once every ten to twelve years.

The island is about 30 miles long (48.3 km) and 4 to 8 miles (6.4 km to 12.9 km) wide. It has an area of approximately 214 square miles (554.26 km²). Geologically it is divided into two parts. The southern end is mountainous and of volcanic origin. The highest point, Mount Lamlam, is 1,336 feet (407.2 m) above sea level. The northern end consists of a high limestone plateau running between 200 and 600 feet (61 m to 183 m) in elevation. The island is surrounded by a coral reef, averaging between 20 and 800 yards (18.3 m to 732 m) in width.

Prehistory. Guam was settled between 3000 and 2000 B.C. The pre-Spanish Chamorros possessed a high Neolithic culture. They were organized into matrilineal clans and lineages and a two-tiered caste system. The clans were grouped into villages and the villages into districts.

The Chamorro economic system consisted of gardening in jungle clearings, gathering in the jungle and on the reef, and fishing. Unlike the peoples of Micronesia, the Chamorros cultivated rice as a ceremonial food. In addition, they engaged in a variety of crafts. Economic relationships were governed by the principles of reciprocity and conspicuous display.

The religious beliefs of the pre-Spanish Chamorros centered around the veneration of the spirits of the dead. The spirits, while no longer a part of Chamorro's physical environment, were still present and had the power to help or hinder the living.

Foreign Contact. Ferdinand Magellan is reputed to have landed on Guam on 6 March 1521. Throughout the sixteenth century, various European navigators visited the island and used it as a source of fresh food and water for their Pacific explorations. Of these, the most important was the Spanish expedition of 1564 headed by Legazpi. This expedition claimed Guam for Spain on 26 January 1565, laid the basis for Spanish control of the Philippines, and discovered a reliable return route to North America.

The discovery of this route led to the establishment of direct trade between Manila and Acapulco by means of the yearly voyage of the Manila *Galleon*. On the eastward leg of its voyage, the *Galleon* stopped at Guam in order to replenish its supplies of food and water. The use of Guam as a source of supplies for the *Galleon* gave the island a strategic significance that would eventually lead to its conquest by Spain.

Initial contacts between Europeans and Chamorros were marked by a great deal of violence. The inability of Europeans to understand the reciprocity system of the Chamorros led to charges of thievery, which were punished by the execution of the Chamorros involved and the burning of their villages. Magellan was so incensed by Chamorro behavior that he named the island chain the Ladrones or the islands of thieves. This name continued in use until 1688 when the Jesuit priest, Diego Luis de Sanvitores, renamed the islands in honor of his patroness, Mariana of Austria, the wife of Philip IV of Spain.

The Spanish Period. Throughout the sixteenth and the first two-thirds of the seventeenth century, Spain made no attempt to establish direct control over Guam. This situation changed in 1662 when Father Sanvitores first arrived on Guam. He was so impressed by the Chamorro people that he decided to devote the rest of his life to Christianizing the Marianas. Upon his arrival in the Philippines, he launched a campaign to establish a Jesuit mission on Guam with himself as the superior. After receiving permission, he left the Philippines in 1667 and returned to Guam the following year.

Initially, the mission was successful. This success

did not last, however, and in 1670 the Chamorros revolted. The revolt was crushed by the end of the year, but nothing was done to alleviate the tension that had developed between the two cultures. In March 1672 violence erupted once again. Sanvitores was killed shortly thereafter by a high caste Chamorro, Matapang, who had forbidden the priest to baptize his daughter.

The death of Sanvitores initiated the Spanish-Chamorro wars of 1672-1700. These consisted of a series of uncoordinated revolts rather than a concerted effort by the Chamorros to oust the Spanish. The lack of unity, the superiority of Spanish weapons, and the inability of the Chamorros to conceive of warfare as something other than a game, eventually led to a Spanish victory.

Between 1694 and 1698 Spain resettled the population of the northern Mariana Islands on Guam. The concentration of the population, except for a handful of families on Rota, led to a series of epidemics. These, coupled with military losses, decimated the population. By the end of the wars, the population had been reduced by more than ninety percent.

The Spanish colonial era on Guam consisted of three major periods. During the first period, 1700-1769, Guam was administered by the Jesuit order. The Jesuits established a prosperous mission and continued the Christianization and Hispanization of the population. The second period of Spanish colonial rule, 1769 to 1825, began with the expulsion of the Jesuits from the island and the confiscation of their property by the Spanish state. With the termination of the mission, a secular government under the viceroy of New Spain was established. The resulting arrival of garrison troops, officials, and clerics from Mexico added a North American dimension to Chamorro culture and society. The expulsion of the Jesuits also initiated a period of economic decline that continued virtually unchecked throughout the remaining years of Spanish control.

The collapse of the Spanish Empire in the western hemisphere ushered in the final phase of Spanish rule in Guam, 1825 to 1898. The administration of the island was shifted from Mexico to the Philippines. This shift, coupled with Spain's decision to utilize the island as a penal colony for both Filipino and Spanish criminals, intensified the Hispanization of the island and introduced Filipino social and cultural traits into the mainstream of Chamorro culture and society. After the smallpox epidemic of 1856 decimated the population, the Spanish authorities opened Guam to settlement by the Japanese and the Carolinians. At approximately the same time, the northern Mariana Islands were opened to settlement by these groups and by Chamorros from Guam.

The American Period. Guam became a United States territory in 1898. In the Treaty of Paris, which ended the Spanish-American War, the island was ceded to the United States and its inhabitants became U.S. nationals. Shortly thereafter, Guam was constituted an unincorporated territory and administrative authority was delegated to the Department of the Navy. The navy administered Guam from 1898 to 1950 with the exception of the World War II period, between 1941 and 1944, when the island was occupied by the Japanese.

During the first period of naval rule, 1898-1941, Guam served as a coaling and cable station. The island was viewed as a single naval station and administered accordingly. Life on Guam during this period continued much as it had during the last fifty years of Spanish rule. What development occurred took place primarily in the fields of health and education. In addition, some progress was made in developing a political awareness within the local population.

During World War II Guam was occupied by the Japanese. The island was incorporated into the Greater East Asia Co-Prosperity Sphere, and administrative control was exercised primarily by the Japanese navy. The island was retaken by the United States between 21 July and 12 August 1944.

The navy resumed sole control of Guam in June 1946. The second period of naval administration, 1946 to 1950, had a greater impact on the island than the first. The destruction caused by the war, the establishment of large military bases on the island, and the influx of large numbers of U.S. citizens and Asiatic construction workers began to alter the nature of island society.

In July 1950 the Congress of the United States passed the organic act of Guam. This act replaced the naval governor of Guam with an appointed civilian, Carlton Skinner, established the twenty-one seat Guam legislature, set up a civilian court system, and granted American citizenship to all Chamorros. While the military no longer controlled the island, it continued to play a large role in local affairs.

In 1962 the security clearance required by the military for entrance to Guam was abolished. In the same year, Guam was struck by Typhoon Karen. The abolition of the security clearance and the rehabilitation program undertaken after the storm radically changed the life-style of the island's residents. Commerce and industry expanded, tourism increased, local and international transportation systems were improved and expanded, media resources were enlarged, the population and immigration continued to increase, and the standard of living of the island's inhabitants rose significantly. To a great extent, these changes have continued into the 1980s.

In 1971 Guam achieved another political milestone with the inauguration of the island's first elected governor, Carlos G. Camacho. One year later the island was given a nonvoting delegate in the United States House of Representatives.

Throughout the period since 1700 Chamorro culture was changed and modified. Its basis, however, remained the culture of the pre-Spanish Chamorros. To this base were added layers of Hispanic, Mexican, Filipino, and American cultural traits which have combined to form the modern Chamorro culture. Since 1970 this culture has come increasingly under attack by the forces of change unleashed after Typhoon Karen. The maintenance and continued development of this culture along with the need to revise the island's political status in light of the growing political sophistication of Guam's population are perhaps the two major issues facing the island in the decade of the 1980s.

RELATED ENTRIES: Calvo, Paul M.; Chamorros (Ancient); Chamorros Peoples, Origin of; Commonwealth of the Northern Mariana Islands; Education in the Pacific, Higher; Guam's Constitutional Conventions; Micronesia; Pease, Benjamin; South Pacific Commission; United States and Pacific Island Bases; United States in the Pacific; War in the Pacific Islands, 1914-1945.

SOURCES AND READINGS: P. Carano and P. Sanchez, *A Complete History of Guam* (Tokyo: Charles E. Tuttle Co., 1964); Guam Department of Parks and Recreation and Department of Anthropology, *Guam Historic Preservation Plan* (Honolulu: Belt, Collins & Associates, 1976).; L. M. Thompson, *Guam and Its People* (Princeton: Princeton University Press, 1947).
George J. Boughton

GUAM'S CONSTITUTIONAL CONVENTIONS (1970-1971, 1976). Guam has held two constitutional conventions: one stemmed from purely local legislation (1970-1971), and the other was created, sanctioned, and governed by federal law (1976). The First Constitutional Convention, held in 1970-1971, was a result of a piece of legislation from the ninth Guam legislature. The goal of this convention was to revamp the organic act of Guam, the basic law of the island which was drafted and given to Guam in 1950 by the U.S. federal government. Several aspects of the organic act were regarded as outmoded or obsolete, and the entire document was in need of reworking. This convention lasted for one year, held forty-three plenary sessions and fifty-four public hearings, and spent a total of $195,000 (U.S.). The resultant document was submitted to officials in Washington, D.C. No response was forthcoming. The Second

Constitutional Convention was held in 1976 as a result of a federal law which authorized the convention and which specified that the general structure of the territory's government be patterned after that of the United States. It also required the constitutional document to recognize the supremacy of the United States over Guam. The convention met for four months, held public hearings, and produced a document which was submitted to President Jimmy Carter. Presidential and congressional approval of the document have been given.

Neither the first nor the second convention produced documents which radically altered the form of government set up by the organic act. There was, however, a position paper concerning Guam's relationship with the United States government which contained substantive suggestions for change, submitted along with the draft constitution of the second convention. It was felt by the delegates that including such changes within the document itself would injure its chances for approval by the federal government.

RELATED ENTRIES: Commonwealth of the Northern Mariana Islands; Guam.

SOURCES AND READINGS: University Seminar on Political Status, *The Political Future of Guam and Micronesia* (Agana: University of Guam Press, 1974).
Ruth Limtiaco

GUILLAIN, CHARLES (1808-1875). Charles Guillain was a French rear admiral who served as governor of New Caledonia from 1862 to 1870. During his administration the first convicts arrived (1864), the Loyalty Islands were annexed (1866), and Nouméa became the chief port and trading center. Guillain offered land grants to encourage colonization and devised a liberal plan to permit well-behaved convicts to work with colonists and eventually own land. Under his military governorship, convicts developed Nouméa and built significant public works. The island's administrative and judicial systems were established. Regarded as efficient, energetic, and progressive, Guillain even supported a utopian community at Yaté until its failure in 1866. He left New Caledonia because of his wife's poor health and died in Lorient on 17 February 1875.

RELATED ENTRIES: New Caledonia.

SOURCES AND READINGS: Patrick O'Reilly, *Calédoniens* (Paris: Musée de l'Homme, 1953).
Russell T. Clement

GUISE, JOHN (1914-). A political leader, former government minister, and first governor-general of Papua New Guinea, Guise was of Scottish and New

Guinean ancestry. He was born in Gedulalaka Village in Milne Bay Province where he attended school through grade four. He worked for several years as a store manager at Samarai until World War II, when he became a signal clerk with the Australian forces. After the war, he joined the territorial police and rose to the rank of sergeant-major. Rebellious but well-liked by his fellow policemen, he left the police in 1955 and worked for a time at the Department of Native Affairs. In 1961 he was elected to the National Council and in 1964 to the first House of Assembly in which he became leader of the Elected Members Group and a member of the Administrator's Executive Council. He was reelected to the House of Assembly in 1968 and chosen speaker. Following the 1972 elections, Guise was appointed deputy chief minister and minister for the interior in the preindependence coalition government. Two years later, after a major cabinet reshuffle, he was appointed minister for agriculture. On Independence Day 1975 Guise was selected as the first governor-general of Papua New Guinea, a post he held until 1977 when he resigned to run successfully for the Milne Bay provincial seat in the national parliament. In 1978 he became deputy leader of the Opposition when the People's United Front, which he had helped to organize, replaced the United Party as the strongest opposition party in Parliament. Long an unyielding champion of national unity, Guise was awarded an honorary LL.D. by the University of Papua New Guinea for his service to his country, named Companion of the British Empire in 1972, and was knighted by Queen Elizabeth in 1975.

RELATED ENTRIES: Papua New Guinea.

SOURCES AND READINGS: Peter Hastings, *New Guinea: Problems and Prospects*, 2d ed. (Melbourne: Cheshire, 1973); David Stephan, *A History of Political Parties in Papua New Guinea* (Melbourne: Lansdowne, 1972).   *Jerome Evans*

GUYON, JOSEPH (1872-1942). A respected and popular governor of New Caledonia from 1925 to 1932, Guyon succeeded in uniting the island politically and vastly improving its economy. His plan was to make New Caledonia self-sufficient. He encouraged economic stability and diversification by improving working conditions and supporting business, particularly small industries. His programs were largely supported and successful. Roads, hospitals, dams, bridges, and other public works were constructed during his administration. Guyon was also concerned with the dwindling Melanesian population. He took some of the first steps toward improving their living conditions, providing education, and preserving their culture. He returned to France and died in Miradoux on 1 June 1942.

RELATED ENTRIES: New Caledonia.

SOURCES AND READINGS: Patrick O'Reilly, *Calédoniens* (Paris: Musée de l'Homme, 1953).
                    Russell T. Clement

HAGERSTEIN (OR HAGGERSTEIN), PETER (ca. 1757-1810). Peter Hagerstein of Helsingfors, Sweden, was a beachcomber in Tahiti from 1793 until his death. Commonly known as "Peter the Swede," he deserted in Tahiti from H.M.S. *Daedalus*, the storeship for Vancouver's expedition. He was of great assistance to the London Missionary Society missionaries after they arrived on the *Duff* in 1797, although they were convinced of his opposition to them, and was prominent in obtaining pork for the New South Wales trade. Hagerstein was thus the principal mediator between the Pomare dynasty and foreign visitors. His primary loyalties were to Pomare II for whom he fought in Tahiti's civil wars.

RELATED ENTRIES: Beachcombers; French Polynesia; London Missionary Society; Pomare Family; Vancouver, George.

SOURCES AND READINGS: John Turnbull, *A Voyage Round the World in the Years 1800 . . . and 1804*, 2d ed. (London: A. Maxwell, 1813). *Ian C. Campbell*

HALL, JAMES NORMAN (1887-1951). Born in Colfax, Iowa, Hall was an adventurer turned writer who had international tastes. During World War I he successively served as a British army private, a pilot in the French Lafayette Escadrille, and, after the United States entered the war, as a captain in the U.S. Aviation Service (predecessor of the Army Air Force). At the close of the war, he and Charles Nordhoff, a friend who served with him in both the Escadrille and the Aviation Service, combined for the first of many collaborations when they wrote *The LaFayette Flying Corps*, a history of that military organization. Returning to the United States, Hall found rapid changes, especially in land development, which displeased him, so he decided to go to the South Pacific in search of tranquility and adventure. Supported by money advanced to them by *Harper's* magazine, Hall and Nordhoff went to Tahiti in 1920 where they were commissioned to write exotic travel articles. The next year many of these articles were combined and published as a book, *Faery Lands of the South Seas*

(1921), the success of which prompted the two to consider further collaboration instead of the separate careers they had planned. Tahiti soon became the permanent home of these American writers. It was here that they collaborated on their famous trilogy concerning the 1787 mutiny aboard the *Bounty*, a British war vessel, and the subsequent experiences of the mutineers and their descendants on Pitcairn and Norfolk islands. The success of these books, *Mutiny On The Bounty* (1932), *Men Against The Sea* (1933), and *Pitcairn Island* (1934), brought fame and some wealth to Hall and Nordhoff. Later the two wrote three adventure novels which are valued today, in part because of their accurate description of Tahiti. These novels, the first of which has been made into a motion picture on two occasions, were *The Hurricane* (1936), *The Dark River* (1938), and *No More Gas* (1940). By 1945 the authors had collaborated to produce three more novels, each of which was well received by both the critical and popular audiences. Nordhoff's death in 1947 ended the partnership, but Hall continued to write. He died 5 July 1951 at his home in Arue, Tahiti.

RELATED ENTRIES: Bligh, William; *Bounty* Mutiny; Nordhoff, Charles.

SOURCES AND READINGS: Paul L. Briand, Jr., *In Search of Paradise—The Nordhoff-Hall Story* (New York: Duell, Sloan and Pierce, 1966); James Norman Hall, *My Island Home—An Autobiography* (New York: Little, Brown & Co., 1952). *Jeffrey J. Butler*

HAMILTON, WILLIAM (1852-1937). A pearl sheller, trader, and planter in the Bismarck Archipelago and the Solomon Islands, Hamilton was born in Scotland and emigrated to Queensland with his family in 1862. His earliest business venture was a shipping service to transport miners and supplies during the rush to the Palmer goldfield of Cape York (1873-1874). He went occasionally on labor trading voyages to the New Hebrides, New Ireland, and New Britain in the 1880s. The following decade he was involved in goldmining and trading in Papua and spent several years pearl shelling at Thursday Island in the Gulf of Carpentaria. After the turn of the century, Hamilton occupied all but the last few years of his life superintending his business interests in the Admiralty Islands and the Solomons.

In 1899 the governor of German New Guinea, granted Hamilton pearl-shelling rights to the Admiralties, Manning Strait (Solomons), and northwest New Britain. The New Britain concession was hardly worked, while that in the Admiralties was abandoned in 1904. By that time Hamilton's attention had shifted eastward to the Solomons with the expectation that his landholdings there would prove more profitable than his pearl-shelling and trading activities.

With the approval of C. M. Woodford, resident deputy commissioner in the British Solomon Islands, Hamilton resumed five thousand acres on islands in the Manning Strait in 1904, of which Vaghena, Salakana, and Carpenter Island were planted immediately. During 1907 he purchased several thousand acres of land on Choiseul for eighty pounds. In 1908, however, inadequate capitalization of his plantations and falling pearl-shell prices on the world market obliged Hamilton to sell his Manning Strait interests to Burns, Philp and Company for eight thousand pounds.

To support his endeavors on Choiseul, Hamilton floated a joint-stock company in 1912. Two years later he acquired land at Inus on Bougainville. During 1918 the joint-stock company's assets were taken over by a partnership of Hamilton and Nathaniel Howes; and in 1923 Associated Plantations, which is still in operation, was formed by Hamilton and Howes to further their plantation interests.

As he consolidated his enterprises in the Solomons Hamilton became involved in the Solomon Islands Planters' Association, formed in 1914, and the council, established about 1920, to advise the resident commissioner on matters of concern to the expatriate white community. But Hamilton's fundamental commitment remained to the development of his business ventures. He died in New South Wales in 1937, undoubtedly a prosperous man.

RELATED ENTRIES: Papua New Guinea, Gold Mining in; Solomon Islands; Vanuatu (New Hebrides).

SOURCES AND READINGS: *Pacific Islands Monthly*, December 1937, p. 7.   *Wil King*

HAWAI'I. Now one of the fifty United States of America, Hawai'i consists of eight major islands all of which are volcanic in origin: (from largest to smallest) Hawai'i, Maui, O'ahu, Kaua'i, Moloka'i, Lana'i, Ni'ihau, and Kaho'olawe. The island of Hawai'i is nearly twice the size of all the others combined and appropriately called the "Big Island." The total landmass is 16,770 km² (6,450 mi²). These islands lie in a rough line running northwest to southeast in the northeastern Pacific Ocean only 3,200 km (2,000 mi) off the west coast of North America, just south of the Tropic of Cancer. The summit of Mauna Kea is 4,205 meters (13,796 ft) above sea level, but it stands between 8,961 to 9,144 meters (nearly 30,000 ft) above the ocean floor at the base of the Hawaiian chain. The total population of approximately 900,000 consists of 39 percent Caucasians, 28 percent Japanese, 12 percent Filipino, 9 percent Hawaiian, 7 percent Chinese, and 5 percent others. Approximately 82 percent of the total population lives on the island of O'ahu where the capital city of Honolulu is located.

Climate. The climate of the Hawaiian Islands provides mild and equable temperatures with moderate humidity and consistent trade winds year-round. Average temperature ranges from 23° C (74° F) in March to 26° C (79° F) in September, although a high of 37° C (100° F) was recorded at Pahala, Hawai'i, in 1931, and the lowest record of −12° C (9° F) was recorded at the summit of Mauna Kea. There are only two seasons: summer (May to October) with its warm, dry climate accompanied with consistent northeast trade winds; and, winter (November to April) with its cooler, wet climate interspersed with variable winds bringing clouds and rain. The average rainfall varies from 23 cm (9 in) a year at Puako on the Big Island to 1,234 cm (486 in) on Mt. Wai'ale'ale on the island of Kaua'i. The average rainfall for Honolulu is 61 cm (24 in) a year.

Flora and Fauna. Hawai'i's isolation from any other landmass permitted the development of over two thousand plants unique to the Hawaiian Islands, most of which are now only found on the remote regions of the islands. The coconuts, orchids, sugarcane, and pineapple so well known to tourists are recent introductions into the islands. Hawai'i's vegetation varies from the lush tropical growth on the windward sides of the islands to the desert cacti on the leeward or dry side of the islands. Land fauna is comparatively scant. The ancient Polynesians introduced the dog, pig, and rat. All other animals have been introduced since European discovery in 1778. The waters around the islands, however, are rich in sea life. Twenty percent of the seven hundred species of fish found in these waters are native only to Hawai'i.

Pre-European History. The first of all the immigrant peoples to arrive were Polynesian voyagers, in all probability from the Marquesas Islands, who settled the northern islands of Kaua'i and Ni'ihau with some expansion to O'ahu. A second arrival of Polynesians came from Tahiti some generations later and these established themselves on Hawai'i and Maui. Though there is much uncertainty concerning the place of origin and the dates of their voyagings and arrivals, the tradition of two migrations is borne out in the study of chants, genealogies, linguistics, and some elements of their material culture. A study of these has led scholars to believe that the first arrival was approximately the seventh or eighth century A.D. and the second about 1200 A.D.

These early settlers lived in family groups in the fertile, well-watered valleys and on the lowlands. Each district was ruled by a chief whose rank and status was determined by his genealogy. Some fourteen generations prior to the discovery of the islands by Europeans, high-ranking chiefs were able to unite districts into single-island kingdoms. Separate lines of ruling chiefs came into being on Hawai'i, Maui, O'ahu and Kaua'i. These kingdoms were the pattern of government at the time of the arrival of the next group of immigrants, the Europeans.

The European Influx. At daybreak on 18 January 1778, the ships H.M.S. *Resolution* and H.M.S. *Discovery*, under the command of Captain James Cook, found themselves in sight of an island and before long had sighted a second one. Cook, the English navigator on his third voyage, had discovered the islands of O'ahu and Kaua'i. Anchoring at Waimea, Kaua'i , and again at the small neighboring island of Ni'ihau, Cook spent two weeks in the northwestern part of the island chain. He christened the group the Sandwich Islands after the Earl of Sandwich, First Lord of the Admiralty of Great Britain, and patron for the voyages of the *Resolution* and *Discovery*.

After exploring the Pacific Northwest in search of a possible water route through North America, Cook's squadron returned to the Sandwich Islands in the fall of 1778 with the intention of wintering in the milder climate. On 26 November, the island of Maui was discovered and later Moloka'i was sighted. Being unable to make a landing on the precipitous windward coast of Maui, the squadron sailed south to Hawai'i and for seven weeks and three days coasted along the shores of that island. The ships finally anchored on the southwest or leeward side of the island at Kealakekua. Two weeks were spent in provisioning and refitting the ship, in engaging in some scientific activity, and in exchanging favors with the ruling chief of the island. Their departure was taken on 4 February 1779, but storm winds damaged the rigging of the *Resolution* before the ships were out of sight of the island. They were forced to return to

Kealakekua for repairs. As the ships returned, numbers of incidents occured which indicated a breakdown in the amicable relations previously enjoyed with the Hawaiians.

The theft of a ship's cutter finally prompted Cook to try to bring the king of the island, Kalaniopu'u, aboard ship as a hostage for its return. In this attempt, Captain Cook was killed and his remains carried away by the Hawaiians. The small squadron sailed away on 22 February but spent three more weeks among the main islands, finally departing again for the Pacific Northwest on 15 March 1779.

One of the lieutenants among Cook's men was George Vancouver who was later to return to the islands with a command of his own. By the time of Vancouver's return in 1791, a young chief, Kamehameha (the "Lonely One"), had replaced the old king on the island of Hawai'i. The new ruler was counselled by Vancouver in matters of government, foreign relations, and the arts of peace. Vancouver was also successful in securing what he called a cession of the island of Hawai'i to Great Britain on 25 February 1794. This was the first arrangement entered into between a European nation and a chief in the islands. No evidence indicates that the cession was accepted or ratified in London or that the chiefs regarded it as any more than placing themselves under the protection of the English monarch. This cession was to play a part in the history of the islands at a later date.

The Rise of the Kamehameha Dynasty. Kamehameha, with the aid of two foreigners, John Young and Isaac Davis, and with the considerable acquisition of foreign weapons, was able to bring the entire island chain under his rule by 1810. Unlike his predecessors, the earlier conquerors, Kamehameha established a government to rule his domain and this government succeeded him. The nine-year reign of this first monarch in the kingdom of Hawai'i was characterized by the pursuit of the arts of peace, by astute and fair dealings with the representatives of the various nations who called at ports in the islands, and by the formation of the council of chiefs. This can properly be called the beginning of the deliberative and policy-recommending functions of government.

Kamehameha died in 1819 and, in a series of events connected with the ascension of his son Liholiho as Kamehameha II, the old religion was thrown off and Ka'ahumanu, the old king's favorite wife, proclaimed herself coruler. The old religion had no sooner been discarded than Christian missionaries— American Protestants—arrived in the spring of 1820. The mission party arrived on the brig *Thaddeus*, having been sent out by authority of the American

Board of Commissioners for Foreign Missions. They were granted permission to remain one year. The new ruler was not much interested in the new religion but was very desirous of learning the skills of reading and writing which the missionaries could teach.

Kamehameha II soon decided to make a voyage to England and left the islands on the ship *L'Aigle* in November 1823. While the purposes of the king's visit are subject for speculation, the visit turned out tragically for the king and his favorite queen, Kamamalu. Both died in London in July 1824. Boki, a chief accompanying the king, was left in charge of the group and in an audience with King George IV on 11 September 1824 renewed the agreement concluded between Kamehameha I and Captain George Vancouver. Instructions regarding this arrangement were included in the secret orders given to Captain George Anson, Royal Navy: Great Britain might claim sovereignty over the islands by right of formal cession in the event of any threat to the islands by any other foreign power.

Ka'ahumanu, the coruler, was left as queen-regent during the voyage of Kamehameha II to England. The king's younger brother was heir to the throne but was only nine years of age. On the death of Kamehameha II, the child was proclaimed king as Kamehameha III, with Ka'ahumanu as regent until the king should reach his majority. Ka'ahumanu had come under the influence of the American missionaries as had many of the other chiefs and the first efforts at law-making in the islands reflected this influence. The first laws, heralded through the streets by crier, required the keeping of the Sabbath and forbade murder, theft, fighting, and gambling. They incidentally encouraged the learning of reading and writing.

On the death of Ka'ahumanu in 1832, the eighteen-year-old monarch exerted himself to overthrow the regency which had passed to his older half-sister, Kina'u. He desired to restore some of the power to the throne which, under the influence of the constitution-minded foreigners, was passing to the council of chiefs. It was apparent, however, that the foreign influences were too well established and troublesome. The number of ships calling at the islands had greatly increased, bringing an increase in the incidents of disorderly conduct of both sailors and islanders. The unpopular arrival of Roman Catholic missionaries from France in 1827 had occasioned a series of incidents in which the Protestant-influenced council of chiefs and the Roman Catholic personnel on French warships were placed in opposing positions. Debts contracted by the chiefs in the sandalwood trade were now a subject of American intervention. The king

was compelled by these circumstances to employ a foreigner as teacher and advisor. He chose his former missionary teacher, William Richards, as teacher, translator, adviser, and chaplain to the council of chiefs and to himself in 1838.

The Beginning of Legal Sanctions. Under the influence of William Richards, a *Declaration of Rights and Laws of 1839* for the Sandwich Islands was published. It was followed soon after by the constitution for the Hawaiian kingdom, adopted in 1840. These two original documents were supplemented by a series of treaties and conventions brought about by the troubles of the 1830s and 1840s. In 1836 a treaty was concluded on behalf of England by Edward Russell who came to Hawai'i in the H.M.S. *Acteon.* The treaty was an effort to secure the interests of British subjects in the islands. The negotiations were flavored by the arrogant behavior of the British consul, Richard Charlton, and the result was a document so imprecise and vague as to be nearly useless. On 24 July 1837, a convention was signed by King Kamehameha III and Captain Dupetit-Thouars of the *Venus.* The most important aspects of this treaty allowed French citizens to come and go freely in the islands and gave France the same status as the most-favored-nation in island foreign relations. Two years later, under threat of war with the French, the king was coerced into signing a third "unequal treaty." This treaty was particularly objectionable in that it placed limitations upon the sovereignity of the king in his own nation.

The climax of Hawai'i's dealings with the major maritime powers came in the 1840s when representatives of the Hawaiian kingdom were in Great Britain, France, and the United States negotiating for a document recognizing Hawaiian independence and national integrity. On 25 February 1843 George Paulet, in command of the H.M.S. *Carysfort,* arrived in the islands and, in response to complaints of Richard Charlton, retiring British consul, and Alexander Simpson, his replacement, set about to exact reparations from the Hawaiian government for insults, both real and imaginary. Simpson openly admitted British acquisition of Hawai'i as his goal. The irascible Charlton was simply eager to do all possible to bring the Hawaiian king to heel. The result was the seizure on 23 February 1843 of the islands, in a provisional cession by George Paulet.

The action was directly contrary to prevailing British policy regarding the Hawaiian Islands and was reversed by Rear Admiral Richard Thomas on 31 July. A result of this seizure, though perhaps unanticipated, was the thwarting of a French action of similar nature. French warships were, in fact, en route to Hawai'i with the same goal in mind. Finding the islands already in British hands, the French withdrew.

Kamehameha III and Landownership. During the mid-nineteenth-century reign of Kamehameha III a change occurred in basic land policy in the islands. The popular term for this change is the "Great *Mahele*" (division). Under the primitive system, the land belonged to the king in a way similar to European feudalism but with the important distinction that the value of land was determined by its use rather than by ownership or governance. The Europeans and Americans who came to Hawai'i arrived with a background of landownership by individuals as a requisite for political, economic, and social status. This conflict in systems brought pressure from foreign traders, missionaries, and immigrants to make land available for private ownership. The *Mahele* of 1840 was the first step in this direction with the king dividing lands between himself and the chiefs. In a second stage, the chiefs divided their lands among their tenants and by 1850 land was made available to foreigners. Time has demonstrated that the old system based on land usage was more appropriate for an island environment since land, once released, is usually divided into smaller and smaller parcels which become higher and higher in price.

King Kamehameha III died in 1854 having ruled the kingdom during its transition from a primitive chiefdom to a constitutional monarchy and through its harrowing first experiences in international intrigues. Since a large number of Americans had become residents of the islands and since the major missionary effort had been American, an early movement for annexation to the United States appeared in 1854. The kings of Hawai'i were to see open trade with the United States as a substitute for annexation and the issue of reciprocity vis-à-vis annexation was to be a recurring issue in the remaining years of the monarchy.

The king's nephew and adopted son, Alexander Liholiho, came to the throne as Kamehameha IV and in a short time married Emma Na'ea Rooke, a chiefess of high rank and granddaughter of John Young, an early foreign adviser to King Kamehameha I. The royal couple became parents of a son and for a short while all Hawai'i enjoyed what have been called the happiest days of the kingdom. The prince of Hawai'i died at an early age, however, and the king was cast into such a deep depression that he himself died shortly thereafter. He was succeeded by his older brother, Lot Kamehameha, with the title of Kamehameha V in 1863. The problems of population, the economy, and the increasing strength of American interests were to occupy the time of the new king throughout his reign.

Population and Economic Problems under the Monarchy. Beginning with the diseases brought by the discoverers and early visitors and continuing with the sterility brought on by the disorientation of cultural shock, the population declined at an appalling rate. A 50 percent decrease occured in fifty years; and by 1890 the Hawaiian population was only one-tenth of the estimated 240,000 at the time of discovery. Four major trends are discernable in island population statistics of which this rapid decline is the first. The second development was immigration for the purpose of supplying a labor force. The newcomers were mostly men and came in largest numbers from China, Japan, Portugal, Korea, Norway, Russia, Puerto Rico, and the Philippines. The third trend in population was intermarriage. The most common intermarriage has been the Chinese with the Hawaiian, with European and Hawaiian being the next most frequent. These developments had produced, by the turn of the century, a population in which single men outnumbered all females, single or married, ten to one; in which there were almost no elderly; and in which foreigners outnumbered Hawaiians two to one.

By the time of Kamehameha V's ascent to the throne, the islands had been through three cycles of economic activity. The provisioning of visiting ships had been the first commercial activity. This was followed by stripping the islands of sandalwood. The hosting of New England whaling ships between 1820 and 1860 was the third activity, but with the discovery and adoption of petroleum in the United States this effort soon ceased. Since as early as 1802 the cultivation and milling of sugar had attracted some attention. In the 1860s this was chosen to be Hawai'i's major economic activity. The climate was ideal for the extended growing season required by sugarcane which, as a plantation crop, presumed ample land, plentiful and low-cost labor living on the premises, and adequate periodic financing.

The land problem had been partially solved in the Great *Mahele* which eventually made land available to foreigners. Through purchase, long-term leases, and simple occupancy of land for which no clear title could be shown, sugar entrepreneurs were able to put together large enough holdings for plantation purposes. The labor problem seemed especially serious in view of the declining indigenous population. It was necessary to consider the importation of laborers. The government preferred to bring in a compatible population which would amalgamate with the disappearing Hawaiian population. The association of planters was more concerned with an immediate supply of workers. Hill coolies from India were the first to be considered, but the first actual laborers actually came from China in 1865. These were followed by a shipment of Japanese in 1868 and the labor problem was thus solved.

The capitalization of the sugar industry also presented unique problems. The growing season was long and bank interest was high on traditional type farm mortgages. The necessary funding was finally secured through mercantile houses in Honolulu. These businesses provided capital, supplies, and equipment and also had the necessary lines of communication for marketing the crop. It was but a short step from this beginning to the agency system whereby the business firms of Honolulu became the agents of all the sugar plantations on all of the islands. They selected managers, set up management boards and made decisions for all local situations. Through their policies in the acquisition of land, importation of labor, and financial underwriting of the industry, they were able to put together a highly centralized economic structure based upon one crop.

The market for Hawaiian sugar was obviously the United States, the closest of the larger nations. Since domestic sugar in that country required protection, tariff barriers had been established for foreign sugar. For Hawaiian sugar growers, two alternatives were immediately obvious—a reciprocal trade treaty or annexation. Annexation was considered preferable and thus Hawai'i's major industry became the major opposition to the monarchy.

The reign of Kamehameha V was also faced with controversy over the constitution of the kingdom. Proposed amendments had been in process for some time and the king called, in early 1864, for a constitutional convention. The convention was deadlocked after six weeks. King Kamehameha V dismissed the convention and issued a constitution of his own devising. This document strengthened the monarchy despite strong opposition from liberals and annexationists, and the constitution of 1864 was to remain the basic law of the kingdom for more years than any other in its history.

Kamehameha V, the last of the dynasty, passed away in December 1872, leaving no heir apparent or appointed. It became necessary to elect a ruler from among the eligible chiefs. William Charles Lunalilo was elected over prince David Kalakaua because of his American sympathies but he ruled only thirteen months. He was replaced in another election which pitted the dowager-queen Emma against David Kalakaua. Although Queen Emma appeared more popular among the Hawaiians, Kalakaua was elected.

As king, Kalakaua faced sufficient pressure from the sugar and business interests to personally take the cause of a reciprocal trade treaty to Washington, D.C. His goodwill tour in the winter of 1874-1875 resulted in the long-sought reciprocity treaty of 1876. A major boom was experienced in the sugar interests and a number of interesting personalities were attracted to Honolulu. Among these was Claus Spreckels who later became known as the "Sugar King." Spreckels came to Honolulu in 1876 and for speculative purposes bought up one half of the sugar crop for that year. Then he proceeded to acquire large land holdings on Maui, became a partner in the largest of Honolulu's sugar agencies, endeavored to purchase an interest in the Crown lands of the kingdom, and bought a steamship line. He offered, in 1886, to advance the kingdom a two-million-dollar public loan. When the legislature failed to approve his proposal he became incensed and left the islands. Returning to California in that year, he became the controlling power in the refining phase of the sugar undertaking.

A second notable personality, Walter Murray Gibson, came to Hawai'i in 1861 as a Mormon missionary though he admitted that his conversion to that faith and the acceptance of the mission call were means with a political end in view. In 1864 he was excommunicated from the Mormon establishment on Lana'i and turned his attention to politics and journalism. Gibson was elected to the legislature from the Lahaina district of Maui and later obtained control of a Honolulu Hawaiian-language newspaper. By May 1882 he had secured for himself the post of premier in the government of King Kalakaua.

The Advent of Annexation. Gibson's "New Departure" in Hawaiian politics was sufficiently visionary and irresponsible as to place even the radical annexationist, Lorin Thurston, and his supporters in the role of patriotic, responsible citizens. These men organized the Hawaiian League in 1887 and with the support of the Honolulu Rifles, a group organized like a drill team, forced the resignation of Gibson and his cabinet and, on Wednesday, 6 July 1887, required the king to sign and support the so-called Bayonet Constitution. This instrument created a king who reigned but did not rule and extended suffrage to aliens while denying the vote to many, if not most, Hawaiians.

King Kalakaua was broken in spirit and deteriorating in health following these years of political turmoil. His reputation as a bon vivant earned him the nickname of the "Merrie Monarch" but in actuality he was a proud and competent ruler defeated by powerful and, in some cases, self-seeking economic interests. In November 1890, the king decided to go to

California to recuperate and while there, died on 20 January 1891. His younger sister, Lydia K. Dominis, came to the throne as Queen Lili'uokalani, Hawai'i's last monarch. The new queen faced a multitude of problems including a strong revolutionary element in island politics, backed with the largest force of armed men in the kingdom, the Honolulu Rifles. Matters were further complicated by the fact that moderates and royalists were divided, making three political parties which were capable, in one coalition or another, of preventing any major move by any single party. Finally, the kingdom was faced with an economic depression brought on by the passage in the United States of the McKinley administration's tariff act which took away the advantageous position enjoyed by Hawai'i's sugar industry. The situation was aggravated by agitation from the Hawaiian population for a new constitution which would restore power to their queen.

Queen Lili'uokalani saw in some radical legislation, an opium bill and a national lottery act, an opportunity to bring in badly needed revenue, and she felt responsive to the pleas of the Hawaiian population for a new constitution, especially since the position of the throne would be strengthened. These intentions served to excite Thurston and members of the Hawaiian League who decided it was finally time to overthrow the monarchy. Counsel was taken with John Stevens, United States minister to Hawai'i, as to whether he would grant recognition to a new government. With his implied agreement, the revolutionaries proceeded, on 17 January 1893, to take over the government building and announce the creation of a provisional government. The queen yielded, as she noted, to the superior force of the United States of America. Minister Stevens had ordered troops landed in Honolulu from the U.S.S. *Boston* the night before.

Immediate efforts at annexation at Washington, D.C., were unsuccessful and it was necessary to create a more permanent government, the Republic of Hawai'i, with Sanford B. Dole as president. It was not until the 1896 U.S. election of President William McKinley, a Republican and an expansionist, that annexation was pursued again. The Hawaiian Islands were annexed as a Territory of the United States by the Newlands Resolution, a joint Senate-House measure, in July 1898. The former revolutionists and annexationists received an unexpected shock, however, when the organic act for the government of Hawai'i was drawn up. Contrary to their needs and expectations, all males born in the islands were given the vote. Local, non-Caucasians had for the first time a strong voting majority. This group formed the Home Rule Party in opposition to the Republican party to which most of the sugar-planter interests belonged.

Hawai'i in the Twentieth Century. The first half of the twentieth century in Hawai'i has been characterized by the efforts of plantation and business interests to consolidate their control over the economy; the efforts of the Republican party to gain control of the governorship, the elected delegate to Congress, and the territorial legislature; and the rise of organized labor. By the end of the first two decades, most aspects of island commerce, industry, and agriculture, including sugar, pineapple, tourism, shipping, construction, banking, and finance were under the control of five major Honolulu firms. Through intermarriages and interlocking directorates, they exercised a benevolent but thorough management of island economic life. Alexander and Baldwin, C. Brewer and Company, Theodore H. Davies and Company, Castle and Cooke, and American Factors were Hawai'i's "Big Five."

Many of the same persons and interests were active in the efforts of the island Republican party. The office of delegate was the first objective. Control of this office was secured by supporting Prince Jonah Kuhio Kalaniana'ole as a Republican candidate. Kuhio, with Republican financial support and the Hawaiian vote, was elected in 1902 and reelected each term until his death in 1922. The legislative majority was obtained through expensive and persuasive campaigning which was not often the subject of close scrutiny. The Republican dominance in the legislature was maintained until 1954. The office of governor of the territory, appointed by the president of the United States was not as easily controlled. During the fifty-nine years of territorial history, Hawai'i was administered by twelve governors, seven being Republican, with the Democratic appointees being usually conservative and friendly to Republican interests at the local level. This was accomplished through very effective lobbying and properly entertaining all Washington visitors to the islands.

The Democratic party was not able to muster a controlling number of votes until 1946 when organized labor made its power felt through that party. Labor organization in the islands had proceeded very slowly, not from lack of effort and strike activity but from lack of financial support and the inability of the various language groups to understand each other. It was not until World War II brought large numbers of union-member shipyard workers that unionism was firmly established. The waterfront was organized under the leadership of the International Longshoremen's and Warehousemen's Union (ILWU). Workers in the sugarcane and pineapple fields and processing plants were to follow. Besides securing wage benefits and independence for workers and forcing the cost of labor up to a point where plantations had to mechanize their operations, the most important activity of the unions was in giving support to endorsed political candidates. The Political Action Committee of the ILWU was, in large measure, responsible for the notable Democratic gains in the election of 1946. Since that time, the Democratic party has continued to grow in influence, and the opposition scarcely exists in many districts.

One of the critical events in Hawai'i's twentieth-century history was the attack on Pearl Harbor by the carrier planes of the Japanese fleet on 7 December 1941. Hawai'i was thus thrust into the very center of the Pacific war effort of the United States. Martial law was imposed in the islands from the very outset and, though it was apparent in a very short time that no further danger of attack existed, civil authority was not restored until 1944 and then only upon an appeal to the Supreme Court of the United States. Among the effects of World War II and Hawai'i's involvement in it was the discovery that Hawai'i's large second-generation Japanese population had been Americanized and was almost fanatically loyal to the United States. This was more than amply demonstrated by the war record of the two military units composed of AJA's (Americans of Japanese Ancestry). A second effect was the advance in unionism among the labor force of the islands and a third was the expansion of federal spending. While the federal contribution to Hawai'i's economy has been substantial in every year since World War II, from 1941 to 1945 it became Hawai'i's economic base.

The economy of the islands had been strongly centralized and under the virtual control of the sugar agencies for an extended period of time. This control began to give way with the advent of the war and by the 1970s much control had been relinquished in favor of diversification and overseas expansion. The new, and apparently the future, economic base in the islands is the rapidly expanding tourist industry. The number of visitors to Hawai'i has risen dramatically since the 1950s. The attraction of ideal climate, romantic island surroundings and island entertainment seems unlimited and the appetite of local purveyors for the tourist dollar seems insatiable. Tourism, while lucrative, does take its toll. More and more, island surroundings are giving way to monolithic hotels and pavement. Many islanders are becoming professional Hawaiians—a state far removed from the stable, productive life of earlier times. It appears conceivable that the Hawai'i which tourists come to see may, in the future, no longer exist.

With the achievement of statehood in 1959, Hawai'i reached full political, economic, and social maturity. Politics are dominated by a liberal Democratic party. Cultural and ethnic groups retain much of their individual character while living as Americans do elsewhere. The economy represents a wide range of businesses of all sizes, both foreign and domestic, and the state is among the upper fifth in the nation in affluence. The problems which are to be faced, while perhaps not peculiar to an island state, are made more critical because of the insularity. Land use, population growth, and water have become the major problems to be addressed by planners, politicians, and citizens.

RELATED ENTRIES: Anglican Missions; Armstrong, Richard; Bingham, Hiram; Bishop, Charles R.; Bishop Museum (Bernice P.); Brigham Young University—Hawai'i Campus; Campbell, Archibald; Cannon, George Q.; Carter, George R.; Cook, (Captain) James; Damien, (Father) Joseph; Davis, Isaac; Dole, Sanford; Ellis, William; Farrington, Wallace; Frear, Walter; Gibson, Walter Murray; Hilo Boarding School; Judd, Gerrit P.; Judd, Lawrence M.; Kalakaua, Prince David; Kamehameha I; Kamehameha II; Kamehameha III; Kamehameha IV; Kamehameha V; King, Samuel W.; Krusenstern, Adam J.; Langsdorf, George H.; Lili'uokalani; London Missionary Society; Long, Oren E.; Lunalilo, William; McCarthy, Charles; Maigret, Louis-Désire; Malo, David; Nimitz, Chester; Obookiah, Henry; Paulet, George; Pinkham, Lucius E.; Poindexter, Joseph B.; Polynesia, Settlement of; Polynesian Culture (Ancient); Quinn, William; Richards, William; St. Julian, Charles; Sandalwood Trade; Spreckels, Claus; Stainback, Ingram M.; Staley, Thomas; Stevens, John L.; Stevenson, Robert Louis; Thomas, Richard; Thurston, Lorrin A.; United States in the Pacific; Young, John.

SOURCES AND READINGS: Hiram Bingham, *A Residence of Twenty-one Years in the Sandwich Islands; or, The Civil, Religious, and Political History of Those Islands*, 3d ed. (New York: Goodwin, 1855); Laurence Fuchs, *Hawaii Pono, A Social History* (New York: Harcourt, Brace & Co., 1961); Ralph Kuykendall, *The Hawaiian Kingdom*, 3 vols. (Honolulu: University of Hawaii Press, 1938-67); William Adam Russ, *The Hawaiian Revolution, 1893-1894* Selinsgrove, Pa.: Susquehanna University Press, 1959).   *Joseph H. Spurrier*

HAWAI'I BLOUNT REPORT. On 11 March 1893 President Cleveland appointed James H. Blount, ex-Congressman from Georgia and former chairman of the House Committee on Foreign Affairs, as special commissioner to Hawai'i to investigate the causes of the recent revolution. Commissioner Blount was given paramount authority in all matters relating to the existing Hawaiian government and could, if necessary, use the naval force at Honolulu to protect American lives and property.

Blount arrived in Honolulu on 29 March 1893. Two days later, he terminated the limited protectorate instituted by the U.S. minister, John Stevens. The American flag was lowered from the government building, and all U.S. forces were withdrawn from Honolulu.

After four months of investigation, Blount concluded that the overthrow of Queen Lili'uokalani would not have occurred without the support of Stevens. Blount reported that Stevens not only improperly ordered U.S. marines ashore to aid the revolutionaries but was also guilty of giving the enemies of the royal government assurances of support prior to the uprising. A Senate investigation in 1894, however, could find no evidence that Stevens had conspired with the revolutionaries beforehand to overthrow the Hawaiian monarchy. Besides Stevens, Blount placed additional blame for the revolution on the desire of Hawaiian sugar planters to secure the sugar bounty through annexation of Hawaii to the United States. Finally, Blount uncovered evidence that the people of Hawai'i did not support the new government which had replaced the monarchy and were opposed to American annexation. Blount's investigation severely damaged annexationist sentiment in the U.S. and strongly reinforced President Cleveland's decision to withdraw the Harrison administration's annexation treaty from the Senate.

RELATED ENTRIES: Hawai'i; Hawaiian Revolution; Lili'uokalani.

SOURCES AND READINGS: John H. T. McPherson, "James Henderson Blount," in Allen Johnson and Dumas Malone, eds., *Dictionary of American Biography*, 20 vols. (New York: Charles Scribner's Sons, 1928-36), 2: 388-89; Allan Nevins, *Grover Cleveland: A Study in Courage* (New York: Dodd, Mead & Co., 1958); U.S. Department of State, *Papers Relating to the Foreign Relations of the United States, 1894* (Washington, D.C.: Government Printing Office, 1895).   *William R. Smith*

HAWAI'I, EDUCATION IN. Education in Hawai'i is constituted of both public and private sectors with the private portion being somewhat larger than in most areas of the United States. Contrary to the usual pattern in America, public education is administered by a single, statewide Department of Education. While there are geographic districts in the system,

most of the administration is centralized in a state office with one superintendent and one elected board of education for the state. Curriculum supervision and some support and special services are handled at the district level but only as a part of the state system. The independent school district does not exist as in other states. Every community in the state is served by one of the thirty-five public high schools and each high school is the keystone of a complex of elementary and intermediate schools. This is to facilitate articulation, or movement from one level to the next.

The organization of the levels of education follows traditional plans. Some complexes have kindergarten through sixth grades as the elementary level, seventh through ninth as the intermediate level, and tenth through twelfth as high school. Others have kindergarten through eighth as the elementary school with ninth through twelfth for high school. In some of the smaller complexes, a kindergarten through twelfth grade organization occurs.

Public higher education consists of three campuses of the University of Hawai'i, the graduate schools, and a system of community colleges. There is postsecondary opportunity for all candidates in this arrangement on all of the major islands. The total number of students enrolled in postsecondary work is about 50,000 with about 12 percent of that number in private institutions.

Private schooling accounts for 17 percent of the total enrollment in the state with the strongest showing in the high schools where 20 percent of enrollments are private. Of the twenty-seven private high schools, twenty are accredited by the local regional agency. Private higher education consists of four small institutions, Brigham Young University—Hawai'i Campus, Chaminade University, Hawai'i Loa College, and Hawai'i Pacific College, ranging in size from 2,400 to just under 200 students.

The high degree of centralization and the strength of the private sector set Hawai'i apart in some measure from the mainland United States. These two characteristics have their origins in the history of island education. In prediscovery Hawai'i, education, as in most primitive societies, was classed as familial (taught in the family) or formal (performed in class or school situations). Basic elements of the culture and most areas of expertise were subjects for familial instruction while only two kinds of formal learning were taught in classes. The largest and most visible formal education was the *halau hula* in which chant and dance were taught. In the absence of a written language, the memorized chant was the vehicle for the transmission of knowledge to the next generation such as would be written in another civilization. The *halau* was a longhouse built and dedicated especially for that purpose to the goddess *Laka*, patron of the dance.

While dancers were not usually organized into formal groups, as in Tahiti, they were a part of every chiefly court and their training was carefully patterned. When a *halau* class was to begin, the *kumu hula* (master of the dance and chant) was selected by the district or island chief. The students were selected on the basis of ability to memorize, grace of movement, and comeliness. Then, directed by their *kumu*, the students set about the building of the *halau*. When the construction was completed, a rectangular block of stone or wood was set up at the entrance, draped with yellow tapa and leis of green vines, and by ritual chant infused with the power of *Laka*. The students were placed under *kapu* for the period of their training, forbidden to chew sugarcane, to become involved in any conflicting activity, or to indulge in any sexual activity. The dances and chants were selected, taught, and a formal graduation ceremony, which included demonstrations of what had been learned, was held. The graduation was called the *uniki*.

Christian missionaries, who arrived in Hawai'i in 1820, had as one of their objectives the teaching of reading and writing and the establishment of schools. The king, Kamehameha II, was interested in these skills and, after giving permission for a one-year stay, encouraged them to form schools and teach. Schools for adults were set up and in the six-year period between 1824 and 1830 almost all of the adult population received some schooling. The attraction of the mission schools was not, however, reading and writing but singing. For generations the chant had represented knowledge and education and it was the hymnody in the missionary schools which was seen as the end of education. As shown by actual attendance figures, those schools which taught music were successful and those which did not languished or failed. The Hawaiians went to school to learn to sing. By 1824 the schools were taught in the native language and the queen-regent, Ka'ahumanu, prescribed, in a law proclaimed through the streets, that all should go to school.

An institution for the training of teachers was established in 1830 at Lahainaluna, Maui. Schools for children were also of missionary origin. After the adults, children attended station schools throughout the islands. An independent school for children was founded at Honolulu in 1833, the O'ahu Charity School. This interesting school had a board of trustees made up of local residents and attracted students from western America, South America, and Russia. A family school for the children of the chiefs was formed in 1836, taught by a missionary couple, and called appropriately, "The Chiefs Childrens School." The Hilo Boarding School was set up in Hilo in the same year and, a half-century before its time, was a successful manual-training or technical school. In 1841 the missionaries established a school for their own children who had been previously forced to return to America for high school and were lost to their parents, usually for the remainder of their lives. This was Punahou, primarily a prep school for university students. The Catholic mission set up Father Maigret's Normal School on windward O'ahu in 1844.

Most of these early institutions continued well into the twentieth century if not to the present. The O'ahu Charity School became, in succession, the Honolulu Free School, the Town Free School, Honolulu High School and is now McKinley High School. Lahainaluna is presently, at the same location, one of the only public, boarding, high schools in the nation. Punahou continues as a prestigious private institution, primarily college preparatory. Father Maigret's Normal School was moved to Honolulu and renamed Saint Louis High School after that cleric's patron saint.

Due to the 1837 depression in the United States, the missionaries were forced to curtail their educational activities and the schools were turned over to the kingdom. William Richards, former missionary turned advisor and chaplain to the Hawaiian government, was made minister of education in 1845. His career was short, however, as he died in 1847. In 1848 his position was filled by the Reverend Richard Armstrong, who also left the mission. Mr. Armstrong had been a schoolmate of Horace Mann in New England and while in Hawai'i was an admirer and a correspondent with that founder of the public schools in America. Under the direction of Mr. Armstrong, the problem-ridden public education system of the kingdom was able to rid itself of sectarian pressures and secure provision for funding. He, himself, provided the sorely needed supervisory and administrative support to bring the public-school system of the kingdom into actuality.

With the passing of Kamehameha III as monarch, much of the missionary influence was cast off by the new ruler as he and his queen were of British sympathy. The newly arrived bishop, Thomas N. Staley, of the mission of the Church of England (Episcopal) was made president of the board of education for the kingdom and the office of minister was replaced with an inspector general—the equivalent of a superintendent. Abraham Fornander was appointed to that position in 1868. Mr. Fornander was a scholar, journalist, and collector of folklore, but as a school administrator he was a failure. His tenure was plagued by vacillation, mistakes, and lack of progress. In 1879 Mr. H. R. Hitchcock was appointed to the position. Hitchcock was a missionary son and had received university training in teaching. He provided a new quality of leadership for the island schools. After seven years Hitchcock was succeeded by Dwight Baldwin, another missionary son and another trained schoolman. The public school system of Hawai'i reached maturity under the leadership of these two men. In 1882 Walter Murray Gibson became premier of King Kalakaua and forced the resignation of most responsible men in Hawaiian government. Indeed, he made himself head of the school system. The ouster of Gibson in 1887 and the overthrow of the monarchy in 1893 resulted in the onset of conservatism which continued into the twentieth century. Paradoxically, it was during this twenty-year period of conservatism that the beginnings of "progressive education" were made in Hawai'i. Under the government of the Republic of Hawai'i in 1895, a Mr. Henry Townsend became inspector general for the schools. Under his administration, a periodical, *Progressive Education*, appeared and a graduate of the Oswego Normal School, birthplace of progressive education, was brought to the islands as a teacher. The first summer schools for teachers were held and leaders of this movement came to Hawai'i as instructors and visiting teachers. Professor Elmer Brown of California came in 1896, followed by Colonel and Mrs. Francis Parker of the University of Chicago, Miss Flora Cook, and finally Dr. John Dewey. Of the latter it is said that all major developments in American education in the first half of the twentieth century were attributable to understanding or misunderstanding of John Dewey.

After Hawai'i was annexed to the United States, the school system had little change to make. By virtue of its formation under a monarchy it was more centralized than was usual for a state or territory but was otherwise totally American. Founded by American missionaries, guided by American educational philosophy, taught from American texts by American teachers, the system had foreshadowed the politics. The organic act under which the Territory of Hawai'i was to be governed provided that the superintendent should be appointed by the governor and inasmuch as the first governor was Sanford B. Dole, the most conservative of the revolutionaries, progressive education was set aside in favor of a more formal and less controversial approach.

By the late 1920s the children of the immigrant labor population were reaching high-school age. The controlling interests in Hawai'i's economy were disturbed by the "over-education" of this group who were expected to continue to provide the labor in the sugar and pineapple fields. With the coming of the depression of 1929 this concern was magnified and Governor Lawrence Judd appointed a committee to make a survey of industry and education. The committee was strongly pro-industry and the report, made in 1930, contained numerous recommendations which were intended to withhold secondary education for children of the labor force lest they be attracted away from the fields to compete for jobs elsewhere. The recommendations of the committee were largely accepted and for eleven years—until the outbreak of World War II—intermediate grades were terminal for non-Caucasians in the islands. The grades seven, eight, and nine were designated "intermediate" since they were not to be thought of as junior high school, which might in turn be thought of as a prelude to senior high school. All of this was done under the guise of coordinating education with the needs of industry on the assumption that the only purpose of education is to prepare for employment. The modern term is "Career Education."

The 7 December 1941 attack on Pearl Harbor by Japanese carrier-based planes marked the entrance of the United States into World War II. More importantly in Hawai'i, the controlling elements of the island community were face-to-face with a large population of Hawaii-born Japanese, the second generation or *nisei* of the labor force. The personal values and loyalties of this group were not really known as it had never seemed important before. As it turned out, they were almost totally American. Their major sport was baseball and their tastes in clothing, popular music, and to some extent even food were American. They had been taught by American teachers, from American texts, in American schools. The educational system had solved the critical problem of the "Mongol Menace," or the "Yellow Peril."

Perhaps the most significant development of the fourth decade of the twentieth century in Hawai'i has been the rise of organization in labor. This has meant a push for equality of opportunity in education and the political power to accomplish it. The most visible change has been the development of higher education. The University of Hawai'i has been able to increase enrollments manyfold and to establish a network of community colleges. Four private institutions have come into being as well as a number of commercial and technical schools.

Through all the history of the schools in Hawai'i, the missionary-established private schools have continued to prosper as children of special groups have sought schooling apart from the conditions of the public schools. The children of the Caucasian, executive, and professional class have entered Punahou and prepared for college on the mainland. Oriental students of means and ability have entered 'Iolani, an Episcopalian-supported high school, while those of Hawaiian ancestry have gone to Kamehameha schools. These schools, which operate on the elementary, intermediate, and high school level, were established by the terms of the will of Bernice Pauahi Bishop, the last princess of the Kamehameha dynasty. Catholic schools, also a major part of the private schooling in Hawai'i, include Saint Louis High School, Damien High School, and Chaminade University. The strength of private education in the islands can be seen then as a reflection of the multiethnic and multicultural population and interests and the efforts of these groups to preserve their peculiar values and interests.

The schools of Hawai'i face problems in common with the rest of the United States but in addition they face the major difficulty of proficiency in language skills. Island children tend to develop communicative skills which employ a low level of verbal demand and as a result they are faced with difficulty in such highly verbal environments as higher education. They score well below national norms in standardized examinations in the verbal problems while performing adequately in other areas. Problems notwithstanding, however, Hawai'i's schools are well developed, well supported, and generally as competent as their counterparts on the mainland of the United States. Their opportunity lies in the multiracial, ethnic, and cultural makeup of the population and the ability to exercise leadership in world citizenship, certainly an inevitable future condition.

RELATED ENTRIES: Cook, (Captain) James; Hawai'i; Hilo Boarding School; Judd, Lawrence M.; Richards, William.

SOURCES AND READINGS: Nathaniel B. Emerson, *Unwritten Literature of Hawaii: The Sacred Songs of the Hula* (Washington, D.C.: Smithsonian Institution, 1909); Benjamin O. Wist, *A Century of Public Education in Hawaii* (Honolulu: Hawaii Educational Review, 1940).   *Joseph H. Spurrier*

HAWAI'I, MAPPING OF. The history of Hawaiian cartography can be divided into three periods, the first beginning in 1778 with the European discovery of Hawai'i by James Cook, a man respected both for mapping and charting abilities and his expert seamanship. For approximately the next ninety years, maps of Hawai'i were produced by cartographers of several nationalities. After Cook, notable British

contributions include George Vancouver's chart of the islands based on surveys conducted in 1792-1794 and detailed plans of Honolulu and Kilauea crater prepared by Lieutenant Malden, the cartographer aboard the H.M.S. *Blonde*, in 1825.

Russians were responsible for the first two known maps of Honolulu. Otto von Kotzebue compiled a chart of the harbor in 1816 which included considerable cultural information, and Vasili Golovnin made a similar but smaller scale chart in 1817-1818.

French mapping of Hawai'i began with the visit of Jean-François de Galaup Lapérouse in 1785, during which time he charted portions of the central islands that Cook's expedition had not examined in detail. In 1819 Louis Isidore Duperrey compiled plans of important harbors in the islands during the visit of the expedition under the command of Louis Claude Desaules de Freycinet. In 1855 Joseph Marie Henri de Lapasse compiled a plan of the Honolulu-Waikiki area, the first to show evidence of Honolulu's growth beyond the immediate vicinity of the harbor.

America's major cartographic contribution in this era was the work of the U.S. exploring expedition (1838-1842), which conducted research in Hawai'i in 1840-1841. In addition to an excellent general map of the kingdom and detailed charts of the harbors, the scientists from this voyage produced the first accurate plans of the craters of Moku'aweoweo (the summit crater of Mauna Loa) and Haleakala (on the island of Maui) as well as an important early map of the crater of Kilauea (on the island of Hawai'i).

Hawaiian-language maps were produced at the school at Lahainaluna, Maui, in the years 1834-1844. Begun by the American missionary Lorrin Andrews, most of the maps were engraved and printed by Hawaiian students. The maps were mostly general and biblical maps for school use and were copied from other school atlases. Several fine maps of Hawai'i, however, were published, including the first map to delineate the major Hawaiian land divisions.

The second era began in 1870 with the establishment of the Hawaiian government survey under the direction of William DeWitt Alexander. The survey's major goal was to provide a geodetic network and base maps from which accurate property surveys could be made. This was, therefore, the beginning of systematic mapping in Hawai'i. Although the survey did not attempt to produce topographic maps per se, its maps of the kingdom and the individual islands compare favorably with the topographic maps produced in other countries at that time. The scientific interests of the survey resulted in important studies concerning tides, the measurement of time, and volcanic phenomena. A number of nautical charts of

Hawaiian harbors were compiled under the direction of Gressy Jackson, most of which were incorporated into U.S. Hydrographic Office and British Admiralty charts.

With annexation to the United States in 1898, Hawai'i entered the third phase of its cartographic history. Established federal agencies assumed many of the tasks begun so well by the Hawaiian government survey. The U.S. post office and the geological survey produced general maps of the islands, and the coast and geodetic survey took over the production of charts. Seven-and-a-half minute topographic maps are now available for all the islands except Ni'ihau, Lana'i, and Kaho'olawe. The *Atlas of Hawaii*, compiled by the geography department of the University of Hawai'i, was issued in 1973. A comprehensive thematic atlas, with text by a host of authorities in different fields, the *Atlas of Hawaii* is a major research tool for modern Hawaiian studies. Also since annexation, an interesting tradition of tourist maps has developed, and the sophisticated use of maps is found in fabric designs, logos, and souvenirs.

It should be noted that many important scientific maps—particulary those relating to Hawai'i's volcanoes—appeared in books and reports rather than as separately published maps.

The maps of Hawai'i by the Lahainaluna school and the Hawaiian government survey were instrumental in recording and preserving aspects of the Hawaiian culture. The survival of Hawaiian place-names after the demise of the Hawaiian language was aided by the fine maps produced prior to annexation.

RELATED ENTRIES: Cook, (Captain) James; Hawai'i; Lapérouse, Jean-François; *Narragansett*; United States Exploring Expedition; Vancouver, George.

SOURCES AND READINGS: Gary L. Fitzpatrick, "Hawaii, A List of Early Maps in the Library of Congress," *Library of Congress Information Bulletin* 38 (1979): 198-204; J. R. Healy, "The Mapping of Hawaii from 1778 to 1848" (Master's thesis, University of Hawaii, 1959).   *Gary L. Fitzpatrick*

HAWAI'I, RELIGIONS OF. The ancient religion of the Hawaiian Islands was well developed and pervasive in the prediscovery culture of the islands. It had an established cosmogony; a pantheon of deities —anthropomorphic and otherwise; an influential priestly class; an extensive ritual literature; and a concept of dynamic power with provisions in the ritual for generation, restoration, and preservation of this power.

The cosmogony exists in various creation chants which, while unwritten, have been remarkably well preserved. Traditions of the creation and of the early generations of chiefs are couched in terms of matings and offspring with only a vague line of demarcation separating the phenomena of physical creation from the creation of the earliest of the chiefs.

The four major deities of the Hawaiians were Kane, the great creator; Ku, the god of war and some forest plant life; Lono, the god of fertility, planting, and the annual celebration of the *makahiki*; and Kanaloa, the god of darkness and the deep sea. An effort was made subsequent to the arrival of Christian missionaries to equate these four with the Christian Trinity plus the lord of darkness, Satan. This was a sincere but overzealous adulteration designed to make the transition from the primitive religion to nineteenth-century Christianity easier for the indigenes.

Two concepts were dominant in the ancient religion. The first was *mana*, the power through which the supernatural was operative in man. It was evidenced in the male procreative power, certain talents, any skill developed to a high degree, specialized knowledge, and even luck. The second concept was that of *kapu*. Usage of the word in early sources indicates it meant sacred or reserved for a sacred person or purpose. The function of *kapu* was the protection of the *mana* of the highest ranking of the chiefs. The higher the genealogical ranking of the chief the more *mana* he possessed and therefore the more rigid the *kapu* surrounding him and his activities. The *kapu* was a universal principal of social control which preserved the power of the chiefly classes through the support and cooperation of the *kahuna* or priestly class. A balance of power was thus created which provided stability in the society. The most onerous and visible aspects of the *kapu* were the eating restrictions. These reserved certain of the best foods for men, forbade men and women to eat together and enjoined women from preparing any but their own foods. It was these restrictions which finally brought an end to the practice of the old religion.

The early religion permeated all phases of life and work. Birth, the passage of boys into the company of men at age seven or eight, mating, and death were marked by prescribed chanting and ritual. Religious chants also accompanied every kind of task.

Many occasions of a more social or political nature, such as the consecrating of a new ruling chief, a preparation for war, or the supplication for better crops, were celebrated in open-air religious structures called *heiau*. The edifices were sacred and usually rectangular in shape consisting of an enclosing stone wall, an altar platform, a thatched house for the sacred drums, and an oracle tower. The larger of the *heiau*, called *luakini*, were dedicated to the god Ku and required human sacrifice in the ceremonies.

In 1819, just six months prior to the arrival of American Protestant missionaries from New England, King Kamehameha II, with the support of his mother, Keopu'olani, his father's favorite wife, Ka'ahumanu, and Kapi'olani, another powerful chiefess, discarded the ancient religion by publicly breaking the rules of the eating *kapu*. This event, one of the most significant of island history, ended most of the stabilizing influence for law and order, the religious character of most tasks which had lent to them a need for quality of performance and product, and the sacred power of the chiefs. The major chiefs now ruled with whatever political power they could muster.

In early April 1820 the first company of Christian missionaries arrived at Kailua, Kona, on the island of Hawai'i. The brig *Thaddeus* carried a party of twenty-two, including children and three Christian Hawaiians. This first company was under the nominal leadership of the Reverend Hiram Bingham. There would be eleven more companies to arrive over the succeeding twenty-eight years and an additional twenty-seven individual arrivals at Honolulu. These were hardy, zealous, well-trained men and women who came to a very primitive Hawai'i and faced the almost insurmountable task of bringing a religion which required the ability to read to a people who had no written language. They were successful, however, in reducing the language to writing and bringing the entire kingdom to a rudimentary state of literacy in just over one decade. The educational effort laid the groundwork for a system of public instruction while the belief in universal equality provided the foundation for a constitutional monarchy and the eventual Americanization of the islands.

The Protestant effort at the Christianization of the Hawaiians received unwelcome assistance when in July 1827 Fathers Alexis Bachelot and Abraham Armand arrived in the ship *Comète* with a mission party of Roman Catholics. This mission was sponsored by the Order of the Sacred Hearts of Jesus and Mary with headquarters at Paris, France. Beginning by landing without formal permission and culminating in a threatened French seizure of the islands in 1842, the French Catholic mission experienced continual difficulty throughout the founding of their work in Hawai'i. The rulers of the islands who were, by 1830, nominally Protestant, were antagonistic to the new religion, and the priests for their part showed almost total disregard for local government authority or tradition.

The most prominent event connected with the Catholic experience in Hawai'i, though not intentionally so, was the ministry of Father Damien desVeuster among the lepers at Kalaupapa. Arriving in Honolulu as Brother Damien, this son of a Flemish peasant family was ordained a priest and eventually assigned to the leper settlement at Kalaupapa on the island of Moloka'i. His work there was, at the same time, the pride and despair of his superiors in Honolulu. The heroic character of his accomplishments was admired by all, but the attention attracted seemed to the church fathers more notoriety than fame. His frequent disregard for policies and procedures of the mission if they seemed to stand in the way of his work was also a constant cause for concern. The fame which came after his death from leprosy, on 15 April 1889, was due largely to the writings of Robert Louis Stevenson and the work of Damien's older brother, Father Pamphile, who had become the historian for the order in Paris. Father Damien is fully deserving of the honor which has since come to him though he was not the only leper priest or Christian minister to labor and die among the lepers at Kalaupapa.

The third mission to be established in Hawai'i was that of the Church of Jesus Christ of Latter-day Saints. Ten elders of this faith arrived at Honolulu on the *Imaum of Muscat* in December 1850. The first baptisms occured in August 1851 and by the end of the year the first branches of the church had been organized on Maui and O'ahu. Within six years the number of converts had grown to 4,500, the *Book of Mormon* had been translated into the Hawaiian language, and branches of the church existed on all major islands. The most influential early missionary for the Mormons was Elder George Q. Cannon who was responsible for the organization of the first branch of the church and the translation mentioned above. Due to the unsettled conditions in Utah in 1858, the mission was closed leaving the local converts to fend for themselves. The unorthodox and colorful Walter Murray Gibson arrived in Hawai'i as a Mormon missionary to the South Seas in 1861 and after a three-year career of church leadership was excommunicated by a deputation from Utah who *reopened* the mission in 1865 with headquarters at La'ie, O'ahu.

The settlement and sugar plantation at La'ie was successful in that it provided opportunity for regularizing life among Hawaiians and returning their self-esteem sufficiently to bring about a reverse in the declining birthrate among the Hawaiians. In 1874, for instance, deaths exceeded births nine to one throughout the kingdom. But at La'ie, births exceeded deaths seven to one. Growth among the Latter-day Saints continued through the end of the nineteenth and into the twentieth century with a present church membership of 32,000. One of the church's temples is located at La'ie as well as a branch of its university and the Polynesian Cultural Center.

In October 1862 at the request of King Kamehameha IV and Queen Emma, Bishop Thomas N. Staley arrived at Honolulu as leader of the mission party of the Church of England (Episcopal). The mission enjoyed generous royal patronage and plans were made for the erection of a cathedral at Honolulu. The work of the mission had proceeded slowly though Bishop Staley was influential in social and political life in Hawai'i. The bishop preferred the High-Church ritual while most of the congregation in Hawai'i were of the Low Church. To complicate matters further, the annexationist sentiments in Hawai'i's business community made the royalist views of the church unpopular. In 1902, after Hawai'i's annexation to the United States, administration of affairs of the mission came under the Protestant Episcopal Church in the United States of America rather than the earlier Anglican authority. Though it seems an unlikely religious contribution, Bishop Staley is best remembered in the minds of many for his introduction of the English celebration of Christmas. Prior to the founding of the Church of England, this holiday had been a solemn holy day with none of the convivial spirit and joyousness which now marks the season.

Other religions were established in Hawai'i at later dates including various Protestant groups, some of the revivalist religions, and a number of important Eastern faiths. With the arrival of large numbers of immigrant laborers from the Far East came the influence of Buddhism. Although the Chinese were the first Buddhists to arrive, little occurred among them in the way of organized effort until the 1950s. Organized Buddhist effort appeared among the Japanese in 1887 when the Reverend Ejun Miyamoto came as the first missionary from Japan. In an effort to prevent the loss of Buddhist and Japanese traditions among children born to the immigrants, the Buddhists established language schools in large numbers around the islands. These were cause for considerable concern among conservative Caucasians, and when World War II came in 1941 the schools were closed, the properties seized,

and the teachers taken to internment camps on the mainland United States. There has been some revival among Buddhist groups since 1950, mostly the Zen which appeals to many Caucasians.

A listing of religious groups presently existent in Hawai'i, in addition to those already mentioned, includes:

Eastern Orthodox Catholic
Baptist
United Methodist
Presbyterian
Lutheran
Society of Friends
Seventh-Day Adventist
Salvation Army
Christian Science
Reorganized Church of Jesus Christ of Latter-Day
    Saints
Unitarian Fellowship
Jewish
Shinto
Baha'i
Christian Church
Jehovah's Witnesses

There are in addition, a number of popular cults of which the Hare Krishna group seems most active.

Religion in Hawai'i since the latter decades of the nineteenth century is marked by the same tolerance and acceptance among faiths as is found with regard to cultural differences among the ethnic groups which form the population of the islands.

RELATED ENTRIES: Bingham, Hiram (both); Cannon, George Q.; Damien, (Father) Joseph; Hawai'i; Staley, Thomas.

SOURCES AND READINGS: Martha W. Beckwith, *Hawaiian Mythology* (New Haven: Yale University Press, 1940); E. S. Craighill Handy, "Perspectives in Polynesian Religion" in *Polynesian Anthropological Series*, issued by the *Polynesian Journal*; Memoirs of the Polynesian Society, no. 17 (Wellington: Thomas Avery & Sons, 1941).   *Joseph H. Spurrier*

HAWAIIAN ANNEXATION, AMERICAN OPPOSITION TO (1893-1898). The attempted annexation of the Hawaiian Islands by the Harrison administration in 1893 and the McKinley administration in 1897 evoked strong opposition from some of America's most prominent politicians and private citizens. Editors Carl Schurz of *Harper's Weekly* and E. L. Godkin of the *Nation* and the *New York Evening Post*, President Grover Cleveland, Secretary of

State Walter Q. Gresham, noted legal authority Judge Thomas M. Cooley, and Yale professor William Graham Sumner, among others, opposed annexation of Hawai'i. They maintained that annexation would violate the principle of nonentanglement laid down by the Founding Fathers and would endanger the security of the nation by placing the U.S. flag in an area where it would be vulnerable to attack by a foreign power. Annexation would also be unconstitutional since it repudiated the basic American concept that all just powers are derived from the consent of the governed. Hawai'i, they pointed out, would probably remain a colony of the U.S. and its people would be denied self-government. Most opponents of Hawaiian annexation favored economic rather than political control of the islands. They believed that annexation would only create additional political, social, and racial problems. Besides, they argued, the U.S. could secure all necessary overseas economic advantages without annexing territory.

In Congress, antiimperialist Republicans and most Democrats steadfastly refused to consent to Hawaiian annexation. On 31 May 1894 the Senate passed a resolution submitted by Senator David Turpie of Indiana which approved the principle of noninterference in Hawai'i's domestic affairs and warned that foreign intervention in the political affairs of the islands would be viewed as an affront to the U.S. Congressional opposition to overseas expansion also prevented ratification of the Hawaiian annexation treaty negotiated by the McKinley administration on 16 June 1897.

The Spanish-American War strengthened expansionist sentiment in the U.S. and focused public attention once again on the question of Hawaiian annexation. In the aftermath of Dewey's victory at Manila Bay, many Americans succumbed to the imperialists' argument that Hawai'i was vital to American security and necessary for the successful completion of the war. The antiimperialists found it impossible to overcome the emotionalism and patriotism generated by the war against Spain. A joint resolution annexing the Hawaiian Islands to the U.S. was overwhelmingly passed by the House of Representatives on 15 June 1898 and by the Senate on 6 July 1898.

RELATED ENTRIES: Hawai'i; Hawai'i Blount Report; Hawaiian Annexation Treaty; Hawaiian Revolution.

SOURCES AND READINGS: Thomas M. Cooley, "Grave Obstacles to Hawaiian Annexation," *Forum* 15 (1893): 389-406; E. L. Godkin, "Hawaii," *Nation* 56 (1893) 96-97; Carl Schurz, "Manifest Destiny," *Harper's New Monthly Magazine* 87 (1893): 737-46;

William Graham Sumner, "The Fallacy of Territorial Extension," *Forum* 21 (1896): 414-19; E. Berkeley Tompkins, *Anti-Imperialism in the United States: The Great Debate, 1890-1920* (Philadelphia: University of Pennsylvania Press, 1970); Hermann E. Von Holst, *The Annexation of Hawaii* (Chicago: Independence Co., 1898); Theodore S. Woolsey, "The Law and the Policy of Hawaii," *Yale Review* 2 (1894): 347-55.   *William R. Smith*

HAWAIIAN ANNEXATION TREATY (1893). Two days after the downfall of the Hawaiian monarchy (19 January 1893) the newly established provisional government of Hawai'i sent a commission of five (four Americans and one Englishman) to Washington, D.C., to negotiate a treaty of annexation with the U.S. On 14 February an annexation treaty was signed by the Hawai'i commissioners and the Harrison administration. The treaty was submitted to the U.S. Senate the next day. The agreement provided for the annexation of the Hawaiian Islands to the U.S., the cession to the U.S. of all rights of sovereignty, and the prohibition of further Chinese immigration to Hawai'i or from the islands to the U.S. In addition, the U.S. would assume the public debt of Hawai'i, would pay an annuity of $20,000 to Lili-'uokalani for life, and would provide for the payment of a lump sum of $150,000 to Princess Ka'iulani.

Democratic opposition in the Senate to President Harrison's hurried annexation attempt made passage of the treaty impossible. President Cleveland withdrew the Hawaiian annexation treaty for reexamination shortly after his inauguration on 4 March 1893. Cleveland decided not to resubmit the treaty to the Senate after reading Commissioner Blount's report on the details of the Hawaiian revolution.

RELATED ENTRIES: Hawai'i Blount Report.

SOURCES AND READINGS: Julius W. Pratt, *Expansionists of 1898: The Acquisition of Hawaii and the Spanish Islands* (Chicago: Quadrangle Books, 1964); U.S. Department of State, *Papers Relating to the Foreign Relations of the United States, 1894* (Washington, D.C.: Government Printing Office, 1895).
                    William R. Smith

HAWAIIAN MUSIC. It is curious that there should be a "Hawaiian Music" in view of the size, population, and relative unimportance of these small bits of land in the middle of the northern Pacific Ocean. It has, however, achieved a worldwide cognizance as an identifiable idiom—Hawaiian music. The appeal is primarily nostalgic and there is a tendency to overvalue it. When it is taken from its island setting, it often seems disappointingly shallow. The themes are simple expressions: love, the beauty of a place, the memorialization of some person or event and, the most recurrent of all, of someone's departure from the islands. The words are unsophisticated, straightforward, earthy, and sometimes explicit while the melodies and harmonies, of modern Hawaiian music at least, are so prosaic as to be clichés. Further, the instruments which accompany the music are not those of serious artistic expression elsewhere. Hawaiian music is a primitive folk music which has preserved its identity through an overwhelming foreign contact and highly compressed acculturation.

In the primitive period of prediscovery Hawai'i, music held a very noticeable and important place in the culture. In the absence of a written language, memorized chant was the means of transmission of knowledge. Originally religious in function, *mele*, which is the Hawaiian term for chant, eventually became the vehicle to transmit all knowledge formal enough to warrant preservation. It was, in accompaniment to the dance, one of the only skills taught in formal, schoollike circumstances. By the time of the arrival of Captain James Cook in 1778, music and dance were not so far removed from their primitive functions as not to be performed on solemn occasions, but they had evolved to a point of being done simply for entertainment and their own artistic significance.

Most scholars of early Hawaiian music classify chant as *mele hula*, that which was to accompany the dance, and *mele oli*, not meant for dancing. The *oli* was solemn, sacred, performed unaccompanied and solo and was much more chant than song. There was one dominant chant tone with very little melodic ornamentation. The function of the *oli* dictated these characteristics. *Pule*, or prayer; *kanikau*, or funeral dirges; *ko'ihonua* which were genealogies; and the *kahea*, which was an announcement or proclamation; these were the uses of the *oli*. The *mele hula*, on the other hand, served a wider variety of functions, was more rhythmic in nature, and had a wider and more varied melodic construction. There was the *inoa*, or name chant; the *mele kou* or song of praise; the *mele ipo*, a song used in the service of love; the *mele ma'i*, an unusual kind of expression in praise of the genitals; and a *mele paeaea* or a taunting song. The list is not exhaustive. These *mele* were usually accompanied by instruments of various kinds.

The musical instruments of prediscovery Hawai'i were mostly percussive or ideophonic though there were examples of stringed and wind varieties. There was even one that might have been harmonic in nature. Small stones played in the manner of Spanish

castanets, goard rattles decorated with feathers or strips of pandanus leaf, hollow gourds of several sizes, and drums ranging in size from a hide-covered half-coconut to very large temple drums were the most common instruments. A version of the musical bow called the *'ūkēkē* was held near the mouth while singing and the strings served as resonators for the sound and gave rhythmic impetus to the words. The only wind instrument seems to have been the nose flute or *'ohe hanu ihu* which was capable of only two or three tones and which gave a plaintive and sometimes ethereal quality. Bamboo tubes, used in pairs, and of various lengths, were held upright and struck, butt first, on the ground. There is conjecture on the matter but it is likely that a rudimentary harmony was perceived in the interval between the tones produced by the two tubes. The list, again, is not exhaustive but rather representative of the instruments used.

The impact of the discovery by Captain Cook was immediate in music. The Hawaiians heard, for the first time, the sound of Western song and of European instruments. Bandsmen with Cook's ships performed on the German flute, the drums, the French horn, and the violin. The new, wider, range of melody was immediately accepted and Hawaiian chants became more songlike, in the modern use of the term. Couple *hulas* in imitation of the sailor's hornpipe appeared very soon also.

In the spring of 1820, American Protestant missionaries arrived in Hawai'i bringing with them the hymns and hymnals of their time. As missionary schools were begun, it became apparent that the attraction of the new learning was largely singing. From prehistoric times, chant carried knowledge and in the new circumstances, learning was learning to sing. Music composed by Hawaiians of this period reflects the influence of the melody and harmony of the New England hymns—a stamp which Hawaiian music was to bear throughout its existence. Compositions were done by students of missionaries and, in the language, by the missionaries themselves.

The next identifiable influence to come to Hawai'i was that of the Mexican cowboys brought to the islands in the 1830s to begin Hawai'i's extensive ranching enterprise. The *vaqueros* brought with them the guitar and the Mexican style of picking the instrument's strings as well as the syncopation of Latin rhythms. The Hawaiians changed the tuning of the guitar so that the unstopped fret on the fingerboard produced a chord when given a full stroke. They named their style "slack key."

Since the days of Captain Cook's ships the Hawaiians had been impressed by the music of the military band and as early as 1832 efforts were made to form a royal band. It was 1872, however, before the band became a continuously functioning unit. In that year Captain Henry Berger arrived from Prussia to form the Royal Hawaiian Band. He began work with a group of young men at the reform school in Honolulu and in a little over a decade was able to win international honors in band competition. The influence of Henry Berger on musical development in Hawai'i is almost incalculable. He headed the Amateur Music Society which was the forerunner of the Honolulu Symphony, taught singing in Sunday schools and began school band work at Kamehameha schools, 'Iolani school, and Saint Louis College. The influence of Berger and his band can also be seen in the mainstream of Hawaiian musical composition. Songs of the period show the influence of martial melodies and, perhaps more importantly, the melodic and harmonic techniques of German romanticism which the band leader exemplified. His settings and the settings of his "boys" for Hawaiian songs form a large body of song material.

During the 1880s there occured the immigration of the Portuguese to Hawai'i. With them came a small guitarlike instrument which the Hawaiians adopted and adapted as the four-string 'ukulele. The strum of this small instrument is not imposing or brilliant but it has flavored Hawaiian music for nearly a century and shows no sign of fading. In the same decade a young man attending the Kamehameha school discovered the idea of stopping the frets of the guitar with the back of his pocketknife, producing a metallic glissando or sliding sound which he turned into the steel guitar. Joseph Kekuku of La'ie, O'ahu, invented the sound which was to dominate Hawaiian music until the 1950s, when the picking and slack key styles were revived.

As Pearl Harbor became a major American naval base, World War II brought hundreds of uniformed tourists to the islands. They brought with them American jazz with its peculiar syncopation and dotted rhythms. Hawaiian music incorporated these elements and the way was opened for a commercial or "Waikiki" music, primarily for consumption by American visitors. To this was added electronic amplification and Hawaiian music followed American music through the phases of popular music from "swing" to "rock," bring a further divergence between the commercial and the reviving folk-style Hawaiian music which purported to be seeking a valid "Hawaiian" expression.

What has survived as Hawaiian music combines language and poetry of the primitive mele with Western hymn-style melodic and harmonic settings, the whole livened with the sound of traditional instru-ments. Still found are the early themes of the glory of the ali'i (chiefs), the beauty and pride of place, and the subtle double meanings of a love song. Added are the sounds of the guitar and 'ukelele and the rhythms of Spanish and American music. Yet, even so, it is identified as Hawaiian music.

RELATED ENTRIES: Hawai'i; Hawai'i, Education in.

SOURCES AND READINGS: Dorothy M. Kahananui, *Music of Ancient Hawaii: A Brief Survey* (Honolulu: 1962); Helen H. Roberts, *Ancient Hawaiian Music* (New York: Dover, 1967).   *Joseph H. Spurrier*

HAWAIIAN REVOLUTION (1893). In the early 1890s, American economic and political influence in Hawai'i was seriously threatened. The McKinley tariff act of 1890 struck an economic blow to the Hawaiian sugar planters, most of whom were of American birth or descent, by placing raw sugar on the free list and providing a bounty of two cents a pound to domestic American producers. The proud and strong-willed Queen Lili'uokalani came to the throne in 1891. She was determined to end foreign influence and reestablish the power of the monarchy. On 14 January 1893 Lili'uokalani announced her decision to promulgate a new constitution which would strip the legislature of its power and give almost absolute authority to the monarch.

The Americans in Hawai'i reacted quickly to news of Lili'uokalani's attempted seizure of power. A revolutionary committee of safety, led by Sanford B. Dole, was organized and plans were made for the establishment of a provisional government. On 16 January the committee of safety asked the U.S. minister to Hawai'i, John L. Stevens, for support. Stevens ordered 160 marines from the U.S.S. *Boston* ashore to protect American life and property. However, the main body was not stationed near American property but took a position across the street from the government building, near the queen's palace. The following day, 17 January, the committee of safety occupied the government buildings and established a provisional government which was immediately recognized by Minister Stevens. The landing of U.S. marines and the prompt recognition of the provisional government by Minister Stevens led Queen Lili'uokalani to conclude that the U.S. officially sanctioned the uprising. Believing she faced overwhelming opposition, Queen Lili'uokalani reluctantly surrendered her power to the revolutionaries.

RELATED ENTRIES: Hawai'i; Lili'uokalani; Stevens, John L.

SOURCES AND READINGS: Julius W. Pratt, *Expansionists of 1898: The Acquisition of Hawaii and the*

Spanish Islands (Chicago: Quadrangle Books, 1964); William A. Russ, Jr., *The Hawaiian Revolution, 1893-1894* (Selinsgrove, Pa.: Susquehanna University Press, 1959); Sylvester K. Stevens, *American Expansion in Hawaii, 1842-1898* (Harrisburg, Pa.: Archives Publishing Co., 1945).   *William R. Smith*

HENRY, TEUIRA (1847-1915). A linguist and scholar of the Tahitian language, Teuira Henry was born in Tahiti on 27 January 1847 to Issac S. and Eliza (Orsmond) Henry. She was the granddaughter of both the Reverend J. M. Orsmond and the Reverend William Henry (missionary of the *Duff*). She was educated at the missionary school in Pape'ete after which she taught French and English in the Viénnot School for nearly twenty years. She then moved to Honolulu and taught in the primary schools for over ten years where she received the First Class Primary Certificate with high credits for her excellent work. She was responsible for the reconstruction of her grandfather's (J. M. Orsmond) lost manuscript dealing with ancient Tahitian society. After many years work on this project, it was finally published in 1928 by the Bernice P. Bishop Museum under the title *Ancient Tahiti*. She died 23 January 1915 in Pa'ea, Tahiti, before seeing her work completed.

RELATED ENTRIES: French Polynesia; Henry, William; Orsmond, John M.

SOURCES AND READINGS: J. W. Davidson and Deryck Scarr, *Pacific Islands Portraits* (Canberra: Australian National University Press, 1970); Teuira Henry, *Ancient Tahiti* (Honolulu: Bernice P. Bishop Museum, 1928); Patrick O'Reilly and Raoul Teissier, *Tahitiens* (Paris: Musée de l'Homme, 1962).
    Brenna J. Rash

HENRY, WILLIAM (1770-1859). A missionary of the London Missionary Society, William Henry was born in Dublin, Ireland, 21 June 1770. He worked as a carpenter by trade and as a joiner in the shipbuilding industry. He studied at Trinity College after which he volunteered for service with the missionary society, founded in London in 1795. He was one of the originals of the *Duff* missionary party sent to Christianize the South Pacific. He was given the title of Reverend after he was named member of the Directing Committee, to regulate the affairs on the course of the voyage. They arrived in Tahiti on 6 March 1797. A year later, he and his family along with two other families moved to Sydney for the safety of the women. He rejoined the mission 30 January 1800 at Matavai Bay (Tahiti) where he lived until 1808. In 1811 he was on Mo'orea. Being dedicated to this mission, he baptized more than 600

adults and 375 children. In 1813 he was named magistrate by Governor Macquire at Pape'ete and in 1842 he again returned to Sydney for his health. He died in Ryde, England, on 1 April 1859.

RELATED ENTRIES: French Polynesia; Henry, Teuira; Orsmond, John M.

SOURCES AND READINGS: J. W. Davidson and Deryck Scarr, *Pacific Island Portraits* (Canberra: Australian National University Press, 1970); Patrick O'Reilly and Raoul Teissier, *Tahitiens* (Paris: Musée de l'Homme, 1962).
    Brenna J. Rash

HERVEY ISLANDS. *See* Cook Islands.

HIGGINSON, JOHN (1839-1904). An Irish entrepreneur and mining industrialist in New Caledonia, Higginson was an important factor in the French annexation of New Hebrides. Raised in Australia, Higginson first came to New Caledonia in 1859. From meager beginnings he advanced to work in James Paddon's enterprises as an early supplier for the island's penal colony. In 1870 Higginson began a bimonthly shipping service between Australia and New Caledonia which was later expanded to coastal villages throughout the region. He also founded sugar and rum factories and became a land agent. His start in mining began with the discovery of copper and gold in 1872-1873 in the Balade district. Higginson soon realized that New Caledonia's real wealth lay in its nickel ore deposits. In 1876, shortly after becoming a French citizen, he formed the *Société le Nickel* and became known internationally as the "Nickel King." He held many business interests in New Hebrides and assured French influence there by founding the *Compagnie calédonienne des Nouvelles-Hébrides* in 1882. A humanitarian, Higginson built churches, schools, orphanages, and hospitals. He died in Paris on 24 October 1904.

RELATED ENTRIES: New Caledonia; Vanuatu.
SOURCES AND READINGS: Patrick O'Reilly, *Calédoniens* (Paris: Musée de l'Homme, 1953).
    Russell T. Clement

HILO BOARDING SCHOOL. A vocational school for native Hawaiian boys, Hilo Boarding School was established by the Reverend David B. Lyman in Hilo, Hawai'i, in 1836. Formed under the auspices of the American Board of Commissioners for Foreign Missions in Boston, the school's original purpose was to train young men for admittance to the Congregationalist seminary at Lahainaluna on Maui. At first consisting of only two grass houses, the Hilo Boarding School was rebuilt in 1839, in 1856 after a fire, and again in 1905.

In its early years the Hilo Boarding School provided the kingdom of Hawai'i with its share of clergy, teachers, and government officials. But from its inception the school had also offered instruction in farming and the crafts. After the closing of the Lahainaluna seminary, and with diminishing financial support from the Missions board after 1850, these vocational programs became of greater significance. Although religious and general education remained important, by the end of the nineteenth century the facilities for vocational education at the Hilo Boarding School also included carpentry, tailor, and blacksmith shops, a printing press, a generator, and an ice plant. The students raised sugarcane, taro, pineapples, other crops, and livestock for their own use.

The Hilo Boarding School continued regular classes until 1925 when the establishment of public junior high and high schools on the island of Hawai'i reduced its usefulness. The Hilo Boarding School antedated by some forty years similar attempts at vocational education in the U.S. and influenced the development of schools for black freedmen in the south after the Civil War.

RELATED ENTRIES: Hawai'i; Hawai'i, Education in.

SOURCES AND READINGS: Ralph C. Canevali, "Hilo Boarding School," *Hawaiian Journal of History* 11 (1977): 77-96.   *Ralph C. Canevali*

HOLCOMB, CRAYTON (1830-1885). A captain and trader from Connecticut, Holcomb undertook a series of whaling voyages during the 1850s and 1860s. Lured by lucrative prospects for trade in copra, *bêche-de-mer*, and shell, he ventured to Yap in 1874 and established one of the first permanent trading stations on the island. With other traders, including David O'Keefe, he helped to establish Yap as a trade center in the late 1870s and thereby exposed the island to later commercial and political influences. As a result of pressure from competitors, however, Holcomb was forced to abandon his own business and to leave Yap in 1880. He returned to the island in 1882 and attempted to rebuild his copra trade with borrowed funds, but was frustrated by stiff competition and his own lack of restraint in dealings with Yapese. In 1883 he was reprimanded by authorities of a British naval vessel for his part in a white mob's attack on a Yapese village. A year later, in hopes of removing the trade advantage of competing German firms, Holcomb personally presented a petition to the governor of the Philippines—signed by himself, his Spanish common-law wife, and some Yapese—requesting that Spanish rule be extended to Yap and Palau. This played into the hands of Spanish authorities who were already looking for a pretext to occupy the Caroline Islands. But, when the formal establishment of Spanish authority in the western Carolines occurred in 1886, Holcomb was not alive to see it. While on a trading voyage in May 1885, Holcomb was killed by islanders of the Saint Mathais group.

RELATED ENTRIES: Micronesia.

SOURCES AND READINGS: Francis X. Hezel, "A Yankee Trader in Yap: Crayton Philo Holcomb," *Journal of Pacific History* 10, no. 1 (1975): 3-19.   *Francis X. Hezel*

HOORN ISLANDS. *See* Wallis and Futuna.

HOPEFUL **SCANDAL (1884).** Perhaps the most notorious and thoroughly documented cases of kidnapping in the Queensland labor trade occurred off the coast of New Guinea and the Bismarck Archipelago in 1884. New Britain, New Ireland, the Louisiade, and D'Entrecasteaux groups in the early 1880s had experienced only minimal and sporadic contact with missionaries, *bêche-de-mer* and pearl-shell fisherman, and copra traders. When the *Hopeful* set sail from Townsville, Queensland, on 3 May 1884 it was in an atmosphere of both anxiety and high expectations. Capitalism in Queensland was experiencing an unprecedented boom, and concomitantly demands for cheap, servile, indentured labor far exceeded the supply. Additionally, traditional recruitment areas such as the New Hebrides (Vanuatu) were exhausted from excessive exploitation. Aside from these structural factors, all was not right specifically with the *Hopeful*. During a previous voyage in 1883, an islander had been abducted and two others shot by the mate, Neil McNeil. All the features of "enlistment" in low contact areas were present. McNeil kidnapped a number of Moresby islanders by dragging them into the boats and securing them in the hold.

At Wararol, off the New Guinea coast, thirty men who had come on board in search of tobacco were detained against their wills, while at Bentley Bay two white sailors who had gone ashore threatened to burn down the village if no "recruits" were forthcoming. The village was burned and men kidnapped. This process was repeated at Hilliwow and Sanoroa where one man was fatally shot and a little lad was drowned. Here, also, another islander had his throat cut by Barney Williams. At Coiawata Island five men were kidnapped after McNeil destroyed their canoe. A Royal Commission probing into widespread kidnapping by at least seven vessels concluded that deceit, cruel treachery, deliberate kidnapping, and cold-blooded murder were rampant.

Subsequently Williams and McNeil were indicted for murder; the captain, Lewis Shaw, the government agent, Henry Schofield, the mate, Freeman, and two seamen, Rogers and Preston, all were charged with kidnapping. All were found guilty, the murderers received the death sentence, and the others substantial terms of imprisonment. The intensely racist Australian public in Queensland was outraged that Europeans could be executed for the murder of mere "blacks." Sixty members of the legislature pleaded for clemency. The executive council relented and commuted the death sentences to "life imprisonment," with the first five years to be spent in irons. The *Hopeful* murderers and kidnappers were discreetly released in 1889, far short of having served their full sentences, when a conservative government was elected.

RELATED ENTRIES: Labor Trade; Melanesian Recruitment to Queensland, Patterns of; Melanesians and Colonial Servitude.

SOURCES AND READINGS: Peter Corris, " 'Blackbirding' in New Guinea Waters 1883-1884: An Episode in the Queensland Labour Trade," *Journal of Pacific History* 3 (1968): 85-106; Raymond Evans, Kay Saunders, Kathryn Cronin, *Exclusion, Exploitation, and Extermination: Race Relations in Colonial Queensland* (Sydney: Australian and New Zealand Book Co., 1975).   *Kay E. Saunders*

HUNT, JOHN (1812-1848). A Christian missionary and translator of scriptures in Fiji, Hunt was born 13 June 1812 in England. He underwent a religious conversion in his sixteenth year and expressed interest in becoming a missionary for the Wesleyan church. He was accepted into the newly opened theological institute at Hoxton. Upon completion of his studies, he married Hannah Summers and sailed to Fiji to assist David Cargill and William Cross, the first permanent Christian missionaries in Fiji. Hunt was sent to Rewa to assist Cross where he rapidly learned the Fijian language. From there, he was sent to a new mission at Somosomo, ruled by Chief Tui Cakau. He spent much of his time learning the customs and history from the older men of the villages.

Conversion to Christianity was extremely slow as these early missionaries witnessed incessant tribal wars, bloodshed, and cannibalism. Hunt moved on to Viwa (two miles from the island of Bau) where he did most of his work in translating the Old and New Testaments. In 1844 he visited the island of Rotuma and recorded the customs and conditions there. Tirelessly, Hunt acted as interpreter for foreign officials, supervised the organization of a native church, and attended to his literary productions. Beloved and greatly respected by the Fijians, he died at Viwa on 4 October 1848 at the age of thirty-six.

RELATED ENTRIES: Fiji.

SOURCES AND READINGS: Norman A. Birthwhistle, *In His Armour: The Life of John Hunt of Fiji* (London: Cargate Press, 1954); Stanley Brown, *Men from Under the Sky: The Arrival of Westerners in Fiji* (Rutland, Vt.: Charles E. Tuttle Co., 1973); G. S. Rowe, *Life of John Hunt* (London: Hamilton Adams, 1868).   *Robert D. Craig*

HUTCHINSON, JOHN (1792-1866). A pioneer Methodist missionary to Tonga, Hutchinson was born in Scarborough, Yorkshire. Hutchinson emigrated to Australia where he set up a farm on the island of Tasmania. In April 1826 he was ordained to the Wesleyan ministry, the first such in Australia. He was appointed to go to Tonga with John Thomas, arriving 26 June 1826. His background and personality were not congenial to the life of a missionary, and his stay in Tonga was neither happy nor successful. He quarreled frequently with Thomas, apparently believing Thomas to be his inferior. In addition, Hutchinson's health broke, and he left Tonga in 1828, vowing to return to his farm. He died in 1866.

RELATED ENTRIES: Thomas, John; Tonga.

SOURCES AND READINGS: Niel Gunson, *Messengers of Grace* (Melbourne: Oxford University Press, 1978); Sione Lātūkefu, *Church and State in Tonga* (Canberra: Australian National University Press, 1974); W. H. Wood, *Overseas Missions of the Australian Methodist Church*, vol. 1 (Melbourne: Aldersgate Press, 1975).   *Ronald Shook*

ISLAND CONFEDERATION MOVEMENTS, 1900-1940. During the nineteenth century there were numerous proposals for wider political associations within Oceania. They often represented outright imperialist ambition, as befitted the times. In the period between 1900 and 1940 the continuing moves for island confederations were the product of yet another mental climate and set of values. Mostly, the sponsors of confederation were planters and traders or those concerned with their interests. Generally, the call for confederation stemmed from economic complaints which were seen to require a political solution. Many of the planters' and traders' grievances stemmed from dissatisfaction with existing arrangements for shipping and marketing island produce and also from concern for future supplies of cheap Indian plantation labor. It was held that the success of European commercial activity in the Pacific depended on its control residing in the hands of those directly concerned. An organizational form was needed to gather together these geographically scattered interests, and a confederation of islands seemed the obvious way of achieving this end.

Most proposals for island confederation also had a pronounced racial component. The idea that the destiny of the islands was for European enterprise lay in the prevalent notion of white superiority and the complementary assumption that Pacific island peoples were either dying out or were no longer "true" islanders but mere shadows of their former selves. The agency of confederation was seen as the means by which this European racial exclusiveness would have an economic underpinning and therefore a continued existence.

Within these limitations, proposals for island confederation differed somewhat in content and emphasis. There was also often a difference beteen a sponsor's stated reasons and his underlying motives. Such was the case with Francis Harman, a plantation manager in Samoa who in 1915 sought a confederation between Samoa and Fiji. Like many other Europeans in Samoa, he wanted to be administered by Britian not New Zealand because the former would, he felt, govern Samoa in a more professional manner.

An association with Fiji was an obvious way of achieving this. But his primary reason for wanting such a union was to secure a cheap and adequate supply of Indian plantation labor.

Henry Milne Scott, the Lord Mayor of Suva and an elected member of the Fiji legislative council, also said one thing but really meant another. He stressed that his 1921 proposal for the unification of British territories in the western Pacific was essentially for reasons of administrative efficiency and coordination. But his underlying reasons were to gain for British subjects in Fiji a greater measure of "popular representation" which at the same time would ensure that the numerically superior Fijians and Indians remained in a state of subservience. Within the wider framework of a confederation of islands centered on Fiji, Scott reasoned, the political and economic ascendancy of its European population would be ensured.

The most influential advocate of island confederation during the interwar years was R. W. Robson, the editor of *Pacific Islands Monthly*. In 1931 he proposed "for the purpose of consultation, so as to secure united action regarding many vital matters of common interest, the formation of a Pacific Islands Association." Robson sought to ensure that all interests in the islands would be represented, but his sympathies lay very much with commercial interests and his arguments were formulated with their wellbeing in mind. In addition, the formation of the Pacific Islands Association would keep "the countless swarming millions of Asia" at bay, thus preserving the Pacific for the "white race."

For the next two decades Robson continued to press for a confederation of islands through the medium of his widely read and influential magazine, but to no avail. In the event, the planters' and traders' idea of a confederation to ensure the future Pacific as their own preserve was overtaken by the events of World War II. Inevitably, perhaps, the initial wartime proposals for confederation were defense-oriented, particulary with reference to the arc of islands lying immediately north and northeast of Australia. As the war progressed and issues of peace began to be discussed, possible options for solving the pressing problems of decolonization and economic development began to be discussed, and the emphasis shifted to one of trusteeship and islander welfare as the basis of regional organization. No longer was confederation seen as the means of according European commercial interests in the islands a freer rein in their exploitation; moreover, the islanders themselves were beginning to develop a definite sense of regional identification. The idea that the Pacific was there for the benefit of its indigenous inhabitants—who were clearly not dying out—was supported not only by many Allied politicians but also by a small yet active corps of European missionaries and academics. That sentiment prevails to this day.

SOURCES AND READINGS: Doug Munro and Richard A. Herr, "Island Confederation and George Westbrook," *Australian National University Historical Journal* 9 (1972): 10-19.

Doug Munro and Richard A. Herr

JALUIT COMPANY. The Jaluit Company was a conglomerate of German trading companies which dominated trade in the Marshall and eastern Caroline islands from the 1870s to the outbreak of World War I. Copra was the basis for Germany's trading activity in the Marshall and Caroline islands. German traders, such as the Hamburg-based Godeffroy und Sohn Company and the Hernsheim company, first moved into the area in the early 1860s. Both companies began operations on Ponape and Kusaie. Godeffroy und Sohn, known for its sponsorship of scientific studies of the Pacific as well as for its commercial enterprises, fell upon hard times. In an effort to save its profitable Pacific ventures, Godeffroy established the *Deutsche Handels und Plantegen-Gesellschaft*. The company soon accounted for almost one-half of all German trading in the Pacific. By 1883 the company had expanded its Micronesian operations to include the Mortlock Islands.

In 1887 Hernsheim and Company and *Deutsche Handels und Plantegen-Gesellschaft* joined with the local Jaluit concern of Capalle and Company in the Marshalls to form the Jaluit Company. In the Marshalls, where Germany held administrative power, the Jaluit Company came to have a monopoly on all trading. The company also controlled trade in the eastern Carolines. In 1899 the German government purchased the Carolines from the Spanish. With the backing of the German government, the Jaluit Company strengthened its position. The trading companies of all other nations were effectively kept out of eastern Micronesia. By 1901 the Jaluit Company stood as the sole trading concern on all but five of the eastern Caroline and Marshall islands. In the western Carolines the persistence of the Japanese and such independent traders as David Dean ("His Majesty") O'Keefe prevented the Jaluit Company from obtaining dominance.

Copra made up 90 percent of the company's exports. The value of the Jaluit Company's import business, however, was twice that of her exports. Iron goods and textiles were brought in from England, canned goods and tobacco from the United States, and hardware and liquor from Germany. In addition, the company supplied the German navy with coal and provided a mail and shipping service for the German administration. In 1905 international pressure forced the German government to allow traders from other nations to return to the eastern Caroline and Marshall islands. Despite the competition, the Jaluit Company showed a dividend of 25 percent as late as 1911. The Jaluit Company ceased operations in 1914 when the Japanese took over control of the islands and forced all German interests out. The company's business was taken over by the *Nanyo Boeki Kaisha* (South Seas Trading Company).

RELATED ENTRIES: German Colonial Empire; Marshall Islands; Micronesia; Ruge and Company, H. M.

SOURCES AND READINGS: Alfred Etens, *Among the Savages of the South Seas: Memoirs of Micronesia, 1862-1868* (Stanford: Stanford Univesity Press, 1958); Florence Mann Spoehr, *White Falcon: The House of Godeffroy and its Commercial and Scientific Role in the Pacific* (Palo Alto: Pacific Books, 1963).
David L. Hanlon

JARNAC, CONVENTION OF. An agreement entered into on 19 June 1847 between the governments of France and Great Britian, the Convention of Jarnac was concerned with the independent status of the Leeward Society Islands (French Polynesia). The treaty is named after the Count of Jarnac, French ambassador to England, who authored the document. For many years British missionaries in Tahiti attempted to gain Britian's political control of the islands, but their efforts were unsuccessful. In 1842 French Admiral Dupetit-Thouars sailed into the Pacific and established a protectorate over Tahiti and the Windward Islands for his country, but anti-French demonstrators continued seeking Britian's support. They openly declared a civil war that lasted until December 1846. In the meantime, diplomatic correspondence between Paris and London ended in a reciprocal agreement—the Convention of Jarnac—that, in general, squelched pro-British sentiment in

Tahiti and outlined the status of affairs in the Windward Islands. In essence, the document states that both countries would recognize the independence of the Leeward Islands (Bora Bora, Huahine, Ra'iatea, etc.), that neither would ever take possession of them, and that no ruler of either the Leeward or Windward islands would ever rule over the entire chain. When France annexed these Leeward Islands in 1880, a flurry of correspondence again passed between the two capitals. Finally in 1888 Great Britian recognized France's outright annexation of the Leeward Islands in consideration of France's military withdrawal from the New Hebrides.

RELATED ENTRIES: Dupetit-Thouars, Abel; French Polynesia.

SOURCES AND READINGS: A. C. Eugène Caillot, *Histoire de la Polynésie Orientale* (Paris: Ernest Leroux, 1910). (Page 277 reproduces the entire agreement.)

Robert D. Craig

JONES, JOHN (1829-1908). A Methodist missionary of the London Missionary Society, John Jones spent over thirty years in the Loyalty Islands. He arrived on Maré in 1854 with Stephen Creagh where they built a successful and prosperous Protestant mission. In 1856 he visited Lifou and started a school for native children. By 1859 he had organized a native teacher's school. He helped Creagh translate and print the New Testament in Maré and journeyed to England in 1868 to publish a second edition. In 1870 he returned to the Loyalty Islands and became entangled in the English-Protestant and French-Catholic disputes. Jones, who had advocated English annexation of the islands since his arrival in 1854, was by now a fairly wealthy landowner. His fight against French influences resulted in the Nouméa administration revoking his commission to preach in 1884. He retired to Sydney until 1887 when he was arrested and expelled from the area. Jones continued missionary work on Aitutaki until his death on 7 August 1908.

RELATED ENTRIES: Creagh, Stephen Mark; Loyalty Islands.

SOURCES AND READINGS: K. R. Howe, *The Loyalty Islands: A History of Culture Contacts 1840-1900* (Honolulu: University Press of Hawaii, 1977); Patrick O'Reilly, *Calédoniens* (Paris: Musée de l'Homme, 1953).

Russell T. Clement

JOSKE, ADOLPH BREWSTER (1854-1937). Joske was a trader, planter, and administrator in Fiji. He migrated to Fiji at sixteen years of age in a brief trading partnership with another settler and then joined his father's extensive trading and plantation interests in the Suva promontory area. Later he established his own wine and spirit, hotel, and plantation business. In 1884 he joined the Crown Colony administration as stipendiary magistrate and inspector of native plantations. After thirty years service, he retired as Commissioner of East and West Colo provinces. He then went to London and published two books of reminiscences, *King of the Cannibal Tribes* (London, 1937) and *The Hill Tribes of Fiji* (London, 1922). He was also known as A. B. Brewster.

RELATED ENTRIES: Fiji.

SOURCES AND READINGS: A. B. Brewster Papers, Museum of Archeology and Ethnology, Cambridge University, Cambridge, England.

Alan Maxwell Quanchi

JUDD, GERRIT PARMEL (1803-1873). A medical missionary and political leader in Hawai'i, Gerrit Judd was born 23 April 1803 in Paris, New York. He arrived in Honolulu on 30 March 1828 to serve as a medical missionary. In 1839 he was appointed by King Kamehameha III to tutor the royal children. Three years later he left the mission to enter Hawaiian politics. He was appointed to the treasury board and became a translator, recorder, and transactor of business with foreigners. In 1843 he was appointed secretary of state for foreign affairs and then minister of finance. From 1845 to 1846 he served as minister of the interior and then in 1849 he was appointed commissioner to France, Great Britian, and the United States. In 1851 he was appointed by the king to help revise the Hawaiian constitution for approval by the legislature in 1852. Many Hawaiians opposed the political views of Judd and his colleague, Richard Armstrong (minister of public education), because they favored Americanization of the islands. When a devastating epidemic of smallpox broke out in 1853 Judd and Richards were blamed for the spread of the disease. They were asked to resign from their positions. After his resignation Judd resumed his medical practice. To supplement his income, he became an active trader in guano. Several years later he turned to the sugar industry where he was instrumental in developing this new industry in the islands during the 1850s and 1860s. After the end of the civil war, a collapse of the sugar industry left Judd jobless. He suddenly died on 12 July 1873 of a paralytic stroke in Honolulu.

RELATED ENTRIES: Armstrong, Richard; Hawai'i.

SOURCES AND READINGS: Gerrit Judd, *Dr. Judd:*

Hawaii's Friend (Honolulu: University of Hawaii Press, 1960); Ralph S. Kuykendall, *A History of Hawaii* (New York: Macmillan Co., 1933).

Brenna J. Rash

JUDD, LAWRENCE McCULLY (1887-1968). Judd, a former senator in the territorial legislature, member of the board of supervisors of the city and county of Honolulu, and president of the Senate, was appointed governor of Hawai'i by President Herbert Hoover on 23 April 1929. He served in this capacity until 1934. Born 20 March 1887, educated in Hawai'i and Connecticut, Judd began his early business career with the Carnegie Steel Company and the Whiting Paper Company. During World War I he served as an aide-de-camp to the brigadier general, first brigade, and in 1920 was made a colonel in command of Hawai'i's national guard and a colonel in the U.S. Army reserves. As governor, Judd improved the public parks and playgrounds in Hawai'i. Also, he took particular interest in state institutions and did much to reduce the cost of administering state programs. Twenty years after his retirement as governor of Hawai'i, Judd was appointed governor of American Samoa. He died 4 October 1968.

RELATED ENTRIES: American Samoa; Hawai'i.

SOURCES AND READINGS: A. Grove Day, *Hawaii and Its People* (New York: Meredith Press, 1968); Edward Joesting, *Hawaii* (New York: W. W. Norton & Co., 1972); Ralph S. Kuykendall and A. Grove Day, *Hawaii: A History* (Englewood Cliffs, N.J.: Prentice-Hall, 1961).

Ned B. Williams

KALAKAUA, PRINCE DAVID (1836-1891). Kalakaua became ruler of Hawai'i on 12 February 1874, after the legislative assembly selected him over Queen Emma, the only other aspirant to the crown. Kalakaua was a champion of the ideas of Kamehameha V, who had given the country the constitution of 1864. Personally, Kalakaua was a man of very pleasing, even impressive manner, who could converse agreeably in English or Hawaiian. He was born 16 November 1836, and was educated at the royal school under the direction of Mr. and Mrs. Amos Star Cooke. Kalakaua was an apt scholar with interests in music, art, writing, archaeology, and public speaking. He contributed to several local newspapers, and through these media he communicated with his people. Politically, Kalakaua believed that the king should be, literally, the ruler of the country, and he lost no opportunity to make his personal influence felt at every turn. He had gained considerable experience in the practical detail of government, both in administrative positions and in the legislature.

One of the most important events which occurred during his reign was his visit in 1874 to the United States, where he was received with the highest honors by President Grant. While there, he brought about the passage of the reciprocity treaty, which was the greatest achievement of his reign. This gave both Hawai'i and the United States duty-free trade, and at once brought about an era of prosperity never before known in the islands.

After his return to the islands from America, Kalakaua and his consort, Kapiolani, crowned themselves king and queen. The purpose of the extravagant ceremony was to confirm the royal family as the ruling dynasty of the kingdom, and to bring the Hawaiian nation to the attention of the world. Kalakaua's popular and noble reign began to decline because of his imperalistic ambitions and his corrupt administrations. It seemed that only the able ministers in his cabinet came and went, while the self-seeking ones, such as Walter Murray Gibson, Claus Spreckels, and Celso Caesar Moreno stayed close to the king. These men, with their schemes to seize land and power, brought the popular opinion against Kalakaua. By the late 1880s the Hawaiians were up in arms because of Kalakaua's suppressive measures and his corrupt dealings with foreign interlopers. Kalakaua was forced to sign a new constitution in 1887 that restricted the power of the throne. Kalakaua naturally resented his loss of authority and prestige, but he soon discovered that he still had some shreds of power, which he used during the remainder of his administration to annoy and sometimes to embarrass the legislative assembly.

After the close of the legislative session in November 1890, King Kalakaua, a sick man, left for California hoping that his health would improve in a different climate. His condition grew worse instead of better, and on 20 January 1891 he died in San Francisco. Although he was a political victim of limited discretion, Kalakaua managed to achieve peace and prosperity for the Hawaiian people, the like of which was never known before.

RELATED ENTRIES: Gibson, Walter Murray; Hawai'i; Kamehameha V; Lili'uokalani; Lunalilo, William; Spreckels, Claus.

SOURCES AND READINGS: A. Grove Day, *Hawaii and Its People* (New York: Meredith Press, 1968); Edward Joesting, *Hawaii* (New York: W. W. Norton & Co., 1972); Ralph S. Kuykendall and A. Grove Day, *Hawaii: A History* (Englewood Cliffs, N.J.: Prentice-Hall, 1961). *Ned B. Williams*

KAMEHAMEHA I (1758-1819). Also known as Kamehameha Nui, the Great, Kamehameha I was born in November 1758, Kohala district, on the island of Hawai'i, the son of Ke'oua Kupuapaikalaninui, a high chief, and of Kekuiapoiwa, a daughter of the former king Alapai. A Hawaiian conqueror and king, Kamehameha by 1810 had united all the Hawaiian islands and had founded the Kamehameha dynasty, the most enduring line of Hawaiian rulers.

In 1779, as a young chief, Kamehameha directed negotiations between his paternal uncle, King Kalaniopu'u, and Captain James Cook, British discoverer of the islands. At Kalaniopu'u's death in 1782, the island of Hawai'i was divided between his sons, Ke'oua and Kiwala'o, and Kamehameha. Despite jealousy between the two cousins, relations were peaceful until July 1782 when a dispute between their chiefs at Keomo led to the death of some of Kamehameha's allies and the outbreak of war. In the ensuing battle at Mokuohai, Kiwala'o was slain, but because the battle was indecisive, Kamehameha was forced to leave some lands to Chief Ke'oua (Kiwala'o's half brother) and other leaders of the opposing camp.

Kamehameha asserted himself more forcefully in 1790, when he invaded the island of Maui and defeated the reigning chief, Kalanikupule. On Maui, Kamehameha acquired Ka'ahumanu, Princess Keopuolani, as his wife. Ka'ahumanu bore him two sons, Liholiho and Kauikeaouli, who each became kings. By 1795 Kamehameha was master of the islands of Hawai'i, Maui, Kaho'olawe, Lana'i and Moloka'i. He crossed over to O'ahu and landed at Waikiki and Waialae. Moving across the plain in the spring or summer of that year, Kamehameha drove the warriors of King Kalanikupule of O'ahu up Nu'uanu Valley and many of them over the Pali. He led frequent campaigns against King Kaumuali'i of Kaua'i but finally acquired the island through peaceful negotiations in 1809. The entire island group was then united under him.

Known among his contemporaries, both European and Hawaiian, for his shrewd business sense, Kamehameha amassed a fortune for his kingdom through a government monopoly on the sandalwood trade and through initiating the collection of port duties from visiting ships. He was an open-minded sovereign who rightfully deserved his title, Kamehameha the Great. His reign was a period of unification, construction, and progress. A man of capable mind and powerful physique, Kamehameha was courageous and skilled in the exercise of war and peace. He was ill for some time before he died on 8 May 1819 on the island of Hawai'i. His bones were concealed in a cave, the location unknown.

RELATED ENTRIES: Cook, (Captain) James; Hawai'i; Kamehameha II; Young, John.

SOURCES AND READINGS: A. Grove Day, *Hawaii and Its People* (New York: Meredith Press, 1968); H. H. Gowen, *The Napoleon of the Pacific, Kamehameha the Great* (New York: Fleming H. Revell Co., 1919); Ralph S. Kuykendall and A. Grove Day, *Hawaii: A History* (Englewood Cliffs, N.J.: Prentice-Hall, 1961).

Ned B. Williams

KAMEHAMEHA II (1797-1824). After the death of Kamehameha I in 1819, his son Liholiho ascended the Hawaiian throne, sharing the realm with Queen Ka'ahamanu, the first *Kuhina Nui* with authority greater than a premier or prime minister. Liholiho, Kamehameha II, who was about twenty-three at the time of his accession, was an amiable prince with some shrewdness but showed serious elements of weakness of character. The first test for the young monarch occurred in 1819 when Kamehameha II, with the support of his able advisers, abolished the ancient *kapu* system which, among other things restricted men and women from eating together. Kamehameha II courageously performed the symbolic act of *'ai noa* (free eating) by eating with the women at a feast he had called at Kailua, Hawai'i. When the meal was ended, he ordered that the pagan carvings and temple idols should be destroyed. However, a number of Hawaiians led by Kamehameha II's cousin, Kekuaokalani, refused to accept this religious revolution, and by December 1819 rebellion against the king had broken out. Kekuaokalani was killed at Kuamo'o by the king's army, thus defeating the last major proponent of the *kapu* system.

American Christian missionaries could not have come at a more opportune moment, for the religious vacuum that had been created could be filled at once by their appeals to the strongly religious-minded Hawaiian people. The first American missionaries to the islands met King Kamehameha II in April 1820, and soon the king granted permission to the missionaries to start a Christian mission at Kailua, the temporary residence of the monarchy. The king and his associates became pupils in the mission's schools and before two years had elapsed, Kamehameha II was reading and writing in Hawaiian and English. Although he has been severely criticized for weakness and vices, credit is due him for the important part he played in the establishment of Christianity and education for the Hawaiian people.

During his reign Kamehameha II not only advanced religious interests, but he encouraged business and political progress in the islands. Sharing the prosperous sandalwood trade with his chiefs, he strengthened domestic unity and generated a more balanced economy. Whaling ships landed in Hawai'i in the early 1820s and with Kamehameha's permission a new industry began to flourish. New foreign business interests in Hawai'i prompted Kamehameha to strengthen diplomatic ties with the United States, Russia, and Britain. Desiring to promote goodwill among his foreign allies and to increase his knowledge of the world, Kamehameha sailed for America and England in November of 1823.

The royal party, including Kamehameha II's favorite Queen Kamamalu, and Governor Boki of O'ahu and his wife, arrived in England 13 May 1824 and proceeded to London. On 8 July of that year, Queen Kamamalu died of measles. Despite every care, Kamehameha II died on 14 July 1824, a royal victim of his desire to know the world beyond his home islands.

RELATED ENTRIES: Hawai'i; Kamehameha I.

SOURCES AND READINGS: A. Grove Day, *Hawaii and Its People* (New York: Meredith Press, 1968); Edward Joesting, *Hawaii* (New York: W. W. Norton & Co., 1972); Ralph S. Kuykendall and A. Grove Day, *Hawaii: A History* (Englewood Cliffs, N.J.: Prentice-Hall, 1961).   *Ned B. Williams*

KAMEHAMEHA III (1814-1854).

Kauikeaouli, a son of Kamehameha I, had more of his father's strong qualities than any of his brothers. Born 17 March 1814 and a minor when he succeeded to the throne (6 June 1825), the young king did not become actual ruler until 1833. During his minority Queen Dowager Ka'ahumanu was regent and *Kuhina Nui*. The reign of Kamehameha III (1825-1854) was the longest in Hawaiian history; and during this thirty-year period, the government and the people made marked progress in domestic affairs, in foreign relations, in social, educational, and cultural achievement, and in the growth of commerce and industry.

There was distinct progress in law enforcement during the regency of Ka'ahumanu, but when she died on 5 June 1832 her strong ruling hand was lost. Her successor as *Kuhina Nui* was Kinau, a daughter of Kamehameha I, who was considerably older than the eighteen-year-old king. The two ruled jointly for a year, but in 1833 the king, resentful of his half sister's control, threw off all restraints and began a two-year course of license and dissipation. The hula and other ancient sports were revived, and many of the people indulged in gambling, drunkenness, and other vices in a reaction against what they felt to have been a puritanical rule.

The need for a new code of laws became necessary, so on 5 January 1835, Kamehameha III proclaimed a penal code which was the result of much consultation among the high chiefs. The numerous chapters of the code included strong penalties for homicide, theft, adultery, divorce, fraud, and drunkenness. In 1839 the king declared the right of religious freedom which, among other things, ended the friction over the establishment of the Roman Catholic church in Hawai'i. In 1840 this liberal monarch gave the people a voice in the government by granting the first writ-

ten constitution, abolishing the old feudal controls, and establishing a limited monarchy with a legislature and a judiciary system. In the late forties, the king presented his subjects with one of their greatest initiatives—the Great *Mahele*—which divided the land, with the people receiving their share. The independence of the kingdom was recognized by America, Britain, and France, and many treaties were entered into during Kamehameha III's reign. In 1852 he gave his people an improved constitution allowing the people of Hawai'i to participate in the making and executing of the nation's laws.

Kamehameha III earned the title of most wise and beloved of all Hawaiian monarchs for supporting the Christian missionary effort, designing the educational pattern for Hawai'i, and taking the lead in putting the finances of the kingdom on a sounder basis. Marked advances in social and cultural life were also achieved during Kamehameha III's eventful reign which ended on 15 December 1854 when the king died at the age of forty-one.

RELATED ENTRIES: Hawai'i; Kamehameha I, II, and IV.

SOURCES AND READINGS: A. Grove Day, *Hawaii and Its People* (New York: Meredith Press, 1968); Edward Joesting, *Hawaii* (New York: W. W. Norton & Co., 1972); Ralph S. Kuykendall and A. Grove Day, *Hawaii: A History* (Englewood Cliffs, N.J.: Prentice-Hall, 1961).   *Ned B. Williams*

KAMEHAMEHA IV (1834-1863).

Prince Alexander Liholiho, born 9 February 1834, the grandson of Kamehameha I was proclaimed Hawaiian king on 15 December 1854, the day Kamehameha III died. Kamehameha IV inherited all the mental keenness of the Kamehameha line as well as the vast family fortune. While Kamehameha III had been extremely democratic in his views and habits, Kamehameha IV was more inclined to be aristocratic, and the etiquette and the ceremonial of the royal court became more noticeable during his nine-year reign.

The new king, a month younger than twenty-one years of age at the time of his inauguration, was one of the sons of Kinau and Governor Kekuanaoa. His high mental ability had been supplemented by a good education in English; he was very fluent in that language as well as in Hawaiian. Kamehameha IV ascended the throne having enjoyed the best educational advantages which his island kingdom afforded and also the benefit of foreign travel. As a result, when he assumed the reins of government, he remodeled the cabinet and made many other institutional changes inspired by his knowledge of foreign governments, especially England's.

In June 1856 the king was married to Emma Booke, a granddaughter of John Young, the English friend and adviser of Kamehameha the Great. Queen Emma was a woman of culture and refinement, with a kindly and lovable character—a gentlewoman in the finest sense of the word. Prince Albert Edward was born to the royal pair on 20 May 1858 and was granted the title of His Royal Highness, the Prince of Hawai'i.

Kamehameha IV's major concern during his reign was the decrease in the native population which had dropped from seventy thousand to fifty-seven thousand between 1853 and 1866. At all times, disease was prevalent, and very little effort was made to prevent it. Kamehameha IV, in a message to the legislature, said the decrease of the population was a subject "in comparison with which others sink into insignificance; for our first and greatest duty is that of self-preservation." In spite of his earnest appeal, the king received little support from the legislature. Finally, in 1859, the king and queen themselves undertook to raise money for a hospital. In the course of a few weeks, they succeeded in obtaining enough pledges for a substantial amount. The Queen's Hospital is the finest monument of the service and loyalty of the royal family to the people of Hawai'i.

During Kamehameha IV's reign, business and foreign relations shifted to a new, more solid foundation in Hawai'i. The whaling industry was booming in the 1850s; the annual average number of arrivals of whaling ships was 400. Soon the sugarcane industry flourished, from several hundred tons exported annually to thousands of tons shipped to various foreign destinations. In government, there was a swing away from the American democratic political ideals to a new constitution in which popular rights were subordinated to the power of the king. In foreign affairs, there was a continuous effort to stabilize and improve relations with other countries and to make secure the independence of Hawai'i. In short, Kamehameha's reign was a period of transition, prosperity, and social progress.

Kamehameha IV's rule ended unexpectedly on 30 November 1863, when he died after a brief illness at the age of twenty-nine. The king's health, undermined by asthma, was further weakened by grief at the loss of his only child who died the previous year, leaving no direct heir to the Hawaiian throne.

RELATED ENTRIES: Hawai'i; Kamehameha III and V; Young, John.

SOURCES AND READINGS: A. Grove Day, *Hawaii and Its People* (New York: Meredith Press, 1968); Ed-

ward Joesting, *Hawaii* (New York: W. W. Norton & Co., 1972); Ralph S. Kuykendall and A. Grove Day, *Hawaii: A History* (Englewood Cliffs, N.J.: Prentice-Hall, 1961).
                                              Ned B. Williams

KAMEHAMEHA V (1830-1872). Prince Lot, Kamehameha IV's elder brother, was born 11 December 1830. Like his brother, Lot was well educated and had traveled widely. As Kamehameha V, Lot's stern character led him to establish a strong government. Among the important changes which he made were a new but less democratic constitution, and the merging of the House of Nobles and the popular assembly of the representatives of the people into one legislative body.

Unlike his younger brother, Kamehameha V did not have brilliant mental attainments but he had a better grasp of practical matters. He had served as minister of the interior during the last six years of his brother's reign, and for more than a year had headed the department of finance. During his reign, he entered personally into all the discussions of important issues; he selected ministers who shared his opinions and gave them full support. Some of his policies aroused fierce opposition, but it is clear that he sincerely believed that his acts were directed to the good of the nation.

Kamehameha V, "the last great chief of the older type," believed that the mantle of his grandfather, the conquering Kamehameha I, gave to the king the right to lead the people firmly into the proper paths. His ways of thinking and acting were despotic, but his was a benevolent despotism. He wished his subjects to be hardworking and thrifty and felt that they must be protected from thoughtless waste and idle temptation.

Like his brother, Kamehameha V reigned for nine years. He was a bachelor. Many suggestions were made that the king ought to marry to provide an heir to the throne. But the king declined to marry. As a single man, Kamehameha was free to dedicate his energies to the welfare of the people. To this ruler, credit is due for many public improvements, among which was the erecting of Ali'iolani Hale, which became the judiciary building in 1893. Many other public improvements were carried out during this ruler's constructive reign.

Kamehameha V's reign ended on his forty-third birthday, 11 December 1872. On his deathbed, Kamehameha V declined to name in the constitutional manner who his successor should be, thus ending the Kamehameha dynasty.

RELATED ENTRIES: Hawai'i; Kamehameha IV; Lunalilo, William.

SOURCES AND READINGS: A. Grove Day, *Hawaii and Its People* (New York: Meredith Press, 1968); Edward Joesting, *Hawaii* (New York: W. W. Norton & Co., 1972); Ralph S. Kuykendall and A. Grove Day, *Hawaii: A History* (Englewood Cliffs, N.J.: Prentice-Hall, 1961).   *Ned B. Williams*

KANAKA REVOLT OF 1878-1879. An uprising in New Caledonia which left two hundred colonists dead and nineteen wounded, the Kanaka insurrection broke out in June 1878 during a famine caused by a severe drought. Directed by a chief named Atai, the Melanesians revolted against the European seizure of their lands, compulsory labor, the removal of sacred objects from tribal burial grounds, the lack of roads in the interior, the widespread destruction caused by colonists' cattle, and the penal regime's neglect of tribal needs and welfare. Military posts and isolated settlers on the western and southeastern coasts were the first attacked. Colonists and some convicts were massacred as islanders ransacked and burned two hundred outposts. The French, led by Governor Jean Olry, retaliated by destroying villages. The fighting ceased in April 1879 and the colonists returned to their holdings in June. Melanesian losses were never calculated. The revolt greatly hindered New Caledonia's colonial development and contributed to its unfavorable penal island reputation.

RELATED ENTRIES: New Caledonia.

SOURCES AND READINGS: Wilfred G. Burchett, *Pacific Treasure Island: New Caledonia*, 4th ed. (Philadelphia: David McKay, 1944); Linda Latham, *La Révolte de 1878* (Nouméa: Société d'études historiques de la Nouvelle-Calédonie, 1978); Virginia Thompson and Richard Adloff, *The French Pacific Islands: French Polynesia and New Caledonia* (Berkeley: University of California Press, 1971).
Russell T. Clement

KAVA. Called *sakau* in Micronesia, *'ava* in Hawai'i, and *yanggona* in Fiji, kava is a nonalcoholic, euphoria-producing beverage made on most Pacific islands from the root of the *Piper methysticum*, a plant of the pepper family with heart-shaped leaves and jointed branches. The plant is cultivated widely, grows to four meters in height, and probably originated at a site west of Fiji.

The active ingredient in kava is alkaloidal in nature and is present as a glycoside which is split into free alkaloid and sugar by one of the enzymes in saliva. The effects of eating or drinking preparations of the yellowish root have been variously described, with agreement on the following: feelings of stimulation followed by sedation; sleepy intoxication of a melan-choly, silent, and drowsy sort. Strong doses of kava cause loss of muscular control and also affect vision.

The *Piper methysticum* root may be used dried or freshly dug. In Polynesia and southern and eastern Melanesia, the root is either chewed or it is pounded and pulverized with a wooden beater. The chewing method appears to be the original method; the pounding method was an innovation originating in western Polynesia. The chewed or pounded kava is then infused in water. It may be mixed by hand in a carved kava bowl or strained through coconut spathe into a bowl or half-coconut shell. In many parts of Micronesia, hibiscus bark fibers are wrapped around the beaten, moist pulp, and then twisted and wrung. The first cup of the resulting ooze is then given to the ranking members of the group.

Kava use has different cultural meanings and relates to various social institutions across the Pacific. In general, kava use in Polynesia displays and reinforces political structure. Kava is drunk in a strict order of social status. It is also enjoyed in a context of social intercourse and conversation. In Melanesia, kava is often a way to communicate with the supernatural world of the ancestors. Absolute silence may be demanded when men are intoxicated. Kava use is also often connected with notions of male and female status. Some cultures allow both sexes to prepare and drink the drug, others restrict kava solely to men.

Although attempts have been made in the past by several island governments to suppress the drug, kava continues to be used and appreciated. In some areas it is a substantial cash crop for rural agriculturalists. Kava has been advocated by some islanders as a traditional and acceptable alternative to alcohol and the problems of alcoholism in the Pacific.

RELATED ENTRIES: Alcohol in the Pacific; Betel Nut Chewing; Kava and Betel.

SOURCES AND READINGS: Beth F. Avery, "Micronesia's Potent Potables," *Glimpses* 18, no. 4 (1978); J. P. Buckley, R. Angelo, and J. Moureen O'Hara, "The Pharmacology of Kava," *Journal of the Polynesian Society* 76, no. 1 (1967): 101-2; Daniel H. Efron, ed., *Ethnopharmacologic Search for Psychoactive Drugs* (Washington, D.C.: Public Health Service Publications, Government Printing Office, 1967).
Lamont C. Lindstrom
Dirk Ballendorf

KAVA AND BETEL. The word *kava* conjures up scenes of Polynesian chiefs seated in a circle round an elaborately carved bowl debating affairs of state, but kava is by no means restricted to Polynesia. Made from the chewed or pounded roots of *Piper methysticum*, the infusion known generally by the Polynesian term *kava* is found as well in island Melanesia and New Guinea and on Ponape and Kosrae in the eastern Caroline Islands of Micronesia. Unlike its use in these other cultural areas, *kava* is known and used all over Polynesia (excepting New Zealand and Easter Island) and the ceremony surrounding preparation and consumption of this indigenous drug has received its greatest cultural efflorescence in the Samoa-Tonga-Fiji area of western Polynesia. Generally speaking, kava use in Melanesia and New Guinea is conspicuous for its lack of ceremonial, although the two Micronesian societies noted above developed the kava ceremony in a manner reminiscent of western Polynesia.

By and large where kava is consumed in Oceania betel is not. Betel usually is prepared as a quid consisting of the nut of the *Areca* palm, the leaves of kava's close botanical relative, *Piper betle*, and some powdered lime, the lot of which is then chewed. While betel chewers often possess handsomely carved paraphernalia for carrying and preparing their concoction, no social ceremony attends betel consumption to rival the kava circle. Kava is made nowhere else in the world; it is the aboriginal Oceanic drug substance par excellence. By contrast, the betel chewing habit is distributed from the east coast of Africa, along parts of the Arabian peninsula, in the Indian subcontinent, through most of mainland and island Southeast Asia, up the China coast, and into the western portions of Oceania. In Oceania, betel chewing is restricted to island Melanesia and (aboriginally) to lowland New Guinea, with the exception of the westernmost islands of Micronesia: Yap, Palau, and the Marianas.

Kava attracted considerable attention from chemists and pharmacologists beginning in the nineteenth century, and pharmacological research on the active ingredients in kava continues. Despite this, a complete pharmacological understanding of kava does not exist, although the drug is known to have diuretic, soporific, anticonvulsant, spasmolytic, analgesic, local anesthetic and antimycotic properties, among others. Unlike beverage alcohol, kava is not fermented, brewed, or distilled, and it must be emphasized that its physiological effects are very different from alcohol. Numerous reports in the literature emphasize that kava consumption does not distort thinking, although heavy indulgence makes it difficult to walk and induces sleep. Fewer pharmacological investigations on betel have been conducted, however. Von Euler and Domeij (1945) carried out such a study on the areca nut and Farnworth (1975, 1976) has provided phytochemical analyses of both *Areca catechu* and *Piper betle*.

Both of these traditional drugs continue to be consumed avidly in many parts of the islands and often they are mixed with introduced drug substances. Kava may be taken together with alcohol or consumed first and followed by alcohol "chasers." Sometimes betel is chewed simultaneously with a wad of chewing tobacco. Kava and betel users often accompany their habit by smoking tobacco. Studies of the interactions among these various substances and how they affect human beings remain to be carried out, although betel has been clearly implicated in the development of oral cancer (e.g., Cooke 1969).

RELATED ENTRIES: Alcohol in the Pacific; Betel Nut Chewing; Kava; Tobacco.

SOURCES AND READINGS: E. E. V. Collocott, "Kava Ceremonial in Tonga," *Journal of the Polynesian Society* 36 (1927): 21-47; R. A. Cooke, "The Pathology of Oral Cancer," *Papua and New Guinea Medical Journal* 12:3 (1969): 84-90; E. R. Farnworth, "*Areca catechu* and *Piper betle* in Papua New Guinea: An Elemental Analysis," *Science in New Guinea* 3, no. 3 (1975): 211-14 and "Betel Nut—Its Composition, Chemistry and Uses," *Science in New Guinea* 4, no. 2 (1976): 85-90; Paul Freund and Mac Marshall, "Research Bibliography of Alcohol and Kava Studies in Oceania: Update and Additional Items," *Micronesica* 13 (1977): 313-17; R. Hansel, "Characterization and Physiological Activity of some Kawa Constituents," *Pacific Science* 22 (1968): 293-313; Mac Marshall, "Research Bibliography of Alcohol and Kava Studies in Oceania," *Micronesica* 10 (1974): 299-306; Robert J. Theodoratus, "Betel Chewing," (Master's thesis, University of Washington, 1953); U.S. Von Euler and B. Domeij, "Nicotine-like Actions of Arecoline," *Acta Pharmacologica* I (1945): 263ff.   *Mac Marshall*

KELLY, CELSUS (1900-1975). A scholar and historian of the Pacific, Kelly was born in Shepparton (Victoria), Australia, 27 June 1900, and joined the Franciscan Order (OFM) in 1918. He studied in Ireland and Rome and then, in 1927, he returned to Australia where he held a number of responsible positions in his province, many involving working with young people. His first historical article appeared when he was managing editor of the *Crusader*. His interest in the activities of the Franciscan friars who accompanied some of the Spanish explorers of the Pacific led him into a long career of search for documents throughout the world, especially in Spain. Father Kelly assiduously collected, classified, and edited many unpublished manuscripts concerning the discoveries in Oceania of Álvaro de Mendaña, Pedro Fernández de Quirós, and Luis Vaéz de Torres, covering the period from 1567 to 1607 and comprising a total of nine volumes. Documented and edited in the original language, mostly in Spanish with English commentaries, his accounts of the Spanish voyages fill the six volumes of his *Austrialia Franciscana* (1963-1973). Volume six was edited jointly with Father Gerard Bushell, OFM, who is continuing the collection mostly with documents collected by Father Kelly. In 1966 the Hakluyt Society published his two-volume work *La Austrialia del Espiritu Santo*, but Father Kelly's crowning work, a book which is of tremendous help to scholars in the field of exploration is his *Calendar of Documents: Spanish Voyages in the South Pacific and Franciscan Plans for its Islanders* (1965). Father Kelly was awarded the decoration of Knight Commander in the Order of Isabella the Catholic by the Spanish government before he died on 5 October 1975. He is buried in the friary of Maryfields near Sydney.

RELATED ENTRIES: Malaspina, Alessandro; Mendaña de Neira, Álvaro de; Quirós, Pedro Fernández de; Spain in the Pacific; Torres, Luis Váz de.

SOURCES AND READINGS: "Fr. Celsus Kelly," *Provincial Chronicle*, Franciscan Province of the Holy Spirit, Sydney, July 1975; "Father Celsus Kelly, OFM," *Provincial Chronicle*, Franciscan Province of the Holy Spirit, Sydney, November 1975. Personal correspondence: Kelly to Gschaedler, 1945-1973.

André Gschaedler

KERMADEC ISLANDS. A dependency of New Zealand, the Kermadec Islands are administered as a wildlife area by the land and survey department. The five principal islands lie between 29° 10′ south latitude and 31° 30′ south latitude. The total land area is 33 km² (12.74 mi²) and the islands are 965 km (599.6 mi) northwards from Auckland. The climate is pleasant and the vegetation is lush. There is a manned meteorological station on Raoul, which is the only inhabited, and largest, island in the group.

Frank P. King

KING, SAMUEL WILDER (1886-1959). Appointed as the Territory of Hawai'i's eleventh governor (1953-1957), King was the only Hawaiian ruler since Lili'uokalani with Hawaiian blood. King was born in Honolulu 17 December 1886 and in 1905 was appointed to the United States Naval Academy, graduating in 1910. He was named to the Territory Tax Commission to the Board of Supervisors of the City and County of Honolulu and later served with the Home Rule Commission. In 1934 he was elected delegate to the U.S. Congress, serving in that capacity until 1942. As governor of Hawai'i, King's major concern was preparing the islands for statehood. He died on 12 March 1959 in Honolulu.

RELATED ENTRIES: Hawai'i.

SOURCES AND READINGS: A Grove Day, *Hawaii and Its People* (New York: Meredith Press, 1968); Edward Joesting, *Hawaii* (New York: W. W. Norton & Co., 1972); Ralph S. Kuykendall and A. Grove Day, *Hawaii: A History* (Englewood Cliffs, N.J.: Prentice-Hall, 1961). *Ned B. Williams*

KIRIBATI. Formerly known as the Gilbert Islands, Kiribati consists of three groups of islands: the seventeen Gilbert Islands, the eight Phoenix Islands, and the eight Line Islands. Although the total land area is only 684 km² (264 mi²), the islands are scattered across more than 5 million km² of ocean. The islands are low-lying coral atolls, many with lagoons, having an elevation of only four meters. The only exception is Banaba (Ocean Island) with a maximum elevation of 78 m (256 ft). The islands are situated in the central Pacific between 169° east and 150° west longitude and between 40° north and 11° south latitude. The climate of the central Gilberts, Banaba, and the Phoenix Islands is maritime equatorial but that of the islands farther north and south is tropical maritime. The mean annual temperature is 27° C (80° F). Vegetation is rather poor, particularly in the Gilbert Islands. The sandy coral soil has little depth or nutriment. Consequently, the indigenous flora has few species and few introduced plants flourish. Prominent are the coconut and the pandanus, a screw pine. Most islands also have breadfruit and pawpaws. The only traditionally cultivated crop is the *cyrto-sperma chamissonis*, a large coarse root known as *babai*. There is no natural fauna apart from birds and the Polynesian rat, but cats, dogs, pigs, and chickens now abound on most islands. The seas around the islands and the lagoons swarm with fish, which form an important part of the islanders' diet.

Kiribati is midway between Polynesia and Micronesia, and the people are of Micronesian stock with Polynesian traces and influences. They are thought to have reached these islands during the course of migratory voyages from the west, possibly from the region of Indonesia. Nothing is known of the original inhabitants of the Phoenix and Line islands. Population is 56,452 (1980 estimate). The only exports are copra, phosphate, which is virtually exhausted, and small quantities of fish and handicrafts.

Pre-European History. Kiribati, the Gilbertese people, appear to have two separate myths about the origin of their race which, although interwoven by the passage of time and the handing down of verbal traditions, are easily distinguishable. The earlier of the two creation myths speaks of a creator, *Nareau*, and a pantheon of gods and goddesses created by him from the void. This tradition appears to have become interwoven with a "Tree of Life" myth, based upon a Samoan legend, with stories of a cannibal race indulging in skull worship on the sacred mountain of Maungatabu. This tree had its own pantheon of heroes and heroines and they, as well as those of *Nareau*, are the subdieties of Gilbertese paganism. These stories tell of civil disturbances in Samoa, of the breaking of the "Tree of Life" and the dispersion of its people to Kiribati, of their meeting there with people of similar ancestry. These stories seem to indicate a Gilbertese belief that their islands were inhabited by Samoans before their arrival. Efforts to trace any substantial reference to the Samoan deity *Tangaroa* have been unsuccessful, and this seems to indicate that the dispersion preceded his rise to preeminence in Samoan religion. This omission from Gilbertese tradition appears to place settlement between 1000 and 1300 A.D. Research into Gilbertese genealogy seems to support such approximate dates.

The islands, though separated by open sea, developed a strikingly similar social order and a unity of tradition, broken only in the north and even there only in the early nineteenth century. Having the same cosmogony gave unity in tradition. The classificatory family, the *utu*, was the social unit ruled by its old men and grouped around its ancestral lands or *kainga*. Interfamily alliances, formed to win power and land, rose and fell so that civil war was endemic. Social behavior was governed by custom and the sanction of public opinion, interpreted by the elders. Fear of the supernatural grew from the cult of hero-ancestor worship; magic was part of the natural order of life and *maka*, superhuman authority and power, was invested in those who were acknowledged as leaders.

There are some outstanding events of the pre-contact era worthy of record. There are stories of northern invaders reaching the southern Gilberts and perhaps more important are the records of the invasions by the southern Gilbertese, emanating from Beru and led by *Kaitu* and *Uakeia* who carried with them to many islands the traditions of the *Karongoa* clan. It is probable that these invasions were responsible for maintaining the uniformity in tradition and social organization. *Kaitu* also conquered Nui in Tuvalu and to this conquest is attributed the Gilbertese patois still spoken on Nui.

In the north and central Gilberts several small kingdoms flourished and those of Butaritari, Abaiang, Tarawa, and Abemama still existed when the islands were annexed by Britain. The most famous kingdom was that of *Tem Binoka* of Abemama, whose story is partly related in R. L. Stevenson's *In the South Seas*. There are also well-authenticated stories of civil wars in the islands about the middle of the nineteenth century which were pagan-religious in origin and later developed into a struggle between Christianity and paganism. Internecine wars are reported from many of the northern islands during the same period, particularly Tarawa, but these appear to have been struggles for temporal supremacy, aided by foreign castaways and traders in arms and liquor.

European Contact. European discovery dates from the sixteenth century; it is thought that Christmas Island and Nonouti were sighted in 1537 by Grijalva's mutinous crew. Quirós is thought to have discovered Butaritari in the northern Gilberts in 1606. After Captain John Byron's visit to Nikunau, in H.M.S. *Dolphin* in 1765, the remaining sixteen islands of the Gilberts were discovered largely as an unintended result of increasing commercial activity in the Pacific. The last islands to be discovered were Onotoa and Beru in 1826. Captain James Cook rediscovered Christmas Island in 1777, and Fanning and Washington were discovered by an American, Captain Nathaniel Fanning, in 1798. In the Phoenix Islands, Manra (Sydney Island) was sighted in 1823, Nikumaroro (Gardner) in 1824, and Canton, Orona (Hull), and Phoenix about 1825.

From the early days of their discovery in the nineteenth century until about 1870, the waters of Kiribati were a favorite sperm whaling ground. With the whalers came the first beachcombers. One of the first Europeans to reside in the islands landed about 1837, and the number steadily grew. Trading ships began to visit regularly from 1850, and a few of the beachcombers became respected residents, traders, and agents for overseas firms. Trade in coconut oil began about 1860 and in ten or twenty years gave way to the sale of copra.

Between about 1850 and 1875, blackbirders raided many of the islands but the warlike Gilbertese are said to have fiercely resisted; there are accounts of several ships being captured and destroyed and the crews being slaughtered. In 1900 phosphate was discovered at Banaba and concessions were obtained to mine and export it. Christianity followed soon after the first traders, and Hiram Bingham of the American Board of Commissioners for Foreign Missions landed at Abaiang in 1857 where he set up his mission headquarters. The London Missionary Society entered the southern Gilberts in 1870. In 1888 two Catholic fathers of the Order of the Sacred Heart began work at Nonouti.

World War II. Within two days of the Pearl Harbor attack, Banaba was bombed and Japanese marines landed on Tarawa and Butaritari but withdrew after only a brief stay. Most of the Europeans escaped by traveling in open boats to Nonouti, 200 miles south of Tarawa, where they were picked up. The Japanese returned in force, and most of the Europeans who had chosen to remain were rounded up and later executed. At Banaba many of the Gilbertese who had been kept there as laborers were killed towards the end of the war. In November 1943 the American forces drove the Japanese from the islands and fought a particularly bloody battle at Tarawa. The Japanese at Banaba were bypassed by advancing American forces and were not forced to surrender until 1945. For the three years when American forces were stationed in the Gilberts, many Gilbertese came into contact with the modern world for the first time. This contact was an education in itself, and the isolation of former years was rudely shattered. The war years brought a realization of modernity which might otherwise have taken a generation to develop.

Government. Britain established the Western Pacific High Commision in 1877 and appointed a high commissioner. Although the high commissioner's jurisdiction was confined exclusively to British subjects, nevertheless all islands where British subjects resided inevitably came within the orbit of British interests. In 1892 Captain E. H. M. Davis of H.M.S. *Royalist* proclaimed Abemama a British protectorate and then visited all of the other islands where he raised the British flag. The Ellice Islands, now Tuvalu, were also visited, and a Gilbert and Ellice islands protectorate was established with headquarters at Tarawa. Banaba was annexed and added in 1900. With the rapid development of the phosphate industry and the increasing importance of Banaba, the headquarters was moved there in 1907. The protectorate became a colony in 1916, and Fanning and Washington islands were included. The Tokelau Islands were also added in 1916 but were placed under New Zealand jurisdiction in 1925. Christmas Island was added in 1919 and the Phoenix Islands in 1937. The islands of Flint, Caroline, Vostok, Malden, and Starbuck in the Line Islands were added in 1972, and the Gilbert and Ellice islands colonies were separated from the Western Pacific High Commission.

A ministerial form of government was established in 1974 and the *Maneaba ni Maungatabu*, the national parliament with elected members, was created. The eight former Ellice Islands separated from the Gilbert and Ellice islands and became, on 1 October 1975, the new state of Tuvalu. This separation came about as a result of a referendum in which the overwhelming majority of the Tuvaluan people voted in favor of separation. The first major step towards Kiribati's independence took place when the first stage of internal self-government was achieved in November 1976. Full internal self-government came in January 1977. Finally, on 12 July 1979, Kiribati became a sovereign independent republic with a president as head of state.

RELATED ENTRIES: Beachcombers; Bingham, Hiram Jr.; Byron, John; Cook, (Captain) James; Line Islands; London Missionary Society; Ocean Island; Pease, Benjamin; Phoenix Islands; South Pacific Commission; South Pacific Forum; Tuvalu; Western Pacific High Commission.

SOURCES AND READINGS: P. A. Crowl and E. G. Love, *Seizure of the Gilberts and Marshalls* (Washington, D.C.: Government Printing Office, 1955); Great Britain, Foreign and Commonwealth Office, *Gilbert and Ellice Islands Colony: Report for the Year 1973* (London: Her Majesty's Stationery Office, 1976); Arthur Francis Grimble, *A Pattern of Islands* (London: John Murray, 1957); Taomati Iuta et al., *Politics in Kiribati* (Suva: Institute of Pacific Studies, 1980); Henry Evans Maude, *Of Islands and Men: Studies in Pacific History* (Melbourne: Oxford University Press, 1968); University of the South Pacific and the Ministry of Education, Training, and Culture, *Kiribati: Aspects of History* (Tarawa: USP, 1979).
Richard Overy

KONG AH BANKRUPTCY. Considered Tahiti's dirtiest political scandal, the Kong Ah bankruptcy occurred in 1933 at the height of the depression in Tahiti when Yune Sing, director of the Chinese-controlled Kong Ah Society (Pape'ete), filed for bankruptcy. Chinese population in Tahiti comprised approximately 11 percent, but the Chinese practically controlled the entire economy, especially the copra trade. Since 1921 the Kong Ah Society had built up an extensive network of "family" members throughout the islands. When the depression came, the company was severely hit and its director Yune Sing filed for bankruptcy in the courts. The French governor proposed that during litigation the company be allowed to continue in the interest of the island economy. For almost a year appointed directors ran the business and presumably pocketed the profits and the money obtained in liquidating assets while engaging in other illegal sales. When this action became public knowledge, the creditors demanded the demise of the arrangement, and several government officials were implicated in the affair. The *Courrier* newspaper was especially sharp in its criticisms whereupon Governor Montagné prohibited its distribution for several months. Colonial pressure in Paris eventually forced the governor's recall and the appointment of a new governor. Chamber of Commerce President Emmanuel Rougier and Privy Council member Armand Hervé were arrested and received prison sentences while Judge Barranger fled the country. The scandal of the Kong Ah bankruptcy and the Rougier affair were closed.

RELATED ENTRIES: French Polynesia.

SOURCES AND READINGS: Robert D. Craig, *History of Tahiti* (Laie, Hawaii: Institute for Polynesian Studies, forthcoming); Philippe Mazellier, ed., *Le Mémorial Polynésien*, vol. 3 (Pape'ete: Hibiscus Editions, 1977).   *Robert D. Craig*

KOTZBUE, OTTO VON (1787-1846). A Russian explorer who led two naval expeditions around the globe in 1815-1818 and 1823-1826, Kotzbue was born in Reval, Estonia, the son of the famous writer, August von Kotzbue. He attended school in St. Petersburg and the naval academy in Krönstadt. Kotzbue was called upon by A. J. Krusenstern to take part in the latter's world voyage of 1802-1806 as mate aboard the *Nadesha*. Having given good account of himself during that expedition, Krusenstern and Count Romanzoff, the imperial chancellor, summoned him to lead another such voyage in 1815. Kotzbue was directed to search for a passage between the Pacific and Atlantic oceans in the vicinity of the Bering Straits. His three-year expedition aboard the *Rurik* took him to the northern reaches of the Pacific, including the coasts of Alaska and Siberia, but he failed to find the mythical Northwest Passage. Instead Kotzbue carried out a detailed investigation of the Pacific islands, visiting Easter and Penrhyn islands, the Carolines and Marianas, with extended stays in Hawai'i and Radak in the Marshalls. Kotzbue circumnavigated the globe yet a third time in 1823-1826, commanding the frigate *Predpriatie* on what was primarily a scientific voyage but was also charged with carrying a cargo to Kamchatka and protecting Russian commercial interests in California from foreign smugglers. In actuality, most of the cruise was spent in the Pacific islands, including the Society Islands, Hawai'i, and Radak. Kotzbue visited Samoa in 1824, entered Pago Pago harbor, but refused to go ashore on account of the ferocity of the inhabitants. Kotzbue was a sharp critic of

the activities of other nations in these regions, particularly of the Spanish colonial administration in California. His attacks on the English missionaries in the Society Islands prompted a bitter response from one of them, William Ellis, who charged Kotzbue with, among other things, serving Russian imperialist interests in the Pacific. Kotzbue published detailed records of his voyages, which included observations of the various Pacific peoples he encountered: *Entdeckungsreise in die Südsee*, 3 vols. (1821) and *Neu Reise um die Welt* (1830). English translations of both appeared soon after. Kotzbue retired from the navy in 1829 and died in Reval in 1846.

RELATED ENTRIES: Krusenstern, Adam Johann von.

SOURCES AND READINGS: *Allgemeine Deutsche Biographie*, vol. 16 (Berlin: Duncker & Humblot, 1969); Heinrich Schnee, ed., *Deutsches Kolonial-Lexikon*, vol. 2 (Leipzig: Quelle & Meyer, 1920).

Ralph C. Canevali

KOUKARE (1848?-1933). An early convert to Christianity in East Tanna, Vanuatu (New Hebrides), Koukare was eventually recognized as paramount chief. He was one of the first involved in copra production on the island and worked as a buyer at Weasisi for trader G. Khyn in the 1870s. He was one of the founders of the Tanna Law (1906-1912), a period of Christian "Big Man" government. Koukare also served as major informant for the anthropologist Charles Humphreys.

RELATED ENTRIES: Tanna; Vanuatu (New Hebrides).

SOURCES AND READINGS: Charles Humphrey, *The Southern New Hebrides: An Ethnological Record* (Cambridge: At the University Press, 1926).

Lamont C. Lindstrom

KRÄMER, AUGUSTIN FRIEDRICH (1865-1941). German ethnologist and explorer of the South Pacific, Krämer studied medicine in Tübingen and Berlin and natural science in Kiel. In 1889 he joined the imperial navy and soon after began a series of expeditions to the German protectorates in the South Pacific where he collected abundant anthropological data. Krämer's first cruise (1893-1895) on the S.M.S. *Bussard* included a twelve-month stay in Samoa. Krämer visited the islands once again, 1897-1899, during which time he was involved in various German intrigues among the rival Samoan chiefs. In 1906 Krämer traveled as anthropologist aboard the S.M.S. *Planet* in the Atlantic and Indian Oceans, and to the Bismarck Archipelago. He also visited Truk, Yap, and Palau in the Carolines in 1906-1907 and led a German naval expedition to New Mecklenburg.

Krämer commanded the second phase of the Hamburg South Sea Expedition to the Caroline and Marshall islands in 1909-1910, gathering much anthropological, zoological, geological, and geographical information along the way. Krämer later became the scientific director of the Linden-Museum in Stuttgart and also published many scholarly works, including *Die Samoa-Inseln* (1902-1903), based on the ethnographical and biological material accumulated during his South Seas travel.

RELATED ENTRIES: American Samoa; German Colonial Empire; Western Samoa.

SOURCES AND READINGS: Hans Meyer, ed., *Das Deutsche Kolonialreich* (Leipzig and Vienna: Bibliographisches-Institut, 1909-10); Heinrich Schnee, ed., *Deutsches Kolonial-Lexikon*, vol. 2 (Leipzig: Quelle & Meyer, 1920). *Ralph C. Canevali*

KRUSENSTERN, ADAM JOHANN VON (1770-1846). The Russian admiral and explorer who led the first Russian expedition to circle the globe, Krusenstern was born in Estonia, and educated in Reval and at the naval academy at Krönstadt. In 1787 his schooling was interrupted by the outbreak of war with the Turks and Swedes in which Krusenstern won great distinction. He served with the British navy in the Atlantic in the wars against France in the 1790s. During these years Krusenstern became increasingly determined to see Russia enjoy a larger share of the trade with the Orient, then dominated by English and Dutch merchants. He urged the Russian minister of trade, Count Romanzoff, to sponsor a naval expedition under his command to the Far East. Russian business interests, especially concerned with strengthening diplomatic and commercial ties with Japan, also lent their support to the mission and vied with Krusenstern for control. Krusenstern's two vessels, the *Nadesha* and *Neva*, set sail in 1802 and reached the Marquesas, Hawai'i, and other Pacific islands in 1804, before proceeding onward to Japan. Although the voyage failed to produce any real commercial benefits, it did result in the accumulation of a wealth of scientific information. Krusenstern was a noted researcher and published many scientific monographs in such fields as hydrography, geography, and philology upon his return to Russia. Together with Count Romanzoff, Krusenstern was influential in sponsoring the Kotzbue expedition around the globe in 1815-1818 and later became involved in the administration of the Russian naval academy at Krönstadt. His publications include an account of his world voyage: *Reise um die Welt* (1811-1812); *Recueil de mémoires hydrographiques* (1824); and *Atlas de l'océan Pacifique* (1829).

RELATED ENTRIES: Kotzbue, Otto von; Langsdorf, George.

SOURCES AND READINGS: Theodor von Bernhardi, *Vermischte Schriften*, vol. 1 (Berlin: G. Reimer, 1879); Heinrich Schnee, ed., *Deutsches Kolonial-Lexikon*, vol. 2 (Leipzig: Quelle & Meyer, 1920). *Ralph C. Canevali*

KUBARY, JOHANN STANISLAUS (1846-1896). The foremost ethnographer of the peoples in the Caroline Islands, especially the Truk Islands, Mortlocks, and Palau, Kubary was born in Warsaw 13 November 1846. He started working on a five-year project in 1869 to collect ethnological materials for the Godeffroy Museum in Hamburg. He first went to Samoa, then to the Marshalls, Ponape, and Yap, accompanied by his Samoan housekeeper, Nosi. In Palau (1871-1873) he helped during the influenza epidemic which claimed the lives of at least 150 people. After a three-month stay in Europe, he returned to the Pacific where he stayed, for the most part, until his death. After the Godeffroy Company failed in September 1879, Kubary was forced to mortgage his plantation on Ponape and to travel around the western Pacific looking for work related to his ethnographical interests. In New Guinea he worked for the Hernsheim company's trading station at Kuragakaul (1885-1887) when he joined up with the New Guinea Company. In 1891 he and his family returned to Germany for a short visit. They returned to New Guinea where Kubary worked until 1895 when the company served notice on him. Back on Ponape, he was beset by Spanish claims on his property at Mpomp and he was forced to live off advances from the firm of Henry Spitz and the generosity of his wife's relatives. Upset by this string of bad luck, Kubary committed suicide on 9 October 1896. Besides his half-dozen writings on Micronesian societies and his fourteen major publications on Micronesia, he is also best remembered as being made the number-five chief of Melekeok village where he attended village council meetings dressed only in a loincloth and large spectacles with tortoiseshell rims and carrying a small handbag full of betel nut.

RELATED ENTRIES: Caroline Islands; Micronesia; Papua New Guinea; Semper, Carl; Western Samoa.

SOURCES AND READINGS: Theodor von Bernhardi, in G. Thilenius, ed., *Ergebnisse der Südsee-Expedition, 1908-1910*, vol. 1 (Hamburg: L. Friederichsen, 1917) and his *Ethnographische Beitrage und Nachbarschaft: Soziale Einrichtungen der Pelauer* (Berlin: Asher, 1885). *Mark L. Berg*

LABOR TRADE. As a result of plantation and mining activities in the semitropical countries of the South Pacific and the abolition of slavery within the British Empire in 1833, labor problems arose for the South Pacific entrepreneur and the sugar-plantation economies of the West Indies and Mauritius. Almost immediately labor trade, the indentured system of labor, developed as a scaled-down but legal replacement of slave labor. In 1847 Benjamin Boyd, a New South Wales entrepreneur, engaged two boatloads of Pacific islanders to work on his sheep runs but the experiment was unsuccessful.

Meanwhile, within the Pacific islands themselves, European sandalwood traders, ship captains, and settlers regularly obtained islander labor and soon found that better work was given by a person who was removed from his home island to work elsewhere. So an informal interisland labor service was developed to supply the muscle power of the growing economy of the islands as they became woven into the European trading network.

In 1862-1863, the most horrendous experiences of the Pacific labor trade occurred when up to twenty ships raided islands in the eastern Pacific for laborers to work in the plantations and mines of Peru. Work conditions were appalling, and few were returned to their homes.

The most significant labor trade was to Queensland, starting in 1863. The European settlers there assumed that arduous work in the more tropical parts of the colony could not be satisfactorily or healthily carried out by Caucasians. At a time when ideas of racial superiority were strongly held, Europeans readily accepted the idea that the more "primitive" peoples from lesser-developed areas were suitable laborers for these areas, and the justification was advanced that through such labor these "savage, pagan" peoples could become "civilized" in the Western fashion. Queensland colonizers generally found the Australian aborigine an unsuitable worker; schemes for bringing in Asiatic coolies were mooted at various times, but the most ready source of cheap labor was the South Pacific. So, in 1863, Robert

Towns brought in a boatload of island laborers and the scheme rapidly spread.

Initially, the southern islands of the New Hebrides (Vanuatu) provided the main supply base; but, by the beginning of the 1870s, the northern islands in that group and the Solomon Islands were also being canvassed. Then, briefly, for eighteen months in 1883-1884, New Britain, New Ireland, and the Louisiade Archipelago off New Guinea became areas of intense labor recruitment where almost six thousand islanders were obtained. In the 1860s and 1870s the islanders worked as stockmen on sheep and cattle runs as well as being agricultural laborers and domestics. Increasingly, however, in the 1870s, sugar became established as the main industry of the coastal wetlands, and it was here that the Melanesian laborer became vital. By the 1880s the Queensland government had prohibited the use of the Melanesian outside this area. The islanders provided the manpower in clearing the land and growing and harvesting the cane as the industry spread north, from the Logan River to Maryborough, Bundaberg, Mackay, Ingham, and Cairns.

The early 1880s saw the peak period of sugar expansion and the peak period of Melanesian importation. Thereafter, increasing doubts and criticisms came to be voiced about this labor system. The British government became concerned when New Guinea was involved, and in Queensland itself some liberally minded people, as well as the growing Labor movement, expressed disapproval of what was considered a cheap, servile, alien, and colored work force. Abuses in recruiting practices in New Guinea and a Royal commission brought legislative moves to end the recruitment system in 1890; but for a variety of reasons, mainly economic, the importation of island labor continued during the 1890s.

There were some cases of kidnapping of islanders and of other devious means used to coax or decoy people aboard a recruiting boat. There were also numerous cases of violence between an island community and a recruiting vessel. Furthermore, areas new to labor-trade practices (or to Western trading generally) could expect to suffer violence and coercive recruiting practices by the Europeans—as in New Guinea in 1883-1884—but after a period of contact a more regular trading system emerged. Instances such as the *Carl*, *Young Australian*, *Hopeful*, *Ceara*, or *Stanley* developed a notoriety about the harsh and brutal aspects of the labor trade. Most missionaries (for example, John Paton) expressed vehement condemnation of the trade, and various humanitarian-minded persons (such as Lord Selborne, lord chancellor in Britain) urged the cessation of the trade which they likened to slavery. Most recruiting trips, however, followed a fairly regular procedure of barter to obtain willing recruits. Presents were exchanged to grieving relatives, and most recruits voluntarily, if not excitedly, set off on this new adventure to obtain money and status, to "grow up" (a new form of initiation), or to escape (for a variety of reasons). The indenture contract provided that the recruit would be paid £6 per year, plus keep, for a period of three years; he would then be returned to his home village, although occasionally this latter condition was not fulfilled. Frequently recruits re-enlisted (over 20 percent in the Solomons) after finding difficulties in readjustment upon their return home.

The British government acted in 1872 and 1875 to regulate the trade with definitions of kidnapping, licensing procedures, and the appointment of a high commissioner for the western Pacific. Meanwhile, the Queensland government acted, more hesitantly, with various regulatory devices. After the creation of the Commonwealth of Australia, however, with the "White Australia" policy fully emblazoned, recruitment ceased in 1904, and the remaining islanders were to be repatriated in 1906. About three thousand islanders protested this policy and petitioned King Edward VII for permission to stay in Queensland; almost one thousand did remain.

About 61,000 islanders were imported to Queensland between 1863 and 1904. Fiji was the second area seeking major recruitment for its sugar plantations. Recruitment from the Solomons to Fiji continued until 1910. The Germans in Samoa also sought Melanesian labor while a local system grew up within German New Guinea. French settlers in New Caledonia initially obtained laborers from the Loyalty Islands and later from the New Hebrides.

RELATED ENTRIES: Fiji; German Colonial Empire; *Hopeful* Scandal; Melanesian Recruitment to Queensland; Melanesians and Colonial Servitude; New Caledonia; Papua New Guinea; Samoa; Vanuatu (New Hebrides); Western Pacific High Commission.

SOURCES AND READINGS: Peter Corris, *Passage, Port, and Plantation: A History of the Solomon Islands* (Melbourne: Melbourne University Press, 1973); R. K. Howe, "Tourists, Sailors and Labourers: A Survey of Early Labour Recruiting in Southern Melanesia," *Journal of Pacific History* 13 (1978): 22-35; Owen Parnaby, *Britain and the Labour Trade in the South West Pacific* (Durham: Duke University Press, 1964).   *W. Ross Johnston*

LACKAWANNA AGREEMENT. Taking its name from the United States naval vessel, *Lackawanna*, on which terms were agreed to, 12 July 1881, the Lackawanna agreement sought to dampen the intermittent warfare between the various Samoan factions struggling for preeminence by establishing a single government in Samoa. This was not the first time an effort had been made, but all previous tries at centralizing the Samoan political system had failed because of strong traditional rivalries between various powerful Samoan factions whose attentions throughout the nineteenth century were focused upon traditional objectives of politics. The parties to the agreement, urged to declare peace by the foreign consuls, were the Tupua and Malietoa factions. Complicating the political scene was the jostling for equal or dominant positions by the representatives of the three powers, the United States, Britain, and Germany, who frequently had recourse to visiting naval commanders to back up their demands and claims upon the Samoans.

Under the agreement, Malietoa Laupepa was to be king and Tupou Tamasese Titimaea was to be vice-king. Malietoa was to rule for seven years. The headquarters of the government was at Mulinu'u, which had become the nineteenth-century seat of Samoan government, although it was of no political significance in the traditional system.

The newly constituted government had a weak beginning and never became really effective as a governing instrument. Tamasese's rivals were slow to accept his position. The *Ta'imua* and *Faipule*, the legislative arm of the government, was months in getting itself organized. Although the government enacted laws, these were indifferently enforced by district chiefs who, for example, refused to forward to Mulinu'u the proceeds from a poll tax which they had collected under the authority of the central government. Much of this money collected on the district level was reserved for the purchase of armaments, obviously in preparation for the next war.

The district leaders were also doubtful of the ability of the Mulinu'u government to resist foreign pressures. Based upon previous experience, this was an understandable feeling. Within the government itself there was continual intriguing for positions on the basis of traditional rivalries and concerns.

German consular and commercial representatives in Samoa campaigned actively against the Malietoa administration. The German objective was to become the dominant Great Power in Samoa. In this they were opposed by the United States. O. W. Steubel, the German consul, and Theodor Weber, the representative of the German firm, *Deutsche Handles-und Plantagen-Gesellschaft*, urged Tamasese to withdraw from the Mulinu'u government, which he did in January 1885. (His Tupua adherents had been intriguing against Malietoa from the beginning of the new government.) Tamasese hoisted his flag at the traditional political center of Leulumoega and declared his renunciation of the *Lackawanna* agreement. The Germans harassed the Malietoa government into virtual ineffectiveness, and with the establishment of the Tamasese puppet government, the Malietoa regime created by the *Lackawanna* agreement effectively came to an end. The Germans deported Malietoa to the Cameroons. By late 1888 his government was a mere shadow and warfare once again resumed in Samoa.

RELATED ENTRIES: American Samoa; *Malietoa*; Weber, Theodor; Western Samoa.

SOURCES AND READINGS: R. P. Gilson, *Samoa 1830 to 1900: Politics of a Multi-Cultural Community* (Melbourne: Oxford University Press, 1970); Sylvia Masterman, *The Origins of International Rivalry in Samoa, 1845-1884* (London: G. Allen & Unwin, 1934).   *Jerry K. Loveland*

LANGSDORF, GEORGE HEINRICH VON (1774-1852). A German naturalist and explorer, born in Wöllstein in Hesse, Langsdorf was educated as a physician in Göttingen, although his real interests were always in natural history. He served as physician for German soldiers in Portugal from 1798 to 1802 and thereafter returned to Göttingen, where he received news of the Russian explorer Krusenstern's planned voyage around the world. He joined that expedition as naturalist, visiting many Pacific islands, including Hawai'i and the Marshalls, between 1802 and 1806. Langsdorf then returned to Russia where he was employed in the civil service until 1820. He left to coordinate German emigration to Brazil, but his stay there so ruined his health that he was forced to return to Germany in 1831. Langsdorf died in Freiburg in 1852. His *Bemerkungen auf einer Reise um die Welt* (2 vols.), a scientific account of his jour-

ney with Krusenstern, remains one of the most important pieces of Polynesian travel literature.

RELATED ENTRIES: Krusenstern, Adam Johann von.

SOURCES AND READINGS: *Allgemeine Deutsche Biographie*, vol. 17 (Berlin: Duncker & Humblot, 1969).
Ralph C. Canevali

LAPÉROUSE, JEAN-FRANÇOIS DE GALAUP, COMTE DE (1741-1788). A French navigator who made significant contributions to Pacific exploration, Lapérouse was born 23 August 1741, the eldest son of a noble family near Albi in southern France. He entered naval service at the age of fifteen. During the Seven Years' War (1756-1763), he was wounded and captured by the British (1759) but later exchanged as a prisoner of war. During the American Revolution, he participated in the Battle of the Antilles (West Indies) against the British (1779) and in successful battles in the Hudson Bay area of North America (1782). In 1785 the French government commissioned Lapérouse to undertake an extensive, scientific voyage to the Pacific to search for all lands which had escaped the vigilance of Cook. The expedition was one of the first massive, scientific voyages ever to be conducted. For three years, Lapérouse crisscrossed the Pacific gathering valuable data on Pacific islands and peoples. At Easter Island (April 1786) he described in detail the Rapanui islanders. On the way to Hawai'i and Alaska, he spent four months at Monterey, California, where he was the first to describe its general coastline and to make complete charts of the area. From California, Lapérouse sailed to Macao (South China coast). From there he sent his journals and scientific observations on to the French Admiralty.

From China, Lapérouse sailed through the northern straits of Japan (Lapérouse Straits), stopped in Kamchatka, and headed once more to the central Pacific. In Samoa, eleven of his men were killed in a skirmish with the islanders. In January 1788 he reached Botany Bay (Australia) where he expedited his last recorded journals to France (published in 1796). Lapérouse and crew were never heard of again, and for forty years his fate remained a mystery. A search expedition in 1791-1792 by Admiral d'Entrecasteaux found nothing. In 1827 Peter Dillon, English navigator-adventurer, found several items on the island of Vanikoro in the Santa Cruz group that indicated that Lapérouse had been there. In 1828 French explorer Dumont d'Urville sailed through the islands in search of further information or remains. On Vanikoro, Dumont d'Urville sighted many other items from the wreckage and learned from the islanders that the two ships had indeed been wrecked on the reef and that the survivors had been massacred. Expeditions in the area in 1901, 1938, and 1956 found no new evidence. The expedition in 1964, however, uncovered two dozen objects all which were identified as belonging to Lapérouse's two ships, the *Boussole* and the *Astrolabe*.

RELATED ENTRIES: D'Entrecasteaux, Antoine; D'Urville, Dumont; Dillon, Peter; France in the Pacific.

SOURCES AND READINGS: Maurice de Brossard, *Lapérouse: des combats à la découverte* (Paris: Editions France-Empire, 1978); Jean F. G. de Lapérouse, *Voyage de La Pérouse autour du monde . . .*, 4 vols. and atlas (Paris: Imprimerie de la République, 1796. (Translations in English, German, and Italian exist.)

Robert D. Craig

LAPITA CULTURE. The archaeological discovery of Lapita culture is of major importance in the study of Polynesian origins. Having its source in the later Neolithic cultures of the Philippines and eastern Indonesia between 1500 and 1000 B.C., Lapita culture penetrated the western Pacific by way of Melanesia, its bearers being Austronesian-speaking voyagers who were probably descendants of a Mongoloid population occupying mainland eastern Asia about six to seven thousand years ago. Highly mobile as a result of developing an advanced maritime technology that included the construction of far-ranging canoes, Lapita colonizers brought to Tonga (via Fiji) a unique style of pottery. Introduced to Tonga about 1300 B.C., the pottery was sand-tempered and open-fired, baked usually with a distinctive red slip. With its basic forms ranging from globular cooking pots to open, round- or flat-based food bowls, the pottery was made up to about 500 B.C., and was outstanding in its geometric and complex anthropomorphic decoration, incised or dentate-stamped with toothed, wooden implements similar to later Polynesian tattoo chisels. Decorative motifs included simple parallel lines and curves, eye-designs, rope and arcade motifs, rectangular meanders, interlocking *Y*'s, and indented circles in a range of motifs that readily identified the pottery within western Oceania and culturally fixed its Philippine-Indonesian origin.

Forming small coastal and offshore island settlements wherever they made landfall in western Oceania, the ancestral Polynesian-Lapitan migrants developed a primitive economy based on marine and shell-fishing with accompanying exploitation of all primary plant foods supplemented by pig and domestic fowl. In addition to carrying untanged adzes of various types into Polynesia, the voyagers also introduced tattoo implements, shell fishhooks (probably) and, most likely, the Polynesian social system characterized by its emphasis on aristocratic ranking. The study of Lapita culture over the past twenty years has considerably increased knowledge of Polynesian origins. Linguistics and archaeological research have broadened understanding of one of man's great maritime achievements—the conquest of the Pacific.

RELATED ENTRIES: Polynesian Culture (Ancient).

SOURCES AND READINGS: Peter Bellwood, *Man's Conquest of the Pacific* (London: Collins, 1977); S. M. Mead, ed., *Exploring the Art of Oceania* (Honolulu: University Press of Hawaii, 1979); James Siers, *Taratai* (Auckland: Millwood Press, 1977).

Alan Taylor

LATIANARA, RATU ASERI S. (1880-1940). A high chief of the province of Serua, island of Vita Levu, Fiji, Ratu Aseri was born 1 February 1880, son of Ratu Isikeli Tubailagi and Adi Kinisimere Tavailagi (from the leading chiefly family of Cuvu Nadroga). In May of 1912 he was installed *Ka Levu* (high chief) and *Vunivalu* (war chief) over four major tribes in twenty-six villages in Serua. As "a chief of the old school" and knowing no English, Ratu Aseri was instrumental in persuading the Fijian government to open the Queen Victoria High School, which had been open exclusively to sons of chiefs, not to children of commoners. He assisted in recruiting labor and supervising the construction of the Queen's Road from Suva to Lautoka. Ratu Aseri was the chief assessor to the Native Lands Commission in the disputes between the high-ranking chiefs of Bau and Verata and also held the same position in Cakaudrove between two ranking chiefs there. Ratu Aseri is remembered by his subjects as being a hard worker, extremely charitable in his daily distribution of food and provisions, an accomplished fisherman, and preserver of the natural environment. Ratu Aseri was awarded the Certificate of Honour for his loyalty and able leadership and he was greatly mourned when he died on 6 February 1940. His eldest son Ratu Tevita Mara Latianara succeeded him.

RELATED ENTRIES: Fiji.

Ratu Penaia L. Latianara

LAUAKI, NAMULAU'ULU MAMOE (?-1915). Samoan chief and orator, Lauaki founded the Mau movement. For generations the movers and shakers of Samoan politics were certain powerful orators, or *Tulafale*, of particular districts on Savai'i and Upolu known as Tumua and Pule. These orators controlled the disposition of several great titles collectively known as the *tafa'ifa*. Lauaki Namulau'ulu Mamoe was one of the most prominent of these powerful orators in the nineteenth and early twentieth centuries. His home was Safotulafai, where he was the chief orator in the Fa'asaleleaga district. One of the Pule districts, its ancestral loyalties were to the Malietoa family, one of the great families in Samoa. The title *Lauaki* is actually a Tongan title and was given to the family during a visit to Safotulafai by King George I of Tonga.

Even in his early twenties, Lauaki established himself as a consummate politician, skilled in oratory and learned in the traditions and history of Samoa which the great orators manipulated to political advantage. His name appears repeatedly as a participant in the great political events in Samoa from the 1860s on. He was intensely Samoan, but he moved freely in and out of the European culture that was being established in Samoa at that time. His loyalties were linked with the fortunes of Malietoa Laupepa during Samoa's time of troubles in the late nineteenth century. His oratorical skills were brought frequently to the service of Laupepa and he was able on occasion to sway the loyalties of wavering groups and individuals to the Laupepa's cause.

He was present during the making of the 1868 confederation at Mulinui. He was a severe critic of the constitution established in 1875 by the American colonel, A. B. Steinberger. He apparently disapproved of the secondary role the Steinberger constitution gave to Laupepa, and he was one of those who urged Laupepa to sign the deportation order by which Steinberger was dismissed from the government and deported from Samoa.

He continued to support the cause of Laupepa, at the same time attempting to uphold the power of Pule. His oratorical and political skills were utilized in the service of both. He was also noted as a skilled adversary on the battlefield. For a time he participated in the German-sponsored government of Tupua Tamasese Titimaea. He became disenchanted with the Tamasese regime, however, when the latter began assuming some of the important *tata'ifa* titles. Lauaki led a group which conferred the Malietoa title upon Mata'afa Iosefa, but later he shifted his loyalties back to Laupepa.

When Germany annexed Samoa at the end of the nineteenth century, Lauaki was disappointed and hoped for the eventual withdrawal of the Germans. He became embroiled in disputes with the German governor, Wilhelm Solf, and even petitioned the kaiser for his removal from Samoa. Solf felt that as long as there were rallying points for dissident Samo-

an groups German rule would be unstable in Samoa, and he began to destroy the remnants of traditional Samoan power. He diminished the authority of the quasi-parliamentary groups, the *Ta'imua* and *Faipule*, as well as the status of the traditional great chiefs. Lauaki was incensed by this action and he toured the country organizing a countermovement to Solf. His following was limited, however, and he failed to rally many Samoans to his cause. His movement was called the *Mau* of *Pule* or the *Mau* of Lauaki. Solf attempted to come to terms with him but Lauaki would not compromise. Finally, in April of 1909, Lauaki with nine other dissidents and their families were exiled to the German colony in Saipan. After World War I began and New Zealand occupied Western Samoa, an Allied vessel picked up the exiles to bring them home, but Lauaki died of dysentery on the journey before reaching Samoa on 14 November 1915.

He died as he had lived, protesting substantive changes in the power structure of the traditional Samoan system. There was scarcely a political event in Samoa for forty years in which he was not a participant. His fame as a brilliant political strategist and orator continues in Samoa today.

RELATED ENTRIES: *Malietoa*; *Mau* of *Pule*; Solf, Wilhelm; Steinberger, Albert; Western Samoa.

SOURCES AND READINGS: J. W. Davidson, "Lauaki Namulau'ulu Mamoe: A Traditionalist in Samoan Politics," in J. W. Davidson and Deryck Scarr, eds., *Pacific Island Portraits* (Wellington: A. H. and A. W. Reed, 1970). *Jerry K. Loveland*

LAVAL, LOUIS (1808-1880). A French Roman Catholic priest of the Order of the Sacred Hearts who accompanied Fathers Caret and Murphy to the Gambier Islands in 1834, Laval was born 9 February 1808. The Christianization of these islands became his life's work. In 1836 Laval and Caret unsuccessfully attempted to establish a Catholic mission in Tahiti. Laval returned to the Gambier Islands where he labored until 1871 except for a two-year mission to the nearby Tuamotu Archipelago (1849-1851). He enjoyed enormous success and became very interested in Gambier's ancient culture and chants. The Roman Catholics gained such control that they drafted and enforced a strict and moral constitution which caused problems with European traders and visitors. In 1871 Laval was accused of wielding despotic powers. Although the investigation cleared him, he was advised to move to Tahiti. Laval returned to Gambier only once, in 1876. Until his death in Tahiti on 1 November 1880, Father Laval wrote about ancient Mangarevan history, culture, religion, and language.

RELATED ENTRIES: Caret, François; French Polynesia.

SOURCES AND READINGS: Patrick O'Reilly, *Tahitiens* (Paris: Musée de l'Homme, 1962).

Russell T. Clement

LAWRY, WALTER (1793-1859). An early Methodist minister and missionary in the Pacific, Lawry was born in Cornwall, England, and sailed to Australia in 1817. In 1818 he was appointed by the British Wesleyan Conference to travel to Tonga as a missionary. Impetuous and headstrong, by turns overoptimistic and depressed, he agonized over whether or not he should go. Finally, he decided to accept the call, and he and his wife departed for Tonga, arriving 16 August 1822. The fourteen months Lawry spent in Tonga were not happy ones; his wife's health was delicate, the mission made seemingly no progress, he was not given a missionary companion, and charges of irregular conduct were laid against him by the London committee. He left Tonga 3 October 1823, sailing first to Sydney and then to England to fight the charges against him. He was successful in defending himself, and from 1825 till 1843 he was a circuit preacher in England, as well as holding several superintendencies. In 1843 he was appointed general superintendent of Wesleyan missions in New Zealand. Energetic and imaginative in the pursuit of his duties, he nevertheless became embroiled in disputes over money, policy, and personalities. Again, charges were laid against him and he was forced to travel to London to refute them. He returned to New Zealand amid a storm of protest because of a cut in missionary allowances and newspaper accounts of his alleged "secular pursuits." Again he was forced to defend himself and was again exonerated. Ill health and near blindness forced him to retire in 1854, and in 1856 he moved to Parramatta where he died in 1859.

RELATED ENTRIES: Tonga.

SOURCES AND READINGS: E. W. Hames, *Walter Lawry and the Wesleyan Mission in the South Seas* (Wellington: Wesley Historical Society, 1967); Lucy Marshall, *Walter Lawry: Cornwall, Australia, Tonga, New Zealand* (Redruth, England: Cornish Methodist Historical Association, 1967); A. Harold Wood, *Overseas Missions of the Australian Methodist Church* (Melbourne: Aldersgate Press, 1975) vol. 1: *Tonga and Samoa*.   *Ronald Shook*

LEENHARDT, MAURICE (1878-1954). A French Protestant missionary and New Caledonia's foremost ethnologist, linguist, and scholar, Leenhardt was sent to the colony in 1902 by the Paris Société des Missions Evangéliques. His first step was to found the mission village of Do Neva at Houlaiou. This later became an important center for native culture and education. Leenhardt returned to Paris in 1926 and spent his life studying, teaching, and writing about Melanesian society and languages. He helped found the *Société des Etudes Mélanésiennes* (1938); occupied the History of Primitive Religions Chair at the Sorbonne (1942-1950); was the first director of the *Institut Français d'Océanie* (1947-1948); and served as president of the *Société des Océanistes* (1944-1954). A prolific writer, his numerous publications remain an invaluable and important part of New Caledonian and Melanesian literature. He died in Paris on 26 January 1954.

RELATED ENTRIES: Melanesia; New Caledonia.

SOURCES AND READINGS: *Journal de la Société des Océanistes* 10 (1954):5-76; Patrick O'Reilly, *Calédoniens* (Paris: Musée de l'Homme, 1953).

Russell T. Clement

LE MAIRE, JACOB (1585-1616). A Dutch navigator and explorer, Le Maire joined with a fellow countryman, William Schouten, to search for another route to the Dutch East Indies via the southern tip of South America without using the passage of the Strait of Magellan. Promoters of this expedition hoped to circumvent the monopoly enjoyed by the vessels of the Dutch East India Company, for this company's charter, granted in 1602, provided that only company vessels could trade with the East Indies by way of the Cape of Good Hope or the Strait of Magellan.

Two vessels, one large and one small, set sail from Texel in June 1615 for the Western Hemisphere. In early December they arrived at Port Desire in Patagonia. Here a fire accidentally destroyed the smaller craft, but no loss of life occurred. Proceeding southward down the eastern coast of South America, the larger vessel eventually came to a short and narrow seaway far below the Strait of Magellan. The Dutch called this passage Le Maire Strait. After passing through this strait, members of the expedition sighted on 29 January 1616 a snow-covered high point of land which they named Cape Horn, after an old town in north Holland. The expedition rounded the Cape, entered the Pacific, and then proceeded in a northwestward direction.

In the course of their voyage across the Pacific, the Dutch visited a number of islands and atolls, including some in the Tuamotu Archipelago and the north Tonga group. By July the northern coast of New Guinea had been reached where some skirmishes occurred with unfriendly islanders. The expedition then proceeded to the Moluccas (or Spice Islands) and from there to Jakarta on the island of Java. Governor Jan Pieterszoon Coen, the top Dutch administrative officer in the East Indies, confiscated the ship and its cargo because in his opinion and that of his council serious infringements upon the special commercial privileges of the Dutch East India Company had been made. In an expedition under the command of Admiral Joris van Spilbergen (or Spielbergen) a number of crewmen together with Le Maire and Schouten were sent back to the Netherlands. Schouten eventually arrived safely in his native land, but Le Maire died at sea during the long passage homeward.

RELATED ENTRIES: Schouten, William C.

SOURCES AND READINGS: John C. Beaglehole, *The Exploration of the Pacific*, 3d ed. (London: A. & C. Black, 1966); W. A. Englebrecht, ed., *De ontdekkingsreis van Jacob Le Maire en Willem Cornelisz. Schouten in de jaren 1615-1617: Journalen, documenten en andere bescheiden* (The Hague: M. Nijhoff, 1945); J. A. J. de Villiers, trans. and ed., *The East and West Indian Mirror* (London: Printed for the Hakluyt Society, 1906).   *Bernerd C. Weber*

LEONORA (1872-1874). The *Leonora* was the best-known ship mastered by the notorious Captain Bully Hayes. She was formerly known as the *Pioneer*, the ship of Captain Benjamin Pease, and had been used for piracy, blackbirding, and head-hunting in the Pacific. Hayes took over the ship in 1872, had it painted white, and renamed it the *Leonora* after one of his twin daughters. The *Leonora* was a brigantine and looked like a yacht. Her master cabin contained a fine gun collection. She also carried four cannons. According to the gossip of that period, Hayes used her in similar gruesome fashion as his predecessor, Pease. However, it is more likely the *Leonora* was used in a slightly more respectable manner than earlier. Hayes had copra stations scattered around the Caroline and Marshall Islands and sold his copra to the German firm of Godeffroy and Company in Apia, Samoa. On 15 March 1874 the *Leonora* was at anchor in Utwe harbor on Kosrae Island, most easterly of the Carolines, when a tropical storm caused her to drag anchor and pile into a reef where she was pounded and sunk by the high surf. The sinking of the *Leonora* led to tales of buried treasure on the island of Kosrae. Frank Clune and Louis Becke wrote that the ship's boats and most of the cargo, including some gold, were removed before the ship sank. Hayes escaped Kosrae in one of the ship's boats to avoid a British man-of-war searching for him. He intended to return to Kosrae, but he was killed by one of the crew on his next ship. In November 1964 an American school teacher, Harvey Segal, and a Kosraen fisherman, Alik Luke, found the wreck of the *Leonora* in nine fathoms of water. This was verified by Scripps Oceanography divers in 1968. Some artifacts of the *Leonora* may be seen in the museum in Kolonia, Ponape, Caroline Islands, and in the Scripps Oceanography Laboratory in La Jolla, California.

RELATED ENTRIES: Labor Trade; Micronesia; Pease, Benjamin; Ruge and Company, H. M.

SOURCES AND READINGS: Frank Clune, *Captain Bully Hayes* (Sydney: Angus and Robertson, 1970).   *Harvey G. Segal*

LEUCAENA LEUCOCEPHALA. A tropical leguminous tree found in many parts of Southeast Asia and Oceania, *Leucaena* is known on Guam and the Marianas as *tangantangan*, as *ēkoa* and *koa haole* in Hawai'i, and as *vaivai* in Fiji. It originated in southern Mexico and Central America and was known to the Mayas. It was transported in the sixteenth century to the Philippines from Mexico as a by-product of the galleon trade. The Philippines was the apparent distribution point for other Pacific areas. *Leucaena* has protein-rich foliage and is widely used as a browse legume. It is also a source for fuel wood, shade, jewelry, charcoal, fences, and for poles. It is famous for being pest-resistant and withstanding grazing, cutting, fire, and drought. *Tangantangan* is especially prominent on Guam, Saipan, and Tinian. Following World War II the United States naval administration used it for the revegetation of these islands to prevent additional soil erosion and to protect watersheds.

RELATED ENTRIES: Commonwealth of the Northern Mariana Islands; Guam.

SOURCES AND READINGS: James L. Brewbaker and E. Mark Hutton, "Leucaena: Versatile Tropical Tree Legume" in Gary M. Ritchie, ed., *New Agricultural Crops* (Boulder, Colo.: Westview Press, 1979), pp. 207-12.   *Russell A. Apple*

LEVUKA. Levuka, on the island of Ovalau, was the first permanent settlement of foreigners in Fiji. Its earliest foreign resident, David Whippy, who was encouraged to settle there by the Fijian chief Tui Levuka arrived in 1825. By the early 1870s at the height of its importance Levuka boasted over two thousand foreigners, four Christian churches, a mechanics institute and numerous mercantile houses and hotels. The economic mainstay of Levuka's early years was the *bêche-de-mer* trade which developed between the late 1820s and the early 1850s. Levuka provided the traders with a safe harbor for repairs, a pool of skilled boat builders, interpreters and pilots, and a depot for mail. During the 1850s despite a hiatus in economic activities, the town grew and acquired Roman Catholic and Wesleyan missionaries, and British and American consular agents. With the cotton boom in the late 1860s Levuka became the center of European economic, political, and social activities. At the same time, race relations between Fijians and foreigners, which had been largely egalitarian and harmonious in the early years, deteriorated markedly. After cession to Britain in 1874 Levuka enjoyed the status of capital of Fiji, but only briefly. British officials in Fiji decided that the narrow coastal plain on which Levuka was situated was not suitable for a capital, and in 1882 the government moved to Suva. Levuka declined rapidly into a political and economic backwater, but in the mid 1960s a Japanese tuna-fishing enterprise was established in the town which is also the administrative and commercial center for the *Lomaiviti* (central Fiji) district.

RELATED ENTRIES: Fiji; Suva; Whippy, David.

SOURCES AND READINGS: R. A. Derrick, *A History of Fiji* (Suva: Government Press, 1963); W. T. Pritchard, *Polynesian Reminiscences* (London: Chapman and Hall, 1866); Caroline Ralston, *Grass Huts and Warehouses* (Canberra: Australian National University Press, 1977).   *Caroline Ralston*

LILI'UOKALANI (1838-1917). Born 2 September 1838, Lili'uokalani was the sister of King Kalakaua. She took the oath of office and was proclaimed queen of Hawai'i on 29 January 1891. A brilliant woman, educated in the Chief's Children's School, her reign of a little less than two years was fraught with trouble almost from the very beginning. The short period during which she was on the throne forms one of the most important chapters in Hawaiian history, for it was then that there was forged the chain of circumstances which led to the abolition of the monarchy and the annexation of the Islands to the United States.

The new sovereign was in the full vigor of mature womanhood when she ascended the throne. Graceful, dignified, educated, Queen Lili'uokalani spoke remarkably pure English and Hawaiian. Like other members of her family, she had a taste for music and a marked talent for composition. Her political ideas were similar to those of her brother, but she had a stronger will than Kalakaua and a resolute purpose to regain for the throne some of the power and prestige that it had lost during his reign.

Persistent struggles between opposing parties caused the legislative session of 1892 to be protracted eight months, and during that period there were four changes in the ministry. The queen endeavored to draw up a new constitution, which was intended to remove the principal checks on the power of the monarch. This caused a political upheaval. Two companies of volunteer troops were placed on duty in the palace grounds, and the queen, upon the advice of her ministers, surrendered her authority under protest. She then appealed to the American government for reinstatement.

As the year 1894 was drawing to a close, a plot was fomented to overthrow the new republic and restore the monarchy. This ended in failure, and on 16 January 1895, Lili'uokalani was arrested on a charge of treason against the Republic of Hawai'i. On 24 January 1895 Queen Lili'uokalani renounced all claims to the throne in order to obtain clemency for those who had taken part in the insurrection.

Queen Lili'uokalani was the last of the royal rulers of Hawai'i. For the rest of her life she lived to put aside bitterness and lead her people, her former subjects, along the difficult path of rectitude and loyalty. Her death on 11 November 1917 brought to an end monarchial days.

RELATED ENTRIES: Hawai'i; Hawaiian Annexation, American Opposition to; Kalakaua, Prince David.

SOURCES AND READINGS: H. H. Gowen, *The Napoleon of the Pacific: Kamehameha the Great* (New York: Fleming H. Revell Co., 1919); Ralph S. Kuykendall and A. Grove Day, *Hawaii: A History* (Englewood Cliffs, N.J.: Prentice-Hall, 1961); H. M. Lyman, *Hawaiian Yesterdays* (Chicago: A. C. McClurg & Co., 1906).   *Ned B. Williams*

LINE ISLANDS. Eleven coral atolls and islands comprise the Line Islands in the central Pacific which lie between longitude 150° and 163° west and latitude 11° south and 7° north. Kingman Reef, Palmyra, Washington, Fanning, and Christmas form the northern Line Islands. Jarvis, Malden, Starbuck, Vostok, Caroline, and Flint form the southern Line Islands. Christmas, the largest in the group, is 1,860 km (1,155 mi) due south of Hawai'i and 2,800 km (1,740 mi) due east of Tarawa in Kiribati.

Physical Description. Each island has a central depression and is not more than 40 meters (131 ft) in height. On Washington this depression forms a freshwater lake. On six others the depression is open to the sea and forms a shallow lagoon. Soil is limited. The islands are characterized by sparse, low vegetation, highly variable monthly and yearly rainfall, consistent temperatures of 24-27° C (75-80° F) and moderate prevailing winds ranging from northeast to southeast. Fringing reefs make access difficult except for natural harbors on Christmas and Fanning and elsewhere where narrow channels have been blasted through the reef. Fauna consists of abundant marine life and seabird colonies.

Prehistory. Stone ruins on Caroline, Malden, Christmas, and Fanning indicate the presence of small communities of less than two hundred to three hundred people. These were probably temporary settlements for longer Polynesian migrations. When Europeans discovered the islands, they were uninhabited.

European Discovery. Russian, American, and British naval captains, traders, and whalers discovered the islands between 1777 and 1825. James Cook discovered Christmas Island in 1777. The four other northern islands, and Caroline, Flint, and Vostok in the south were discovered between 1795 and 1802. The remaining southern islands were discovered between 1820 and 1825.

Modern History. The southern Line Islands, excepting Vostok, were mined extensively for phosphate. J. T. Arundel Limited (later the Pacific Islands Phosphate Company of Australia) mined guano on Flint, Caroline, and Starbuck between 1870 and 1895. Malden was mined between 1860 and 1927 by two Melbourne companies. Jarvis was mined by the American Guano Company between 1858 and 1879. Companies from Tahiti, New Zealand, the Australian colonies, and the United States developed mining and coconut plantations for shorter periods on other islands.

Coconut oil and, later, copra production were developed in the northern Line Islands, excepting Kingman Reef. Extensive coconut planting continued until World War II on Flint, Caroline, Palmyra, Washington, Fanning, and Christmas. In the postwar period, copra remained as the only economic resource of the islands. Deep-sea and coastal fishing have not been developed. Mineral wealth is now considered negligible. In 1902 Fanning briefly assumed an important role as a mid-Pacific cable station. During World War II and after, air travel and the transpacific cable service led to flying-boat facilities and landing strips being constructed on several islands.

Postwar Developments. Atomic and nuclear testing and occasional scientific expeditions have led to further contact with the outside world. Christmas and Malden were developed for the British test "Operation Grapple" in 1956-1957. Kingman Reef has been a restricted-access, strategic area of the United States since 1941. Attempts have been made to develop tourist facilities on Palmyra and Christmas islands. The latter island, a declared flora and fauna reserve, has the most potential as a tourist site. Jet-plane air services link Christmas with Tarawa and Honolulu. Palmyra has been suggested as a potential site for nuclear waste-dumping.

Political Status. Kingman Reef, Palmyra, and Jarvis are possessions of the United States. The United States took possession of Palmyra in 1898, Kingman Reef in 1922, and Jarvis in 1930. Great Britain took possession of the remaining islands between 1866 and 1889. After 1877 they were governed by the Western Pacific High Commission. In 1916 Fanning and Washington were included by Britain in the Gilbert and Ellice Island colony; Christmas was added to the colony in 1919. Malden, Starbuck, Caroline, and Vostok were leased for varying lengths of time to phosphate and plantation companies. The southern eight islands were included in the Republic of Kiribati upon its independence in 1979. In 1978 the estimated population of Christmas was 1,288, Fanning 434, and Washington 417. The remainder are currently uninhabited. Occupational leases have been granted to private persons and companies for Caroline, Vostok, and Flint; Palmyra is in private possession by an American family.

RELATED ENTRIES: Canton Island Question; Kiribati; Western Pacific High Commission.

SOURCES AND READINGS: Stuart Inder, *Pacific Islands Year Book*, 13th ed. (Sydney: Pacific Publications, 1978), pp. 243-44.   *Alan Maxwell Quanchi*

LOCKERBY, WILLIAM (1782-1853). A sandalwood trader in the Fiji Islands, Lockerby was born 6 January 1782 in Ashbridge near Lockerby, Scotland. He subsequently moved to Liverpool, England, where he established his business. In 1807 he sailed from Liverpool to Boston where he boarded an American vessel, the *Jenny*, for a voyage to New South Wales and Canton. At Port Jackson, he heard of sandalwood just having been discovered in the Fiji Islands. He went there with the other crew members and between 1808 and 1809 he became involved not only in this lucrative trade but in Fijian politics as well. He gained the friendship and confidence of the Tui of Bua who conferred a royal title upon him. For months Lockerby lived among the Fijians and was present at the first full-scale use of firearms in Fijian wars. After one battle hundreds of Fijians lay dead. Having sold his services as mediator between other sandalwood traders and the Fijians, he left the islands to return to his home in England where he wrote his memoirs of his stay among the islanders, a valuable journal not published until 1925. Lockerby died at his residence in Liverpool on 29 June 1853.

RELATED ENTRIES: Fiji; Sandalwood Trade.

SOURCES AND READINGS: Stanley Brown, *Men from under the Sky: The Arrival of Westerners in Fiji* (Rutland, Vt.: Charles E. Tuttle Co., 1973); Sir Everard im Thurn, ed., *The Journal of William Lockerby* (London: Hakluyt Society, 1925).

Robert D. Craig

LOGAN, ROBERT W. (1852-1887). A prominent Protestant missionary in Truk (Ruk), Caroline Islands, in the 1870s and 1880s, Logan was ordained in 1870 and joined the American Board of Commissioners for Foreign Missions (ABCFM) mission in 1874 at Ponape, Caroline Islands. There he began to learn a dialect spoken by visitors to Ponape from the Mortlock Islands southeast of Truk. He visited the Mortlocks with fellow missionary Albert Sturges in 1877 and was stationed on Oneop Island in 1879. He translated a hymnbook, some readers, and the New Testament into Mortlockese. After spending time in the United States, he and his wife joined the Ponapean lay "teachers" who had been placed in Truk by Sturges and established the mission station on Moen Island in 1884. Logan died of fever in Truk after having established a reputation as a staunch campaigner against the custom of closing lands to exploitation after a death in the kin group, use of turmeric in dancing, and interclan feuds.

RELATED ENTRIES: American Board of Commissioners for Foreign Missions; Sturges, Albert.

SOURCES AND READINGS: D. Crawford and L. Crawford, *Missionary Adventures in the South Pacific* (Rutland, Vt.: Charles E. Tuttle Co., 1967).

Craig Severance

LONDON MISSIONARY SOCIETY IN THE PACIFIC, 1797-1901. The last decade of the eighteenth century produced a current of revolutionary development in Europe. The Seven Years' War, the loss of the American colonies, and the excesses of the French Revolution effected varying degrees of pessimism in the minds of many European Christians. At the same time, however, the spirit of maritime discovery which characterized the three voyages of Captain James Cook excited evangelical interest in the islands of the Pacific.

The Pentecostal movement in Great Britain began in earnest with the formation in 1795 of the Missionary Society, better known after 1818 as the London Society (LMS). Under the auspices of the Reverend

Thomas Haweis, the rector of All-Saints Church at Aldwinkle, and with the support from his benefactress the Countess of Huntington, the society sought to send a company of missionaries to Hawai'i, Tonga, the Marquesas, and the Society Islands. Hawai'i was quickly eliminated as a destination shortly before the departure of the mission packet *Duff*. The arrival of the missionaries in Tahiti in 1797 commenced the evangelical enterprise in the Pacific. Though mission efforts in the Marquesas and Tonga soon proved to be failures, the Tahitian mission was considerably more successful after almost eighteen years of trial. In 1815 the traditional religion of Tahiti had been unceremoniously discarded by Pomare, paramount chief of the Windward Islands, who then accepted Protestant Christianity under his patronage. LMS contributions to Tahitian society focused primarily on education and literacy. By 1810 the Tahitian alphabet had been transcribed into the Roman alphabet and published material was soon thereafter introduced into the mission curriculum. Subsequent translations of several books of the Bible were completed in 1837. In more secular matters, a European-style code of laws was printed in 1819 and a Tahitian-English dictionary appeared in 1851, the first such endeavors in the Pacific.

The LMS enterprise in the Windward Islands was curtailed in 1842 when France proclaimed a protectorate over the area. Though many LMS missionaries continued in service, by 1855 the London directors formally terminated financial support to the Windward Islands mission. During this brief period, Protestant Christianity had become an important factor in Tahitian politics and society.

LMS expansion into the western Pacific continued. With the important aid of Polynesian teachers, LMS missions were successfully established in the Cook Islands (1821-1852). In Samoa, likewise, the LMS extended their pastorates, which continued from 1835 to 1845. Similar efforts in the Marquesas, however, were frustrated after several brief attempts between 1798 and 1833. In Tonga the evangelical initiative was lost to the Wesleyans beginning in 1822, though the LMS managed to maintain a nominal presence in the islands. LMS movement into western Melanesia proved to be tragic. The violent death of John Williams in 1839 in the New Hebrides suspended formal LMS activity, though several stalwart Polynesian teachers maintained residences until the arrival of a European minister in 1842. Mission activity in the Loyalty Islands was successful, supported by the political ambitions of the Naisseline chiefs of Maré. By 1871 the LMS had commenced efforts in southern New Guinea. The missionaries were subject to considerable travail. The complexity of local languages, tribal hostilities, and above all the presence of malaria subjected the LMS missionaries to difficulties not normally encountered elsewhere in the Pacific.

Missionary enthusiasm was founded on righteous optimism and deep commitment to spread the gospel. Antimissionary movements in the islands were denounced or discredited, often with the aid of sympathetic chiefs and colonial officials. The lack of sufficient funds from the London directorate compelled many missionaries to undertake supplemental forms of commercial activities and secular pursuits. Small sugar and tobacco plantations were favored pastimes. In Tahiti, missionary George Pritchard accepted a post as British consul, much to the consternation of his colleagues. Occupation with the daily routine tasks of material survival often detracted from the hard trade of evangelism.

LMS proprietary interests in their clerical duties were jealously guarded. While amicable dialogue existed between the LMS and their Wesleyan and American Protestant counterparts, the LMS steadfastly opposed Roman Catholic intrusion into their field of labor, though New Guinea appears to have been the notable exception. Such policies led to severe disputes in Tahiti (1836-1841) and the Loyalties (1864-1873). In these two areas support from loyal island constituencies forced diplomatic confrontations across a broad front between the LMS and their Roman Catholic rivals. The LMS, moreover, became indirect and often unknowing agents of colonialism and settlement in the frontier areas of the Pacific. Particularly in southern New Guinea and the Cook Islands, the missionaries prepared the way for more direct means of control by British colonial administrations by properly cultivating friendly relations and opening lines of communication between Europeans and indigenous peoples. The LMS, however, did not hesitate to oppose colonial policies when the interests of their following were threatened.

The important by-products of LMS activity in the Pacific rests primarily in their useful accounts of island societies, particularly in Polynesia. Works by John Davies (*History of the Tahitian Mission, 1799-1830*), William Ellis (*Polynesian Researches*), Robert Thomson (*The Marquesas Islands: Their Description and Early History*), John Williams (*A Narrative of Missionary Enterprises in the South Sea Islands*), and James Chalmers (*Pioneering in New Guinea*) are among the published histories which are part of the vast LMS legacy in the Pacific. The archives of the LMS (now known as the United Church of Christ Board of World Ministries) are currently housed in the School of Oriental and African Studies, University of London.

RELATED ENTRIES: Catholic Church in the Pacific; Hawai'i, Religions of; Mormons in the Pacific.

SOURCES AND READINGS: Niel Gunson, *Messengers of Grace: Evangelical Missionaries in the South Seas, 1797-1860* (New York: Oxford University Press, 1978); Richard Lovett, *The History of the London Missionary Society, 1795-1895*, 2 vols. (London: H. Frowde, 1899); Colin Newbury, *Tahiti Nui: Change and Survival in French Polynesia, 1767-1945* (Honolulu: University Press of Hawaii, 1980); Patricia A. Prendergast, "A History of the London Missionary Society in British New Guinea, 1871-1901" (Ph.D. diss., University of Hawaii, 1968).

William Tagupa

LONG, OREN E. (1889-1965). Born 4 March 1889, a former school teacher, principal, and superintendent of public instruction of Hawai'i, Long was appointed governor of Hawai'i (1951-1953) by President Harry S. Truman. An outspoken advocate of immediate statehood for the territory, Long figured closely in the work of the constitutional convention. Before he assumed the governorship, Long was acting governor; and in that position he is credited with the advancement of public welfare, the promotion of the Punchbowl Memorial (national cemetery of the Pacific), and with the early settlement of labor strikes on the islands in 1947. He served the U.S. Navy, heading its advisory committee on education for trust territories, visiting educational facilities on Guam, Truk, and the Marshall and Caroline islands. His brief administration was one of continued effort on the statehood issue. He died 6 May 1965.

RELATED ENTRY: Hawai'i.

SOURCES AND REFERENCES: A. Grove Day, *Hawaii and Its People* (New York: Meredith Press, 1968); Edward Joesting, *Hawaii* (New York: W. W. Norton & Co., 1972); Ralph S. Kuykendall and A. Grove Day, *Hawaii: A History* (Englewood Cliffs, N.J.: Prentice-Hall, 1961).   *Ned B. Williams*

LORD HOWE ISLAND. Located 5° 20' south latitude and 159° 30' east longitude, Lord Howe Island is a dependency of New South Wales, Australia. The island lies 702 km (436 mi) northeast of Sydney, is volcanic in origin, wooded, and has an area of 17 km² (7 mi²). Sighted in 1788 by Lt. Henry L. Ball of the British navy, the island has high coastal cliffs rising to a mountain in the south. It was named after Admiral Lord Howe. The island was settled in 1834 and served as a supply station for whalers. It is now governed by a local council and a board in Sydney and has a population of about 300 persons. To the northeast side of Lord Howe Island lie the Admiralties, a group of rocky islets on which innumerable sea birds nest. To the southeast lies a visually striking outcropping of rock called Ball's Pyramid.

RELATED ENTRY: Admiralty Islands.

Frank P. King.

LOTI, PIERRE (1850-1923). Pierre Loti was the pen name for Louis-Marie-Julien Viaud, a French writer born 14 January 1850. He popularized the South Seas and especially Tahiti through his romantic novel *Le Mariage de Loti* (1890). As a sailor aboard the *Flore*, Viaud arrived in the Pacific in January 1872. He spent some sixty-four days tied up in Pape'ete harbor. Eight years later, the novel he wrote concerning his Tahitian experiences made him famous. No other single author has ever created the mirage of an exotic South Seas island as compelling as did Viaud in this one solitary work. This semiautobiographical work describes a warm, sensual love affair between an Englishman, Harry Grant, and the Polynesian *vahine* Rarahu who was attached to the royal court of Queen Pomare IV of Tahiti. The overly sentimental quality of the book made it popular in the late nineteenth century. It comments concerning the customs and character of the Polynesians and its descriptions of court life make it an invaluable source for Tahitian customs and history of the time. Loti died 10 June 1923.

RELATED ENTRIES: French Polynesia; Pomare Family.

SOURCES AND READINGS: Pierre Loti, *The Marriage of Loti* (Honolulu: University Press of Hawaii, 1976); Patrick O'Reilly, *Tahitiens* (Paris: Musée de l'Homme, 1962).

Robert D. Craig

LOUISIADE ARCHIPELAGO. The Louisiade Archipelago is an offshore island group which is part of Papua New Guinea and lies about 160 km (100 mi) southeast of it at 11° 12' south latitude and 153° 00' east longitude. The islands are scattered over an area of about 97 km by 257 km (60 mi by 160 mi) in the Coral Sea. The main islands are Tagula (Sudest), Rossel, Misima, and the Calvados chain. The total land area is 1,790 km² (691 mi²). The population is about 15,500 (1978 est.) persons, with about half that number of persons on Misima.

Visited by Luis Vaéz de Torres (1606), Louis Antoine de Bougainville (1768), and Antoine de Bruni d'Entrecasteaux (1793), it is unclear whether the islands were named for Bougainville or Louis XV of France. For years the dangerous waters around the islands were bypassed by ships; but after 1860 copra and slave traders (blackbirders) from Australia were active in the area. In 1888 and afterwards small gold deposits on Sudest and Misima were worked.

RELATED ENTRIES: Bougainville, Louis; Melanesians and Colonial Servitude; Melanesian Recruitment to Queensland, Patterns of; Papua New Guinea; Papua New Guinea, Gold Mining in.   *Frank P. King*

LOYALTY ISLANDS. A chain of limestone coral islands in the French Overseas Territory of New Caledonia, the Loyalty Islands are located about 105 km (65 mi) northwest of New Caledonia. The group extends 241 km (150 mi) with a total land area of 1,970 km² (760 mi²). The largest islands are Ouvéa, Lifou, and Maré. The indigenous people are Melanesian although there is a marked Polynesian admixture resulting from mid-eighteenth-century migrations from the Wallis Islands. The population was 14,518 in 1976. The islands consist of low-lying plateaux formed by upraised coral which rise no higher than 90 m (300 ft). There are no rivers so the inhabitants rely upon rainfall and deep wells. The soil is thin yet fertile. Taro, yams, bananas, and coconuts are grown with copra the chief export.

D'Entrecasteaux sailed near the group in 1793 and named its northern reef after his hydrographer, Beautemps-Beaupré. In 1827 and 1840 Dumont d'Urville explored and roughly charted the group but did not land. Members of the London Missionary Society arrived in 1841 and were joined by the Marist (French Roman Catholic) missionaries in the 1850s. At the time of European contact, the population was estimated between 12,000 and 15,000. Areas on each island were soon designated as either Protestant or Catholic missions, usually according to the ruling chief's preference. These settlements have become permanent divisions. Traders in sandalwood and other goods began frequenting the islands in the 1840s. Alarmed at tribal fighting between native Catholics and Protestants, and by English commercial influence near New Caledonia, the French sent a military expedition in 1864. France secured the islands by 1866. In 1946 the Loyalty Islands became a dependency of New Caledonia. Loyalty islanders have responded well to European contact and influences beginning with early trade relations, and they have continued to hold possession of their lands. Although most islanders farm and fish, some work in New Caledonia's nickel industry.

RELATED ENTRIES: Jones, John; London Missionary

Society; MacFarlane, Samuel; Melanesian Recruitment to Queensland, Patterns of; Naisseline Chiefship; New Caledonia; Sandalwood Trade; Selwyn, George; South Pacific Commission.

SOURCES AND READINGS: K. R. Howe, *The Loyalty Islands: A History of Culture Contacts 1840-1900* (Honolulu: University Press of Hawaii, 1977); Jean Le Borgne, *Géographie de la Nouvelle-Calédonie et des Iles Loyauté* (Nouméa: Ministère de l'Education, 1964). *Russell T. Clement*

LUNALILO, WILLIAM CHARLES (1835-1874). The king of Hawai'i from 1873 to 1874, Lunalilo was born on 31 January 1835 and was descended from a brother of Kamehameha I. His mother was Kekauluohi, who had been *Kuhina Nui* of the kingdom until she died in 1845. Lunalilo was the first Hawaiian to leave his property to a benevolent institution. He is best remembered for the Lunalilo Home, erected under the terms of his will "for the use and accommodation of poor, destitute, and infirm people of Hawaiian blood or extraction, giving preference to old people."

For several weeks after the death of Kamehameha V, Hawai'i had no king. The members of the cabinet, on the day after the death of Kamehameha V, ordered the legislature to meet on 8 January 1873, for the purpose of electing a new ruler of Hawai'i. Lunalilo, a candidate for ruler of Hawai'i, was favored over David Kalakaua to take the reins of government. Lunalilo recommended that a vote should be taken on 1 January to make the people's wishes known. A week later, members of the legislative assembly cast their votes. Every one was in favor of Lunalilo. Although it was believed that Lunalilo supported American ideas at the time of his election, he had a remarkable popularity among all classes of his subjects. Unfortunately, by the end of his brief reign he had lost much of this support.

King Lunalilo was undoubtedly the most extravagant chief and, having been well educated at the Royal School, his mental abilities both natural and acquired were far above the average. As a child he was brought up as a spoiled prince living in idleness, yet he was intelligent and witty with an unusual gift for mimicry. By disposition he was fair-minded and truthful, but his indecisiveness might well have resulted in harm to the nation.

Like his three predecessors, Lunalilo sought to conclude a reciprocity treaty with the United States.

The need for such a treaty was greater than ever due to the serious financial depression Hawai'i underwent in 1872. However, Lunalilo was ineffectual in promoting stronger ties with America because the indigenous Hawaiians were reluctant to release strategic sections of the islands to American military and business interests. Also, the sugar trade with America decreased during Lunalilo's reign due to the high tariffs imposed by the United States government.

Then awkward incidents at home, including the mutiny of his own household troops, increased pressure on the ailing king. Under the strain of governing Hawai'i, Lunalilo died on 3 February 1874, one year and twenty-five days after he mounted the throne.

RELATED ENTRIES: Hawai'i; Kalakaua, Prince David; Kamehameha V.

SOURCES AND REFERENCES: A. Grove Day, *Hawaii and Its People* (New York: Meredith Press, 1968); Edward Joesting, *Hawaii* (New York: W. W. Norton & Co., 1972); Ralph S. Kuykendall and A. Grove Day *Hawaii: A History* (Englewood Cliffs, N.J.: Prentice-Hall, 1961). *Ned. B. Williams*

LYTH, RICHARD BURDSALL (1809-1887). An early Wesleyan missionary to Fiji, Lyth was born in 1809 to a famous Methodist family. He trained for the medical profession but then turned to religion and was sent to Tonga where he spent his first two years as a missionary. He was then sent to the relatively new mission in Fiji where he spent the next sixteen years as "the carpenter of sickness." He was one of the earliest qualified medical missionaries of Methodism. Lyth became attached to the stations at Lakeba and Viwa where he helped train Fijian preachers in the seminaries he helped establish there. His linguistic ability supplied valuable criticism in the translations of the Scriptures and other works into Fijian. After sixteen years of work, his illness forced his retirement to New Zealand. He returned to England in 1858, and from 1869-1873 he was chaplain to the British forces at Gilbraltar. He died 17 February 1887 in York.

RELATED ENTRIES: Calvert, John; Fiji; Hunt, John.

SOURCES AND READINGS: George G. Findlay, *The History of the Wesleyan Methodist Missionary Society*, vol. 3 (London: Epworth Press, 1921); Richard B. Lyth, "Journal 1836-1854," 9 vols., Mitchell Library, Sydney, Australia. *Robert D. Craig*

MAASINA RULE. A nationalist movement, the Maasina Rule (also called the Marching Rule) flourished in the Solomon Islands from 1944 to 1950. While precedents can be traced back over half a century, *Maasina* Rule itself sprang directly from World War II. The Japanese invasion wrecked the English colonial administration. The Americans, after halting the advance of the Japanese at Guadalcanal, built a major base there. Many laborers from the populous southern island of Malaita worked for the Americans who treated them more generously and warmly than Europeans had done before. Malaitans, many of whom were Christians, were also impressed by the way in which the Americans' behavior accorded with New Testament values. Consequently, they were reluctant to return to the poverty and subordination that had been their lot under colonial rule and sought to control their own affairs for their own benefit.

Maasina ("brotherhood") Rule, beginning in south Malaita in 1944, spread through the rest of the island during 1945 and to San Cristobal in 1946. In 1945 its leaders forbad Malaitans to recruit for work elsewhere and in 1946 the people began organizing themselves into new large villages where they could live the new life of brotherhood. The strength of the movement was demonstrated in 1947 when seven thousand people gathered at Auki to inform the district commissioner that they intended to set up their own courts, presided over by experts in native custom. The carrying out of this policy over the next few weeks, in defiance of the administration, was tantamount to a declaration of independence. The government responded by arresting the leaders and imprisoning them for sedition. But new leaders took their place and civil disobedience continued. So did the arrests. In June 1949 there were two thousand men in jail.

By that time popular enthusiasm for resistance was beginning to fade. No material benefits had been achieved and the large-scale jailings had upset village economies and domestic arrangements. In June 1950, therefore, the resident commissoner released the nine principal chiefs on condition that they urge their followers to support the government. The offer was accepted. By the end of the year, laborers were recruiting for plantation work, and people were paying their taxes, which was a sign of submission.

Maasina Rule is important because it generated much evidence of the political consciousness of the Solomon Islanders, something that was not taken seriously under colonial rule, and because by creating a mass movement it demonstrated that despite their traditional social fragmentation Melanesians were capable of combining on a large scale for a common purpose. It was sign that eventual nationhood was possible. Nevertheless, the independence of the Solomon Islands in 1978 was not achieved by *Maasina* Rule. Independence was the result of a program of political development initiated by British authorities in 1960 and carried out with the cooperation of the Solomon people generally.

RELATED ENTRIES: Solomon Islands; War in the Pacific Islands.

SOURCES AND READINGS: Hugh Laracy, "Maasina Rule" in Alex Mamak and Ahmed Ali, eds., *Race Class and Rebellion in the South Pacific* (Sydney: Allen & Unwin, 1979), pp. 98-107; Hugh Laracy, *Marists and Melanesians: A History of Catholic Missions in the Solomon Islands* (Canberra: Australian National University Press, 1976).

Hugh Laracy

McCARTHY, CHARLES J. (1861-1929). Born in Boston, 4 August 1861, McCarthy began his political career in the Territory of Hawai'i when he was elected to the Senate, serving until 1912. In that year, McCarthy was elected treasurer of the City of Honolulu, an office he held until 1914. McCarthy served as territorial treasurer until 1918 when President Woodrow Wilson appointed him governor of Hawai'i. During Governor McCarthy's three-year post (1918-1921), his most important contribution to Hawai'i's economy was his work connected with the Waikiki reclamation project. Also important was Governor McCarthy's influence in Washington where he promoted Hawai'i's commercial growth during the two years he lived in the nation's capital. McCarthy died in Honolulu on 26 November 1929.

RELATED ENTRIES: Hawai'i.

SOURCES AND REFERENCES: A. Grove Day, *Hawaii and Its People* (New York: Meredith Press, 1968); Edward Joesting, *Hawaii* (New York: W. W. Norton & Co., 1972); Ralph S. Kuykendall and A. Grove Day, *Hawaii: A History* (Englewood Cliffs, N.J.: Prentice-Hall, 1961). *Ned B. Williams*

MacFARLANE, SAMUEL (1837-1911). MacFarlane was a Scottish Methodist missionary sent to the Loyalty Islands by the London Missionary Society in 1859. Under his direction the Protestant mission on Lifou developed rapidly and prospered. The islanders built large houses, churches, workshops, and storehouses. MacFarlane drafted a set of laws based on Christian principles and enforced them with a police force organized by Lifouan chiefs. In 1863 he began a teacher's school and worked on a translation of the New Testament. One year later he was accused by the French of ruling Lifou. They demanded his departure. MacFarlane, characterized as witty and arrogant, managed to stay in the Loyalty Islands until 1871. Once expelled, he traveled to New Guinea and founded a mission there. He returned to England in 1871, then labored in New Guinea until 1886. He died in England on 27 January 1911.

RELATED ENTRIES: Loyalty Islands; Papua New Guinea.

SOURCES AND READINGS: K. R. Howe, *The Loyalty Islands: A History of Culture Contacts 1840-1900* (Honolulu: University Press of Hawaii, 1977); Patrick O'Reilly, *Calédoniens* (Paris: Musée de l'Homme, 1953). *Russell T. Clement*

MacGREGOR, WILLIAM (1847-1919). The last British colonial administrator of British New Guinea, MacGregor was born at Towic in Aberdeenshire, Scotland, the son of a farmer. MacGregor received a medical degree at Aberdeen, did his residency at Glasgow, and later entered the British colonial service. He served in a variety of administrative posts in the Seychelles, Fiji, Mauritius, and as acting high commissioner and consul general for the western Pacific before being appointed administrator (later lieutenant governor) of the Crown Colony of British New Guinea in 1888. A student of geology, botany, chemistry, statistics, astronomy, and surveying, he devoted the early years of his administration to formalizing legislation for the government of the colony, establishing a small but effective administration, and

initiating a program of exploration and pacification. Convinced that exploration of the colony should be led by administration officials rather than private individuals seeking personal gain, he sought to make contact with villagers throughout the colony. Recognized as a man with an extraordinary capacity for work and great physical strength, he himself led patrols up the Mambare and Palmer rivers, far up the Fly River, and to the top of Mount Victoria, the highest point (4,076 m) in the Owen Stanley Range. He was also responsible for establishing an indigenous police force in 1890 and for the early application of British institutions and administrative forms to the indigenous culture. MacGregor left New Guinea in 1898 at the end of the joint agreement between Britain and Australia for the government of the colony, eight years before it was renamed Papua and became a territory of Australia. He subsequently served as governor of Lagos (1899-1904), Newfoundland (1904-1909), and Queensland (1900-1914), and received many medals and honors for his overseas service to Britain.

RELATED ENTRIES: Papua New Guinea.

SOURCES AND READINGS: Gavin Souter, *New Guinea: The Last Unknown* (Sydney: Argus and Robertson, 1963). *Jerome Evans*

MAGELLAN, FERDINAND (ca. 1480-1521). A Portuguese navigator and explorer, Magellan was a member of a noble Portuguese family of French descent. He served during his youth as a page at the Portuguese court. In 1505 he left Lisbon for the Far East in the service of D. Francisco de Almeida, the first Portuguese viceroy to India. Magellan participated in Portuguese maritime activities in the waters east of India during the years that he lived in the Far East. Returning to Portugal in 1511 as a veteran soldier and sailor, Magellan next joined as a volunteer in a Portuguese army which fought the Moors in Morocco. While there he received a lance wound which lamed him for life. He was also accused of various financial irregularities. Although these charges were later dropped, Magellan lost the favor of the king of Portugal, Manuel I. Feeling thwarted at home, Magellan left for Spain where he took out naturalization papers. Through the influence of friends he eventually received a commission from Charles I (later the Emperor Charles V) to search for a passage to the Moluccas by using a western route.

After many months of preparation, Magellan sailed from the port of Sanlúcar at the mouth of the Guadalquivir River in Spain on 20 September 1519 in command of five ships carrying a diverse crew with a large number of junior officers. Toward the end of November the easternmost part of Brazil had been reached. Sailing southward with a sharp lookout for the strait which would carry them to the South Seas, the ships took up winter quarters in Port Saint Julian in the area which Magellan named Patagonia. Here a serious mutiny occurred which Magellan put down quickly and harshly. Proceeding southward again, Magellan discovered on 21 October 1520 the water passage which he named *Todos los Santos* ("All Saints' Strait") which now bears his name. Navigation through this perilous passage took thirty-eight days, but finally on 28 November the expedition reached an open sea which Magellan called the "Pacific" because of its calmness. The fleet, now reduced to three vessels (the *Trinidad*, the *Concepción*, and the *Victoria*), continued northward and then in a northwesterly direction across the vast expanse of the world's largest ocean. Supplies ran so low that crew members had to eat rats and leather chaffing-gear. Many suffered greatly from scurvy, and Antonio Pigafetta, the Italian gentleman from Vicenza who accompanied Magellan in this enterprise, has left a vivid narrative of the hardships which all had to endure. After great difficulties the expedition reached the southernmost part of the island group now known as the Marianas. Magellan did not long remain here because of the thievery of the islanders, commemorated in the name of *Ladrones* which he gave to the archipelago. In mid-March Magellan reached a new archipelago which he named in honor of Saint Lazarus, and which a later explorer renamed the Philippines. Magellan visited several islands, exchanged gifts with the local people, and with the assistance of his Malay slave Enrique who served as interpreter, converted many to Christianity. To please the ruler of the island of Cebu the newcomers undertook hostile operations against the population of the small neighboring island of Mactan. In a skirmish on 27 April 1521 Magellan and a number of his men lost their lives. After Magellan's death and the loss of further men because of the treachery of the ruler of Cebu, the survivors decided to abandon the *Concepción* and sail away in the two remaining vessels. Eventually they reached the Moluccas and obtained large quantities of cloves and other spices on the island of Tidore. The *Trinidad* unsuccessfully attempted a homeward journey across the Pacific and then returned to the Moluccas where the Portuguese took control. Only the *Victoria*, commanded by Juan Sebastián de Elcamo, a Basque navigator, eventually reached Spain by sailing to Timor, then across the Indian Ocean, around the Cape of Good Hope, and up the west African coast to the port of Sanlúcar in September 1522. The first circumnavigation of the globe had been completed, and the profit realized from the sale of the spices brought back was more than enough to pay the expenses of the entire voyage.

RELATED ENTRIES: Mariana Islands.

SOURCES AND READINGS: Samuel Eliot Morison, *The European Discovery of America: The Southern Voyages, A.D. 1492-1616* (New York: Oxford University Press, 1974); Charles E. Nowell, ed., *Magellan's Voyage around the World: Three Contemporary Accounts* (Evanston, Ill.: Northwestern University Press, 1962); George E. Nunn, "Magellan's Route in the Pacific," *Geographical Review* 24 (1934): 615-33; Charles M. Parr, *Ferdinand Magellan, Circumnavigator* (New York: Thomas Y. Crowell Co., 1964); Antonio Pigafetta, *Magellan's Voyage: A Narrative Account of the First Circumnavigation*, ed. and trans. R. A. Skelton, 2 vols. (New Haven: Yale University Press, 1969); Martin Torodash, "Magellan Historiography," *Hispanic American Historical Review* 51 (1971): 313-35.   *Bernerd C. Weber*

MAIGRET, LOUIS-DÉSIRE (1804-1882). A Roman Catholic bishop in Hawai'i, Maigret was born 14 September 1804 at Maillé, county of Vienne, France. In 1829 he became a priest and joined the Congregation of the Sacred Hearts. He was sent to the Pacific in 1834. While serving on Mangareva in 1840 he was sent to Hawai'i in the first organization of an apostolate. Seeing the need for more help in Hawai'i, Bishop Rouchouze, the Vicar Apostolic, sailed to France to recruit sisters and priests. Father Maigret was left in charge of the church during the bishop's absence. The bishop and his party boarded the *Marie-Joseph* for their return journey to Hawai'i on 15 December 1842. The ship was last seen at Cape Horn but then vanished and was never heard of again. As a result, Father Maigret was made bishop of Arathia (1846) with the responsibility for the church in Hawai'i. He went to Rome and was consecrated 30 October 1847. His first year was one of conflict with the Protestants who opposed the Catholic plans to increase their schools in the islands. David Malo, as superintendent of schools in the kingdom, was one of the bishop's chief opponents. Vandalism and violence became part of the conflict. King Kamehameha III, though a Protestant, expressed the wish that all Christian denominations tolerate one another in Hawai'i. He appointed an American, Richard Armstrong, as minister of public instruction, and he exempted all schools from taxation. Bishop Maigret sent for ten sisters of the Congregation of the Sacred Hearts who arrived in Honolulu from France on 4 May 1859 to aid in teaching in the schools. Bishop Maigret took Father Damien, a volunteer, to the Kalawa'o leper colony on Maui, Hawai'i. He died 11 June 1882.

RELATED ENTRIES: Armstrong, Richard; Damien, (Father) Joseph; Malo, David.

SOURCES AND READINGS: Sister Adele Marie Lemon, *Lei of Islands: A History of Catholic Hawaii* (Honolulu: Tongg Publishing Co., 1956); *A Century in Hawaii, 1859-1959* (Honolulu: Sisters of the Sacred Hearts, 1959).   *Vernice W. Pere*

MAILO, PETRUS (1902-1971). A traditional and modern leader in Truk (Caroline Islands), Mailo was born to a chiefly clan of Moen island. He became the most important political figure in Truk during the early period of American administration (1947-1968) and was known and respected throughout Micronesia. Mailo acquired traditional knowledge of *itang* (esoteric powerful military and religious knowledge), oratorical ability, and political astuteness. He effectively combined the authority of traditional and elected political office. Mailo was educated at a Protestant elementary school in the German period of occupation and became secretary of the island of Moen in 1932. He was appointed adviser on island affairs for the Japanese civil and military governments and he coordinated the relocation of Moen's people during the war. When the American government was formed in 1947 he became magistrate and chief of Moen municipality. He was elected mayor when Moen became charted in 1957 and held the post until his death. He served in the Truk District Congress from 1957 until 1962 and was also a member of the Inter-District Advisory Council to the high commissioner. He was elected from Moen to the House of Representatives of the First Congress of Micronesia and served as vice-speaker until his resignation in 1968. Petrus traveled to both Japan and the United States on leadership tours, but is remembered best for his efforts to serve Truk in both public and private capacities. He was responsible for establishing savings institutions based on traditional forms of contribution and was president of the largest trading company with local shareholders. He arbitrated disputes between different islands, convened magistrates' conferences, and argued that Trukese should combine the good things of traditional and Western culture.

RELATED ENTRIES: Micronesia.

SOURCES AND READINGS: Jim Manke and Tom Gladwin, "Petrus Mailo: A Micronesian Chief," *Micronesian Reporter* 19, no. 4 (1971): 25-29.
                    Craig J. Severance

MALASPINA, ALESSANDRO (1754-1809). An Italian who was the most important scientific explorer to sail under the Spanish flag, Malaspina departed from Cádiz in August 1789 with his two ships, the *Descubierta* and the *Atrevida*. He sailed to the coast of South America, Panama, Sandwich Islands, the west coast of North America, Alaska, the Philippines, New Zealand, and Australia. Malaspina made detailed surveys of the Galapagos and the Tongan islands. He returned to Cádiz in September 1794. Malaspina brought back hydrographic, ethnographic, and biologic data. Malaspina's jealous enemies in the Spanish court suppressed his scientific studies and had him imprisoned. In 1803 Napoleon Bonaparte was instrumental in having him freed and sent to Milan. He died in 1809. In 1885 a few of his studies were published. Some scholars consider his achievements as great as those of Lapérouse or Captain James Cook.

RELATED ENTRIES: Galapagos Islands; Spain in the Pacific; Tonga.

SOURCES AND READINGS: J. C. Beaglehole, *The Exploration of the Pacific* (London: A. & C. Black, 1947); H. R. Friis, *The Pacific Basin* (New York: American Geographical Society, 1967); Hectór R. Ratto, *La Expedición de Malaspina* (Buenos Aires: Emecé Editores, S.A., 1945); R. L. Silveira de Braganza and C. Oakes, *The Hill Collection of Pacific Voyages* (San Diego: University of California, 1974).
                    Joseph A. Montoya

MALIETOA. *Malietoa* is one of the two highest-ranking family titles in Western Samoa. Its origin dates ca. A.D. 1200 when young Samoan chiefs Tanu and Fata defeated their Tongan overlords. The departing Tongan king called from the sea: "*Malie tau, malie toa,*" ("excellently fought, brave warriors"). The title *Malietoa* was bestowed upon their eldest brother Savea by their people. It has continued in direct line down to the present *Malietoa*, Tanumafili II, head of the state of Western Samoa. Although a lesser title than the Tui A'ana and Tui Atua, the Malietoa family became prominent in 1831 when Malietoa Vai'inupo gained all five major Samoan titles and reigned as *Tupu'o* Samoa (king of Samoa). Upon his death in 1841, the titles were again divided. *Malietoa* went first to his half brother Taimalelagi, then to his sons Moli (d. 1858) and Talavou

(d. 1880), and then to his grandson Laupepa (d. 1898) each of which attempted by war, intrigue, and foreign support to gain the title *Tupu'o* Samoa once again. (The title *Tupu'o* Samoa has not been used in Samoa since German control in 1900.) Laupepa's son Tanumafili I was granted the title *Fautua* ("adviser"), shared with his rival Tuimaleali'ifano Si'u. When Malietoa Tanumafili I died in 1939, he was succeeded in office by his son Tanumafili II who became sole head of the Western Samoan state in 1963 upon the death of Tupua Tamasese Mea'ole, the successor to Tuimaleali'ifano Si'u.

RELATED ENTRIES: American Samoa; Tui Manu'a; Tupu'o Samoa; Western Samoa.

SOURCES AND READINGS: J. W. Davidson, *Samoa Mo Samoa* (New York: Oxford University Press, 1967); Augustin Krämer, *Die Samoa-Inseln*, 2 vols. (Stuttgart: E. Nägele, 1902); *Pacific Islands Monthly*, August 1939, p. 29; July 1940, p. 15.

Robert D. Craig

MALIETOA TANUMAFILI II (1913-). The head of state of Western Samoa, Tanumafili II was born 4 January 1913, son of Malietoa Tanumafili I (d. 1939). A descendant of one of the two highest chiefly families in Samoa, he was educated at Saint Stephen's College and Wesley College, Auckland, New Zealand. In 1940 he was elected to the title *Malietoa* and became *Fautua* (one of the two leading high chiefs) to the New Zealand governor in Western Samoa. In 1958 he appeared before the United Nations as a member of the delegation to discuss Samoan independence. He was joint chairman of the constitutional convention in 1959, and when Western Samoa became independent on 1 January 1962, he became joint head of state with the late Tupua Tamasese Mea'ole (d. 1963). He married secondly Tiresa Patu Tauvela Hunter (1962). He is to hold the position of *Malietoa* for life, after which the position will be subject to election by the legislative assembly and the term will be limited to five years.

RELATED ENTRIES: *Malietoa*; Western Samoa.

SOURCES AND READINGS: James W. Davidson, *Samoa Mo Samoa: The Emergence of the Independent State of Western Samoa* (New York: Oxford University Press, 1967). *Robert D. Craig*

MALO, DAVID (1793?-1853). An author and collector of Hawaiian lore, Malo was born around 1793 to Aoana and Heone Malo in Keauhou, North Kona, Hawai'i. As a young man he learned the old Hawaiian traditions. He later moved to Maui where he met the Reverend William Richards and was converted to Christianity. In 1831, at the age of thirty-eight, he entered Lahainaluna High School to study for the ministry. He dedicated himself to the study and writing of Hawaiian legends and to the ministry to the Hawaiian people. His book, *Hawaiian Antiquities*, written around 1840, tells the history and traditions of the Hawaiian people. In 1843 he was ordained a minister and in September 1852 was installed as a pastor in Keokea, Maui. Malo became a personal friend and advisor to King Kamehameha II and his chiefs. Between 1841 and 1845 he served as the first superintendent of schools in Hawai'i. He served as pastor of the Congregational church in Kalepolepo, Maui, until his death on 21 October 1853.

RELATED ENTRIES: Hawai'i; Kamehameha II; Richards, William.

SOURCES AND READINGS: R. S. Kuykenall, *The Hawaiian Kingdom 1778-1854* (Honolulu: University of Hawaii Press, 1968); David Malo, *Hawaiian Antiquities* (Honolulu: Bernice P. Bishop Museum, 1951). *Brenna J. Rash*

MANGAIA, COOK'S VISIT TO (1777). The island of Mangaia was sighted from the *Discovery* on 29 March 1777 in the tenth month of Captain James Cook's third Pacific voyage. Though a fringing reef prevented a landing, it was there Cook first encountered people of the island group now bearing his name. Voyagers' journal accounts of the contact are supplemented by Mangaian historical traditons recorded in the mid-nineteenth century.

Traditions tell of the great ship of Tute (Cook) and Ma'i (Omai, from Huahine, Society Islands, who acted as Cook's interpreter). These names were discovered by the warriors Kavoro (also known as Mourua, as he appears in the journals) and Makutu, who bravely approached the ships in a canoe and spoke with Ma'i. Later, Mourua and other Mangaians boarded the ships' boats as they sought a reef passage. Cook did not realize that these included the island's warrior leader, the temporal lord, Kirikovi.

Kirikovi received a crude iron axe. Although Edgar's log suggests that Mangaians failed to appreciate iron hatchets, this axe was greatly treasured, used in woodworking such as weapon making, and in taking human sacrifice for the god Rongo. Other goods dispersed included cloth, nails, a knife, and some highly prized glass beads subsequently buried with a high-ranking woman.

Mourua visited the *Resolution*. The Mangaian account suggests that he hoped for personal political advantage, alliance, and perhaps a marriage for his daughter. He made an unceremonious departure from the ship after falling over the first goat seen in the Cook Islands. Cook's visit was positively viewed by Mangaians and was celebrated in a dance drama. Clearly potential material advantages had been seen by the islanders while dangers were not revealed until later contacts.

RELATED ENTRIES: Cook Islands; Cook, (Captain) James.

SOURCES AND READINGS: J. C. Beaglehole, ed., *The Journals of Captain James Cook: The Voyage of the Resolution and Discovery, 1776-1780*, vol. 3 (Cambridge: At the University Press, 1967); William Wyatt Gill, *From Darkness to Light in Polynesia* (London: Religious Tract Society, 1894).

Christian C. Clerk

MANGAIAN CHIEFS AND COLONIAL AUTHORITIES (1903-1965).

Friction between the colonial administration and members of the *aronga mana*, a body of chiefs, is a repeated feature of twentieth-century Mangaian politics. A resident agent, Major J. Large, was appointed to Mangaia in 1903, two years after New Zealand's annexation of the Cook Islands. Local leaders saw his arrival as a serious threat to their authority. The British protectorate had allowed the chiefs considerable administrative and judicial freedom. With a resident agent heading the island council and magistrate's court, freedom of action was curtailed. Chiefly fears and Large's determined assertion of his personal authority led to conflicts in many areas, from government building plans to canoe cargo rates. But two central problems appeared which persisted under successive resident agents: the relative roles of the island council and the *aronga mana* and the control of land matters.

Administrators hoped to promote an elected island council at the expense of the intractable *aronga mana*. To some extent, resident agents took advantage of factionalism and intervillage tensions in pressing their policies. However, after an initial boycott by John Trego Ariki and other senior chiefs, the *aronga mana* exerted their influence to gain effective control of the council which was to last until the 1950s.

With the erosion of the judicial powers of the chiefs, their rights in determining distribution of lands became crucial to their influence and a central point of contention. All attempts to establish the land courts operating elsewhere in the group were strongly resisted by the *aronga mana* with considerable popular support. Such courts could not operate without detailed land surveys. These were consistently opposed, and fears of surveying were involved in opposition to other government schemes such as the replanting program of oranges in the 1940s and 1950s.

The *aronga mana* survived the colonial administration and maintained considerable influence in land affairs. Despite a decline in authority after some financial mismanagement in the 1940s and some doubtful appropriations of land, popular opinion still supported a fully Mangaian institution against an administration centered on Rarotonga. Curiously, Mangaian independence has consistently been asserted by an appeal to the days of British control, and Mangaians have earned themselves the name of *Peretane* ("Britishers") among other Cook Islanders.

RELATED ENTRIES: Cook Islands.

SOURCES AND READINGS: Mangaia Files, Cook Island Archives, Rarotonga, Cook Islands. *See* especially, L. H. Trenn, report: *The Aronga Mana of Mangaia*, April 1946; *see also* Appendixes to the *Journal of the New Zealand House of Representatives* for the relevant period.

Christian C. Clerk

MANGAIA'S NEW ORDER (1824-1830).

The early period of mission activity on Mangaia saw revisions of the political order with the emergence of hereditary district and subdistrict chieftainships under a supreme secular *ariki* ("chief"). These arrangements followed from the battle of Putoa in 1828, where antimission forces, weakened by internal divisions, were defeated by mission supporters. The island's new leader was Numangatini *Ariki* who four years earlier, when high priest of the pan-tribal god Rongo, had taken the newly arrived London Missionary Society teachers under his protection. Traditionally, a new, land-holding warrior leadership was selected after warfare. But the selection of Numangatini ended a division between priestly and warrior authority. The mission had provided a new focus for Mangaia's power struggles. With the cessation of intertribal warfare, the titles established in 1828 became hereditary.

RELATED ENTRIES: Cook Islands; London Missionary Society; Mangaian Chiefs and Colonial Authorities.

SOURCES AND READINGS: William Wyatt Gill, *From Darkness to Light in Polynesia* (London: Religious Tract Society, 1894); John Williams, *A Narrative of Missionary Enterprises in the South Sea Islands* (London: John Snow, 1838).

Christian C. Clerk

MARAU, JOANNA (1860-1934). The last queen of Tahiti, Joanna Marau was born on 24 April 1860, the third daughter of Alexander Salmon, a prosperous merchant, and his Tahitian wife, Ari'i Ta'ima'i, the great chiefess of Papara (Tahiti). Marau married the heir apparent Teri'i Tari'a (1839-1880) in 1875, but they never got along. When Queen Pomare IV died in 1877, Teri'i Tari'a became King Pomare V but not without some opposition. The English Protestant party attempted to have Marau chosen monarch rather than her husband. She was popular, talented, Protestant, and a descendant of a most famous ancient family. The move was stopped by a quick maneuver by French Governor Serre. The royal couple finally divorced in 1888. Her memory of ancient Tahitian lore was prodigious, and much of that knowledge was recorded by the American historian Henry Adams who visited this family in 1891. She was greatly loved by all her subjects. Before her death, the French government bestowed upon her the distinguished citation, the Legion of Honor. Marau left three children all of whom were disinherited by the king upon his coronation. He claimed that they were not his. When Marau died on 2 February 1934 it seemed to many Tahitians that a glorious chapter in Tahitian history had closed.

RELATED ENTRIES: Ari'i Ta'ima'i; French Polynesia; Pomare Family; Salmon, Alexander.

SOURCES AND READINGS: Henry Adams, *Tahiti: Memoirs of Arii Taimai* (1901; reprint ed. Ridgewood, N.J.: Gregg Press, 1968); Takao Pomare Vedel, *Resumé d'histoire tahitienne des Éstablissements Français de l'Océanie* (Paris: Société d'éditions géographiques, 1931); "Tomb of Ex-Queen Marauta-'aroa," *Pacific Islands Monthly* 20 (1935):46.
Robert D. Craig

MARCHAND, ÉTIENNE (1755-1793). The French explorer and navigator Étienne Marchand sailed to the northwest coast of America (1790-1792) to investigate the possibility of establishing a lucrative fur trade for the Maison Baux, a commercial house in Marseille (France). On his way to the northwest coast, he came upon the Marquesas Islands (1791) which he named "Revolution Islands." Although he is credited in having "discovered" them, the islands were actually visited before by Mendaña (1595), Cook (1775), and Ingraham (1791). Marchand's journal (ms. 49025-26 in the Bibliothèque de Marseille) consists of some 633 pages and has never been fully published. Marchand arrived back in France during the height of the French Revolution where he died in an accident in 1793.

RELATED ENTRIES: France in the Pacific; Marquesas Islands.

SOURCES AND READINGS: Charles Claret de Fleurieu, *A Voyage Round the World...by Étienne Marchand*, 2 vols. (London: Longman & Rees, 1801); Robert Juteau, "Journal de bord du capitaine Étienne Marchand," *Bulletin de la Société d'études océaniennes* 11 (1961): 247-60. (Marquesan portion of Marchand's journal).
Robert D. Craig

MARCHING RULE. *See* Maasina Rule.

MARIANA ISLANDS. Situated between 13° and 20° north latitude, at 140° east longitude, the Marianas are volcanic and coral islands. Guam is the largest and southernmost island and Farallon de Pájaros is the northernmost. There are fifteen islands in all, with 795 km² (307 mi²) of land area stretching over 724 km (450 mi) of ocean, about 2,414 km (1,500 mi) east of the Philippines. The 1980 (census) population was 16,758 (excluding Guam). The important islands in the group besides Guam are Saipan, Tinian, Rota, and Pagan. Asunción and Farallon de Pájaros are active volcanos. The Marianas are in the wet tropics. Temperatures range from 25-30° C (the mid-70s to the mid-80s F) all year round. Humidity is 80 percent on the average, with about 254 cm (100 in) of rainfall per year.

The only presumably native land animals are two species each of insect-eating bats and fruit bats. Domestic and farm animals were introduced by the Spanish in the seventeenth and eighteenth centuries. Carabao (water buffalo) and deer were brought from the Philippines. Geckos, iguanas, and snails are common. Marine and shore birds abound. A rich marine fauna exists in the open sea, reefs, lagoons, and shore areas. Vegetation varies in tropical form from high to low areas; coconut and breadfruit trees are very common, and there are flowers of many varieties. Bananas and taro, as well as kasava, are common food crops.

Discovered in 1521 by the Portuguese navigator Ferdinand Magellan working for Spain, the islands were not colonized until 1668 when their name was changed by Jesuit missionaries from *Los Ladrones* ("Thieves Islands") to Mariana, to honor Maria Anna of Austria, then regent of Spain. When the Spanish arrived, they found islanders living on Guam whom they called Chamorros. After much intermarriage and racial mixing through the years, there are no full-blooded Chamorros left today. The ancient Chamorros were subsistence farmers and fishermen with great skill as outrigger-canoe (called *proas*) builders and navigators. They were a peaceful people living in a matrilineal society.

In the more than three hundred years of Spanish colonization, there were numerous wars and rebellions. The Marianas lay on the galleon routes and were a regular stop. Over the years, many Filipinos were brought to the islands as well as Mexicans from Guadalajara and Acapulco.

Guam was ceded to the United States in 1898 following the Spanish-American War and has remained an American territory to the present. The rest of the Marianas were sold to Germany in 1899. In 1914 Japan seized the Marianas from Germany. Subsequently, Japan was awarded the islands as a League of Nations mandate. After a series of difficult battles at Saipan, Tinian, and Guam in 1944, the Americans wrested all the Marianas from Japan. Guam had been seized by Japan in 1941 at the start of World War II.

After the war all the Marianas, except Guam, became part of a United Nations strategic trusteeship administered by the United States. This status continues, but in 1973 the people of the Northern Marianas entered into political-status negotiations with the United States. This led to a plebescite which in turn led to commonwealth status for the islands with the United States. The first elected governor of the Northern Marianas was installed on 9 January 1978. The Northern Marianas will officially become an American commonwealth when the trusteeship is terminated.

Guam continues as an unincorporated territory of the United States by the organic act of 1950. Guamanians are American citizens with a nonvoting representative in the U.S. House of Representatives. Future political status for Guam and a united Mariana Islands is a lively political issue.

RELATED ENTRIES: Chamorros (Ancient); Chamorros Peoples, Origin of; Commonwealth of the Northern Mariana Islands; Guam; *Leucaena Leucocephala*; Micronesia.   *Dirk Anthony Ballendorf*

MARINER, WILLIAM (1791-1853). An Englishman who lived for four years among the Tongans (1806-1810) Mariner was regarded as the adopted son of the powerful and cunning chief Finau Ulukalala II. At fifteen, Mariner sailed on the *Port-au-Prince*, an English privateer vessel, which was overwhelmed and taken in November 1806 by Finau Ulukalala who wanted firearms and men to make him the *hau* (paramount ruler) of Tonga. Saved from death, Mariner was taken into Finau's household where he was placed in the care of Mafi Habe, one of Finau's wives, by whom he was carefully educated in the language and customs of Tonga. His skill with the language, his superb memory, and his special position in

the royal household helped Mariner to learn extensively about Tongan society. Upon his return to England, Mariner related his experiences to John Martin who published them in *An Account of the Natives of the Tongan Islands*. This publication contained Mariner's own original grammar and vocabulary of the Tongan language. Touching nearly every aspect of the Tongan culture and owing to its accuracy, Mariner's valuable record remains a standard by which modern study of ancient Tongan society can be checked. In England he became a prosperous stockbroker. He died of drowning in the River Thames after a boating accident.

RELATED ENTRIES: Beachcombers; Tonga; Ulukalala II, Finau; Vason, George.

SOURCES AND READINGS: John Martin, *An Account of the Natives of the Tongan Islands in the South Pacific Ocean*, 2 vols. (London: For the author, 1817). (Several editions have appeared.)

Ian C. Campbell
Eric B. Shumway

MARQUESAS ISLANDS. One of the five island groups which make up French Polynesia, the Marquesas consist of some twelve high islands lying in the South Pacific approximately 140° west longitude and 10° south latitude about 1,191 km (740 mi) northeast of Tahiti. Population is estimated to be near 6,000. The windward sections of the islands contain lush tropical vegetation while the leeward sides are practically barren. The Polynesians who inhabit these islands came from western Polynesia, possibly from Samoa or Tonga in the second century, B.C. From the Marquesas, these early Polynesian navigators sailed the Pacific and settled Tahiti, the Tuamotus, Hawai'i, and Easter Island. The Marquesas Islands are generally regarded as the "womb of eastern Polynesia."

The Ancient Marquesans. Several centuries before European contact, inhabitants of these islands had created a high stage of neolithic culture. Their houseforms, temples, and carvings in stone and wood are unsurpassed in Polynesia. They placed heavy emphasis on military prowess, and oral tradition from the Marquesas relates a long history of bitter, intertribal warfare. These incessant wars prevented any one valley or community from exercising much political authority over the rest.

European Contact. The Marquesas were the first of the Polynesian islands to be discovered by European navigators. The Spanish commander Mendaña came upon them in 1595, but they were not visited again until Captain James Cook anchored in Vaitahu Bay, Tahuata, in 1774. Their geographical location made them a favorite stopover for the whaling ships whose numbers soared during the nineteenth century. Each visit to the Marquesas in one way or another seemed to end in bloodshed and death for the Marquesans. Once an extremely heavily populated archipelago, by 1887 the first census placed their population at 5,246. By 1920 only 1,500 people remained in the islands.

Christianization. The Protestant Missionary Society from London sent its first ship of missionaries to the South Pacific in 1797. Of their number, William P. Crook and John Harris chose the Marquesas. Harris spent only two weeks on the islands and Crook left early in 1798. Several other attempts were made, but all ended in failure. French Roman Catholics arrived in 1833 and had more success than the English Protestants. Their work helped pave the way for French political authorities when they arrived in 1842.

French Control. Between 1834 and 1842 the French sailed into the southeastern Pacific and established a protectorate over the Society Islands, the Tuamotus, and the Marquesas. In 1880 the Marquesas became a direct possession of the French government along with the other island groups in French Polynesia called the *Établissements Français de l'Océanie* (EFO) under a French governor appointed from Paris to Pape'ete, the recognized capital of French Polynesia. The Marquesas sent two representatives to a general council in Tahiti until 1899 when it was deemed necessary to have their own council. Local governments in these islands were dominated by the French gendarmes who took over much of the functions of the district councils.

After World War II the French government granted them full-fledged citizenship and allowed a representative assembly (later called the territorial assembly) to be elected by adult suffrage of all the islanders. This assembly met in Pape'ete on the island of Tahiti. Two of the ten representatives came from the Marquesas. In 1956 a new law allowed the territorial assembly to elect a vice-president whose powers resembled those of a premier and allowed a greater degree of internal self-government. By 1977 the vice-president and territorial assembly gained their goal of internal autonomy with two representatives being elected to the French senate in Paris. The Tuamotus and the Marquesas together elect one of the senators.

Resources, Economy. Copra has been the islands' main export product, but this market fluctuates so radically that it appears it will no longer be a desired commodity. Air Polynesia connects the islands now with weekly flights from Pape'ete and the Tahiti tourist development board hopes to bring needed income through tourism. The islands are fertile and capable of supporting a larger population than the few white traders and Marquesans who mostly still maintain marginal living conditions.

RELATED ENTRIES: Crook, William; French Polynesia; Mendaña de Neira, Álvaro de.

SOURCES AND READINGS: Bengt Danielsson, *Forgotten Islands of the South Seas* (London: G. Allen & Unwin, 1957); Louis Rollin, *Les Iles Marquises* (Paris: Société d'éditions Géographiques, Maritimes et Coloniales, 1929); Robert Thomas, *The Marquesas Islands: Their Description and Early History*, ed. Robert D. Craig (La'ie, Hawai'i: Brigham Young University—Hawai'i Campus Press, 1978).

Robert D. Craig

MARSDEN, SAMUEL (1765-1838). Anglican chaplain, pioneering missionary, and innovative grazier, Marsden was born at Farsley near Leeds in England. In 1793 he left his studies at Cambridge to become assistant chaplain to the convict colony of New South Wales, Australia. The arrival in 1798 of eleven London Missionary Society (LMS) refugees from Tahiti began Marsden's contact with Pacific evangelism. Some of the LMS missionaries became firmly involved with farming, teaching, and itinerant preaching in New South Wales; others were temporarily supported by Marsden and other officials before returning to the Society Islands. From 1804 Marsden was the agent, and later the foreign director, of the LMS operations in the Pacific. Although he did not visit the Society Island stations, his role was sometimes decisive in ensuring that the task was not abandoned by lonely and frustrated missionaries. Many of the early Tahitian texts were printed by Marsden in Sydney. As in his own New Zealand mission, Marsden stressed civilization before conversion, aiming to convince the Polynesians of their inferiority in material terms and then wean them from idleness to sobriety and industry. Although he was a cultural chauvinist, his efforts by legislative and executive action to protect the islanders from the barbarities of Sydney adventurers and Nantucket whalers should be recognized.

RELATED ENTRIES: French Polynesia; London Missionary Society.

SOURCES AND READINGS: N. Gunson, *Messengers of Grace: Evangelical Missionaries in the South Seas* (Melbourne: Oxford University Press, 1978); A. T. Yarwood, *Samuel Marsden: The Great Survivor* (Melbourne: Melbourne University Press, 1977).

A. T. Yarwood

MARSHALL ISLANDS. The easternmost group of islands in the Trust Territory of the Pacific Islands, the Marshall Islands lie at 9° north latitude and 168° east longitude, about 4,184 km (2,600 mi) northwest of Auckland, New Zealand.

There are two parallel chains, the Ratak, or sunrise islands, to the east, and Ralik, or sunset islands, to the west. Their total land area is about 202 km² (70 mi²). They are all atolls or coral caps, almost a mile deep, set upon dome volcanos rising some 5,486 m (18,000 ft) from the ocean floor. Temperatures range from 25-30° C (75-85° F) with approximately 203 cm (80 in) of rainfall. The 1980 population is estimated at 32,427 with less than two percent foreigners. Majuro is the capital and district center for administration.

A great variety of fish and marine life is found in the lagoons and open ocean: tuna, barracuda, sea bass, sharks, and eels are common. There are also many starfish, lobsters, and sea cucumbers. Shore birds are plentiful, and there are a number of domestic animals. Coconut, breadfruit, bananas, and pandanus are found. Papayas and avocados grow wild, and vegetables are cultivated.

The Marshalls were discovered by the Spaniard, Alvaro Saavedra, in 1529. The British captain, John Marshall, partially explored them in 1788 and gave them his name. Russian expeditions under Adam Johann Krusenstern did much mapping in 1803, as did Otto von Kutzbue in 1815 and 1823. A Spanish claim was recognized in 1886, but Spain sold the group to Germany in 1899 after the Spanish-American War together with the northern Marianas and the Carolines. The Japanese occupied them in 1914 when World War I broke out. The United States took them from the Japanese in 1943 during World War II with a major battle at Kwajalein. In the 1950s, Bikini and Eniwetok became test sites for American thermonuclear devices.

Protestant missions were established in the nineteenth century, and many preachers arrived from Boston to teach the English language and the Gospel. Marshallese is a common language throughout the island groups. In prehistoric times, a number of petty, warring, and unstable feudal states arose accompanied by stratification into several social classes that persist today.

Sailing trips to the islands and atolls were made throughout the area as well as to Kosrae. The Marshallese were noted as sailors and for the development of bamboo navigational charts (stick charts) to assist in sailing over vast ocean distances.

In 1979, after some ten years of political status negotiations with the United States, together with neighboring islands in the Carolines and Northern Marianas, the Marshallese established their own parliamentary democracy with Amata Kabua elected as first president. Their "freely-associated" status with the United States will take effect when the United Nations trusteeship is terminated.

RELATED ENTRIES: Krusenstern, Adam Johann von; Micronesia; Saavedra Cerón, Alvaro de; Spain in the Pacific.   *Dirk Anthony Ballendorf*

MATA'AFA, FIAME FAUMUNIA MULINU'U II (1921-1975). The first prime minister of Western Samoa (1959-1969, 1972-1975), Mata'afa was born in 1921, the son of the distinguished Mata'afa (d. 1948) and descended from one of the four royal families of Western Samoa. Educated at the Marist Brothers School in Apia, he first appeared in politics as a member of the 1954 constitutional convention where he spoke out for support of universal suffrage rather than the traditional *matai* ("chiefly") vote. He became minister for agriculture in 1957, and in 1959 was surprisingly elected prime minister. Only thirty-eight years of age, he was a newcomer to politics. He had, however, gained the respect of all his close associates and had kept in touch with the needs of his *'aiga* ("extended family"). He was generally regarded as conservative regarding Samoan ideas and values. To create and maintain unity within the government, he chose as his first cabinet most of the outgoing ministers of state. In December of 1960 he spoke before the United Nations General Assembly in New York regarding Samoan independence and the role of New Zealand in that new independence. Mata'afa was prime minister for thirteen years (1956-1969 and again from 1972-1975). During his term in office Western Samoa gained its independence (1962) and made rapid social, economic, and political progress while at the same time becoming more involved in regional and international affairs. He died in 1975 leaving his wife Fetauimalemau La'ulu, who, after her husband's death, was pro-chancellor of the University of the South Pacific (1970-1976) and member of parliament (1975, 1979-). They have one daughter, Naomi.

RELATED ENTRIES: Western Samoa.

SOURCES AND READINGS: James W. Davidson, *Samoa Mo Samoa: The Emergence of the Independent State of Western Samoa* (New York: Oxford University Press, 1967); Felise Va'a, *Pacific Islands Monthly*, August 1975, pp. 15, 73.   *Robert D. Craig*

MAU OF PULE. Precursor of the *Mau* movement of the 1920s and 1930s, the *Mau* of *Pule* ("opposition of Savai'i'') was organized to oppose German administration in Western Samoa. The chief figure in the movement was Lauaki Namulau'ulu Mamoe, the most prominent of the chiefs of Tumua and Pule, orator chiefs who represented particular districts on the islands of Upolu and Savai'i. Tumua and Pule had been the prime forces in Samoan politics throughout the nineteenth century, and this was the role to which they aspired in the twentieth century as well. They were opposed in this by the newly established (1900) German administration of Western Samoa, headed by Governor Wilhelm Solf.

When Samoa was partitioned between the United States and Germany in 1900, the leaders of the traditional Samoan political system assumed that essential political power would be left in their hands, as had always been the case, and that Germany would assume the role of protector. Perhaps, they hoped, the Germans might even withdraw from Samoa. This was definitely not what Solf had envisaged for himself or his administration. To establish the authority of the colonial administration and to demoralize and disorganize his opposition, Solf pursued a divide-and-conquer policy. Traditional rivalries were always simmering in the Samoan polity, and it was these rivalries that Solf exploited to isolate his opposition from Tumua and Pule. Mata'afa Iosefa was given the title, *Ali'i Sili*, by the Germans, who reserved to themselves the right to confer the title. Mata'afa's supporters assumed that he and his party were the *malo*, the rightful government of Samoa, but Solf was unwilling to accord them this authority and he began appointing Mata'afa's old rivals to positions of promise in the government.

Resentment at the political implications of German policy was compounded by certain economic grievances the Samoans had. They resented the poll tax. European settlers and half-castes in the contemporary economic mainstream felt their interests were being ignored by the administration's policies. In 1904 a Samoan trading company was organized with Lauaki as one of its founders, which hoped to produce copra to support the Samoan dissidents. Solf ordered the company to cease operations; in 1905 the company closed down after its leaders abandoned it.

That same year the governor disbanded the *Ta-'imua* and *Faipule*, the Samoan parliament, as part of his program to discourage the political pretensions of Tumua and Pule. He created a new representative group, the *fono* of *Faipule*, which consisted of individuals more acceptable to Solf. In January of 1905 Lauaki petitioned the German kaiser for changes in the administration of Western Samoa, to the further annoyance of the governor. Lauaki saw his role as

the restorer of the traditional political order to Samoa, and he continued to press the claims for a primary role for Tumua and Pule. To this end he organized the *Mau* in December 1908 and began a campaign to secure support for his movement from among the Samoan villages. At the request of the German governor he visited Mulinu'u in January 1909, accompanied by a fleet of canoes filled with his followers. Solf, who seems to have had a genuine admiration for the political capacity of Lauaki, forgave him for the greater part of his offenses. In fact, however, the point of reconciliation was past. Solf persuaded the *fono* to request Lauaki's deportation. (There were many in the *fono* who were Lauaki's political enemies.) Warships were dispatched to Samoa; and after a final, dramatic and emotional meeting with Governor Solf, Lauaki and nine of his followers and their families were sent to Saipan in April 1909. The *Mau* of *Pule* was ended; Lauaki himself never saw Samoa again. He died in the Gilbert Islands of dysentery in November 1915 on his way home.

RELATED ENTRIES: Lauaki, Namulau'ulu Mamoe; Western Samoa.

SOURCES AND READINGS: J. W. Davidson, ''Lauaki Namulau'ulu Mamoe: a Traditionalist in Samoan Politics'' in J. W. Davidson and Deryck Scarr, eds., *Pacific Islands Portraits* (Wellington: A. H. and A. W. Reed, 1973).   *Jerry K. Loveland*

MEAD, MARGARET (1901-1978). Regarded as a leading American anthropologist, Margaret Mead concentrated her early work on ten islands of the Pacific, although she also conducted research in modern American culture and the culture of native Americans in the Great Plains. The principal sites of her fieldwork in the Pacific were eastern Samoa (1925-1926), Manus in the Admiralty Islands (1928-1929, 1953, 1964-1965, 1975), New Guinea (1931-1933, 1939, 1967), and Bali (1936-1938) which, though not in the Pacific, has cultural relationships with islands on the western edge of the Pacific. For most of her career, she held an appointment as a curator of Pacific ethnology at the American Museum of Natural History in New York. From 1954 on she also served as adjunct professor of anthropology at Columbia University. She traveled much within the United States and was a popular public speaker.

Mead was an effective spokesperson for anthropology to the general public. She believed that antrhopological knowledge of remote cultures, including the Pacific cultures, deserved wide dissemination. She held that one of the values of ethnographic research was to provide models of alternate ways of life for consideration by her own society. In her autobiography *Blackberry Winter* (1972), she wrote, "I have spent most of my life studying the lives of... faraway peoples, so that Americans might better understand themselves." Thus, she suggested that Samoa demonstrated that adolescence could be a time of little psychic stress and gradual, regular psychosocial development. Manus at the time of her first field trip suggested to her the futility of permissive child-rearing in a competitive society. On her later trips, Manus showed that some kinds of major social change were easier to achieve by a sudden sweeping reform than by piecemeal change over a long period.

Mead was especially interested in the psychological significance of culture. She tried in her writings to describe the people she studied as understandable fellow humans: understandable partly in terms of their particular cultural background and partly in terms of the unique life histories of each. Some of her writing for general audiences has been characterized as "novelistic" for this reason, as well as for its general clarity and avoidance of unnecessary technical terms.

Mead received wide recognition both within and outside the field of anthropology, as indicated by some of the offices she held: president, Society for Applied Anthropology (1949); president, World Federation for Mental Health (1956); president, American Anthropological Association (1960); chairman of the board, American Association for the Advancement of Science (1976).

With her quick wit, extensive knowledge and experience, and direct mode of expression, she could be a formidable adversary in public and scholarly debate, especially toward opponents whom she perceived as rigid, self-satisfied, or arrogant. At the same time, she was a warm and generous friend to many and took time to encourage promising junior colleagues. As she grew older, young people were especially attracted to her as someone who could communicate across generations. Much of her research was directed at childhood and youth in the societies she studied.

In most of her research, she showed a great sensitivity to the current problems of the living people she studied. She was sympathetic with the strivings of the peoples of the Pacific for self-determination, as is manifest especially in her later research on Manus with Theodore Schwartz. While some of her early work seems to assume a stability of non-Western cultures (Samoa, Manus), as she returned repeatedly over many years to some of the societies she studied, she was led to an ever-growing interest in problems of social and cultural change, in Pacific societies as well as in American society.

Mead's lively descriptions of the people she studied sometimes offended them as they acquired literacy in English, but she tried to heed their criticism. She held it as a goal to describe people accurately, yet in terms that they would find acceptable. That she could strive for such a goal is evidence of her deep faith in humanity.

Her writings are voluminous and many deal with her work in the Pacific. Her best known works on the Pacific include *Coming of Age in Samoa* (1928), *Growing Up in New Guinea* (1930), *Sex and Temperament* (1935), and *New Lives for Old* (1956). These books all sold widely in paperback to the general public as well as being read by fellow anthropologists and academics.

RELATED ENTRIES: Admiralty Islands; American Samoa; Papua New Guinea; Roheim, Geza; Semper, Carl; Western Samoa.

SOURCES AND READINGS: Joan Gordon, ed., *Margaret Mead: The Complete Bibliography 1925-1975* (The Hague: Mouton, 1976); Margaret Mead, *Blackberry Winter: My Earlier Years* (New York: Morrow, 1972).
J. L. Fischer

MELANESIA. The term *Melanesia* is nothing more than an academic construction. The area referred to is thought to lie in a 5,600 km (3,500 mi) arc, north and northeast of Australia, from Papua New Guinea and the Bismarck Archipelago to the Solomons, New Hebrides, and Torres Straits Islands, through New Caledonia and Fiji, with all intermediate groups included. Total land area comes to about 525,475 km² (202,886 mi²). There are more than 200 languages spoken in this area, most of which are distinct and mutually unintelligible; they are of the Malayo-Polynesian family.

The peoples of these islands tend to be dark-skinned, hence the descriptive name Melanesia: μέλας *melas*, black; νῆσος *nesos*, island. The term became popular with anthropologists and other students who were preoccupied with racial types after it was first used in 1832 by the French navigator Dumont d'Urville. Today the description is often thought to be antiquated rather than precise.

SOURCES AND READINGS: H. C. Brookfield, *Melanesia, A Geographical Interpretation* (London: Methuen, 1971); B. A. Cranstone, *Melanesia: A Short Ethnography* (London: British Museum, 1961).
Frank P. King

MELANESIAN RECRUITMENT TO QUEENSLAND, PATTERNS OF (1863-1904). It has been imagined popularly that the pattern of recruitment of indentured servants from Melanesia (predominantly the Loyalty group, the New Hebrides, the eastern Solomons and the offshore Niugini islands) for sugar plantations and pastoral stations in Queensland, Australia, from 1863 to 1904 only involved blackbirding, a contemporary euphemism for kidnapping, reminiscent of the initial African slave trade. Certainly, this did occur in the initial stages of contact, but to presume that Melanesians could be duped for over forty years belies their intelligence and self-determination. Several distinct patterns do emerge.

In low-contact areas where Melanesians had experienced little intercourse with Europeans such as missionaries, planters, traders, and itinerant labor agents, the enlistment process was consistently illegal and even, at times, approached some aspects of slave trading. These nefarious methods declined significantly in the transitional period when Pacific islanders gained more experience of white intruders until in the high-contact areas enlistment became almost totally voluntary.

In March 1868 the Queensland government ratified the *Polynesian Labourers Act* which legally defined recruitment as the process whereby "labourers have voluntarily engaged themselves and entered into their agreements with full knowledge and understanding of its nature and conditions." During the previous five years, there had been no official monitoring of the system whereby private individuals could procure laborers. This innocuous legislation, however, hardly contained any real safeguards against abuse. In 1867 the crew aboard the *King Oscar* kidnapped many Loyalty islanders; in the process, several resisting villagers had been shot, their homes burnt, and their crops destroyed. Furthermore, evidence suggests that canoes had been rammed or destroyed by dropping large weights from the barque's bow (a device popularly termed "the eye-drop"). In cases like these, kidnapped men and women would be kept chained for the entire voyage of several months below deck. In November 1871 the captain, mate, and four seamen of the *Jason* were indicted for assaulting and kidnapping New Hebrideans. The latter charge could not be legally substantiated, for it was deemed in the Queensland supreme court that kidnapping could only be said to occur when a person was deprived of the protection of English law. Since Melanesians were regarded as "savages" they could not therefore be deprived of their freedom, a state which pertained only to supposedly "civilized" individuals.

Melanesian society altogether lacked the social structure which alone could have ensured a reliable slave trade. For instance, unlike these Pacific islander communities, coastal west African societies were often rudimentary nation states, where rulers exerted total authority over their subjects and could pillage weaker people farther inland. Small-scale societies—for instance, a tribe in the New Hebrides numbering several hundred persons—could never display this organized, internal control over recruitment. Without this complex organization *within* the indigenous society itself, kidnapping essentially could remain only an isolated mode of procurement. Unlike in Africa, kidnapping in Melanesia thus relied upon the actions of a small number of white labor-traders capitalizing upon the ignorance of low-contact people.

A far more extensive method could be termed *covert coercion*, for it involved trickery and fraud rather than outright abduction. On occasions the ships' crews would disguise themselves as itinerant missionaries. In 1869 a Melanesian named Narufu informed the British naval captain, George Palmer, that the recruiting agent off the *King Oscar* had enticed men on board at Dillon's Bay, Eromanga, in the New Hebrides, with the promise of pigs and tobacco. When the hapless men attempted to leave, they were all imprisoned in the hold. Frequently islanders coming to barter food in return for trade goods would be informed that they could go to "place belonging to the white men" for periods varying from one to three months. In reality, indentured servants in Queensland worked for three years for their master. Three fingers would be held up to indicate the length of servitude or else a grotesque and totally novel pantomime depicting cane-cutting was enacted. Certainly, too, those Melanesians who were employed as interpreters had no moral compunctions in aiding and abetting these nefarious and fraudulent practices. They were, in fact, highly adept collaborators.

The third illegal procedure which was used could be termed *unwitting self-commitment*; this occurred when people of their own volition agreed to sign on without fully comprehending the obligations and strictures. For this common category, violence, deceit, or fraud were not necessary or desirable accompaniments. It would have been difficult, perhaps impossible without direct experience, to convey accurately the nature of colonial servitude to people coming from small-scale, precapitalist societies.

These factors effectively established the basis for legal recruitment. Extensive knowledge of Queensland and other colonial centers such as Fiji, French New Caledonia, and German Samoa which also competed for the same labor could be verbally transmitted by those who were returning, so that the recent arrival had a more comprehensive understanding which surpassed actual experience. Patterns of coercion, fraud, and deceit could hardly continue as viable methods in high-contact areas. Here only legally defined recruitment or voluntary contract was observed. William Matson, a Queensland official on board the *May Queen*, in 1874 described the procedure whereby the second officer would go ashore and call for recruits for Queensland. After negotiation, the local "big men" would indicate their choice of recruits. Trade goods, usually muskets and ammunition, would be offered to compensate for the community's loss of its labor force. Symbolically, the venue where individuals were engaged had irrevocably and permanently shifted during the trade's various phases from the deck of the labor vessel to the beach, where the Melanesians could control the proceedings.

Other factors also altered the nature of the procedures. Initially, all recruits originated from the coastal tribes, for only they had direct access to the itinerant labor vessels. As one of the primary incentives to sign on was to procure a rifle and ammunition, these saltwater people held an unprecedented advantage over the bushmen. Around 1880 in the New Hebrides and Solomons this pattern was to change significantly. With the increasing loss of man power (caused by depopulation directly attributable to the introduction of new virulent diseases by Europeans and returnees, and the temporary absence of the young men—and to a far lesser extent women—in the colonies) fewer coastal dwellers were recruited. With increasing frequency those who remained acted as middlemen in various capacities: as boat's crew, victualers, and intermediaries between the recruiters and the inland bushmen. By the 1890s laborers for Queensland's sugar industry were obtained from Malaita and Guadalcanal while New Hebrideans acted in the ultimately more remunerative and less arduous capacity as boat's crew. The procedures here differed substantially from those involving saltwater people. Labor vessels were forced to anchor for several days as messages were transmitted to the inland. In the New Hebrides, the premier anchorages were Port Resolution, Tanna, Vila and Havannah Harbors, Efate, Dillon's Bay, Eromanga, Port Sandwich, Malekula, Hog Harbor, and Espiritu Santo. The Solomons, being more populous and increasingly more lucrative, contained more anchorages, notably Estrella Bay, Ysabel, Makira, Eponi, Wainoiu and Maru Bays, San Christobal, Talisi and Taisimboko Bays, Guadalcanal, Malu'wu, Urassi, Alete and Port Adams Bays, and Malaita. Here, recruiting proceeded with the invaluable assistance of passage masters who were invariably former recruits and also men of rank within their own communities. They were thereby able to influence, though not truly coerce, their compatriots.

The patterns formed were thus sometimes subtle, complex, and often brutal.

If the nexus of power ultimately always resided with Europeans, what we can discern is the gradual modification of these controls from total supremacy, in the case of kidnapping, to the collaboratory activities of the passage masters.

RELATED ENTRIES: *Hopeful* Scandal; Labor Trade; Loyalty Islands; Melanesians and Colonial Servitude; Solomon Islands; Tanna; Vanuatu (New Hebrides).

SOURCES AND READINGS: Peter Corris, *Passage, Port and Plantation: A History of Solomon Islander Labour Recruitment, 1870-1914* (Melbourne: Melbourne University Press, 1974); J. W. Davidson and Deryck A. Scarr, eds., *Pacific Islands Portraits* (Canberra: Australian National University Press, 1970).

Kay E. Saunders

MELANESIANS AND COLONIAL SERVITUDE (1863-1904).

Between 1863 and 1904 some 62,000 Melanesians disembarked in Queensland, Australia. This figure does not include those who died on the often hazardous, morbid voyage or those who were killed by recruiters. Though Queensland took the largest number, Fiji, New Caledonia, and Samoa were also competing for labor, so that in the second half of the nineteenth century well over 100,000 people from the islands of the southwest Pacific engaged in some form of colonial servitude.

If the labor trade in Melanesia initially was characterized by kidnapping, murder, fraud, and endemic violence, this was not totally characteristic. Ultimately, it was far easier and more profitable to induce Pacific islanders willingly and eagerly to enlist for indentured service. Concurrently, a distinct pattern showing the diminution of coercion and fraud from low- to high-contact regions can be traced. This transformation did not depend upon the moral reformation of the white labor-traders but upon the assertiveness and shrewd negotiations of the Melanesians. The introduction of Western technology, particularly steel knives and muskets since the 1830s and 1840s, produced severe economic ramifications. Almost imperceptibly, the peoples of the southwestern Pacific were drawn into the nexus of capitalism. If initially their position was formidable vis-à-vis the isolated European trader, for most Melanesians colonial servitude was the only avenue through which Western goods could be obtained.

The prospect of a three-year indenture on an Australian sugar plantation with its rigid class and caste structures does not seem particularly inviting, and yet the majority of Pacific islanders who assumed this status did so of their own volition. This is not to say the experience was, in any respect, enjoyable. By working as an indentured laborer for three years, those who survived received £18 sterling which could buy all manner of desirable European goods. Chief among these was the rifle. Particularly in areas like Tanna, there was an enormous socioeconomic pressure upon the very limited resource of land, and warfare between competing groups was endemic. The seasonal recurrence of hurricanes and cyclones, which might destroy a year's crop and injure valuable livestock causing famine, exacerbated existing tensions.

This in turn created an increased demand for superior weaponry such as rifles, steel knives, and tomahawks. It was no mere coincidence that the preponderance of recruits were single males between the ages of fifteen and thirty. Enlistment to Queensland thereby provided the means of securing this weaponry. It was not only the recruits who would be involved in this process. Local "big-men" negotiating between the local community and the labor-traders were also presented with rifles as compensation for the loss of kinsmen.

This was not the sole incentive to enlist. Peter Corris argues that since the period between puberty and marriage in the Solomon Islands was usually uneventful, indenture became a type of initiation. It must have proven, moreover, a traumatic *rite de passage*. A labor vessel also provided an ideal avenue of escape for the individual who committed a crime such as adultery or murder.

Another powerful incentive to enlist was to obtain urgent medical treatment. The dilemma facing Melanesians here was indeed difficult: those returning from colonial indenture introduced unfamiliar and virulent diseases, such as venereal infection, tuberculosis, amoebic and bacillary dysentery, scurvy, influenza, and measles for which there were no traditional cures. This placed the sufferer in a hopeless and vulnerable position, for it was only in the colonies that any medical treatment was available. Though medication and hospitalization in Queensland were grossly deficient, a modicum of relief might be afforded.

The individual who had completed his colonial service found himself in a unique position on returning home. Highly prized trade goods brought prestige. If initially the returnee possessed status, however, his subsequent experience was unenviable after excitement abated. Frequently, his house, gardens, and canoes were in disrepair, his animals dispersed, and his wife remarried. He had become an alien, an interloper clad in ill-fitting European clothes disrupting the traditional structure and mores, particularly if he had been converted to Christianity. Youths baulked at resubmitting to the authority of their elders. More seriously, those returning were suspected of being the harbingers of disease and death. As the problems of readjustment to village life often proved insurmountable, many reengaged.

Overall, however, Melanesians were not hapless victims. They were able to make rational and determined decisions as to whether to enlist or not, as they became aware of the ramifications implicit in signing on to a labor vessel bound for the sugar plantations of distant Queensland.

RELATED ENTRIES: *Hopeful* Scandal; Labor Trade; Melanesian Recruitment to Queensland, Patterns of; Tanna.

SOURCES AND READINGS: Peter Corris, *Passage, Port and Plantation: A History of Solomon Island Labour Migration 1870-1914* (Melbourne: Melbourne University Press, 1974); Kay Saunders, "The Pacific Islander Hospitals in Colonial Queensland: The Failure of Liberal Reform," *Journal of Pacific History* 11 (1976).   *Kay E. Saunders*

MELVILLE, HERMAN (1819-1891). One of America's great novelists, Herman Melville set sail for the Pacific as a twenty-two-year-old crew member of the *Acushnet*, a whaling ship. He and a shipmate, Tobias Green, deserted the whaler eighteen months later when it finally put into port at Nukuhiva in the Marquesas Islands. In Melville's book *Typee* (1846) these adventures are embellished with fictional license. Nevertheless, it is true that Melville and his companion did spend a month among the Marquesan Taipis who were cannibals. Melville escaped the Marquesas aboard another whaler, the *Lucy Ann*, and went to Tahiti where, for a time, the crew was placed under technical arrest. After working for a short while as a plantation laborer on a neighboring island in 1843, he joined the crew of another whaler which carried him to Honolulu. There Melville enlisted as an American sailor aboard the U.S.S. *United States* where he served until discharged fourteen months later in Boston.

While he did not return again to sea, Melville's most significant novels almost all reflect his background in the Pacific. Further, he was the first American novelist to draw upon his ocean experiences and South Pacific geography for his material. *Typee* was an immediate success, as was *Omoo* (1847), his second novel which told of his sojourn in Tahiti and the nearby island on which he labored. Later, the

Galapagos Islands became the setting for the *Encantadas* (Enchanted Isles), ten fictional sketches of people who could have come to the islands. Public indifference to *Moby Dick* (1851), a remarkable account of whaling which was later recognized as Melville's masterpiece, and some hostility toward *Pierre* (1852) diminished Melville's reputation and, subsequently, his literary career. Consequently, he became a customs inspector in New York City where, from 1865 until his death, he lived in relative obscurity. Melville's last writing, *Billy Budd*, a novelette about discipline at sea, was unpublished until 1924. Critics then began to give him belated recognition as one of America's great writers.

RELATED ENTRIES: French Polynesia; Marquesas Islands.

SOURCES AND READINGS: Charles R. Anderson, *Melville in the South Seas* (London: Oxford University Press, 1939); Sculley Bradley, et al., eds., *The American Tradition in Literature*, 3d ed. (New York: W. W. Norton & Co., 1967); Herman Melville, *Typee* (Clinton: Colonial Press, 1965).   *Jeffrey Butler*

MENDAÑA DE NEIRA, ÁLVARO DE (ca. 1542-1595).

The Spanish navigator and explorer Mendaña, a native of Galicia, left Spain and came to the New World in 1567. In November 1567 Alvaro de Mendaña sailed with two ships from Callao, Peru, to search for those Pacific islands where according to Incan legends one could obtain easily much gold and silver. Mendaña also hoped to find the great southern continent usually marked on Renaissance maps as Terra Australis Incognita. Mendaña crossed the vast expanse of the Pacific and sighted only one small island in the Ellice group. Not until early February 1568 did this expedition land on Santa Isabel in the central Solomons. Using this island as a base for their activities, the Spaniards continued their explorations. For some six months the Spaniards remained in the Solomon Archipelago, where they explored and named various islands in this group, including Guadalcanal, Malaita, and San Cristóbal. In August Mendaña made preparations for the long and arduous journey to western America. After great hardships the expedition reached the coast of lower California in mid-December, but not until 11 September 1569 did the vessels finally arrive at the port of Callao, Peru, so slow was the passage down the western coast of the Americas.

Mendaña hoped to establish a colony in the newly discovered Solomon Islands, but he was over fifty years old before he obtained another opportunity to sail across the Pacific. In April 1595 Mendaña again left from Callao in an expedition that included his wife, her three brothers, and 378 other persons including soldiers, sailors, and a number of women, many of ill repute. Pedro Fernández de Quirós, a young, courageous, and competent Portuguese navigator, served as the chief pilot.

In July they landed on a group of beautiful and rather heavily populated islands which they named *Las Marquesas de Mendoza* in honor of the viceroy of Peru. Clashes between the Spaniards and the Marquesans left hundreds of islanders dead. Leaving this area and proceeding further westward, the Spaniards finally established a settlement on an island they named Santa Cruz (now Ndemi). Bitter quarrels and dissensions among the Spaniards, the breakdown of order and discipline, and bloody conflicts with the islanders destroyed any hope that this colonization effort might be successful. Food became scarce and sickness rampant. Many died from tropical fever, and on 18 October 1595 Mendaña himself succumbed.

In November Quirós, now in actual charge of operations, managed to bring the starving survivors to Manila where they arrived in February 1596. After arriving in the capital of the Philippines, Doña Isabel (Mendaña's widow) married Don Fernando de Castro, a relative of her late husband. The *San Jeronimo*, refitted and repaired, sailed from Manila in August 1596 bringing Doña Isabel, her husband, the pilot Quirós as well as others to Acapulco, Mexico, on 11 December. Mendaña had failed to achieve his goal of establishing a Spanish colony on a firm and lasting foundation, but his exploration efforts did contribute to a better understanding of the geography of the central Pacific.

RELATED ENTRIES: Marquesas Islands; Quirós, Pedro Fernández de; Spain in the Pacific.

SOURCES AND READINGS: William A. Amherst and Basil Thomson, eds. and trans., *The Discovery of the Solomon Islands by Álvaro de Mendaña in 1568*, 2 vols. (London: Printed for the Hakluyt Society, 1901); John C. Beaglehole, *The Exploration of the Pacific*, 3d ed. (London: A. and C. Black, 1966).
Bernerd C. Weber

MÉTRAUX, ALFRED (1902-1963).

An anthropologist active in research on Easter Island, Métraux was born 17 June 1902 in Lausanne, Switzerland, was educated in France and Sweden, and specialized in Oriental languages and anthropology at the University of Paris. In 1934 he joined the Franco-Belgium scientific expedition to Easter Island. For a year, he investigated the old religion and customs by interviewing the oldest inhabitants. Interested in the hypothesis that the Easter Island culture may be linked with the Chinese and Southeast Asian civilizations, he compared ancient Easter Island scripts with ancient Chinese writings. Other scientific trips took him to the Bolivian Highlands, central Brazil, Haiti, Mexico, and Africa. He was director of the Institute of Anthropology of the University of Tucuman from 1928 until 1934. From 1936 to 1938 he was a fellow of the Bernice P. Bishop Museum. After spending a year as a Guggenheim Fellow, he became a visiting professor at Yale University until 1941. He served from 1941 to 1945 as a member of the American Bureau of Ethnology at the Smithsonian Institution. At the writing of *Easter Island: A Stone Age Civilization of the Pacific*, he was a member of the social sciences division of UNESCO. His work is the best single book on the "mystery" of Easter Island. He died 11 April 1963.

RELATED ENTRIES: Easter Island.

SOURCES AND READINGS: Alfred Métraux, *Easter Island: A Stone Age Civilization of the Pacific* (London: Oxford University Press, 1957); Alfred Métraux, *Ethnology of Easter Island* (Honolulu: Bernice P. Bishop Museum, 1940).   *David Welch*

MICRONESIA. A collection of island groups in the north Pacific Ocean lying between 13° and 20° north latitude and stretching from 130° to 180° east longitude. Included are the Marianas, Carolines, Marshalls, Kiribati (Gilbert Islands), and the island nation of Nauru. In all, there are some 2,106 islands covering 2,851 km² (1,104 mi²). The population is 123,000 (1978 est.), including some 700 expatriates from America, England, and Australia.

Climate and Land. The climate is tropical with small seasonal changes. Temperature, barometric pressure, and relative humidity are fairly uniform. The average daily temperature ranges between 21° and 29° C (70° to 85° F). The humidity is high. Rainfall is heaviest in a belt between 1° and 8° north latitude where the annual precipitation averages over 3.048 m (120 in) a year. On the high islands within this zone, the precipitation often is considerably greater. On the northern islands and atolls of the Marshalls group, there is a pronounced dry season. From August to December storms are prevalent. The western part of Micronesia is subject to typhoons, particularly between July and November. In the main, the islands in the eastern section lie outside the normal track of typhoons, but from time to time severe storms of typhoon proportions occur. In general, the climate of Micronesia is pleasant and healthful. Epidemic diseases frequently found in tropical

areas, such as cholera, yellow fever, and malaria, do not occur.

In spite of the general shallowness and relatively low fertility of the rain-leached soil, the tropical vegetation is thick and diverse. On some of the high islands, which have both limestone formation and volcanic soil areas, two distinct types of plant formations are found, consisting of forests on the limestone area and grassland or scrub forests on the volcanic soil areas. On the coral atolls, the predominant vegetation is the coconut palm and its related plant associates of breadfruit, pandanus, and plants of a shore character. The high volcanic islands have mangrove swamps on the tidal flats, coconut vegetation on the slopes, and mixed forest growth on the uplands. Certain of the forest trees of the uplands are valuable as a source of building material.

Flora and Fauna. Three main groups of animals are found in the islands today: indigenous types, those introduced by the migrating Micronesians prior to European contact, and types introduced subsequently. The only indigenous animal is the bat, and even this is not found on some of the coral atolls. Ethnologists do not agree as to whether the dog, pig, and rat were introduced by the migrating islanders. Such original strains, if they were brought in, either have become crossbred or were replaced by later species brought in through Western contact. The water buffalo, or carabao, was introduced to the Marianas from the Philippines in early Spanish times and subsequently spread to Ponape and the Palaus. Deer were introduced into the Marianas by the Germans and later carried to Ponape where they thrived. Horses, cattle, goats, and cats also were introduced in the post-European period.

Marine and shore birds characteristic of the tropical Pacific are found in sizable numbers, but land birds are relatively scarce. Among the many sea and shore birds are the tern, albatross, booby gannet, frigate bird, golden plover, duck, and heron. On the high islands, land birds include the pigeon, dove, kingfisher, cuckoo, starling, finch, flycatcher, purple swamp heron, reed warbler, rail, and woodcock. In the Marianas and Palaus, a species of megapode or moundbuilder similar to that found in New Guinea and Australia is found.

A sea crocodile, monitor lizards, and certain species of poisonous snakes are found in the Palaus. There are also two species of land snakes in Palau, and a blind, burrowing snake is found in the Marianas, the Carolines, and the Marshalls.

The tropical waters of the sea, reef, and lagoons have a large, marine fauna. There are bonito, tuna, barracuda, sea bass, sharks, eels, flying fish, porcupine and scorpion fish, octopuses, sea slugs, many kinds of crustaceans and mollusks, such as crabs, lobsters, shrimps, langouste, oysters, clams, and others. Sea animals are represented by the porpoise and the dugong, or sea cow, although the latter is found only in Palau.

Insects are numerous, and it has been estimated that there are 7,000 species of insects of which perhaps 15 percent have been introduced by human beings. Of the total, some 45 percent are distributed throughout the islands, and the rest are endemic to specific areas. Few are dangerous.

Natural Resources. Copra and fish are the two most important Micronesian exports. Land under cultivation for agriculture was 600 hectares (1,282.6 acres) in 1978; mostly for subsistence farming. About 33,500 hectares (82,779 acres) are planted with trees such as coconuts, breadfruit, and pandanus. Much land remains uncultivated. Copra is the only important cash crop with a 1978 export value of $5 million. Small quantities of taro, yams, sweet potatoes, and bananas are exported. No minerals are presently mined in the islands, although in the past the Germans and Japanese took phosphate from the Palaus.

Foreign Discovery and Colonization. Micronesia was peopled, probably, from eastern Asia and Indonesia about ten thousand years ago, but it was not until the sixteenth and seventeenth centuries that the Pacific Ocean area, including Micronesia, was opened to the knowledge of the European nations. By the middle of the latter half of the eighteenth century, most of the puzzling geographic problems of the area had been solved, and from the late seventeenth century to the end of the nineteenth century, European powers began to colonize the region.

Ferdinand Magellan was the first to open Micronesia to the Western world when he stopped briefly at Guam during his circumnavigation of the globe in 1521. He named the islands he had discovered *Los Ladrones* ("the thieves") because some Chamorros stole a skiff that was trailing one of his ships. The group was later renamed the Marianas in honor of Queen Maria Anna of Spain.

In 1564 Manuel Lopez de Legaspi landed at Saipan and proclaimed Spanish sovereignty over the group, but the Spanish during these years were too occupied with conquests in the Americas, the Philippines, and the Moluccas, to devote much attention to Micronesia.

Thomas Cavendish, the British adventurer, was next to arrive in 1588 in his ship, *Desire.* He traded briefly and left. These early explorers brought gifts of ironware which they traded for fresh fruits and vegetables to combat scurvy on long voyages. They also brought a variety of infectious diseases including influenza, smallpox, leprosy, venereal disease, and tuberculosis, which severely depleted the island population.

The actual Spanish colonization of Micronesia began with the arrival of Fray Diego Luis de Sanvitores in 1668. He brought with him priests, laymen, and Filipino soldiers. They entrenched themselves and established churches and religious schools. A series of revolts attended the effort as the islanders only reluctantly embraced Christianity, which did not fit with their traditional beliefs. At one point, the Spanish, in order to control the people more effectively, moved the population of the Marianas into enclaves and segregated them into villages. In addition to being an unpopular move among the islanders, this also had the effect of further decreasing the population since many were killed in the process of relocation, and others died during their adjustment to strange and new environments. Father Sanvitores was martyred in 1672 by some islanders when he forced his way into a house to baptize an infant. He founded eight churches, established three seminaries, and baptized a reported fifty thousand Chamorros.

In 1680 the Spanish returned in greater force led by Don Jose Quiroga who was governor of the Marianas three times from 1680 to 1696. He subdued the islanders after a series of revolts, sieges, murders of missionaries, burnings of churches, and the fleeing of the islanders to the hills. Finally the people of Guam took the oath of allegiance to the king of Spain, took on Spanish customs, wore clothes, cultivated corn, and learned to eat meat. Artisans were sent out to the villages to teach sewing, spinning, weaving, hide tanning, iron forging, stone masonry, and other crafts.

But fighting flared up again, and in 1684 some sixty soldiers and missionaries were killed in a revolt and the governor was wounded. Reprisals were brought to bear. The entire population was brought to Guam in 1698, and the subjugation was then complete.

The Spanish branched out into the rest of Micronesia with only mild persistence. The major town on Guam, Agana, was made a regular stop for their ships traveling between the Philippines and Mexico. By the nineteenth century the islands had become involved in European colonial rivalries. The Germans were interested in Micronesian trade, particularly copra. The Spanish at this time had their weakest claim in the Marshalls, and the Germans assumed a protectorate there in 1885. The British also had a claim to the Marshalls, so the Germans had to contend with them as well as the Spanish. In 1886, however, the two countries ceded the islands formally to Germany.

But the Germans did not stop with the Marshalls. They pressed claims in the Carolines as well. The Spanish reacted violently and a serious conflict was averted by having the issue referred to Pope Leo XIII, who confirmed Spain's claim to the Carolines, but allowed Germany the right to fish and trade and also to establish coaling stations.

Spain's empire, however, was weakening and by 1898 war with the United States was at hand. Commodore George Dewey seized Manila Bay on 1 May, and the Americans also took Guam. In 1899 Spain made the decision to withdraw from the Pacific entirely and sold the Carolines and the Marianas—except Guam which the Americans continued to hold—to Germany for 25 million pesetas.

The Germans were intent on developing Micronesia as a basis for a lucrative copra trade. Using indigenous labor and setting enforced quotas, large numbers of coconut palms were planted. Administrative centers were established at Ponape, Yap, Saipan, and Jaluit.

German control in Micronesia ended abruptly with the outbreak of World War I. In October 1914 the Japanese navy took military possession of all the islands and after the war received them by League of Nations mandate on 20 December 1920. The United States gave its consent to this on 11 February 1922. Following this action, Japan instituted civil rule in Micronesia and began immediately to develop the islands economically.

Japanese rule in Micronesia was complete, direct, and allowed little use of Micronesians in local government. The basic laws of Japan were extended to the mandate, and only necessary modifications were allowed to meet local conditions. Formal educational facilities were restricted and emphasis was placed on the teaching of the Japanese language. Considerable attention was also placed upon the health of the people, and one medical doctor was stationed in each district. Under the Japanese administration, Micronesia and its people were made more productive than they ever had been before.

With the outbreak of World War II, Japan immediately took Guam from the United States and made its domination of the area complete. All of the islands became bases for aggression to the south and east. In turn, the islands served as a great barrier to the liberation of the Philippines, Wake, and Guam. Not until November 1943, when the Gilberts were invaded, did the United States forces begin to break through the barrier. In January and February of 1944 the Marshalls were seized; in June and July the Marianas were invaded; by August the eastern and central Carolines were neutralized; in September Angaur and Peleliu in the western Carolines were captured.

Many of the individual islands were bypassed, and with most of these communication was not reestablished until the war was over.

American Period in Micronesia. The American invasion of Micronesia during World War II completely destroyed the economy. America began the task of rebuilding. The United States was very interested in keeping the islands under its jurisdiction after the war, and on 18 July 1947 President Harry Truman delegated responsibility for the civil administration of the islands, on an interim basis, to the secretary of the navy. Then, on 1 July 1951, administrative responsibility was transferred to the secretary of the interior. A trusteeship was established with the United Nations. A special designation of "strategic" trusteeship was made which placed ultimate jurisdiction of the islands under the United Nations Security Council. This arrangement continues today.

The United States pledged to promote the development of the inhabitants of the Trust Territory towards self-government or independence as may be appropriate to the particular circumstances of the Trust Territory and its peoples, and the freely expressed wishes of the people concerned. In 1969 serious future political status talks began between the Micronesians and the Americans. At the time, six administrative districts—Marianas, Yap, Palau, Truk, Ponape, and the Marshalls—existed, covering an area larger than that of the continental United States.

In 1972 the people of the Northern Marianas (excluding Guam), started separate negotiations of their own with the United States. This led to a plebiscite in which the people chose a commonwealth status with the United States. Although the trusteeship remains technically in effect, the new commonwealth government, led by an elected governor, began operations in January 1978.

The other islands—the Carolines and the Marshalls—drafted a constitution at Saipan in 1975. In addition, they negotiated a political status of "free association" with the United States. After some conflicts over the political "fit" of the free-association status with the proposed constitution had been worked out, all the people in the Carolines and the Marshalls voted on the acceptance of the proposed constitution on 12 July 1978. The results were that four districts—Truk, Yap, Kosrae, and Ponape—accepted the constitution, and two districts—Palau and the Marshalls—did not. Kosrae, mentioned above, was a new district carved out of Ponape.

The governing rules called for the constitution being approved by a majority of voters in at least four of the six districts; and also that if four or more of the districts accepted the constitution, it would be effective within one year after the election. Hence, the Federated States of Micronesia (FSM)—Truk, Yap, Ponape, and Kosrae—officially came into being on 10 May 1979. The new capital is on Ponape. A president and vice-president preside over the new government. Each state elects a governor of its own.

In December 1978 the Marshalls drafted and had accepted by the people a constitution which was passed in referendum in March 1979. In April of the same year an election was held for their new legislature, called the *Nitijela*. At the same time the Palauans held a constitutional convention which was ratified in 1980. A presidential election was held in November 1980, and Palau became the Republic of Belau, formulating their own freely associated status with the United States.

As it now exists, Micronesia—the Trust Territory of the Pacific Islands—consists, not of seven districts, but of four separate government entities: the Northern Marianas, effective 9 January 1978; the Marshall Islands, effective 1 May 1979; the Federated States of Micronesia, effective 10 May 1979; and the Republic of Belau, effective 1 January 1981. All of these government entities will be part of the trust territory until the trusteeship is formally terminated by the United States and the United Nations.

RELATED ENTRIES: Betel Nut Chewing; Bishop Museum; Caroline Islands; Chamorros (Ancient); Chamorros Peoples, Origins of; Commercial/Economic Importance of the Pacific Islands; Commonwealth of the Northern Mariana Islands; Earhart, Amelia; Education in the Pacific, Higher; German Colonial Empire; Guam; Jaluit Company; Kubary, Johann; *Leonora*; Mariana Islands; Marshall Islands; Micronesia (all entries); Micronesian Area Research Center; *Morning Star*; Nimitz, Chester; Peace Corps; Regionalism; Sokehs Rebellion; Solomon Report; South Pacific Commission; Spain in the Pacific; Stick Charts; Strategic Importance of Oceania; United States and Pacific Island Bases; United States in the Pacific; United States Congress and Micronesia; War in the Pacific Islands 1914-1945; Whaling in the Pacific; World War II Battles for the Gilbert and Marshall Islands; Xavier High School.

SOURCES AND READINGS: Emme Helen Blair, ed., *The Philippine Islands* (Cleveland, Ohio: A. K. Clark Co., 1909); E. H. Bryan, *Life in Micronesia* (Honolulu: Bishop Museum Press, 1972); F. W. Christian, *The Caroline Islands* (London: Cass, 1967); Paolo Giordani, *The German Colonial Empire* (London: Bell and Co., 1916); Henry H. Jackman, "Economic Development in Micronesia" (Master's thesis, Aus-

tralian School of Pacific Administration, 1958); Alice Joseph and V. F. Murray, *Chamorros and Carolinians of Saipan, Personality Studies* (Cambridge: Harvard University Press, 1951); Yanaihara Tadao, *Pacific Islands Under Japanese Mandate* (London: Oxford University Press, 1940); Trust Territory of the Pacific Islands, *Annual Reports*, Washington, D.C., Department of the Interior, 1948-1979.

Dirk Anthony Ballendorf

MICRONESIA, CONSTITUTION OF THE FEDERATED STATES OF. The constitution was adopted in a United Nations observed referendum on 12 July 1978 by the districts of Yap, Kosrae, Ponape, and Truk of the Trust Territory of the Pacific Islands. The districts of Palau and the Marshalls rejected the constitution and now form their own autonomous governments under their own constitutions.

The constitution of the Federated States of Micronesia was written by a convention held between 12 July and 8 November 1975 on Saipan, Mariana Islands. It was made up of delegates from Yap, Ponape, Truk, the Marshalls, Palau, and the Northern Marianas. Sixty delegates were authorized including twelve traditional leaders, six members of the Congress of Micronesia, and forty-two delegates elected from the districts by population. Some districts failed to send their full delegations (Mariana Islands and the Marshalls). The convention was chaired by Tosiwo Nakayama (Truk) with University of Hawaii Professor of Political Science Norman Meller heading up the staff.

After the constitution was written, the Northern Marianas separated from the rest of the trust territory through the adoption of their own covenant to establish a commonwealth with the United States and their own constitution in 1976. Kosrae became a separate district on 1 January 1977 thus replacing the Northern Marianas as the sixth district at the 12 July 1978 constitutional referendum.

The constitution establishes a presidential government with parliamentary overtones and a decentralized federal structure. The central government consists of a president and vice-president, a congress of the Federated States, and a supreme court. The president and vice-president are elected from the congressional membership elected at large, one from each of the four member states. The congress is composed of two types of senators: one each from each state elected at large for a four year term and ten elected on the basis of population, one from Kosrae and Yap each, three from Ponape, and five from Truk, all for two-year terms. In order to balance the large and small districts, all legislation will be passed on second reading by each district delegation casting one vote.

The national government is restricted in its authority to international affairs, matters involving more than one state, and those "of a national character." Its taxing authority is restricted to import and income taxes. The district governments retain all other powers. A bill of rights is included in the constitution guaranteeing the civil liberties of the citizens, protecting traditions and customs, and universal suffrage is provided. Each district or state is guaranteed its own constitution in conformity with provisions of the national constitution. In addition, states have exclusive rights over land matters in recognition of the importance of land in these small islands. The right of eminent domain is not mentioned at all in the national constitution.

The constitution defines the boundaries of the Federated States to be at twelve miles from an archipelagic baseline with an exclusive economic zone extending to two hundred miles. An added provision, however, permits adjustments of this line to conform with international treaties of the law of the sea. In fact, instead of the archipelagic principle, each island now has a three-mile territorial water boundary, a twelve-mile exclusive fisheries zone, and an additional 188-mile fisheries jurisdiction for a total of two hundred miles of jurisdiction. The outer boundaries of the nation are the intersecting lines. States control resources within the twelve-mile zones, and the national government controls the 188 miles with a 50 percent revenue-sharing principle applying to the contiguous state and the national government for any returns on exploitation of the waters between twelve and two hundred miles.

Political status is not dealt with directly in the national constitution although independence is the basic theme. A status less than independence is provided for in Article IX, Section 4 which permits the delegation of major governmental authorities to another government with the consent of two-thirds of the state legislatures. This provision has been accepted as compatible with the principle of free association with the United States which is the status being negotiated; and it is expected to be in force when the trusteeship with the United Nations is terminated in or about 1981.

The constitution became partially effective on 12 July 1979, one year following the referendum, in those states that ratified it. It will become fully effective upon the termination of the trusteeship agreement.

The first Congress of the Federated States was elected on 27 March 1979, with the election of the executive branch in mid-May, following the organization of the congress beginning on 10 May at the new capital of the Federated States in Ponape.

RELATED ENTRIES: Commonwealth of the Northern Mariana Islands; Micronesia; Solomon Report.

SOURCES AND READINGS: P. F. Kluge, "The Micronesian Constitutional Convention," *Micronesian Reporter* 23, 4 (1975):38-44; Samuel McPhetres, "Micronesia's Islands Headed for New Future," *Micronesian Reporter* 26 (1978):2-9.   *Sam McPhetres*

MICRONESIA, FOREIGN INVESTMENT IN. Since 1945, when the United States first began administering the scattered islands in the three million square miles of western Pacific Ocean known as the Trust Territory of the Pacific Islands (Micronesia), foreign investment has been strictly regulated. From 1945 to 1974 foreign investment was allowed only by American citizens under the United States administration's interpretation of Article 8 of the United Nations Trusteeship Agreement, "the most-favored nation" clause. In 1974 the secretary of the interior reversed this policy in an attempt to attract other members of the community of nations to invest. As of 1979 the bulk of foreign investment in Micronesia remained that owned by U.S. citizens.

Under the military/naval administration of the territory (1945-1951), policy on foreign investment was promulgated by directive with the aim of keeping the inhabitants of Micronesia from being exploited by any outside interests. Under the Department of the Interior administration which began in 1951, a code of laws was promulgated which continued the navy's regulations of business. Under Section 1100(b), the high commissioner was authorized to license noncitizen business. In 1962 a major policy change allowed U.S. citizen investment, but the prohibition against other investment continued. The result of these policies was to limit alien investment in Micronesia to less than ten businesses, most of which were owned by persons who had lived and done business in Micronesia under the Japanese administration.

In 1970 the Congress of Micronesia enacted the Foreign Investors Business Permit Act which provides a general formula under which foreign investment applications can be screened and business permits issued. The act is regulatory in nature and does not provide development incentives.

Foreign investment in Micronesia has remained at about $17 to $18 million in its entities, excluding the Northern Marianas, since 1973. With the establishment of a separate government in the Northern Marianas in 1978, U.S. individuals or companies are no longer required to obtain foreign business permits. The area with the most significant growth, outside of the Marianas, has been Palau which increased its investment by $5 million during the last half of the 1970s.

The trusteeship agreement under which Micronesia is administered is not considered a permanent arrangement and upon its termination, presently proposed for 1981, the governments of the Commonwealth of the Northern Mariana Islands, the Marshalls, Palau, and the Federated States of Micronesia will become separate entities. There is every indication that the strict regulatory policies, laws, and regulations which have been in force for many years will be continued by these new governments, with the exception of the Northern Marianas.

RELATED ENTRIES: Commonwealth of the Northern Mariana Islands; German Colonial Empire; Micronesia; Micronesia, Constitution of the Federated States of; Ruge & Company, H. M.; Solomon Report; Vaitupu "Company"; War in the Pacific Islands.

SOURCES AND READINGS: Robert Klitzkie, "U.S. Policy Regarding Foreign Investment in Micronesia," *Micronesian Reporter* 24, No. 3 (1976). Trust Territory of the Pacific Islands, *Annual Reports on the Administration of the Foreign Investors Business Permit Act*, 1974, 1975, 1976, 1977, 1978.

Elizabeth S. Udui

MICRONESIA: A GEOGRAPHICAL DEFINITION. Micronesia encompasses an enormous area of the tropical, western Pacific Ocean. Land constitutes a mere 2,740 km² (1,054 mi²) within an oceanic region of well over five million square kilometers. Micronesia is one of three major geographical regions, or designations of the Pacific, or Oceania.

The Region. There are several island groups and individual islands in Micronesia: μικρός , *mikros*, small; νῆσος, *nēsos*, island, whose proposed name was submitted by Domeny de Rienzi to the Société de Géographie de Paris in 1831. The island groups of Micronesia consist of the former Trust Territory of the Pacific Islands (TTPI), Guam, Nauru, Ocean, and Kiribati. The TTPI contains three major archipelagic areas: the Caroline Islands (this vast east-west archipelago includes five TTPI districts—Kosrae, Ponape, Truk, Yap, and Palau, respectively, of which the first four districts have formed a new political entity called the Federated States of Micronesia) which numbers 957 islands, islets, and reefs totaling 1,195 km² (461 mi²); the Marshall Islands, numbering 1,225 islands, islets, and reefs, totaling 180.8 km² (69.8 mi²); and the Mariana Islands, exclusive of

Guam, now known as the Commonwealth of the Northern Marianas numbering twenty-one islands, islets, and reefs totaling 477.8 km² (184.5 mi²).

Guam, the southernmost island of the Marianas archipelago, and its associated reef complexes, is approximately 554.2 km² (214 mi²). Guam has been a U.S. territory (unincorporated) since 1898 and politically is separated from the other Mariana Islands and Micronesia.

The remaining Micronesian islands are Kiribati (formerly the Gilbert Islands) consisting of 295.57 km² (114.12 mi²), Nauru Island (an independent republic) 21.2 km² (8.2 mi²), and Ocean Island (a United Kingdom dependency) 5.95 km² (2.3 mi²). Kiribati, Nauru, and Ocean Island together total 322.7 km² (124.6 mi²). Therefore, Guam and the islands of the former TTPI account for 2,408 km² (929.8 mi²) which constitutes approximately 88 percent of the total land area of Micronesia.

Since Edwin H. Bryan's areal compilations of 1971 were published, a TTPI territorial survey by R. G. Perry revealed several adjustments of these land figures. The overall Perry land-area size of 707.442 square miles constitutes a downward adjustment of Bryan's 715.789 square miles by 8.347 square miles. This difference does not seem significant until one compares the land sizes of individual "high" islands, that is, Ponape Island proper, and Babelthuap in Palau. While Perry measured them to be about the same size (140 square miles with Ponape slightly larger) Bryan found their sizes in square miles much different: Ponape at 129.04 and Babelthuap with 153.24 square miles.

Ocean Floors. There are other physiographic characteristics of Micronesia that further distinguish the region from other areas of Oceania. Micronesia borders on East Asia and is part of a structural province known as the Western Margins. These "margins" refer to land divisions within the Pacific proper and the continental areas of Asia and Oceania.

In Micronesia the most significant physiographic distinction is established by the boundary between the Pacific Basin floor and the island structures (volcanic mountains) of the Philippine Sea. The Palau Islands, Yap Islands (excluding Ulithi and the other outer islands and atolls of the Yap District), Guam and the Marianas, Kazan (formerly Volcano), Ogasawara (Bonin), and the Izu Islands to Honshu, Japan, constitute a section of the Andesite Line which differentiates the deeper Pacific from the partially submerged continental areas on its margins.

The Western Margins designate the complex area also known as the Pacific "Rim of Fire," where the Pacific Basin meets the trenches adjacent to the island archipelagos that convexly face the western Pacific along the Asian continent from Fiji to Palau to Japan. Therefore, Micronesian archipelagoes, that is, the Palaus, are located on the extreme eastern edge of Asia. Along this "edge," at or near the meridian 135° east longitude, Koror and Tokyo are separated by 3,200 km and provide a focus for a regional distinction. There is the Far East, including the countries of Indonesia, the Philippines, and Japan on the one hand, and the western Pacific areas of Micronesia, including the outer islands of Yap, Truk, the Marshalls, and Nauru on the other.

RELATED ENTRIES: Bernart, Luelen; Betel Nut Chewing; Boo, Lee; Caroline Islands; Chamorros (Ancient); Chamorros Peoples, Origin of; CIMA; Commonwealth of the Northern Mariana Islands; Doane, Edward; Ellis, Earl; German Colonial Empire; German South Seas Expedition; Gibbon, James; Guam; Guam's Constitutional Conventions; Holcomb, Crayton; Jaluit Company; Kubary, Johann; Langsdorf, George H.; *Leonora*; *Leucaena Leucocephala*; Logan, Robert; Mailo, Petrus; Mariana Islands; Marshall Islands; Micronesia; Modekngei; *Morning Star*; Nan Madol; Nanpei, Henry; Nauru; Ocean Island; Ogasawara (Bonin) Islands; Pease, Benjamin; Semper, Carl; Sokehs Rebellion; Solomon Report; Soumadau; South Pacific Commission; Spruance, Raymond; Swanston, Robert; Tuba; United States in the Pacific; Xavier High School.

SOURCES AND READINGS: Edwin H. Bryan, Jr., *Guide to Place Names in the Trust Territory of the Pacific Islands* (Honolulu: Bernice P. Bishop Museum, 1971); Kenneth B. Cumberland, *Southwest Pacific: Australia and New Zealand and their Pacific Island Neighborhoods* (London: Methuen, 1956); Bruce G. Karolle and D. C. Jones, "Territoriality: A Basic for Determining the Future of Micronesia," *Pacific Asian Studies* 2 (1977); Raymond E. Murphy, "High and Low Islands in the Eastern Carolines," *Geographical Review* 39 (1949); Ronald G. Perry, *Department of Lands and Surveys* (Saipan: Trust Territory of the Pacific Islands, 1973); William L. Thomas, Jr., "The Pacific Basin: An Introduction" in Herman R. Friis, ed., *The Pacific Basin: A History of its Geographical Exploration* (New York: American Geographical Society, 1967).   *Bruce Karolle*

MICRONESIA: A POLITICAL DEFINITION.

The small islands of Micronesia have a geographic, cultural, and political significance. Geographically they encompass the Marianas, Carolines, Marshalls, Kiribati (Gilbert Islands), and Nauru.

Culturally Micronesia includes generally the same groups, although there is a heavy Polynesian influence at Kapingamarangi Atoll, which is near the equator south of Truk and Ponape, and a Melanesian influence at Tobi in Palau. Some ethnographers have considered Tuvalu (Ellice Islands) to be culturally Micronesian.

Politically, the definition is more complicated. Until recently Micronesia was usually considered as synonymous with the United States administered Trust Territory of the Pacific Islands which included all the Marshalls, Carolines, and Marianas except Guam. Guam has been a U.S. possession since 1898 and an unincorporated territory of the United States since 1952.

In 1969 the people of the Trust Territory of the Pacific Islands entered into formal future political-status negotiations with the United States. In 1972 the people of the Northern Mariana Islands broke away from the rest of the island groups and entered into separate negotiations. After a plebiscite and election of a government, the Commonwealth of the Northern Mariana Islands (CNMI) was formed. The first governor, Carlos Camacho, took office on 9 January 1978 at Saipan. Hence, the Mariana Islands now contain two political entities: Guam, a territory, and the commonwealth which is all the rest of the Mariana Islands.

The other island groups in the trust territory held a constitutional convention in 1975. All the people voted on the adoption of this document on 12 July 1978. Four districts ratified: Yap, Ponape, Truk, and Kosrae. Two did not: Palau and the Marshall Islands. The four ratifying formed the Federated States of Micronesia (FSM) and their government, with an elected president, Tosiwo Nakayama, and a vice-president, Petrus Tun, came into being officially on 10 May 1979. Elected as governor in each of the four states in the federation were: Leo Falcam of Ponape, John Mangafel of Yap, Erhart Aten of Truk, and Jacob Nena of Kosrae.

The Marshall Islands drafted and had accepted by their people a constitution which was passed in referendum in March 1979. In April an election was held for their new legislature, called the *Nitijela*. It has thirty-three members and provides for the election of one president, who is also a member of the legislative branch as well. There is no vice-president. Amata Kabua was chosen as the first president and was inaugurated on 1 May 1979.

In April 1979 the Palauans also held a constitutional convention. Their document, not yet approved, provides for a general election of president and vice-president.

As it now exists, the Trust Territory of the Pacific Islands consists of four separate government entities: the Northern Marianas (CNMI), the Marshall Islands, the Federated States of Micronesia (FSM), and Palau (Belau). All of these government entities are in transitional status and are technically still part of the Trust Territory of the Pacific Islands until the official termination of the trusteeship by the United Nations which is scheduled for 1981.

RELATED ENTRIES: Micronesia; Micronesia, Foreign Investment in; Micronesia: A Geographical Definition.

SOURCES AND READINGS: Dirk A. Ballendorf and Frank P. King, eds., *Towards New Directions and Political Self-Actualization* (Mangilao, Guam: Micronesian Area Research Center, 1980).

Dirk Anthony Ballendorf

MICRONESIAN AREA RESEARCH CENTER (MARC). Created by an act of the ninth Guam legislature in 1967, the Micronesian Area Research Center is situated at the University of Guam where it is an integral part of the academic community. MARC conducts social science research of various kinds to acquire a better understanding of the area. It assists the various governments and agencies in the region in the preparation of special reports and surveys. It acquires historical and cultural relics for study and display. It publishes materials of relevance to the area which will enhance cultural and historical understanding, as well as understanding within the various social sciences, and also publishes materials in support of instructional programs. MARC possesses a large (40,000 volume) collection of archival materials, books, manuscripts, documents, microfilms, photographs, and other material related to Micronesia. The center also transcribes, translates, and prepares analytical bibliographic listings of important Spanish, German, French, Japanese, and other foreign-language documents. *Dirk Anthony Ballendorf*

MICRONESIAN MISSION (1852-1909). The Micronesian Mission was organized by the Hawaiian Missionary Society and the American Board of Commissioners for Foreign Missions (ABCFM), both of them arms of the Congregational Church in America with headquarters in Boston, Massachusetts.

In 1852 the first missionary couples, three American and two Hawaiian, arrived in Micronesia to establish stations on the islands of Ponape and Kosrae (Kusaie) in the eastern Carolines. Five years later the mission had expanded to Ebon in the Marshalls and Apaiang in the Gilberts. At the end of twenty-five years, it could claim thirty-six churches and nearly two thousand members on islands ranging from the westernmost outpost of Truk to the easternmost in the Gilberts. A series of vessels named *Morning Star* aided immeasurably in the work.

By 1874 three large training schools and several smaller ones were producing teachers, preachers, and mission workers from among island church members. These teachers were very effective in establishing new mission stations, and they reduced the need for American recruits, although the latter continued to hold supervisory positions. Printed translations of all or parts of the New Testament in four island dialects were available by the mid-1870s.

Obstacles faced by the missionaries ranged from indifference to outright enmity, usually from chiefs who felt endangered by the new ideas. Opposition often came from whalers and traders and from the small but influential beachcomber colonies. Nevertheless, mission influence grew, sometimes extending to civil matters. Soon after Spanish occupation of Ponape in 1886, missionaries were accused of fomenting rebellion among the islanders. One was arrested. In 1890 all Americans were expelled from the island. After the Spanish-American War established German rule in the Carolines and Marshalls, the German *Liebenzeller* mission society assumed responsibility for Protestant missions in those groups, and by 1909 the ABCFM withdrew from them. Great Britain had claimed the Gilbert Islands in the meantime, where the London Missionary Society took full responsibility for missions in 1917. Although the Micronesian Mission, as such, was dissolved, the ABCFM temporarily entered the islands again following World War II, but only long enough to help the old mission churches reestablish themselves in the islands. When they had become self-sufficient, the ABCFM once again withdrew.

RELATED ENTRIES: American Board of Commissioners for Foreign Missions; *Morning Star.*

SOURCES AND READINGS: David and Leona Crawford, *Missionary Adventures in the South Pacific* (Rutland, Vt. and Tokyo, Japan: Charles E. Tuttle Co., 1967); Clifton J. Phillips, *Protestant America and the Pagan World: The First Half Century of the American Board of Commissioners for Foreign Missions, 1810-1860* (Cambridge: East Asian Research Center, Harvard University, 1969). *Mary Browning*

MICRONESIAN SEMINAR. A Jesuit pastoral research institute located at Xavier High School on the island of Moen, Truk, Federated States of Micronesia, the Micronesian Seminar was founded in 1957 in Woodstock, Maryland. Its principal function at that time was to aid Jesuit students in preparation for their future work in Micronesia while they pursued general theological studies. A newsletter and small library were established, and its activities, including English translations of early accounts of life in the islands, were carried on under the direction of Father Tom McGrath. In 1969 the Micronesian Seminar library and its activities were transferred from Woodstock to its present site at Xavier High School. Father Francis X. Hezel at Xavier assumed directorship, and in 1972 the Micronesian Seminar was formally designated as the pastoral-research institute of the Caroline-Marshalls mission. Since that time, its library and activities have grown apace with its added responsibilities. Ties have been forged with social scientists, historians, and pastoral research groups throughout the Pacific, the United States, and Europe as well as with individuals in all parts of Micronesia.

A principal objective of the Micronesian Seminar since 1972 has been to stimulate sociotheological reflection, that is, to raise questions relative to the islands today in light of the Gospel's teachings and to help both Catholic and Protestant pastors bring these problems to the attention of their parishioners. This is accomplished through a series of mimeographed publications and through seminars for both church and Micronesian government personnel. Publications have focused upon such things as the educational system in Micronesia, population migration into district centers, the disparity between people's acquired tastes and their pocketbooks, and the suicide rate among young Micronesians, among others. These articles have found their way into newspapers, magazines, and journals throughout the Pacific. Conferences, with a cross-section of English-speaking Micronesian leaders in attendance, have also been sponsored almost annually. Topics have included Micronesia's political future, education, economic development, youth problems, and effects of the U.S. federal program bonanza.

A second major objective, continued from the Micronesian Seminar's early days, has been to carry out and promote historical research and to make the results of this work available not only to Jesuits and scholars, but to Micronesians as well through various educational programs and publications. Thus, translation work has continued and articles on the early contact period of Micronesia have appeared in the *Journal of Pacific History*. Two social studies textbooks, coauthored by Father Hezel and a Peace Corps teacher, are being used in high schools through-

out Micronesia. Moreover, in the near future, two book-length publications will appear to help fill the gap on material on Micronesian history for island students and teachers.

RELATED ENTRIES: Micronesia; Xavier High School.
Francis X. Hezel

MIDWAY ISLANDS. An unincorporated American territory in the central Pacific, the Midway Islands are situated 28° 13′ north latitude, 177° 22′ west longitude, 2,100 km (1,300 mi) northwest of Honolulu. A coral atoll with a circumference of about 24 km (15 mi) encloses the two islands, Eastern (Green) and Sand, with a land area of about 5 km² (2 mi²).

These uninhabited islands were claimed by the United States in 1859 when Captain N. C. Brooks discovered them. They were first called Middlebrooks and then the Brooks. When the United States formally annexed the islands in 1867 the name was changed. The islands were placed under the control of the Department of the Navy by President Theodore Roosevelt in 1903. Sand Island became a station on the Hawai'i-Luzon submarine cable in 1905. In 1936 it became an air stop on the San Francisco-Manila mail run. The famous Battle of Midway was fought nearby on 3 to 6 June 1942 and was a turning point in World War II. The islands have had greatly reduced strategic and communication importance since that time.

RELATED ENTRIES: Spruance, Raymond; War in the Pacific Islands.   *Frank P. King*

MIGRATION TRENDS. The rapid rise in population and the extensive rural-to-urban migration of the last twenty-five years have had their dramatic effect on the islands of the Pacific Ocean. No major part of this region has remained unaffected by these two closely interrelated phenomena.

Most of the Pacific island populations are relatively youthful. Throughout the region, from Micronesia through Papua New Guinea to central Polynesia, the median ages are between fourteen and seventeen years, making this one of the youngest average populations of the world. In most places, high birth rates accompanied by moderate-to-low infant mortality rates combine to give Oceania one of the world's most rapidly growing populations. And, with the exception of Melanesia and the extremities of Polynesia (Hawai'i and New Zealand), the generally small landmasses of the Pacific island groups produce some of the world's highest population densities. These factors, coupled with an overall poor natural resource base and the handicap of great distances from potential market outlets, have created social and economic conditions which tend to produce abnormally high migration rates. In the past generation, the urban centers (principally port towns) of the Pacific have grown at extremely rapid rates and, where politically and economically possible, there have been some of the most dramatic international mass migrations in modern history: for example, over half of the population of an island group (Wallis and Futuna or the Cook Islands) have migrated to a new area.

The phenomenon of large movements of population is certainly not new to the Pacific. In fact, the islands themselves were settled by migrating groups of seafarers who conquered the vast reaches of this ocean. There has never been, however, a period of time in the Pacific when so many migration episodes have taken place over such vast distances involving such a large number of persons. This movement of people involves both internal migration within a specific island group or political unit and external migration involving a basic severance of immediate physical ties with a specific home region, island, or archipelago.

The internal movement is generally from a hinterland or outer island (rural) area to the port towns which are usually also administrative, economic, and communication centers for the island group or region. This migration within the island group involves persons who are seeking occupational opportunities—especially in the fields of government employment and service occupations although opportunities for work in tourism and air transportation fields are available in places such as Pape'ete, Noumea, and Suva. Educational opportunities, a second important reason for rural to urban migration, are related to the first. There is now a widespread awareness that some technical and professional skills require a basic education and the best educational training facilities are located in the administrative centers. Many people choose to relocate in these urban places for either their own educational advancement or for the benefit of their children. Other reasons for moving include health and medical attention, being near to relatives, social and economic disputes in the home village, and simply the desire to live in a place which offers a wider variety of activities and diversions.

External (international) migration is undertaken for the same basic reasons. The external migrant follows political and economic routes which were established (or still exist) when outside nations had established colonial control over the various island groups of the Pacific. Thus, areas which were (or are) dependencies of New Zealand account for the largest number of Oceanic immigrants entering that country.

American Samoans, Guamanians, and Micronesians (from the trust territory) account for the largest number of Pacific islanders entering the United States (principally Hawai'i and California). French Polynesians and Wallisians migrate to New Caledonia, and Easter Islanders are now moving to Chile. Those areas of the Pacific which had no clear lines of immigration established in their preindependence period account for fewer international migrants. Also, because of immigration requirements of the various receiving nations, the emigrants from these newly independent states tend to migrate in the direction of least resistance rather than following any well-defined immigration channels. Thus, while there are persons and families leaving Fiji, Nauru, Papua New Guinea, and the Solomon Islands (all areas which had not established clear-cut immigration routes before independence) the flow of migration out of these countries is, as of now, generally multidirectional to the various urban and residential areas of the Pacific Basin and the west coast of North America.

Another type of migration which has had a significant impact on some of the Pacific island communities has been the relocation of entire villages or island populations—often to points outside the traditional culture area of the persons involved. In some cases, this process has been brought about because of circumstances beyond the control of the islanders themselves. Such cases include the resettlement of the Bikini Atoll dwellers of the Marshall Islands to Rongerik Atoll and ultimately to Kili (both atolls also being in the Marshalls) because of the selection of their homeland, Bikini Atoll, as a nuclear test site by the United States government. Another example is the relocation of communities because of the threat of natural disasters, such as the evacuation of the village of Maat on Ambrym Island in the New Hebrides because of the threat of a fairly active pair of volcanoes.

One episode in the history of relocated communities which had a tremendous effect on the impacted populations was the forced removal of workers (mostly young adult males) to work in copra plantations or to work in the cotton and sugar plantations of Queensland or to extract guano from the coastal areas of Peru and northern Chile. This practice was called blackbirding. It had its most significant effect on the populations of the islands of Melanesia (especially in the Solomon Islands and New Hebrides) and in some of the eastern Polynesian areas, most notably Easter Island. This practice took place throughout the latter half of the nineteenth century. Many persons did not survive the bitter treatment of blackbirding and by 1907 when the last "recruits" were returned to their home islands a large number of communities in the Pacific were ruined and destroyed.

In some cases, large numbers of persons have been resettled because of religious, political, or cultural differences, most often the result of postcolonial contacts. Examples of this type of relocation would be the establishment of the village of Iosepa in the desert of Utah (which was abandoned by 1920) by Hawaiian members of the Church of Jesus Christ of Latter-day Saints and, more recently, the settlement of Independence, Missouri, by Samoan Latter-day Saints. After the Indonesians formally took control of Irian Jaya (West New Guinea) in 1963 a large number of Papuans, especially in the Sepik River drainage basin, fled Indonesian control and settled across the border in what is now the independent nation of Papua New Guinea.

The most common type of resettlement in the Pacific, however, has been as a response to population pressures, economic and educational needs, or both, as in the movement of persons from what is now the Republic of Kiribati (Gilbert Islands) including the Banabans (Ocean Islanders), to the Solomon Islands, the Phoenix Islands, and Fiji. Other examples include the migration to Ponape of the Polynesian atoll-dwellers of Kapingamarangi and Nukuoro and New Zealand's plan to relocate Tokelau islanders in the rural farming-dairy Taupo-Rotorua area of the North Island of New Zealand. As the Pacific islands continue to increase in population and as changes occur in the traditional economic order, other resettlement schemes may arise.

In the past twenty-five years social institutions in Oceania have had to undergo major revisions in order to adjust to the mass displacement of people. Two types of adjustments become necessary.

The first adjustment must be made by the migrant who, arriving in the new urban social environment, must make some important changes quite rapidly. The most frequent means of adjustment lies in finding relatives and close friends who have previously settled in the area. Other mechanisms include seeking out religious congregations serving persons from one's home area, frequenting social clubs and bars or night clubs which cater to persons from a specific area, or settling in a part of town which is inhabited by a large number of persons coming from the same general district or island group. Far less frequently a person will move to an area and settle there simply because it is conveniently located or because it provides an affordable rent regardless of its proximity to kinsmen, friends, or other persons from one's home area.

The second type of adjustment is that of the home area due to the emigration of a person. A large num-ber of migrants are either older adolescents or young adults, people at the most vital and productive stage of their life with regard to physical abilities. Their absence, especially in the labor-intensive, extended-family and rural-agrarian communities, can have a dramatic impact on the economic and political conditions of an area. Their absence also diminishes the number of youths learning how to assume the responsibilities of mature adulthood, thus depriving the extended families and villages of mechanisms necessary for an efficient and fully functioning community order.

The outflow of migrants to the port-town administrative centers and international ports has coincided quite closely with improvements in communication and travel in the Pacific areas. Nearly all major islands have adequate all-weather roads and telephone contacts, either by direct wire or shortwave radio connections, are now available to even the most remote village. Interisland surface connections are still important but air travel has now become the principal mode of transportation in most areas. International jets and modern turboprops can now land at a large number of points in the Pacific thus making it possible to span vast distances in a very short time. This revolution in communication and transportation has produced a large number of persons who are involved with circular migration which enables them to return to their home areas with relative ease on a frequent basis if they so desire. It has also made it possible for families to keep in close contact—even to the point that younger married migrant couples are able to send their children to their parents or older relatives in their home village for a few years, to be raised partly in the traditional social environment of these relatives and partly in the urban environment of their parents.

The fact that a person may return to a home community at nearly any time can be a potential threat to the stability of that place. The economic, political, and kinship networks which had to be adjusted because of the departure of a person or a family must, at the return of a long-absent individual, be readjusted.

Three very positive consequences of high rates of out-migration have served to benefit the hinterlands, port towns, and in general, whole island groups. The first is the reduction of population pressures. Nearly all Oceanic island areas have had quite high rates of population growth. By moving to areas which provide a wider range of occupational opportunities, the home villages are spared the task of providing homes and a livelihood for the adults, schools for their children, and general social services for all members of the family. A second advantage is the fact that much-needed capital, real-cash currency, can be generated in the home village in the form of remittances from the emigré to his family or to members of his extended kinship-group. Also, because of the availability of relatively easy and rapid transportation networks, it is possible for a person to move to an urban area to obtain employment while living with relatives or close friends and then return to the home village with cash earned while away. Sometimes a person living away from the home village will finance projects (such as the building of a meetinghouse or construction of a seawall) by sending cash to the persons involved with the construction rather than by providing the expected physical labor.

It is also a common practice to return to one's home village at the time of an important event such as a marriage, birthday, funeral, or church dedication and contribute cash to the proper recipients. The third positive consequence of large-scale out-migration is the skills learned by the migrant. Having been to the urban areas and having been exposed to a wide variety of ideas and techniques enabling him to cope with the advanced technology and the complex social, political, and economic conditions of the urban world, on his return he is often able to serve as a culture broker to facilitate contacts between the rural, tradition-oriented village and the change-oriented outside world.

RELATED ENTRIES: Commercial/Economic Importance of Pacific Islands.

SOURCES AND READINGS: Edward Wybergh Docker, *The Blackbirders* (Sydney: Angus and Robertson, 1970); Alan Kay, "Population Growth in Micronesia," *Micronesian Reporter* 22, no. 2 (1974); Hal B. Levine and Marlene Wolfzahn Levine, *Urbanization in Papua New Guinea* (New York: Cambridge University Press, 1979); Michael D. Lieber, ed., *Exiles and Migrants in Oceania*, Association for Social Anthropology in Oceania, Monograph no. 5 (Honolulu: University Press of Hawaii, 1977); Cluny Macpherson, Bradd Shore, and Robert Franco, eds., *New Neighbors: Islanders in Adaptation* (Santa Cruz, Calif.: Center for South Pacific Studies, 1978); Alexander Spoehr, ed., *Pacific Port Towns and Cities* (Honolulu: Bishop Museum Press, 1963); Robert Trumball, *Tin Roofs and Palm Trees* (Seattle: University of Washington Press, 1977). *Max E. Stanton*

MILLER, WILLIAM THOMAS (1899-1944). Born 8 August 1899, educated at the University of Michigan, William Miller served as a pilot in the Naval Air Service. About 1928 he joined the aeronautics branch (later the Bureau of Air Commerce) of the Depart-

ment of Commerce. He became superintendent of airways for the bureau and, in 1935, was given charge of the colonization of Howland, Baker, and Jarvis Islands and the surveying of other islands in the area for their aeronautical value. When the Department of the Interior took control of the islands in 1936, Miller was replaced after he had trained his successor, Richard Black. In early 1937 he served as the liaison official to Amelia Earhart in the launching of her first attempt to fly around the world. Afterwards, he was sent to Australasia to investigate the volume of business that would ensue if there was an airline connection between the United States and that area. He continued to serve in government regulatory agencies connected with aviation until his death in 1944.

RELATED ENTRIES: Central Pacific Air Route; Earhart, Amelia; Equatorial Islands, U.S. Aeronautics in.

SOURCES AND READINGS: Fred Goerner, *The Search for Amelia Earhart* (Garden City, N.Y.: Doubleday & Co., 1966); Record Group 126, Records of the Office of Territories, File 12-17, National Archives, Washington, D.C. *Francis X. Holbrook*

MODEKNGEI. Modekngei is a religion in the Palau Islands of the western Carolines, founded in the early 1900s by a Palauan named Temedad of the village of A'ol (or Ochl) in northern Babelthuap. Modekngei means "to bring them together" referring to both the ancestral spirits and the Palauan people. Religious authority is derived from the ancient Palauan god, Ngiromokuul. Modekngei began as a political movement as well as a religious doctrine. It was always antiforeign. Temedad began his preachings at the end of the German administration and continued into the Japanese occupation of Micronesia. He was believed to have occult powers through the performance of various feats and the experiencing of strange occurrences. Early in 1916 Temedad had what was probably an epileptic seizure and communicated with Ngiromokuul whom he claimed empowered him to dictate taboos. Subsequently, he declared that all traditional Palauan money was "contaminated" due to Japanese presence. Many brought their money to Temedad to be cleansed, for which he exacted a fee; some "unpurifiable" money he kept. He soon gained prestige and considerable wealth.

Soon A'ol became the center of Modekngei authority. People in other villages paid homage and tribute. Temedad recalled old political rivalries, settled arguments, cast out demons, and reportedly raised one woman from the dead. Soon the Japanese hospital in Koror became unpopular, and medical patients were brought to A'ol instead. In 1918, on Temedad's orders, a Japanese school at Ngaraard was burned. Through the advocacy of Modekngei, Temedad proposed to unite the Palauans against all foreigners. His revitalizing of old Palauan political disputes, the burning of the school, and the purification and enhancement of the value of Palauan money, were all attempts to assert a conception of the old order of Palau—a society that the Japanese sought to change.

In modern times, Modekngei survives and reportedly has up to one third of the population as followers. In 1974 a secondary school was founded at Ibobang, in Ngatpang municipality, on Babelthuap for teaching vocational, practical, and traditional Palauan arts. The history of the movement has indicated a remarkable adaptability to issues of the day, and its influence is still felt at election times.

RELATED ENTRIES: Cargo Cults; Micronesia.

SOURCES AND READINGS: Arthur J. Vidich, *Political Factionalism in Palau* (Washington, D.C.: Department of the Navy, Report no. 23, CIMA, 1949); Interview with John Sadao Tarkong, relative of Temedad, in Kolonia, Ponape, 1 October 1978.

Dirk Anthony Ballendorf

MOERENHOUT, JACQUES-ANTOINE (1796-1879). Moerenhout was the United States consul and then the French consul to Tahiti during the turbulent years of the Franco-Anglo conflict over control of the island (1836-1844). A Belgian by birth (17 January 1796), Moerenhout fought in the French army under Napoleon (1812-1814). Afterwards, he became a merchant and sailed to Chile (1826). He arrived in Tahiti in 1828 on a commercial venture that took him through the Tuamotus and then back to Tahiti where he established his business. During his visit to the United States (1835), he was named U.S. consul to Tahiti. The next year Moerenhout openly supported the French Catholic priests who landed in Tahiti to convert the Protestant Tahitians to Catholicism. For the next eight years (1836-1843) Moerenhout was the prime person involved in the complex conflict between Protestant versus Catholic and English versus French factions for control of the island. His chief adversary was the Protestant minister George Pritchard who at that time dominated the Tahitian queen, Pomare IV. Because of his pro-French stand, Moerenhout suffered physical threats on his life. In fact, his wife was murdered in 1838 in such a scuffle. Pritchard and some of the Protestants hoped to gain English annexation and thus protection from the French and the Catholics. In 1842 he visited England for this purpose but was unsuccessful. While he was gone, French admiral Dupetit-Thouars arrived in Tahiti and declared it a French protectorate. He named Moerenhout French consul and general administrator of the provisional government until a permanent one could be established. Pritchard returned in February 1843. He attempted to undermine the French again (the ''Pritchard Affair''), but he was arrested and expelled from the country (1844). Because of the strong opposition to Moerenhout by various factions on the island, the French government decided to relieve him of his duties (1848). He was reassigned to California as French consul, first to Monterey (1852) and then to Los Angeles (1859) where he lived until his death in 1879. Moerenhout's two-volume work, *Voyages aux îles du Grand Océan*, printed first in 1837, provides a wealth of primary sources for ancient Tahitian culture as well as the political developments in Tahiti up to that time. He knew most of the first-generation missionaries as well as the important Tahitian chiefs and priests who formed the basis of his work.

RELATED ENTRIES: Dupetit-Thouars, Abel; French Polynesia; Pomare Family; Pritchard, George.

SOURCES AND READINGS: Jacques-Antoine Moerenhout, *Voyages aux îles du Grand Océan*, 2 vols. (Paris: Bertrand, 1837; reprint ed., Paris, 1959); Léonce Jore, *J. A. Moerenhout* (Paris: Adrien Maisonneuve, 1944).   *Robert D. Craig*

MONCKTON, CHARLES ARTHUR WHITMORE (1873-1936). A resident magistrate in British New Guinea and an author, Monckton was born on 30 May 1873 at Invercargill, New Zealand. He went to New Guinea in 1895; and after two years prospecting, pearling, and trading, he became a magistrate. He served in the eastern and southeastern divisions, then took the new northern division. Because of his success, he was also given the northeastern division in 1903. He saw magisterial work as a quasi-military operation and was said to be successful because of his readiness to kill. He resigned in 1907, went farming in New Zealand, married M. Arkwright and, going to England in 1914, enlisted. He served in India throughout World War I. He published *Some Experiences of a New Guinea Resident Magistrate* (1921), *Last Days in New Guinea* (1922), *New Guinea Recollections* (1934), and *Further Adventures of a New Guinea Resident Magistrate* (1936). All are intensely readable though unreliable.

RELATED ENTRIES: British New Guinea; Papua New Guinea.   *H. J. Gibbney*

MONTROUZIER, XAVIER (1820-1897). An ordained priest, scientist, and missionary, Montrouzier spent more than twenty years among the various Melanesian groups. Born 3 December 1820 near Clermont, France, he distinguished himself in the study of natural sciences. In 1841 he entered the seminary and was ordained a priest. Four years later, Montrouzier left Europe as provicar. Reaching Sydney in June 1845 he spent four months busily collecting botanical specimens. In October 1845 he embarked with colleagues for various places in Melanesia. Shortly before leaving Sydney, however, he resigned as provicar. His first major assignment was to work in the Solomons and New Caledonia. He also worked on Murua (Woodlark) and Tikopia Island. Montrouzier complained about the islanders and their interpretation of the gospel. His "overbearing manner" created friction with his colleagues; and in June 1851 when the Marists chose a perfect apostle, Montrouzier was not named. Instead, he was appointed as guide to six young people bound for Sydney. There he occupied himself with natural history. He wrote his *Essai sur la faune de l'île de Woodlark*, published in Lyons in 1857. The last part of his mission was spent in New Caledonia where the Marists played a significant role in bringing about French annexation on 25 September 1853. Montrouzier last served as convict chaplain to New Caledonia's penal colony. In 1876 his health began to fail. He retired in 1893 and died at Saint Louis, near Noumea, on 16 May 1897.

RELATED ENTRIES: Catholics in the Pacific; New Caledonia.

SOURCES AND READINGS: J. W. Davidson and Deryck Scarr, eds., *Pacific Islands Portraits* (Wellington: A. H. and A. W. Reed, 1973); Patrick O'Reilly, *Nouvelle Calédoniens*, (Paris: Musée de l'Homme, 1955).

Michael P. Singh

MORMONS IN THE PACIFIC. The Church of Jesus Christ of Latter-day Saints, commonly referred to as the Mormon church, was formally established by Joseph Smith in the state of New York in 1830. The early activities of the church were concentrated in Ohio, Missouri, Illinois, and finally, Utah where the church headquarters is located today. The first overseas mission of the church began in England in 1837; the second occurred seven years later when missionaries first visited Polynesia.

As a result of interest stimulated by conversations with former sailors among his converts, Joseph Smith planned to send missionaries from Mormon headquarters in Nauvoo, Illinois, to the Sandwich Islands in 1843. Unable to find a ship going to Hawai'i, the four men assigned to the mission journeyed instead to the Society Islands, left one of their number at Tubuai, about four hundred miles south of

Tahiti, and began an association in the Pacific that has continued to the present.

Missionary work continued in what is now French Polynesia only from 1844 until 1852 when non-French religious groups were expelled from the islands, but by then Latter-day Saint missionaries had finally reached Hawai'i and Mormonism in the Pacific continued unabated. In 1850 ten missionaries had arrived and active proselyting continued until it was temporarily stopped in 1857. New Zealand experienced a short-lived exposure to Mormonism in 1854, but serious activity in that country did not begin until the 1880s when missionary work began among the Maori people.

Events in Hawai'i in the early 1860s brought some interesting changes of direction by the church. Beginning in 1854 church membership in Hawai'i had become concentrated on the island of Lana'i where missionaries from Utah had directed farming and ecclesiastical activities; this continued until 1857 when all the Americans returned to the United States. For four years, Hawaiian elders led the Mormons until the arrival in 1861 of Walter Murray Gibson, an adventurer who had recently joined the Mormon church. He soon persuaded the Hawaiians that he had been commissioned by Brigham Young—then presiding over the church—to assume the leadership of the Sandwich Islands mission. Complaints about his methods and practices soon prompted an investigation, and Gibson was excommunicated in 1864.

Two of Gibson's activities, however, were to have long-range implications for the Mormons. By the time he was excommunicated the property on Lana'i was in his own name, forcing the Mormons to seek another "gathering place," so the following year a tract of six thousand acres was purchased at La'ie near the northern tip of O'ahu and there Mormons soon began raising sugarcane and other crops. The community of La'ie today is still almost entirely Latter-day Saint.

Gibson's other significant activity was in sending two Hawaiians to Samoa to serve as missionaries. Unknown to the church after Gibson's fall, the two men managed to gather a small band of converts which drifted in and out of church involvement until 1881. That year, in response to a letter from the sole surviving Hawaiian, American missionaries arrived in Samoa to further the church program along more stable lines. Samoa became a center of Mormon activity in the South Pacific and local gathering places were established at Vaiola on Savai'i, Sauniatu and Pesega on Upolu, and Mapusaga on Tutuila. Today, Western Samoa is unique in that it is the only country in the world completely covered by Mormon stakes (the formal administrative and ecclesiastical

MORMONS IN THE PACIFIC   195

subdivisions of the church, each of which usually contains between 2,500 and 3,000 Latter-day Saints). Although Mormon-owned Mapusaga High School in American Samoa was discontinued in the early 1970s, the Mormons still sponsor Church College of Western Samoa at Pesega as well as elementary and intermediate schools elsewhere on Upolu and on Savai'i.

Samoa, in turn, became the "mother of missions" for other areas in that part of the Pacific. Samoan missionaries traveled to Tonga in 1891 but the progress in that country was slow. A school was started the following year and the first conversion to Mormonism took place about fourteen months after the arrival of the missionaries. The Tongan mission was created from the Samoan mission in 1916 as the missionaries found their greatest success through the medium of conducting schools. In 1925 the church established a high school at Makeke on Tongatapu which educated Mormons and non-Mormons alike until it was replaced by Liahona High School in 1948. Twelve "middle schools" are also operated by the church and a second high school was added in 1978 when Saineha High School was dedicated on Vava'u.

The *Book of Mormon* was translated into Tongan in 1939, and after the interruption of World War II, missionary work was renewed more vigorously. A great surge of activity took place in the 1950s as chapels were constructed throughout the kingdom and today Tonga has the highest percentage of Mormon citizens of any country in the world with over 15,000 members, approximately 16 percent of the population.

In addition to Tonga, Samoa was also the base from which missionaries returned to Tahiti in 1892 after a forty-year absence to reestablish the church in French Polynesia. A stake and an elementary school now are located in the capital city of Pape'ete. Missionary work is conducted by the Tahiti-Pape'ete mission which also includes the Cook Islands. Within this mission there are approximately 5,500 Latter-day Saints among the total population of 288,000.

The Mormons did not begin formal missionary work in Fiji until 1954 and for several years after that work was carried on by missions located in either Samoa, Tonga, or New Zealand. In 1971, however, the Fiji mission was created and with 2,595 members as of July 1978, there will probably be a stake established within the country before the end of the decade. In addition to two primary schools the Latter-day Saint church sponsors the Fiji Technical College which opened its doors in 1975.

The new nation of Kiribati began its official existence in 1979. Here, in the Gilbert group, is found one of the newer Mormon establishments, Moroni Community School, with just over one hundred students. Most of the Mormon teachers and missionaries in the country had been converted to Mormonism while attending school at Liahona College in Tonga. Micronesia is currently part of the Hawai'i-Honolulu mission. In 1979 there were approximately forty missionaries serving on Palau, Yap, Truk, Majuro, Ponape, Saipan, and Guam. Branches of the church are located on Kwajalein and Guam and two wards (larger, more self-sustaining units than branches) are also found on Guam.

So far, very little effort has been put forth by the Mormons in Melanesia although for several years the church's translation office in Auckland, New Zealand, has been preparing materials for use in the Solomon Islands and New Hebrides. New Caledonia is now part of the Fiji-Suva mission. Within the Mormon church both missionaries and local leaders are part of a lay ministry. Bishops, branch presidents, and stake presidents serve in their ecclesiastical callings while meeting the demands of regular employment in the secular world. Young men and women—usually in their early twenties—are called to serve full time as unpaid missionaries in various parts of the world, the young men for two years, the women for eighteen months. Although some missionaries are assigned to serve in their homelands most are sent elsewhere, producing the somewhat strange circumstance of Tahitians serving in Alaska, Samoans teaching on Indian reservations in the American Midwest, Hawaiians preaching in Central America while missionaries from the United States might be sharing the concepts of Mormonism with others on the islands of the Pacific.

With the exception of the British Isles, the Pacific has received more Mormon attention over the years than any other overseas area. The most sacred of Latter-day Saint buildings are the temples, only seventeen of which are to be found in the world. The first to be built outside Utah was dedicated in Hawai'i in 1919 and in 1958 another was constructed in New Zealand. In October 1977 church authorities announced plans for a third such structure—although much smaller—to be built in American Samoa. La'ie, Hawai'i, the site of the Hawai'i temple, is also the home of Brigham Young University—Hawai'i Campus. Including Hawai'i, nearly half of the student body of 1,800 come from the islands of the Pacific. To provide employment for approximately 800 students and to help preserve elements of their heritage, the Mormon church built the Polynesian Cultural Center in 1963 which has since become world famous and one of Hawai'i's most popular tourist attractions. Mormon interest in the Pacific is further illustrated by the fact that the church's medical missionary program also began here, with the first doctor serving in Samoa; subsequent medical missionaries were sent to Tonga.

The interest of the Mormons in the Pacific is based on the belief that at least some of the prehistoric migration into the Pacific originated in the Western Hemisphere, whose residents had previously migrated from the eastern Mediterranean and whose story is told in the *Book of Mormon*. This spiritual kinship has resulted in a special tie between the peoples of the Pacific and the rest of the 4,000,000 members of the Church of Jesus Christ of Latter-day Saints.

RELATED ENTRIES: Brigham Young University—Hawai'i Campus; Gibson, Walter; Polynesian Cultural Center; Pratt, Addison.

SOURCES AND READINGS: Kenneth W. Baldridge, "Sauniatu, Western Samoa: A Special Purpose Village," *Journal of the Polynesian Society* 87 (1978): 165-93; George S. Ellsworth, *Zion in Paradise: Early Mormons in the South Seas* (Logan, Utah: Utah State University, 1959); Andrew Jenson, comp., "History of the Hawaiian Mission of the Church of Jesus Christ of Latter-day Saints" (Unpublished typescript, Archives of the Church Historical Department, Salt Lake City, Utah).   *Kenneth W. Baldridge*

MORNING STAR (1856-1958). Four years after the Micronesian mission had been established, the sponsoring American Board of Commissioners for Foreign Missions (ABCFM) acquired a vessel in Boston, christened it *Morning Star*, and sent it to Hawai'i in 1856 to become its link with Micronesia. The missionary packet carried mail, freight, and passengers on yearly cruises from its home port of Honolulu to all stations in Micronesia and, for a time, to those in the Marquesas as well. It was the first of seven ships to carry the name and to perform a similar service. The vessels were paid for—in part at least—by Sunday school children. Shares cost ten cents and entitled the shareholders to certificates. The ships were not immune to problems faced by others in those waters. *Morning Star I* simply wore out and was sold in 1866. A new one was built in East Boston, but in 1869, midway through its third cruise, *Morning Star II* drifted onto a reef at Kosrae (Kusaie) where a squall finished it off. *Morning Star III* was launched at East Boston in 1871. It served thirteen years before wrecking in nearly the same spot as its predecessor. The distance covered during its 1881 cruise was logged at 15,783 miles. Another generation of Sunday school children provided enough dimes to build *Morning Star IV*, launched at Bath, Maine, in 1884. It was nearly twice as large as the last, and its passengers no doubt welcomed such innovations as a hurri-

cane deck and auxiliary engines. The ABCFM hoped it would be the last, for expenses increased yearly. Nevertheless, *Morning Star V* had to be purchased in 1904. Home station was now in Micronesia, but it was more costly than ever to maintain this ship, and it was sold in 1906. Under German rule, commercial shipping in Micronesia improved and allowed the ABCFM to go out of the *Morning Star* business—for good, it hoped. Following World War II, however, the ABCFM assumed temporary responsibility for churches in Micronesia until they could become self-sustaining. The Reverend Eleanor Wilson accepted delivery at Kosrae in 1948 of *Morning Star VI*, a used schooner purchased in Maine. In 1952 the vessel was condemned and sank at sea while being towed. *Morning Star VII* arrived in 1956, but, like its predecessor, was not sound enough to perform well. In 1958, too battered to be dependable, this last of the *Morning Stars* was sold.

RELATED ENTRIES: American Board of Commissioners for Foreign Missions; Micronesian Mission.

SOURCES AND READINGS: Hiram Bingham, Jr., *Story of the Morning Star: The Children's Missionary Vessel* (Boston: American Board of Commissioners for Foreign Missions, 1866); Maribelle Cormack, *The Skipper Was a Lady* (New York: Hill & Wang, 1956); Creston D. Ketchum, *His Path is in the Waters* (New York: Prentice-Hall, 1955); Ralph E. Turner, "Missionary Says 'Yokwe Kom'," *Micronesian Reporter* 10, no. 6 (1962): 5-7.   *Mary Browning*

MORRIS, BASIL MOORHOUSE (1888-1975). A soldier and administrator, born and educated in Melbourne, Morris served in the Royal Australian Garrison Regiment during World War I and was awarded the Distinguished Service Order in 1919. Between the wars, Morris commanded artillery units in New South Wales, Victoria, and South Australia. On the outbreak of World War II, he was sent to the Middle East; and in May 1941 he was given the command of the newly formed Eighth Military District which embraced the Australian territories of Papua and New Guinea.

As general officer commanding the New Guinea force, Morris' first duty after the rapid southward advance of the Japanese in 1942 was the absorption of former colonial officials into a new unit of government. After consultation with army headquarters in Melbourne, he ordered the departure of some of the senior officials of the Papuan government including H. Leonard Murray, the administrator. He brought to an end what had become known as the "Murray government," the rule over Papua by Murray and his uncle and predecessor, Sir Hubert Murray.

After February 1942 the Japanese established bases at Lae and Salamaua on the mainland of New Guinea. In April while the Japanese forces prepared to move southwards, the Papuan Administrative Unit (PAU) established by Morris was combined with remnants of the two civil governments to form the Australian New Guinea Administrative Unit (ANGAU). Although relieved of some of his duties by the arrival of Lt. Gen. S. F. Rowell and Brig. D. M. Cleland as deputy adjutant and quartermaster general, Morris remained in New Guinea as general officer commanding ANGAU and in that position continued to occupy a role which most nearly approximated that of administrator until the end of the war.

Morris was still in New Guinea in February 1946 when the formations of the Australian army were repatriated, and by that time he had about 110,000 Japanese prisoners under his command. In 1946 an approach was made to the Australian government to have Morris reappointed as civilian administrator of the combined territories. It was argued that his progressive policies, personal integrity, and strong humanitarian principles fitted him for the post. But he was recalled. His final wartime broadcast to the Papuan people in July 1946 ended with the bidding that they should do everything they could to keep their country. Morris retired from the army in 1946 and stood as the endorsed Liberal candidate in two Victorian elections. He died near Melbourne in 1975.

RELATED ENTRIES: Murray, John Hubert; Papua New Guinea; Port Moresby; War in the Pacific Islands, 1914-1945.

SOURCES AND READINGS: J. V. Barry, *Report of Commission of Inquiry into the Suspension of the Civil Administration of the Territory of Papua in February, 1942* (1945, mimeo.); D. M. Horner, *Crisis of Command: Australian Generalship and the Japanese Threat, 1941-1943* (Canberra: Australian National University Press, 1978); Dudley McCarthy, "South-West Pacific Area, First Year: Kokoda to Wau" in D. P. Mellor, ed., *Australia in the War of 1939-1945* (Canberra: Australian National University Press, 1949); Basil Moorhouse Morris, private papers 1888-1975, in possession of the writer; *Stand-To* (Canberra: September 1957-October 1958), pp. 46-48.   *David Wetherell*

MORUROA ATOLL (erroneously spelled Mururoa). The main site of France's nuclear testing, Moruroa Atoll is located 1,247 km (775 mi) southeast of Pape-'ete in the southeastern end of the Gambiers (French Polynesia). In 1963 the French government an-

nounced its intent to begin such tests; and between 1966 and 1974, nuclear devices were exploded in the atmosphere above the atoll. Worldwide protest pressured France to transfer their testing to Fangataufa, another uninhabited atoll nineteen miles south of Moruroa. Tests on Fangataufa have been underground. Despite continued protest, the tests have continued.

RELATED ENTRIES: French Polynesia; Tuamotu-Gambier Archipelago.

SOURCES AND READINGS: Bengt Danielsson, *Moruroa, Mon Amour* (Paris: Stock, 1974).   *Robert D. Craig*

MOSES, TEIKOROI (1848?-1920?). Revered throughout Truk as the man who "planted" Christianity in the Truk Lagoon, Moses was born to Gilbertese parents stranded on the island of Ponape. He was orphaned in early childhood by the murder of his parents and was at first fostered by a family of the Kitti district, Ponape. Later, he lived for some time in the home of Albert Sturges, a Protestant missionary on Ponape. Upon completion of training for the Christian ministry, Moses and his Ponapean wife, Jepora, were stationed in 1876 on Etal in the Mortlocks. In 1878 he was ordained a minister by Sturges and transferred to the "Upper" Mortlocks where he oganized the first church on Nama. There he befriended a visiting chief from Uman in the Truk Lagoon. Since Sturges had long dreamed of missionizing the populous Truk Atoll, he seized upon the opportunity and accompanied Moses and the visiting Uman chief to Truk. Moses was settled on Uman in 1879 and by 1881 had formally organized a church there—the first in the Truk Lagoon. His tact and good character soon won him the respect of chiefs on other islands. As a result, he was able to pave the way for four additional Ponapean couples who were dispatched by Sturges to islands in the lagoon. When Robert Logan, an American Congregationalist missionary, arrived on Truk in 1884, Moses had already secured a foothold for Christianity in the islands. On Uman, he helped to reconcile differences between rival districts and thereby reduced the incidence of warfare. For many years, Moses' advice and support on mission matters was actively sought by resident foreign missionaries. Although he had no children of his own, he adopted five Trukese children—several of whom became Christian teachers in their own rights. Moses remained on Uman until his death in the early years of the Japanese administration of Micronesia.

RELATED ENTRIES: Logan, Robert; Sturges, Albert; Truk.

SOURCES AND READINGS: American Board of Commissioners for Foreign Missions, *Letters and Papers of the American Board of Commissioners for Foreign Missions: Mission to Micronesia, 1852-1909*, vols. 5, 7, 8, 12 (Cambridge: Harvard University, Houghton Library); David and Leona Crawford, *Missionary Adventures in the South Pacific.* (Rutland, Vt.: Charles E. Tuttle Co., 1967).

Charles B. Reafsnyder

MOSS, FREDERICK JOSEPH (1829-1904). A New Zealand journalist, politician, author, planter, and administrator, Moss began a forty-five year association with the islands in 1868 when he migrated to Fiji during the cotton boom. His two books, *A Month in Fiji* (Melbourne, 1868) and *A Planter's Experience in Fiji* (Auckland, 1870) and a series of articles in New Zealand newspapers were responsible for much of the migration during the rush to Fiji of 1868-1872. After returning to New Zealand, he entered provincial politics and joined Julius Vogel (1835-1899) and others campaigning for the expansion of New Zealand influence in the Pacific. He served on trade reciprocity commissions to Tahiti, Tonga, and Fiji and commissions to investigate union with Fiji in 1885 and 1901; he was also a member of the commission investigating Vogel's Pacific Island Confederation and Annexation Bill of 1888. He wrote *Through Atolls and Islands* (London, 1889) and further books on New Zealand education, politics, and the Maoris.

When a British protectorate was established in the Cook Islands (1891) Moss became administrator. He worked energetically organizing legislative, judiciary, education, and land-claims procedures. Ill health and disputes with an *ariki*-dominated legislature led to his dismissal and return to New Zealand in 1898. Two articles he wrote on the Cook Islands remained standard works long after his death.

RELATED ENTRIES: Cook Islands; Fiji.

SOURCES AND READINGS: A. H. McIntosh, *An Encyclopedia of New Zealand*, vol. 2 (Wellington: Government Printer, 1966); A. Ross, *New Zealand Aspirations in the Pacific in the Nineteenth Century* (Wellington: Oxford University Press, 1964); G. H. Schofield, *A Dictionary of New Zealand Biography* (Wellington: Whitcombe & Tombes, 1940).

Alan Maxwell Quanchi

MURRAY, JOHN HUBERT PLUNKETT (1861-1940). A lieutenant governor of Papua from 1908 to 1940, Murray had been appointed chief judicial officer of British New Guinea in 1904. Hubert Murray was then forty-three and without experience in colonial administration. As a barrister, parliamentary draftsman, Crown prosecutor, and acting judge in New South Wales, he had not exploited his outstanding physical and mental talents. Born in Sydney, the son of Sir Terrence Murray, he graduated from Oxford University with first-class honors, won the amateur heavyweight boxing championship of England, and qualified in law before returning to Australia. There he endured the "living death" of mundane legal work broken only by heavy drinking and distinguished service in the Boer War.

In 1906 his cleverly marshalled criticism of many of his colonial colleagues was accepted by a Royal commission. The commission's report made Murray one of the most hated men in Port Moresby, but left the Australian government free to establish a new administration at the same time as it accepted responsibility for British New Guinea, now renamed the Australian Territory of Papua. Made acting administrator in 1907, Murray was appointed lieutenant governor in 1908.

Attempting to fulfill Australia's optimistic expectations for its new northern frontier, Murray tried both to promote plantation settlements and protect Papuan rights. While aborigines could not obtain redress before courts in northern Australia and punitive expeditions were frequent in German New Guinea, Murray ensured that the Papuan laborer could give evidence against his employer in court and that government officers would use guns against hostile tribesmen only in the last resort. When the slight "boom" petered out before World War I, Murray was left with a small, often disgruntled, planter community, a few alluvial gold miners, and a minuscule revenue; but the Papuan landowners were safe from foreign investors. Over the next twenty years, Murray advanced modest schemes to educate, provide better health, and increase the cash incomes of Papuans. Restrained by lack of funds, hostile white settlers, and fear that sudden change would lead to depopulation, Murray's reforms resulted in little change in most villages.

Cold and aloof, but unpretentious and abstemious in later life, Murray outlived his enemies. Given close loyalty by his field staff and respected, even revered, by many Papuans, he was acknowledged as a great Australian at the time of his death, still in office, in 1940. Married to Sybil Jenkins (died 1929) and then to Mildred Vernon, he was survived by two sons and one daughter. He was knighted in 1925.

Measured against changes after 1945, his policies show a paternalistic lack of confidence in Papuans; and he introduced and administered much petty discriminatory legislation. But, compared with nearly all other white men in the territory, he was better read in anthropology and colonial administration, and he was much more enlightened in his attitudes to other races. Few others could have done so much in the face of aggressive white settlers in Papua and indifferent politicians in Australia.

RELATED ENTRIES: Bromilow, William E.; Grimshaw, Beatrice E.; Morris, Basil M; Newton, Henry; Papua New Guinea.

SOURCES AND READINGS: B. Jinks, P. Biskup, and H. Nelson, eds., *Readings in New Guinea History* (Sydney: Angus and Robertson, 1973); Francis West, *Hubert Murray: The Australian Pro-Consul* (Melbourne: Oxford University Press, 1968); Francis West, ed., *Selected Letters of Hubert Murray* (Melbourne: Oxford University Press, 1970).

Hank Nelson

MURUROA ATOLL. *See* Moruroa Atoll.

NAISSELINE CHIEFSHIP. A line of influential chiefs on the Loyalty Island of Maré, the Naisseline chiefship began in the late eighteenth century with a great chief named Yiewene who ruled the Si Gwahma and Si Waeko regions until his death in 1848. Yiewene was the first Maréan chief to accept members from the London Missionary Society (LMS) in 1841, although he was mainly interested in their technical skills and in increased trading opportunities. His youngest son, Yiewene Kichini Bula (ca. 1835-1853), was appointed heir with two older brothers, Nidoish and Alakuten, as regents. By 1855 Nidoish Naisseline had gained power and established a political administration with LMS missionaries John Jones and Stephen Creagh. Under their leadership the Protestant mission flourished and Protestant Maréans were directed to attack the fledgling Catholic villages. Nidoish and the LMS ruled Maré until his death in 1880 when his son, Yiewene Dokucas Naisseline (1846-1916), became great chief. A ferocious Catholic persecutor, Yiewene Dokucas joined forces with a French Protestant missionary named Cru in 1883. This intensified the English-French hostilities on Maré and promoted French influence throughout the Loyalty Islands. He was succeeded by his son, Henri Naisseline (1874-1918) in 1916. Henri died two years later and the chiefship was transferred to his son, Henri Nawossé Naisseline (1911-). Henri Nawossé was advised by regents until 1936 when he became great chief of the Guahua (Maré) district. He has been active as a conservative in New Caledonian politics and has encouraged agricultural and economic development of the Loyalty Islands.

RELATED ENTRIES: Loyalty Islands.

SOURCES AND READINGS: R. K. Howe, *The Loyalty Islands: A History of Culture Contacts 1840-1900* (Honolulu: University Press of Hawaii, 1977); Patrick O'Reilly, *Calédoniens* (Paris: Musée de l'Homme, 1953); Deryck Scarr, ed., *More Pacific Islands Portraits* (Canberra: Australian National University Press, 1979).   *Russell T. Clement*

NAMBAS (1900?-1968). A "big man" from the village of Ipikil, who institutionalized the John Frum cargo cult on Tanna, Vanuatu (New Hebrides), Nambas was arrested and deported first in 1942 and then three other times. After the government recognized the cult as a religion in 1956, he returned to Tanna and organized a John Frum church with a day of worship, annual ceremonies, and recognized symbols. Nambas was featured in a film by David Attenborough, the British film actor and director. He was buried, amid much speculation of sorcery, at Ipikil on Sulphur Bay.

RELATED ENTRIES: Cargo Cults; Cargo Cult, John Frum; Tanna; Vanuatu (New Hebrides).

SOURCES AND READINGS: Jean Guiart, *Un Siècle et demi de contacts culturels à Tanna, Nouvelles Hébrides* (Paris: Musée de l'Homme, 1956); Monty Lindstrom, *Bigman or Chief? Knowledge in Political Process on Tanna*, Kroeber Anthropological Society Papers 57/58, 1981.   *Lamont C. Lindstrom*

NAN MADOL. The prehistoric city of man-made islands, Nan Madol is located at the mouth of Madolenihmw Harbor on the island of Ponape in the eastern Carolines. The name *Nan Madol* translates as "the place between the spaces" and refers to the watery channels which flow among the more than one hundred individual islets. Called the "Venice of the Pacific," the site is spread over an area of .65 km² (.25 mi²). High-walled, rectangular structures made from prismatic boulders of columnar basalt rock enclose the remains of old houses and administrative structures. On many of the islands are found tombs, tunnels, and underground chambers.

According to Ponapean tradition, two magicians from outside of Ponape built the site and established a dynasty of rulers known as the Saudeleurs. The Saudeleurs ruled Ponape from Nan Madol for several centuries until invaders from the island of Kusaie, (Kosrae), 563 km (350 mi) to the east, conquered the city and established the existing system of *Nanmwar-*

kis ("kings"). Nan Madol continued to serve as the capital of Ponape until the eighteenth century A.D. Depopulation due to disease and wars increased the difficulties of supporting a population on Nan Madol to which food was brought from the other areas of Ponape. Excessive flooding of the structures by a series of heavy storms finally forced the Nanmwarki and his people to move to the nearby islands of Temwen. The Nanmwarki of Madolenihmw, the bloodline descendant of Isokelekel, the commander of the invading forces, still holds authority over Nan Madol to this day.

James F. O'Connell, an Irish seaman shipwrecked off Ponape, first described Nan Madol in 1836. The American Protestant missionary, Luther H. Gulick, wrote down his observations in 1857. More scientific treatment of the area was given by anthropologists Johann Kubary in 1874, F. W. Christian in 1899, and Paul Hambruch in 1911. Excavations of selected sites within the complex were conducted by German officials in 1908 and by the Japanese anthropologist, Yawata, during the Japanese administration of the island (1921-1945). A Smithsonian Institution study in 1963 obtained a radiocarbon date of 1180 A.D. for the construction of the artificial islets.

RELATED ENTRIES: Kubary, Johann; Micronesia.

SOURCES AND READINGS: F. W. Christian, *The Caroline Islands* (London: Frank Cass and Co., 1899); Luther H. Gulick, "The Ruins of Ponape or Ascension Island," *Journal of American Geographical Statistical Society* 1 (1857): 129-37; Paul Hambruch, *Ponape. Ergebnisse der Südsee-Expedition: 1908-1911*, 3 vols. (Hamburg: Friederichsen, DeGruyter and Co., 1932-36); Johann Kubary, "Die Ruinen von Nanmatal auf der Insel Ponape (Ascension)," *Journal des Museum Godeffroy* 3 (1874); 123-31.

David Hanlon

NANPEI, HENRY (1862-1928). The richest and most prominent Ponapean of the late nineteenth and early twentieth centuries, Henry Nanpei was the son of the *Naniken* ("prime minister") of the Kitti kingdom of Ponape Island. He attended school first at the American Protestant mission school at Oa on Ponape and later at a religious training school in Hawai'i. Returning from Hawai'i, Nanpei used his father's wealth and position to set up a trading business with the growing number of foreign commercial vessels plying the Pacific. The business prospered, and Nanpei soon opened a store in the Rohnkitti section of Kitti. With the goods received in

return for supplying the foreign merchant ships, Nanpei was able to add to his already large holdings of land. Nanpei sold these goods to Ponapeans who had nothing to offer in exchange except their land. Such transactions soon made Nanpei the single, largest landholder on Ponape and provided him with power equal to that of the *Nanmwarkis* ("kings"). The name *Nanpei* is actually the sixth title in the *Nanmwarki's* line of succession. So powerful was Henry that he simply took the title and made it his last name.

As protector and pastor of the Protestant church on Ponape, Nanpei proved overly zealous. Accounts of the period identify Nanpei as the instigator behind the Protestant-Catholic wars which raged on Ponape between 1887 and 1899. Spanish authorities arrested Nanpei several times with the intent to banish him from the islands. All attempts to punish him failed when it became painfully obvious that Nanpei was the only man who could quell the disturbances. In 1910 Nanpei urged on the people of Sokehs in their rebellion against the German administration. Nanpei hoped that the rebellion would put an end to the German road-building project which he feared would give the Germans access to Kitti and ultimately result in the elimination of his unlicensed trade with the foreign ships.

A man of extraordinary wealth, Nanpei made numerous trips across the Pacific to such places as San Francisco, Honolulu, Hong Kong, China, and Japan. In 1905 he journeyed around the world. Nanpei is credited with the introduction and dissemination of many foreign goods on Ponape. No friend of the Spanish, German, or Japanese administrations, Nanpei espoused an American protectorate for Ponape, governed by a congress which he, himself, desired to lead.

RELATED ENTRIES: Bernart, Luelen; Micronesia; Sokehs Rebellion.

SOURCES AND READINGS: John L. Fischer and Ann M. Fischer, *The Eastern Carolines* (New Haven: Human Relations Area Files Press, 1957); Paul Hambruch, *Ponape. Ergebnisse der Südsee-Expedition: 1908-1911*, 3 vols. (Hamburg: Friederichsen, DeGruyter and Co., 1932-36); A. Cabezo Pereiro, *La Isla de Ponape* (Manila: Tipo-Litografia de Chofre y Comp., 1895).

David Hanlon

NARRAGANSETT (U.S.S.), CRUISE OF (1871-1873). The cruise of the U.S.S. *Narragansett* under Commander Richard W. Meade III, USN (1837-

1897) exemplifies American Pacific policy before the Spanish-American War. The ship was attached to the American Pacific Squadron but operated independently of it, and throughout 1872 Meade received virtually no communication from his superiors.

At sea for 431 days (mainly under sail because of government limits on the use of coal), the *Narragansett* voyaged a record sixty thousand miles. The ship touched most regions of the central and southern Pacific, including Hawai'i, Samoa, Australia, and the Phoenix, Marshall, and Gilbert islands. Meade overcame the crew's lack of discipline, the ship's poor sailing qualities, and the government's parsimony.

Meade's diplomatic activities demonstrate the "gunboat diplomacy" of America's "Old Navy" and were shaped by: his general orders to visit and survey islands and locate coal, his vision of American mission, and the interests of American commercial agents. In Samoa, which was threatened by political disruption and Anglo-German economic domination, Meade temporarily stabilized warring tribes to ensure American strategic and economic interests. He promulgated articles of confederation, a commercial treaty (suggested by the Wilkes' expedition), and a treaty granting the American navy exclusive use of Pago Pago. His civilian superiors approved the harbor treaty which, although rejected by the U.S. Senate, helped avert German annexation of Samoa and led to the 1878 LeMamea treaty. Meade warned that the nascent labor trade (frequently slave labor) was a threat to American commerce and the economic health of Oceania, and he captured (but released because of lack of evidence) the notorious labor-trader and pirate, William H. ("Bully") Hayes. At Abaiang, Meade fired his ship's guns and forced Tarawan invaders to evacuate and pay an indemnity. In July 1872 Meade took formal possession of Christmas Island, occupied by the American Guano Company.

The crew charted harbors and islands, collected hydrographic information, and prepared sailing directions. Inaccurate charts were revised, including the Wilkes charts of the Phoenix Islands. Meade recommended sources of coal for steamships, described native life, and named Canton Island. He forwarded to Washington political and economic intelligence, frequently contrasting foreign naval strength with American naval impotence.

Meade's initiative suited American policy well. Lacking an extensive diplomatic corps, but wishing to further its strategic and commercial interests in the Pacific, the government relied on the independent actions of commanders like Meade to implement and shape foreign policy.

RELATED ENTRIES: United States Exploring Expedition; Wilkes, Charles.

SOURCES AND READINGS: *Narragansett* Log Books (Record Group 24) and Commanders Letters (Record Group 45) at the National Archives, Washington, D.C.; Richard W. Meade III Papers at the New-York Historical Society, New York City; and personal papers in possession of the Meade family.

Kenneth John Blume

NAURU. The smallest and richest (per capita) independent republic in the world, Nauru lies 166° 56' east longitude and approximately 40.2 km (25 mi) south of the equator. The present population numbers approximately 7,500 of which 4,400 are indigenous Nauruans of Micronesian extract. Approximately 1,900 are Gilbertese or Tuvaluans, 650 are Chinese, and there is a small number of Europeans. The climate is tropical with a variable rainfall that annually averages approximately 20 cm (8 in) falling mainly between November and February. Lacking in arable land, the island makes up for it in its rich phosphate deposits—the highest grade known in the world. Extensive phosphate production provides employment and royalties for the Nauruans. Some coconuts, bananas, and pineapples are grown, but for the most part food, services, and other material commodities are imported.

History. This small atoll, Nauru, was settled by various Micronesian peoples from the Gilbert, Caroline, and Marshall islands. There is also Melanesian influence from the Solomons. Anciently, the island was divided into twelve districts presided over by tribal chiefs whose languages and racial extracts were more evident in pre-European history. The first European to visit the island was John Fearne in 1798, but it was not until 1830 that Nauru became a popular stop for food and water for whaling ships sailing the Pacific. European beachcombers—John Jones (1841), William Harris (1842), Ernest M. H. Stephens (1881), and others—acted as intermediaries between the Nauruans and the Europeans in gaining firearms, tools, and alcohol, all of which led to incessant civil war between 1878 and 1888. German merchants who settled there petitioned their government to annex the island into their Marshall Island protectorate. In October 1888 the gunboat *Elber* landed troops who surrounded the island and forced the Nauruans to surrender all their arms. German administration, usually under the direction of a trader, lasted until World War I. The Reverend P. A. Delaporte, an American minister, arrived in 1899 and most Nauruans were converted to Protestantism. Father Kayser introduced Catholicism in 1903 but with much opposition by the Protestants.

Economic Importance. In 1898 H. E. Denson of the Pacific Islands Company in Sydney sent samples of a "fossilized tree" to his home office. When it was examined by Albert F. Ellis, he found it to contain 78 percent phosphate of lime. Britain, thereupon, sent Ellis to Nauru's neighboring Ocean Island and he found that it, too, contained similar quantities of phosphate. As a result, Britain signed an agreement with the local inhabitants for a 999-year treaty. On Nauru, the German Jaluit Company signed an economic agreement with the British for mutual assistance in mining the mineral. Hundreds of islanders from the Carolines and many Chinese were imported to work the mines.

When World War I broke out, Germany established martial law and deported the British citizens to Ocean Island. An Australian force under Major General W. Holmes intervened and captured Nauru. The British were returned and the Germans were arrested and deported to Australia. In 1919 the League of Nations awarded a mandate for the administration of the island to Great Britain, Australia, and New Zealand. The British Phosphate Commissioners, primarily under the direct administration of Australia, continued the monopoly of the phosphate industry with profits divided 42 percent to Australia, 42 percent to Great Britain, and 16 percent to New Zealand. Agreements reached by the first Australian administrator, General T. Griffiths, allowed Nauruans some royalties and part of the profits.

World War II and Its Aftermath. When World War II broke out in Europe, German ships sailed into the Pacific and in December 1940 they attempted to retake Nauru. They sank five shipping vessels and halted the mining. A year later on 9 December 1941 Nauru was bombed and then in August it was occupied by the Japanese. They deported most of the population to Truk and built an airstrip to aid their Pacific defense line. American bombing began in March 1943 and continued throughout the year. These attacks prevented any further Japanese exploitation of the island. On 13 September 1945 Australian forces regained the island and on 31 January 1946 the Nauruans who had survived on Truk were returned to their homes.

After the war, a United Nations mandate was established awarding administration again to Australia, Great Britain, and New Zealand, while the British Phosphate Commissioners reorganized their activities. Nauruans became more and more vocal in their wish for local autonomy and control of the phosphate industry. In December 1951 the Nauruans assumed some of the administration of the island. A formation of a local government council replaced a former, weak council of chiefs. Strong leaders such as Timothy Detudamo and Hammer DeRoburt made Nauruan wishes for independence known to the United Nations. Increase of royalties to the Nauruans continued through 1967 as they negotiated with the foreign governments. Finally on 25 October 1967 an independence charter was signed, and on 31 January 1968 the independent Republic of Nauru was established as an associate member of the British Commonwealth.

Nauruan Government. The government consists of an elected eighteen-member parliament chosen for a three-year term from the various districts around the island. Parliament selects a president who chooses a five- or six-man cabinet and together they act as the executive head of state. Their first president was Hammer DeRoburt who served until December 1976 when he was defeated by Bernard Dowiyogo. His government lasted only until April 1978 when DeRoburt's supporters forced his resignation and DeRoburt was reelected president.

The government owns its own shipping lines, air lines, and collectively it owns expensive real estate in Australia. It is predicted that the phosphate industry will die out by 1990. The government, in order to seek means to continue the high standard of living when the phosphate proceeds run out, has created the Nauru Phosphate Royalties Trust.

SOURCES AND READINGS: Nancy Viviani, *Nauru: Phosphate and Political Progress* (Canberra: Australian National University Press, 1970).

Robert D. Craig

NAVIGATORS' ISLANDS. *See* American Samoa; Western Samoa.

NAVOSAVAKADUA (?-1897). Navosavakadua, whose real name was Dugumoi, was a hereditary priest from Ra coast of Viti Levu in Fiji. He was the focus of the *Wai-ni-tuka* ("elixir of life") cult, a syncretist movement in the 1870s and 1880s which promised the imminent return to earth of the *Kalou Vu* ("deified ancestors") Nacirikaumoli and Nakausabari, whom Dugmoi identified with Jehovah and Jesus in order to take account of the newly introduced Christian consciousness of the Fijians. As much directed against "foreign" Fijians from other part of Fiji as against Europeans, *Tuka* lay behind the Ra plot of 1878 to overthrow the colonial government's Fijian provincial administration in Ra. Dugumoi as a result was exiled to Lau at the behest of the council of chiefs and was kept there until 1883, some time after other exiled plotters were allowed home to Ra. This was a wise precaution on the part of the chiefs. Within a few months of Dugumoi's return, *Tuka* rites were being practiced once more—the graves of dead local chiefs stamped on at night to arouse the occupants, *yanggona* (kava) poured out in libations to the *Vu* ("ancestors"), all this in order that the men of Ra and its hinterland, the fabled Kauvadra range of hills, should be free to act independently of colonial administration and coastal chiefs alike. These latter both concurred that separatism actually meant sedition; accordingly Dugumoi was first sent to jail, then in 1887 was deported to Rotuma. He died on his return to Levuka in 1897, but there are Fijians who would say that he, like the *Vu*, still lives on.

RELATED ENTRIES: Fiji.

SOURCES AND READINGS: Deryck Scarr, "A Roku Tui for Lomaiviti: The Question of Legitimacy in the Fijian Administration 1874-1900," *Journal of Pacific History* 5 (1970); Files relating to the Deportation of Natives, National Archives, Suva, Fiji.

Deryck Scarr

NAWAI, APOLOSI R. (1876?-1946). Born into a family of no traditional rank in Narewa, Nadi, on Viti Levu, Fiji, Apolosi received some training in carpentry and a thorough knowledge of the Bible from the Wesleyan mission's single high school at Navuloa and later in Davuilevu near Suva. In 1911 or 1912 he began to fire the imagination of banana-growing villagers on the tributaries of the Rewa river with a scheme to launch the Fiji Company (*Viti Kabani*) to cut out rapacious white middlemen and buyers and even shippers.

The response was overwhelmingly enthusiastic and extended to copra growers as well. Apolosi and his agents collected a few thousand pounds. Despite his flagrant abuse of the trust he evoked in his followers and his total managerial ignorance, the colonial government was not wholly unsympathetic to his modernizing mission and hesitated long enough for most Fijians to assume its tacit approval. The paramount chiefs in the ranks of the Fijian administration, however, correctly perceived the mounting challenge to their privileged and unimaginative leadership, and with Ratu Sukuna in the lead, successfully exposed the anticolonial undertones of the movement and the reckless claims of its leader. By 1914 Apolosi was reworking his genealogy to upgrade his own origins, and developing a colony-wide organization to bypass the administrative system established by the first British governors but now increasingly under the supervision of European district commissioners.

Apolosi was jailed for eighteen months in 1915, just long enough to earn the mantle of the "Suffering Servant" of his people. His appeal became a colony-wide call to the ordinary village Fijians to take command of their destiny. The authorities and local Europeans residents feared an all-out race war and at the end of 1917 had him exiled to Rotuma for seven years.

In the late 1920s Apolosi refurbished his somewhat tarnished image with arcane allusions to occult powers and a messianic mission to bring about a new era of which he and/or his brother Jesus would be king. In 1930 expectation was running high that the day of salvation was nigh; even ranking chiefs of the Nadi area were beginning to waver, and the eccentric Wesleyan missionary Arthur D. Lelean urged the government to at least acknowledge the mandate given to Apolosi at the enormous inaugural meetings of the company's foundation years. Instead, Apolosi was exiled to Rotuma for another ten years.

Released on strict probation in 1940, the aging "Pacific Island Rasputin" soon showed that he had lost none of his now legendary oratorical and sexual prowess. The governor exiled him yet again to Rotuma for fear that he would spike the war effort. Later, he was considered a potential Quisling and was removed from possible Japanese rescue on defenseless Rotuma to a New Zealand jail.

After the war he was confined to Yacata. He died unrepentant in 1946 knowing full well that he had opened a deep vein of discontent in the neotraditional structures protected by the Fijian administration. The Viti Company bared the receptivity of Fijians to new initiatives that would bring their labor and their social and natural resources into a more productive relationship with the capitalist economy.

RELATED ENTRIES: Fiji; Sukuna, Ratu Josef L. V.

SOURCES AND READINGS: Deryck Scarr, ed., *More Pacific Islands Portraits* (Canberra: Australian National University Press, 1978), pp. 173-92.

Timothy J. Macnaught

NELSON, OLAF FREDERICK (1883-1944). Patriot, trader, and educator, Olaf Nelson was born 24 February 1883, in Savai'i, Samoa, of a Swedish father and a high-ranking Samoan mother. At age seventeen he took over the A. Nelson and Son Company which later became O. F. Nelson and Company. Nelson was an affluent member of the Samoan and European communities. After World War I Nelson was outraged at the League of Nations' decision to have New Zealand administer the Samoan mandate.

He voiced his protest to the League on behalf of Samoa but to no avail. In 1923 Nelson became a member of the new Samoan legislative council. Then he became the leader of the *Mau*, a Samoan nationalist movement, and fought the New Zealand government for fifteen years. In 1927 Nelson was banished and sent to New Zealand because of his political activities. In 1933 he returned home only to be banished again. In 1936 the newly elected Labour government rescinded the decree and brought Nelson and his family honorably back to Samoa. Nelson contributed much to the new Samoan government. He wrote a small book on *Legends of Samoa*, and in 1925 he was elected life member of the Polynesian Society. Nelson died in Western Samoa on 21 February 1944.

RELATED ENTRIES: *Mau* of *Pule*; Western Samoa.

SOURCES AND READINGS: S. Masterman, *An Outline of Samoan History* (Apia: Department of Education, 1955); "Death of Mr. O. F. Nelson," *Pacific Islands Monthly*, March 1944, pp. 10 and 30.

Joseph A. Montoya

NEW CALEDONIA. New Caledonia consists of a large island with adjacent, smaller island dependencies which comprise a French Overseas Territory in the southwest Pacific Ocean. New Caledonia lies at the crossroads of Melanesia and Polynesia about 1,207 km (750 mi) northeast of Australia. Its dependencies include the islands of Chesterfield, Huon, Surprise, Bélep, Loyalty, Pine, Walpole, and Matthew. The group lies between 19° and 23° south latitude and between 163° and 168° east longitude. New Caledonia stretches 400 km (248 mi) in length with a maximum width of 50 km (31 mi). With a land area of 16,900 km² (6,530 mi²), it is one of the largest islands in Oceania. The territory's total area is 19,050 km² (7,358 mi²). Nouméa, the capital and chief port, is situated on the southwest coast and has a population of 74,335 (1978).

Population. While the indigenous people of New Caledonia are Melanesians, their origins are obscure. In the mid-eighteenth century, large numbers of Polynesians from Wallis Island migrated to the Loyalty Islands and to New Caledonia. Early Europeans numbered the population between 60,000 and 90,000. The first official French census in 1887 counted 41,874. By 1911 it had dropped to 28,075. The Melanesian population, however, stablized during the 1920s and has increased to 58,400 (1978). Most continue to live in rural areas. New Cale-

donia's European population, most French, has steadily increased to 51,400 (1978). Other Oceanic groups, particularly Wallisians and Tahitians, along with approximately 10,000 Indonesians and Vietnamese immigrants, have boosted the territorial population to 139,600 (1980).

Climate, Geography, and Natural Resources. New Caledonia enjoys one of the most favorable tropical climates in the South Pacific. Temperatures average 22°C (72°F) in summer (December to May) and 18°C (65°F) in winter (June to November). The island is cooled by southwest trade winds. Rainfall is heaviest on the east coast (80 in or 200 cm annually) with the west coast receiving about one half that amount. Tropical hurricanes are common. A rugged volcanic mountain chain gives the island its basic form. The eastern coast is forested with kauri pine. The western coast is low and broken with marshes and grasslands. It is estimated that less than 10 percent of the total area is arable. New Caledonia is rich in mineral deposits, notably nickel. The highest point is Mont Panié (5,412 ft or 1,628 m). Native varieties of flora are the *niaouli* or cajeput tree (a eucalyptus from which medicine is made), mangroves, coconut palms, ferns, acacias, and pines. Fauna include deer, cattle, birds, and an abundant and varied marine life. The most interesting species is the *kagu*, a flightless bird found only in New Caledonia and nearing extinction.

Economic Resources. Nickel mining and smelting is by far the leading industry. New Caledonia has about one third of the world's known nickel ore deposits, the second largest after Canada. Nickel comprises more than 90 percent of all exports. Iron, manganese, coal, and gypsum are also mined and the island has large chromium ore deposits. Tourism is a lesser major industry. Other local industries include lumbering, brick making, soap making, and bottling. Agricultural produce is marketed locally although some coffee and copra are exported.

Pre-European Culture. The islands' Melanesian society was divided into families, clans, and tribes. The clan was the strongest unit. Several clans were grouped into a loosely structured tribe which shared a common, isolated area. Clan members claimed descent from a common ancestor (*totel*) who was highly revered in legends, chants, and religious ceremonies. Families followed a male hierarchial order. The closest relationships were between relatives of the same age. Polygamy existed but was not widely practiced. Women were considered inferior and had traditional tasks of rearing children and cultivating crops. Each tribe was headed by a chief whose role was priest and statesman. The main island was inhabited by an estimated forty tribes at Cook's arrival.

History. Bougainville sighted the island in 1768, but the first European to visit was James Cook in 1774. Cook named it New Caledonia after his native Scotland. Searching for the lost Frenchman Lapérouse, d'Entrecasteaux explored the Isle of Pines and the eastern coast of the islands in 1792. During the next fifty years, New Caledonia was visited by navigators, sandalwood traders, runaway seamen, and whaling ships. Members of the London Missionary Society reached the area in 1840. By 1843 a French Roman Catholic mission was founded. France's seizure of New Caledonia in 1853 ended a growing rivalry for the islands with Great Britain. France annexed it for a penal colony (following England's example in Australia) and for a naval and trading base. The French sent between 30,000 and 40,000 convicts to New Caledonia from 1864 to 1897. Following the Franco-Prussian War, many political prisoners (*communards*) were deported to Ile Nou, Ducos, and the Isle of Pines. Efforts toward colonization began in the early twentieth century but were hampered because of local hostilities and the islands' penal history. During World War II the United States built a huge military and naval base on New Caledonia for staging Pacific battles. In 1946 the island acquired the status of a French Overseas Territory.

Government. From 1853 to 1884 New Caledonia was administered by French military governors. After 1885 a civilian governor, assisted by an elected advisory council, ruled the island. After 1946 an elected territorial assembly was established and its executive powers vested in the high commissioner, a public servant appointed from Paris. France has been reluctant to grant internal self-government. New Caledonia is represented by two deputies in the French National Assembly and one seat in the French Senate.

RELATED ENTRIES: Bouarate; Cook, (Captain) James; Creagh, Stephen; Defense Planning for Oceania between the Wars; D'Entrecasteaux, Antoine; Feillet, Paul; France in the Pacific; French Polynesia; Guillain, Charles; Guyon, Joseph; Higginson, John; Jones, John; Kanaka Revolt of 1878-1879; Leenhardt, Maurice; Montrouzier, Xavier; Paddon, James; Sandalwood Trade; Selwyn, George; South Pacific Commission; Thompson, William K.

SOURCES AND READINGS: Patrick O'Reilly, *Bibliographie Méthodique, Analytique et Critique de la Nouvelle-Calédonie* (Paris: Musée de l'Homme, 1955) and *Calédoniens: Répertoire bibliographique de la Nouvelle-Calédonie* (Paris: Musée de l'Homme, 1953); Virginia Thompson and Richard Adloff, *The French Pacific Islands: French Polynesia and New Caledonia* (Berkeley: University of California Press, 1971).
                                    Russell T. Clement

NEW GUINEA. *See* Papua New Guinea.

NEW HEBRIDES. *See* Vanuatu.

NEWTON, HENRY (1866-1947). A bishop of New Guinea (1922-1936), Newton was born in Victoria, Australia, on 5 January 1866. Educated at the University of Sydney and Merton College, Oxford University, after serving a curacy in London he returned to Australia where he was instituted priest-in-charge of the parish of Esk in the diocese of Brisbane. In 1899 he joined the staff of the Anglican mission which had been established in British New Guinea (Papua) eight years earlier. Following an absence from the mission of six years as bishop of Carpentaria from 1914, he was elected third bishop of New Guinea in 1921.

Newton became bishop of New Guinea at a time when the social and economic circumstances of Papua were stagnating, and when the culture of Melanesian villages in the area claimed as part of the sphere of the Anglican mission appeared to be decaying. In his numerous addresses and articles, and particularly in his book *In Far New Guinea* (1914), Newton argued for the maintenance of the Papuans' traditional usages although the erosion of clan authority had led partly to the return of the indentured laborers from the plantations. In order to foster the development of authority among mission-educated Papuans, he ordained Papuan clergy and convened an annual gathering of Papuan Christians known as the *Oga Tara*. He considered the training of Papuan priests to be his primary responsibility, and in 1903 he began instructing the first Papuan theological students. Every Papuan clergyman ordained between 1914 and 1947 was trained by him. As bishop of Carpentaria, Newton created St. Paul's theological college on Moa Island and ordained the first two Torres Strait islanders to the diaconate.

By virtue of his association of forty-eight years with the mission, Newton played a significant part in shaping the distinctive qualities of the Anglican church in Papua. The attitude of the mission towards traditional customs and its emphasis on the sacrificial nature of the missionary vocation bore the stamp of Newton's personal influence. While lacking formal anthropological expertise, Newton and other Anglican missionaries helped in the preparation of C. G. Seligmann's major text, *The Melanesians of British New Guinea* (1910). His outlook was characterized by a liberal intellectual tolerance and sympathy, but it cannot be said that he was a notably original thinker. Though he held a broad respect for Melanesian customs, Newton criticized some younger anthropologists for advocating, as it seemed to him, the wholesale preservation of Papuan culture. The theological college bearing his name near Popondetta and the Anglican cathedral at Dogura, at the time of its completion in 1939 probably the largest ecclesiastical building in the South Pacific, may be regarded as fitting monuments to Newton's contribution to mission education and the indelible mark he left on the development of the Anglican church in Papua New Guinea.

RELATED ENTRIES: Anglican Missions; Labor Trade; Melanesian Recruitment to Queensland, Patterns of; Melanesians and Colonial Servitude; Papua New Guinea.

SOURCES AND READINGS: English Committee of the New Guinea Mission, *Occasional Papers*, London: 1903-1947; New Guinea Mission (Anglican) *Annual Reports*, 1899-1940 (Dogura); Henry Newton, *In Far New Guinea* (London: Seeley, Service and Co., 1914); Montagu Stone-Wigg and Henry Newton, *The Papuans: A People of the South Pacific* (Sydney: Australian Board of Missions, 1933); David Wetherell, *Reluctant Mission: The Anglican Church in Papua New Guinea 1891-1942* (Brisbane: University of Queensland Press, 1977).   *David Wetherell*

NIMITZ, CHESTER WILLIAM (1885-1966). Commander in chief (1941-1945) of the United States Pacific Fleet during World War II after Japan's attack on Pearl Harbor in Hawai'i in December 1941, Nimitz helped to shape the American tactic of "island hopping"—fighting only for key islands which would serve as bases for future actions of strategic importance. He was promoted to admiral of the fleet in 1944 and signed in behalf of the United States at the surrender ceremonies in Tokyo Bay in 1945. He then became chief of naval operations (1945-1947).

RELATED ENTRIES: Spruance, Raymond; War in the Pacific Islands, 1914-1945.   *Frank P. King*

NIUE. A small coral island approximately 58 km (36 mi) in circumference with an area of 260 km², Niue is a self-governing British Commonwealth country in free association with New Zealand and with New Zealand citizenship. It lies 19° south latitude and 169° west longitude, approximately 480 km (300 mi) due east of Vava'u, Tonga, and 560 km (350 mi) southeast of Samoa. The population (1979) numbers

3,578 of which 75 percent are of Polynesian extract and the remaining are Europeans. The climate is tropical but cooled by the southeast trade winds. The average mean temperature is 24.7° C (76.5° F), and the average annual rainfall measures 217.7 cm (87 in). The volcanic soil is fertile but not abundantly so. The main crops of copra, passion fruit, and limes are generally exported to New Zealand. The island's imports far exceed its exports.

Niue was originally settled by Samoans or perhaps eastern Polynesians over a thousand years ago, and two other migrations from Tonga settled there in more modern times. Tribal chieftans controlled the various districts around the island. The language in the north differed from that in the south. The first European to visit the island was Captain James Cook (24 June 1774) and because of the ferocious nature of the islanders he nicknamed it "Savage Island." Missionaries John Williams and Charles Barff attempted to land in 1830 and again in 1842, but they too were expelled. In 1846 the missionaries H. Nishet and W. Gill from Samoa landed Peniamina, a Niuean who had been trained in the seminary in Samoa, and he persuaded the islanders to accept the missionaries. Finally in 1849 the Samoan missionary Paulo landed and introduced Christianity. By 1854 most Niueans had been converted. The Reverend W. G. Lawes and his brother F. E. Lawes were the two prominent resident English missionaries during the last half of the nineteenth century.

During the first half of the nineteenth century, the ferocity of the islanders had generally kept the blackbirders and whalers from landing on the island; but in 1863 a slave ship from Peru captured 130 men, and in 1868 "Bully" Hayes kidnapped about sixty men and thirty women and took them to Tahiti. Later, other Niueans volunteered to leave and work in the phosphate mines on Malden Island owned by Grice, Sumner and Company of Melbourne. The chief products of Niue during the nineteenth century were cotton, arrowroot, coconut fiber, and fungus. The chief trader was an Englishman by the name of Henry Head who had been shipwrecked on Niue in 1867 and who had married the daughter of a paramount chief. He exercised great influence in the island.

In 1876 the Niueans selected Mataio Tuitoga as their king and his successor, Fataaiki, petitioned Queen Victoria for an English protectorate in 1898 and again in 1899 but was refused. On 10 October 1900, however, Britain granted their request; and in September 1901 Niue was formally annexed to New Zealand as part of the Cook Islands. S. Percy Smith became its first governor. A local administrative council was selected in 1904 and little change in government occurred until 1960 when a Niuean assembly was established giving representation to the fourteen villages on the island. Other powers were gradually granted to the assembly until on 19 October 1974 Niue gained self-government within the British Commonwealth with free association with New Zealand who is chiefly responsible for its defense and foreign affairs.

The government consists of fourteen legislative assemblymen elected by proportional representation from the villages and six members who are elected at large. The assembly chooses a president who in turn selects three ministers from the assembly as his cabinet. The government is the major employer on the island, hiring about 90 percent of all wage workers through its government development board.

Niuean economy, however, is characterized by a flexible combination of wage work and growing taro and other crops by rotating cultivation. Niuean population has declined over the past decade as more and more islanders move to New Zealand. This has relieved any local overpopulation problem, but at the same time, has drained Niue of its more highly trained manpower to New Zealand.

RELATED ENTRIES: Cook Islands.

SOURCES AND READINGS: Edwin M. Loeb, *History and Traditions of Niue* (Honolulu: Bishop Museum Press, 1926); Nancy J. Pollock, "Work, Wages, and Shifting Cultivation on Niue," *Pacific Studies* 2 (1979): 132-43.   *Robert D. Craig*

NORDHOFF, CHARLES BERNARD (1887-1947). The grandson of Charles Nordhoff, an American author who wrote accounts of his adventures at sea, Charles Bernard Nordhoff, perhaps inspired by his namesake, also sought a life of adventure and writing. He first joined the French Lafayette Escadrille as a pilot before World War I and then became a commissioned officer in the United States Aviation Service during the war. While in Europe, Nordhoff met another budding author, James Norman Hall; and shortly after their release from the service, the two collaborated to write *The LaFayette Flying Corps* (1920). Later that year, Nordhoff and Hall went to Tahiti on a salary advance from an American magazine and began writing travel stories about the South Pacific. Originally printed in *Harper's* magazine under individual titles and authors, the articles were soon combined into one book, *Faery Lands of the South Seas* (1921), which brought the writers modest success. Between 1922 and 1928 Nordhoff wrote three novels of his own, all of which used the South

Pacific for a major part of their substance. But it was not until 1932, again in collaboration with Hall, that Nordhoff gained international recognition as a successful writer. In this collaboration, Nordhoff wrote the epic episodes and most of the passages relating to ships, fishing, and the sea, while Hall provided the lyrical and emotional descriptions. Combining their skills at fictionalization with some research, the two authors wrote their famous trilogy which describes the 1787 mutiny on the *Bounty*, a British warship, and the subsequent lives of those involved. *Mutiny On The Bounty* (1932) describes the events leading to and culminating in the mutiny. *Men Against The Sea* (1933) tells of the miraculous voyage of Captain Bligh and the seventeen nonmutinous members of his crew. *Pitcairn Island* (1934) narrates the Pacific wanderings and settlement of those who mutinied. The success of these writings brought a measure of financial security to Nordhoff and Hall, as did the six subsequent novels they were to coauthor, the last of which, *The High Barbaree*, was written in 1945. While these novels were being collaborated upon, Nordhoff also continued to write pieces of his own. Among these were the edited journals of his grandfather which he published in 1940 as *Yankee Windjammers*. Near the end of his career Nordhoff returned to live in the United States and eventually died in Santa Barbara, California, on 11 April 1947.

RELATED ENTRIES: Bligh, William; *Bounty* Mutiny; Hall, James Norman.

SOURCES AND READINGS: Paul L. Briand, Jr., *In Search of Paradise—The Nordhoff-Hall Story* (New York: Duell, Sloan and Pierce, 1966); James Norman Hall, *My Island Home—An Autobiography* (New York: Little, Brown and Co., 1952).   *Jeffrey Butler*

NORFOLK ISLAND. Lying 29° south latitude and 168° east longitude, about 1,287 km (800 mi) northeast of Sydney, Norfolk Island has a land area of 34.5 km² (13.3 mi²) and is low-lying except for Mounts Pitt and Bates. The climate is pleasant with mean annual temperatures of about 16° C (61° F) and about 132 cm (52 in) of annual rainfall, and has recently had a population of about 1,600 persons. Discovered by James Cook in 1774, the island was a penal station during the years 1788-1813, 1825-1855. In 1856 nearly two hundred descendants of the mutineers from the *Bounty* relocated from Pitcairn Island. At that time, Norfolk was made a separate settlement under the jurisdiction of the governor of New South Wales. With the passage of the Norfolk Island Act in 1913, it became a territory of Australia in 1914. The island is administered locally by a local representative of the Australian Minister for the Capital Territory. The Norfolk Island Council has eight members and has advisory and consultative functions; there is also a local Court of Petty Sessions. Currently about 18,000 tourists visit Kingston, the main town and Norfolk each year.

RELATED ENTRIES: Bligh, William; Pitcairn Island.

SOURCES AND READINGS: Merval Hoare, *Norfolk Island: An Outline of its History, 1774-1968* (St. Lucia, Queensland: University of Queensland Press, 1969).
                                                      Frank P. King

NOTT, HENRY (1774-1844). A member of the London Missionary Society (LMS), Nott arrived in Tahiti in the first Christian contingent aboard the *Duff* in 1797. He quickly mastered Tahitian and preached the first sermon in that language in August 1801. During the troubled times of civil war between the various districts on Tahiti and Mo'orea, all of the other missionaries left except Nott. He remained with chief Pomare. He came to exercise great influence over the king, but it was not until 1815 that he had any conversions to the Christian faith. When high priest Pati'i and then Pomare converted to the Christian faith, most of the island followed their examples. Nott advised King Pomare in the promulgation of Tahiti's first law code (1819) and exercised great influence over the royal family. He was the first to translate the Scriptures into Tahitian and published them in 1836. He personally presented a copy to Queen Victoria. He retired from mission service in 1840 and died 2 May 1844 at Papara (Tahiti). A solitary stone with an appropriate inscription marks his tomb at Matavai, a short distance from the burial grounds of the Pomare family.

RELATED ENTRIES: French Polynesia; London Missionary Society; Pomare Family.

SOURCES AND READINGS: Richard Lovett, *History of the London Missionary Society*, 2 vols. (London: H. Frowde, 1899); James Sibree, ed., *Register of the Missionaries of the London Missionary Society* (London: London Missionary Society, 1923).
                                                      Robert D. Craig

NOUVELLE-BRETAGNE. The ship *Nouvelle-Bretagne* left Barcelona on 7 April 1881 for the colony of Port Breton (Nouvelle France) where she arrived in August 1881 to find the settlement totally abandoned and the colony nonexistent. She carried on board a number of families from Belgium and Alsace-Lorraine as well as a few representatives of the Marquis de Rays sent to administer, survey, and organize the colony. Disease, death, and shortages of supplies afflicted the would-be colonists, and in September the captain, Henry, left for Manila where he hoped to find the necessary funds to buy essential supplies. Instead, the ship was impounded by the Spanish authorities. Determined to return to the settlement, the captain disregarded official orders. The news he brought back to the colonists only accentuated the difficult situation which had developed during his absence. The immediate arrival of a Spanish man-of-war to arrest the captain brought partial relief to the plight of the settlers. *Nouvelle-Bretagne* was escorted back to Manila with the most distressed settlers, while the remaining ones made arrangements with a local trader to be taken to Australia. In Manila the captain of *Nouvelle-Bretagne* was tried and acquitted, and the ship was sold to an Australian trader.

RELATED ENTRIES: *Chandernagor*; *Genil*; Nouvelle France; Rays, (Marquis) Charles de.

SOURCES AND READINGS: P. Baudouin, *L'Aventure de Port Breton et la colonie libre dite Nouvelle France* (Paris: M. Dreyfous, 1883); J. B. O. Mouton, *Personal and Business Papers*, (Pacific Manuscript Bureau, microfilm 603. Public Records Office: General Correspondence, France, F027).
                                                      Anne-Gabrielle Thompson

NOUVELLE FRANCE. A "free" colony of Port Breton, Nouvelle France was envisaged by Marquis Charles de Rays to encompass eastern New Guinea, New Britain, and New Ireland. The proposed colony was to be above all Catholic and a profitable enclave of the old, aristocratic France.

In reality, conditions in the Pacific were vastly different from the propaganda distributed in Europe. Only three locations were briefly occupied at various times between January 1880 and February 1882: Port Breton and Likiliki on the south coast of New Ireland, and the Laughlan Islands at the southern tip of eastern New Guinea. No productive enterprises in precious woods and sugarcane were ever launched, and only a lay missionary and a priest, both of dubious reputation, advanced the cause of the Catholic church. During its brief existence Nouvelle France was peopled mainly by non-French settlers and was abandoned three times: in October 1880 by the survivors from *Chandernagor*; in February 1881 by the survivors from *India*, who eventually founded a thriving settlement in Australia; and finally in February 1882 when the forty remaining members from *Nouvelle Bretagne* bargained with the local trader,

Thomas Farrell, and Queen Emma for safe transport to Australia.

Nouvelle France was only one of the numerous "South Sea Bubbles" which burst during the nineteenth century. Its more peculiar feature is the fact that it acted as a cover for an ingeniously conducted embezzlement. Its sensationalist aspects have given rise to much fantasy literature.

RELATED ENTRIES: *Chandernagor*; *Genil*; *Nouvelle-Bretagne*; Rays, (Marquis) Charles de.

SOURCES AND READINGS: J. Lucas-Subreton, *L'Eden du Pacifique* (Paris: Gallimard, 1929); J. Niau, *The Phantom Paradise* (Sydney: Angus and Robertson, 1935); A. G. Thompson, "'New France,' the Free Colony of Charles Marie Bonaventure du Breil, Marquis de Rays. A Dream or a Fraud?" (Master's thesis, University of Queensland, 1975).

Anne-Gabrielle Thompson

O

OBOOKIAH, HENRY (1792?-1818). A Hawaiian who inspired the first missionaries of the American Board of Commissioners for Foreign Missions to come to Hawai'i, Obookiah was born about 1792 on the island of Hawai'i and was orphaned at the age of twelve. Surviving the tribal wars on the island, he signed aboard a visiting ship captained by Caleb Brintnall. In 1809 he reached New Haven, Connecticut, where he was taught to read and write by several pious New Englanders including Edwin W. Dwight, president of Yale University. He later studied Christian theology at Bradford Academy, became a member of the church of Torringford, and on 1 January 1817 became a member of the Foreign Mission Society in Cornwall, Connecticut. There he began the translation of the Bible into Hawaiian. On 17 February 1818 Obookiah died of typhus fever. Shortly after his death his *Memoirs of Henry Obookiah* was published. This one work greatly influenced the Foreign Mission to send its first missionaries to Hawai'i (1819-1820), a dream Obookiah was never able to see realized in his own life time.

RELATED ENTRIES: Hawai'i; Hawai'i, Religions of.

SOURCES AND READINGS: A. Grove Day, *Books About Hawaii* (Honolulu: University Press of Hawaii, 1977); D. B. Eberhart, *Memoirs of Henry Obookiah* (Los Angeles: D. B. Eberhart, 1959); Edward Joesting, *Hawaii: An Uncommon History* (New York: W. W. Norton & Co., 1972).   *Brenna J. Rash*

OCEANIA, STRATEGIC IMPORTANCE OF SINCE 1945. The islands of Oceania derive their strategic significance from their interior position within the Pacific, the world's largest ocean. In an eastward direction, the Micronesian islands in particular lie astride major air and maritime routes leading to the east Asian mainland and Japan. In a westward direction, the Polynesian islands lie across sea and air passages to the west coast of the American continents; and to the southward, the Melanesian islands stand athwart routes leading to Australia and New Zealand. Strategically, these small islands may act either as bases for defensive or offensive operations across the Pacific.

The Pacific Ocean, covering approximately a third of the earth's surface, presents special strategic problems in terms of the immense distances involved: for example, the distance from Singapore to the Panama Canal is over 16,100 km. In such a huge oceanic environment, island bases in a conventional war strategy can be of crucial importance, as the progress of World War II in the Pacific demonstrated. In the event of nuclear war, however, bases can be quickly destroyed: thus nuclear strategy places less emphasis upon the importance of island bases. But the oceans themselves are of particular significance in a nuclear age since they provide highly important opportunities for the concealment, in the sea itself, of strategic land-attack weapon systems such as nuclear missile-firing submarines. Oceanic islands can provide valuable bases for the missions conducted by such vessels, though by the late 1970s this function was beginning to decline.

Since the end of World War II, because of the momentous political and military events in east and southeast Asia, the western Pacific has been a much more active strategic area than the eastern Pacific. In 1945, following the defeat of imperial Japan, the Pacific Ocean was in strategic terms an "American lake." No other country could challenge American air and sea dominance. Having occupied the islands of Micronesia—the Marianas, the Carolines, and the Marshalls—at heavy cost during World War II, the United States was determined to maintain effective strategic control of this important area. American strategic interests in Micronesia were recognized by the United Nations in 1947 with the creation of the Trust Territory of the Pacific Islands as a United Nations strategic trust administered by the United States. In effect, this arrangement provided for continuing American military control of Micronesia. Guam, as an unincorporated territory of the United States, remained outside the trust arrangement so that the United States exercised complete sovereignty over this island with its important naval and air bases.

Throughout the immediate postwar period, American strategic influence in Oceania was overwhelming; Japan was vanquished, the Soviet Union was not at this stage a rival, and both Britain and France (with their numerous possessions in the Pacific) acquiesced in American dominance. Britain, the once mighty mistress of the seas, was excluded from the Pacific Security Treaty of 1951, which linked together the defense interests of the United States, Australia, and New Zealand.

The onset of cold war rivalry between the United States and the Soviet Union did not initially lead to any effective challenge by the latter to the predominance of American power in the Pacific Ocean. Nor did the establishment of a communist regime in China in 1949 change this situation. The United States was able to maintain and supply across the Pacific its large army fighting in the Korean War (1950-1953) without interference by the Soviet or Chinese naval and air forces. Even following the deepened American military involvement in the Vietnam War during the 1960s, American control of the Pacific was not challenged by the Soviet Union or the People's Republic of China. During the Vietnam War, Guam acted as a completely secure base for the air bombardment by American B-52 bombers of Vietnamese targets.

Towards the end of the 1960s the dramatic growth of the Soviet navy began to create new strategic problems. With a naval base near Vladivostock and an estimated 100 submarines plus other vessels operating in the Pacific, the Soviet Union had the capacity to penetrate what had been an American lake. But American strategic capability in the Pacific still outweighed that of the Soviet Union because of the American aircraft-carrier fleet and American strategic bases in the Asian-Pacific area gave a range of surveillance and strike capacity not available to the Soviet Union. However, both the United States and the Soviet Union possessed an ultimate deterrent against one another in the form of nuclear missile-firing submarines as well as intercontinental ballistic missiles.

The Soviet Union did make demonstrations of its naval power in the Pacific during the 1968 crisis when North Korea seized the American ship *Pueblo* and after the American mining of the North Vietnamese ports of Hanoi and Haiphong in 1972. On both occasions, these naval demonstrations took the form of the massing of Soviet naval forces in proximity to American naval units in the western Pacific but at sufficient distance to maintain a "low-risk" profile. In the event, neither of these Soviet displays of naval strength escalated and the Soviet-American rivalry continued in the form of peaceful confrontation. But the era of unquestioned American dominance in the Pacific was coming to an end.

The failure of American intervention in the Vietnam War led to a major reassessment of American global strategy and called forth the Nixon Doctrine of 1969 in which the limits of American power in Asia were recognized. A central feature of Richard Nixon's new policy was the desire to exploit the open rift between the Soviet Union and the People's Republic of China. Thus by the 1970s, although the most important Great Power relationship globally was between the United States and the Soviet Union, in the east Asian-western Pacific area there was a three-way balance between these two powers and China (which had also become a nuclear power). The most significant factor for the western Pacific of this new triangular balance was the intense rivalry between the Soviet Union and China. The United States thereby gained a valuable flexibility in its relations with these two competing communist states. Japan, the other major east Asian state, has become an economic superpower but has remained weak militarily: she does not possess nuclear weapons and has stayed in the sphere of American strategic protection.

By the end of the 1970s the United States remained the predominant, though no longer unassailable, power in the Pacific. Aside from the United States Second Infantry Division in South Korea, whose eventual withdrawal was under consideration, the principal United States forces immediately available for action in the western Pacific were: ten squadrons of land-based fighter/attack aircraft; two brigades of the Third Marine Amphibious Force including its Air Wing in Okinawa; and the Seventh Fleet which included two attack carriers. In addition, the Twenty-fifth Infantry Division, stationed in Hawai'i, was available for possible commitment. To maintain the Seventh Fleet in the western Pacific, the United States Navy used bases at Subic Bay in the Philippines, Yokosuka in Japan, and at Guam. The Seventh Fleet's immediate backup force was the remainder of the United States Pacific Fleet.

The Soviet military challenge to American power in the Pacific continues to grow, though at a moderate pace. The threat posed by these forces to the United States is limited by three major considerations: 1) the bulk of Soviet military power in the Asian-Pacific area is directed at the People's Republic of China; 2) the Soviet Pacific Fleet is much less active than other Soviet fleets or the United States Pacific Fleet; 3) there are problems associated with both of the Soviet Pacific Fleet's two main bases: Vladivostock has restricted access to the open sea and Petropavlovsk on the remote Kamchatka Peninsula is difficult to support and resupply.

Although the Soviet Pacific Fleet possesses a formidable force of nuclear missile-firing submarines, it exhibits a serious lack of capability in conducting sustained antisubmarine warfare at any great distance away from home waters; whereas the bulk of American nuclear missile-firing submarines are likely to be located far out in the Pacific Ocean. Hence the Soviet Pacific Fleet remains at a considerable disadvantage when compared with the capability of the United States Pacific Fleet.

The navy of the Chinese People's Republic is large, ranking third in the world in 1978, but it is weak in open-ocean experience. The Chinese navy is primarily designed for coastal defense in which it possesses a massive capability, but it has not attempted to conduct extended operations beyond immediate territorial waters.

While Britain virtually completed her withdrawal from the Pacific during the 1970s, France still kept a military presence in Oceania. After the United States (which had 10,000 men stationed on Guam), France in 1979 maintained the second largest armed force in the area with 3,000 troops in French Polynesia and 2,500 on New Caledonia. France has a particular military interest in maintaining use of her nuclear testing facilities on the island of Moruroa. In terms of visible military presence, at the end of the 1970s the United States and France were the powers most directly involved in the security of Oceania. But the Soviet Union (which has made overtures to Tonga) and the People's Republic of China (which has opened a mission in Western Samoa) have both displayed long-range interests in establishing a more effective presence in Oceania.

Given the conditions prevailing at the end of the 1970s, any future changes in the strategic situation in Oceania seemed likely to be governed by American policy. It appeared unlikely that the Soviet Pacific Fleet would be able effectively to challenge American predominance. The Soviet position compared with that of the United States could worsen still further because of the development of the American strategic "Cruise" missile. Such missiles could be retrofitted to existing United States surface vessels, aircraft, and attack-submarines, vastly increasing the number of strike platforms with which the Soviet navy has to contend. Also, the dispute between the Soviet Union and the People's Republic of China is likely to embroil the two major communist states in an essentially land-based confrontation in East Asia.

A key factor in the superiority of the United States in the western Pacific is her possession of bases in the Philippines, Japan, and Micronesia. The focus of the American strategic position in Micronesia is the American island of Guam, which has important naval and air base facilities. In 1978 Guam still acted as a base for American *Polaris* and *Poseidon* nuclear-powered ballistic missile-firing submarines deploying in the Pacific, though the new *Trident*-class submarines, which are to enter service in the next few years, were to be based on the West Coast of the continental United States itself. The United States also has a strong military interest in maintaining the use of the facilities of the Missile Test Center on Kwajalein in the Marshall Islands.

In responding to political pressures for self-determination in the Trust Territory of the Pacific Islands during the 1970s, the United States has made arrangements to protect its military interests in Micronesia. The Northern Mariana Islands became a commonwealth of the United States and the other parts of the trust territory formed the Federated States of Micronesia in free association with the United States, but allowed full American authority in defense matters for fifteen years. Despite criticism of official United States policy that retention of bases on these Micronesian islands was no longer essential to American security, the American government continued to regard access to and use of such facilities as a valuable part of its strategic posture in the western Pacific.

When assessing likely trends for the future, it appears that the need for continued American protection of Japan in particular will require the United States to maintain its strategic predominance in Oceania. The negotiations over the future political development of the Pacific trust territory suggests that the United States is determined to preserve such superiority at least into the 1990s. However, some very long-term trends likely to disturb American dominance are becoming discernible. The Soviet Union is showing a willingness to increase the intensity of its strategic challenge in the western Pacific; and the People's Republic of China is also seeking to increase its presence in the area. Such developments pose the question of the cost and long-term political value to the United States of maintaining a major strategic presence in the western Pacific. This is especially the case when the new *Trident* class of ballistic missile-firing submarines (with their range of 4,000 miles) can be deployed near the North American continental shelf, thus reducing or eliminating the need for forward bases in the western Pacific.

In the event of a long-term retraction of American power in the western Pacific, Japan would have to undertake more responsibility for her own defense. The United States could in turn concentrate on maintaining her strategic superiority in the eastern Pacific, from Hawai'i to the West Coast of the American mainland. If the United States withdraws her Pacific defense line to Hawai'i, the western Pacific would then seem destined to become an area of strategic competition between the USSR, China, and Japan. Such a development would involve considerable dangers since the existing relative stability of strategic conditions in Oceania, associated with American predominance, would give way to a much more volatile and unstable situation.

RELATED ENTRIES: Commonwealth of the Northern Mariana Islands; Guam; Micronesia.

SOURCES AND READINGS: H. W. Baldwin, *Strategy for Tomorrow* (New York: Harper & Row, 1970); Michael Godley, "China as a Pacific Power," *Pacific Studies* 3 (1979):41-50; D. F. McHenry, *Micronesia: Trust Betrayed: Altruism vs Self-Interest in American Foreign Policy* (New York: Carnegie Endowment for International Peace, 1975); T. B. Millar, *The Indian and Pacific Oceans: Some Strategic Considerations* (London: Adelphi Papers, no. 57, Institute for Strategic Studies, 1969); "The Pacific Basin: Forces of Unity and Division," *Proceedings of the Pacific Basin Conference* (Washington, D.C.: Center for Strategic Studies, Georgetown University, 1976); U.S. Congress, Report to the Congress by the Comptroller General of the United States, 26 January 1979 (LCD-78-426A), *Observations on Fleet Support Provided by the Navy's Shore Installations in the Western Pacific and Indian Ocean*; J. H. Webb, Jr., *Micronesia and U.S. Pacific Strategy: A Blueprint for the 1980s* (New York: Frederick A. Praeger, 1974).
Geoffrey F. Matthews

OCEANIC NITRATES CORPORATION. Incorporated in Delaware on 1 June 1935 by Samuel D. Robins, F. L. Crocker, and E. E. Carlys, all of New York, the Oceanic Nitrates Corporation allegedly was to deal in nitrates and fertilizers. The company was really a front for Pan American Airways which desired to keep the equatorial islands of Howland, Baker, and Jarvis out of the hands of competing airlines using land planes. Oceanic sent out an expedition in late July 1935 on the yacht *Kinkajou*. The expedition was under the nominal leadership of Francis Dana Coman of Johns Hopkins University but the real leader was Harold Gatty, Pan American's agent, who paid the expedition's expenses, contacted the necessary government officials, and selected the personnel for the trip. The expedition landed several men on each of the islands to establish a claim and went on to examine the flying-boat potential at other islands in the general area. Later, Pan American acted as the go-between in presenting Oceanic's application for a guano license to United States federal departments. Once the inadequacies of the three islands for aeronautical use had been proven, the company was allowed to drop from sight and its incorporation was declared inoperative on 1 January 1940.

RELATED ENTRIES: Canton Island Question; Equatorial Islands, U.S. Aeronautics in; Gatty, Harold; South Seas Commercial Company; Southwest Pacific Air Route, Creation of the.

SOURCES AND READINGS: Articles of Incorporation of Oceanic Nitrates Corporation, 1 June 1935, filed in the office of the Secretary of State, Dover, Delaware; Harold Charles Gatty correspondence, Library of Congress, Washington, D.C.; Francis X. Holbrook, "Commercial Aviation and Colonization of the Equatorial Islands, 1934-1936," *Aerospace Historian* 17, no. 4 (1970): 144-49; *New York Times*, 21 July 1935, p. 13, and 1 September 1935, p. 1.
Francis X. Holbrook

OCEAN (BANABA) ISLAND. Located in the west central Pacific at 0° 52' south latitude and 169° 35' east longitude, Ocean Island is part of the independent republic of Kiribati. It is low-lying, has a circumference of 10 km (6 mi) and a land area of 5 km² (2 mi²). Unlike most Pacific islands, it has rich mineral deposits. The population is about 2,200 persons.

Discovered in 1804 by the British ship *Ocean*, the island was annexed by Britain in 1900 and administered by the newly formed Gilbert and Ellice Islands Protectorate. The headquarters of the protectorate was moved from Tarawa to Ocean Island in 1907. The protectorate with Fanning and Washington Islands added (with the Tokelaus following in 1917 and the Phoenix group in 1937) became a colony in 1917.

Phosphate has been mined in significant amounts since 1900. The British Phosphate Commission, which also ran operations in Nauru, exports most of the phosphate to Australia, New Zealand, and Japan. Since the 1970s more than half a million tons have been extracted annually.

The island was occupied by the Japanese during World War II, and the Banabans were forcibly sent by the Japanese to islands in the Marshalls and Carolines. In part because of the heavy damage during the war, the Banabans were relocated in 1947 to the island of Rabi near Fiji, which was purchased with royalties from the mining operations.

RELATED ENTRIES: Kiribati; Nauru; New Caledonia; Phoenix Islands.
Frank P. King

OGASAWARA (BONIN) ISLANDS. Ninety-seven volcanic islands, the Ogasawaras, at 27° north latitude and 142° 10 ′ east longitude, lie about 966 km (600 mi) southeast of Japan with a total area of 106 km² (41 mi²) and a population of less than 1,000. Chichi-jima is the largest with 39 km² (15 mi²). The Kuroshio Current runs between the islands and Japan and the climate consequently is relatively mild. It sustains the growth of cacao, cattle, fruits, sugarcane, and trees. Whaling by factory ships is also common. The islands were visited in 1543 by the Spaniard, Ruy López de Villalobos, vaguely claimed by the United States and Britain in 1823 and 1825, unsuc-cessfully colonized by Hawaiian adventurers in 1830, annexed by Japan in 1876, and then named *Ogasawara-gunto*. Prior to World War II nearly 6,000 persons lived on the islands. After the war, the United States removed all of the survivors, and administered the islands. In 1968 control was re-turned to Japan. Currently the islands, which were designated a National Park in 1972, have a popula-tion (1978) of 1,562 persons, including 1,240 on Chichi-jima and 322 on Haha-jima.

RELATED ENTRY: Ryukyu Islands.   *Frank P. King*

OKINAWA. The best known of the Japanese Ryu-kyu Islands, Okinawa lies in the far western Pacific. In size, 1,434 km² (554 mi²), and population, 1,059,000 persons (1976 est.), it is the largest island in the chain. Naha is the capital. The climate is subtrop-ical with an average temperature of 22° C (72° F) and 211 cm (83 in) of rain per year. Tourism, agriculture, and crafts (ceramics, lacquerware, cloth) are impor-tant elements of the economy. Pottery has been made on the island since the seventeenth century. Okinawa and the other Ryukyus became a prefecture (district) of Japan in 1879. The island and its people suffered heavy damage in World War II after American troops landed in April 1945. It was heavily militarized by the United States after the People's Republic of China was formed in 1949 and after the outbreak of the Korean War in 1950. The United States retained administrative control until 1972 when, by an agree-ment with Japan, the United States was permitted to keep military bases on the island but no nuclear weap-ons without Japan's consent. Okinawa has an elected governor, an assembly of forty-four members and its citizens elect seven representatives to the na-tional parliament (*Diet*) in Tokyo.

RELATED ENTRIES: Defense Planning for Oceania be-tween the Wars; Oceania, Strategic Importance of; Ryukyu Islands; War in the Pacific Islands.

Frank P. King

OMAI (ca. 1753-1784). A Polynesian from Ra'iatea (Society Islands), Omai joined Captain James Cook's crew as interpreter and guide. He returned to England with them in July 1774, one of the first Polynesians to visit Europe. He was courted by Lon-don's high society, including King George III, painted by the artists of the day, especially Sir Joshua Reynolds, visited museums, attended ballets, and generally was well entertained by a people who had never seen such a "noble savage" before. As Cook prepared a third-voyage itinerary, the British Admi-ralty charged him with returning the homesick Omai to his native land. Cook sailed from England and landed on Huahine (Society Islands) in 1777 where Omai disembarked with all his European goods. A European-type house, various forms of livestock, and firearms were left with him. As Cook surmised, Omai quickly returned to his former ways. His animals died, his house was abandoned, and not long after he died, having been the first Tahitian to have seen England. Some of his souvenirs and artifacts from England were still around when the first Chris-tian missionaries arrived there in 1797.

RELATED ENTRIES: Cook, (Captain) James; French Polynesia.

SOURCES AND READINGS: Eric H. McCormick, *Omai, Pacific Envoy* (Auckland: Auckland University Press, 1977). *See also* his article "Captain Cook and Omai," *Pacific Studies* 1, no. 2 (1978): 97-118.

Robert D. Craig

ORGANISASI PAPUA MERDEKA. A guerrilla movement active on the border separating Papua New Guinea from Irian Jaya, the *Organisasi Papua Merdeka* (OPM) has condemned the Indonesian gov-ernment for acts of political repression and ethno-genocide against the indigenous people of Irian Jaya.

The formation of the OPM has its origins in the Dutch-Indonesian conflict over West New Guinea. After World War II, following the defeat of the Japanese, Indonesian nationalists proclaimed inde-pendence on 17 August 1945 and claimed the western half of the New Guinea island as part of the new state since it was part of the Netherlands East Indies. The Dutch government wanted to retain West New Guin-ea, arguing that the culturally different people should be given self-determination. This Dutch attempt led to a prolonged period of confrontation with the Indonesians. The dispute was finally settled in 1962 in what became known as the "New York Agree-ment" which permitted immediate Indonesian administrative control of West Irian but required that the will of people concerning their political fu-ture be ascertained not later than 1969. The "Act of Free Choice," as the referendum was labeled, was so devised in 1969 that the outcome was foreclosed before the ballots were cast. The OPM has called the exercise the "Act of No Choice" and has continued to challenge the legitimacy of Indonesia's authority over what became known as Irian Jaya, Indonesia's seventeenth province.

Since it was formed in 1963, the OPM has witnessed the consolidation of Indonesian control over Irian Jaya. Over 250,000 non-Irianese from various parts of Indonesia have migrated to Irian Jaya converting the capital, Jayapura, from a Melanesian town to a predominantly Asian city. The OPM has built its appeal among Irians around four complaints: (1) loss of land; (2) cultural imperialism; (3) forced incorporation of Irian Jaya as a part of Indonesia; and (4) political repression. The OPM is composed entirely of indigenous Irian Jayanese citizens, many of whom are among the most educated.

Papua New Guinea's independence in 1975 has encouraged the OPM to believe that it too can achieve independence. Indeed, the OPM viewed Papua New Guinea as its most important ally in this purpose and proceeded to establish bases on Papua New Guinea territory from which to launch military attacks against the Indonesians. Consequently, a substantial amount of OPM activity is concentrated around the border shared with Papua New Guinea. The border, lacking clear demarcation lines and poorly guarded, is a seamless web through which a flow of men, medicines, and small weapons move to support the guerrillas. About 10,000 Irianese refugees, most sympathetic to the OPM, reside in various parts of Papua New Guinea, mainly in Port Moresby. Most refugees have come across the border as a consequence of Indonesian search-and-destroy missions against Irianese villages suspected of harboring OPM guerrillas. Papua New Guinea's policy towards the Irianese is to accept them if they are bona fide refugees but permissive residence is given only after they agree not to become involved in politics affecting Indonesia. Despite this pledge, most refugees covertly provide moral and material support to the OPM.

The OPM has two segments. One group, based outside Irian Jaya, is almost entirely engaged in political propaganda activities. A public relations office is allowed to operate openly in Dakar, Senegal. The other group, based in Irian Jaya and areas contiguous to the Papua New Guinea border, is both political and military in focus. The military arm is called the *Tentara Nasional Papua* (TNP). Estimates of the OPM's active guerrilla force ranges from 2,000 to 20,000. The ideological orientation of the OPM is pro-Western; it has indicated its preference for a Christian-Democratic government. However, since

no Western state has offered assistance, the OPM has threatened to turn to communist sources.

Overall, the OPM has grown much larger than it was in the 1960s. It has become increasingly bold in its politico-military offensives but has been hampered by internal schisms. Under Indonesian pressure, the Papua New Guinea government has agreed to clean up its side of the border. The OPM leader and his deputy were arrested and jailed by the Papua New Guinea government for illegal entry in September 1978. All this attests to a new phase in the border conflict. The Indonesians do not take the OPM for granted any more. President Suharto of Indonesia requested that the prime minister of Papua New Guinea demonstrate his commitment to Indonesia's territorial integrity by taking action against the OPM. The prime minister obliged him during June and July 1978 when the Papua New Guinea Defence Force launched a large anti-OPM operation on the Papua New Guinea side of the border.

RELATED ENTRIES: Papua Besena; Papua New Guinea.

SOURCES AND READINGS: Peter Hastings, "The Papua New Guinea-Irian Jaya Border Problem," *Australian Outlook*, August 1977, pp. 52-59; Ralph R. Premdas and Kwasi Nyameky, "Papua New Guinea-Indonesian Relations Over Irian Jaya," *Asian Survey* 19 (1979): 927-45.   *Ralph R. Premdas*

ORSMOND, JOHN (1788-1856). A London Missionary Society (LMS) member, Orsmond lived in the Society Islands (French Polynesia) from 1817 until his death. In 1824 he became director of the South Seas Academy, a school established on Mo'orea for the children of the missionaries and of the Tahitians. In 1831 he headed the Protestant church at Mataoae (Taiarapu, island of Tahiti). During the French-English struggle over control of the island (1836-1842), it appeared that he favored French control, and as a result he was afterwards named head of the French Protestant Mission Church in Pape'ete, the capital. Tahitian language, customs, and history fascinated him from the beginning of his ministry, and during the years from 1824 to 1834 he recorded volumes of legends, stories, and genealogies from the old priests and scholars. In 1848, he passed his monumental manuscript on to the French Commander, Lavaud, but apparently it became lost in Paris. Fortunately, his granddaughter Teuira Henry, who inherited his notes, reedited them and saw them published for the first time in 1928. The *Tahitian Dictionary*, published by the LMS in 1851, is almost totally his work. Later in life, Orsmond bought land in New Zealand where he planned to retire. On his journey there in 1856 he died on 23 April and was buried at sea.

RELATED ENTRIES: French Polynesia; Henry, Teuira; London Missionary Society.

SOURCES AND READINGS: Teuira Henry, *Ancient Tahiti* (Honolulu: Bernice P. Bishop Museum, 1928; reprint ed., New York: Kraus Reprint Co., 1971); James Sibree, ed., *Register of the Missionaries of the London Missionary Society* (London: London Missionary Society, 1923).

Robert D. Craig

PACIFIC STUDIES, INSTITUTE FOR. The University of the South Pacific in Fiji established the Institute for Pacific Studies in 1976 to carry out research and publication in five major subject areas within the social sciences: land tenure and rural development, government and politics, history and biography, social and cultural studies, language and communication. Its primary focus is on the eleven English-speaking countries of the central south Pacific which are served by the university, but the various projects concerned with the Pacific region cover a wider area (Papua New Guinea, New Caledonia, French Polynesia, and the U.S. Trust Territory among others). The institute sees its primary task as the development of skills and confidence and the production of useful research data and publications, primarily by citizens of the region served. This is achieved by facilitating their undertaking research, writing, consultancy, and teaching, with the Institute for Pacific Studies' participation as appropriate. Their success can be measured by the number of important publications that have appeared to date. Over three hundred Pacific islanders have written and published, or are in the course of doing so, in association with the institute. Much of the institute's work is carried out in cooperation with extension centers, schools and other institutes, or with member governments, regional organizations, and individuals.

RELATED ENTRIES: Fiji; University of the South Pacific.

SOURCES AND READINGS: University of the South Pacific, *Report of the Institute of Pacific Studies*, Suva, Fiji, March 1979.   *Robert D. Craig*

PADDON, JAMES (1812-1861). An Irishman, James Paddon was a trader, entrepreneur, and colonist who developed commerce in southwest Oceania, particularly New Caledonia. His early life was spent in the Royal Navy. By 1839 he was involved in China's opium and sandalwood trade. He arrived at the Loyalty Islands in 1843 where he lost seventeen crewmen in a skirmish with the islanders. Paddon established a lucrative commercial station in the New Hebrides. He built a shipyard, traded sandalwood, copra, and mother-of-pearl and was instrumental in providing land for the first Roman Catholic mission there. In 1847 he opened a station on the Isle of Pines and another on New Caledonia. A few years earlier he had acquired Ile Nou (near Noumea) where, in 1853, he moved his enterprises and built a large trading center. He greatly aided the French administration in developing New Caledonia by encouraging colonization and agriculture (he introduced the first cattle to the area). In 1857 he traded Ile Nou for a tract of land on New Caledonia which he tried to colonize. Paddon had a reputation for honesty and generosity. One of New Caledonia's foremost pioneers, he died on Ile Nou on 13 February 1861.

RELATED ENTRIES: New Caledonia; Vanuatu (New Hebrides).

SOURCES AND READINGS: Patrick O'Reilly, *Calédoniens* (Paris: Musée de l'Homme, 1953).
                Russell T. Clement

PAGO PAGO HARBOR. *See* American Samoa.

PAPEHIA (PAPEIHA) (ca. 1791-1867). Papehia was a member of the London Missionary Society (LMS) from the Society Islands (French Polynesia) who introduced Christianity to the Cook Islands. Born probably on Bora Bora, Papehia sailed to Ra'iatea where the LMS missionary the Reverend John Williams was preaching the Christian faith. In 1821 Williams sailed to Sydney. On the way, he brought Papehia and another Ra'iatean, Vahapata, to Aitutaki Island where they labored for two years. When Williams returned in 1823, Papehia moved to Rarotonga, Cook Islands, where he remained until his death. Papehia's success was phenomenal compared to the hard go the English missionaries had in Tahiti. His ethnic background and his understanding of the language and the people no doubt had much to do with his success. His procedure of conversion was to argue with the priests regarding the potency of their old gods and to show them that with the burning of their idols no great calamity would befall them. He also convinced several weaker chiefs that his Jehovah would bring prosperity and peace among them. Most of them were converted; and as conversion came, Papehia encouraged the new converts to settle in the village of Avarua for instruction and mutual protection. Sometime between 1825 and 1826 Papehia marred Te Vaerua, a daughter of chief Tinomana, and assumed a chiefly title which no doubt strengthened his missionary effort among the people. By 1827 most of the idols had been burned and "heathen" practices suppressed. Churches were built, the language reduced to writing, and laws established to enforce the new religious beliefs. In 1828 Papehia moved to Arorangi station on the west side of the island where he spent the remainder of his life among his wife's relatives. He and his wife had eight children, seven of whom left descendants in the islands. He died in May 1867, and his son Isaia, educated and trained in England, took his place as minister of the Arorangi church.

RELATED ENTRIES: Cook Islands; French Polynesia; Williams, John.

SOURCES AND READINGS: Richard Gilson, *The Cook Islands, 1820-1950* (Wellington: Victoria University Press, 1980); Taira Rere, *Genealogy of the Papehia Family* (Suva: Institute of Pacific Studies, 1974).

Robert D. Craig

PAPUA BESENA. Led by Josephine Abaijah, the Papua Besena movement seeks self-determination for Papua which was integrated with New Guinea to form the independent state of Papua New Guinea in 1975. Papua was an Australian colony acquired in 1906, while New Guinea was a United Nations trust territory acquired originally by Australia from the Germans in 1914 during World War I. Until World War II the two entities were administered separately by Australia; the war, however, forced the Australians to unite them under a single military government called ANGAU (Australian New Guinea Administrative Unit). In the immediate postwar period, the joint administrative arrangement was continued until 1949 when it was legally formalized by an act of the Australian parliament. Expressions of fear that the Papuan identity would be lost in this joint administration were met by repeated official assurances during the 1950s and 1960s that the Papuan people would be consulted about their political destiny. To symbolize this commitment, the new country was called the Territory of Papua and New Guinea.

After the 1972 general elections, however, it became evident that Australia had decided to grant internal self-government to the country united as a single entity without consultation with the Papuans. Josephine Abaijah, the Papuan member of the House of Assembly, spearheaded an organized effort to forestall this eventuality. On 3 June 1973 the Papua Besena movement was formally launched. On 16 March 1975 Abaijah unilaterally declared Papua's independence from Australia. A provisional government was named and even though independence within a united Papua New Guinea occurred on 16 September 1975, the Papuan separatists still seek to break away. Abaijah asserts that she plans to pursue her objectives by peaceful means.

The supporters of Papua Besena say that it is an anticolonial nationalist movement. The phrase *Papua Besena* in the Motu language means "Papuan Nation" or "Papuan Tribe." Abaijah argues that because old promises were not honored, Papua was arbitrarily united with New Guinea which continues the condition of oppression via internal colonialism. To her, colonial control by New Guinea, which has a population almost three times that of Papua's 750,000 people, is worse than Australian colonialism.

Papua Besena asserts its claim for Papuan self-determination not only on the basis that Papua was historically a separate colony from New Guinea, but on a claim that its people are different. The separatists argue that Papuans speak a unique language and possess different cultural values from New Guineans. Like the rest of Papua New Guinea, Papua consists of small, economically self-sufficient communities, most speaking mutually unintelligible languages. The biggest anomaly in the separatists' claims can be seen with reference to the Southern Highlands, a Papuan province containing 200,000 people, that is, almost one third of Papua's total population; but in many respects, this province is geographically and culturally more a part of New Guinea than Papua.

Papua Besena's popularity is most intense in the Capital District Province and the adjoining Central Province where its candidates in both national and local elections have scored impressive victories. In this area, which includes the capital city of Port Moresby, large agglomerations of migrants have settled. Although New Guineans number only about 25 percent of the migrant population, and New Guinean Highlanders account for only 8 or 9 percent, the latter in particular are blamed for local law and order problems. Papuans, particularly the Motuan groups in the city, regard Highlanders as barbaric. Competition from New Guineans for economic benefits in Port Moresby is also a significant source of Papuan animosity. Periodically, as in 1968 and 1973, rugby games between Papuan and New Guinean teams spilled over into citywide riots.

Another base on which Papua Besena asserts its case for self-determination in the economic neglect of Papua during the colonial period. On the whole, economic development has been skewed in favor of New Guinea. The separatists visualize that even with an independent, combined Papua and New Guinea, because of the New Guinea majority in Parliament and the logic of development programs to allocate projects in areas that are already developed, the economic disparities will continue, with Papua becoming even poorer in the years ahead.

Papua Besena has increased its base of popular support to other Papua provinces particularly since independence. It presently has nine members in the national parliament. A new leadership has, however, emerged to challenge the demand by Abaijah for complete independence. Many prominent Papuans, even among Papua Besena's contingent in Parliament, support the establishment of a separate government for Papua but within the context of a larger Papua New Guinean nationhood. The central government is determined to prevent the fragmentation of its territory. It has made concessions to compensate for the earlier neglect of Papua to keep the country united. It is a matter of speculation whether economic incentives will appease or encourage Papuan ethnonationalism to seek the more limited end of maximum internal autonomy or complete self-determination as a separate state.

RELATED ENTRIES: Morris, Basil M.; Organisasi Papua Merdeka; Papua New Guinea; Papua New Guinea, Government and Political System.

SOURCES AND READINGS: Josephine Abaijah, "Papua's Colonial Experience with Australia and New Guinea" (Paper delivered at the New Guinea Research Unit, Waigani, Papua New Guinea, 2 April 1975); Ralph R. Premdas, "Secession and Political Change: The Case of Papua Besena," *Oceania* 4 (1977): 266-83.   *Ralph R. Premdas*

PAPUA NEW GUINEA. Covering 461,693 km² (178,260 mi²), Papua New Guinea lies between the equator and 12° south latitude and between 141° and 160° east longitude. The island of New Guinea, divided between Indonesia in the west and Papua New Guinea in the east, provides most of the landmass, but significant areas are contained on the numerous islands scattered through the Bismarck Archipelago in the north, Bougainville (part of the Solomon group) in the east, and the Louisiade Archi-

pelago in the southeast. New Britain, with nearly 40,000 km² (15,444 mi²) is the biggest of the outer islands.

Geologically young, New Guinea has many mountains over 4,000 m (13,100 ft) and even on the smaller islands numerous peaks rise over 2,000 m (6,500 ft). By contrast, the flood plains of the Fly, Sepik, and Markham rivers are extensive swampy grasslands. The grassed highland valleys probably result from slash-and-burn agriculturalists clearing the primary forest.

Uniformly hot on the coast, the climate is modified by altitude and the quantity and season of rainfall. Small areas at over 4,000 m (13,100 ft) have the tussock grasses, ferns, and mosses of alpine and tundra zones. Wide areas of the highlands' subsistence and cash crops are vulnerable to frost. While most of the country receives over 2,500 mm (98 in) of rain in a year, Port Moresby suffers a pronounced dry season from May to November reducing the annual total to 1,000 mm (39 in). At the other extreme, Gasmata on west New Britain is deluged with over 6,000 mm (236 in) with both the southwest trades and the northwest monsoon bringing heavy falls. Although floods and mud slips are frequent hazards for village gardeners, hot suns and the failure of rain-bearing winds cause periodic local famines even where the normal rainfall exceeds 2,000 mm (78 in).

Prehistory. More than forty thousand years ago, man probably crossed the narrow seas dividing southeast Asia from a vast continent including the present areas of Australia, New Guinea, and Tasmania. With limited archaeological research completed, it is not yet possible to say when and where people first inhabited New Guinea, but there is evidence that they were living at Kosipe, a mountain site northwest of Port Moresby, twenty-seven thousand years ago and had obviously occupied coastal sites well before that. Exciting recent research indicates that ten thousand years ago people in the central highlands were transitory cultivators and pig keepers. This places the growing of crops and the domestication of animals at an earlier date than established for some centers previously accepted as points of origin for cultivation and sedentary village life.

The drowning of Torres Strait about eight thousand years ago, and the arrival of migrants speaking Austronesian languages and bringing the skills of pottery and ocean voyaging increased the divergence between the prehistories of Australia and New Guinea. By the early nineteenth century 1.5 million Melanesians inhabited east New Guinea and the neighboring islands. Distinguishable as a group from the Australian aborigines to the south, Polynesians to the east, and the Malays to the west, they were still culturally and physically diverse. House styles varied from small, leaf shelters, to tree houses, and the giant *erave* of the Papuan Gulf and the *haus tambaran* of the Sepik with their upward-sweeping front gables. Some people used the bow and arrow, others were spearmen, rock slingers, or axemen. On the Trobriand Islands leadership was inherited. In other areas leadership was partly inherited and partly achieved, and in some highland communities men were almost entirely dependent on their own abilities to make themselves "big men." Fragmentation is most apparent in the 700 languages, many with less than 5,000 speakers and the largest, Enga, having only 130,000. Some of the coastal and island languages can be grouped together as Austronesian and many mainland languages belong to the trans-New Guinea phylum, perhaps representing two major migrations; but several smaller, isolated groups and single languages have not been shown to have any generic relationship to other languages. Complex trade and ceremonial cycles, such as the *kula* in the southeastern islands and the *hiri* along the south coast, connected disparate communities, but most people felt no bond to those outside their descent group and village. At best a coalition of villages, or sections of villages, might unite for festival or war.

Foreign Contact. Coastal peoples, living alongside safe anchorages and accustomed to trading with peoples of different cultures, quickly became accustomed to ship-to-canoe transactions. From the 1790s when ships from the eastern Australian colonies began passing through the islands on their way to Asia to the 1830s when whalers started working nearby grounds, foreign boats were frequent in the area. Villagers at points in the eastern islands often encountered sailors looking for water, food, men to work, and women for pleasure. After foreigners were killed in sudden attacks, perhaps as reprisals for the actions of previous visitors, and many sailors had died of malaria, the islands acquired a reputation for fever and the islanders for savagery. That reputation was strengthened when the first Catholic missionaries to settle on Woodlark and Umboi islands in the 1840s and 1850s were forced to abandon their stations. Dense vegetation and broken terrain further deterred foreigners, leaving Papua New Guineans as latecomers to colonial rule and the cash economy.

Annexation. From the 1870s Polynesian and European Christian missionaries established coastal stations; labor recruiters from Fiji and Queensland engaged men from Bougainville and briefly exploited the unknowing islanders farther north and west; pearlers and *bêche-de-mer* fishermen worked the shallow waters; copra traders established regular contacts; scientists and adventurers mounted expeditions that had trouble passing beyond the coast; and gold prospectors made an abortive rush inland from Port Moresby. The Australian colonists, fearful that another power would occupy the area, urged a reluctant Britain to annex the islands. Just as she agreed in 1884, Germany raised her flag to claim a share. After some shuffling of outposts of empire the European powers decided on a threefold division: the Dutch with a long-standing claim retained all of west New Guinea to the 141st meridian; Germany took the northeast mainland, the Bismarck Archipelago and Bougainville; and Britain declared a protectorate over the southeast mainland and the Louisiade Archipelago.

German New Guinea. Entrusted with government, the New Guinea Company aimed to build a prosperous plantation colony on the mainland. Inexperienced officials, reluctant laborers, malaria, and isolated, ill-chosen sites destroyed optimism and capital. By 1899 when the company handed administrative responsibility back to the imperial government little had been achieved. But in the Bismarck Archipelago other foreigners operating independently had succeeded. From 1875 and 1882, Australian Methodists and French Catholics respectively had established missions in the islands. Adventurers made the shift from recruiting and trading in shell and copra to planting. Most notable was the American-Samoan, Emma Coe-Forsayth (Queen Emma), who established her plantation "empire" on the Gazelle Peninsula. By 1914 pockets of plantations had been established on Bougainville, through the Bismarck Archipelago to Manus, and on to the mainland. They employed 17,500 New Guinean laborers, not all of whom survived the harsh experience. The more active imperial administration established coastal stations to impose peace, gather head tax, force villagers into road work, and make plantation recruiting easier. Punitive expeditions employing New Guinea police attacked communities offering resistance. Each year incidents occurred in which fifty or so villagers were shot in a series of small wars progressively subjecting New Guineans to central government authority. Albert Hahl, governor from 1902 to 1914, tempered severity by his interest in indigenous cultures, by recognition of basic rights to land, and by closing some areas crudely exploited by recruiters. Hahl gave a small measure of authority to government-appointed village leaders, the *luluais.*

German rule ended in 1914. The Australian government sent a naval and military expeditionary force north to occupy the area soon after the outbreak of war in Europe. The coastal plantations, the problems of land and labor, and an interior little known except along the rivers were now Australian. The foreigners who knew most about the inland were probably the Lutheran missionaries who had begun work at Finschhafen in 1886.

British New Guinea. Having declared a protectorate to placate the Australian colonies in 1884, Britain had no plans and no desire for active involvement in the internal affairs of New Guinea. With their own underdeveloped frontiers, the Australians had few resources for overseas expansion: British New Guinea was left to those few officials, missionaries, traders, planters, and prospectors prepared to venture north of Torres Strait. To increase the legal power of the administration to direct internal affairs, the protectorate was changed to a possession in 1888. Divided authority between the British government and the eastern Australian colonies continued, but Sir William MacGregor, a tough, experienced administrator, made the cumbrous system work. He passed basic land and labor legislation, appointed resident magistrates to administer divisions, and began a program of exploratory patrols.

After MacGregor left, the colony entered a period of administrative stagnation as officials waited for the newly formed federal government of Australia to assume control. Finally brought into effect in 1906, the Papua Bill transformed British New Guinea into the Australian Territory of Papua. Confident that the territory could be "another Java," the Australian government encouraged Australian settlers to take up land. When returns on copra, rubber, and hemp failed to meet expectations, settlers began abandoning leases. The number of white settlers scarcely increased in the 1920s and 1930s, and few of the plantation companies paid dividends. In the early years of British New Guinea and Papua, gold was the most important export and the main reason why foreigners went inland beyond the beaches.

Encouraged by MacGregor, Methodist and Anglican missionaries joined the London Missionary Society and the Sacred Heart communities that were already operating in the area. As in German New Guinea, the missionaries were the first Europeans to enter some villages, and they were responsible for much of the health care and formal education. Operating in "spheres of influence" the missions rarely competed directly for converts.

Under the guidance of Sir Hubert Murray (lieutenant governor 1908-1940) the administration acquired a reputation for a generous "native policy." It did protect Papuan land rights, prevented gross abuse of laborers, and endeavored to extend government control peacefully. But, limited by funds, it did little that was positive to advance Papuans in the government or the economy. By 1940 the most highly educated Papuans, except for one ordained priest, had passed grade six in the mission primary schools, and the highest positions open to them were as sergeants of police, captains of small boats, labor overseers (boss boys), mission teachers, and medical assistants. Although some of the government-appointed village constables wielded local power, they did it more through their own authority than as agents of the central government. The few elected village councils had limited funds and power.

Australian Mandated New Guinea. With few men experienced in colonial administration and restricted by ambiguous international law, the Australian garrison in German New Guinea pursued a policy of maintaining a going concern. German laws, and the punitive patrols, were generally retained and German planters were encouraged to increase production; the exports now went via Australia rather than to Hamburg. The indentured laborers needed to service the plantations and other industries increased to 28,000 by 1921. At the end of the war, Australia was granted administrative control of a richer prize than she had occupied in 1914. Apart from agreeing to outlaw slavery and trade in drugs and arms, guarantee freedom of religion, and render an annual report, Australia was unimpeded by the Class "C" League-of-Nations mandate awarded her in 1920.

Civil administration of the Australian Mandated Territory of New Guinea began formally in 1921. While anti-German feeling was still high, Australia expropriated the assets of German companies and planters. The Australian ex-servicemen who took up the plantations with high hopes suffered the depression of the 1930s, and the few survivors were heavily in debt to trading companies. Other sections of the cash economy and government revenue were protected only by the investment and production on the Morobe goldfields.

Preceded by New Guinean and European Lutheran missionaries, gold prospectors entered the eastern edge of the central highlands. In 1930 Michael Leahy and Michael Dwyer, two prospectors, crossed New Guinea from the eastern highlands to the Papuan Gulf, and in 1933 James Taylor, a government officer, and Michael and Daniel Leahy went west across the highlands to Mount Hagen. At the same time, government officers from Papua were exploring the southern highlands. The valley homelands of nearly one million people were now known to the outside world, but only a few of the inhabitants had accepted central government control or the teachings of missionaries before World War II.

World War II. The sudden southward movement of the Japanese in 1941-1942 changed the scale of foreign intervention. Where 1,500 white residents had lived in Papua and 4,500 whites and 2,000 Asians had lived in New Guinea in 1939, by the end of the war 300,000 Japanese, 1,000,000 Americans, nearly 500,000 Australians, and smaller numbers of Chinese, Indonesians, Indians, Malays, Fijians, and New Zealanders had passed through the two territories. Nearly all the towns were destroyed, and massive army camps, aerodromes, hospitals, roads, assembly plants, and store sites had been built. By mid-1942 the Japanese, having occupied the New Guinea islands and the north coast of the mainland, had reached the zenith of their power. Defeated at the Battle of the Coral Sea, at Milne Bay, on the Kokoda Trail, and in the Solomons, Japanese troops began three years of desperate retreat. The Allies advanced along the north coast through a series of battles at Buna, Wau, Salamaua, Lae, Finschhafen, in the Markham and Ramu valleys, and the Sepik. In the islands, they landed on Bougainville, New Britain, and Manus. At the end of the war, New Ireland, small parts of the Sepik, north New Britain, and the extremities of Bougainville remained in Japanese control.

The wartime experiences of Papua New Guineans varied greatly. Perhaps one third of the population living in the highlands knew almost nothing of the war beyond rumors and hearing of crashed aircraft. On the south Papuan coast, all able-bodied men were conscripted into the labor force or served voluntarily in the army, but the people at home saw no violence and few soldiers. At Milne Bay, villagers were caught in savage, brief fighting and then had to learn to live alongside massive military establishments; in parts of the Sepik they endured protracted and confused guerrilla warfare; and on New Ireland they suffered four years of Japanese rule and Allied bombing. More men went into the cash economy than ever before. They were given chances to acquire skills as drivers, mechanics, and construction workers; and they were likely to see the old "master-boy" relationships broken. Australians emerged from the war with a new awareness of their responsibilities in New Guinea and a sense of debt to the "Fuzzy Wuzzies" who had fought and worked alongside the Allies.

The Postwar Era. Combined under the Australian New Guinea Administrative Unit (ANGAU) during the war, the two territories continued under one civil

government with its headquarters in Port Moresby. Separate statistics were kept for the old mandated territory, which now became a trust territory of the United Nations. Australian government grants, never over $100,000 a year before the war, rose to $9 million in 1950, $30 million in 1960, to over $100 million in 1970. Significant advances in taking health care to the villagers were not matched in education. Aiming to provide universal primary education, the greatly expanded mission and government school systems still provided places for only half the children of primary-school age in 1970. The foundation of the University of Papua New Guinea in 1966 had been a significant step in the development of higher education. Attempts to encourage Papua New Guineans to enter the cash economy at above the level of unskilled laborers also had limited success in spite of the spread of cooperative societies and the willingness of villagers to plant coffee and cocoa. Twenty-five years after the war, banks, insurance companies, large retail stores, plantations, major transport companies, and importing and exporting activities were still controlled by foreigners.

The legislative council formed in 1951 had three nominated Papua New Guinean members, but it was not until the House of Assembly was established in 1964 that elected Papua New Guineans held a majority in the legislature. Even then business in the House was dominated by Australians. When Michael Somare, leader of the *Pangu Pati*, was able to form a coalition pressing for self-government after the 1972 elections, few of his supporters had had any experience in executive government. Australia, eager to forgo final responsibility, handed internal administration to the Somare government in 1973 and granted full independence on 16 September 1975. Reelected in 1977, the Somare government survived shifts in the coalition to provide stable administration and modest reform.

Independent Papua New Guinea. Under the constitution adopted in 1975, power rests with the single-house National Parliament of 109 members representing provincial and smaller local or "open" electorates. The nominal head of state is the queen of England, whose ceremonial role is taken by the governor-general who is appointed on the advice of the parliament. Ministers drawn from the National Parliament exercise power as the National Executive Council under the chairmanship of the prime minister. In a major change from the Australian administration, the national government has devolved power to elected provincial assemblies.

Three years after independence, Papua New Guinea had increased its economic self-reliance but still received nearly one-third of all government revenue from Australia. The giant copper mine at Panguna, where Conzinc Riotinto began production in 1972, has contributed to national growth at the same time as it has provided a stronger economic base for those Bougainvilleans who wish to express their physical and cultural differences from other Papua New Guineans by loosening political ties to the central government. No other area exerts as much centrifugal force as Bougainville. Papuan separatism, unable to attract support in all Papuan provinces, sustains a political movement without hope of achieving an independent Papua. Although still lacking a coherent political voice, the populous, landlocked highlands could become a political power center. Moving quickly from traditional village life through an Australian-imposed peace, to cash coffee-farming and independence, many highland communities are rent by violent clan fighting. The Papua New Guinea government inherited from the Australian administration a lawlessness that has worsened with increased cash, mobility, and alcohol.

With little experience in international affairs at independence, the Somare government began defining Papua New Guinea as a South Pacific nation while valuing its membership in the Commonwealth and the United Nations and seeing itself as a link between the Pacific and Southeast Asia. Unlike most ex-colonies, Papua New Guinea is a neighbor of the former metropolitan power and must continue to negotiate with Australia over defense, migration, quarantine, territorial seas, and transport; but its most delicate negotiations have been about aid and relocating the Torres Strait border. Other important bilateral relations are maintained with Japan, a buyer of natural resources and seller of manufactured goods, and with contiguous Indonesia. Difficulties of administering the long Papua New Guinea-Indonesian border are increased by west New Guineans who resist Indonesian rule and win sympathy from Papua New Guineans. With a lightly equipped defense force of about three thousand, Papua New Guinea must look to negotiation and goodwill to secure her borders.

RELATED ENTRIES: Anglican Missions; Australian Projects for Annexation in the Pacific Islands; Barton, Francis; Bismarck Archipelago; British New Guinea; Bromilow, William E.; Cargo Cults; D'Albertis, Luigi M.; Defense Planning for Oceania; German Colonial Empire; German South Seas Expedition; Grimshaw, Beatrice; Guise, John; Hamilton, William; *Hopeful* Scandal; Labor Trade; London Missionary Society; MacFarlane, Samuel; MacGregor, William; Mead, Margaret; Melanesians and Colonial Servitude; Melanesian Recruitment to Queensland, Patterns of; Monckton, Charles; Morris, Basil M.; Murray, John; Newton, Henry; Organisasi Papua Merdeka; Papua Besena; Papua New Guinea, Gold Mining in; Papua New Guinea, Mental Health Services in; Papua New Guinea, Mixed-race People in; Port Moresby; Rays, (Marquis) Charles de; Roheim, Geza; Scratchley, Peter; Selwyn, George; Sepik River; Solomon Islands; Somare, Michael; South Pacific Commission; South Pacific Forum; Squatter Settlements; Thomson, (Sir) Basil; War in the Pacific Islands, 1914-1945; Western Pacific High Commission.

SOURCES AND READINGS: Paul Hasluck, *A Time for Building: Australian Administration in Papua and New Guinea 1951-1963* (Melbourne: Melbourne University Press, 1976); B. Jinks, P. Biskup, and H. Nelson, eds., *Readings in New Guinea History* (Sydney: Angus & Robertson, 1973); P. A. Ryan, ed., *Encyclopaedia of Papua and New Guinea*, 3 vols. (Melbourne: Melbourne University Press, 1972); Michael Somare, *Sana: An Autobiography of Michael Somare* (Port Moresby: Niugini Press, 1975); Gavin Souter, *New Guinea: The Last Unknown* (Sydney: Angus & Robertson, 1963); J. L. Whitaker et al., eds., *Documents and Readings in New Guinea: History Prehistory to 1889* (Brisbane: Jacaranda, 1975).
Hank Nelson

PAPUA NEW GUINEA, DECENTRALIZATION AND PROVINCIAL GOVERNMENT. With the formation of political parties, the rise of a nationalist leadership, and the advance towards independence, a major political debate was launched on the appropriateness to Papua New Guinea of the structure of government developed during the colonial period. Australia had ruled through a highly centralized bureaucracy located in the capital city, Port Moresby. In the 1970s, momentum began to be generated in favor of decentralization, that is, the transfer of political and administrative powers of decision-making from the central government to provincial governments. This movement in favor of decentralization reflected an indigenous Papua New Guinean response to the problems of governing an ethnically, linguistically, and regionally diverse country. With decentralization, Papua New Guinea has embarked on an interesting experiment in structural change within the confines of a unitary system of government.

Early attempts by Australia to bring government closer to the people were first initiated in 1951 through the creation of local government councils. By 1969 there were 156 councils covering approximately 90 percent of the population. However, as in other colonial settings, the introduction of local councils from above served in practice only to reinforce administrative control rather than to expand popular participation and responsibility for decision-making. In the 1960s, the colonial authorities created district coordinating committees and district advisory committees ostensibly to solicit local participation in widening development efforts. The former were composed of officials of the specialized departments operating at the district level and were chaired by the district commissioner; the latter were appointed by officials and tended to reflect expatriate and plantation interests. In 1970 district political assemblies, or area authorities, as indirectly representative bodies, were provided for in the Local Government Authorities Ordinance. Implementation did not begin until 1972 with the coming to power of the Somare government. By the end of 1974 the only districts without area authorities were Bougainville, East New Britain, and Central, East, and West Sepik. However, the area authorities had a diverse record largely due to their advisory position, lack of financial power, and weak administrative support.

The real momentum for provincial government developed in 1972 with the grant of internal self-government to an indigenous leadership committed to local democracy. An eight point plan outlining the future goals of Papua New Guinea was articulated; it included the devolution of decision-making to local communities. A Constitutional Planning Committee (CPC) appointed by the House of Assembly was assigned the task of touring the country to ascertain the wishes of citizens in formulating a constitution for an independent Papua New Guinea. A key issue that preoccupied their efforts concerned central-regional-local government relations. In its several reports, the CPC revealed that an overwhelming majority of witnesses that came before it demanded that the machinery of government be brought closer to the people. Decentralization of both political and administrative power was seen as the appropriate response both to increase participation in collective community decision-making as well as to make services more accessible to the majority of citizens who lived in rural areas. The recommendations of the CPC, however, were so sweeping in devolving power to the provinces that they were perceived as a threat to the power of politicians and bureaucrats who had inherited the central government institutions from Australia. Defiant activities by the Bougainville secessionists, who originally sought substantial autonomy for their island, convinced the House of Assembly to reject the section on provincial government for inclusion in the country's constitution passed in August 1975.

Intense confrontation between the Bougainville secessionists and the Somare government was finally resolved peacefully by a concession that accorded Bougainville maximum autonomy in governing its own affairs within the larger context of a Papua New Guinea nationhood. The provisions conceded to Bougainville were incorporated in an organic law on provincial governments extended to all provinces passed by Parliament in February 1977.

Provincial government that includes substantial devolution of political and administrative powers to Papua New Guinea's subordinate regional units is a controversial experiment partly inspired by the view that such an arrangement can best keep this country with seven hundred different linguistic groups united. The record to date shows mixed performance with successes in enhancing local participation offset by local corruption and inefficiency. The experiment in decentralization has been called "a bloodless revolution" in democracy by the Minister for Decentralization, John Momis. Detractors claim that it is the first step in the fragmentation of the country. They argue further that Papua New Guinea cannot afford to pay the financial overhead to maintain such an establishment: twenty provincial premiers; twenty provincial houses of assembly each with about twenty to twenty-five members, that is, 600 to 700 paid politicians; twenty cabinets with each containing to eight ministers each with special privileges; and twenty provincial bureaucracies. Beyond the financial burden, however, Papua New Guinea's experiment with decentralization has yet to demonstrate the extent to which a newly independent country can both diffuse power and responsibility and maintain a strong and legitimate central government.

RELATED ENTRIES: Bougainville (North Solomons) Secessionism; Papua New Guinea; Papua New Guinea, Government and Political System; Solomon Islands; Somare, Michael T.

SOURCES AND READINGS: Ralph Premdas and Stephen Pokawin, eds., *Decentralization in the Pacific* (Waigani: University of Papua New Guinea Press, 1979); W. Tordoff and R. L. Watts, *Report on Central-Provincial Government Relations* (Port Moresby: Government Printery, 1974).   *Ralph R. Premdas*
Jeffrey S. Steeves

PAPUA NEW GUINEA, ECONOMY OF. At least two-thirds of the people of Papua New Guinea remain within the subsistence economy, living on taro, yams, sweet potatoes, and a few green vegetables from their village gardens, as well as sago and small amounts of pig, fish, chicken, and wildfowl. Yet as a growing number of villagers have learned to sell their produce in the towns so that they can purchase clothing, tools, cigarettes, beer, and canned foods, the market sector of the gross domestic product has risen by an average of 9.5 percent from 1972 to 1978. It continues, however, to be dominated by public services, large-scale mining, and the production of export crops. Since the opening of the mine at Panguna on Bougainville in 1972, Papua New Guinea has become the world's fourth largest producer of copper, and a second large mine is being developed at Ok Tedi in the western province. Coffee, which is mostly grown in the highlands on large plantations and in village gardens, has nonetheless replaced copper as the country's leading earner of foreign exchange. Other important exports are cocoa, coconut products, and palm oil, which are produced chiefly on New Britain, New Ireland, and Bougainville, and timber, tuna, and rubber, which are produced in many parts of the country.

The government is encouraging a variety of commercial and agricultural projects throughout the nation by means of technical assistance, credit expansion, and direct investment so as to extend economic development to poorer areas, reduce dependence on imports, and broaden its export capacity. This has helped to stimulate a modest increase in private investment, a key ingredient in the government's development plan. Other than the highway connecting Lae with the highlands, however, the country has few paved roads outside of the larger towns, and it has no railroads. Thus, while truck transport is increasing rapidly where there are roads, people and goods still move largely by foot, by canoe and small boat, and by air (Papua New Guinea has 150 public and eighty private airstrips as well as thirteen major airfields).

Because of its heavy reliance upon exports and imports, the country is highly vulnerable to international business cycles and inflation. Yet the *kina* has remained strong—stronger than the Australian dollar that it replaced and to which it is pegged—since it was adopted as the national currency in 1975. The government has been successful in combating inflation with a combination of wage restraints, price controls, export commodity stabilization funds, and controlled government spending. Public expenditures amount to one-third of the gross domestic product but are being held to annual increases of about 3 percent. At the same time, however, Papua New Guinea continues to rely heavily upon Australian aid. In 1978 the government obtained about 43 percent of its income from Australian aid, 7 percent from other foreign aid, and 50 percent from internal revenues.

The World Bank estimated Papua New Guinea's gross national product to be $490 per capita in 1977, indicating that although it is certainly not a wealthy country, neither is it among the most impoverished. With the continuation of Australian aid and governmental budget restraint, an active program to slow population growth, and further encouragement for private investment, the nation's long-term prospects for modest but sustained economic growth appear good.

RELATED ENTRIES: Commercial/Economic Importance of the Pacific Islands; Papua New Guinea.

SOURCES AND READINGS: International Bank for Reconstruction and Development, *The Economic Development of the Territory of Papua and New Guinea* (Baltimore: Johns Hopkins Press, 1965); *The National Public Expenditure Plan* (Waigani: National Planning Office, 1978); *Quarterly Summary of Economic Conditions: 1977 and 1978* (Waigani: Department of Finance, 1977-1978); *Papua New Guinea: Its Economic Situation and Prospects for Development*, A World Bank Country Report (Washington, D.C.: World Bank, 1978).   *Jerome Evans*

PAPUA NEW GUINEA, GOLD MINING IN. Attracting support or expressing hope, early European navigators spoke of gold in New Guinea. The Spaniard Alvaro de Saavedra sailed along the north coast of New Guinea in 1528 and named it *Isla del Oro*. The discovery of gold in eastern Australia rekindled speculation that New Guinea's forested valleys would yield high profits for prospectors. But it was not until rushes to the north Queensland fields in the 1870s that experienced miners began testing the most accessible areas.

Finding a trace of gold stimulated a brief rush to the Laloki River inland from Port Moresby in 1877. No worthwhile gold was found, and the disappointed men, suffering from malaria and hampered by rain, heat, dense undergrowth, steep slopes, and hostile villagers realized that New Guinea's gold would be hard-won.

Sudest Island, the first field to return findings worth more than the cost of travel and stores, attracted nearly 400 foreign men by the end of 1888. The next year another find on nearby Misima Island increased the number of white miners in the Louisiade Archipelago to 700, then the highest concentration of foreigners anywhere in New Guinea. As the Louisiades declined, a strike was made in 1895 to the north on Woodlark Island. Companies formed to sink shafts and crush lodes located by the early alluvial miners continued in production until 1918. The

Murua field on Woodlark was the richest of the early finds. Undeterred by the killing of four early prospectors who trespassed on the grounds of the indigenous peoples, miners continued to press up the mainland rivers. By 1896 a few were obtaining gold on MacLaughlin's Creek on the upper Mambare, and from there they opened fields on the northern rivers: the Gira in 1898, the Yodda in 1899, and the Waria in 1906. At their height in 1901, only about 150 white men and 750 Papuan laborers were on the Yodda and Gira. With all stores and equipment being carried on men's backs through the lands of hostile peoples to wet, isolated sites, the northern fields were marked by disease and violence. In some years, nearly one-third of the men died, many laborers deserted in fruitless attempts to escape, and local villagers fought desperately against miners, government officers, and police to rid their land of foreigners.

Small finds took miners to Milne Bay in 1899 and Keveri in 1901; and, as the mining population was again declining, the veteran prospectors Matt Crowe and Frank Pryke found gold on the Lakekamu River in 1909. Marred by a dysentery epidemic in which 250 laborers died in six months, the Lakekamu was the last field opened in Papua. For twenty years after 1895, gold was the most valuable export from British New Guinea and Papua, and it was again important in the 1930s when a company worked lodes on the old Misima field. Until World War II, gold was responsible for bringing more foreigners to the territory than any other cause, and the search for it had induced them to go beyond the beaches. The miners forced the government to open inland stations at Ioma, Kokoda, and Nepa. The miners had taken thousands of Papuans into the cash economy and enabled or pressed them to enter new relationships with other villagers.

Apart from the prospectors who crossed from the Gira and Waria, no miners worked in German New Guinea; but soon after 1921, when Australia assumed control of northern New Guinea under a mandate from the League of Nations, William ("Sharkeye") Park began exploiting a find on Koranga Creek in the Morobe district. A trickle of interest became a rush in 1926 when Bill Royal, one of the Big Six syndicate, found the rich alluvials of Edie Creek. In spite of the difficulties of reaching the field, over 200 white miners and 1,300 laborers had walked in from Salamaua by the end of the year. Quickly surpassing the production of the individual miners, companies moved in to exploit major reefs and alluvial deposits. Particularly successful were the huge dredges that churned the deep, auriferous ground of the Bulolo Valley. With high profits and no alternative method of travel other than using foot-paths, aircraft became the common means of transport. Lae was the busiest airport in the world as airline companies pioneered the shifting of dredge components and basic stores to the mining centers at Wau and Bulolo.

While mining companies exploited New Guinea's richest finds in the Morobe district, individual diggers worked smaller fields on the upper Ramu, farther west in the highlands, in the Sepik district, and on Bougainville. As in Papua, the prospectors were in the forefront of foreign penetration of much of the interior. Notable among many pioneering expeditions was that of the Leahy brothers, Michael and Dan, who joined government officer James Taylor on the first patrol to Mount Hagen.

By 1939 over 7,000 New Guinean laborers were employed in mining in the mandated territory, and the industry was returning six million dollars, more than 80 percent of all exports. Gold had enabled the government and many of the foreign community to pass through the depression with much less difficulty than the neighboring territory of Papua.

Completely closed down by the Japanese invasion of 1942, the industry failed to recover to its prewar heights. In 1953, the peak postwar year, over four million dollars worth of gold was produced, but it was a declining proportion of total exports. More recently output has increased again as gold is a major by-product of the giant copper mine on Bougainville.

Within three years of the arrival of the first white miners in the Louisiades, islanders were working gold for themselves, and villagers have continued to work most fields long after the foreigners have left. Requiring no capital from those able to live off the land and with a low level of technology, alluvial mining was one of the few industries open to illiterate villagers. Mining has continued to be an important source of income for some communities, and it has enabled a few individuals to become wealthy.

RELATED ENTRIES: Papua New Guinea; Papua New Guinea, Economy of; Port Moresby; Sepik River; Solomon Islands.

SOURCES AND READINGS: A. M. Healy, "Bulolo: A History of the Development of the Bulolo Region, New Guinea," *New Guinea Research Bulletin* 15 (1967); Hank Nelson, *Black, White and Gold: Goldmining in Papua New Guinea, 1878-1930* (Canberra: Australian National University Press, 1976); James Sinclair, *Wings of Gold: How the Aeroplane Developed New Guinea* (Sydney: Pacific Publications, 1978).   *Hank Nelson*

PAPUA NEW GUINEA, GOVERNMENT AND POLITICAL SYSTEM. The form of government in

Papua New Guinea, as is true for a number of other governments in Oceania, is based on the Westminster model in which the parliament is the supreme lawmaking body. A written constitution adopted at independence on 16 September 1975 defines the component parts of the formal governmental machinery including their respective roles and relationships. Parliament is a unicameral body consisting of 109 seats. From it a cabinet and a prime minister are derived. The cabinet is collectively responsible to parliament and, as the dominant body, provides executive direction for the country. An independent judiciary adjudicates conflicts and ensures that the executive branch conforms to the rule of law. Civil liberties, including the traditional freedoms of speech, association, and religion are embedded in and protected by the constitution. Other noteworthy aspects of the governmental system include an ombudsman commission, a leadership code, and a system of highly decentralized provincial governments. As a member of the Commonwealth of Nations, Papua New Guinea accepts the queen of England, represented locally by a governor-general, as the titular head of state.

Underlying the formal government structure is a political culture traditionally adapted to small-scale village democracy in which decisions are made by discussion and consensus. The Papua New Guinean state encompasses over seven hundred linguistic groups and covers extensive territory very unlike the small, egalitarian village-settings that characterized traditional Papuan and New Guinean society. Grave doubts exist as to whether the precolonial political and cultural habits can readily adapt to the requirements of a democratic, institutional framework imported from the West.

Papua New Guinean colonization by Australia witnessed the imposition on local society of Western forms of political organization. Initially, imperial conquest was consolidated by a nonconsultative, hierarchical, administrative organization that emphasized law and order. It was not until after World War II that Australia grudgingly introduced legislative councils to accommodate the views of local residents. A countrywide legislative council was first established in 1951. It consisted of twenty-nine seats dominated by sixteen official, or appointed, members and presided over by the administrator of the territory. The first council was mainly advisory in nature; it lasted until 1960 when a new legislative council was inaugurated. The new council possessed a nonofficial majority, but, while it contained twelve Papua New Guineans, nine more than in the first council, it still did not engage the broad popular consent of indigenous Papua New Guineans. The wind of change that swept through Africa and Asia heralding independence for numerous colonies also critically affected Papua New Guinea. In 1962 a United Nations trusteeship mission, headed by the British jurist, Sir Hugh Foot, visited the territory and submitted a report sharply critical of Australian colonial control; it demanded that the pace of political advancement be increased dramatically. The Foot Report called on Australia to establish a new legislative assembly selected by elections and consisting of a majority of indigenous Papua New Guineans. In response, universal adult suffrage was introduced, and members of a house of assembly of sixty-four seats were elected in 1964. National elections were repeated in 1968 and 1972 by which time a full-blown party system had evolved, a national leadership had been recruited, and a body of experience in parliamentary democracy had been accumulated by indigenous Papua New Guineans. During the life of the third house of assembly (1972-1977), self-government was conceded in December 1973, and full independence was granted in September 1975. The country's first prime minister, Michael Somare, led the Pangu Pati party in a coalition arrangement with the People's Progress Party, the National Party, and the Mataungan Association to form a government. The first postindependence elections were held in 1977 when the political stability of the 1972-1977 period was quickly broken. Somare's leadership has been repeatedly challenged as mounting problems of modernization such as urbanization, unemployment, tribal fighting, and union strikes beset the new nation. Old partycoalition arrangements disintegrated, and the political climate became more fluid. In mid-1979 a government bedeviled by grave problems and a fierce parliamentary opposition, promulgated a state of emergency covering the highlands provinces. The main concern since then is whether the democratic institutions inherited from Australia are adequately anchored in a supportive and relevant political culture to ensure their survival in the face of the crises of development.

RELATED ENTRIES: Guise, John; Papua New Guinea; Somare, Michael T.

SOURCES AND READINGS: Ralph R. Premdas, "Internal Problems of Rapid Political Change," *Asian Survey*, December 1975, pp. 1054-76; David Stone, ed., *Prelude to Self-Government* (Canberra: Australian National University Press, 1976). *Ralph R. Premdas*
Jeffrey S. Steeves

PAPUA NEW GUINEA, MENTAL HEALTH SERVICES IN. A culturally based mental system or service has existed in each of the hundreds of discrete cultural-linguistic groups in Papua New Guinea probably since time immemorial. Village studies of traditional groups with minimal overseas contact show that not only do such systems exist, but there is very little in the systems of industrialized countries overseas whose principles could not be paralleled in some way here. In its simplest form such a system consists of three people, firstly the *disturbed person*, secondly the concerned *observer* of the disturbance, and thirdly the *helper*, who is called in because of his or her experience of previous disturbances. Such a triad is the nucleus upon which all the subsequent mental health services have developed. This, however, does not negate the importance of cultural factors which are inextricably interwoven with all other aspects of the medical enterprise. Melanesian medico-historical data such as books, scientific papers, personal documents, archaeological findings, and other unpublished materials reveal a continuity of psychiatrically based issues as well as techniques for their superintendence since the dawn of human prehistory, clearly testifying to the need for provision of such facilities. In addition, world affairs, local events, and imported psychiatric ideologies have all played a part in molding policies related to the administration of clinics and hospitals for mentally disturbed people.

In line with the prevailing values in 1914, the chief medical officer budgeted for two detention cells which he felt was all that was necessary for any unmanageable persons of this sort. But it was not until 1959 that the government set up its own mental health services headed by a psychiatrist. Insufficiency of funds at all times and, in the immediate preindependence period, the system of preferred diseases buttressed by the euphemism of priorities and the notion that psychiatric services were a luxury all tended to delay progress. During their terms of office as general health administrators, Sir John Gunther and Dr. Roy Scragg were outstanding in the sympathy they showed for the mental health services and needs of the people. Despite the difficulties mentioned, slow progress was made over the years so that today major action programs are directed towards community mental health, mental health education and promotion, psychiatric social work, clinical anthropology, clinical psychology, training of all categories of health workers, forensic psychiatry as an instrument of prophylaxis, and transcultural psychiatric research.

In the earlier years of the service (after 1959), the work was carried out under difficult conditions. A small hospital was erected at Bomana 15 km from Port Moresby. This consisted of a few galvanized iron sheds and an airing court. Rats and other pests damaged hospital records. It was later abandoned and a new site selected on the Laloki River. The first buildings were subject to flooding and higher ground was sought which ultimately developed into Laloki Psychiatric Center, the only state mental hospital in the country. In the area, a village was established along traditional lines. Here the convalescing patients recreate their own lives in the way they would wish, determine their own government with minimal low-profile nurse surveillance, grow their own food such as taro, yams, and *kaukau*, and husband their own chickens, ducks, pigs, and goats. They also do their own fishing. The community gladly supports this project. Psychiatric wards have been set up in the major general hospitals throughout the country. The first psychiatric clinic in Port Moresby, Le Hunte Clinic—where there is a concentration of technical expertise made up of psychiatrists, clinical psychologists, a clinical anthropologist, psychiatric social workers, and psychiatric nurses—maintains contact with all parts of the country through visits, telephone, and radio. Forty mental health officers have been trained in the psychiatric nursing school since 1968 and are now posted throughout the country. Medical officers and nurses from other countries now come to Papua New Guinea for postgraduate training.

RELATED ENTRIES: Papua New Guinea.

SOURCES AND READINGS: C. Bell, *The Diseases and Health Services of PNG* (Port Moresby: Department of Public Health, 1973) and *PNG National Health Plan* (Madang: Kristen Press, 1974); B. G. Burton-Bradley, "PNG Psychiatry: An Historical Sketch," *PNG Medical Journal*, March 1976.

Burton G. Burton-Bradley

PAPUA NEW GUINEA, MIXED-RACE PEOPLE IN. Nonindigenous genes have been introduced into Papua New Guinea for many centuries. The list of explorers who have visited the country is very large since the first contact with Europeans attributed to the Portuguese in 1511. A story is told by the elders of Hood Point Peninsula concerning their area. They say that before the Europeans came a Chinese boat was wrecked and two of the crew were allowed to marry two widows. They say that the rest of the crew were eaten. Descendants of these people with marked epicanthic eye folds are often seen in the market at Koki to this day. The list of countries from which the mixed-race people claim ancestry is extensive. It embraces Australia, Ceylon, China, Eire, England, Fiji and other South Pacific islands, France, Germany, Greece, India, Indonesia, Italy, Malaysia, Micronesia, the Middle East, New Zealand, Portugal, and Russia. Intermarriage and interracial liaisons have characterized a small component of Papua New Guinea social life since the early nineteenth century, and the innocent products of these unions are the people to whom the name "mixed-race" has been assigned by others and by themselves as well.

The increase in health, size, and beauty among the first generation through heterosis is marked and many of these people occupy significant places in the life of the country. From the early part of the nineteenth century the area attracted whalers, sailors, traders, and political prisoners following the failure of revolutions in Europe. The children of those people were not recognizable as a discrete group in society until the country was annexed by England and Germany. A French absconder from the prison settlement of Devil's Island was well known to the administrator, Sir Hubert Murray, during his term of office. The Frenchman married a Kiwai woman, and their daughter was sent to an Australian school. She experienced no difficulties there but ran into the problems of discrimination on her return. An earlier administrator, Sir William MacGregor, brought in two Fijians and twelve Solomon islanders, provision having been made for a national constabulary. He also retained Fijians for his boat crew and settled them on blocks of land. The Christian missions brought in Filipinos. Foreigners came to the gold fields up until the 1920s and some of these people remained. Along with European traders, they established liaisons with local women. The Murray administration was characterized by a high degree of efficiency, considering the limited funds available and the context in which it operated, but it was unfortunately a period in which the mixed-race person found himself in a caste relationship to the white group.

Later, for a time at least, a similar relationship was to develop with Melanesians generally, as they received more education. Most mixed-race persons are Roman Catholics; a few are apostates. The Catholic attachment ensues from the fact that the indigenous women were not often supported adequately by their mates, and the Roman Catholic church in particular exhibited a generous and kindly approach to their problems. These people also had the additional benefit that their knowledge of English gave them a marked advantage over the Papuans and New Guineans.

Indicative of the status accorded to mixed-race people in the rapidly changing scene are the various phases of mixed-race drinking laws. There was total prohibition for all, other than Europeans, prior to 1948 when the mixed-race people indulged in illegal drinking. This was followed by the permit era, 1948-1956, based on an arbitrary, selective process whereby some mixed-race people were given a permit by the government secretary on the basis of their application and a character report by the police. The permit license had to be shown on demand when buying liquor in hotels. Compared with the third era, where no discrimination against mixed-race people was made, the total prohibition and permit eras were, strangely enough, looked back upon with nostalgia by many mixed-race people. The elders say that there was more interest in sporting activities, more community and church functions, and better-managed, strife-free picnics and dances. All this disappeared with the third period (from 1956 onward) of complete freedom for drinking by mixed-race people, when there was a marked increase in consumption. Finally, with the fourth period in 1962, prohibition was lifted for everyone, which had the effect of removing the status-conferring attribute of the discriminatory liquor right from the mixed-race people.

During the mid-1950s, the mixed-race person's aspiration to belong to European society, with which he was in constant contact and for membership in which there was no way to promote eligibility, was liable to frustration. At that stage, he was unwilling to be identified with the indigenous culture. He was often in a state of tension because of this. Slowly the situation changed. Six mixed-race persons were selected to meet the queen in Cairns, Australia, in 1954. A year later the Mixed-Race Association was formed, the Women's Island Social Club appeared in 1959 and the Youth Club in 1960. Greater interaction among children and teenagers in schools made its appearance, and mixed-race youth became more aware of the European way of life. Adequate housing began replacing the earlier self-constructed dwellings with its inevitable effect of promoting a greater degree of solidarity in family life. The former friction between mixed-race and Papua New Guinean employees is much less in evidence, and now that the latter have caught up in education in many areas there is more leveling when all eat together, go out to entertainments together, and share activities of all kinds.

Independence in 1975 has had a further effect. Whereas before the mixed-race person often tended to lean towards Western society, his aspirations are now directed, quite correctly, towards the burgeoning new nationalism of which he is a part, having been born in the country. This, superimposed upon better educational standards, improved economic conditions, and the greater mixing of everybody holds great promise for the so-called dual-identity groups of yesterday.

RELATED ENTRIES: Catholic Church in the Pacific; MacGregor, William; Papua New Guinea; Papua New Guinea, Gold Mining in.

SOURCES AND READINGS: B. G. Burton-Bradley, *Mixed-Race Society in Port Moresby* (Canberra: Australian National University Press, 1968); H. F. Dickie-Clark, *The Marginal Situation* (London: Paul Kegan, 1966); C. Dover, *Half-Caste* (London: Martin Secker and Warburg, 1937).

Burton G. Burton-Bradley

PAPUA NEW GUINEA, POLITICAL PARTIES IN. Papua New Guinea has a multiparty system; however, no one party is sufficiently strong by itself to command a majority of votes in Parliament. Party government has been constructed, then, around coalition arrangements. The emergence of party politics in Papua New Guinea coincided with the grant of universal adult suffrage and the inauguration of the first House of Assembly in 1964. Two major and common factors contributed to the introduction of political parties. The organization and mobilization of voters in elections could be done most effectively by an extraparliamentary mechanism endowed with greater resources than an individual candidate. Moreover, once candidates are elected, an organizing force is required within Parliament to weld together a majority to run the government. The transfer of a Westminster model of government in its full expression necessitated the existence of parties to bring coherence, order, and responsibility to the political process.

The first attempts to establish political parties in Papua New Guinea faltered badly. Partly this was due to a lack of familiarity with the operation of parties. More importantly, the difficulties can be traced to widespread distrust of the party institution per se. It must be remembered that when universal suffrage was introduced nothing less was contemplated than eventual self-government and ultimate independence for Papua New Guinea. Hence, the party apparatus as a vital ancillary institution that tends to accompany mass, democratic politics was opposed by powerful conservative local interests that did not want self-government. Several attempts were made between 1964 and 1968 to launch political parties. One notable example was initiated by Oala Oala Rarua, a young Papua New Guinean nationalist who formed his New Guinea United National Party (NGUNP) in September 1965. He did so in an atmo-

sphere of strong antiparty sentiments. Concerted efforts were quickly mounted to discourage him and to disband the party. Conservative members in the House of Assembly began the harassment. Oala and the executive members of his party were labeled communists. Further, the party institution was depicted as a means by which expatriates would be driven out of Papua New Guinea taking their skills and capital with them. Ironically, the most offensive aspect of Oala's party was its explicit demand for internal self-government by 1968. Fear of victimization deprived the NGUNP of extending its membership; the party continued to exist on paper until 1967 when it was dissolved.

Lessons were learned. Oala Oala Rarua had several young contemporaries, a group of Westernized Papua New Guinean intellectuals who were studying in 1965 at the Administrative College in Port Moresby. These young men, called the "Group of Thirteen," included Michael Somare and Albert Maori Kiki; the former would become prime minister and the latter deputy prime minister of an independent Papua New Guinea. From the "Group of Thirteen" open criticisms would be heard for the first time against the tardy process of Australian decolonization. These angry young men demanded that Australians must no longer be masters, but advisers, assistants, and guides. In June 1967, with the help of certain Australian friends, they organized the Pangu Pati, the mass-based, nationalist party that would eventually lead Papua New Guinea into independence.

The Pangu Pati faced intense opposition from anti-independence, conservative forces. Not only were the activists within the Pangu Pati labeled cargo cultists, but strenuous efforts were systematically launched to discredit the party institution altogether. When in 1968 the Pangu Pati decided to select candidates to compete for votes in the general elections, it decided that it would permit its endorsed candidates to conceal their Pangu connections and let them run as independent persons. In the 1968 elections the Pangu Pati won only ten seats. It faced a formidable force in the House of Assembly, called the Independent Members Group (IMG). The IMG was led by conservative European planters who viewed the Pangu Pati as anathema. This opposition was the first to crack. Internal differences within the IMG split the group asunder, and from the disintegrated parts there emerged several groups which would become formal parties by the time of the 1972 general elections. These included: (1) the United Party which constituted the largest and most conservative segment (its key program and raison d'être was to postpone self-government indefinitely); (2) the People's

Progress Party which supported self-government but wanted it much later than the Pangu Pati; and, (3) the National Party which identified strongly with the program of the Pangu Pati.

Thus, the 1972 elections witnessed for the first time electoral campaigns waged by several political parties. The negative sentiments previously associated with the party institution, held particularly in the New Guinea highlands where the United Party was strongest, still persisted. Consequently, many candidates who identified with or were supported by parties concealed their party sympathies until after the elections. When the 1972 elections were completed, all but a few of the elected members declared their association with one of the parties. The United Party won forty-one seats, the largest bloc but less than the majority required to form the new government by itself. At that time, the House of Assembly had 104 members composed of 100 elected and four nominated members. The other parties stood as follows: the Pangu Pati gained twenty-seven seats; the People's Progress Party twelve seats; the National Party eleven seats; and the Mataungan Association from the Gazelle Peninsula gained three seats. Together with six independents, the small parties coalesced to form the first party government in Papua New Guinea's history forcing the United Party into opposition. Michael Somare became leader of the coalition parties and was designated chief minister in the first full-fledged cabinet government. The Pangu Pati coalition government would lead Papua New Guinea to internal self-government in December 1973 and ultimate independence in September 1975.

The basis of party support has remained the same since parties were introduced in Papua New Guinea. Citizens tend to identify first and foremost with candidates sharing a common ethnic or regional bond. Even in city elections, "the primordial ethnic belly button" is the primary determinant of voter preference. Political parties, therefore, recruit candidates who are the most likely to draw the largest number of ethnically or regionally determined votes. In the simple-plurality, single-constituency electoral system adopted, in place of the original preferential proportional-representation system, candidates can win over their several ethnic-based competitors by slim margins. In the 1977 general elections, the typical candidate won with only 29 percent of the popular vote on a constituency basis. The ethnic factor, although dominant as the primary determinant of voter preference, is reinforced in most cases by other leadership characteristics such as education, ownership of property, or religion. Party competition for votes then tends to be more sophisticated than the

appeal merely to ethnic identity. In a modernizing country, factors other than ethnicity may gain greater importance in future elections.

Coalition party politics is inherently unstable. The coalition of Pangu, People's Progress, National, and Mataungan Parties in 1972 has since fallen apart, but not before it provided a measure of stability for the new government that lasted until the 1977 general elections. In contemporary Papua New Guinea, the Pangu Pati has grown to be the largest party superseding the United Party; in the 109-member parliament, it commands thirty-eight committed votes. Both the People's Progress Party and National Party, which in 1972 joined Pangu to form the government, have since abandoned that relationship and become part of the opposition. In the case of the National Party, it left the coalition in 1976 because of disputes between Somare, the Pangu leader, and Kavali, the National Party leader. The old National Party has since dissolved. The People's Progress Party rejoined the Pangu Pati after the 1977 elections to form the new coalition government. However, by November 1978 the leader of the People's Progress Party, Julius Chan, left the government and joined the opposition, charging that Pangu had consistently failed to consult it on policy matters. The United Party of 1972 has disintegrated into smaller units. Part of its membership retained the title "United Party" with twelve seats and joined the Pangu Pati in forming the government when Chan and his followers defected in November 1978. The remaining part of the United Party became at first the People's United Front and then later converted to a new National Party becoming the official Opposition Party in parliament led by Iambakey Okuk. The Pangu-led coalition consisting of Pangu, the United Party, the Mataungan Association, and a number of independents is pitched in parliament against the National Party and the People's Progress Party. Several votes of no confidence in 1978 and 1979 have demonstrated that the Somare-led government can count on approximately sixty-four seats out of 109. Yet, because party discipline is weak, it is not a stable system. In each of the no-confidence votes, it was never certain what the outcome was likely to be until the last moment.

Finally, the programs and ideologies of the parties require comment. No firm or established ideology pervades the programs of any of the parties. The Pangu Pati is regarded as liberal-to-socialist, but in practice it endorses a mixed economy with a pivotal role assigned to free enterprise. The United Party, People's Progress Party, and National Party all stand to the right of Pangu. They are more firmly in favor of a greater role for the capitalist, free-enterprise system. None of the parties, however, can be said to be doctrinaire. All of the parties are weakly organized at the grass roots. During the period between elections, grass-roots organizations are practically nonexistent. During elections, however, branches are established everywhere. Parties rarely depend on their members for funds. Generally, parties obtain finances from large contributors and from holding social functions. The Pangu Pati, People's Progress Party, and the United Party also own businesses from which revenue is obtained to pay full-time activists and to sponsor candidates.

Political parties constitute an integral part of the imported, Westminster, democratic system. The multiparty system has worked well for Papua New Guinea up to this period. The fates of parties may be determined, however, by the capability of party government to meet the needs of citizens increasingly subjected to the forces of modernization.

RELATED ENTRIES: Papua Besena; Papua New Guinea; Papua New Guinea, Government and Political System; Somare, Michael T.

SOURCES AND READINGS: Ralph R. Premdas, "Towards a One Party System in Papua New Guinea: Problems and Prospects," *Australian Outlook* 29 (1975): 161-79; Ralph R. Premdas and Jeffrey S. Steeves, *Elections in a Third-World City* (Waigani: University of Papua New Guinea Press, 1978); D. Stephen, *A History of Political Parties in Papua New Guinea* (Melbourne: Lansdowne Press, 1970).

Ralph R. Premdas
Jeffrey S. Steeves

PASCUA ISLAND. *See* Easter Island.

PATEL, AMBALAL DAHYABHAI (1905-1969).
A lawyer, educator, and the founder of the National Federation Party in Fiji, Patel was born 15 March 1905 in Mahij, Gujarat State, India. "A. D.," as he was popularly known, attended Middle Temple Law School in London. While there in 1928, he was influenced by Ghandi's associates to go to Fiji. In Fiji he stressed the importance of education to the Indian people, and he helped establish several schools to improve education among them. During World War II, the British kept him under house arrest because of his support of equal pay for Indian soldiers and his involvement in sugar farmers' strikes. Between 1944 and 1950, and again from 1963 until his death, he served as a member of the government legislative council. He was also selected as a member of the executive council and social services. In 1966 he participated in talks in London to bring about Fijian na-

tional independence. During the 1966 general election, he became the leader of the opposition, the National Federation Party, a position he held until his death on 1 October 1969.

RELATED ENTRIES: Fiji.

SOURCES AND READINGS: G. J. A. Kerr and T. A. Donnelly, *Fiji in the Pacific: A History and Geography of Fiji* (Brisbane: Jacaranda Press, 1969); *Pacific Islands Monthly*, November 1969, p. 135; Judy Tudor, *Pacific Islands Year Book and Who's Who* (Sydney: Pacific Publications, 1968).

Michael P. Singh

PATTESON, JOHN COLERIDGE (1827-1871).
An Anglican bishop, Patteson was born in London into a prominent High Church family which was deeply involved in assisting the overseas expansion of the Church of England. Educated at Eton and Balliol College, Oxford University, he was ordained in 1853. Two years later he went to New Zealand to work with Bishop George A. Selwyn in the Melanesian mission and in 1861 was consecrated as the first bishop of Melanesia. Patteson was responsible for planting the Anglican church at many places in the northern New Hebrides and Solomon Islands. He encouraged the early development of an indigenous ministry and sought to adapt Christianity to the needs of Melanesian societies. His violent death on 20 September 1871 at the island of Nukapu in the Santa Cruz group has generally been regarded as an act of revenge for the abduction of several young men from Nukapu by a labor recruiter. As one of the best-known Anglican missionaries of the nineteenth century, Patteson is commemorated widely throughout the Anglican Communion and has been the subject of many popular biographies.

RELATED ENTRIES: Anglican Missions; Selwyn, George.

SOURCES AND READINGS: John Gutch, *Martyr of the Islands: The Life and Death of John Coleridge Patteson* (London: Hodder and Stoughton, 1971); David Hilliard, "John Coleridge Patteson: Missionary Bishop of Melanesia" in J. W. Davidson and Deryck Scarr, eds., *Pacific Islands Portraits* (Canberra: Australian National University Press, 1970); Charlotte Mary Yonge, *Life of John Coleridge Patteson: Missionary Bishop of the Melanesian Islands*, 2 vols. (London: Macmillan & Co., 1874).

David L. Hilliard

PAULET, GEORGE (1803-1867). An English naval captain who temporarily seized the Hawaiian Islands for Britain in 1843, Paulet was born 12 August 1803. In 1833 he was made captain of the frigate *Carysfort* and was assigned to the Pacific. When complaints reached the British naval commander in the Pacific concerning the mistreatment of Englishmen in Hawai'i, Captain Paulet proceeded to the Sandwich Islands for their protection. Arriving in Honolulu on 10 February 1843, he assessed the situation and fearing that France would soon annex the islands (as they were during in Tahiti), he sent notice to King Kamehameha III to cede the islands to Great Britain. On 25 February 1843 it was decided that the kingdom should be placed under British rule and, thereupon, Paulet took possession of the islands. Because Paulet had taken it upon himself to annex the islands without his government's approval, Paulet's actions were not sanctioned by his superiors. When Admiral Richard Thomas, commander of the British Pacific Squadron, learned of Paulet's actions, he immediately set sail from Valparaiso and arrived in Honolulu on 26 July. After his interview with the Hawaiian king, independence of the kingdom was again restored. One month after Thomas' arrival, Paulet quietly left the Hawaiian Islands. By 1854 he was in command of a seventy-eight-gun vessel. In 1867 he retired from the British navy with the rank of full admiral and then died at the age of seventy-six.

RELATED ENTRIES: Hawai'i; Thomas, Richard.

SOURCES AND READINGS: Edward Joesting, *Hawaii, An Uncommon History* (New York: W. W. Norton & Co., 1972).   *Brenna J. Rash*

PAUMOTU ISLANDS. *See* Tuamotu-Gambier Archipelago.

PEACE CORPS. An international project of the United States government, the Peace Corps' objections are: (1) to furnish needed manpower to developing countries, (2) to give foreign people the opportunity to know and understand Americans, and (3) to give Americans the opportunity to share their knowledge with less affluent societies. Begun in 1962-1963 under the direction of President John F. Kennedy, it was not until 1966 that some 350 Peace Corps volunteers arrived in Micronesia and the Pacific. In 1967 volunteers also began service in Tonga, Fiji, and Western Samoa. Later, groups were requested and sent to the Solomon Islands. Volunteers also served in the Cook Islands and in the New Hebrides under the auspices of the South Pacific Commission.

In all Pacific area countries, the initial program emphasized elementary school education and public health. By 1968 there were some 800 volunteers and trainees in Micronesia alone, which represented the Peace Corps' largest program strength per capita of any place in the world. In some Pacific countries, school enrollments rose dramatically with the arrival of primary-school English teachers. From 1966 to 1971 about 3,500 Peace Corps volunteers from the United States served in the Pacific in some twenty different programs in nearly every major activity.

Most of the program concentrations in the Pacific have been in the human services areas. The Peace Corps has never been charged with economic development per se. All Pacific area volunteers receive training in local languages and cultures. Altogether, they have served as teachers, health workers, nurses, public works engineers, tourism and small business advisers, lawyers, civil engineers, journalists, agricultural workers, fisheries development workers, community development aides, transportation assistants, land management and forestry officers, sanitation specialists, and in other areas.

The United States bears most of the cost for training and maintaining the volunteers in the field, although each host country in the Pacific also contributes some share for their support. Although some of the volunteers have been trained and certified as professionals in their areas of expertise, most are interested generalists who have recently graduated from college and who have received brief, intensive training in a specialized area. There are also a number of older volunteers, both men and women, serving in the Pacific. Methodologies employed to assess the impact of the Peace Corps on a country or population have been generally more descriptive than empirical. During the years of the Peace Corps service in the Pacific, every governing group has commended the efforts of the volunteers.

RELATED ENTRIES: Cook Islands; Fiji; Micronesia; Solomon Islands; Solomon Report; South Pacific Commission; Tonga; Vanuatu (New Hebrides); Western Samoa.

SOURCES AND READINGS: Dirk A. Ballendorf and Howard Seay, "Catalysts or Barnacles in Micronesia: The First Five Years of the Peace Corps," in Frank P. King, ed., *Oceania and Beyond* (Westport, Conn.: Greenwood Press, 1976); Roy Hoopes, *Complete Peace Corps Guide* (New York: Dial Press, 1965).
                    Dirk Anthony Ballendorf

PEASE, BENJAMIN (?-1874). An American trader in coconut oil, timber, and other island commodities, Pease attempted between 1866 and 1870 to establish a commercial empire in the northern Gilberts, southern Marshalls, and eastern Carolines. Best known as a sometime companion of William Henry ("Bully") Hayes, Pease acquired personal notoriety during his own time.

The Vermont-born Pease appeared in Micronesia in 1866. C. A. Williams, an American merchant in Honolulu, supplied trade and the brig *Blossom* for Pease's first voyage in 1867 during which he placed traders on several atolls. By mid-1868, however, Pease was commanding the heavily armed brig *Water Lily*. He also had formed a partnership with the British firm of Glover and Company of Shanghai. The new venture, the Island Trading Company, was intended to trade in timber from Ponape. It was more than Pease could handle, however. At least one established atoll trader accused him of stealing oil. His own agents, not the most experienced or reliable, created further problems. Pease's temper exploded more than once, and his reputation as a wily barbarian became fixed. At Ponape, agents sent from Shanghai proved incompetent to manage the laborers sent out to cut and mill timber. His atoll traders often went without trade and complained of neglect.

The U.S.S. *Jamestown* was dispatched in 1870 to investigate the situation. Statements were taken from Pease's atoll traders, from missionaries, and from the demoralized group at Ponape, most of whom returned to China. Pease was not there to present his case. In fact, he was just returning from aiding Bully Hayes in escaping authorities at Samoa, assisted, there is reason to believe, by the American consular agent. When the pair reached the Carolines and learned of the visit of the *Jamestown* they went their separate ways. Hayes left for Shanghai.

Pease retained some of his old crew, picked up his wife at Ponape, and retired to temporary obscurity at Port Lloyd in the Bonins. In February 1871 he was arrested by Spanish authorities at Guam, sent to Manila, and then on to Shanghai to face the U.S. consul. Had not the prime witness against him died, the U.S. consul said, Pease would have been sent to California to stand trial. Pease was released and left Shanghai in May 1871. He lived in the Bonins where he traded as the Bonin Company, quarrelled with his neighbors, and is believed to have been murdered in October 1874.

RELATED ENTRIES: Caroline Islands; Kiribati; Micronesia.

SOURCES AND READINGS: Lionel B. Cholmondeley, *The History of the Bonin Islands From the Year 1827 to the Year 1876* (London: Constable, 1915); Dispatches from U.S. Consuls, Kanagawa, Japan, vol. 8, December 1874-February 1878, General Records of the Department of State, Record Group 59, U.S.

National Archives Microfilm Publication M 135, roll 8; Dispatches from U.S. Consul in Shanghai, China, February 23-October 7, 1871, General Records of the Department of State, Record Group 59, U.S. National Archives Microfim Publication M 112, roll 12; H. E. Maude, *Of Islands and Men, Studies in Pacific History* (Melbourne: Oxford University Press, 1968); *North China Herald & Supreme Court & Consular Gazette* 6 (1871): 523-26.   *Mary Browning*

PERRY, MATTHEW CALBRAITH (1794-1858). Matthew Perry was the American naval commander who sailed the first warships into Tokyo Bay on 8 July 1853 and thus altered both Japan's and the United States' perception of the outside world and Oceania. Perry arranged a treaty with Japan in 1854 that protected American property and sailors in Japanese waters. His *Narrative of the Expedition of an American Squadron to the China Seas and Japan* was published in 1856 and stimulated American interest in the Pacific and Far East.

RELATED ENTRIES: United States in the Pacific.

SOURCES AND READINGS: F. L. Hawks, *Narrative of the Expedition of an American Squadron to the China Sea and Japan*, 3 vols. (Washington, D.C., n.p., 1856); Robert Tomes, *The Americans in Japan* (New York: Appleton & Co., 1857); Joseph B. Icenhower, *Perry and the Open Door to Japan* (New York: Watts, Franklin, 1973).   *Frank P. King*

PHOENIX ISLANDS. An uninhabited group of coral atolls in central Oceania, the Phoenix Islands include Phoenix, Sydney (Manra), McKean, Gardner (Nikumaroro), Birnie, and Hull (Orono) which are part of the newly formed Republic of Kiribati (1979). Since April 1939 Canton and Enderbury islands have been administered separately and jointly by Britain and the United States. Discovered by American whaling ships in the nineteenth century, all of the islands were annexed by Britain in 1889; they were incorporated, excluding Canton and Enderbury, into the Gilbert and Ellice colony in 1937 and then into the new, independent Republic of Kiribati in July 1979.

RELATED ENTRIES: Kiribati.

SOURCES AND READINGS: Alaima Talu et al., *Kiribati: Aspects of History* (Tarawa, Kiribati: Ministry of Education, Training & Culture, 1979).

Frank P. King

PINKHAM, LUCIUS EUGENE (1850-1922). Pinkham was nominated governor of the Territory of Hawai'i (1913-1918) by President Woodrow Wilson after the resignation of Governor Walter Frear in 1913. Pinkham is generally credited with the expansion of the National Guard, the Waikiki reclamation movement, the Workman's Compensation Act, and the Teachers Pension Bill, measures that rightfully labeled him as the champion of social betterment in Hawai'i. Pinkham was born in Massachusetts on 19 September 1850 and was educated in the Boston public school system. He came to Hawai'i as a businessman in 1892 to oversee the erection of mining and drilling operations on O'ahu. In 1904 Pinkham was appointed president of the Board of Health, a position he retained for four years. After his confirmation as governor in 1913, he forcefully promoted various projects that benefited the people of the territory, including several homestead bills, and transportation and water improvements that aided development and progress on the outer islands. He died in San Francisco 2 November 1922 after several years of illness.

RELATED ENTRIES: Hawai'i.

SOURCES AND READINGS: A. Grove Day, *Hawaii and Its People* (New York: Meredith Press, 1968); Edward Joesting, *Hawaii* (New York: W. W. Norton & Co., 1972); Ralph S. Kuykendall and A. Grove Day, *Hawaii: A History* (Englewood Cliffs, N.J.: Prentice-Hall, 1961).   *Ned B. Williams*

PITCAIRN ISLAND. Located in south central Oceania, 25° 04′ south latitude and 130° 05′ west longitude, Pitcairn Island lies about 2,170 km (1,350 mi) southeast of Tahiti. The main island has a land area of nearly 5 km² (2 mi²). It is an irregular semicrater with fertile soil rising to about 300 m (1,100 ft) surrounded by steep coastal cliffs. The population is about one hundred persons. The outer islands of Oeno, Henderson, and Ducie are uninhabited.

Discovered by a British naval officer, Philip Carteret, in 1767, Pitcairn was populated by Fletcher Christian and other mutineers from H.M.S. *Bounty* and a number of Polynesian women in 1790. Despite intrusions by American whalers after 1807 and unsuccessful attempts by British officials to relocate them in Tahiti, they and their descendants endured. Some of the islanders, threatened with overpopulation, migrated to Norfolk Island in 1856. Most of the islanders have become Seventh-Day Adventists since 1877.

The Pitcairn settlement was placed under the jurisdiction of the High Commissioner for the Western Pacific in 1898. After Fiji became independent on 10 October 1970, Pitcairn was put under the administrative control of the British High Commissioner in New Zealand. The inhabitants of the island also have their own elected island council in Adamstown, the Main settlement, and an island court.

RELATED ENTRIES: Bligh, William; *Bounty* Mutiny; Norfolk Island; Western Pacific High Commission.
                                              Frank P. King

POINDEXTER, JOSEPH BOYD (1869-1951). Poindexter served two full terms as the eighth governor of Hawai'i from 1934 to 1942. In no other administration did the cause of equal rights for Hawai'i receive greater encouragement than during the more than eight years under Governor Poindexter. Born 14 April 1869, he arrived in Hawai'i in 1917 after President Woodrow Wilson appointed him United States District Judge for Hawai'i. He practiced law in Honolulu until his appointment as governor in 1934. During his first administration, Poindexter promoted social and educational rights for the inhabitants of the islands. His major efforts during his second administration centered around Hawai'i's defense against the gradual threat from Japan. After the Japanese bombed Pearl Harbor in 1941, Poindexter declared martial law in Hawai'i. As governor, he successfully directed territorial affairs during a time of turmoil and fear. Upon expiration of his second term, Poindexter resumed practice of law until his death on 3 December 1951.

RELATED ENTRIES: Hawai'i.

SOURCES AND READINGS: A. Grove Day, *Hawaii and Its People* (New York: Meredith Press, 1968); Edward Joesting, *Hawaii* (New York: W. W. Norton & Co., 1972); Ralph S. Kuykendall and A. Grove Day, *Hawaii: A History* (Englewood Cliffs, N.J.: Prentice-Hall, 1961).   *Ned B. Williams*

POLYNESIA. The term *Polynesia* comes from two Greek words: πολής, *polys*, many; νῆσος, *nesos*, islands. This rather loose name is applied to a very large triangular area in east central Oceania ranging between the Tropics of Capricorn and Cancer which extends along the base from Easter Island about 9,200 km (5,700 mi) to include the Maori population of New Zealand and then about 7,600 km (4,700 mi) north to include the indigenous Hawaiians. The best-known island groups within this so-called triangle are Tuvalu (Ellice), Phoenix, Tokelau, the Samoas, Tonga, Line, Cook, Marquesas, Tuamotu, Society, and Tubuai (Austral). The peoples of Tikopia and Rennell in Melanesia and Kapingamarangi and Nukuoro in Micronesia are also thought to be Polynesians, as are the native Fijians in some aspects of their culture. The whole area covers about 39 million km² (15 million mi²) with a population of about 450,660 persons, excluding New Zealand and Hawai'i.

The term *Polynesia*, like *Melanesia*, and to a lesser extent *Micronesia*, is a generalization that increasingly becomes less useful as an intellectual tool. The term originally was favored by nineteenth-century anthropologists and others who were preoccupied with racial types and classifications. Increasingly, Oceanic scholars realize that the exceptions to these generalizations are legion.

RELATED ENTRIES: Melanesia; Micronesia.

Frank P. King

POLYNESIA COMPANY. An organization to deal in land development, speculation, and investment schemes in Fiji, the Polynesia Company was incorporated in Melbourne, Australia in 1868. Based on a charter signed by Ratu Seru Cakobau (1817-1883), the company claimed 200,000 acres and banking, trading, and taxation privileges. It was responsible for much of the favorable press reporting about Fiji's prospects as a planter's El Dorado. Shares sold quickly, and land titles were conveyed to prospective settlers throughout the Australian colonies, particularly in Victoria. More than a hundred shareholders joined the several thousand settlers who rushed to Fiji from 1868 to 1872. Some plantation development took place at Viti Levu Bay and Natewa Bay. The main focus was on Suva promontory where forty shareholders established cotton and sugar plantations, market gardens, and cattle grazing. A settlement at Nabukalo Creek served as a provisioning center for the south coast of Viti Levu. Later it became the seat of government and the modern city of Suva. By 1873 cotton and sugar production had failed, and the company virtually collapsed. At cession in 1874 the company's charter was declared invalid, and the Land Claims Commission (1879-1883) rejected all claims derived in its name, excepting where occupation or capital improvement had occurred. Most shareholders returned to the Australian colonies. Due to a failure to attract permanent settlers to develop the land, involvement in an American annexation movement, alleged involvement in the formation of a colonial militia for Fiji, and agents' activities in other speculative ventures and political intrigues, the company acquired a bad reputation. John Bates Thurston (1836-1897) was the company's most bitter opponent, and he used his position in the Cakobau and Crown Colony governments to frustrate attempts to salvage a return for its investors.

The company was never liquidated. Disgruntled investors maintained a dialogue with British and Fiji Crown Colony authorities until the late 1880s trying to secure land titles or monetary compensation.

RELATED ENTRIES: Fiji; Fiji Planting and Trading Company; Fiji Trading Company; Thompson, William K.; Thurston, John Bates.

SOURCES AND READINGS: R. A. Derrick, *A History of Fiji* (Suva: Government Printer, 1946, 1968); A. M. Quanchi, "This Glorious Company: The Polynesia Company in Fiji and Victoria" (Master's thesis, Monash University, 1977).   *Alan Maxwell Quanchi*

POLYNESIA, SETTLEMENT OF. Sometime in the remote past, people who came to be known as Polynesians settled the islands in the area between and including Hawai'i, New Zealand, and Easter Island. How those intrepid seafarers populated the Polynesian islands has stirred Western man's thoughts since first coming upon these places in the sixteenth century. The Polynesians, themselves, had shown a similar interest in their heritage by preserving in chants, genealogies, legends, and myths their own beliefs as to their origins, but they are known to have changed their histories in order to enhance certain relationships. Thus a study of their claims, while informative, would reveal other things in addition to their origin beliefs.

Through recent research in linguistics and archaeology we are able to trace the Polynesians' probable migration route from Melanesia into western Polynesia and from there to all areas of the Polynesian triangle. Settlement was likely the result of planned migrations, although Andrew Sharp (1957) suggests that the Polynesians lacked the ability for making prepared, long-distance, two-way voyages, and that settlement of new and distant islands would therefore have been the result of an accidental discovery by a group of exiles or by those whose canoe had been blown off course. Others who have studied Polynesian maritime skills (Lewis, Finney) believe that such long-distance, two-way voyages were possible and that they played an important part in the settlement of Polynesia. Each of these views merits discussion.

Other theories for Polynesian homelands are advanced by Thor Heyerdahl, Robert Langdon, and Barry Fells. Heyerdahl maintains that Polynesia was settled in part from the Americas, not from Melanesia as most scientists believe. Langdon and Fells are authors of less accepted theories. Langdon believes that some Polynesians are the descendants of Spaniards whose ship was wrecked in the Pacific in 1526; and Fells has suggested that central Polynesia was settled by Libyans serving under an Egyptian king, Ptolemy III, who had ordered a voyage of circumnavigation and a search for gold in the third century B.C.

Earlier theorists had considered that the Pacific people might have originated on a continent, now subsided, but once believed to have existed in the Pacific; that theory was disproved in the nineteenth century when geographical knowledge showed that no such continent had ever existed.

More recently, Buck (1938) and Spoehr (1952) raised the possibility that Polynesia was settled by people from Indonesia traveling through Micronesia; but the Micronesian route is no longer accepted in light of the overwhelming evidence which shows that the main group of people who became Polynesians traveled through Melanesia and from there into Polynesia. Bellwood (1978:20) suggests that the Polynesians' more distant origins lie somewhere in eastern Indonesia or the Philippines.

In earlier times, Westerners proposed major theories of worldwide population shifts that would have resulted in a people being forced, or moving voluntarily, into the Pacific region. That classical approach also accepted a wave theory of migrations, in which it was believed that, over time, groups of migrants successively brought different traits to the same area. Today's scholars adopt an approach that deals with the immediate Oceanic origins of the Polynesians without considering what might have caused those people to exodus from Asia; at the same time future research in Melanesia and in southeast Asia could indicate the ultimate origins of the Polynesians.

Anthropologists now accept that cultures develop and change through time, so that the wave theory is not necessary to explain all changes within a culture; yet some island groups, such as Hawai'i, probably did receive successive waves of immigrants who introduced new traits, while other areas, such as Easter Island, were likely settled by one migration group.

Modern study of Polynesian migrations has been aided by archaeological research which has uncovered Lapita pottery and other remnants of early habitation. These material artifacts can be compared and dated, thus indicating the migration routes of a people. Lapita was first discovered on Watom Island, near Rabaul, New Britain, in 1908-1909, but its discovery did not generate great excitement until further findings were made in the widespread areas of New Caledonia, Fiji, and Tonga in the 1940s and 1950s. Since that time continued research has shown that the first people to enter Polynesia were the makers of this pottery.

Only infrequently have enough pieces of Lapita been found to reconstruct whole pots, but the existing fragments show that the most common form was a globular or shoulder cooking pot which was sand-tempered and fired in open bonfires; there were also open bowls, some of which were red slipped, with the rims decorated by incision or by a stamping made with a tattoolike comb.

It is not clear where the makers of Lapita pottery came from. It may have been from Island South East Asia, or from eastern Melanesia. But by 1500 B.C. these people had established themselves as coastal traders living on the small islands offshore of, or on the coasts of, the already populated, larger islands in eastern Melanesia. In those areas, these purveyors of pottery practiced horticulture and made widespread use of their marine environment. Most importantly they serviced trade networks with voyages farther than 600 km, perhaps trading their canoes or navigational knowledge for rocks to be used as tools, or for pottery, or for the materials needed to manufacture it (Green, 1973: 335). With time they expanded their trade networks. Pieces of their pottery have been found and dated and show that by 1300 B.C. they were the first settlers in Tonga. They settled in Fiji at the same time, where they may also have been the first people.

Three hundred years later, by 1000 B.C., makers of this pottery moved, probably through the northern islands of Tonga, to the unsettled areas of western Polynesia, especially Samoa. Because of the distance between Tonga and Samoa there was infrequent contact between those groups so that the languages gradually separated into what linguists call the Tongic and the nuclear-Polynesian subgroups. Following isolation in Samoa, where the Lapita people apparently made their earliest settlements in interior valleys and developed a fully fledged horticultural economy of a Polynesian type (Bellwood, 1978:56), production of pottery was abandoned by about 300 A.D., but not before some settlers had reached the Marquesas where a few tiny shards of the pottery have been found at the earliest levels. The Society Islands may have been settled at the same time, and there, and in the Marquesas, there was further isolation and eventual dispersal to the rest of Polynesia.

What of the Lapita potters? In Melanesia, probably as their trade networks grew too long to service, they were absorbed into the larger Melanesian groups, while in Polynesia their descendants were the founding population. Although pottery making was abandoned in Samoa and Tonga by 300 A.D. and the eastern Polynesian islands had always lacked the clay for its manufacture, the maritime skills of the Lapita people and of their descendants did lead, over hundreds of years, to the eventual settlement of these islands. The migrations within Polynesia were probably the result of expanding populations being forced to seek new homelands because of overpopulation, warfare, and famine, as well as a curiosity as to what islands might exist over the horizon.

The trail of Lapita pottery ends in the Marquesas, but the dispersal of people to, and within, Polynesia has been studied by archaeologists who have compared and dated other artifacts, and by linguists who attempt to show how today's language groups evolved from reconstructed protolanguages.

Archaeological evidence shows that in eastern Polynesia, the Marquesas, Society Islands, Hawai'i, and Easter Island were all settled between 300 and 700 A.D., while the Cooks, Austral Islands, and New Zealand were probably settled between 700 and 1100 A.D. These early east Polynesian cultures were fairly homogeneous. Bellwood (1978:57-58) believes that settlement began with a very small group of people in either the Marquesas or Society groups who made cultural adaptations different from Samoa which they carried with them as they expanded farther into Polynesia. Those cultural adaptations consisted mainly of tanged rather then untanged adzes and the development of a range of shell and bone fishing gear that was virtually absent in western Polynesia.

Linguistic evidence reveals that a proto-Tahitic language, perhaps located in Tahiti, developed into the languages of New Zealand, the Tuamotus, Austral Islands (Tubai), the Cooks, and Tahiti. From a proto-Marquesic language developed the languages of the southeast Marquesas, northwest Marquesas, Mangareva, and Easter Island; Hawaiian may have been in either group.

Both the proto-Marquesic and the proto-Tahitic languages had evolved from a protoeastern Polynesian which itself had split with a proto-Samoic outlier from a proto-nuclear Polynesian. The proto-Samoic outliers included the languages of Samoa and those of the Polynesian outliers located in Melanesia and Micronesia. Bellwood (1978:28) suggests that the outliers were settled from the Ellice Islands (Tuvalu) and from east Futuna, both in western Polynesia, and that the outlier populations are not, as once believed, remnants of the earliest migrating Polynesians left behind in Melanesia.

On the basis of linguistic and archaeological evidence, it appears that the initial settlement of Easter Island was made around 400-500 A.D. from eastern Polynesia, perhaps from the Marquesas, although Green (1973:22) believes that Easter Island was settled from some island nearer than the Marquesas,

and that all the island groups in central east Polynesia (such as the southern Cooks, Society Islands, Marquesas, and Tuamotus) were probably settled by 700 A.D. and presumably could have served as the impetus for the settlement of Easter Island. There is general agreement among archaeologists that after initial settlement Easter Island was completely isolated from the rest of Polynesia.

Hawai'i was apparently settled from the Marquesas about 500-600 A.D. with later influence, as indicated by archaeology and oral histories, from the Society Islands. Based on linguistic research the northern Cooks were settled from Samoa, while traditions and archaeology imply that the southern Cooks were settled from the Society Islands by the end of the first millennium A.D., with a possible secondary settlement from Samoa to Rarotonga (Bellwood, 1978:89-90). New Zealand was settled from the area of the Marquesas, Society, or Cook groups by 1100 A.D. (Bellwod, 1978:130-132). This was the last major region of Polynesia to be settled.

While most research shows that the people who settled Polynesia traveled west to east through Melanesia and from there into Polynesia, Thor Heyerdahl, in a number of popular books and articles, has written that Hawai'i and Easter Island were settled from the Americas and that those populations scattered and mixed with a lesser group from Melanesia. His evidence is based on: (1) the pre-European presence in Polynesia of the sweet potato, a plant that has South American origins; (2) knowledge that the oceanic winds and currents are mainly east to west, thus voyages would more easily have occurred in that direction; (3) linguistic evidence which he felt showed that the Polynesian languages were not related to those of the Malay-Indonesia area; and (4) what he believed to be earlier dates of settlement for east Polynesia than for west Polynesia, which would indicate an east-to-west movement of people.

Yet Heyerdahl's archaeological dating was disproved when more recent work showed that sites in west Polynesia do predate those of the eastern islands, and, in fact, Bellwood (1978:126-28) writes that there is no archaeological or linguistic evidence to support a major American settlement of Easter Island or anywhere else in Polynesia. Finney (1977) and Lewis (1972) also disagree with Heyerdahl and point out that to sail eastward the Polynesians could have made use of the equatorial countercurrent or occasional westerlies. As for the sweet potato, it does have South American origins and was introduced from there either by Polynesians who reached the American continent and returned with the tuber, or by South American Indians who voyaged from that continent. Even if voyages from South America did occur, their influence, limited mainly to the introduction of the sweet potato, was minor when compared to what other research has shown was the western origins of the Polynesian people, their languages, and the animals and most plants which they carried with them.

In recent years there has been a controversy as to the manner in which Polynesia was settled. Andrew Sharp (1957, 1963) has written that the Polynesians, once having discovered an island more than 350-450 km distant, would not have had the maritime skills to return to their homeland, organize a colonizing expedition, and retrace their course to settle on the new land. Therefore, according to Sharp, those distant places were settled either by exiles randomly searching for a new home or by accidental drift voyages.

Others maintain that Polynesians were able to make purposeful, long distance voyages of settlement and their research has included a test of the sailing ability of Polynesian canoes and of the effectiveness of traditional navigation. In 1976 a voyage from Hawai'i to Tahiti and back, a distance of nearly 5,000 km one way, was successfully undertaken by the Hōkūle'a, a canoe built to model the ancient Polynesian voyaging canoes. Those trips showed that traditional craft could travel into the wind and that methods of traditional navigation could result in a successful long-distance voyage. In addition, the research of David Lewis (1972) and continued long-distance voyaging in Micronesia (Lewis, 1972; Gladwin, 1970) have shown the effectiveness of traditional Pacific sailing. As for the problem defined by Sharp as the poor target areas of single islands, Lewis (1972) and others have noted that the voyagers would have aimed for a whole island chain and upon reaching that larger area would have been able to island-hop to their destination.

Planned voyages must have played some part in the settlement of Polynesia; computer simulations have shown that accidental drift voyages could not have accounted for the initial movement of people from western to eastern Polynesia and had no chance of reaching Hawai'i, Easter Island, and New Zealand from other parts of Polynesia (Levison, Ward, and Webb, 1973). Still, the difficulties of those long voyages would have been such that Finney (1977:1284) believes they were never extensive.

If limited, two-way contact, over long distances had once occurred it had terminated by the time of European penetration of the islands, although such people as Captain James Cook in the eighteenth century were impressed by Pacific navigators who re-

called the paths to distant islands (Beaglehole, 1974). Climatologists suggests that long-distance voyages might have ceased when a climate favorable for voyaging (that had lasted from 450 A.D. to 1100-1300 A.D. and consisted of mild trade winds and more frequent and enduring westerly wind shifts) changed to a little Ice Age from 1400-1800 A.D. This change brought strong trade winds and more storms and could have made long-distance voyaging more hazardous. Finney (1977:1284) also proposes that such voyages might have ended as the Polynesians desired to concentrate scarce personnel and resources on local development.

In conclusion, infrequent two-way contact between distant areas of Polynesia may at one time have occurred. In spite of the objections of Andrew Sharp, studies by Lewis (1972) and Finney (1977) indicate that the Polynesians had the skills to navigate and sail over such distances.

Thor Heyerdahl's theory of a major settlement of Polynesia from the Americas has been refuted, although there must have been some contact with that continent since the sweet potato, found in Polynesia, had its origins there.

The majority of linguistic and archaeological evidence shows that the Polynesians moved west to east through Melanesia, into Polynesia, spending long periods in Tonga and Samoa, eventually settling the Marquesas and Society Islands, and from there dispersing to the rest of Polynesia. The most recent research has been aided by the discovery of Lapita pottery and the material artifacts associated with it from which archaeologists have been able to reconstruct the movements of the Polynesians.

Surely, however, there can be no resolution as to how Polynesia was settled, for the answers are hidden in the mists of time. Our research can only indicate what we believe to be the settlement routes and we must be willing to accept new theories and added evidence that may indicate other alternatives.

RELATED ENTRIES: Austronesian Languages; Lapita Culture; Polynesian Culture (Ancient).

SOURCES AND READINGS: J. C. Beaglehole, *The Life of Captain James Cook* (Stanford: Stanford University Press, 1974); Peter Bellwood, *The Polynesians: Prehistory of an Island People* (London: Thames and Hudson, 1978); Peter Buck, *Vikings of the Sunrise* (Philadelphia: J. B. Lippincott Co., 1938); Barry Fells (as reported by G. Kraus), "New Evidence of Egyptian Presence in the Pacific," *New Diffusionist* 5, no. 18 (1975); Ben Finney, "Voyaging Canoes and the Settlement of Polynesia," *Science* 196, no. 4296

(1977); Thomas Gladwin, *East Is a Big Bird* (Cambridge: Harvard University Press, 1970); Roger Green, "Dating the Dispersal of the Oceanic Languages," *Oceanic Linguistics* 12 (1973) and "Lapita Pottery and the Origins of Polynesian Culture," *Journal of Australian Natural History* (1973); Thor Heyerdahl, *Aku-Aku, The Secret of Easter Island* (Chicago: Rand McNally and Co., 1958) and *American Indians in the Pacific: The Theory Behind the Kon-Tiki Expedition* (London: G. Allen & Unwin, 1952); Robert Langdon, *The Lost Caravel* (Sydney: Pacific Publications, 1975); M. Levison, R. G. Ward, and J. W. Webb, *The Settlement of Polynesia: A Computer Simulation* (Minneapolis: University of Minnesota Press, 1973); David Lewis, *We, The Navigators* (Honolulu: University of Hawaii Press, 1972); Andrew Sharp, *Ancient Voyagers in the Pacific* (Baltimore: Pelican Books, 1957) and *Ancient Voyagers in Polynesia* (Auckland: Paul's, 1963); Alexander Spoehr, "Time Perspective in Micronesia and Polynesia," *Southwestern Journal of Anthropology* 8, no. 4 (1952).   *Robert Graham*

POLYNESIAN CULTURAL CENTER. A nonprofit and educational institution, the Polynesian Cultural Center (PCC) is located in La'ie, Hawai'i. As the state's largest paid tourist attraction, the PCC draws more than one million visitors annually. The center is sponsored by the Church of Jesus Christ of Latter-day Saints (Mormon) and its main purpose is to perpetuate the music, dances, history, and arts and crafts of the island groups it represents (Fiji, Hawai'i, Marquesas, New Zealand, Samoa, Tahiti, and Tonga). In addition, it provides jobs and scholarships for students attending the adjoining Brigham Young University—Hawai'i Campus. More than 60 percent of the center's 1,200 employees are BYU—HC students. Construction of the center began in April 1962. More than one hundred labor missionaries volunteered their skills and energy to build the center. A year-and-a-half later, the center opened on 12 October 1963. In each of the center's seven villages are typical family dwellings and other buildings. Villagers demonstrate ancient practices such as tapa construction, poi production, coconut husking, songs, music, dances, and history. Tours and demonstrations take place continuously throughout the day. The evening show, "Invitation to Paradise," is staged in a 2,750-seat amphitheater. The center also has a curio shop, a large restaurant, and various snack areas. The center attributes its success to the knowledge, talent, and enthusiasm of its employees who come from all over the Pacific and who enable

visitors to fully experience the rich and vibrant cultures of Polynesia.

RELATED ENTRIES: Institute for Polynesian Studies; Mormons in the Pacific.   *Robert D. Craig*

POLYNESIAN CULTURE (ANCIENT). Classical Polynesian culture as observed by early European navigators was essentially derived from Lapita culture, a western Oceanic culture characterized by an advanced Neolithic tradition in social organization and complexity of material culture. Carried first to Tonga and Samoa about 1000 B.C. by sea-borne, Austronesian-speaking colonists, Lapita culture not only introduced into Polynesia the concept of social stratification, but also various arts and crafts, in addition to horticulture and deep-sea voyaging in remarkable double-hulled canoes.

Of the several arts practiced in early Tonga and Samoa, pottery making was perhaps the most intriguing as it did not extend beyond the two island groups. Decorated with a wide range of geometric designs, Lapita pottery took the form of finely shaped food bowls and containers. Both the puncture or dentate technique in decoration and the pottery designs, most likely, had their origins in western Oceanic tattoo.

Almost universal throughout Polynesia, tattoo symbolized courage and was invariably regarded as an art sacred to the gods. Consequently, it was highly ritualized and its practitioners generally were of hereditary priestly status. Marked by feasts, ceremonial dancing, and even on occasion by human sacrifice, tattooing was an art of intricate design. Its motifs included spirals, abstract birds and fish, and naturalistic plant forms. The finest tattoo was reserved for chiefs and proven warriors who often paid tattoo experts in decorative mats, tapa cloth, and carvings.

Among the nonceramic artifacts dating from early Tonga and Samoa, were untanged stone adzes and shell chisels, gauges, and scrapers. Of excellent craftsmanship in themselves, these tools were used in the creation of an art tradition that reached as far as Hawai'i and remote Easter Island. This art embraced sculpture in wood, bone, and even stone—the beautifully shaped adzes were used in tree felling and house and canoe construction.

An outstanding achievement aesthetically, Polynesian figure carving in wood and bone gave form to gods, tribal ancestors, and a highly imaginative range of supernatural beings. Regionally differing in style, carving varied from plain, naturalistic figures to images of considerable complexity in surface detail. The decoration of tribal assembly houses, war and fishing canoes, weapons, and domestic utensils with carving was also common throughout Polynesia. So too was the decoration with vegetable dyes of tapa cloth, floor mats, and basket work; the motifs normally were strictly geometric studies in imaginative design based on tattoo and naturalistic motifs such as the palm leaf. Usually, within the dispersed village communities of volcanic and atoll Polynesia, domestic architecture was simple in design; its materials ranged from thatch to adzed planks and roughly hewn posts. Only in such religious and communal architecture as assembly houses and *marae* (sacred enclosures) was there accomplished craftsmanship. The *marae* were religious centers characterized by stone-paved plazas, stepped-altar platforms, god houses, and often high, worked stone walls. The almost exclusive domain of priests, serving tribal ancestors and a complex hierarchy of gods and demons who dominated the life of classical Polynesian man, *marae* were centers of ceremonial ritual and the focal point in community life. Here tribal politics were debated and various seasonal festivals held. Here also, decisions were made relating to war, important tribal marriages, and the election of chiefs or the confirmation of chiefly status. And within these sacred compounds, men died: slaves, prisoners, criminals, sacrificed to gods equal in their ferocity to the warrior societies that created them.

Warfare was institutionalized in Polynesia. Its weaponry and ritual, its organization and leadership were of a high order. To die in battle was the ambition of all warriors. It was the ultimate sacrifice to tribal gods of war. To be a successful warrior often meant elevation to tribal leadership even to *ariki* (high chieftainship status). Warfare could arise out of overpopulation. However, there were many other less serious causes: simple revenge, suspicion of witchcraft, tribal insult, disputes over fishing and hunting grounds. Invariably, war commonly involved cannibalism and enslavement of defeated enemies.

Enslavement of war prisoners in Polynesia was closely connected with, for example, tribal economic systems. Slaves were automatically integrated into the horticultural labor force and employed in fishing and shellfish harvesting. As well as being domestic workers for chiefs and priests, slaves frequently accompanied their masters to the grave to serve them in the underworld.

Religion in Polynesia was a complicated system of beliefs, revolving around a multitude of gods and creation myths with religious practice being unique in its extent and imaginativeness. The gods included such cosmic deities as Tangaroa (in some island groups, creator of man); Rongo, whose domain was generally peace and horticulture; and Tane, god of fertility. Other minor gods, both tribal and domestic, included patron deities who were benefactors and, usually, governed man's everyday activities. Priests or *kahuna* (in Hawai'i) were the depositories of temple ritual, oral wisdom, and history. They were also well-versed in incantation and death-dealing magic, as well as being healers and communicants with both gods and the dead who existed in an underworld which essentially was much the same in character as the world they had lived in in life. Teachings differed on the afterlife, as they did on the nature and function of the gods. However, there was little variation in the structure of society for the living. Throughout Polynesia, society was generally clearly stratified: high chiefs (*ari'i* in Hawai'i) were the masters, supported in power by secondary chiefs, commoners, and slaves, with outstanding craftsmen, priests, and warriors of merit enjoying a status almost equal to chieftainship; a system common to several other island groups in the degree of its *inflexibility*. Much of the finest art of Polynesia was created for chiefs. So too, was much of the finer craftwork, that included in the Hawaiian Islands remarkable decorative feather cloaks and helmets; and in the Austral Islands, magnificently carved ritual drums and canoe paddles.

The games and pastimes of classical Polynesia expressed in their wide variety an aspect of character revealing a nature not wholly given up to violence and ambition. To take Hawai'i again, as an example, the people played a large number of games or *pa'ani kahiko* which numbered among them: the making of string figures (*hei*); checkers or *konane*; bowls (*'ulumaika*); javelin throwing or *pahe'e*; sledding (*holua*); and surfing (*he'e nalu*). All Polynesians were enthusiastic in the pursuit of entertainment. Dancing and singing to drums and flutes was an integral part of life. So too, was listening to storytellers who gave life to legend and reality to folktales in which ghosts, ogres, and mysterious fairy people rampaged through the imagination of captive audiences. In some island groups, kava stimulated both mind and spirit on festive occasions.

Horticulture was a science in many parts of Polynesia. For example, the cultivation of the sweet potato (*kumura*), yam, and taro was more than simple planting. It involved considerable knowledge of soils, fertilizers, seasons, and irrigation. Also, horticulture involved (in some areas) a great deal of planned and coordinated labor in draining and terracing cultivations under the supervision of priestly experts who possessed knowledge not only of the science of horticulture but of its religious rituals during planting and harvesting.

Polynesian navigational skill was excellent within the framework of known horizons. Trading was fairly common throughout the volcanic islands and atolls of both the western and eastern groups as were war expeditions. Ranging the seas in double-hulled canoes, masterfully designed and constructed, priestly navigators carried cargos and migrants to islands discovered (more often than not) by accident by explorers of courage and perseverance; the canoes usually had large crews, the "Vikings of the Pacific."

Women played a subservient role to men in classical Polynesian society unless the women were of chiefly status, in which case they were often influential in tribal councils. From birth, men were conditioned to the role of superiority; while women, from nativity, were destined to serve them. Man was created by the gods, woman was formed of common clay. Political and religious power was the prerogative of men. Women possessed only procreative powers. She was also considered spiritually unclean and a part of her symbolized death. Yet, in truth, she *was* life, survival, and love; she was the symbol for earth, she took possession of men's souls, she was the spiritual goddess of the underworld.

In addition to horticultural resources, classical Polynesians exploited forest and sea. Vast numbers of birds were snared, speared, and netted, and around this economic enterprise arose a considerable body of lore combined with wide technical expertise. The implements of the hunters often were beautifully made and decorated. Fishermen, in lagoon and open sea, were experts who created a wide range of bone and shell hooks and different types of net. Fine canoemen, they too drew on a long tradition of lore and practical knowledge. Neolithic Polynesian culture was highly advanced at the time of the first European contact. It was also broad in scope and still in the process of development. It was a living, vital force of remarkable possibilities that were ultimately unrealized as a result of confrontation with an intrusive European culture dominated by a superior technology and a predisposition towards conquest and colonization.

RELATED ENTRIES: Lapita Culture; Polynesia, Settlement of.

SOURCES AND READINGS: Terrence Barrow, *Art and Life in Polynesia* (Wellington: A. H. and A. W. Reed, 1972); Peter Buck, *Arts and Crafts of Hawai'i* (Honolulu: Bernice P. Bishop Museum, 1957); R. C.

Suggs, *The Island Civilizations of Polynesia* (New York: Mentor, 1960).
Alan Taylor

POLYNESIAN STUDIES, INSTITUTE FOR. Located at the Brigham Young University—Hawai'i Campus, the Institute for Polynesian Studies was chartered in 1978 by action of the directors of the Polynesian Cultural Center and the Board of Education of the Church of Jesus Christ of Latter-day Saints. The institute is charged with assisting the Polynesian Cultural Center in meeting its objectives of presenting a quality program of traditional Polynesian culture on the grounds of the center and with expanding the scope and quality of Pacific-island scholarship. The institute is headed by a director who is assisted by an executive committee consisting of individuals appointed from the staff of the Polynesian Cultural Center, the Brigham Young University —Hawai'i Campus, the community, and the Bishop Museum in Honolulu. The institute publishes a semiannual journal, *Pacific Studies*, as well as other scholarly monographs, pamphlets, and books. The institute is also engaged in a program to document various aspect of island life and has produced a film, "Fiji: The Great Council of Chiefs," which was filmed on Lakeba in 1978. Other films are planned. The institute sponsors seminars, symposia, and special classes and lectures on the university campus or at the Polynesian Cultural Center.

RELATED ENTRIES: Brigham Young University— Hawai'i Campus; Mormons in the Pacific; Polynesian Cultural Center; Polynesian Culture (Ancient).
Jerry K. Loveland

POMARE FAMILY. The Pomares were a Tahitian royal family who ruled in the Society Islands and the Tuamotus from the time of the arrival of the first European navigators until 1880. Pomare I (ca. 1751-1803) held one of the highest social, religious, and political titles in all of eastern Polynesia. When the European powers landed on Tahiti, Pomare's position was strengthened by the navigators' gifts and firearms. The Christian missionaries, likewise, regarded him as "king" over all the Tahitian islands. Pomare's political position was threatened throughout his rule and incessant wars broke out between Pomare's forces and his rival chiefs on the island of Tahiti. He saw the arrival of the London Missionary Society missionaries in 1797, and he generally supported their work. At the peak of his power, he died in 1803. His son, Pomare II, assumed the position of his father and through the zealous work of the missionaries, he finally accepted Christianity. He was responsible for bringing about many reforms in Tahiti, and he established the first legal code in 1819. His excessive drinking caused his death in December of 1821. His one-year-old son, Pomare III, was crowned in regal fashion by the London missionaries who exercised great control over the family. The young child died in 1824, leaving as next heir his sister who took the title Pomare IV (1813-1877). Her reign was marked by drastic changes that came to Tahitian politics, culture, and social order. The attempt to land French Catholic missionaries in Tahiti in 1834 began a struggle between the English missionaries on the island and the French government. It was finally resolved when the French gained a protectorate over the islands in 1845. Little by little, Tahitian control of the government fell to the French. When the queen died in 1877, she left a position that exercised no great authority in the islands. Her son, Pomare V (1839-1891), saw the islands become an overseas French possession. He was persuaded by the French to cede Tahiti to them in 1880 for cancellation of his heavy debts and for a pension for the rest of his life. He retained his title as king, but it died with him in 1891. There are a few Tahitians today who still claim descent from this old family.

RELATED ENTRIES: Ari'i Ta'ima'i; French Polynesia; Marau, Joanna.

SOURCES AND READINGS: A. C. Eugène Caillot, *Histoire de la Polynésie Orientale* (Paris: Ernest Leroux, 1910); Patrick O'Reilly, *Tahitiens* (Paris: Musée de l'Homme, 1962). *Robert D. Craig*

POMARE LAW CODE. The first law code to be set down in writing in Oceania was the Pomare Code of 1819. In 1797 the first missionaries of the London Missionary Society (LMS) arrived in the Pacific. Their first destination for proselyting was Tahiti. It was only after sixteen years, however, that they received their first converts. In 1819 Pomare II, king of Tahiti, was converted; and on 13 May he promulgated a code of laws written primarily by the Reverend Henry Nott in collaboration with the other missionaries. Its nineteen points prohibited the usual Christian transgressions: murder, infanticide, theft, bigamy, adultery, false witness, divorce, not keeping the Sabbath day holy, and so on. The infractions of the law brought severe punishment usually in the form of hard labor for the king. The punishment for men disregarding the Sabbath, for example, was to construct one hundred yards of roadway and for women, to make a piece of tapa cloth sixty yards long. Commenting on these peculiar punishments, Chateaubriand, a French writer of the time, wrote

that if "such equal laws existed in France, we would have the most beautiful roads in Europe" (p. 53). Punishment for thievery was retribution fourfold: twice the value of the stolen article to the owner and twice to the king. On Ra'iatea, one of the laws imposed the death penalty for anyone found guilty of idolatry. Since Pomare's central government consisted of hardly a handful of retainers, the task of enforcing the new laws was assigned to the district chiefs and judges around the island. Copies of the law code were printed and distributed to the missions in the Pacific where it became the model on which the later law codes in Oceania were based.

RELATED ENTRIES: French Polynesia; Nott, Henry; Pomare Family.

SOURCES AND READINGS: Louis J. Bouge, "Première législation tahitienne. Le Code Pomare de 1819," *Journal de la Société des Océanistes* 8, no. 8 (1952): 5-26 (includes facsimile and translation into French); François August Chateaubriand, *Travels in America and Italy* (London: H. Colburn, 1828); Colin Newbury, "A Note on Missionary Codes of Law; With a List of Codes and Regulations of Eastern Polynesia," in John Davies, ed., *History of the Tahitian Mission* (Cambridge: At the University Press, 1961), pp. 365-76. *Robert D. Craig*

POMPALLIER, JEAN-BAPTISTE FRANÇOIS (1801-1871). One of the first Catholic missionaries to the Pacific, Pompallier was born 11 December 1801 in Lyons, France. Ordained a priest in 1829, seven years later Pompallier was appointed bishop to head a group of Marists (Society of Mary) to evangelize the western part of Oceania (including Micronesia, Melanesia, and Polynesia west of the Cook Islands). In 1836 the group left Le Havre, arrived in Tahiti in September 1837, and then landed missionaries on Wallis and Futuna islands. Despite Protestant opposition, Pompallier finally established his see in New Zealand. The isolated and abandoned life of the Marists was difficult and Father Chanel, one of the Marists, was killed on Futuna in 1841. Disagreement with his superior general over the affairs of the mission caused a division of Pompallier's vicariate although Pompallier had reported a large number of conversions. In 1846 Pompallier returned to Rome to plead his case, but his superiors decided instead to divide New Zealand into two dioceses (Wellington under Philip Viard and Auckland under Pompallier). Maori wars, inability to retain priests in the islands, and an economic depression during the 1860s prevented any further progress. Pompallier finally returned to Europe and resigned his see (1869). He died at Puteaux, near Paris, on 21 December 1871.

RELATED ENTRIES: Catholic Church in the Pacific; Chanel, Pierre.

SOURCES AND READINGS: Jean-Baptiste François, *Notice historique at statistique de la mission de la Nouvelle-Zélande* (Anvers: P. J. Van Aarsen, 1850); Lillian Keys, *The Life and Times of Bishop Pompallier* (Christchurch: Pegasus Press, 1957).

Robert D. Craig

POPPE, ALFRED (?-?). Poppe was the German acting consul and agent of the Hamburg based J. C. Godeffroy trading house in Samoa in the early 1870s. Poppe temporarily replaced Theodor Weber in these posts while the latter was in Germany on business. Poppe was less forceful and influential than his predecessor and maintained a relatively low profile during the Steinberger episode in Samoa. Poppe held private discussions with the American adventurer Steinberger that were a prelude to Steinberger's trip to Germany in 1874 to arrange an agreement with the Godeffroy company. According to this settlement Germany would support Steinberger's regime in exchange for close political and economic ties with Godeffroy interests. During the next two years Poppe did maintain strong links with Steinberger, thereby alienating the American and British consuls and ultimately bringing about Steinberger's downfall in 1876. But Steinberger failed to fulfill all of his committments to the Germans, especially a resolution of the volatile land claims issue, prompting Poppe to withhold credit from his government. Nevertheless, Poppe played no major role in either attempting to bring down or to save Steinberger. Soon thereafter Weber returned to Samoa to replace Poppe and resume his position as consul.

RELATED ENTRIES: German Colonial Empire; Steinberger, Albert; Weber, Theodor; Western Samoa.

SOURCES AND READINGS: R. P. Gilson, *Samoa 1830 to 1900* (Melbourne: Oxford University Press, 1970); Sylvia Masterman, *The Origins of International Rivalry in Samoa, 1845-1884* (London: G. Allen & Unwin, 1934).   *Ralph C. Canevali*

PORT MORESBY. The capital of Papua New Guinea, Port Moresby is situated on the southeastern coast, 9° 29′ south latitude and 147° 08′ east longitude. In 1980 the population stood at 122,761. While roads are steadily being extended along the coast, Port Moresby is cut off from main centers of population by the cordillera which extends along the length of the New Guinea mainland. A deep, landlocked harbor was discovered by Captain John Moresby in 1873, and the London Missionary Society mission established a station on its shores in the same year. It became the headquarters of British New Guinea soon after a protectorate was declared in 1884. Until 1942 the town was confined to the small peninsula at the mouth of the harbor; the expatriate population did not exceed four hundred and the resident indigenous population was negligible. Port Moresby became the capital of Papua and New Guinea when the territories were united under a single administration in 1945. The population then increased rapidly as a result of a large injection of Australian funds into the economy. There has been some development of secondary industry, but the presence of government headquarters still provides the city's economic base. At first immigrants were drawn from the Papuan coast but later they came from the highlands and elsewhere in New Guinea. Although expatriates formed only a quarter of the town population throughout the postwar period, until recently Port Moresby remained an Australian town in character. As Papua New Guineans take over jobs from expatriates, it is gradually assuming a more Melanesian character.

RELATED ENTRIES: British New Guinea; London Missionary Society; Papua New Guinea.

SOURCES AND READINGS: C. S. Belshaw, *The Great Village* (London: Routledge and Kegan Paul, 1957); Murray Groves, "Dancing in Poreporena," *Journal of the Royal Anthropological Institute* 84 (1954): 75-90; N. D. Oram, *Colonial Town to Melanesian City: Port Moresby 1884-1974* (Canberra: Australian National University Press, 1976); A. W. Rew, *Social Images and Process in Urban New Guinea* (New York: American Ethnological Society Monograph, 1975).   *Nigel Oram*

PORT RESOLUTION. A harbor in southeast Tanna, Port Resolution was named by James Cook after his flagship in August 1774. The port was a major refueling and watering site for whalers and sandalwood traders from 1820 to 1860 and later was frequently visited by Pacific labor recruiters. The British man-of-war *Curacoa* bombarded villages around the port in 1865 in retaliation for the rout of the missionary J. G. Paton. An earthquake in 1888 raised the floor of the port and ruined the harbor for all but small ships and yachts.

RELATED ENTRIES: Labor Trade; Tanna; Vanuatu (New Hebrides).   *Lamont C. Lindstrom*

POUVANA'A A OOPA, MARCEL (1895-1977). A political leader and ardent nationalist in French Polynesia, Pouvana'a A Oopa was born 10 May 1895 on Huahine (Society Islands). He served in the Pacific battalion of the French army during World War I. Between then and World War II he became the head of a Tahitian nationalist movement for which he was exiled back to his native island by the French government. In 1947 his followers founded the *Comité Pouvana'a*, later called the *Rassemblement Démocratique des Populations Tahitiennes* (RDPT) party. After two years of conflict with the French officials in Tahiti, he was elected in 1949 as deputy of French Oceania to the French Parliament. He was reelected in 1951 and 1956, while his party won a majority of seats in the local territorial assembly in 1953 and 1957. After a vigorous campaign in 1958 for independence from France, he gained only 36 percent of the votes. Pouvana'a and his followers were arrested on charges of attempting to burn down the city of Pape'ete. He served an eight-year prison term and fifteen years in exile until he was pardoned and amnesty granted. In 1971 he was elected to the French senate for a nine-year term, but by that time Pouvana'a was seventy-six and too old to become the active leader of the autonomous movement he once had been. He died on 10 January 1977.

RELATED ENTRIES: French Polynesia.

SOURCES AND READINGS: Patrick O'Reilly, *Tahitiens* (Paris: Musée de l'Homme, 1962); Robert Langdon, *Pacific Islands Monthly*, March 1977, pp. 68-69.
Robert D. Craig

POWELES, (SIR) GUY RICHARDSON (1905-). Poweles was appointed high commissioner of Western Samoa and prepared that state for political independence in 1962. Born 5 April 1905 in Otaki, New Zealand, Poweles was educated at Wellington University and was a lawyer and solicitor in Wellington from 1927 to 1940. He served in World War II as a brigadier-major and immediately after the war he entered political service as counselor at the New Zealand embassy in Washington, D.C. (1946-1948). Returning home, he was appointed high commissioner of Western Samoa with the United Nations charge to prepare the country for self-government. He deviated from the pattern of previous high commissioners by resisting New Zealand's habit of intervening in minor local matters and by insisting that Samoan department heads work out internal problems without relying continually on their counterparts in Wellington. He took an active part in major debates and discussions on Samoan affairs and helped guide the various factions of Samoan politicians to a mutual compromise. Gradually the position of high commissioner became less important as Samoans assumed more control over their affairs. As a result, Poweles relinquished his office in April 1960, assured that independence would be obtained smoothly and effectively. After his Samoan experience, he was appointed New Zealand high commissioner to India (1960-1962) and then ombudsman to the New Zealand government in 1962.

RELATED ENTRIES: Western Samoa.

SOURCES AND READINGS: James W. Davidson, *Samoa Mo Samoa: The Emergence of the Independent State of Western Samoa* (New York: Oxford University Press, 1967).
Robert D. Craig

PRATT, ADDISON (1802-1872). An early Mormon missionary in French Polynesia, Pratt served two missions there, from 1844 to 1847 and from 1850 to 1852. Pratt, who gained early nautical experience aboard American whaling ships in the 1820s, arrived at Tubuai Island in 1844 with three other Mormons. While the others traveled to Tahiti, he experienced immediate success with the conversions of a chief named Nabota, his wife Telii, and several Europeans. In July 1844 a Mormon branch (local group) was formed which soon numbered sixty members out of an estimated population of two hundred people. Pratt traveled to Tahiti in 1846 and later preached on Ana'a Island. On 24 September 1846, the first Mormon conference in Polynesia was held on Ana'a. Membership totalled 866. After organizing other branches, Pratt left Tahiti in 1847 to join his family in Utah. He encouraged missionary work in Oceania and raised sufficient interest to teach a Tahitian language class. In 1849 Pratt led a group of Mormons to California. He and a few missionaries sailed on to Tahiti. A second group, including his wife and four daughters, soon followed. During his absence, the Mormon mission in French Polynesia had declined. Discouraged by a revival of ancient religion coupled with increasing religious competition, Pratt left in 1852. He tried several times (in 1853 and 1856) to reestablish the mission but was unsuccessful. He died in Anaheim, California, on 14 October 1872.

RELATED ENTRIES: French Polynesia; Mormons in the Pacific.

SOURCES AND READINGS: George S. Ellsworth, *Zion in Paradise: Early Mormons in the South Pacific* (Logan: Utah State University Press, 1959); Patrick O'Reilly, *Tahitiens* (Paris: Musée de l'Homme, 1962).
Russell T. Clement

PRITCHARD, GEORGE (1796-1883). A missionary of the London Missionary Society and a British consul to Tahiti and Samoa, Pritchard was born 1 August 1796. In 1824 Pritchard sailed to Tahiti as an ordained missionary. By 1832 he had become the most influential counselor to Queen Pomare IV who appointed him British consul to Tahiti. When French Catholic missionaries attempted to land on Tahiti in 1836 Pritchard intervened and forced the queen to expel them. The French demanded retribution. Pritchard and the queen had to concede and the French left. He entered into a lengthy correspondence with the British government in London asking for their protection and for annexation. Between February and August 1842 he visited England in hopes of persuading the government to annex the islands. During his absence, the Tahitian chiefs agreed to a French protectorate. Returning to Tahiti in February 1843 and learning what had occurred while he had been gone, Pritchard again unsuccessfully attempted to undermine the French and to gain British control over the islands ("The Pritchard Affair"). He was finally arrested in 1844 and expelled from Tahiti by the French government. In 1845 the British government appointed him consul in Samoa. Even here he exercised more than consular authority. He dreamed of establishing a British colony complete with governor and a garrison of soldiers to protect the British subjects who would immigrate and develop the unoccupied land. His rival commercial interests and quarrels in the European community in Samoa frequently forced British naval commanders to arbitrate the matters. Finally in 1857 he resigned and returned to England as director of the London Missionary Society for Scotland and Ireland, a post he occupied until 1872. He died at Hove near Brighton on 6 May 1883.

RELATED ENTRIES: French Polynesia; London Missionary Society; Pomare Family; Western Samoa.

SOURCES AND READINGS: Léonce Jore, *George Pritchard, l'adversaire de la France à Tahiti, 1796-1883* (Paris: Société de l'histoire des colonies françaises, 1939); Patrick O'Reilly, *Tahitiens* (Paris: Musée de l'Homme, 1962); James Sibree, ed., *Register of the Missionaries of the London Missionary Society* (London: London Missionary Society, 1923).   *Robert D. Craig*

PRITCHARD, WILLIAM (1829-1909). Born in Tahiti, William Pritchard was the son of George Pritchard, the British consul in Tahiti and later in Samoa. In 1856 William succeeded his father as acting consul of Samoa and nine months later was appointed to the same position in Fiji. While fulfilling this responsibility, Pritchard became the first British consul to live in Fiji. At the time Pritchard assumed his duties, King Cakobau of Fiji was required to satisfy claims of $45,000 by the United States. Under conditions negotiated by Pritchard, Great Britain paid the claims in return for Fiji's agreement of cession of 200,000 acres of island lands, in fee simple, to England. However, the cession was never realized, largely because of political pressure from Wesleyan missionaries in Fiji who opposed the introduction of other churches which they feared would come about had the agreement been ratified by the English parliament. During Pritchard's administration he established a British form of law and a mercantile court for the adjustment of all disputes involving English subjects in Fiji. He also mediated conflicts between Wesleyans and Catholics, defused efforts by Tonga to take over Fiji, and used his leverage to keep Cakobau in power in spite of numerous internal attempts to dethrone him. Further, Pritchard was influential in aiding Fijian economics by encouraging sheep farms and sugar manufacturing. But the rejection of the cession in 1862 undermined his political base and led to his resignation in January 1863. That year Pritchard returned to England where he remained until his death in 1909.

RELATED ENTRIES: Fiji; Pritchard, George; Western Samoa.

SOURCES AND READINGS: William Pritchard, *Polynesian Reminiscences* (London: Chapman and Hall, 1866); Isobel Whippy, *Pritchard: A Play* (Honolulu: Pacific Manuscript Bureau, 1971).   *Jeffrey Butler*

QUINN, WILLIAM F. (1919-). Appointed governor of Hawai'i (1957-1959), Quinn became the first elected governor of the new state of Hawai'i (1959-1962). Born 13 July 1919, a Harvard Law School graduate and a U.S. Naval officer, Quinn came to Hawai'i in 1947 to practice law. Much of his time as a private citizen was devoted to numerous civic and religious programs, serving as a member of the Executive Committee of the Bar Association, as a member of the Advisory Membership Committee, and as president of the Honolulu Community Chest. As governor, Quinn participated in the opening of the transpacific cable on the morning of 8 October 1957. In July 1959, a month after Hawai'i accepted statehood, Quinn was elected the first governor of the fiftieth state, thereby achieving the unique distinction of also being the last governor of the Territory of Hawai'i.

RELATED ENTRIES: Hawai'i.

SOURCES AND READINGS: A. Grove Day, *Hawaii and Its People* (New York: Meredith Press, 1968); Edward Joesting, *Hawaii* (New York: W. W. Norton & Co., 1972); Ralph S. Kuykendall and A. Grove Day, *Hawaii: A History* (Englewood Cliffs, N.J.: Prentice-Hall, 1961).   *Ned B. Williams*

QUIRÓS, PEDRO FERNÁNDEZ DE (ca. 1565-1615). Quirós was a Portuguese navigator, a native of Evora, who served the Spanish state in maritime enterprises in the Pacific. He held the post of chief pilot of Alvaro de Mendaña's ill-fated expedition of 1595 which discovered the Marquesas and the island of Santa Cruz (in the Santa Cruz group). The attempt to establish a settlement on Santa Cruz by Mendaña failed miserably, and after his death in October 1595 Quirós had the responsibility of bringing the disheartened and starving survivors of that expedition to Manila.

Despite the formidable obstacles which confronted him, Quirós successfully completed this arduous task, returned to Acapulco, and went from there to Peru. A keen student of both the art of navigation and of cartography, Quirós hoped to discover the great southern continent (*Terra Australis Incognita*) which some believed might extend from the Strait of Magellan to New Guinea. Quirós unsuccessfully attempted to interest the viceroy of Peru (Don Luis de Velasco) in subsidizing an expedition to discover this continent, but Velasco referred Quirós to the Spanish Court in Madrid for assistance.

Quirós returned to Spain and from there went to Rome as a pilgrim on the occasion of the Jubilee Holy Year of 1600. He was a man of deep religious convictions. Through the assistance of the Duke of Sesa, Spanish ambassador to the Holy See, Quirós had an audience with Pope Clement VIII. Both the pope and the Duke of Sesa supported the project of Quirós to continue his Pacific exploration and to bring about the conversion of the people he might find in that area. Provided with letters of recommendation from the pontiff and the Spanish ambassador, Quirós returned to Madrid, and these letters moved King Philip III to act favorably. Eventually a royal order to the viceroy in Peru commanded that Quirós be provided with ships to continue his Pacific exploration.

In the summer of 1603 Quirós sailed for Peru, but a shipwreck in the Caribbean delayed him so that he did not arrive in Lima until March 1605. After additional delays and some opposition, Quirós finally sailed from Callao on 21 December 1605 in command of an expedition of three vessels, with a complement of nearly three hundred soldiers and sailors, six Franciscan friars, and four nursing brothers of the Order of John of God. During the course of the next few months various islands were visited, principally in the Tuamotu Archipelago, the Duff and Bank groups, and the New Hebrides. In May 1606 the vessels arrived at one of the islands of the New Hebrides group and anchored in a large bay which Quirós named Saint Philip and Saint James. Believing that the land he saw before him was the tip of the southern continent he had been seeking, Quirós called the area *La Austrialia del Espíritu Santo* (The South Land of the Holy Spirit). Quirós remained on this island for thirty-six days, although on two occasions he did attempt to leave in order to continue his exploration, The strong southeast trade winds thwarted these plans, and the ship which carried Quirós finally became separated from the other two vessels. Driven out to sea by strong winds and a swift current, Quirós decided to sail back to America and abandon further exploration efforts. The long return journey finally ended at Acapulco on 23 November 1606.

Lacking financial resources at this time, Quirós benefitted from the generosity of a sea captain who provided him with a passage to the Spanish port of Cadiz. On 9 October 1607 Quirós arrived in Madrid where he received a mixed reception from court officials. Not until September 1614 did Quirós obtain authorization to return to Peru in the company of the newly appointed viceroy, Francisco de Borja. Accordingly, Quirós sailed for the New World from San Lúcar in April 1615. He did not live, however, to carry out his great dream of discovering a southern continent and of proselyting for Christianity, for he died a few months later in Panama.

RELATED ENTRIES: Mendaña de Neira, Álvaro de; Spain in the Pacific.

SOURCES AND READINGS: John C. Beaglehole, *The Exploration of the Pacific*, 3d ed. (London: A. & C. Black, 1966); Celsus Kelley, ed. and trans., *The Voyage of Pedro Fernández de Quirós, 1595 to 1606*, 2 vols. (London: Printed for the Hakluyt Society, 1904).
                                                    Bernerd C. Weber

R

RAPANUI. *See* Easter Island.

RAYS, (MARQUIS) CHARLES DE (1832-1893). A land speculator and a romantic, Rays was born at Quimerc'h in Finistère, France, and baptized Charles-Marie Bonaventure de Breil. Rays, who inherited his father's title in 1838, possessed an inordinate taste for the grandiose. The sad state of France after the Franco-Prussian War of 1870 and the journals of various navigators stirred his imagination and led him to attempt to restore the ancient glory of France by establishing a personal empire in the Pacific. In 1877 he declared himself "King Charles of New France," an area that extended from eastern New Guinea to the Solomon Islands. He then organized a colonizing expedition to what he called the "Free Colony of Port Breton" at Port Praslin in southern New Ireland. Governments denounced his scheme but the promise of a new life appealed to many people who had little to hope for in Europe.

In 1880 and 1881 he sent four ships to Port Breton with about 570 colonists, mostly French, German, and Italian. Supplies were inadequate, malaria was rife, and the death rate high. Most of the colonists soon fled to Australia, New Caledonia, and the Philippines. Rays, who did not join his subjects, was sentenced by a French court in 1882 to six years imprisonment for criminal negligence.

"New France" contributed to the Australian sensitivity to the danger of a threat from the north which led to the declaration of the British New Guinea protectorate in 1884. It also brought the Catholic church back to New Guinea. Two chaplains had accompanied the settlers; in 1881 the missionaries of the Sacred Heart took over the vicariate of Melanesia. One of the few to benefit from the colony was the pioneer, Rabaul-based trader and planter, "Queen" Emma Coe. With her partner, Thomas Farrell, she obtained much iron ware, building material, and even a steamship from it at little cost. Today a mill-stone brought by the expedition stands in Rabaul as a memorial to "New France."

RELATED ENTRIES: France in the Pacific; Nouvelle France; Papua New Guinea.

SOURCES AND READINGS: P. Biskup, ed., *The New Guinea Memoirs of Jean Baptiste Octave Mouton* (Canberra: Australian National University Press, 1974); Eugénie and Hugh Laracy, *The Italians in New Zealand and other Studies* (Auckland: Società Dante Alighieri, 1973); J. H. Niau, *The Phantom Paradise* (Sydney: Angus and Robertson, 1936); R. W. Robson, *Queen Emma* (Sydney: Pacific Publications, 1965).   *Eugénie and Hugh Laracy*

REGIONALISM. The concept *regionalism* has been defined in various ways at different times in order to satisfy the requirements of a specific usage or to emphasize a particular attribute. In the South Pacific, regionalism has tended to revolve around three basic interpretations. Perhaps the most general usage centers on intergroup identification: defining regionalism as the sentiment of belonging which leads groups of neighboring nations to perceive a sense of commonality. In political terms, regionalism denotes the attempt to coordinate government policy across national boundaries. Regionalism, in the context of international affairs, refers to the instruments of transnational cooperation (governmental and nongovernmental), especially the formal organizations and associations of this cooperation.

Despite a contemporary myth of a universal pan-Pacificism prior to the advent of European colonialism, there is little evidence of extended geographical knowledge among precontact Pacific islanders. This is not to say that no sentiment of commonality existed before European contact, but rather that it was limited in scope and modest in intensity. The vagaries of the colonial dismemberment no doubt did have a detrimental effect on indigenous attitudes towards intergroup identification, but in terms of the modern phenomenon this influence must be considered marginal.

The first genuine attempt to coordinate government policies across political boundaries occurred in the late nineteenth century with the establishment of the Western Pacific High Commission. This institution sought primarily to achieve the administrative aspirations of the British Colonial Office, but it also created an environment in which other, more localized, forms of cooperation could develop. During the years between the two world wars, regionalism became a political issue with several proposals being offered to confederate or federate the Pacific islands, usually around the nucleus of the Western Pacific High Commission. Often these proposals were little more than thinly disguised attempts to entrench the control of resident Europeans. While nothing came of these efforts at political integration, this era witnessed the strengthening of nongovernmental ties among the islands. Two especially important influences were the establishment of the Central Medical School in Suva, Fiji (1928), and the appearance of a regional planters' journal, the *Pacific Islands Monthly* (1931).

The slow but steady growth of interterritorial linkages before World War II encouraged the development of a regional consciousness among island elites, but no vehicle for a political expression of this sentiment existed until 1947. The formation of the South Pacific Commission (SPC) under the Canberra Agreement finally drew all the threads of regionalism together, albeit with some inherent weaknesses. For the first time, an organization for the coordination of substantive policy united the entire breadth of the South Pacific. Its powers were solely advisory, however, and they were limited to nonpolitical technical matters such as health and social development. Nonetheless, by establishing a triennial auxilliary assembly for Pacific islanders, the SPC provided the means for a direct input by islanders into the regional process.

The pressure for decolonization during the 1960s greatly expanded the opportunities for regional relationships in the South Pacific. Among the more important of these were the South Pacific Games (the first games were held in Suva in 1963), the Pacific Islands Producers Association (1965-1974), the University of the South Pacific (opened in 1968), and the South Pacific Arts Festival (the first festival was staged in Suva in 1972). Although the SPC played an important role in the development of most of these organizations, its failure to keep pace with the movement towards decolonization within the region led to increasing criticism of the regional body. Reform to allow greater indigenous participation and control came too slowly and incompletely for leaders such as Fiji's then chief minister Ratu Kamisese Mara. When the 1970 review of the SPC decided against a political role for the SPC, the independent states were forced into other avenues to achieve their regional aspirations.

The establishment of the South Pacific Forum in Wellington, New Zealand, in August 1971 gave the independent and autonomous island states the political outlet which they sought initially through reformation of the SPC. However, it denied them the geographic completeness which the SPC retained. Much of the controversy surrounding regionalism in the 1970s can be traced to this distinction between the two regional bodies. While the forum felt some frustration at its restricted membership, it did achieve a number of noteworthy breakthroughs in regional cooperation. Perhaps the most significant ramifications from the forum to date have been the establishment of the South Pacific Bureau for Economic Cooperation (now the forum's secretariat under the acronym SPEC), the Forum Shipping Line, and the South Pacific Regional Fisheries Agency.

Although the course of regionalism in the South Pacific has been very uneven in recent years, the basic rationale for regional cooperation continues to attract support from island elites. There appear to be few alternatives to some form of regionalism if the virtually ubiquitous problems of small populations, limited resources, and widely scattered islands are to be surmounted. Economies of scale are not guaranteed through regional cooperation, but such economies are impossible for microstates of the South Pacific individually.

RELATED ENTRIES: Fiji, Federal Movement in; Island Confederation Movement; South Pacific Commission; South Pacific Forum; Western Pacific High Commission.   *Richard Herr*

RICHARDS, WILLIAM (1793-1847). An American Board of Commissioners for Foreign Missions (ABCFM) Pacific missionary and later a political leader in Hawai'i, Richards was born 22 August 1793 in Plainfield, Massachusetts. As an ordained minister, he set sail from New Haven, Connecticut, 19 November 1822, on the ship *Thames* and arrived in Honolulu on 27 April 1823. In 1838 he resigned his missionary post to enter the employ of King Kamehameha III as a chief adviser. As the king and his ministers formulated laws for the state, Richards was given the responsibility of being their adviser and interpreter. Because of American, English, and French intervention in the islands, he was sent to England to obtain British recognition of the independence of the Hawaiian kingdom. On 1 April 1843 Richards received an official statement that the British government was willing to recognize the independence of the Hawaiian Islands. After an absence of nearly three years, he returned to Honolulu and was appointed to the board of the land commission to handle land claims for the Hawaiians. Two months later (1846) Richards became Minister of Public Instruction and was charged with establishing an educational system in Hawai'i. He died in Honolulu on 7 November 1847, revered and respected by the Hawaiian people.

RELATED ENTRIES: Armstrong, Richard; Hawai'i; Kamehameha III.

SOURCES AND READINGS: Edward Joesting, *Hawaii, an Uncommon History* (New York: W. W. Norton and Co., 1972); Ralph S. Kuykendall, *The Hawaiian Kingdom, 1778-1854* (Honolulu: University of Hawaii Press, 1938); Hawaiian Mission Children's Society, *Missionary Album* (Honolulu: Hawaiian Mission Children's Society, 1937).   *Brenna J. Rash*

ROBARTS, EDWARD (ca. 1771-1832). Robarts, a beachcomber in the Marquesas, deserted from the whaler *Euphrates* at Tahuata in 1798. He soon moved to Nukuhiva where he lived with the chief, Keattonnue, in Taiohae valley. He was the self-appointed mediator between vessels calling for refreshment and the Marquesans, and assisted the Russian explorers Adam Johann Krusenstern and Yuri Lisiansky in 1804 in their circumnavigation of the globe (1803-1806). He left on the *Lucy*, commanded by Captain Ferguson, in 1806 because of divided local loyalties at a time of impending civil war. He lived mainly in India in poverty and obscurity until his death. His autobiography is the principal source for Marquesan history at the time of early Western contact.

RELATED ENTRIES: Beachcombers; Krusenstern, Adam Johann von; Marquesas Islands.

SOURCES AND READINGS: Greg Dening, ed., *The Marquesan Journal of Edward Robarts* (Canberra: Australian National University Press, 1974).

Ian C. Campbell

ROGGEVEEN, JACOB (1659-1729). A Dutch lawyer, explorer, and navigator, Roggeveen was a native of Middelburg in the Dutch province of Zeeland. He received academic training in law and in 1693 became a notary in Middelburg. In 1706 he left his native land to go to the Dutch East Indies where he had an appointment to the Council of Justice in Batavia, Java. After a successful but relatively brief career in the Far East, he returned to the Netherlands, arriving there early in 1715. At the age of sixty-two Jacob Roggeveen sought and obtained permission to arrange an expedition to the Pacific Ocean for the Dutch West India Company, thereby reviving a project which his scholarly father Arend Roggeveen (d. 1679) unsuccessfully had sought to undertake many years before. The expedition had as its purpose a search for a southern continent, supposedly located between South America and Australia.

In August 1721 Jacob Roggeveen left the Netherlands with three vessels, the *Eagle*, the *Thienhoven*, and the *African Galley*. After rounding the southernmost end of South America, the vessels entered the Pacific and stopped at Más á Tierra (February 1722), the main island of the Juan Fernández group. Then proceeding in a northwestward direction, Roggeveen "discovered" on Easter Sunday in the area of eastern Polynesia a small inhabited island which he appropriately named Easter Island. As Roggeveen noted in his journal he found the area dotted with "high erected stone images" which the islanders appeared to worship. After departing from Easter Island, the search for the southern continent continued, but without success. In May 1722 among the islands and islets of what is now known as the Tuamotu Archipelago, Roggeveen lost one of his vessels (the *African Galley*), wrecked on a coral atoll. In further exploratory efforts, islands were discovered in the north of the western sector of what is now designated as the Society Islands and in the eastern Samoa group. Early in October 1722, the two vessels of the original expedition arrived at Batavia. Officials of the Dutch East India Company confiscated the ships and eventually sent the personnel back to the Netherlands where they arrived in July 1723. A long series of negotiations ensued between the Dutch West India Company and the Dutch East India Company as a result of these incidents. Meanwhile, Roggeveen went to live again in Middelburg where he died in 1729.

RELATED ENTRIES: Easter Island.

SOURCES AND READINGS: F. E. Mulert, ed., *De reis van Mr. Jacob Roggeveen* (The Hague: M. Nijhoff, 1911); Andrew Sharp, ed., *The Journal of Jacob Roggeveen* (Oxford: Clarendon Press, 1970).

Bernerd C. Weber

ROHEIM, GEZA (1891-1953). A psychoanalytic anthropologist, Roheim was born in Budapest. After studying geography and anthropology in German universities, he took his Ph.D. at the University of Budapest and was later psychoanalyzed by Sandor Ferenczi. Roheim was a prolific writer. He published fifteen books and scores of articles and reviews every year from 1911 to 1951, with the single but significant exception of 1931. This surprising lacuna denoted a momentous change in his theoretical ideas. It was the year following the impact of fieldwork in Bwaruada, Sipupu, and Boasitoraba on Normanby Island, Papua New Guinea, where he was greatly assisted by M'a'a Baloiloi. He abandoned the theory of primal parricide, then a doctrinal requirement of Freudian psychoanalytic theory, in favor of explanations of behavior in terms of stages of individual development, reminiscent of Shakespeare's "Seven Ages of Man." He also replaced the theory of racial unconscious or memory traces with the theory of the persistence of juvenile physical and psychological characteristics into adult life. Roheim left an enormous amount of valuable data relevant to Papua New Guinea and also to the world at large. The work of Erik Erikson, a leading figure in the field of human development, owes much to Roheim who was not appreciated during his lifetime. The once prevailing view, environmentalism, referred to the belief that the environment almost exclusively determined the development of human behavioral patterns. Now that the current values surrounding excessive forms of this doctrine show early erosion with the advent of modern psychosomatic medicine and sociobiology, Roheim's work might well be coming into its own. He died in New York.

RELATED ENTRIES: Papua New Guinea.

SOURCES AND READINGS: Erik Erikson, *Childhood and Society* (New York: W. W. Norton & Co., 1950); W. B. Wilbur and W. Muensterburger, *Psychoanalysis and Culture* (New York: International Universities Press, 1951).   *Burton G. Burton-Bradley*

ROPITEAU, ANDRÉ (1904-1940). A Pacific savant, scholar, and friend to Pacific islanders, Ropiteau was from a well-to-do family in Bourguignon (France). He first came to the Pacific and Tahiti in 1928. He returned frequently between the years 1930-1938 where he established a residence on the island of Maupiti in the Leeward Society Islands. Ropiteau was eager to seek out documents, books, and manuscripts concerning the history of the islands. After his death, his great collection became the basis for the monumental reference work *Bibliographie de Tahiti* by Patrick O'Reilly (Paris: Musée de l'Homme, 1967, 1046 pages). His frequent articles on mythology, Tahitian life, and Pierre Loti appeared in scholarly journals throughout the Pacific and France. He served in the 227th French Infantry Regiment in World War II and was killed on 20 June 1940 just two days before the armistice was signed between France and Germany.

RELATED ENTRIES: French Polynesia; Loti, Pierre.

SOURCES AND READINGS: Patrick O'Reilly, *Portrait d'André Ropiteau, 1904-40* (Dijon: Darantière, 1940).   *Robert D. Craig*

ROTUMA. A volcanic island of approximately 44 km² (17 mi²), Rotuma is located at 12° south latitude and 177° east longitude on the western fringe of Polynesia. Physically, Rotumans show traces of Micronesian, Polynesian, and Melanesian influence. A Caucasian influence was also introduced by visiting European sailors early in the nineteenth century. The Rotuman language has some unique features that distinguish it from others in the region, but it also shows evidence of extensive borrowing from Polynesia. Rotuman legends suggest strong Samoan and Tongan influences, which may account for the Polynesian character of Rotuman culture.

The island was discovered by Captain Edwards in H.M.S. *Pandora* during 1791 while searching for the *Bounty* mutineers. Contact intensified rapidly in the early nineteenth century with whalers and labor recruiters making frequent stops. Wesleyan and Catholic missionaries established themselves soon after mid-century, resulting in a factionalism following traditional political divisions. Antagonisms continued to mount until 1878 when the Catholics were defeated in a skirmish by the numerically superior Wesleyans.

The unrest following this religious conflict induced the paramount chiefs of Rotuma's seven districts to petition England for annexation; in 1881 the island was officially ceded to Great Britain. It was decided that Rotuma be administered as part of Fiji which, being 480 km (300 mi) to the south, was the nearest Crown colony. A resident commissioner was appointed to govern it with the seven paramount chiefs forming an advisory council. Economically, copra became the main source of income.

As a result of contact with Europeans, the Rotuman population declined from an estimated 5,000 at the time of discovery, to less than 2,000 following a measles epidemic in 1911. Since then it has risen steadily, primarily as a result of improved public health and medical conditions. The Fiji census of 1976 recorded 7,389 Rotumans, with 2,805 residing on Rotuma. The majority now live in urban centers in Fiji, where they had made a remarkably successful adaptation. Rotumans are well represented in the professions and other high-status positions, with many attaining senior positions in the government bureaucracy. The relationship between Rotuma and Rotuman enclaves in Fiji is maintained by considerable mobility back and forth, as well as letters, remittances, and other forms of exchange.

For much of the time following cession, physicians were appointed as resident commissioners and later, following an administrative reorganization, as district officers. The first Rotuman, Josefo Rigamoto, was appointed district officer in 1945. Political and economic ties with Fiji have become increasingly strong, until currently Rotuma is inextricably part of the recently founded Republic of Fiji. Rotuma is represented in the upper house of the Fiji legislature by a senator, but its representation in the lower house is as part of a larger regional division. Rotumans today are thus in the position of a minority ethnic group within Fiji's pluralistic society.

RELATED ENTRIES: Fiji.

SOURCES AND READINGS: William Eason, *A Short History of Rotuma* (Suva: Government Printer, 1951); J. Stanley Gardiner, "Natives of Rotuma," *Journal of the Royal Anthropological Institute* 27 (1898): 396-435, 457-524; Alan Howard, *Learning to be Rotuman* (New York: Columbia Teachers College Press, 1970); Chris Plant, ed., *Rotuma: Split Island* (Suva: South Pacific Social Sciences Association and the Institute of Pacific Studies, 1977).

Alan Howard

ROUTLEDGE, KATHERINE PEASE (1866-1935). Katherine Routledge was born in Darlington, Australia, and received her higher education in Oxford and Dublin. In 1906 she traveled through South Africa and Rhodesia to research the conclusion of the Boer War for the South Africa Colonization Society and Guild of Local Women. In the same year, she married anthropologist Scoresby Routledge. In 1914 she undertook the first archaeological expedition to Easter Island on her yacht, the *Mana*. During seventeen months on Easter Island, she interviewed the older islanders who remembered the legends passed down through generations. The 1914 Routledge expedition succeeded in making a detailed study of the large Easter Island statues, petroglyphs, and ancient scripts and tablets. A detailed genealogy from the gods to modern Easter Island was also published as a result of this expedition. From 1921 to 1923 she led an expedition to French Polynesia. Besides the *Mystery of Easter Island*, she wrote several other articles. She planned to write a large, scientific volume on Easter Island but died before it was completed.

RELATED ENTRIES: Easter Island.

SOURCES AND READINGS: Katherine Routledge, *The Mystery of Easter Island: The Story of An Expedition* (London: Sifton, Prael and Co., 1919).

David Welch

RUGE & COMPANY, H. M. Ruge and Company was an important and ill-fated trading firm in Fiji, Samoa, Tonga, and Wallis and Futuna islands in the 1870s and 1880s.

In the early 1870s Heinrich Martin Ruge arrived in Fiji and bought into the firm of F. C. Hedemann and Co., agents of the Hamburg shipping company of Wachsmutt and Krogmann. He had previously conducted a large mercantile enterprise in South America, based at Valparaiso. In 1874 the partnership expanded into Samoa. Hedemann remained in Fiji and Ruge went to Apia and set himself up in direct opposition to J. C. Godeffroy und Sohn, another Hamburg shipping company whose Pacific branch controlled the largest trading and plantation network in Oceania.

After Godeffroys, Hedemann-Ruge was the most extensive trading company operating in Samoa. Between them, these two firms exercised a dominating influence over the commerce of Samoa and Tonga. By 1879 they had cornered 87 percent of the export trade from these two groups and 79 percent of imports passed through their hands. Ruge's tactics emulated those of his larger rival. As the representative of an extraterritorial company, he too could call on heavy overseas capital backing to underwrite his expansion. The Ruge company also imported large quantities of debased South American currency, the use of which disadvantaged their competitors since it lost much of its face value on export. Ruge also involved himself in local politics for the sake of his business interests and was at one with the Godeffroy management in calling for the German annexation of Samoa. Lastly, Ruge established an interisland trading network along the same lines as Godeffroys'. These two companies keenly contested the lucrative Tongan copra trade, the area in which Ruge was most actively involved. His ships also plied nearby island groups, such as Wallis and Futuna islands. A lesser interest was the copra trade of the island groups to the northwest of Samoa.

For the next decade the two German firms maintained their dominant position in Samoa and Tonga. In 1879-1880 Godeffroys exported 5,000 tons of copra to Ruge's 2,400 tons; by 1884-1885 these figures had risen to 7,050 tons and 3,200 tons respectively. The extent of German interests exceeded those of all other nationalities combined. In 1880, for example, the value of German exports from Apia reached £44,000 as against a figure of £8,000 for other nationalities.

Nevertheless, Hedemann-Ruge's Apia establishment did not survive the difficult years of the 1880s when the European market price for copra spiralled ever downwards. A combination of personal extravagance and poor management compounded Ruge's difficulties. He was a man of considerable personal charm who entertained generously and who sought creature comforts for himself. His first concern upon arriving in Apia was the construction of a handsome and costly residence with a wide pathway leading up from the harbor. He was also absent in Europe for eighteen months from December 1877, instead of taking care of his affairs in Apia. Neglect of this sort played a part in the financial troubles within the partnership of Hedemann, Ruge and Company, resulting in the formation of a separate firm in Apia called H. M. Ruge and Co. Subsequent financial difficulties also led Ruge to sell off some of his Tongan interests —the backbone of his enterprises—to one of his competitors, Wm. and A. McArthur and Co.

Against this background of contradiction, Ruge sought to repair his fortunes. He did so not only when world copra prices were falling but when the buying price of copra from the indigenous producer was rising as a result of increasing competition among trading companies. Ruge and Company struggled on until finally forced to close down following the withdrawal of a large shareholder in Hamburg in 1888. Martin Ruge did not long survive the collapse of his company; he died two years later.

RELATED ENTRIES: German Colonial Empire; Tonga; Wallis and Futuna; Western Samoa.

SOURCES AND READINGS: Stewart Firth, "German Firms in the Western Pacific Islands, 1857-1914," *Journal of Pacific History* 8 (1973):10-28; Kurt Schmack, *J. C. Godeffroy & Sohn, Kaufleute zu Hamburg: Leistung und Schicksal eines Welthandelshauses* (Hamburg: Broscher and Co., 1938); Reingold Segebrecht, "Aus den Tagebuchern von Kapitan Nils Simson Michelsen," *Hamburger Wirtschafts-Chronik* 1 (1956): 285-322; Thomas Trood,

Island Reminiscences: A Graphic Detailed Romance of Life Spent in the South Sea Islands (Sydney: McCarron, Stewart & Co., 1912).   *Doug Munro*

RYUKYU ISLANDS. More than a hundred in number, the Ryukyu Islands (*Nansei-Shoto* or Luchu Islands) stretch from Japan to Taiwan between the East China Sea and the Pacific, 26° 30′ north latitude and 128° 00′ east longitude, and properly belong historically and culturally to the Orient rather than to Oceania. The land area amounts to 3,120 km² (1,205 mi²) and supports a population of more than 1.15 million. The temperature averages 21° C (70° F), and the rainfall annually averages 135 to 305 cm (53 to 120 in). Typhoons are not uncommon. These islands may have been inhabited since the Ice Age by wandering tribes from China, Japan, the Philippines, and Taiwan. Certainly both Chinese and Japanese explorers had visited the islands by the seventh century A.D.; and by the fourteenth and fifteenth centuries, Okinawa, the most important of these islands, was part of the trading network that linked China, Japan, Korea, and southeast Asia. In 1874 China relinquished its claims to the islands; and in 1879 Japan annexed them as a prefecture. After World War II (1941-1945), during which there was heavy fighting in the islands, the United States administered the Ryukyus north of Okinawa until 1953 and the remainder until 1972 when sovereignty was restored to Japan.

RELATED ENTRY: Okinawa.   *Frank P. King*

SAAVEDRA CERÓN, ALVARO DE (d. 1529).

A Spanish navigator and explorer, Saavedra has the distinction of being the first European navigator to sail across the Pacific from the North American coast to the East Indies. Hernándo Cortés, the conqueror of the Aztec empire, received an order from the emperor Charles V to send forth an expedition to discover the fate of the *Trinidad*, one of the vessels in Magellan's voyage. Accordingly, three vessels, the *Florida*, the *Santiago*, and the *Espiritu Santo*, were made ready and placed under the command of the hidalgo Alvaro de Saavedra Cerón, a kinsman of Cortés. These vessels sailed from the little harbor of Zihuatanejo on the western coast of New Spain on 31 October 1527. Early in December a heavy squall separated the *Florida* (the flagship) from the other two vessels which were swept forward and not seen again by anyone on the flagship. Late in December the island now known as Guam was sighted, but the crew made no landing there. In February, the Philippines were reached and anchorage made off a small island near the north coast of Mindanao. While in the Philippines Saavedra rescued a few men who were survivors from the earlier voyage of Loaysa. From the Philippines Saavedra proceeded to the Moluccas, reaching the tiny island of Tidore by the end of March 1528. Subsequently Saavedra made two northern cruises in an effort to find a suitable return route to the western coast of North America, but his efforts failed. In the course of these expeditions Saavedra sailed along the coast of New Guinea, and he also discovered islands in the Marshall and Caroline groups as well as the Admiralty Islands off the north coast of eastern New Guinea. During the second expedition Saavedra died and was buried at sea. Survivors of his company eventually returned to Tidore (December 1529) and surrendered themselves to the Portuguese who kept them in detention for several years before finally sending them back to Spain.

RELATED ENTRIES: Spain in the Pacific.

SOURCES AND READINGS: Ione Stuessy Wright, "The First American Voyage Across the Pacific, 1527-1528: The Voyage of Alvaro de Saavedra Cerón," *Geographical Review* 24 (1939): 472-82; Ione Stuessy Wright, *Voyages of Alvaro de Saavedra Cerón, 1527-1529* (Coral Gables: University of Miami Press, 1951).
Bernerd C. Weber

ST. JULIAN, CHARLES JAMES HERBERT DE COURCY (1819-1874).

A journalist and propagandist of Pacific expansion, St. Julian was born on 10 May in either 1818 or 1819, probably in London. St. Julian appears to have deliberately obscured the details of his early life, but according to his own account, he left an apprenticeship as a wood and ivory turner to join an exploratory expedition up the Niger River in Africa, volunteered as a junior officer in the Circassian Mountains in support of Armenian rebels against Tsarist Russia, and then fought for the Queen of Spain in the Carlist Wars.

St. Julian arrived in Adelaide, South Australia, 15 May 1838, and during the 1840s worked as a journalist, editor, and finally newspaper proprietor. He also established a reputation in New South Wales as being an authority on the Pacific.

On 29 April 1848 St. Julian had begun a regular correspondence with R. C. Wyllie, Hawaiian minister of foreign relations. In 1853 he became King Kamehameha III's "Commissioner to the Independent States and Tribes of Polynesia." St. Julian gained Wyllie's tacit support for his scheme to encourage the development of island kingdoms modeled on the Hawaiian constitution, with the intention of ultimately forming a confederation of Polynesia under the patronage of the Kingdom of Hawai'i. With this in mind, he drafted a constitution for Samoa and corresponded on constitutional matters with King George of Tonga, thereby arousing the antagonism of the Wesleyan missionaries there. Although unsuccessful in his grand design, some of his proposals were later incorporated in the 1862 code of laws of Tonga.

St. Julian published extensively in New South Wales newspapers on Pacific matters. Many of his articles were later published in Sydney as books or pamphlets, including *Notes on the Latent Resources of Polynesia* (1851), *The Productions, Industry and Resources of New South Wales* (1853, with E. K. Silvester), and the *Official Report on Central Polynesia*, with a *Gazetteer* by Edward Reeve (1857), which republished his "Constitution for Upolu" (Samoa) and his correspondence with King George of Tonga.

St. Julian acted as consul general for Hawai'i in New South Wales and advised Governors Fitzroy and Denison on Pacific matters. His main concern was that a power vacuum in the Pacific, which to him was synonymous with Polynesia, would lead to an expansion of French influence. Ideally, in his view, Britain should fill that vacuum, but if, as seemed likely, the British government refused to act, then independent Polynesian governments under the nominal suzerainty of Hawai'i would perform a comparable stabilizing role. However, by the late 1850s, Wyllie's responses to St. Julian's initiatives had become desultory and St. Julian had become disillusioned with the Hawaiian association.

The Wesleyan missionaries successfully opposed St. Julian's application for the position of British consul at Tonga on the ostensible grounds of his Catholic faith, although his influence over King George clearly lay at the base of their resistance. However, a printed paper by St. Julian of "Suggestions as to the Policy of Her Britannic Majesty's Government with Reference to the Various Groups of Central, Western, and North-Western Polynesia," (May 1855) forwarded to the British government by the governor of New South Wales was acted on by the Foreign Office, particularly in relation to the establishment of new British consulships in the Pacific.

During the 1860s St. Julian's active interest in the Pacific waned, as he became more involved in municipal government and other issues of more local interest. However, he remained as Hawaiian consul general and appointed Robert Swanston as Hawaiian consul in Fiji.

In 1870 he sent an exploratory letter to the new Hawaiian minister of foreign relations, Charles Harris, suggesting that the unstable situation in Fiji might be resolved if Fiji were to become a protectorate of Hawai'i. In 1871 he made a similar suggestion to Lord Belmore, governor of New South Wales, but the suggestion was rejected by the Foreign Office. Hawai'i however, while giving St. Julian no special instructions, was prepared to support him to the extent of giving him £200 with which to visit Fiji as "His Hawaiian Majesty's Special Commissioner to the Fijis

and Chargé d'Affaires to the Independent Chiefs and Governments of the South Pacific." St. Julian arrived in Levuka on his first trip to Fiji—or indeed to any part of the Pacific—in August 1871.

The Hawaiian proposal met with no favor in Fiji, but on his return to Sydney St. Julian wrote the *International Status of Fiji* (1872) in which he argued in support of the recognition of the Cakobau government by the Great Powers. This pamphlet was widely circulated. As a result, the Cakobau government offered St. Julian the position of chief justice and chancellor of the Kingdom of Fiji. On his arrival there in May 1872, he posed as Sir Charles S. Julian, Knight of the Order of Kamehameha I, and subjected himself to criticism which tended to obscure his real talents as chief justice.

The Cakobau government was short-lived. Annexation was the aim of its European subjects, but the existence of a Fijian government allowed for a negotiated annexation rather than an unconditional transfer of sovereignty. St. Julian was involved in these negotiations and Sir Hercules Robinson, governor of New South Wales who accepted the annexation on 10 October 1874, recommended to the British government that St. Julian be given a pension, to be paid from the revenue of the colony. Unfortunately, he did not live to receive this compensation, for he died, possibly of dysentery, on 26 November 1874.

RELATED ENTRIES: Fiji; French Polynesia; Hawai'i; Kamehameha III; Samoa; Tonga.

SOURCES AND READINGS: Marion Nothling, "Charles St. Julian—Alternative Diplomacy in Polynesia" in Deryck Scarr, ed., *More Pacific Island Portraits* (Canberra: Australian National University Press, 1978); St. Julian-Wyllie Correspondence, Foreign Office and Executive Files, Hawai'i State Archives, Honolulu, Hawai'i.   *Marion Diamond*

SALMON, ALEXANDER (1820-1866). A landowner, wealthy merchant, and confident of Tahitian royalty, Salmon was born in London to a Jewish banking family. He left England for San Francisco and then went to Australia where he was named British consul to Tahiti. He arrived during the conflict between France and England over control of the islands (Pritchard Affair). He rapidly learned Tahitian and ingratiated himself with the royal court of Queen Pomare IV. He married the granddaughter of high chief Tati, the Princess Ari'i Ta'ima'i, and as a result inherited one of the richest districts on the island. Sensing England's loss of Tahiti, he quickly acknowledged French control, an act which economically benefited him in the end. He frequently acted as liaison between the French government and the queen, often acting as her secretary. His wealth came from the produce of his vast lands: coconuts, coffee, oranges, pigs, and, later, cotton and sugarcane. He was appointed vice-president of the tribunal of commerce and later became a member of the governor's administrative council. Of his ten children, his son Tati (1850-1918) inherited the title of chief of Papara while his daughter Marau married Teri'i Tari'ia, who became King Pomare V in 1877. During his life, Salmon converted to Protestantism. He died on his estates along Pape'ete harbor on 6 August 1866.

RELATED ENTRIES: Ari'i Ta'ima'i; French Polynesia; Marau, Joanna; Pomare Family; Tati.

SOURCES AND READINGS: Patrick O'Reilly, *Tahitiens* (Paris: Musée de l'Homme, 1962); Eric Ramsden, "Alexander Salmon, An English Jew who made History in Tahiti and his Family," *Australian Jewish Historical Society* 1 (1940): 57-71.   *Robert D. Craig*

SALOTE, (QUEEN) MAFILI'O PILOLEVU (1900-1965).

A daughter of Tongan king George (Siaosi) Tupou II and Queen Lavinia Veiongo, Salote was born 13 March 1900. She succeeded her father on 5 April 1918 and was crowned queen 11 October. Earlier in her life, she attended the Church of England Diocesan School for girls in Auckland. On 19 September 1917 at the age of seventeen, she married Prince William Tupoulahi Tungi and they had three sons: Tungi, Tuku'aho and Tu'ipelehake. Her reign saw many improvements come to Tonga. In 1919 a wireless station was established at Nuku'alofa. The exportation of bananas to New Zealand began in 1931. The first Tongan students to be sent abroad on scholarships went to Fiji and Australia in 1928 and 1929. In 1955 she set up the Tradition Committee with the object of recording customs and genealogy for posterity. In 1960 the first radio station was opened. Queen Salote was not only known and loved by the Tongan people but by others, including the monarchs of Great Britain. Queen Salote was awarded the Commander of the British Empire (CBE) in 1945 by King George VI, was made a Dame Commander of the Order of the British Empire (DBE) in 1952 by King George VI, and received a Knight Grand Cross of Royal Victorian Order (GCVO) in 1953 from Queen Elizabeth II. She also received the honor of Dame Grand Cross of the Order of Saint Michael and Saint George, the first woman in history to be so distinguished. Queen Salote died at Aotea hospital in Auckland on 16 December 1965. She was put to rest together with her ancestors in the Royal Burial Grounds Mala'ekula at Nuku'alofa.

RELATED ENTRIES: Tonga.

SOURCES AND READINGS: Kenneth Bain, *The Friendly Islanders* (London: Hodder and Stoughton, 1967); Noel Rutherford, ed., *The Friendly Islands: A History of Tonga* (Melbourne: Oxford University Press, 1977); A. H. Wood, *History and Geography of Tonga* (Victoria: Border Morning Mail, 1972).
Etta Harris

SAMOA. *See* American Samoa; Western Samoa.

SANDALWOOD TRADE.

Sandalwood has been in demand in China since the introduction of Buddhism. Most has been burnt as offerings in temples and at funerals, but some has gone into the production of inlaid boxes, perfume, and other products. Trees of the genus *Santalum*, from which the aromatic wood comes, are found scattered from India's Malabar Coast to Hawai'i and the Marquesas Islands, but they do not grow in China. The result has been the sandalwood trade, a commerce dating back at least to the sixth century A.D.

Timor, in the Lesser Sundas, early became the main source of supply. As merchants in Malacca put it, "God made Timor for sandalwood." By the thirteenth century, Chinese merchants were trading regularly in Java for sandalwood from Timor; but as nearby Malacca rose in power, they were squeezed out. Thereafter they went directly to Timor. Most of their purchases went to Canton, but occasional shipments found their way to Manila or Japan.

The Portuguese seized a large share of the trade beginning in the sixteenth century, but neither they nor the Dutch who supplanted them in the East Indies were able to drive the Chinese from the trade. Nor were the Dutch successful in eliminating the Portuguese from their toehold in the Lesser Sundas. The acquisition of Macao in 1557 made possible a direct commerce between Timor and the China coast that kept the Portuguese in the Orient long after the power they had enjoyed in the sixteenth century had faded.

While Chinese, Dutch, and Portuguese were carrying sandalwood from Timor to China, the British East India Company was transporting it there from India. From the late seventeenth through the early nineteenth century, it was a regular item of commerce for both East Indiamen and privately owned "country" ships operating under license from the company. Profits fluctuated wildly in the easily glutted markets of China: wood carried in 1795 earned but 3.4 percent profit, that taken five years later earned 72 percent. Amounts shipped varied almost as much as profits.

The nineteenth century brought great changes to the trade. Sandalwood was finally growing scarce in Timor, but new sources—and new competitors—appeared. In 1789 an American, Captain John Kendrick, discovered sandalwood in the Hawaiian Islands. Efforts to exploit the find were unsuccessful, and for the moment it was all but forgotten. Then Fiji entered the picture. Since the seventeenth century, Tongans had been going to the Fiji Islands for sandalwood and other local products which they used. Perhaps it was from them that Westerners first learned of the wood's presence in the unexplored Fijis. In any case, shortly after the turn of the century a ship-wrecked sailor, Oliver Slater, was rescued from Vanua Levu, where he had seen sandalwood growing in abundance. The news was soon out. Americans, Australians, and others quickly dispatched vessels to the islands. Initial successes generated a rush for sandalwood that extended from 1804 to 1816 and which peaked in 1808-1809. Profits were often enormous. Although Fijian sandalwood was poorer in quality than that from India and Timor, and thus brought less in Canton, it could be obtained far more cheaply. At first cargos could be obtained for small quantities of hoop iron and other cheap goods, but Fijians drove increasingly hard bargains, eventually demanding firearms and assistance in fighting their enemies. As a result, internal wars soon brought unprecedented destruction.

Deceit and treachery marked the trade. One sea captain even turned his cannon on a village where he had just traded with success so as to embitter its residents and thus ruin any chance his competitors might have of obtaining sandalwood there. Fijian actions were often as bad. Contacts between the cultures could hardly have begun less auspiciously.

Fiji's sandalwood rush was followed by others. Hawai'i had a sandalwood boom from 1811 to 1828, the Marquesas Islands from 1813 to 1817, and southwestern Melanesia—the New Hebrides (Vanuatu), Loyalty Islands, and New Caledonia—from the late 1820s to 1865. Australians dominated the trade in Melanesia, especially after 1834 when termination of the East India Company's monopoly opened China to colonial vessels. In Hawai'i and the Marquesas, Americans were the most frequent traders; but in 1817 Georg Anton Schäffer, acting in behalf of the Russian-American Company, wrung from Kaumua-li'i, king of Kaua'i, exclusive rights to his island's sandalwood. The Russians, however, were unable to maintain their position. Americans dominated the waning years of the Hawaiian trade, as they had the early ones.

Each rush had its deleterious effects. The sandalwood trade, coupled with whaling and other sources of Western contact, nearly depopulated the Marquesas, leaving only a disease-ridden remnant of a once vital culture. In Hawai'i the impact was less severe, especially under Kamehameha I who used restraint in selling the wood for Western goods. His successor, Liholiho, was both less wise and less politically secure. He turned over the trade to local chiefs in an effort to win their support and in the process unleashed an orgy of cutting and credit buying that had disastrous social and economic effects. Purchases so outstripped the capacity to repay with Hawai'i's dwindling supplies of sandalwood that in 1829 Governor Boki of O'ahu dispatched an expedition to the New Hebrides to gather sandalwood for creditors. The effort ended in disaster; only a handful of the 479 participants lived to return to Hawai'i.

In southwestern Melanesia the worst aspects of the trade were moderated by the presence of missionaries; by the relative permanence of the trade, which put a premium on good relations with the indigenous population; and by the presence of permanent trading stations in the islands that would have been endangered by some of the tactics used in Fiji. Even here, however, the sandalwood trade was a grim business. Through it Melanesians collided violently with the outside world.

With the decline of sandalwood gathering in southwestern Melanesia in the 1860s, the trade returned to its earlier channels. India again became the main source. Experimental plantings of sandalwood were made on O'ahu in the 1830s, but an important—and destructive—chapter in the history of the Pacific islands was over.

RELATED ENTRIES: Fiji; Hawai'i; Marquesas Islands.

SOURCES AND READINGS: C. R. Boxer, *Francisco Vieira de Figueiredo: A Portuguese Merchant-Adventurer in Southeast Asia, 1624-1667* (The Hague: Nijhoff, 1967); Theodore Morgan, *Hawaii: A Century of Economic Change, 1778-1876* (Cambridge: Harvard University Press, 1948); Dorothy Shineberg, *They Came for Sandalwood* (Melbourne: Melbourne University Press, 1967); Everard im Thurn, L. C. Wharton, eds., *The Journal of William Lockerby . . .* (London: Cambridge University Press for the Hakluyt Society, 1925).   *Thomas R. Cox*

SANDWICH ISLANDS. *See* Hawaiian Islands.

SANFORD, FRANCIS (1912-). A political leader of the United Front Party in French Polynesia, Sanford was born 11 May 1912 in Pape'ete, Tahiti. He was a school teacher and master up to World War II when he was named liaison officer between the French government and the six thousand American soldiers stationed on Bora Bora during the war, a duty that earned him many distinguished citations. After the war, he reentered his teaching profession but then turned to politics in 1959. In 1964 he became the first mayor of the newly incorporated city of Fa'a'a (Tahiti). Two years later, his political battle brought him to the foreground of politics in French Polynesia. Sanford's position has always been one of internal autonomy for French Polynesia, a position he maintained during his four consecutive terms as deputy to represent French Polynesia in the government in Paris. After several years of sometimes angry dialogue with Paris, Sanford's party won. On 14 July 1977 French Polynesia gained internal autonomy and in August Francis Sanford's party gained a clear majority of seats in the new assembly. He, therefore, became the first head (vice-president) of the new French Polynesian government.

RELATED ENTRIES: Bora Bora, U.S. Military Life during World War II; French Polynesia.

SOURCES AND READINGS: Patrick O'Reilly, *Tahitiens Supplément* (Paris: Musée de l'Homme, 1966).

Robert D. Craig

SARMIENTO DE GAMBOA, PEDRO (1530?-1592?). Sarmiento, a Spanish explorer, soldier, and historian, was given credit jointly with Mendaña for the discovery of the Solomon Islands. Born in Spain, he had a career as a soldier and a seaman in Europe before crossing to the New World. While in Peru, he became interested in the past of the Inca rulers, especially Tupac Yupanqui who was reported to have sailed to some Pacific islands and brought back gold. Sarmiento suggested to Lope G. de Castro, governor of Peru, to send out an expedition to rediscover the islands. Two ships sailed in November 1567 under the command of Alvaro de Mendaña, Castro's nephew, with Sarmiento in charge of navigation. The island of Santa Isabel in the Solomons was discovered on 7 February 1568. While the Spaniards were in the Solomons, Sarmiento's chief task was to command expeditions by the soldiers. As a result of exploration by a brigantine, the ships moved on to the island of Guadalcanal, where they anchored in the vicinity of present-day Honiara, the capital of the Solomons. In Guadalcanal, a watering party was massacred and Sarmiento was entrusted with punitive expeditions. He attended a meeting held on the island of San Cristobal to decide what to do next. Sarmiento was in favor of starting a settlement, but the majority of the men wanted to leave.

The return voyage which started on 11 August 1568 was difficult. The California coast was sighted on 19 December. Mendaña had to use force to prevent Sarmiento from complaining to officials in Mexico about the way the expedition had been managed. Back in Peru, Sarmiento gained the favor of Francisco de Toledo, the new viceroy, while Mendaña experienced many difficulties when he wanted to prepare another expedition.

Sarmiento was entrusted with several important missions. One of them was the establishment of a fortified settlement in the Strait of Magellan to prevent a recurrence of Drake's raid into the Pacific. While returning to Spain to obtain help for the struggling settlement, Sarmiento was captured by the English and then later by the French for ransom. Nothing is known for certain about the end of Sarmiento's life. His writings include a *History of the Incas* and a report on his voyage to the Solomons.

RELATED ENTRIES: Mendaña de Neira, Álvaro de; Solomon Islands; Spain in the Pacific.

SOURCES AND READINGS: Stephen Clissold, *Conquistador: The Life of Don Pedro Sarmiento de Gamboa* (London: Derek Verschoyle, 1954); Colin Jack-Hinton, *The Search for the Islands of Solomon, 1567-1838* (Oxford: Clarendon Press, 1969); Celsus Kelly, ed., *Australia Franciscana* (Madrid: Franciscan Historical Studies in Cooperation with Archivo Ibero-Americanao, 1967), vol. 3, *Documentos sobre la expedición de Álvaro de Mendaña a las Islas de Solomón en el Mar del Sur, 1567-69.*

André Gschaedler

SAVAGE, CHARLES (ca. 1785-1813). A beachcomber in Fiji, Charles Savage was of Swedish nationality. He worked as a seaman out of Sydney from 1804 before being wrecked in the American brig *Eliza* on Nairai reef in Fiji in 1808. He became a favorite of Naulivou, the *Vunivalu* (dominant chief) of Bau and enjoyed some prestige for his fighting. Legends grew up around Savage, attributing Bau's eminence to his prowess. He was killed in an affray between sandalwood traders and Fijians at Wailea, Vanua Levu, in 1813. This was the famous "Dillon's Rock" affair in which Peter Dillon was also involved.

RELATED ENTRIES: Beachcombers; Dillon, Peter; Fiji; Whippy, David.

SOURCES AND READINGS: I. C. Campbell, "The Historiography of Charles Savage," *Journal of the Polynesian Society* 89 (1980); Everard im Thurn and L. C. Wharton, eds., *The Journal of William Lockerby: Sandalwood Trader in the Fijian Islands during the Years 1808-1809* (London: Cambridge University Press for the Hakluyt Society, 1925).

Ian C. Campbell

SCHOUTEN, WILLIAM CORNELISON (ca. 1567-1625).

A Dutch navigator and explorer, Schouten was born in Hoorn, North Holland. He became a master mariner with three successful voyages to the East to his credit. He joined with Isaac Le Maire, a wealthy Dutch merchant, to form an association to trade with the East Indies. The Dutch East India Company (chartered in 1602) had obtained the commercial privilege that allowed its company ships sole use of the sea routes around the Cape of Good Hope and through the Strait of Magellan in order to trade in east Asian waters. William Schouten and Isaac Le Maire decided to challenge this monopoly by discovering an alternate passage to the East Indies by going completely around South America. Two vessels were equipped for the projected voyage. Schouten held the position of skipper and chief pilot of the *Unity* while Jacob Le Maire, the son of Isaac, served as supercargo. John Schouten, William's brother, became the skipper of the *Hoorne*.

On 4 June 1615 the two vessels sailed from the Texel. In the course of their outward-bound voyage they made a call at Sierra Leone on the west coast of Africa, where they obtained large quantities of lemons to prevent the possible ravages of scurvy. On 7 December the Dutchmen arrived at Port Desire on the coast of Patagonia. On 19 January 1616, while the vessels were being careened, the *Hoorne* accidentally caught fire and burned to the water's edge. All the crew members, however, were transferred to the *Unity* and thence proceeded down the coast, passed by the entrance to the Strait of Magellan, and on 24 January came to a short and narrow seaway between southeastern Tierra del Fuego and an island to the east which the Dutch called Staten Land. The waterway they named Le Maire Strait. Sailing southward, the Dutch sighted on 29 January the southern extremity of South America which according to Schouten's report consisted of high mountains covered with snow with an ending like a sharp corner. The Dutch named this point Cape Horn in honor of Schouten's birthplace. In proceeding toward the Pacific, the *Unity* sailed in a more southerly latitude than had any other Europeans before them.

While crossing the Pacific, the Dutch visited part of the Tuamotu Archipelago, some northern outliers of the Tonga group, and Futuna and Alofi which they named the Hoorn Islands. In July the *Unity* sailed along the northern coast of New Guinea where they experienced skirmishes with some unfriendly islanders. Several islands at the entrance of a large bay off the northwest coast of New Guinea were named after Schouten. In late October, the ship arrived in Jakarta where the Dutch governor-general of India condemned Schouten's voyage and confiscated his ship and cargo. Schouten, Le Maire, and several crew members were sent back to the Netherlands in an expedition commanded by Admiral Joris von Spilbergen (or Spielbergen). On 1 July 1617 Schouten finally arrived home safely, but Jacob Le Maire died at sea during the course of the long voyage. In the Netherlands Schouten and Isaac Le Maire, after a long period of litigation, ultimately received justice in the Dutch courts and obtained compensation for the loss of *Unity* and its cargo. Schouten continued his maritime activities by making further journeys to the Dutch East Indies. While returning from his last voyage, bad weather forced him to take refuge in a harbor on the east coast of Madagascar, and there he died in 1625.

The voyage of William Schouten and Jacob Le Maire in the years 1615-1616 did much to stimulate further interest in Dutch voyages to the South Pacific. Moreover, these two Dutch navigators made one of the truly significant geographical discoveries of the early seventeenth century, for the sea route which they found around the end of South America became an important ocean highway for more than two centuries.

RELATED ENTRIES: Le Maire, Jacob.

SOURCES AND READINGS: John C. Beaglehole, *The Exploration of the Pacific*, 3d ed. (London: A. & C. Black, 1966); "The Sixth Circum-Navigation by William Cornelison Schouten of Horne...." in Samuel Purchas, ed., *Hakluyt Posthumous or Purchas his Pilgrims...*, vol. 2 (Glasgow: James MacLehose and Sons, 1905).   *Bernerd C. Weber*

SCRATCHLEY, PETER HENRY (1835-1885).

A soldier and administrator in New Guinea, Scratchley was born in Paris 24 August 1835. He obtained a commission as second lieutenant in the Royal Engineers in 1854 and later fought in the Crimea and in the Indian Mutiny. He played a significant role as military adviser in the creation of defense systems in the Australian colonies in Victoria (1861-1863) and later as commissioner for defenses to the colonies (1878-1883) before returning to England. Appointed special commissioner to the new protectorate of British New Guinea in 1884, Scratchley arrived in Melbourne in January 1885, but he was delayed for some months in Australia by difficulties in arranging financial backing from the colonies for the protectorate. He arrived in Port Moresby in August 1885 and promptly formulated plans for an administration, adopting the principle that the government of British New Guinea should be primarily for the benefit of the indigenous people themselves. Port Moresby was chosen as the center of government. Coastal ships were to be registered, customs dues arranged, and a mail service established. Scratchley carefully examined the land claims of European settlers in order to protect the interests of the villagers. He made several voyages of exploration. He laid down an elementary pattern of local authority by arranging for the appointment of government chiefs. His brief term as special commissioner was sufficient for him to inaugurate policies which were of some use to successive administrations. After contracting malaria, Scratchley died at sea on 2 December 1885.

RELATED ENTRIES: Murray, John H. P.; Papua New Guinea.

SOURCES AND READINGS: Clement Kinloch-Cooke, *Australian Defences and New Guinea* (New York: Macmillan Co., 1887).   *J. D. G. Whitmore*

SELWYN, GEORGE AUGUSTUS (1809-1878). Selwyn was consecrated New Zealand's first Anglican bishop in 1841. Owing to a mistake in letters patent, Melanesia became part of Selwyn's diocese. While amused at this clerical error, he took seriously Archbishop Howley's valedictory exhortation to bring salvation to this area. This mission was to be one of the first Anglican missions directed by a bishop from its beginnings. Selwyn's enthusiasm was not shared by most New Zealanders, who thought him neglectful of his primary charge.

Selwyn firmly believed that only through an indigenous ministry would the mission be active and successful. He aimed to quickly develop a ministry in every island group which he hoped would form a church structure capable of being in communion with the English church in New Zealand.

In 1843 Selwyn founded Saint John's College at Waimate in New Zealand as a school and theological institution. Christianity from there was expected to spread throughout New Zealand and eventually to Melanesia. He planned annual journeys around the islands to build up mutual trust by personal contact. The bishop expected the young to be entrusted to him to spend short periods aboard his ship and, in some cases, at Saint John's to be trained in "all social and civilized habits" along with the basic doctrines of Christianity. Then, they were to be returned to pass on knowledge gained. If these scholars showed promise, further instruction would follow until they were ready for baptism and hence ready to systematically undertake the work of conversion.

Selwyn first visited Melanesia in December 1847. From Samoa and Tonga, he sailed to the New Hebrides (Vanuatu) and New Caledonia where contact was mainly with whalers and traders. After sandalwood was discovered there in large quantities, European contact increased.

The bishop's attitude to the sectarian bodies he found in the field was one of encouragement, but as they represented schism he would take no part in their public services. He greatly respected the Wesleyan mission in Tonga, likewise the Presbyterian Church of Nova Scotia, this being a truly independent colonial effort. He saw the London Missionary Society as free of any particular form of church government and approved of their developing local churches, but Selwyn tended to underestimate all other missionary bodies in this respect, believing them to be paternalistic. Contact with the Roman Catholics was made purely in the spirit of Christian charity.

In 1849 Selwyn visited the southern New Hebrides, New Caledonia, and the Loyalties; he returned with five Loyalty islanders. By 1851 thirteen youths from six different islands had come to Saint John's, now established in Auckland. In 1850 the synod of Australasian bishops set up an Australasian Board of Missions to convert and civilize the Australian aborigines and the heathen in the western Pacific. However, the Melanesian mission soon became the responsibility of New Zealand. Between 1847 and 1851, Selwyn had travelled 24,000 miles.

During Selwyn's visit to England in 1854-1855, an endowment of £10,000 was raised for a Melanesian diocese. Bishop Selwyn chose well when he enlisted the Reverend John Patteson, a first-class linguist and a man who could endure. From 1856 Patteson served his apprenticeship which led to his consecration in 1861. While Selwyn continued to visit Melanesia from 1856 to 1859, he was soon happy to hand over to Patteson the responsibility for the organization of the mission and for the scholars who came to Auckland. After 1861 Selwyn's direct link with the mission ceased though his concern continued even after his return to England. There he became the bishop of Lichfield in 1868 and had one of the colleges at Cambridge University named after him.

RELATED ENTRIES: Anglican Missions; London Missionary Society; Loyalty Islands; New Caledonia; Patteson, John C.; Samoa; Tonga; Vanuatu (New Hebrides).

SOURCES AND READINGS: J. H. Evans, *Churchman Militant: George August Selwyn, Bishop of New Zealand and Lichfield* (London: G. Allen & Unwin, 1964); D. Hilliard, *God's Gentlemen: A History of the Melanesian Mission 1849-1942* (St. Lucia, Queensland: University of Queensland Press, 1978); G. A. Selwyn, papers and documents 1842-1867, 17 folders,

Auckland Institute and Museum, MS 273; letters and documents 1848-1860, correspondence to and from Selwyn re Melanesian mission, London Missionary Society, Norfolk Island mission, and colonial bishops. Auckland Institute and Museum, micro #38, Auckland, New Zealand; H. W. Tucker, *Memoir of the Life and Episcopate of George Augustus Selwyn, D.D.*, 2 vols. (London: William Wells Gardner, 1879).   *Noeline V. Hall*

SEMPER, CARL GOTTFRIED (1832-1893). A German zoologist and ethnographer who inaugurated an era of German scientific research in the Caroline Islands, Semper was born in Altona, Germany, 6 July 1832. He received his doctorate from Würzburg University (1856) and two years later reached the Philippines where he lived from 1858 to 1865. Here, he compiled many notes on the ethnography of the people and on the plant, animal, and insect life as well. He left Manila in 1861 and arrived at the village of Ngabuked on Babeldaob Island in northern Palau on 23 March 1862. For ten months he traveled to all major island groups where he studied the coral reefs as well as the marine and terrestrial life of Palau. He also transcribed many Palauan legends and wrote an eyewitness account of the indigenous religion and customs. The results were published under the title *Die Palau Inseln im Stillen Ocean*. After departing Palau in January 1863, Semper returned to Würzburg where he joined the faculty of zoology. In 1871 he became the head of the Würzburg Zoological Institute. He died in May 1893 leaving a legacy of seven books (one on Palau and six on the Philippines) and numerous articles, all of which exhibit his keen observations, his intelligence, and his sympathetic understanding of the Pacific peoples among whom he had lived.

RELATED ENTRIES: Caroline Islands; Micronesia.

SOURCES AND READINGS: W. H. Scott, ed., *German Travelers on the Cordillera, 1860-1890* (Manila: New Day, 1975); C. Semper, *Die Palau Inseln im Stillen Ocean* (Leipzig: F. A. Brockhaus, 1873).
     Mark L. Berg

SEPIK RIVER. One of Papua New Guinea's two largest rivers, (1,126 km), the Sepik rises in the Victor Emanuel Range near the center of New Guinea. It first flows northwestward to the border with Irian Jaya which it crosses and recrosses several times and then eastward along a great intermountain valley to the island's north coast. Fed by heavy rainfall along its upper section and a number of large tributaries, it

cuts a serpentine, braided, and ever-changing course along a floodplain that in some places reaches a width of seventy kilometers and is marked by frequent oxbows, lagoons, and natural and man-made *barats* (valley or canal), as well as several large, permanent swamps. In its middle and lower stretches, the river drops less than one meter in fifty kilometers, but it moves at an average of three knots per hour and carries an immense load of silt, organic debris, and floating grass. At its mouth, the Sepik is more than one and one-half kilometers wide, and it discharges its load of silt into the Bismarck Sea with such force that from the air the sea can be seen to be discolored for as far as thirty-five kilometers from shore.

Although the object of extensive exploration by German scientists between 1885 and 1913 and traversed by Champion and Karius in their famous crossing from the Fly River in 1928, much of the river above Ambunti remained untouched by Western influences until after World War II. Yet the Sepik has long served as a major trade route for the people living along its banks, who move up and down its course in large dugout canoes carrying yams, taro, and sago from garden to village and, more recently, from village to town. The plains and foothills on either side of the river are leached by the heavy rainfall and often flooded for months at a time, but they have nevertheless supported a vigorous culture famous especially for its ceremonial houses and for its wood carvings, which have been collected by museums around the world. In stylistic sophistication and volume of output, the Sepik basin has been ranked second only to the Congo basin as a center of "primitive" art.

RELATED ENTRIES: Papua New Guinea.

SOURCES AND READINGS: Diana R. Howlett, *A Geography of Papua and New Guinea* (Melbourne: Thomas Nelson, 1967); Ernst Löffer, *Geomorphology of Papua New Guinea* (Canberra: Australian National University Press, 1977); Douglas Newton, *Crocodile and Cassowary* (New York: Museum of Primitive Art, 1971).   *Jerome Evans*

SOCIETY ISLANDS. *See* French Polynesia.

SOKEHS REBELLION (1910-1911). The last major uprising against foreign rule in Micronesia, the Sokehs rebellion took place on the island of Ponape during the German administration of the island (1899-1914). Resentment against foreign domination peaked during the second half of the German period. Opposition to German land policies, dislike of the labor tax, the institution of corporal punishment, long-standing political feuds among the island's kingdoms, and sectarian religious struggles all contributed to the uprising. Successful skirmishes against the Spanish twenty years earlier encouraged the violence.

The rebellion occurred in the Sokehs section of Ponape where the Germans were attempting to build a road linking the southern and western parts of the island to the German capital in the north. The work had been marred by a series of disputes over wages and compulsory labor. The beating of a Ponapean laborer by a German supervisor for alleged laziness sparked the final confrontation. Seeing the marks on his body, the man's fellow clansmen and relatives decided upon a course of war. On 18 October 1910 the Ponapeans refused to work on the road. Threats were made against the German supervisor. Notified of the incident, German Governor Boeder tried to settle the dispute. Arriving at the scene of the dispute, he was met with two shots to the abdomen and a death shot to the head delivered by the rebellion's leader. The governor's secretary, two road overseers, and five Mortlockese members of the boat crew were also killed.

The Germans, aided by Ponapeans from the other four kingdoms, managed to hold the colony until reinforcements arrived in early December. The Germans then took immediate steps to contain the rebellion and reclaim the island. The Germans pursued the rebels for more than two months over the island's mountains and inland terrain. The Germans' advance firepower and superior numbers won out. The refusal of the other kingdoms to come to the aid of the rebels sealed the fate of the rebellion.

A trial was held, and seventeen of the rebellion's participants were sentenced to death. The execution was carried out on 24 February 1911. The rest of the rebels along with their families were exiled to Palau. This action, in effect, removed almost the entire Ponapean population from the Sokehs kingdom. The German governor took possession of the land and distributed a portion of it to 1,250 immigrants from the typhoon-devastated islands of Mokil, Pinglap, Ngatik, and the Mortlocks. Descendants of the rebellion's participants were allowed to return to Ponape during the period of Japanese administration; they were not permitted, however, to reclaim their land.

RELATED ENTRIES: German Colonial Empire; Micronesia; Nanpei, Henry; Soumadau.

SOURCES AND READINGS: William Bascomb, *Ponape: A Pacific Island Economy in Transition* (Berkeley: University of California Press, 1965); John L. and Ann M. Fischer, *The Eastern Carolines* (New Haven: Human Relations Area Files Press, 1957); Willy Gartzke, *The Rebellion on Ponape*, trans. Ivan Tilgenkamp (Saipan: Trust Territory Printing Office, 1974).   *David L. Hanlon*

SOLF, WILHELM HEINRICH (1862-1936). A German colonial official who served for over ten years as governor of Western Samoa, Solf was the son of a wealthy merchant. Solf was educated in London, Berlin, and Calcutta, studying philology and Sanskrit. Solf entered the diplomatic service after 1885 and was attached to the general consulate in Calcutta for two years. In 1896 he became employed by the colonial department of the German Foreign Office. After a stint in German East Africa, Solf was appointed president of the municipal council in Apia, Western Samoa, in 1899 and in the following year became governor of the islands. Solf was among the ablest and most respected of Germany's colonial officials. Arriving in a land torn by decades of intertribal strife and conflicts among the white settlers, Solf became known for his firm but fair treatment of both groups. Through his toleration of Samoan customs and experimentation with self-government, Solf restored harmony to the colony and overcame much of the Samoan hostility to German rule. Solf also furthered German economic interests in Samoa by encouraging the expansion of copra and cocoa production and importing Chinese indentured laborers for the plantations. In view of his services Solf was promoted to state secretary of the German colonial office in December 1911, a post he held until 1918. Solf was also a publicist on German colonial affairs, having authored *Kolonialpolitik* in 1919.

RELATED ENTRIES: German Colonial Empire; Western Samoa.

SOURCES AND READINGS: Hellmuth Rössler and Günther Franz, eds., *Biographisches Wörterbuch zur deutschen Geschichte*, vol. 3 (Munich: Francke, 1975); Wilhelm Kosch, ed., *Biographisches Staatshandbuch*, vol. 2 (Berne: A. Franke, 1963); Eberhard von Vietsch, *Wilhelm Solf* (Tübingen: Wunderlich, 1961).   *Ralph C. Canevali*

SOLOMON ISLANDS. One of the major island groups of Melanesia, the Solomon Islands were the largest of Great Britain's tropical dependencies in Oceania until the achievement of their independence on 7 July 1978. The core of the archipelago consists of six large, mountainous continental islands or island clusters of volcanic origin. Many of them are overlaid by marine sediments and fringed with coral reefs. The islands are subject to high levels of rainfall (average 30-35 cm or 11.8-13.8 in) and are clad in tropical rain forest, though the northern flank of Guadalcanal has extensive grasslands on a broad coastal plain.

The central islands are arranged in the form of an attenuated *V*, oriented in a northwest-southeast direction between 5° and 12° south latitude, roughly 1,931 km (1,200 mi) from the Queensland coast of Australia. Along the northern flank lie the islands of Choiseul, Santa Isabel, and Malaita (Lauru, Boghotu, and Mala as they are known traditionally); along the southern, the New Georgia Islands, Guadalcanal, and San Cristobal (Makira). Approximately 708 km (240 mi) east of San Cristobal lies Nendö, the principal island in the Santa Cruz group, while around the core lie a number of outliers inhabited by Polynesian peoples: The large atoll of Ontong Java north of Santa Isabel, the tiny atoll of Sikaiana east of Malaita, and the elevated atolls of Rennell and Bellona south of Guadalcanal. The distance from Choiseul in the northwest to Vanikolo in the southeast is approximately 1,448 km (900 mi) while the total land area of the archipelago is roughly 29,785 km² (11,500 mi²). The population of the Solomons is roughly 200,000 of which 95 percent are people of Melanesian stock.

Prehistoric Times. It is difficult to determine with precision how and when the Solomons were occupied in prehistoric times. Our linguistic and archaeological knowledge of that period is extremely limited, but it seems likely that the central Solomons were occupied by hunters and gatherers about 10,000 years before the present (B.P.). Then about 4,000 B.P. the aborigines were overrun by Neolithic peoples who spoke a variety of languages belonging to the widely spread Oceanic branch of the Austronesian language family. The newcomers were agriculturalists. They planted taro and domesticated chickens, dogs, and pigs. Moreover, they possessed a high enough level of marine technology to allow them to cross the open ocean between San Cristobal and the Santa Cruz group in their outriggers. The inhabitants of the latter islands were part of the Lapita culture which flourished in various parts of the southwest Pacific from the Bismarcks to Samoa. That culture was characterized by the production and wholesale distribution of decorated pottery in the earliest of the long-range, Oceanic, Melanesian trade networks. Archaeological fieldwork elsewhere (Fotoruma Cave, Poha River, Guadalcanal) suggests that Solomon Islands cultures enjoyed a remarkable degree of continuity over time.

Exploration. The Spanish were the first Europeans to visit the Solomons. An expedition, under the command of Alvaro de Mendaña, made landfall on the east coast of Santa Isabel (Estrella Bay) in February 1568. Mendaña sailed throughout the central Solomons, skirmished with the islanders in a desperate attempt to obtain food, and retired to Peru. Several of his officers kept detailed accounts of their sojourn which are invaluable for their descriptions of Solomon Islands societies. The discovery of fool's gold, exaggerated by sailors' talk, led to the islands being officially described as the Isles of Solomon in 1574. Mendaña established a brief-lived settlement at Graciosa Bay, Nendö, in 1595, but when he died the remnants of the expedition departed for the Philippines. The Dutchman, Abel Tasman, visited and named Ontong Java in 1643. A number of European explorers sailed through the Solomons in the late eighteenth century: Philip Carteret visited Santa Cruz in 1767; Louis Bougainville, the shores of Choiseul and Bougainville in 1768; Jean Surville, the islands of Santa Isabel and San Cristobal; Jean, Comte de Lapérouse, Vanikolo in 1788; Shortland, the islands of Guadalcanal, New Georgia, and the Shortlands in the same year; and Sir Alexander John Ball the coast of Malaita in 1792. Finally, in 1838, the French navigator Dumont d'Urville confirmed that the Solomons, the existence of which had long been in doubt, were Mendaña's Isles of Solomon.

Traditional Societies. The Melanesian societies which the European explorers encountered were highly fragmented linguistically and geographically. Broadly speaking, the islanders were interior-dwelling, up-country, swidden agriculturalists (later known as "bush people") or coastal-dwelling fisher folk (known as "saltwater people"). In kinship terms, they might be matrilineal or patrilineal depending on the island or part of the island where they lived. Most of the Solomon islanders lived in small villages or hamlets seldom exceeding two hundred people. Their wood carving, canoe making, and other crafts were highly developed and artistic. They indulged in fairly constant interclan warfare of a largely ritualistic, honor-readjusting variety on a small scale, though fairly large head-hunting raids did take place in and from the New Georgian archipelago until early in the twentieth century. The islanders inhabited a world of ghosts, spirits, sorcery, and magic and many of their activities involved the propitiation of spirits or the enactment of appropriate rituals.

European Contact. Contact between Europeans and Solomon islanders was fleeting prior to 1870. *Bêche-de-mer* fishers, sandalwood cutters, and whalers visited the Solomons bringing with them trade goods such as fishhooks, calico, axes, and tobacco. Imported iron implements had a dramatic impact on the lives of the Neolithic agriculturalists who were able to clear jungles, prepare gardens, and wage war more efficiently than before. Unfortunately contact was often marred by cultural misunderstanding, murder, and reprisals and the Solomons soon came to enjoy a reputation for being dangerous and malarial.

During the last quarter of the nineteenth century, thousands of Solomon islanders were recruited, principally from Malaita, to work on the sugarcane estates in Queensland and the coconut plantations in Fiji. The recruiting process led to the further spread of European goods and firearms in particular. The indentured experience led to acculturation and the return to the islands of men and women accustomed to European ways and religion.

Captain H. W. M. Gibson of H.M.S. *Curaçao* declared a protectorate over the central Solomons in 1893 in a move by Great Britain to forestall any French annexation plans. In accordance with the Anglo-German demarcation agreement of April 1886, the islands of Buka, Bougainville, Choiseul, and Santa Isabel fell within the German sphere of influence. Choiseul and Isabel were united with the remainder of the British Solomon Islands Protectorate (BSIP) in 1899. Buka and Bougainville, by an accident of history, became part of Papua New Guinea.

Charles Morris Woodford was the first resident commissioner for the BSIP. He took office in 1896 and established the colonial capital of Tulagi on an island of the same name in the Florida group. He had two mutually reinforcing responsibilities: to bring law and order to the islands and to render the BSIP economically self-sustaining. He and his successors were largely successful in these objectives by the late 1920s. At the same time, various missions commenced their labors. The Anglicans had been in the Solomon group since 1865. The Roman Catholics arrived in 1898, having attempted unsuccessfully to establish missions on Santa Isabel and San Cristobal in the 1840s, the Methodists in 1902 (their activities contributing to the termination of head-hunting on New Georgia), the South Sea Evangelical Mission (an outgrowth of the Queensland Kanaka Mission which had ministered to Solomon Island laborers in Queensland) in 1904, and the Seventh-Day Adventists in 1914.

The missions encouraged the movement of bush people to the seacoast, eroded traditional cultures and customs, further divided Solomon Island societies by adding a religious dimension, and provided almost all of the education and most of the medical facilities prior to World War II.

The Woodford administration leased large blocks of land to Lever's Pacific Plantations Limited to develop as coconut plantations. Copra became the protectorate's main export. The European community was very small and consisted principally of government officers, missionaries, planters, and traders. Chinese carpenters, mechanics, and cooks were recruited prior to World War I and formed a Chinatown at Tulagi. The Great Depression dealt a severe blow to the Solomons. The copra trade collapsed, plantations were mortgaged, and the administration eked out a precarious existence, exercising its influence through a handful of district officers. Few of these changes, however, had a marked effect on the Solomon islanders, most of whom, particularly in the outlying regions or in the hilly interiors of islands, went on with their lives much as their forefathers had done.

The Pacific War. Following their attack on Pearl Harbor on 7 December 1941, the Japanese occupied Tulagi in May 1942 and began the construction of an airstrip on the Guadalcanal plains. Completion of this airstrip would have permitted the Japanese to attack and occupy New Caledonia and Fiji, which lie astride the major trade routes to Australia.

The Americans reoccupied Tulagi and invaded Guadalcanal on 7 August 1942. Fierce fighting ensued as the Japanese tried to recapture the newly completed Henderson airfield. The Americans and their allies drove the Japanese from Guadalcanal and northward through the archipelago. They were assisted heroically by individual Solomon islanders, by a supportive populace, and by a handful of "Coastwatchers." The last mentioned were principally district officers and planters who remained behind the lines to report on the movement of Japanese forces. By October 1943 the fighting had moved out of the BSIP to the island of Bougainville.

The Postwar Period. The war left the BSIP economy in ruins. Plantations were war-damaged, abandoned, or overgrown. The missions, administration, and commercial sector were obliged to rebuild the prewar infrastructure almost entirely. They were hindered in this task by a quasi-nationalist, indigenous movement called Marching Rule which had begun to develop in the closing years of the Pacific war. It manifested itself, at first, in passive resistance, particularly on the island of Malaita, to the reimposition of British rule. Followers of Marching Rule, a transliteration of *maasina* or "brotherhood," organized themselves in a paramilitary fashion, built new villages, promoted custom, and not infrequently obstructed British census and tax-collecting efforts. When passive resistance turned to active resistance, the British administration resorted to force and compromise to quell the opposition. Marching Rule alerted the British to the need for local government, and from 1952 onwards local councils were established throughout the BSIP.

The Move to Independence. Two major features characterized the period 1952 to 1978: a commitment to development projects and an advance towards independence. The administration developed schools, improved health services, and encouraged new development schemes in cocoa, timber, mining, oil palm, rice, and fishing. At the same time the Western Pacific High Commissioner, who had been headquartered in Fiji since 1877, moved his office to Honiara, the new postwar capital on Guadalcanal, and acting in his capacity as governor of the BSIP established a legislative council in 1960. That council underwent a number of permutations as Solomon islanders took a greater share in the government and on 2 January 1976 the Solomons were granted internal self-government. On 14 July 1976, following a general election for the legislative assembly, Peter Kenilorea from Malaita, was chosen to be the chief minister. He held that position until 7 July 1978, when, on the occasion of independence, he became the first prime minister of the Solomon Islands. Baddeley Devesi became the first governor-general, and the Solomon Islands became the 150th state to be admitted to the United Nations.

RELATED ENTRIES: Bougainville (North Solomon) Secessionism; Britain in the Pacific; Codrington, Robert; Cook, (Captain) James; Diaper, William; Hamilton, William; Labor Trade; Maasina Rule; Melanesian Recruitment to Queensland, Patterns of; Melanesians and Colonial Servitude; Montrouzier, Xavier; Patteson, John; South Pacific Commission; South Pacific Forum; War in the Pacific Islands, 1914-1945; Western Pacific High Commission.

SOURCES AND READINGS: British Solomon Islands Protectorate, *Annual Reports* (Honiara, Solomon Islands: HMSO, London or Government Printer, published annually); Charles E. Fox, *The Threshold of the Pacific: An Account of the Social Organization, Magic, and Religion of the People of San Cristoval in the Solomon Islands* (London: Kegan Paul, 1924); R. C. Green and M. M. Cresswell, eds., *Southeast Solomon Islands Cultural History: A Preliminary Survey* (Wellington: Royal Society of New Zealand, 1976); H. Ian Hogbin, *Experiments in Civilizations: The Effects of European Culture on a Native Community of the Solomon Islands* (London: Routledge, 1939); Colin Jack-Hinton, *The Search for the Islands of Solomon, 1567-1838* (Oxford: Clarendon Press, 1969); Charles M. Woodford, *A Naturalist Among the Headhunters of the Solomon Islands, 1886, '87 and '88* (London: Philip, 1890).

James Boutilier

SOLOMON REPORT. The Trust Territory of the Pacific Islands (Micronesia) was established in 1947 by the United Nations Security Council which assigned the administration of the area to the United States as the administering authority. It was one of eleven trust territories created after World War II in Asia, the Pacific region, and Africa to bring former colonies and possessions of the defeated Axis powers to self-government or independence. Only Micronesia was declared a "strategic trust," which permitted the United States to utilize the islands for military purposes and to give it the sole authority to determine the appropriate time for the termination of the trusteeship. During approximately the first fifteen years, the area was administered generally without firm direction or goals from Washington, first by the Department of the Navy and then by the Department of the Interior. There was a very low budgetary subsidy from the United States government, starting out at about $5 million annually.

Following a severely critical report by a visiting mission of the United Nations Trusteeship Council in 1962, there was an increasing awareness in Washington of the obligation to prepare the islands for eventual self-government and the termination of the agreement with the United Nations. The major question was under what circumstances the trusteeship could be ended while still preserving the perceived defense interests of the United States.

President John F. Kennedy issued National Security Action Memorandum No. 243 on 9 May 1963 appointing Professor Anthony N. Solomon of the economics department at Harvard University (who later became assistant secretary of state for economic affairs) to head a government survey mission to the trust territory to review the major political, economic, and social problems facing the people. The mission was mandated to gather information and make recommendations needed in the formulation of federal policies and programs for a greatly accelerated rate of political, economic, and social development in line with the United States' obligations as a charter member of the United Nations. Part of the mission's task was also to examine means for implementing National Security Action Memorandum No. 145 (18 April 1962) which envisaged moving Micronesia into a permanent relationship with the United States in a manner acceptable to the member nations of the United Nations.

In addition to Solomon, the survey mission consisted of representatives of the president's Council of Economic Advisors, the Bureau of the Budget, the Maxwell School at Syracuse University, the Peace Corps, and the Department of Education in the American Virgin Islands.

The mission surveyed the conditions in Micronesia for about six weeks during July and August 1963 and issued their report, entitled "A Report by the U.S. Government Survey Mission to the Trust Territory of the Pacific Islands," on 9 October 1963. This later became known widely as the "Solomon Report."

Although classified for many years, significant parts of the document were leaked to the staff of the *Young Micronesian*, a student newsletter in Hawai'i, and were later reprinted in the *Micronitor*, a weekly newspaper (later called the *Micronesian Independent*) published in the Marshall Islands on 10 July 1971.

The report itself, in three volumes, was critical of past American policies and mismanagement, and it called for an "integrated master plan for action." It was hoped that improved conditions, on a broad front, would influence Micronesians and make them choose a political status in 1968 as an American territory similar to that of American Samoa, Guam, and the American Virgin Islands.

Despite enormous increases in American budgets for the trust territory after the Solomon mission, substantial efforts by the Peace Corps, and occasional disavowals by American officials of the thrust of the Solomon Report itself, the unofficial publication of the report created a climate of distrust among many Micronesians and their leaders that has not been totally dispelled since. Ironically, the sentiment for complete independence in Micronesia in the 1960s and early 1970s was never strong.

Commonwealth status, similar to that of Puerto Rico, was offered to Micronesians by the United States in 1969. It was rejected by all the districts except the Northern Mariana Islands which have since negotiated, in 1975, a commonwealth agreement with the United States. The remainder of the districts are preparing, some separately, for a free association status (similar to the one the Cook Islands have with New Zealand) with the United States which is a loose, terminable relationship just short of independence.

RELATED ENTRIES: Commonwealth of the Northern Mariana Islands; Cook Islands; Micronesia; Peace Corps.

SOURCES AND READINGS: Noel Grogan, "Dependency and Nondevelopment in Micronesia" in F. P. King, ed., *Oceania and Beyond: Essays on the Pacific Since 1945* (Westport, Conn.: Greenwood Press, 1976); Donald F. McHenry, *Micronesia: Trust Betrayed, Altruism or Self-Interest in American Foreign Policy* (New York and Washington: Carnegie Endowment for International Peace, 1975).

Sam McPhetres

SOMARE, MICHAEL THOMAS (1936-). A former prime minister of Papua New Guinea, Somare was born 9 April 1936 at Rabaul the son of a policeman. Somare returned to his father's village of Karau in the Murik Lakes area at the outbreak of World War II. His formal education began at age ten when he was enrolled in primary school at Wewak. He went on to postprimary school at Finschhagen in 1951 and to the teacher-training course at Sogeri High School in 1956. After teaching high school for several years and serving in other educational posts, he became a radio newsreader for the territorial information department. Although active in employee organizations critical of policies favoring Australian public servce workers, he received a scholarship in 1965 to the Administrative College in Port Moresby where he met others of the small, emerging, educated elite who were becoming increasingly restless under Australian rule and impatient for self-government. After issuing a public demand for home rule, Somare and a number of other "radicals" formed Pangu Pati, the first of the territory's political parties of consequence. Elected to the House of Assembly in 1968 from the East Sepik provincial seat, he was chosen parliamentary leader of Pangu and served on several important committees, but with other Pangu members refused to accept a ministerial post. Following the election of 1972, Somare and his allies formed a coalition government made of Pangu, the People's Progress Party, the National Party, and several independents with Somare as chief minister. Having led the drive for independence, Somare became prime minister of the new nation of Papua New Guinea when independence came in 1975. He overcame challenges to his leadership in 1978 that produced a major realignment of his parliamentary support but left his government as strong as ever. Nondoctrinaire and extraordinarily skilled in democratic politics, Somare remains a preeminent popular leader of his country.

RELATED ENTRIES: Papua New Guinea.

SOURCES AND READINGS: Michael Somare, *Sana* (Port Moresby: Niugini Press, 1975); Don Woolford, *Papua New Guinea: Initiation and Independence* (Brisbane: University of Queensland Press, 1976); "Somare—The Great Survivor," *Pacific Islands Monthly* 50, no. 1 (1979): 15-18.   *Jerome Evans*

SOUMADAU (d. 1911). Soumadau was a leader and tactician in the Sokehs rebellion against the German colonial administration on Ponape (Caroline Islands) in 1910. Soumadau was a high-ranking noble from the district of Sokehs hired by Governor Boeder to supervise the free Ponapean labor drafted to build roads. Tension existed between the administration and the Sokehs Ponapeans and traditional "signs" had indicated that the Sokehs district would soon suffer annihilation. On 17 October 1910 a German supervisor severely beat a laborer and Soumadau and others agreed to avenge the dishonor. When approached the following day by the governor and aides the Ponapeans killed him, raided the colony for guns, and retreated to a mountaintop fortification. Both sides apparently refused to negotiate, and beginning on 13 January 1911 combined naval bombardments and pincer attacks by German and Melanesian troops eventually drove the rebels into the interior. Dispersed and receiving little aid, groups of rebels gradually surrendered. Soumadau surrendered on 13 February to a neighboring Ponapean chief and was executed on Ponape on 24 February 1911 along with fourteen others held responsible for the governor's death. Two others involved in the rebellion were reported to have been executed on Yap shortly thereafter.

RELATED ENTRIES: Sokehs Rebellion.

SOURCES AND READINGS: John L. Fischer and Ann M. Fischer, *The Eastern Carolines* (New Haven: Human Relations Area Files Press, 1957).

Craig J. Severance

SOUTH PACIFIC COMMISSION (SPC). The first contemporary manifestation of regionalism in the South Pacific, the South Pacific Commission (SPC) originated from the trauma and ensuing reconstruction of World War II. Convinced by the war that the Pacific islands were essential to their defense, the governments of Australia and New Zealand determined to devote more attention to the islands lying athwart their northern approaches. They also shared the humanitarianism of the Western allies who were determined to restore a more compassionate moral order after the defeat of the Axis Powers. The two aspirations were linked in the Australia-New Zealand Agreement of January 1944 which proposed two types of regional organization for the South Pacific: one a military alliance, the other a welfare association for the peoples of the region.

Although the Australian foreign minister, H. V. Evatt, probably attached a higher priority to the military association, the return of peace irretrievably dampened the enthusiasm of other states for this aspect of regional cooperation in the South Pacific. Support for a welfare organization also diminished, but there was sufficient residual interest among the Western states holding territorial claims in the South

Pacific to convene a meeting in January 1974 to discuss the ANZAC allies' proposal for a South Seas regional commission. After more than a week of negotiations, the six participants—Australia, France, the Netherlands, New Zealand, the United Kingdom, and the United States—agreed to establish an advisory organization to be called the South Pacific Commission. The Canberra Agreement, as the charter for the new association became commonly known, took full effect from July 1948, and shortly afterwards the SPC's permanent headquarters opened in Anse Vata, a resort suburb in Nouméa, the capital of New Caledonia.

The establishment of the SPC created two fundamental preconditions for the development of South Pacific regionalism. In the first instance, it defined the boundaries of the region. The original members of the SPC included: American Samoa, the Cook Islands, Fiji, French Polynesia, the Gilbert and Ellice Islands Colony (now Kiribati and Tuvalu), Nauru, New Caledonia, the New Hebrides (now Vanuatu), Niue, Norfolk Island, Papua New Guinea (at first separately), the Pitcairn Islands, the British Solomon Islands Protectorate (now the Solomon Islands Republic), the Tokelau Islands, the Kingdom of Tonga (by invitation), Wallis and Futuna, and Western Samoa. This initial definition has been subsequently amended only twice. In 1951 the United States added Guam and the Trust Territory of the Pacific Islands (TTPI) to the ambit of the SPC, and in 1962 West New Guinea was excluded when the Netherlands surrendered the territory to Indonesia, making it thereby ineligible for continued membership in the regional organization.

The second important innovation of the Canberra Agreement was the creation of the South Pacific Conference, an auxiliary body to be composed of delegates from the Pacific islands who would meet triennially to advise the commission on aspects of its work program. Although formally limited to a purely advisory role in a consultative organization, the conference gradually developed an image of itself as the legitimate voice for the regional aspirations of the Pacific peoples. This perception was given an enormous fillip in 1965 when Western Samoa, independent since 1962, won a seat on the commission itself. Several metropolitan governments had had reservations about localizing the SPC's decision-making arm and had opposed Western Samoa's entry into the commission, which hitherto had been restricted to the six European countries. Encouraged by the Samoan success in the commission, the conference determinedly applied itself to winning further concessions for islander influence in the SPC throughout the latter half of the 1960s.

The first serious volley by the South Pacific Conference against European domination of the SPC was fired by the future Fijian prime minister, Ratu Kamisese Mara, in the politically charged atmosphere of the July 1965 conference in Lae, Papua New Guinea. The accession of Western Samoa to the Canberra Agreement, the move to autonomy by the Cook Islands, the negotiations in London on Fijian independence, and the absence of a West New Guinea delegation were among the more important events during the year which pointed up both the prospects and hazards of decolonization in the region. Ratu Mara felt that if the SPC could become a politically effective vehicle for South Pacific regionalism, it would help the emerging island states to more satisfactorily manage their relations with extra-regional influences. For the SPC to assist in moderating the strains of decolonization, however, it was vital in Ratu Mara's view that the SPC itself be decolonized.

Between 1965 and 1970 significant changes occurred in the operation of the SPC. Two additional island countries successfully sought to join Western Samoa on the commission—Nauru (admitted 1969) and Fiji (1971)—thus further weakening the European dominance of this important element of the organization. Papua New Guinea (1975), the Solomon Islands and Tuvalu (1978), the Cook Islands and Niue (1980) have also since acceded to the Canberra Agreement. The conference not only secured more control over its internal affairs, but it also won the right to influence more directly the SPC's work program. In 1967 the commission agreed to annual meetings of the conference, to the automatic referral of the work program to the conference, and to voluntary contributions to the budget from the territories. The conference obtained control of its agenda and rules of procedure and the authority to elect its own chairman in 1970. Even the secretariat of the SPC was drawn into the process of reform when it was decided in 1969 to appoint an islander, Afioga Afoafouvale Misimoa of Western Samoa, to the post of secretary-general for the first time in the organization's history.

Although the European founders of the SPC had yielded on many points, the failure of the general review of 1970 to achieve a political role for the SPC came as a particularly bitter blow to many island leaders. Their frustration in this matter, probably more than any other single cause, led to the establishment of the South Pacific Forum in the following year. France, with some support from the United Kingdom and the United States, argued against a politicized SPC on the grounds of legal competence, but most observers considered France to have been motivated by a desire to prevent criticism of its colonial policies and nuclear testing in the South Pacific. The decision of the 1970 review committee to deny the SPC a political function was undoubtedly a watershed for the organization. Much of the controversy surrounding regionalism in the 1970s stemmed from this crucial decision.

The emergence of the South Pacific Forum did not deter attempts to further reform the SPC. Three additional general reviews were instituted between the years 1972 and 1980. Australia, embarrassed by the strong tactics of France during the Apia Conference of 1972, found ready support from New Zealand for an enquiry into reducing the responsibility of the commission in the affairs of the SPC. This was largely achieved through a memorandum of understanding signed at the Rarotonga Conference of 1974, which created a de facto merger of the commission and the conference. Even at the signing ceremony, however, it was suggested that another review would be needed to resolve relations between the SPC and the forum.

The foreshadowed review convened on Nauru in May 1976. Although a number of forum members argued that the SPC had become redundant, the smaller territories convincingly countered that the SPC was a valuable organization for village-level development. The subsequent conference ratified both the reduced role for the SPC and the elimination of the weighted voting formula which had given the European states exaggerated influence since its introduction in 1965 as part of the compromise to admit Western Samoa to the commission. Relations between the SPC and the forum (and especially its executive arm, the South Pacific Bureau for Economic Cooperation) nonetheless continued to be subject to demarcation disputes.

The Tahiti Conference of 1979 accepted the invitation of the forum to participate in yet another review in 1980 to attempt a final resolution of all remaining issues between the two regional organizations. The report of the review committee established to examine the problem of organizational duplication found few concrete examples of overlap but recommended nonetheless that the two bodies be merged within three years. Both the forum and the conference considered the committee's report during their 1980 meetings, but each appears to regard its principal recommendation as unacceptably precipitate. It now seems that a less formal, more evolutionary *modus vivendi* will be sought to pursue interorganizational cooperation between the SPC and the forum.

While the historical significance of the SPC will undoubtedly be assessed primarily from the perspective of its centrality in the development of South

Pacific regionalism, the impact of the organization extends well beyond the role of the conference as a training ground for regional cooperation. Financed by a modest budget (approximately $4 million Australian in 1979) from the member states, the work program of the SPC has included such highly regarded, long-term projects as the Samabula Community Education Training Centre, the Tate School Readers Program, and the Skipjack Survey and Assessment Program. It has also encompassed a myriad number of short-term projects spanning such diverse areas as atoll sanitation, boat building, crop disease, nutrition, and vocational training. Beyond the intended repercussions of its own work program, the SPC has also influenced the course of Pacific affairs through less direct means. It had an instrumental role in the development of other regional bodies such as the South Pacific Games, the South Pacific Arts Festival, and the University of the South Pacific.

RELATED ENTRIES: ANZAC; Defense Planning for Oceania between the Wars; Fiji, Federal Movement in; Island Confederation Movements; Regionalism; South Pacific Forum; War in the Pacific Islands 1914-1945; Western Pacific High Commission.

SOURCES AND READINGS: W. D. Forsyth, "South Pacific: Regional Organisation," *New Guinea and Australia, The Pacific and South-East Asia* 6 (1971): 6-23; R. A. Herr, "A Child of its Era: Colonial Means and Ends," *New Guinea and Australia, The Pacific and South-East Asia* 9 (1974): 2-14; T. R. Smith, *South Pacific Commission: An Analysis after Twenty-Five Years* (Wellington: Price Milburn, 1972).   *Richard Herr*

SOUTH PACIFIC FORUM. An intergovernmental organization, established August 1971 in Wellington, New Zealand, the South Pacific Forums's originating members included Fiji, Western Samoa, Tonga, the Cook Islands, Nauru, Australia, and New Zealand. Membership has expanded to include Papua New Guinea (1974), Niue (1975), the Solomon Islands and Tuvalu (1978), and Kiribati (1979).

Created to provide a needed setting where the heads of government of independent and self-governing island states could consult fully with each other and Australia and New Zealand, this political function has been harnessed towards attempts to further regional cooperation, especially in economic and related fields.

A major development in 1972 was the establishment and location in Suva of the South Pacific Bureau for Economic Cooperation (SPEC). Its major task has been to investigate and then advance regional economic projects for South Pacific Forum members, especially in trade, investment, shipping, air services, telecommunications, technical cooperation (such as plant disease eradication), marketing and aid. As well, it has assisted in consultations between South Pacific Forum members and external organizations, including the Association of South East Asian Nations (ASEAN), the United Nations Economic and Social Commission for Asia and the Pacific (ESCAP), and the European Community's Lomé formula arrangements with African, Caribbean, and Pacific (ACP) states. Working in close conjunction with forum governments, it has been a key task of SPEC to process and monitor the information necessary to identify the choices open to the forum's annual heads-of-government meeting where most major decisions are reached.

It was on this basis that the forum's 1976 meeting established a regional shipping venture, the Pacific Forum Line, involving New Zealand, Nauru, Western Samoa, and Tonga. Commencing operations in 1978, this line has faced problems of finance, organization, and the utilization of new technology. Although hesitant, this progress stands in marked contrast to the failure of attempts to further regional cooperation in civil aviation where national commercial interests have remained decisive.

In 1977 a key development occurred when the forum adopted a "Declaration on the Law of the Sea" through which members agreed to establish 200-mile fishing, or exclusive economic, zones as soon as possible. This was given added point by a joint decision to establish a South Pacific Fisheries Organization. This is intended to coordinate the joint interests of members and all countries in the South Pacific, supporting the sovereign rights of coastal states to conserve and manage living resources, including highly migratory species, within their respective 200-mile economic zones.

This reference to highly migratory species has proved contentious, given the strong American commercial interest in harvesting skipjack tuna. At the 1978 forum meeting, the Cook Islands and Western Samoa were prepared to envisage American participation within the planned arrangement, subject to appropriate license and royalty payments, but this was opposed by Papua New Guinea and Fiji. These differences need to be viewed against a background of forum attempts to establish a comprehensive environmental management program for the region. This was clearly in evidence in 1979, when the forum decisively rejected tentative American proposals for the utilization of remote South Pacific island locations as possible nuclear waste storage facilities.

Since its establishment, the South Pacific Forum has expressed its opposition to atmospheric nuclear weapons testing, supported the principle of a nuclear weapons free zone in the South Pacific, helped provide a focus in the Commonwealth for the international needs of very small states, and stressed the advantages of a partnership based on easy, often informal, consultation.

RELATED ENTRIES: Cook Islands; Fiji; Kiribati; Nauru; Niue; Papua New Guinea; Solomon Islands; South Pacific Commission; Western Samoa.

SOURCES AND READINGS: A. Haas, ed., *New Zealand and the South Pacific* (Wellington: Asia-Pacific Research Unit, 1977); A. Haas, ed., *New Zealand Foreign Affairs Review* 21-29 (1971-79).

Roderick M. Alley

SOUTH SEAS COMMERCIAL COMPANY. Incorporated 30 July 1934 at Los Angeles the South Seas Commerical Company had Donald W. Douglas of Douglas Aircraft, T.C. McMahon, and Moe M. Fogel as directors. Its purpose was to construct landing fields and flying-boat facilities at certain Pacific islands to create a western air route to the Philippines and a southwestern air route to American Samoa or beyond to Australia. The company's general agent at Washington, D.C., was Harold Gatty who had gained the support of President Franklin Roosevelt's son Elliott in the venture. In turn, the son had interested his father in the plan. The younger Roosevelt's part was to get Pan American Airways, Matson Navigation Company, and Inter-Islands Airways of Hawai'i to work together, setting up the actual airline to operate through the facilities to the Philippines and American Samoa. Gatty attempted to negotiate with the U.S. Navy for long-term leases to the needed islands but lost out to Pan American Airways on the western route. The company merged with Pan American in May 1935 to create the southwestern route, with Douglas becoming a Pan American director and Gatty becoming Pan American's New Zealand agent. The company was not legally dissolved until June 1940.

RELATED ENTRIES: Equatorial Islands; Gatty, Harold; Oceanic Nitrates Corporation; Southwest Pacific Air Route.

SOURCES AND READINGS: Articles of Incorporation of South Seas Commercial Company, 30 July 1934, filed in the office of the Secretary of State, Sacramento, California; Harold Charles Gatty Correspondence, Library of Congress, Washington, D.C.; Francis X. Holbrook, "Commercial Aviation and the Colonization of the Equatorial Islands, 1934-1936," *Aerospace Historian* 17, no. 4 (1970): 144-49; U.S., Department of the Navy, Correspondence of the Secretary of the Navy, Record Group 80, National Archives, Washington, D.C.

Francis X. Holbrook

***SOUTHERN CROSS* (1856-1860).** Bishop George A. Selwyn's first specially designed and English-built mission vessel was the *Southern Cross*. The money for this ship was raised by supporters of the Melanesian mission on the bishop's visit to England in 1854-1855. This mission schooner was regarded as a floating headquarters, and it was equipped with teachers, a school, and a printing press. This arrangement aimed to avoid costly construction on the islands and to prevent missionaries being subjected to an unhealthy climate, along with other hazards of established contact. During 1856 to 1859, Selwyn sailed in this vessel four times in annual visitations around his Melanesian diocese. Although the original *Southern Cross* was wrecked in June 1860, subsequent mission ships have retained this name.

RELATED ENTRIES: Anglican Missions; Selwyn, George A.

SOURCES AND READINGS: J. H. Evans, *Churchman Militant: George August Selwyn, Bishop of New Zealand and Lichfield* (London: G. Allen & Unwin, 1964).

Noeline V. Hall

SOUTHWEST PACIFIC AIR ROUTE, CREATION OF THE (1934-1942). In March 1935 the United States landed colonists on Howland, Baker, and Jarvis islands and began to mark out runways. Pan American Airways set up Oceanic Nitrates Corporation, allegedly a guano company, to block competition from other airlines. That July, Oceanic sent an expedition, which included Pan American's agent Harold Gatty, to land several men on each of the islands. Palmyra Island, Kingman Reef, and Pago Pago were investigated by Gatty for flying-boat facilities. Later Pan American sought an exclusive guano permit for Oceanic which would have prevented any competition. The Department of the Interior rejected the request, but it made no difference as the islands proved too difficult for landplane operations.

Gatty recommended Palmyra Island as the best stopover after Hawai'i but that the island was privately owned. As an alternate, he suggested using a tender alongside Kingman Reef as there was unsufficient land area for a shore establishment. Pago Pago in American Samoa would be the second stop, with Auckland as the terminal. In November 1935 Gatty obtained a permit from New Zealand for an airmail service conditional on reciprocal rights being granted a parallel British service when ready. The British planned a global airmail service and wished to force the United States to open Hawai'i to them. The United States refused to grant such an important commercial privilege in exchange for the minor New Zealand route. Throughout 1936 the company unsuccessfully attempted to renegotiate the permit to remove the reciprocity clause. In March 1937 Pan American flew a survey flight to Auckland and, in December, inaugurated its commercial route. On the second trip, 11 January 1938, the plane blew up. The company lost its chief pilot, Edward Musick, and an S-42B flying boat which could not be replaced. The southwest route had to await the arrival of the Boeing 314s which were ordered in 1936.

Pan American also concluded that Kingman Reef and Pago Pago were too dangeorus for flying-boat operations. In February 1938 Juan Trippe of Pan American asked the State Department for a permit to use Canton Island. The State Department was already involved in an ownership dispute with England over Canton. The United States landed colonists there and on Enderbury in March to strengthen its claim to these islands and granted a permit to Pan American. England countered with an offer of joint occupation and use on condition that aeronautical reciprocity was granted, meaning Hawai'i. The United States rejected the condition and, in August 1938, both sides agreed to a joint occupation and use on the stipulation that Pan American's permit would be a joint grant, which was made in April 1939. In August 1939 Pan American flew its survey flight using a Boeing 314 and, in July 1940, the route was put into commercial operation.

Pan American sought an Australian terminal but this was held up by the reciprocity question. The Allied collapse in Europe and the worsening situation in the Far East caused Australia to yield. Unfortunately for Pan American, Pearl Harbor came before the service could be started. It began in 1942 as a Navy contract service.

RELATED ENTRIES: Canton Island Question; Equatorial Islands, U.S. Aeronautics in; Gatty, Harold; Oceanic Nitrates Corportion; South Seas Commercial Company.

SOURCES AND READINGS: Francis X. Holbrook, "Aeronautical Reciprocity and the Anglo-American Island Race, 1936-37," *Journal of the Royal Australian Historical Society* 57 (1971): 321-35; "The Canton Island Controversy," *Journal of the Royal*

Australian Historical Society 59 (1973): 128-47; and "The Road to Down Under," *Aerospace Historian* 22 (1974): 225-30.   *Francis X. Holbrook*

SPAIN IN THE PACIFIC (1513-1899). The Pacific has been called a "Spanish lake." This was true to some extent in the middle of the sixteenth century. Spain's presence in and around the ocean had five main aspects. First, after Balboa's discovery of the "South Sea," Spain gradually extended her domination along nearly the whole eastern rim of the Pacific. Second, starting with Magellan's voyage, Spain explored the possibility of reaching the coveted Spice Islands (Moluccas) by crossing the ocean. Third, after the discovery of the return route from the western Pacific to the Americas, Spain established her domination over the Philippines and later over Micronesia. Fourth, Spanish expeditions in the South Pacific resulted in discovery of some islands of Melanesia and Polynesia. Fifth, Spain also took part in the last phase of Pacific exploration starting in the eighteenth century and remained present in the ocean until the end of the nineteenth century. The first aspect of Spain's great endeavors can only be covered in a text on Latin American history. The other four aspects can be dealt with here.

There were three main Spanish voyages to the Spice Islands, two from Spain and one from Mexico. Magellan emerged into the Pacific in 1520 after going through the strait which bears his name. Crossing the ocean was a terrible ordeal; no refreshments could be obtained before reaching Guam. Magellan was killed in the Philippines, but one of his ships, the *Victoria*, under the command of Elcano, reached Spain in 1522 having sailed around the world. The next expedition under Loaysa entered the Pacific in 1526. Its purpose was to establish Spanish rule over the Spice Islands in spite of Portuguese objections. Loaysa and Elcano, who had gone with him, died while crossing the ocean. According to a theory exposed by Robert Langdon of Canberra, castaways from one of the ships intermarried with Polynesian women and even today Spanish features may be detected in their descendants. Following a request from Emperor Charles V who ruled Spain, Cortés sent Saavedra from Mexico in 1527 to rescue Spaniards who had remained in the area of the Spice Islands. Saavedra found some of them fighting the Portuguese. He died unable to return to Mexico. Conflict over the Spice Islands was settled by the Treaty of Saragossa (1529) when Charles V renounced his claims in exchange for money.

A number of Spanish vessels had made the crossing of the ocean from east to west, but attempts to recross it had failed. The last one had been made by the *San Juan* of Villalobos' fleet in 1545. Unless a return route could be found, Spain could not hope to keep settlements in the western Pacific. A northern route was finally found in 1565 mainly through the skill of Urdaneta, a survivor of Loaysa's expedition. Spain started colonization of the Philippines under Legazpi's leadership. The islands were actually in Portugal's sphere, but Spain ignored Portuguese protests. Anyway, for several decades, Spain and Portugal were ruled by the same monarch and some Spaniards wanted to conquer parts of the Asian mainland. Possession of the Philippines gave Spain a share in the wealth of Asia through Manila galleon trade. Missionary work led Spain reluctantly to extend her rule over Micronesia starting in the second half of the seventeenth century. Up to that time, only Guam had served as port of call for ships. Spain's sway over Micronesia was never as firm as over the Philippines and she had to reckon more and more with attacks from her European rivals.

While Spain was consolidating her rule in the Philippines, three Spanish expeditions left Peru for the southwest Pacific. The purpose of the first one, under the leadership of Mendaña and Sarmiento de Gamboa was to rediscover islands whereto an Inca ruler was supposed to have sailed and brought back some gold. The result of this expedition was the discovery of the Solomon Islands in 1568; no gold was found. The two ships succeeded in recrossing the Pacific by the northern route, arriving in Peru in 1569. Mendaña wanted to start a settlement in the area discovered, but he was unable to do so until 1595, and then he could not find the islands again; Santa Cruz was discovered instead. The settlement was unsuccessful and Mendaña died. Thanks to the skill of Quirós, the chief pilot, Mendaña's widow brought the remnant of the expedition to the Philippines. In 1605 Quirós undertook to continue exploration but was unable to rediscover either the Solomons or Santa Cruz. He reached Espíritu Santo in the New Hebrides. The vessels got separated as they were about to leave the island. Quirós returned to the Americas on a larger unit, the other two vessels under Torres and Prado discovered in 1606 the passage between Australia and New Guinea now called Torres Strait. Quirós' insistence that Spain should settle islands in the South Pacific to forestall occupation by the other powers fell on deaf ears in the seventeenth century.

The situation changed in the following century. Spain became concerned about the activities of others in the Pacific, and an attempt was made to settle missionaries in Tahiti as a first step towards

occupation. This failed. Spain also participated in final stages of exploration of the ocean. Her greatest navigator of the time was Malaspina who sailed all over the Pacific between 1790 and 1793. His discoveries were few on account of the work by previous explorers, but the scientists who accompanied him collected data which filled many volumes. After the loss of her American colonies, Spain discontinued the Manila galleon trade between Mexico and the Philippines but continued to communicate with the islands through other sea lanes. Towards the middle of the nineteenth century, there was restlessness in Spain and in the Philippines and some liberals were deported to Micronesia. Spain had a serious revolt on her hands in the Philippines when the Spanish-American War broke out. She lost the archipelago and Guam to the United States in 1898. The following year, she sold the islands of Micronesia she had claimed to Germany.

After 1899 Spain's flag was not flying any longer on land owned by her in and around the Pacific Ocean, yet Spain's record in that part of the world was considerable. The eastern rim of the ocean from Mexico to Chile is still inhabited by Spanish-speaking peoples. Spain has made the Philippines the only predominately Christian nation in the area; most of the inhabitants still have Spanish surnames although only a few speak the language of Spain. Spanish navigators discovered many islands in Micronesia, Melanesia, and Polynesia, but only in a few cases, such as Guadalcanal, have the Spanish names been preserved.

RELATED ENTRIES: Guam; Magellan; Mendaña; Micronesia; Polynesia; Sarmiento de Gamboa, Pedro; Vanuatu (New Hebrides).

SOURCES AND READINGS: Antonio Del Campo Echeverria, *España en Oceanía* (Santander: Blanchard y Arce, 1897); William L. Schurz, *The Manila Galleon* (New York: E. P. Dutton, 1939); Oskar H. K. Spate, *The Spanish Lake* (Minneapolis: University of Minnesota Press, 1979).   *André Gschaedler*

SPRECKELS, CLAUS (1828-1908). A sugar manufacturer and businessman, Spreckels was born in Lamstedt, Hanover, Germany, in 1828. He immigrated to the United States in 1846 and made his first fortune in the grocery business, operating stores in Charleston, South Carolina, New York City, and San Francisco. In 1863 he founded the Bay Sugar Refining Company which he sold two years later at a substantial profit. Interested in learning more about the sugar industry, he returned to Germany in 1865 to work in a refinery at Magdeburg where he studied every detail of processing refined sugar. He returned to America in 1867 and established the California Sugar Refinery Company. In subsequent years, he invented a process which greatly reduced the time required to manufacture hard sugar, constructed the largest refinery on the West Coast, and helped develop California's sugar beet industry. Fearful of competition from Hawai'i's high-grade sugar, Spreckels had originally opposed commercial reciprocity with the islands. Once reciprocity with Hawai'i became a reality, however, he became a strong advocate of the new economic arrangement. His conversion was due in part to the fact that the Hawaiian reciprocity treaty omitted the importation into the United States of high-grade sugar and his belief that reciprocity could be made to work to his advantage. Shortly after Senate ratification of the reciprocity treaty in 1875, he invested heavily in the Hawaiian sugar industry. He established the Hawaiian Commercial Company which eventually became the largest sugar producer in the islands. In 1883 Spreckels and one of his sons founded the Oceanic Steamship Line which transported most of the sugar grown in Hawai'i to the United States. His ownership of the California Sugar Refinery Company also gave him great control over the price of Hawaiian sugar. Spreckels was a strong opponent of American annexation of Hawai'i. His opposition stemmed from the fact that annexation would place Hawai'i under U.S. immigration laws, thereby restricting the number of foreign laborers imported to work in the sugar fields. He died in San Francisco on 26 December 1908.

RELATED ENTRIES: Hawai'i; Hawaiian Annexation Treaty.

SOURCES AND READINGS: Jacob Adler, *Claus Spreckels, the Sugar King in Hawaii* (Honolulu: University of Hawaii Press, 1966); P. O. Ray, "Claus Spreckels" in Allen Johnson and Dumas Malone, eds., *Dictionary of American Biography*, 20 vols. (New York: Charles Scribner's Sons, 1928-36) 17: 478-79; Claus Spreckels, "The Future of the Sandwich Islands," *North American Review* 152 (1891): 287-98.

William R. Smith

SPRUANCE, RAYMOND AMES (1886-1969). Spruance was the American admiral who was the tactical and operational commander of the victorious forces during World War II at the Battle of Midway, and in the campaigns in the Gilbert, Mashall, Caroline, Mariana, and Bonin islands. At the end of the war in 1945, he succeeded Chester Nimitz as commander-in-chief of the U.S. Pacific fleet (1945-1946).

RELATED ENTRIES: Nimitz, Chester; War in the Pacific Islands, 1914-1945.

SOURCES AND READINGS: *National Cyclopedia of American Biography* (Clifton, New Jersey: James T. White & Co., 1974) 55: 172-173, photo facing page 172.

Frank P. King

SQUATTER SETTLEMENTS. Human settlement in Oceania traditionally involved kin and language-related peoples living in relatively small communities. The trend since European contact, and particularly since World War II, has been towards towns and cities. Hand in hand with this socio-ecological-economic shift is the growth of settlements within or around such core locations, usually termed *squatter settlements*. Often these communities are of one ethnic group, but sometimes they are mixed. They are usually in areas and cul-de-sacs not immediately evident and on land not owned by the settlers, who build their own shelters. This component of the Pacific population is growing rapidly: Port Moresby, the capital of Papua New Guinea, experienced a 10 to 15 percent annual increase in its squatter population in the 1970s. Associated social problems include school dropouts, unemployment, vagrancy, juvenile delinquency, lawlessness, and other symptoms of the larger process of rural-to-urban migration. Government concern for these settlements in Papua New Guinea is intense for they also represent concerted efforts by people to improve their lives. Efforts to stabilize such settlements have sometimes proven successful, especially if done at the community level of contact.

RELATED ENTRIES: Contemporary Stress Syndromes; Micronesia; Papua New Guinea; Port Moresby.

SOURCES AND READINGS: J. L. Murphy, "Under Thirty in the Third World," *Australian and New Zealand Journal of Psychiatry* 8 (1974): 229-37; K. J. Pataki-Schweizer, "Transcultural Coping: Psychiatric Aspects of Squatter Settlements," *Papua New Guinea Medical Journal* 21 (1978): 270-75.

Kerry J. Pataki-Schweizer

STAINBACK, INGRAM MACKLIN (1883-1961). Born 12 May 1883, Stainback was appointed governor of Hawai'i by President Franklin Delano Roosevelt in 1942 when the territory was the main stronghold in the front line of the Pacific defense. From the day he took office as governor, Stainback faced vital problems that affected the war effort, civil economy, and the prosperity of the territory. He reorganized the Office of Civilian Defense that unified the various races on the islands towards common emergency preparedness. His "Work to Win" campaign encouraged greater participation in the war effort from the Hawaiian citizens. At the same time, he instituted the Postwar Planning Division to aid Hawaiians at the end of the war. Upon leaving the governorship on 8 May 1951 he had served in Hawai'i's highest office for nearly nine years, the longest of any governor. He died 12 April 1961.

RELATED ENTRIES: Hawai'i; War in the Pacific Islands 1914-1945.

SOURCES AND READINGS: A. Grove Day, *Hawaii and Its People* (New York: Meredith Press, 1968); Edward Joesting, *Hawaii* (New York: W. W. Norton & Co., 1972); Ralph S. Kuykendall and A. Grove Day, *Hawaii: A History* (Englewood Cliffs, N.J.: Prentice-Hall, 1961). *Ned B. Williams*

STALEY, THOMAS NETTLESHIP (1823-1898). On 15 December 1861 the Reverend Thomas N. Staley, fellow of Queen's College, Oxford, and a tutor of St. Mark's College, Chelsea, was consecrated an Anglican bishop for Honolulu, Hawai'i. He came to Hawai'i 11 October 1862 at the request of King Kamehameha IV and Queen Emma amid American press charges that his mission was political on the part of the English government and that he was, in fact, a "political missionary." The king gave land for a church and parsonage and a yearly gift of £200 towards the support of the Anglican mission in Hawai'i. However, relations between the English missionaries and their American critics were strained. In 1865 Staley appealed to England for help in establishing schools in Hawai'i. Three Sisters of the Society of the Holy Trinity were sent to Lahaina and there organized the Saint Cross Industrial School for girls. That same year, he attended the General Convention of the Protestant Episcopal Church in America in Philadelphia and addressed the delegates on the need for a joint mission of the American and English churches in Hawai'i. The Protestant Board of Missions agreed and assigned two men to Hawai'i, pledging one half their salaries. In 1867 Bishop Staley left for England and his wife and children followed that same year. He remained in England two years. Upon his return to Hawai'i in 1870 he resigned his office. He had become discouraged by the difficulties of procuring funds for the mission needs and by the insufficiency of his private means to support his large family. The mission had not progressed as rapidly as hoped and the bishop's own style of Anglo-Catholic worship had its critics in his congregation. He returned to England where he worked in a parish until

his death 1 November 1898. He was buried in Saint Clement's churchyard, Boscombe, Bournemouth.

RELATED ENTRIES: Anglican Missions; Hawai'i; Hawai'i, Religions of.

SOURCES AND READINGS: John F. Mulholland, *Hawaii's Religions* (Rutland, Vt.: Charles E. Tuttle Co., 1970); Henry Bond Restarick, *Hawaii 1778-1920: From the Viewpoint of a Bishop* (Honolulu: Paradise of the Pacific, 1924). *Vernice W. Pere*

STEINBERGER, ALBERT BARNES (1840-1894). Cut in the pattern of other Pacific island foreign adventurers, A. B. Steinberger was a prominent figure on the Samoan political scene for only a brief period, 1873 to 1876, but he created much excitement and anticipation and controversy during his short relationship with Samoa.

Born 25 December 1840 in Minersville, Pennsylvania, Steinberger first went to Samoa in 1873 as a special agent of the United States government. His appointment was certainly engineered in part by persons, notably W. H. Webb, who had a financial interest in Samoa and wished to secure it by having the U.S. government assume a more active role in Samoa, even to the extent of annexing the islands or establishing a protectorate over them. In any event Steinberger, a friend of President Ulysses S. Grant, was given a presidential order to proceed to Samoa where, according to the instructions issued him by Secretary of State Hamilton Fish, he was to collect data on the islands, including information about possible harbors for utilization by ocean-going vessels. He was to caution the chiefs about disposing of their lands to individual foreigners. He was further instructed to avoid any conversation with anyone regarding relations between the United States and any foreign government. He was not, Fish told him, a regular diplomatic agent. His appointment was an informal one, and his sole task was to obtain full and accurate information on Samoa. He was given $12 a day for expenses, but no salary.

His reception in Samoa could hardly have pleased him more. The chiefs appreciated his position on the alienation of land. They asked him to review a proposed legal code which he did in consultation with the foreign consuls and the Catholic and Protestant missionaries. He met with all of the important Samoan dignitaries, some of whom attempted to involve him in their political disputes with each other. He was asked to read the proposed 1873 constitution, which he did and which he claimed the credit for establishing.

Steinberger left for the United States after three

months, carrying with him letters from the leading missionaries and chiefs to President Grant. The latter asked that Steinberger be returned to Samoa as the American governor. The missionary letters requested that the United States establish a protectorate in Samoa with Steinberger as the American representative. Steinberger definitely created the impression in Samoa that he expected to return to Samoa as an official representative of the United States. Secretary of State Fish, nonetheless, attempted to dampen Steinberger's enthusiasm for the creation of an American protectorate in Samoa.

In the meantime, Steinberger sailed for Hamburg where he negotiated an agreement with Godeffroy and Son in September 1874, under which he agreed to virtually turn over the Samoan economy to the German firm. In return for this arrangement, Steinberger, who it was understood would become premier of Samoa, would share in the company's profits from the exploitation of Samoa and the Samoans.

Although Steinberger told the State Department of his meeting with the Godeffroy company, he did not give them the details of his private arrangement with them. He received permission from the State Department to return to Samoa as a special agent. His assignment was to observe and report back on Samoan affairs. He was to assure the Samoans of the interest that the United States had for their welfare, but no more. He arrived back in Apia 1 April 1875 aboard an American naval vessel bearing arms and ammunitions as a gift to the Samoan government.

He immediately immersed himself in Samoan politics. He rewrote the constitution, providing for the position of premier in the new government. He plainly saw himself playing this role and he was appointed premier 4 July 1875.

Steinberger's involvement in Samoan politics raised some anxieties in the foreign community, and doubts about his status began to be heard. The American consul, S. S. Foster, took a dislike to Steinberger's activities and wrote to the State Department for clarification of Steinberger's official role in Samoa. The missionaries likewise began to be concerned about the rise of Steinberger's star. Fish rebuked Steinberger for the role he was playing in Samoa, particularly for encouraging the Samoans to believe that United States annexation of Samoa was imminent. Steinberger evidently wished to retain some form of official status with the U.S. government, and he did not resign his position as special agent until 29 October 1875, more than three months after he had accepted the premiership.

In January 1876, in a letter to Consul Foster, the State Department indicated that Steinberger no longer had any official status with the U.S. government. Steinberger's old friends, the British consul, S. F. Williams, and Dr. George A. Turner, the medical missionary, in company with Captain C. E. Stevens of the *Barracouta* then in port, conspired to have Steinberger deported. They took the nominal head of state, Malietoa Laupepa, aboard the *Barracouta* and persuaded him to request the deportation of Steinberger, although Malietoa wondered what business it was of theirs who governed Samoa.

Steinberger was arrested by a party of armed marines and sailors from the *Barracouta*. He was kept aboard the ship for two months before being finally put ashore in Levuka, Fiji. From there he went to New Zealand where he continued to attempt to play a role in Samoan politics, writing letters to the chiefs advising them on particular political actions. From New Zealand he went to London in an effort to vindicate himself with the support of the U.S. State Department and to press a claim for damages against the British government. Stevens was dismissed from the Royal Navy for his role in the Steinberger deportation and Consul Foster was also removed. The British government, nonetheless, refused to indemnify Steinberger on the grounds that Captain Stevens had acted as he had done on the request of the U.S. consul. Steinberger never again saw Samoa. He died 2 May 1894 in Massachusetts.

RELATED ENTRIES: American Samoa; Stevens, Charles E.; Webb, William H.; Western Samoa.

SOURCES AND READINGS: George H. Ryden, *The Foreign Policy of the United States in Relation to Samoa* (reprint ed., New York: Octagon Books, 1933).   *Jerry K. Loveland*

STEVENS, CHARLES E. A British naval captain, Stevens was involved in the Steinberger affair in Samoa, 1875. On 12 December 1875, Stevens aboard the British man-of-war *Barracouta* sailed into Pago Pago harbor, Samoa, on request of the acting British consul to give military support in ousting Albert B. Steinberger, a U.S. citizen who had assumed almost absolute power in Samoa. Captain Stevens persuaded King Malietoa to board the ship and sign a letter requesting the arrest of "Special Agent" Steinberger, whereupon he was brought aboard and detained. The *Ta'imua* and *Faipule* (types of legislative assemblies) forcefully deposed King Malietoa for his actions. On 13 March, an armed party from the *Barracouta* attacked the rebellious Samoans, and in the skirmish three marines and eight Samoans were killed. On 30 March, Stevens sailed with Steinberger aboard and landed at Levuka, Fiji. On 5 April, Steinberger was released, but he never returned to Samoa. All three major participants in the Steinberger affair (Captain Stevens and the British and American consuls) were dismissed. Stevens was court-martialed in England and dismissed from service for grossly exceeding his authority although Stevens pleaded that he was merely acting according to the wishes of the consuls and the king of Samoa.

RELATED ENTRIES: American Samoa; Britain in the Pacific; Steinberger, Albert B.; Western Samoa.

SOURCES AND READINGS: James W. Davidson, *Samoa Mo Samoa: The Emergence of the Independent State of Western Samoa* (New York: Oxford University Press, 1967); W. P. Morrell, *Britain in the Pacific Islands* (New York: Oxford University Press, 1960).   *Joseph Montoya*

STEVENS, JOHN LEAVITT (1820-1895). A clergyman, journalist, and U.S. diplomat, Stevens was born at Mount Vernon, Maine, in 1820. He attended Maine Wesleyan Seminary and Waterville Classical Institute. In 1845 he entered the ministry and served as pastor in the Universalist church for ten years. He was owner, along with James Gillespie Blaine, of the *Kennebec Journal* of Augusta, Maine, which he edited from 1855 to 1869. He was minister to Paraguay and Uruguay from 1870 to 1874, to Norway and Sweden from 1877 to 1883, and to Hawai'i from 1889 to 1893.

While he was U.S. minister to Hawai'i, Stevens sent numerous reports to the State Department. He warned that the steady importation of Oriental labor coupled with the growing discontent among sugar growers in Hawai'i over the McKinley tariff of 1890 would destroy American influence in the islands. Stevens called for the annexation of the Hawaiian Islands as soon as possible.

In mid-January 1893, a small group of American Hawaiians, led by Sanford B. Dole, revolted against the islands' monarchical government. An attempt by Queen Lili'uokalani to replace the existing Hawaiian constitution with an autocratic new one that would return greater power to the Hawaiians, precipitated the uprising. On 16 January 1893, the revolutionaries asked Minister Stevens to land troops from the cruiser *Boston* to protect American lives and property. Stevens complied with the revolutionaries' request and ordered over 150 sailors and marines ashore. They took up positions which intimidated the queen's forces and protected the revolutionaries in their occupation of Honolulu's public buildings. On 17 January 1893 the revolutionaries proclaimed the monarchy abolished and established a provisional government which Stevens immediately recognized.

The extent to which Stevens supported the overthrow of the Hawaiian monarchy is still open to question. There is no doubt that he strongly advocated American annexation of Hawai'i and used his position as minister to aid the revolutionaries. However, his actions prior to the Hawaiian revolution are unclear. James H. Blount, sent to Hawai'i by President Cleveland to investigate the causes of the revolution, alleged that the revolt would not have occurred without Stevens' promise to support the revolutionaries with U.S. naval forces. In 1894 Stevens denied under oath, before a Senate committee, Blount's accusation that he conspired with the revolutionaries to overthrow the Hawaiian monarchy. Furthermore, all of the leaders of the revolution swore that Stevens was innocent of the conspiratorial charges made against him by Blount. Stevens returned to Maine after the Hawaiian affair, where he died on 8 February 1895.

RELATED ENTRIES: Dole, Sanford B.; Hawai'i; Hawaiian Revolution; Lili'uokalani.

SOURCES AND READINGS: William A. Russ, Jr., *The Hawaiian Revolution, 1893-1894* (Selinsgrove, Pa.: Susquehanna University Press, 1959); Thomas M. Spaulding, "John Leavitt Stevens" in Allen Johnson and Dumas Malone, eds., *Dictionary of American Biography*, 20 vols. (New York: Charles Scribner's Sons, 1928-36) 17: 618-19; John L. Stevens, "A Plea for Annexation," *North American Review* 157 (1893): 736-45; U.S. Department of State, *Papers Relating to the Foreign Relations of the United States, 1894* (Washington, D.C.: Government Printing Office, 1895).   *William R. Smith*

STEVENSON, ROBERT LOUIS (1850-1894). An author, essayist, and writer, Stevenson was born in Edinburgh on 13 November 1850. He studied engineering and later law. He devoted the rest of his time to writing. Handicapped from youth by tuberculosis, he traveled widely in Europe, America, and the South Pacific in search of better health. During the 1870s, he contributed numerous articles and stories to magazines. His first popular success as a writer came with *Treasure Island* (1882) and *Kidnapped* (1886). He married an American, Fanny Van deGrift Osbourne, a divorcée several years his senior. In June 1882 Stevenson and family left for the South Pacific visiting the Marquesas, Tahiti, Hawai'i, Micronesia, and Australia before settling permanently in Samoa. In 1889 he built a home at Vailima ("five waters") about three miles outside of Apia. He opposed Western imperialism and stood against white colonialism which nearly resulted in his deportation from Samoa. Life in Samoa was certainly the happiest and perhaps the most creative time in his life. He wrote

The Beach of Faleia (1892), one of the best South Seas stories ever written. His other work, *Weir of Hermiston* (1896), contains some of his most brilliant narrative writing. Stevenson died suddenly of a cerebral hemorrhage on 3 December 1894 and was buried on famous Mount Vaea, overlooking Apia Bay.

RELATED ENTRIES: Western Samoa.

SOURCES AND READINGS: Graham Belfour, *The Life of Robert Louis Stevenson* (New York: Charles Scribner's Sons, 1915); David Deaches, *Robert Louis Stevenson* (Norfolk, Conn.: New Directions Books, 1947).   *Michael P. Singh*

STEWART, WILLIAM (1820-1873). Stewart was an Irish entrepreneur and wine merchant who settled in Tahiti (1864) to raise cotton and compete in the soaring prices on the world markets. Stewart obtained prime land called Atimaono at Teahupo'o (Tahiti) for his Polynesian Plantation Company, later called the Tahiti Cotton and Coffee Plantation Company, directed from London by his brother-in-law Auguste Soarès. Local permission was granted to import nearly one thousand Chinese and three hundred other Polynesian laborers to cultivate the land (1867). Under Stewart's management, the company at first profited, but with the end of the U.S. Civil War, demand on the world market declined and the company could no longer compete. After rumors of human atrocities being committed at Atimaono, a French government investigation team found Stewart innocent of charges. Later, his brother swindled him out of a large sum of money and attempts were made to save the collapsing business. Stewart finally declared bankruptcy on 24 September 1873. That night he died of a violent hemorrhage. The plantation fell into disuse and decay. The Chinese "club," theaters, and homes no longer stand. Today, the only visible legacy of Stewart's enterprise is the industrious Chinese population that dominates the economic life of the island.

RELATED ENTRIES: French Polynesia.

SOURCES AND READINGS: Robert Langdon, *Tahiti: Island of Love* (Sydney: Pacific Publications, 1949) (esp. chap. 41); Eric Ramsden, "William Stewart and the Introduction of Chinese Labour in Tahiti, 1864-74," *Journal of the Polynesian Society* 55 (1946): 187-214.   *Robert D. Craig*

STICK CHARTS. Stick charts are navigational aids made and used by Marshall islanders. Each chart is fashioned of thin strips of wood, often coconut leaf midribs, which are laid out in the manner which best suits the individual navigator. They are tied with twine where they cross. The resulting open framework is usually of an irregular square or rectangular shape. Small shells are tied at strategic points on the strips to designate islands, while certain of the strips themselves represent whichever patterns of ocean swells the navigator wishes shown. The Marshallese themselves have no generic term for the charts, but categorize them either as *mattang*, *medo*, or *rebillib*. The *mattang* is a generalized representation of swell patterns which form around the typical single island or atoll. It is used to teach a novice navigator the fundamentals of the navigational system and to demonstrate theoretical problems. *Mattang*, with their decorative and symmetrical lines, are often produced for the tourist trade. The *medo* is specific, representing patterns formed by swells around a given group of neighboring atolls, probably the navigator's own, those he visits most often, or those he must pass to travel farther. The *medo* is perhaps the chart tailored most carefully to individual requirements. The *rebillib* usually represents one chain of the archipelago (or, more rarely, both the Ralik and Radak chains), showing the directions from which the primary swells approach them. Spatial relationships between atolls are also depicted, although not to an accurate scale. A saying, "the navigator wears the atolls like a wreath," confirms that the important knowledge is in the seaman's head. The charts serve only as general guides and even then as only part of a complex system of navigation which uses all the more ordinary observations of natural phenomena. *Mattang*, *medo*, and *rebillib* have been subjected to misinterpretation since first observed by outsiders. Their use has also been attributed to other islanders. Nevertheless, the invention, manufacture, and use of these navigational aids is unique to the Marshalls.

RELATED ENTRIES: Micronesia.

SOURCES AND READINGS: Mary A. Browning, "Walab im Medo: Canoes and Navigation in the Marshalls," *Oceans* 5, no. 1 (1972): 25-37.
Mary Browning

STURGES, ALBERT (1819-1887). A graduate of Wabash College and Yale Seminary, Sturges arrived on the Micronesian island of Ponape in 1852 as a Congregationalist missionary of the American Board of Commissioners for Foreign Missions (ABCFM). Albert and his wife Susan were a part of the first band of Christian missionaries to arrive in Micronesia.

The Sturgeses established the first mission station on Ponape in Kitti district. They remained on Ponape until 1870 when they were forced to return to the United States for medical reasons. During these first eighteen years, the Sturgeses led other ABCFM missionaries and Ponapean converts in the work of Bible translation, establishment of a training school for pastors, and the pioneering of new churches in other districts of Ponape. Opposition to their efforts, which continued for many years, came from a number of island chiefs as well as from the colony of white beachcombers and traders on Ponape.

Albert Sturges returned to the island from his visit in the United States in 1871. In the next two years he extended mission activities to the islands of Mokil and Pingelap and began preparations for Christianizing the islands to the west of Ponape. In January 1874 he accompanied three Ponapean couples whom he had trained as missionaries to the Mortlock Islands for the establishment of the first mission stations there. Later, in 1879, he also assisted in the settlement of the first missionary within the Truk Lagoon—a Ponapean named Moses who had been aided by Sturges when orphaned as a child. Sturges remained based on Ponape throughout the 1870s, making yearly visits to the mission stations on Truk and in the Mortlocks. After a furlough to the United States in 1882, he returned to Ponape and continued his work until a stroke forced his retirement in 1885. He died in 1887 having played an instrumental part in the missionization of the central Carolines.

RELATED ENTRIES: American Board of Commissioners for Foreign Missions; Moses, Teikoroi.

SOURCES AND READINGS: American Board of Commissioners for Foreign Missions, *Letters and Papers of the American Board of Commissioners for Foreign Missions: Mission to Micronesia, 1852-1909*, vols. 1-3, 5, 8, 9, Houghton Library, Harvard University, Cambridge, Mass.; David and Leona Crawford, *Missionary Adventures in the South Pacific* (Rutland, Vt.: Charles E. Tuttle Co., 1967).

Charles B. Reafsnyder

SUKUNA, RATU JOSEF LALABALAVU VAANIALIALIA (1888-1958). "Statesman, Soldier, Paramount Chief, Leader of Men," as the legend on Sukuna's statue in Suva has it. Born 22 April 1888 to Ratu Jone Madraiwiwi and Adi Litaiana Maopa, Ratu Sukuna was descended from the Fijian chiefly families of Lau and Bau in particular. He was given a British tutor from childhood, then he studied in Wanganuia, New Zealand, and after matriculation in 1906, he was brought back to Fiji to be a fifth-class clerk in the secretariat. He was a brilliant translator. Under the anthropologist A. M. Hocart, he taught at Lau Provincial School; in 1913 he was sent away to Oxford at the instigation of Fijian chiefs who wanted an educated spokesman. When World War II broke out, Ratu Sukuna joined the French Foreign Legion after the British Army rejected him as a colored man. Being wounded and winning the *Médaille Militaire*, he was brought back to Fiji, but he did not rest until he could return to France in 1917, if only as quartermaster sergeant with the Fijian Labour Corps. Graduating from Oxford after the war, called to the Bar, he served as chief assistant to the Native Lands Commission. Able now to deal on equal terms with British colonial rulers, Ratu Sukuna saw as his role returning Fijian affairs, then in the hands of European district commissioners, to Fijian hands, but not by confrontation. A gentle, humorous man, behind a formidable reserve, he hid his feelings well; they nonetheless appear in his comment that he was supposed to be "loyal and amiable" in legislative council when he was forced to accept a seat there in 1932 as being "a native in whom there is a sufficient veneer of education to conceal the savage." In 1932 he became additionally provincial commissioner for Lau and sat in legislative council too, breaking his silence there when Fijian orthography was attacked or when he felt it expedient to join conservative European members in the late 1930s in seeking to stop Indian demands for common roll, which would have led to Indian domination, by trying to return to a wholly nominated council. Acknowledged leader of those Fijians who did not incline towards the messianic Apolosi R. Nawai, Ratu Sukuna came into the center of national politics in 1943-1944 when Sir Philip Mitchell put Fijian affairs back into Fijian hands. Ratu Sukuna at that time was recruiting officer for the Fiji military forces and reserves commissioner, whereby he implemented the new policy of setting aside Fijian land reserves while making the rest of Fijian land available for leasing through a trust board. Sukuna also was made secretary for Fijian affairs. In that role, he attempted to advance Fijian economic development—the main postwar task, as he saw it, far more important than political change—by building on the corporate strength of Fijian society. Independent farmers, *galala*, had no great friend in him. He believed in organic growth in society, education for a basically agricultural environment, big villages as counterpoises to check urbanization, respect for and observance of tradition, and common decency—a man whose public persona sometimes obscured the witty human being, but who, again, sometimes put home truths over by humor, as when he told the Defense Club in Suva what Europeans thought of Fijians. He was awarded the Knight of the British

Empire (KBE) in 1946 and the Knight Commander of Saint Michael and Saint George (KCMG) in 1958. He died off Colombo on 10 May 1958.

RELATED ENTRIES: Fiji; Nawai, Apolosi R.; Thurston, John.

SOURCES AND READINGS: Alan Burns, *Fiji* (London: Her Majesty's Stationery Office, 1963); "Sukuna, Famous Fijian, Loved by all, Dies at Sea," *Pacific Islands Monthly*, June 1958, pp. 61-63.

Deryck Scarr

SWAIN'S ISLAND. *See* American Samoa.

SWANSTON, ROBERT SHERSON (1825-1892). A trader, planter, and political activist in the islands for forty years, Swanston was born in India and moved with his family to the Australian colonies in 1824, where the Swanstons became one of the established pioneering families. Between 1844 and 1856 he worked in the colonial service in South Africa, on his family's properties in Tasmania and Victoria, and took on several merchant ventures on the American West Coast. He visited Samoa, Tahiti, and Pitcairn on transpacific voyages. In 1856, en route for Australia, he called at Samoa to act as temporary American consul for nine months. He then changed plans and joined a plantation venture in Fiji. This began a long sojourn in the islands.

In Fiji, Swanston tried planting, sheep breeding, trading and finally became involved in local politics, as secretary to Ma'afu in the Lau Confederation, as acting British consul 1859, as minister for native affairs in the Cakobau government, and as a key figure in the precession political debates. After cession, he served as secretary for native affairs and later as stipendiary magistrate.

After disputes with the Crown Colony administration, he moved back to Australia and then Samoa. There he disagreed with Sir Arthur Gordon (1829-1912), governor of Fiji and Western Pacific high commissioner, over an offer to serve as British consul in Samoa. After returning briefly to Fiji, he then joined the German firm of J. C. Godeffroy and Son in Jaluit, Ponape, and Yap. Eventually, he settled in Rotuma Island with his married daughter from 1885 to 1887 and finally retired to Fiji.

RELATED ENTRIES: Fiji; Gordon, Arthur; Micronesia.

SOURCES AND READINGS: A. B. Brewster Papers, Museum of Archaeology and Ethnology, Cambridge University, Cambridge, England; R. A. Derrick, *A History of Fiji* (Suva: Government Printer, 1968).

Alan Maxwell Quanchi

TAHITI. *See* French Polynesia.

TAHITIAN ANNEXATION BY THE FRENCH, 1880. The annexation of Tahiti by the French in 1880 can best be understood by an examination of international European politics during the late nineteenth century. By 1880 France had lost most of her overseas colonies and, in 1871, she had suffered a humiliating defeat by the German army, followed by a bloody civil war with the Paris commune. Up to then, the French had generally been apathetic concerning their overseas possessions, and in the 1870s internal problems prevented any increase of these interests. One of her few surviving overseas interests was Tahiti where, in 1842, she had established a protectorate under the rule of Queen Pomare IV. With a change in the French government in 1879, Jules Grévy became the new Republican president. His council members favored the establishment of a French colonial empire to match the growing empires of other European states: Russia, Belgium, Holland, Great Britain, and especially Germany who had humiliated her in 1871. They hoped to gain some compensation for their loss of Alsace and Lorraine as well as to keep pace with the colonial gains being made by their neighbors. Tahitians never knew that in desperation to keep her states of Alsace and Lorraine in 1871, France offered Germany all of her overseas possessions, including Tahiti, if she could only retain these two eastern French provinces. Germany refused, and as a result, France grew to hate the growing, powerful German state. It is not surprising, therefore, that the new French Republican government in 1879 was alarmed about news of German infiltration into Samoa and of German gunboats sailing into Tahitian waters. Other considerations, no doubt, influenced their decisions, such as the opening of the Panama Canal which they thought would make Tahiti an important commercial landfall in the Pacific. French patriotic imperialism now became coupled with Pacific commercial interests. It was vital to France not to allow her Pacific islands to fall into competitive hands and, in 1880, the Pacific islands belonged to anyone who cared to raise a flag. The new French government made no little haste in dispatching Commander Isidore Chessé to the Pacific. When he arrived in Tahiti and heard of King Pomare V's dissolute living and bankruptcy, of the various schemes to change the line of succession, of the power of the English Protestants, and of the fact that German gunboats were nearby, he concluded that something decisive must be done. Chessé convinced the king that it would be advantageous for him and for France if he would simply agree to French annexation. After "negotiations" with the council of chiefs on Tahiti and Mo'orea, the document was drawn up, signed by the king and the island chieftans on 29 June 1880 and was then ratified by the French National Assembly in Paris on 30 December. Under its provisions, Pomare retained his title, and he and members of his immediate royal family received government pensions for life. (Pomare and his title died in 1891.) The new executive power in Tahiti became a governor named from Paris who held virtually absolute authority over the islands, although he was assisted by a five-man ministerial board called the privy council and a larger elected body called the general council, but by 1903 these councils had essentially lost all but their advisory powers.

RELATED ENTRIES: Ari'i Ta'ima'i; French Polynesia; Jarnac, Convention of; Marau, Joanna; Pomare Family.

SOURCES AND READINGS: A. C. Eugène Caillot, *Histoire de la Polynésie Orientale* (Paris: Ernest Leroux, 1910); Bengt Danielsson, *Le Mémorial Polynésien*, vol. 3 (Pape'ete: Hibiscus Editions, 1978). *Robert D. Craig*

TANNA. Tanna lies 169° 19′ east longitude in the New Hebrides (Vanuatu) Archipelago. Approximately 25 km × 30 km long (15.5 mi × 18.6 mi), the land rises from a central plateau (Middle Bush) to two peaks in the south: Mount Tukosmera (1,084 m, 3,556 ft) and Mount Melen (1,047 m, 3,435 ft). A small cinder cone (361 m, 1,184 ft) near White Sands is in continuous volcanic eruption. The island is populated by Melanesians although it has experienced significant Polynesian influence. Earliest evidence of human occupation is dated about 500 B.C. Cook named the island during his visit in August 1774. In the nineteenth century it became a popular watering spot for whalers and sandalwood traders, and later it provided a large proportion of the men and women recruited to work the plantations of Queensland, Fiji, and New Caledonia. Christian missionaries arrived in 1839, and the island was eventually two-thirds converted by the Presbyterian mission. A period of Christian "big-man" government, beginning in 1906, is known as the Tanna Law. A cultural revitalization movement, the John Frum Cargo Cult, emptied the churches in 1941. The population, of about 16,202 (1980 estimate), remains divided into Christians, pagans, and cultists. Copra is the economic mainstay although market gardens and tourism are increasingly important resources.

RELATED ENTRIES: Cargo Cult, John Frum; Koukare; Melanesian Recruitment to Queensland, Patterns of; Port Resolution; Vanuatu (New Hebrides); Yasur Volcano.   *Lamont C. Lindstrom*

TASMAN, ABEL JANSZOON (1603-1659). A Dutch explorer of the Pacific, Tasman was born in the Dutch province of Groningen and started service with the Dutch East India Company in 1634. After gaining much experience in matters of the sea as a captain, the opportunity came for him in 1642 to undertake the voyage which was to make him famous in the annals of exploration. The East India Company speculated that there might be very rich lands south and east of the points on the coast of New Holland (now the western half of Australia) which had been sighted by Dutch navigators. Governor-General Anthony van Diemen selected Tasman to command two ships to explore that part of the ocean. First, Tasman sailed from Java to the island of Mauritius in the Indian Ocean. From there, on 8 October 1642, he started sailing south to nearly 50° south latitude. Weather conditions obliged him to return to about 44° south latitude. Remaining in about the same latitude and steering northeastward, he sighted land on 24 November. When the Dutch landed, they noticed the land was inhabited but did not see anyone. Tasman called the new land Van Diemen's Land (now Tasmania). Tasman continued his voyage eastward, crossing what is now known as the Tasman Sea. On 13 December 1642, he "discovered" the South Island of New Zealand which he

called Staten Land. Maoris killed some of his men in Murderers' Bay (now Golden Bay). Tasman skirted the North Island. He did not realize that New Zealand was actually two islands, but a chart made by Visscher, Tasman's chief associate, shows an opening where Cook Strait is located. After leaving New Zealand, Tasman sailed north and in January 1643 he "discovered" some Tonga islands. Then in February he sighted some islands of the Fiji group. After a loop in what is now the Bismarck Archipelago where New Britain was "discovered," the Dutch ships skirted the northern coast of New Guinea. The voyage ended in Batavia on 15 June 1643.

Tasman's achievement had been momentous. Sailing from a great distance he had circumnavigated Australia, but Van Diemen and the directors of the East India Company were not satisfied, and in 1644 Tasman was sent on a number of missions. In 1648 around the Gulf of Carpentaria, north of Australia. He failed, however, to discover the strait through which Torres had passed. After his return to Java, Tasman was sent on a number of misions. In 1648 he nearly succeeded in capturing one of the Manila galleons, but he was brought to trial following a complaint by one of his men and was suspended from duty. He was reinstated and left the company between 1651 and 1653. He stayed in the Indies and died some time before October 1659. Tasman's journal of his 1642-1643 voyage is richly illustrated, and his charts greatly influenced the development of cartography of the Pacific.

SOURCES AND READINGS: J. C. Beaglehole, *The Exploration of the Pacific*, 3d ed. (Stanford: Stanford University Press, 1966); Herman R. Friis, ed., *The Pacific Basin: A History of its Geographical Exploration* (New York: American Geographical Society, 1967); A. Sharp, *The Discovery of the Pacific Islands* (Oxford: Clarendon Press, 1962) and *The Voyages of Abel Janszoon Tasman* (Oxford: Clarendon Press, 1968).   *André Gschaedler*

TATI (ca. 1770-1854). A great high chief of Tahiti's western district of Papara, Tati was born around 1770. He remembered having seen Captain James Cook during his last visit to the island in 1777. Descended from an ancient family that generally rivaled the rising power of the Pomares in the north, Tati surprisingly supported Pomare II's rule. When Pomare II died in 1824, ancient custom would have transferred these royal privileges to Tati. However, the London missionaries insisted upon crowning young Pomare III as king of Tahiti, a ceremony in which Tati himself carried the royal crown. When

Queen Pomare IV revolted against the rule of the missionaries, Tati opposed her religious and political supporters (called the *Mamaia*). Tati supported French intervention to avoid anarchy in Tahiti and he and the regent, Paraita, signed the document for a French protectorate in September 1842. When Queen Pomare IV finally returned to her position and to Pape'ete, Tati became the president of the legislative assembly from 1848 to 1852. All contemporary accounts describe him as one of the handsomest in all the islands, as one having the best manners, as one who was law-abiding, honest, and sincerely attached to the Christian religion. He was considered one of the most brilliant orators in modern Tahitian history. Two drawings of this great chief are extant: one in Moerenhout's famous work, and one by Sébastien-Charles Giraud which appeared in *Illustration* (January 1948), p. 328. When Tati died on 16 July 1854 the chieftainship passed to his famous granddaughter Ari'i Ta'ima'i.

RELATED ENTRIES: Ari'i Ta'ima'i; French Polynesia; Pomare Family.

SOURCES AND READINGS: Jacques-Antoine Moerenhout, *Voyages aux îles du Grand Océan*, 2 vols. (Paris: Adrien Maisonneuve, 1837); Patrick O'Reilly, *Tahitiens* (Paris: Musée de l'Homme, 1962).
Robert D. Craig

TAUFA'AHAU, GEORGE TUPOU I (?-1893). The first king of Tonga, Tupou united the islands as one kingdom in the 1850s and ruled them securely and peacefully. He crusaded for Christianity in his youth and formed a lasting friendship with the Reverend Shirley Baker of the Wesleyan mission. His later efforts were to keep Tonga for the Tongans and outside influences under strict control. In June 1862 Tupou passed a new law code for the islands which forbade the sale of land to foreigners. A later "Act to Regulate Hereditary Lands" was passed by the parliament in October 1882 by which all land was declared to belong to the king. This act further established the concept that every Tongan had a right to earn a living by working his own land. He also initiated the radical Emancipation Edict which abolished the traditional payment of goods by the lower classes to higher-ranking chiefs. It successfully replaced the kinship system of commerce with a cash system supported by a new, cash, poll tax levied on every Tongan over the age of sixteen. The poll tax provided the government with salaries and the chiefs with compensating pensions for the loss of their kinship payments. Sweeping economic changes accompanied these new laws, resulting in Tonga be-

coming one of the Pacific's major producers of copra and other agricultural products. Prosperity gave rise to the development of public facilities and a new era of modernization for Tonga. Tupou built a royal palace and installed a throne. A crown, flag, great seal, and national anthem of Tonga were prepared and a constitution was written by Baker. The immediate results of the new constitution were treaties with both Germany (1876) and England (1879) which recognized and protected Tonga. The kingdom suffered civil unrest when a large faction of the people opposed Baker's strong influence on the king and government. Later discord arose out of the king's dissatisfaction at relations between the Wesleyan church and the government. Tupou established a Free Church of Tonga by proclamation and then exercised harsh judgment on those who refused to join the new church. The Wesleyans became targets of personal violence throughout the islands and were eventually exiled to Fiji. The British government conducted an investigation of the kingdom which resulted in Baker's forced removal from Tonga. Tupou died of pneumonia three years later, and was mourned by his people for six months. The accomplishments of his reign attest to the wisdom of his rule, as Tonga has enjoyed prosperity and well-being due to his sweeping vision.

RELATED ENTRIES: Baker, Shirley; Tonga.

SOURCES AND READINGS: Noel Rutherford, ed., *The Friendly Islands: A History of Tonga* (Melbourne: Oxford University Press, 1977).   *Vernice W. Pere*

TE MOANA, CHARLES (1821?-1863). Te Moana, chief of the bay of Taiohae in Nuku Hiva (Marquesas), later was recognized as "king" by the French (1842). While still a young man, Te Moana was sent to the Methodist school on Rarotonga by the missionaries. He later signed on as cook on an English whaling ship and in each port the sailors would show him off for a few pennies a head. Herman Melville called him "Mowanna" and said that his tattoos resembled the spirals on Trajan's columns in Rome. After spending seven years at sea, Te Moana returned to the Marquesas in December 1839. Within a few months he attempted to exert his authority over the other chiefs of the island. Civil war raged for six months. The Catholic church was burned and the missionaries left the island. Only through intermediaries were the hostile forces finally reconciled. The French commander, Dupetit-Thouars, coming to take possession of the Marquesas for France, signed a treaty with Te Moana on 31 May 1842 and recognized him as "king" of Nuku Hiva. The French agreed to aid him in his attempt to rescue his wife, Vahekehu, who had been stolen by the Taioa tribe. Finally, through gifts and negotiations by the missionary Baudichon, she was returned. Both she and her husband were baptized Catholics in 1853. In September 1862 Te Moana died in the great smallpox epidemic that was brought from Peru. Within six months almost half of the population of Nuku Hiva had been wiped out. Having had no natural children from his wife, Te Moana had adopted Stanislas Moanatini and willed his rights to him.

RELATED ENTRIES: Dupetit-Thouars, Abel; French Polynesia; Marquesas Islands; Vahekehu, Elisabeth.

SOURCES AND READINGS: Robert D. Craig, *The Marquesas Islands: Their Discovery and Early History by Reverend Robert Thomson* (Laie, Hawai'i: Brigham Young University—Hawai'i Campus Press, 1978).
Robert D. Craig

TERAUPO'O, WAR OF (1880-1897). In 1880, chief Teraupo'o from the island of Ra'iatea, French Polynesia, refused to recognize French annexation of the leeward Society Islands or the authority of his island king, Tamatoa V. Teraupo'o and his followers fled to Avera valley where they would not accept the government's demands for allegiance nor the payment of taxes. For ten years he refused to negotiate with the French governors in Pape'ete. Finally in January 1897, the French organized a military expedition under Captain Boyle to force the rebels from the valley. Six weeks later the French captured Teraupo'o and his followers. He and many of them were either exiled to New Caledonia or sent to the Marquesas. Amnesty for them all finally came in 1905, and Teraupo'o and his family returned to Ra'iatea where he lived until his death.

RELATED ENTRIES: French Polynesia.

SOURCES AND READINGS: Auguste Caillot, *Les Polynésiens orientaux au contact de la civilisation* (Paris: Ernest Leroux, 1909).
Robert D. Craig

TERI'IERO'O A TERI'IERO'OTERAI (1875-1952). The illustrious chief Teri'iero'o came from the district of Papeno'o, Tahiti. Under his administration, public works and agriculture on the eastern coast of Tahiti were all intensified: the eastern road was completed, a bridge built at Papeno'o, and a rapid increase made in the cultivation of coconuts, coffee, vanilla, and vegetables. His commanding appearance and oratory made him a popular public figure. He entertained international figures who visited the islands. For his meritorious duty in both

war and peace, he was highly decorated and respected by both the French and the Tahitians. He died at Papeno'o on 19 August 1952.

RELATED ENTRIES: French Polynesia.

SOURCES AND READINGS: Martial Iorss, "Teriieroo a Teriierooterai, 1875-1952," *Bulletin de la société des études océaniennes* 100 (1952): 454-57; Patrick O'Reilly, *Tahitiens* (Paris: Musée de l'Homme, 1962.
Robert D. Craig

TEVITA 'UNGA (?-1879). A member of the Tongan royalty, Tevita 'Unga was the son of George Tupou and Kalolaine, a secondary wife of the king. Although his mother was cast off by the king upon his conversion to Christianity, Tevita 'Unga was nevertheless named heir to the throne in the constitution of 1875. 'Unga died in 1879 while still crown prince and premier. His grandson, George Taufa'ahau, succeeded to the throne.

RELATED ENTRIES: Taufa'ahau, George Tupou I; Tonga.

SOURCES AND READINGS: Noel Rutherford, ed., *The Friendly Islands, A History of Tonga* (Melbourne: Oxford Univesity Press, 1977).   *Vernice W. Pere*

THOMAS, JOHN (1795-1881). Although not the first Christian missionary to Tonga, nor the first Wesleyan, John Thomas founded with John Hutchinson the first permanent mission, and it was during his stays (1826-1850 and 1855-1859) that most of Tonga became Christian. Though hampered in the early years of his mission by inadequate training (he had been a blacksmith), and by a certain amount of enthnocentrism and lack of tact, Thomas was able to accomplish through diligence and perseverence what other, perhaps more brilliant, men had not been able to do: establish and maintain a Christian mission in Tonga. He arrived in Tonga 26 June 1826 and settled at Hihifo on the island of Tongatapu. After three frustrating and unsuccessful years, during which Hutchinson had to leave because of ill health, Thomas moved to Nuku'alofa, and in 1830 to Ha'apai, where he was instrumental in the conversion to Christianity of Taufa'ahau—later King George Tupou I, the first king of all Tonga. By 1850, when he returned to England, he was regarded as the elder statesman of the Wesleyan missionaries. Finding England not to his liking, he traveled to Tonga again in 1855, but his second trip proved too much for him and his wife and their health suffered. He retired to England for good in 1859, living the remainder of his life in the village of Stourbridge near his birthplace in Clent. He died 29 January 1881.

RELATED ENTRIES: Hutchinson, John; Taufa'ahau, George Tupou I; Tonga.

SOURCES AND READINGS: Sione Lātūkefu, *Church and State in Tonga* (Canberra: Australian National University Press, 1974); G. S. Rowe, *A Memoir of the Reverend John Thomas* (Canberra: Kalia Press, 1976); Noel Rutherford, ed., *The Friendly Islands: A History of Tonga* (Melbourne: Oxford University Press, 1977); W. H. Wood, *Overseas Missions of the Australian Methodist Church*, vol. 1 (Melbourne: Aldersgate Press, 1975).   *Ronald Shook*

THOMAS, (REAR ADMIRAL) RICHARD (1777-1857). A British naval commander in chief in the Pacific from 1841-1844, Thomas sent the frigate *Carysfort* to the Hawaiian Islands to investigate a complaint concerning the mistreatment of Englishmen and their property. Captain George Paulet aboard the *Carysfort* arrived in Honolulu on 10 February 1843 where he interviewed King Kamehameha III and forced him to cede the Hawaiian Islands to Britain. When Rear Admiral Thomas learned of Paulet's action, he at once set sail from Valparaiso to Hawai'i. After arriving in Honolulu on 26 July 1843, he immediately talked with the king and reestablished the independence of his kingdom. On 31 July 1843 official restoration was announced at a place east of town now known as "Thomas Square." Thomas' actions were fully approved by his government in London. He was later promoted to vice admiral, a position he held until his death on 21 August 1857 in Stonehouse, Plymouth.

RELATED ENTRIES: Hawai'i; Kamehameha III; Paulet, George.

SOURCES AND READINGS: Ralph S. Kuykendall, *Hawaii: A History* (Englewood Cliffs, N.J.: Prentice-Hall, 1948); Ralph S. Kuykendall, *A History of Hawaii* (New York: Macmillan Co., 1933).
                Brenna J. Rash

THOMPSON, WILLIAM KERR (1832-1896). A merchant, investor, and founder of Suva, Fiji, Thompson's firm financed Fiji's first sugarcane experiment on Suva Promontory. In 1875 he personally assumed all the assets of the Suva partnership of Brewer and Joske including stores, freight, postal services, plantations, and timber mills. He invested heavily in other Fiji plantations as well as banking and mining companies in New Caledonia and acted as Fiji's representative in the Australian colonies for conferences and exhibitions. He acquired the title to several thousand acres on Suva Promontory and after cession negotiated with the British government over subdivision and development of the land. The final agreement allocated two-thirds of the blocks to the Fiji Crown Colony government. Thompson donated several blocks to churches and sold the rest privately, many through a well publicized Suva Land Quest in 1880. In the depressed economic climate of the 1880s, Thompson lost heavily on his Fiji investments. His Melbourne firm, James McEwan and Company, continued to trade in Fiji until selling out to Fiji and New Zealand buyers in the 1890s. A main thoroughfare in Suva is named after him. Thompson committed suicide in Melbourne in 1896.

RELATED ENTRIES: Fiji Trading Company; Joske, Adolph B.; New Caledonia.

SOURCES AND READINGS: Weston Bate, *History of Brighton* (Melbourne: University Press, 1962).
                Alan Maxwell Quanchi

THOMSON, (SIR) BASIL HOME (1861-1939). Basil Thomson was a British colonial aministrator in Fiji, Tonga, and New Guinea between 1883 and 1893. In Fiji, he held various posts including commissioner of the Native Lands Court and stipendiary magistrate. In 1890 Thomson was sent to Tonga by the British High Commissioner as the deputy prime minister for the purpose of reestablishing peace and order after the forcible removal of Shirley Baker from his post as prime minister. Thomson accomplished his mission and left Tonga in 1891, but returned nine years later to a more chaotic Tonga, this time to negotiate the treaty of 1900 which made Tonga a British protectorate and gave Britain control over Tonga's foreign relations and much of its domestic policy. Thomson had to exert considerable pressure on King George Tupou II to sign the treaty. The rest of his life was spent in the administration of prisons and police work in London. A prolific writer, Thomson has left vivid, though controversial, accounts of Tonga and Fiji as the two island countries existed around the turn of the century. These accounts appear in such books as *Diversions of a Prime Minister* (1894), *South Sea Yarns* (1894), and *The Fijians* (1908). Born 21 April 1861, Thomson died 26 March 1939.

RELATED ENTRIES: Baker, Shirley; Fiji; Papua New Guinea; Taufa'ahau, George Tupou I; Tonga.

SOURCES AND READINGS: Sione Lātūkefu, *Church and State in Tonga* (Canberra: Australian National

University Press, 1974); Noel Rutherford, ed., *The Friendly Islands: A History of Tonga* (Melbourne: Oxford University Press, 1977).   *Eric B. Shumway*

THOMSON, ROBERT (1816-1851). A missionary of the London Missionary Society, Robert Thomson sailed to the South Pacific in 1839. He first worked in the Marquesas (1839-1841) without success and then sailed to Tahiti where he headed the Protestant church in Tahiti after the French takeover in 1842. He was well respected by both Tahitians and the French. He married Louisa Barff in 1842. Illness forced his retirement from the ministry in 1850. While on his way to Australia, he died at sea on 1 January 1851. Thomson left two journals, his *History of the Marquesas* and his *History of Tahiti*, both of which are used as important documents for Pacific scholars.

RELATED ENTRIES: French Polynesia; London Missionary Society; Marquesas Islands.

SOURCES AND READINGS: James Sibree, ed., *Register of the Missionaries of the London Missionary Society* (London: London Missionary Society, 1923); Robert Thomson, *The Marquesas Islands: Their Description and Early History*, ed. Robert D. Craig, 2nd ed. (Laie, Hawai'i: Institute for Polynesian Studies, 1980).   *Robert D. Craig*

THURSTON, JOHN BATES (1836-1897). A governor of Fiji, a consul general and high commissioner for the western Pacific from 1888 to 1897, John Thurston was born in London January 1836. He died at sea off Port Melbourne in February 1897. At age thirteen he was apprenticed in Liverpool to ships bound for India and later Australia, where he settled briefly as a farmer before returning to the sea until 1865. He entered the British consulate as a clerk and in July 1867 became acting consul. He was awarded the title *Na Kena Vai* ("bayonet, spearpoint") by Ratu Apenisa Seru Cakobau for championing the Fijian cause against the Polynesian Company. He upheld the sovereignty of the Fijian chiefs against European settlers. After being a planter on Tavenui between 1869 and 1872, he reluctantly entered King Cakobau's government as chief secretary and minister for foreign relations.

Cession of Fiji to Great Britain being achieved virtually under duress in 1874, Thurston devoted the rest of his life to nurturing the fiction that cession was actually by free consent of the Fijians and that they were in a special, close, personal relationship with the sovereign whose representative, the governor, they formally installed as *vakaViti* ("supreme chief"). Thurston was saved from political oblivion after cession by the understanding of the first resident governor, Sir Arthur Hamilton Gordon. Gordon regarded Thurston as a very able man who had incurred the hostility of settlers because he championed Fijians. Thurston became auditor-general, then colonial secretary, administrator, and lieutenant governor before being made governor in 1888. Working from pre-cession principles, Thurston established a native tax system, provided a central marketing system for Fijian produce and enabled Fijians to participate directly in the cash economy without becoming wage labor for Europeans. Taxes were paid in produce which the government sold to the highest bidder, returning any surplus cash above assessment to the producers—a system later forgotten but thereafter remembered and admired by his intellectual heir, Ratu Josef Lalabalavu Sukuna.

Under the Western Pacific High Commission, Thurston was influential in conducting British relations with Samoa, Tonga, the New Hebrides, and the Gilbert, Ellice, Solomon, and other islands. He was frequently employed on international commissions, and was regarded as the chief British South Seas expert. He supported the Reverend S. W. Baker as premier of Tonga until he became convinced that Baker was leading the Kingdom of Tonga into civil war, whereupon he deported Baker in 1890. He regarded German activity in Samoa as deplorable and motivated solely by a concern for commercial interests. Thurston, however, felt Germany too well-entrenched to be dislodged—and certainly not by New Zealand, whose adventurers he held responsible for German measures to seize control. He established protectorates over the Solomon, Gilbert, and Ellice islands in the 1890s, saying privately that he did not know what a protectorate was and could not find any constitutional lawyer who knew either. He felt it was generally a pity that Pacific islanders could not be left very much alone.

In his later years in Fiji, he was at odds with the newly proselyting Marist mission whose attempts to break the established hold of Wesleyanism he thought more likely to produce alienated communities than good Christians. Thurston had also to deal with Tuka and with the Seaqaqa "revolt"—really a separatist movement aimed at local provincial authorities rather than at the central government (Fijians having accepted the latter as one of the facts of life). His old enemies, the Europeans, sat cowed under his rule, waiting for him to retire or die in harness—which he did, of muscular atrophy, a little after his term as governor had been extended (an event which prompted one of his Fijian provincial heads to say *Na Kena Vai* should stay until all the old men were dead). Thurston was imaginative and temperamental, a believer in an iron hand within a velvet glove, in consultation, and personal rule. He had a mordant wit and no respect for British departments of state. Upon his death, Fijians wanted his body brought back for burial in Fiji, but they were denied.

RELATED ENTRIES: Baker, Shirley; Fiji; Gordon, Arthur C. H.; Polynesia Company; Sukuna, Ratu Josef Lalabalavu.

SOURCES AND READINGS: Deryck Scarr, ed., *More Pacific Islands Portraits* (Canberra: Australian National University Press, 1979). *Deryck Scarr*

THURSTON, LORRIN ANDREWS (1858-1931). Lorrin Thurston was a lawyer, businessman, and political leader whose grandparents had emigrated from New England to Hawai'i in the 1820s. He was born in Honolulu, Hawai'i, in 1858. He was educated at Punahou (O'ahu) College and Columbia University School of Law. In addition to practicing as an attorney, he was elected to the Hawaiian legislature in 1886 and 1892. He was also one of principal owners of the Halakala Ranch Company, serving as its director and secretary. In 1887 Thurston helped lead American businessmen in a bloodless revolt against the Hawaiian government. This uprising resulted in the formation of a new ministry and the adoption of a constitution that curtailed the royal government's power. He was appointed minister of the interior under this new government. Three years later, the leaders of the reform ministry were forced to resign because of growing opposition from native Hawaiians. With the succession of Queen Lili'uokalani to the Hawaiian throne in 1891, royalist sentiment greatly increased in the islands. Thurston became convinced that the overthrow of the monarchy followed by annexation to the United States offered the best chance for economic security and political stability in the islands.

The end of the Hawaiian monarchy finally came in 1893 when Lili'uokalani attempted to replace the constitution of 1887 with one which strengthened her control of the government. Thurston was the leading force behind the overthrow of the monarchy and headed the annexation commission sent to Washington, D.C. He served as Hawaiian envoy to the United States from 1893 to 1895 and helped write the Republic of Hawai'i's constitution in 1894. Following the annexation of Hawai'i by the United States in 1898, he retired from public service and became part owner of the *Honolulu Advertiser*. In 1904 he edited the *Fundamental Law of Hawai'i*, which contained Ha-

wai'i's constitution and related public documents. He died on 11 May 1931.

RELATED ENTRIES: Hawai'i; Hawaiian Annexation Treaty; Hawaiian Revolution; Lili'uokalani.

SOURCES AND READINGS: Ralph S. Kuykendall, "Lorrin Andrews Thurston" in Allen Johnson and Dumas Malone, eds., *Dictionary of American Biography*, 20 vols. (New York: Charles Scribner's Sons, 1928-36) 18: 517-18; Lorrin A. Thurston, *A Handbook on the Annexation of Hawaii* (St. Joseph, Mich.: A. B. Morse Co., 1897); Lorrin A. Thurston, *Memoirs of the Hawaiian Revolution*, ed. Andrew Farrell (Honolulu: Advertiser Publishing Co., 1936). *William R. Smith*

TOBACCO. Tobacco is a New World drug substance that was seized upon by some of the first Europeans to make contact with the peoples of North and South America in the late fifteenth and early sixteenth centuries. Both the drug and methods of consuming it were taken back to Europe by these early explorers where the demand for tobacco mushroomed almost overnight. Although the historical details remain to be worked out and may never be known completely, it does seem clear that this plant was transported by Portuguese and Spanish seamen to the western border of the Pacific during the sixteenth and early seventeenth centuries. Magellan's sailors were most likely familiar with tobacco when they embarked in September of 1519. Tobacco then could have reached Guam and the Philippines by 1521. It was introduced into Java by 1601 and to the Moluccas very soon thereafter, into Japan by 1605, into Korea from Japan by 1608-1618 and into China from Luzon via Chinese traders. It is likely that tobacco spread to the island of New Guinea from the west, probably from the Moluccas, in the sixteenth century. Despite this apparent early contact with tobacco by some New Guineans and the Chamorro of the Marianas, it took two centuries or more for tobacco to be introduced over the remainder of the Pacific.

The anthropological literature on tobacco in Oceania is richest for New Guinea and the surrounding area and poor to nonexistent elsewhere. Haddon's massive volume, *Smoking and Tobacco Pipes in New Guinea*, is the most thorough compendium of information available as of the late 1930s for that culturally diverse region. However, his work was preceded by several other useful articles: Laufer (1931), Lewis (1924 and 1931), Merrill (1930), and Zimmer (1930).

Once the islanders became addicted to nicotine, the demand for tobacco knew no bounds and it was widely used all over the Pacific in the late eighteenth and nineteenth centuries as a major trade item. In many places (Ponape, New Britain, Truk) it became, for all practical purposes, the main currency in which trade was conducted. In addition to its place in trade, renunciation of tobacco smoking often was made a condition of church membership by Christian missionaries to the Pacific, a practice which continues to the present in at least some locations.

Recent research suggests that tobacco's pharmacologically active ingredients—especially nicotine—may possibly produce or facilitate altered states of consciousness. In this regard, it is interesting to note that tobacco is possibly implicated (along with certain mushrooms) in "ritual madness" among the Kuma of the Western Highlands, New Guinea. A great deal remains to be learned not only about the pharmacological effects of different varieties of tobacco on human beings but also about the myriad cultural beliefs and practices associated with this substance. Given the frequent statements in the Pacific literature like Lessa's assertation that "about 90 percent of the population" on Lamotrek smoke cigarettes, and given the well-documented affinity of many Pacific islanders for nicotine, serious scholarly research on all aspects of tobacco use in Oceania is long overdue.

RELATED ENTRIES: Alcohol in the Pacific, Betel Nut Chewing; Kava and Betel.

SOURCES AND READINGS: A. C. Haddon, *Smoking and Tobacco Pipes in New Guinea* (London: Cambridge University Press for the Royal Society, 1947); Oscar Janiger and Marlene Dobkin de Rios, "Suggestive Hallucinogenic Properties of Tobacco," *Medical Anthropology Newsletter* 4 (1973): 6-11; Berthold Laufer, "Tobacco in New Guinea: An Epilogue," *American Anthropologist* 33 (1931): 138-40; William H. Lessa, "Traditional Uses of the Vascular Plants of Ulithi Atoll with Comparative Notes," *Micronesica* 13 (1977): 129-90; Albert B. Lewis, *Use of Tobacco in New Guinea and Neighboring Regions* (Chicago: Field Museum, 1924) and "Tobacco in New Guinea," *American Anthropologist* 33 (1931): 134-38; Mac Marshall and Leslie B. Marshall, "Holy and Unholy Spirits: The Effects of Missionization on Alcohol Use in Eastern Micronesia," *Journal of Pacific History* 11 (1976): 135-66; E. D. Merrill, "Tobacco in New Guinea," *American Anthropologist* 32 (1930): 101-5; Marie Reay, "Ritual Madness Observed: A Discarded Pattern of Fate in Papua New Guinea," *Journal of Pacific History* 12 (1977): 55-79; Harold M. Ross, "Competition for Baegu Souls: Mission Rivalry on Malaita, Solomon Islands" in James A. Boutilier, Daniel T. Hughes and Sharon

W. Tiffany, eds., *Mission, Church, and Sect in Oceania* (Ann Arbor: University of Michigan Press, 1978); John Rublowsky, *The Stoned Age, A History of Drugs in America* (New York: G. P. Putnam's Sons, 1974); G. F. W. Zimmer, "A New Method of Smoking Tobacco in Papua," *Man* 30 (1930): 133-34.

Mac Marshall

TONGA. The Kingdom of Tonga is located between 15° and 23° south latitude and 173° and 175° west longitude and consists of about 150 islands, forty of which are inhabited. These islands are divided into three main groups: Tongatapu, Vava'u, and Ha'apai. Made up of both volcanic and coral islands, Tonga has a population of over 105,000. Bananas and copra are its principal export items. Vegetables, peanuts, melons, and vanilla are also marketed abroad. Most Tongans engage in some sort of subsistence farming, the staple foods being taro, *'ufi* (yam), *kumala* (sweet potato), and bananas.

The Kingdom of Tonga is a constitutional monarchy, having remained united and largely autonomous in its internal affairs since King Taufa'ahau George Tupou I came into power in 1845. In 1970 its protectorate status under Great Britain was dissolved and it became independent as a member of the British Commonwealth.

History and Legend. Tonga was part of the western Polynesian complex and shared much of its history and many cultural traits with the islands in this area, especially Samoa and Fiji. These areas, plus Uvea, Futuna, and the Tokelaus, figure in ancient Tongan legends and history. Present archaeological investigations indicate people were living in Tonga five hundred to one thousand years before the beginning of the Christian era.

Tongan legends contain virtually no accounts of migration. Rather, there are numerous stories of a special creation through the exploits of the Maui and Tangaloa gods. According to the most popular Tongan myths, Tangaloa 'Atulongolongo created the first humans from a worm and called them Kohai, Koau, and Momo. From the ocean floor, Maui fished up Tongatapu, Tangaloa Tufunga dropped stone chips from the sky to form the high islands, and Tangaloa Eitumatupu'a cohabited with a woman descended from the worm to produce 'Aho'eitu (ca. 950 A.D.), the first king of Tonga, the *Tu'i Tonga.* Although the distinctions between history and myth are not always clear in early accounts of ancient Tonga, according to the preserved Tonga genealogies, 'Aho'eitu was a real person and founder of the principal Tongan royal dynasty that lasted nearly one thousand years. It ceased to exist with the death of the *Tu'i Tonga* Laufilitonga in 1865.

Although not much is known of the different men who held the title *Tu'i Tonga*, it is obvious they had immense power, being supreme spiritual as well as temporal rulers over the people. Best known among these kings are the eleventh *Tu'i Tonga*, Tuitātui (ca. 1200), the alleged builder of the famous trilithon *Ha-'amonga 'a Maui*, and Talakaifaiki (ca. 1250) who invaded and temporarily conquered Samoa. It is clear, however, that the authority of the *Tu'i Tonga* waxed and waned over the centuries. In the fifteenth century, the court of the *Tu'i Tonga* was plagued by intrigue, treachery, and assassination. For personal safety's sake Kau'ulufonuafekai (ca. 1470), the twenty-fifth *Tu'i Tonga*, bestowed upon his younger brother, Takalaua, the temporal rule of the kingdom, while he retained for himself the sacred part of his office. The title of *hau* (temporal ruler) was given to Takalaua who became the head of the *Tu'i Ha'atakalaua* clan, the second royal dynasty in Tonga. Again, the sixth *Tu'i Ha'atakalaua*, feeling the weight and the danger of absolute rule, bestowed upon his younger brother Ngata, the kingly title *Tu'i Kanokupolu* as well as the office of *hau* and founded the third collateral line of kings (ca. 1610). Although the *Tu'i Kanokupolu* was in rank the inferior title, it was destined to become the most powerful. The political complexities involved in the relationships of these three kingly titles inevitably led to a collapse of traditional lines of authority, which in turn led to political opportunism and finally civil war, beginning with the murder of the *Tu'i Kanokupolu*, Tuku-'aho, in 1799.

The first Europeans to arrive in Tonga were Dutch explorers, Le Maire and Schouten (1616) and Abel Tasman (1643). Later explorers came from Britain, France, and Spain. The most notable of these was the British captain, James Cook, whose journals of his three voyages to Tonga in the 1770s recorded extensive information about the early Tongan society. Other equally valuable early accounts were provided by William Mariner, a captive British seaman who survived the *Port au Prince* massacre and lived four years (1806-1810) as the adopted son of Finau 'Ulukalala II, George Vason, renegade London Missionary Society missionary who also lived several years among the Tongans, and John Thomas, the first successful, long-term, Wesleyan minister to Tonga (ministry from 1826-1850).

The early Tongan society as described by European visitors was rigidly stratified, the population being subjected to the rule of chiefs who had total sovereignty over the person and property of those in their district. A handsome, energetic people, the Tongans did not live in villages, but in meticulously kept residences and teeming garden plots enclosed by reed fences. Generally monogamous (except for the chiefs) and family centered, they believed in a multiplicity of gods. These gods were served by an extensive "priesthood" who generally belonged to high-ranking families. The chiefs were assured of a happy afterlife in a paradise called *Pulotu* no matter what their behavior as mortal humans had been. The commoners were considered to be without souls and therefore without consequence except insofar as they obeyed and comforted the chiefs (*hou'eiki*). Before the civil war, notwithstanding occasional hostilities toward some foreign ships, the Tongans generally demonstrated both a friendly behavior to visitors and a social tranquility among themselves.

Civil War (1799-1852). Among the principal causes of the Tongan civil war was the long decline of the traditional prestige and power of the *Tu'i Tonga*. With the emergence of the power of the *Tu'i Ha'atakalaua* and especially the *Tu'i Kanokupolu*, not to mention the real political power of the lesser chiefs, such as Finau 'Ulukalala II who claimed sole sovereignty over Vava'u, there was fertile ground for the seeds of ruthless ambition and tyranny. Specifically, it was the fatal clubbing of the despotic Tuku'aho that ignited widespread conflict which did not completely end until Taufa'ahau suppressed the final rebellions against his authority in 1852.

The outbreak of the war removed all chances for the success of the struggling little Christian mission established by the London Missionary Society in 1797 and abandoned in 1800. For over two decades thereafter, Tonga was a forbidding place, not only because of the factious chiefs but also because of unscrupulous aliens who had turned "savage." The Christian cause in Tonga was again established with the coming of the Wesleyan minister William Lawry in 1822 and John Thomas and John Hutchinson in 1826. The chiefs of Tongatapu gave these and other missionaries a mixed reception. They longed for the white man's technology but dreaded his doctrine. They feared that the white man's form of worship (*lotu*) eventually would undermine the prerogatives of the chiefly system. This fear, complicated by mistakes of ignorance and problems of communication on the part of the missionaries, made the success of the Wesleyan mission precarious indeed. The assurance of success came largely with the conversion of the *Tu'i Kanokupolu*, Aleamotu'a, and the brilliant soldier-warrior, Taufa'ahau, who finally succeeded his uncle to the title *Tu'i Kanokupolu* in 1845.

The Rise of Taufa'ahau King George Tupou I. Taufa'ahau, the grandson of Tuku'aho and son of Tupouto'a (both of whom had held the title *Tu'i*

Kanokupolu) showed early signs of great leadership. Athletic and physically powerful, he was eager to learn new ideas, including those of the new *lotu*. He was baptized in 1831, announced his name to be King George, and immediately took up the cause of universal conversion to Christianity. The missionaries realized that the spiritual fortunes of the Wesleyan mission were significantly linked to the political fortunes of Taufa'ahau. Having already proved himself a formidable warrior in his defeat of the *Tu'i Tonga*'s army at Velata, Ha'apai, in 1826, he showed his diplomatic and oratorial powers in his persuasion of Finau 'Ulukalala Tuapasi, ruler of Vava'u, to accept Christianity. This Finau did and then assisted King George in destroying many of the heathen gods at various places of worship.

In 1833 the dying Finau 'Ulukalala declared King George to be the ruler of Ha'apai, thus consolidating his powers in the two northern groups. In 1845, with the encouragement of the Wesleyan missionaries and an ever-widening Christian following, King George succeeded to the *Tu'i Kanokupolu* title which gave greater validity to his designs on Tongatapu and the unification of all the islands under his authority. He was met with strong resistance by his traditional enemies, the Ha'a Havea chiefs, who were encouraged in their dissatisfaction by the newly arrived Catholic missionaries. However, in 1852 the last armed resistance by the Ha'a Havea chiefs was successfully overcome. Instead of punishing these rebellious chiefs, King George wisely granted them amnesty on condition of their loyalty to him. He also allowed them to continue in their traditional positions of power over their people.

In 1855 George signed a treaty with France in which he guaranteed religious freedom to Catholics. Likewise, France recognized his sovereignty over all the Tongan islands. Thus, under King George, Tonga became Christian, subject to one ruler, and to the rule of law, even though the traditional chiefs still exercised much power over their own districts.

The Making of Modern Tonga. The accomplishments of King George during his long reign (1845-1893) justify the appellation frequently given to him "The Maker of Modern Tonga." Not least among these accomplishments was the preservation of the kingdom's autonomy and the Tongan identity even in the face of European imperialism. In view of the heavy European involvement in Fiji, Samoa, Tahiti, New Zealand, and Hawai'i, King George's fears of annexation were real. His strategy was to demonstrate Tonga's capacity for self-rule, modeling his government after venerable British institutions. Already having established the rule of law in the 1850 Code of Law, and the 1862 Code of Law (in which the people were freed from "serfdom and all vassalage" to the chiefs), King George granted the Tongan constitution in 1875. The constitution, plus a flourishing economy, the widespread success of the Wesleyan mission, the establishment of schools, and the construction of roads and buildings—all manifested an order and political stability that persuaded the foreign powers of Tonga's capacity for self-rule. Tonga was finally secure in its autonomy when friendship treaties were signed with Germany (1876) and Britain (1879), the two largest imperial forces in the South Pacific.

It is unlikely that King George would have succeeded in his efforts to keep Tonga for Tongans without the help of Shirley Baker who came to Tonga in 1860 as a Wesleyan minister. In 1869, he was made chairman of the Wesleyan mission, by which time he was clearly the most influential *pālangi* (white man or European) in King George's court. Baker drafted the Tonga constitution of 1875 and advised the king on matters foreign and local. His loyalty and support of Tupou in carrying out the "Tonga for Tongans" policies won him many enemies among the Europeans. An accusation of monetary irregularities in 1879 brought about his release from active missionary duty and his removal to Australia. He returned, however, the following year to become the premier of Tonga, minister of external affairs, and the minister of lands.

Although Baker benefited King George and Tonga in many ways, he did become a liability to the peace and tranquility of the country. At least he became the professed source of much discontent. In his official government role, Baker proved to be unrelentingly thorough in gathering taxes and implementing the land laws. His tactics as well as the laws themselves infuriated certain powerful segments of society who petitioned for his release as premier. The petition, begun in Mu'a, was tantamount to rebellion and Tupou dealt with it severely. This disturbance was increased in 1885 by the culmination of a longtime quarrel between King George and the Wesleyan church which was controlled largely by the Wesleyan conference in Australia. King George resented this foreign control. In 1885 he proclaimed the Free Church of Tonga and exercised considerable force in persuading his people to join. Persecution followed those who refused to join the "free" church. This persecution increased when an assassination attempt against Baker was perceived to be a Wesleyan plot. In 1887 the core Wesleyan resisters were allowed to seek exile in Fiji.

Thus, the church was "united," and the Mu'a "rebellion" suppressed, but the image of Tongan political stability was tarnished in British eyes. This led to an important British involvement in Tonga's internal affairs and Shirley Baker was finally removed from Tonga on a British ship in 1890. His replacement was the *Ha'atakalaua* chief, Tuku'aho, largely the choice of the British high commissioner for the western Pacific. Tuku'aho was now shadowed by a British deputy premier, Basil Thompson.

Angered at first by this imposition of a new government upon him, King George was finally reconciled to it. When he died in 1893 having outlived the first two generations of his heirs, tranquility appeared to reign throughout the kingdom. He was formally mourned by his people for six months.

The Reign of King George Tupou II (1893-1918).
The succession of George Taufa'ahau Tupou II to the throne of his great-grandfather was accomplished without serious difficulty, although there were other claimants to the title of *Tu'i Kanokupolu*. Descended from King George Tupou I through both his maternal and paternal lines, Tupou grew up suave and self-indulgent. As king he seemed to be preoccupied more with his social prerogatives and recreation than with sound government. His otherwise competent premier, Siosateki Veikune, seemed more intent on indulging his sovereign than in maintaining a solvent treasury. Tenaciously thorough in tax gathering, Sateki (as he was called), like Baker, satisfied his king, but brought cries of outrage from powerful segments of both the European and the Tongan community. These cries increased among many of the nobles when Tupou II inexplicably married Lavinia, daughter of Kupu, in violation of a long-standing family agreement that he marry Ma'atu's daughter, 'Ofa.

Thus, with the government's financial problems getting worse, with Sateki acting independently of the advice of the deputy premier and the British consul, with the accusations of corruption in all levels of government, and with Tupou's popularity at its lowest ebb, the British government in 1901 forced a treaty upon the Tongan kingdom by which it would become a protectorate of the British crown. The treaty gave Britain control of Tonga's external relations and the right to try all foreigners in British courts and under British law. With British pressure, new government leaders were selected. In 1905 a modified treaty gave Britain even more power over Tonga, including the right to approve all appointments and dismissals of high government officials. Total annexation was just one step away.

But the tiny kingdom held together, even prospered, in the years following the treaty. By 1911 the relationship between the British consul and the leaders of government was fairly well defined and Tongan autonomy, though somewhat circumscribed, was reaffirmed.

Queen Sālote Tupou III (1918-1965). When Tupou II died in 1918, his only daughter and heir, Sālote Mafile'o Pilolevu, was just eighteen years old. She was invested with the title *Tu'i Kanokupolu* on 9 October 1918 in a traditional kava ceremonial (*taumafa kava*), and crowned queen of Tonga on 11 October by the Reverend J. B. Watkins. A beautiful, pious woman with a congeniality unmatched in either of her predecessors, Sālote was married to William Tupoulahi Tungi, son of Tuku'aho, and direct descendant of the *Tu'i Ha'atakalaua*, the second of three royal lines of Tonga. This meant that their issue would indisputably lay to rest any lingering wonderment about the rightful heirship to the Tongan throne. She was to have three sons: Taufa'ahau (the present king), Tuku'aho, and Tu'i Pelehake (the present premier). Tuku'aho died at the age of sixteen.

In the forty-seven years of her reign, Queen Sālote dominated the love and the imagination of her people. She was queen of the personal touch, perhaps more a mother to her people than a monarch. If King George Tupou I pursued a political ideal of Tonga for Tongans, it was Sālote who espoused the love of being Tongan among her subjects. Her many acts of charity, her obvious self-sacrifice, and her vast abilities as a poet endeared her to her people in a way that insured a public sense of well-being that no material prosperity could ever produce. It was these qualities, plus a pious determination, that helped her in 1924 to achieve the legal union of the Free Church of Tonga (proclaimed by King George in 1885) and the Wesleyan church.

But guiding her tiny kingdom into the twentieth century, into contact with the world community, and developing human and material resources for a sound nation were tasks not easily accomplished. The principal concerns were those of education, health, and agriculture.

The Education Act of 1927 made primary-school education mandatory, government scholarships for overseas education were instituted in 1929, and a teacher-training college was established in 1944. The queen vigorously supported campaigns for better health, having seen the death by flu of approximately 8 per cent of her kingdom's population in 1918-1919. The establishment of the Central Medical School in Suva in 1929 was to provide for the medical education of numerous Tongan practitioners. Sālote also encouraged diverse and better commercial agriculture. Tonga had depended too long on a single export, copra, which was too vulnerable to the frequent hurricanes.

Queen Sālote's government inspired the confidence of the British administration in Tonga. Whereas the treaty of 1905 had bestowed considerable authority upon the British consuls to regulate Tongan affairs, the successive agreements with Sālote's government reduced that authority, until in 1970, five years after she died, Tonga's protectorate status was lifted altogether.

Sālote's congenial qualities were publicized worldwide during her visit to London for the coronation of Queen Elizabeth in 1953. She captured the hearts and the imagination of the British people by standing uncovered in her carriage in a heavy downpour during the coronation procession. When King Tupou I died in 1893 all of Tonga mourned. When Queen Sālote died in 1965 the entire British Commonwealth mourned.

The Reign of King Taufa'ahau Tupou IV (1965-). Much of Tonga's development during Queen Sālote's reign was due to the progressive notions of her son, Taufa'ahau. Born on 4 July 1918, Taufa'ahau took his B.A. (1939) and LL.B. (1942) from Sydney University in Australia, becoming the first Tongan to receive a university degree. As the crown prince, he returned to Tonga to become the minister of education in 1943. He married Mata'aho 'Ahome'e in 1947. The royal couple became the parents of four children, Crown Prince Tupouto'a, Princess Pilolevu, Prince Alaivahamama'o, and Prince 'Aho'eitu. In 1949 Taufa'ahau became the prime minister of the kingdom, a position he held until the death of Queen Sālote in 1965. He was crowned king of Tonga in 1967.

The achievements of Taufa'ahau Tupou IV as an educator are of singular importance to the Tongan kingdom and to all of Polynesia. He was a principal founder of Tonga High School to prepare students for university matriculation abroad. He also strengthened the scholarship system to send Tonga's brightest students to Commonwealth universities. Recognizing the need for better schools at home, he also established the Government Teachers Training College (1944) and implemented standardized leaving exams for secondary schools. In 1969 he became the first chancellor of the University of the South Pacific in Fiji.

King Taufa'ahau has been a scholar as well as a government administrator for education. He is a student of the Chinese, Russian, and Japanese abacuses, and the inventor of an efficient formula for teaching addition and subtraction in the Tongan primary schools. Through mathematical calculations he discovered that an original purpose of the renowned *Ha'amonga 'a Maui* trilithon was to measure the summer and winter solstices.

King Taufa'ahau has made substantial contributions to the field of music in Tonga. He has transcribed and arranged for Tongan voices and brass the works of Bach, Handel, and Mozart. His book is the first scholarly treatise on Tongan music ever published.

As prime minister, and now as king, Taufa'ahau has labored to give stability and prosperity to a growing nation caught in the tensions between a traditional life and the rush of foreign influence and technology. To help provide this stability and prosperity he established the Tonga Electric Power Board, the Tonga Water Board, the Tonga Construction Company, and the Tonga Shipping Company. He negotiated the building of the Dateline Hotel, the new Queen Sālote wharf, and the new Vaiola Hospital. Also, the Tonga Broadcasting Commission and the *Government Weekly Newspaper* were established while he was prime minister. Finally, in 1970, under the leadership of His Majesty, the Kingdom of Tonga ended its dependent relationship with Britain and entered the comity of nations as a completely sovereign state.

The tensions of change are everywhere apparent in Tonga today. The constant burgeoning of population, the scarcity of land, the lack of private industries, unemployment, inflation, poor roads, increased dependence on foreign aid, and the conflict between modern democratic notions about government and those of traditional monarchy, are a few of the problems facing Tupou IV and his people. But Tonga remains rich in pride, strong in its national identity, and sure of its own capacity to bring about a peaceful change without sacrificing the basic values of its society—which are epitomized in the national slogan *"Ko e Otua mo Tonga ko Hoku Tofia"* ("God and Tonga Are My Heritage").

RELATED ENTRIES: 'Atenisi Institute; Baker, Shirley; Bataillon, Pierre-Marie; Chevron, (Father) Joseph; Cook, (Captain) James; Crocker, W.; Defense Planning for Oceania between the Wars; Diaper, William; Fiji, Tongan Imperialism in; German Colonial Empire; Huchinson, John; Lapita Culture; Lawry, Walter; London Missionary Society; Mariner, William; Polynesia, Settlement of; Polynesian Culture (Ancient); Ruge and Company, H. M.; St. Julian, Charles; Sālote (Queen); Selwyn, George; South Pacific Commission; South Pacific Forum; Taufa'ahau, George Tupou I; Tevita'unga; Thomas, John; Thomson, Basil H.; Tongan Code of 1862; Tongan Constitution; Tu'i Ha'atakalaua; Tu'i Kanokupola; Tu'i Tonga; Tungi, William; Ulukalala II; Vason, George; Western Pacific High Commission.

SOURCES AND READINGS: E. W. Gifford, *Tongan Myths and Tales* (Honolulu: Bernice P. Bishop Museum, 1924) and *Tongan Society* (Honolulu: Bernice P. Bishop Museum, 1929); Sione Lātūkefu, *Church and State in Tonga* (Canberra: Australian National

University Press, 1974); Noel Rutherford, ed., *The Friendly Islands: A History of Tonga* (Melbourne: Oxford University Press, 1977).   *Eric B. Shumway*

TONGAN CODE OF 1862. A document of emancipation, the Tongan Code of 1862 marked a significant milestone in the development of government by law in the Kingdom of Tonga. Expanding upon two previous sets of law, the Vava'u Code of 1839 and the Code of Laws of 1850, the Code of 1862 was granted by King George Tupou I and became the primary ruling document of the kingdom until the constitution was granted in 1875. The Vava'u Code of 1839 was King George's first attempt to subject the Tongan people to a rule of law. While this code did not terminate the rule of the chiefs (*hou'eiki*), it did limit some of their arbitrary powers. It forbade stealing, murder, theft, adultery, fornication, idolatry, the sale and drinking of spirits, and the wanton cutting of timber—all upon the pain of confinement or fines. The code also provided a simple judicial method for handling disputes and grievances among the common people. The Code of Laws of 1850 expanded upon the Vava'u Code by limiting further the powers of the chiefs and by consolidating the prerogatives of the king. This code laid out a rather stringent set of laws governing domestic living as well as public responsibility. Among other things it forbade any kind of slothfulness. The Code of 1862 contained more comprehensive constitutional measures, subjecting the king to the rule of law, securing the emancipation of the common people (*me'a vale*) from virtual slavery by the chiefs (*hou'eiki*), setting up a workable state-revenue system, and providing for the allotment of land to the common people. The code also allowed for the payment of salaries to those in the service of the government. The annual festival celebrating the Code of 1862 and the emancipation of the Tongan people is held on the fourth of June.

RELATED ENTRIES: Taufa'ahau, George Tupou I; Tonga; Tongan Constitution.

SOURCES AND READINGS: Sione Lātūkefu, *Church and State in Tonga* (Canberra: Australian National University Press, 1974) (contains the full text of the Code of 1862).   *Eric B. Shumway*

TONGAN CONSTITUTION. Written by the Reverend Shirley Baker, the Tongan Constitution was granted by King George Tupou I in 1875. It was the crowning effort of a series of progressive attempts by the Tongan monarch to achieve a respected, serviceable, Christian legislation for Tonga. The earliest laws in Tonga containing any constitutional measures were laid down in the Vava'u Code of 1839.

The Code of Laws of 1850 expanded upon the Vava'u Code, but was itself made more comprehensive in the landmark Code of 1862 in which the common people (*me'a vale*) were freed from serfdom under the chiefs (*hou'eiki*). But it was not until the acceptance of the constitution that there was a full, carefully planned set of guidelines and guarantees for the governing of Tonga. This document consists of three main sections: the Declaration of Rights, the Form of Government, and the Lands. The Declaration of Rights proclaims the equality of all men before the laws of the country and assures the freedoms of the press, speech, and worship. The freedom of worship, however, is modified by the insistence that the Sabbath would be sacred in Tonga forever. The Declaration of Rights also granted to all Tongans the right to vote for the representatives to the legislative assembly. The Form of Government section describes the functions and prerogatives of the king, the privy council, the legislative assembly, and the judiciary. The Lands section details the way land is to be distributed as *tofi'a* (estates) to twenty nobles of the kingdom, which in turn are divided into smaller allotments and leased to the people. This section of the constitution forbids the sale of any land by chief or commoner. Notwithstanding the turbulence of changes and social forces within the country, the constitution has helped to secure a peaceful existence and a stable self-government in Tonga for over a hundred years.

RELATED ENTRIES: Baker, Shirley; Taufa'ahau, George Tupou I; Tonga; Tongan Code of 1862.

SOURCES AND READINGS: Sione Lātūkefu, *Church and State in Tonga* (Canberra: Australian National University Press, 1974) (contains the full text of the constitution); Noel Rutherford, ed., *The Friendly Islands: A History of Tonga* (Melbourne: Oxford University Press, 1977).   *Eric B. Shumway*

TONGAN ORAL CULTURE. The oral culture of Tonga is still richly alive, and consists of a wide variety of local histories, legends, and stories of the past as well as songs, poems, and dances composed for present events. Early visitors to the Tongan islands discovered people highly developed in singing, dancing, and storytelling. Unlike some Polynesians who merely chanted their poetry and genealogies, the Tongans frequently sang in parts. Mariner and Labillardiere have left notation fragments that demonstrate harmonic singing. Generally, Tongan poetry is put to music and dance. The integration of these three elements constitutes the special delight of Tongan *faiva* (performance).

Some of the principal expressions of Tongan oral culture are in the following *faiva*: (1) The *lakalaka*—a grand *faiva* performed by up to 250 people in several rows. Women, graceful and controlled, are on the right, the men, energetic and aggressive, are on the left. A group of singers, or *langi tu'a*, stands and sings from behind the dancers. The *lakalaka* evolved in the nineteenth century probably from the ancient group dance, the *me'elaufola*. (2) The *mā'u-lu'ulu*, also performed in a large group, is a sitting-down dance. It is the Tongan version of a Samoan dance with touches of the ancient Tongan *faiva*, *'otuhaka*. The *mā'ulu'ulu* is always seen at major festivals. (3) The *tau'olunga*, or solo dance, was borrowed from Samoa around 1900. It is usually accompanied by guitars and ukuleles. (4) The *me-'etu'upaki* is apparently an ancient religious dance whose meaning is lost to us now. It is performed with wooden paddles. (5) *Hiva kakala* ("sweet smelling songs") is a musical genre which includes love songs and songs of praise for country, special people, and special events. *Hiva kakala* frequently provides the accompaniment to a *tau'olunga*. (6) The *tau'a'alo* is the most ancient musical genre still preserved in Tonga. It is melodious yet chantlike, and sung as an accompaniment to various kinds of ceremonial work such as dragging litters of gifts to the royal compound. (7) The *tangi* (royal: *tutulu*) is a melodic lament which combines elements of wailing and singing. (8) An *'upē* is a lullaby for small children. (9) *Ta'anga* is the lyrics of any song that is given *haka* (dance movements) or described in a dance, particularly in a *lakalaka* or *mā'ulu'ulu*. (10) A *maau* is any poem composed for recitation rather than for singing. (11) A *fananga* is a legend or fabulous tale. Tonga preserves hundreds of *fananga*. (12) A *pal-ōvepi* (proverb) is a wise, concise Tongan saying.

Tongans have also cultivated to a high degree the arts of formal oratory (*malanga*), storytelling (*fai talanoa*), and humor (*hua*). The vastly popular kava parties provide a forum for the perpetuation and enrichment of most of the above *faiva*. Queen Sālote (1900-1965) more than anyone else, has been both Tonga's finest composer and most enthusiastic custodian of Tongan traditions. In 1952 she established the Tongan Traditions Committee for the study and preservation of Tongan culture.

RELATED ENTRIES: Mariner, William; Polynesian Culture (Ancient); Sālote (Queen), Mafile'o Pila-levu; Tonga.

SOURCES AND READINGS: E. E. V. Collocot, *Tales and Poems of Tonga* (Honolulu: Bernice P. Bishop Museum, 1928); Edward Winslow Gifford, *Tongan Myths and Tales* (Honolulu: Bernice P. Bishop Museum, 1924); Adrienne L. Kaeppler, "Aesthetics of Tongan Dance," *Ethnomusicology* 15 (1971): 175-85 and "Tongan Dance: A Study in Cultural Change," *Ethnomusicology* 14 (1970): 266-76; Eric B. Shumway, "Ko e Fakalāngilāngi: The Eulogistic Function of the Tongan Poet," *Pacific Studies* 1 (1977): 25-35.

Eric B. Shumway

TORRES ISLANDS. Located at 13° 15' south latitude and 166° 37' east longitude, the Torres Islands are the northernmost group of the New Hebrides. These low-lying islands comprise Hiw (Hiu), Tegua, Loh, Metoma, and Toga. The approximately two hundred inhabitants are Polynesians.

RELATED ENTRY: Torres, Luis Váez de.

Frank P. King

TORRES, LUIS VÁEZ DE (d. early 1600s). A Portuguese navigator and explorer in the service of Spain, Torres played a major role in Pedro Fernández de Quirós' voyage of 1605-1606 which sought to discover a southern continent in the South Pacific. Two ships and a launch made up this expedition which departed from Callao, the harbor of Lima, Peru, in December 1605. Torres commanded the *San Pedro* (also known as the *Almirante*), a ship of 120 tons burden. In May they reached the island group later called the New Hebrides and to which Quirós gave the name of *Austrialia del Espíritu Santo*. Suitable anchorage was found in a large bay on the north side of one of the islands. After a stay of several weeks in this area, the vessels resumed their voyage on 8 June, but the strong southeast trade winds made sailing difficult. On 11 June the *San Pedro* and the launch returned to their previous anchorage, but Quirós failed to do so. This rather enigmatic commander had decided to return to the coast of western America, and in November 1606 he and his men reached the port of Acapulco.

Torres, after waiting in vain for fifteen days for the return of Quirós, decided to continue exploration activities, and the *San Pedro* and the launch eventually reached New Guinea. Slowly the two vessels sailed westward along the southern coast of this large island, finding the area inhabited by many people and fringed with islets, atolls, and innumerable reefs. Torres discovered the strait which separates New Guinea from northern Australia and which later would bear his name. Passing through this strait, Torres continued northward finally arriving at the Moluccas (where the launch was left on the island of Ternate), and then the Philippines. Torres disembarked at Manila in May 1607, and from this port city he sent his formal account of the expedition to

King Philip III. Thereafter nothing further is heard about Torres. He disappears from view. Captain James Cook rediscovered Torres Strait during the course of his first voyage in 1768-1771.

RELATED ENTRIES: Quirós, Pedro de; Spain in the Pacific.

SOURCES AND READINGS: Francis J. Bayldon, "Voyage of Luis Váez de Torres from the New Hebrides to the Moluccas, June to November, 1606," *Royal Australian Historical Society: Journal and Proceedings* 11, pt. 3 (1925): 158-94.   *Bernerd C. Weber*

TORRES STRAIT ISLANDS. Some seventy in number, the Torres Strait Islands lie between Queensland and the Papua New Guinea mainland. The population in 1971, which was heavily weighted in favor of females, was 6,100. In 1976 it was estimated that 60 percent of all the islanders, who are Australian citizens, lived on the Australian mainland. There are three administrative districts—Western, Eastern, and Central—with Thursday Island acting as the center. The following are the best known of the islands: Thursday, Friday, Prince of Wales, Tuesday, Wednesday, Goode, Moa, Badu, Mabuiag, Murray, Darnley, Yorke, Saibai, Dauan, and Boigu. The history of these islands is related to their location. Captain Luis Váez de Torres took a month to work through the strait bearing his name in 1606. Since then the islands have been visited by innumerable explorers, traders, missionaries, pirates, and scoundrels. The population is mixed.

RELATED ENTRY: Torres, Luis Váez de.

SOURCES AND READINGS: Margaret Lawrie, *Myths and Legends of Torres Strait Islands* (St. Lucia: Queensland University Press, 1970); D. Walker, ed., *Bridge and Barrier: The Natural and Cultural History of Torres Strait Islands* (Canberra: Australian National University Press, 1971).   *Frank P. King*

TROBRIAND ISLANDS. One of Papua New Guinea's offshore island groups (the others being the D'Entrecasteaux, Woodlark, and Louisiade islands), the Trobriand Islands lie about 241 km (150 mi) northeast of the island of New Guinea. The Trobriands cover an area of 544 km² (210 mi²) and have a population of about 15,500 of both Melanesian and Polynesian peoples. Kiriwina is the largest island. The chief exports are pearls and pearl shells.

RELATED ENTRY: Papua New Guinea. *Frank P. King*

TRUST TERRITORY OF THE PACIFIC ISLANDS. *See* Commonwealth of the Northern Mariana Islands; Marshall Islands; Micronesia, Constitution of the Federated States of; Palau.

TUAMOTU-GAMBIER ARCHIPELAGO. The Tuamotu-Gambier Archipelago, also called Paumotu Archipelago, is one of the five island groups of French Polynesia. It consists of one large coral island, Makatea, and countless smaller atolls or low islands scattered immediately east and south of the Society Islands in the South Pacific. Total land mass measures 922 km² (356 mi²). Because of the treacherous nature of the islands and their reefs, they were nicknamed the "Dangerous Islands." The land that is exposed grows tropical coconut palms, pandanus, and breadfruit trees, but because of the nature of the soil it cannot support a wide range of plant life. Population is estimated to be 7,023 (1980 estimate).

Ancient History. Because of the nearness of the Society Islands, these two groups have had navigation contact for centuries. As a result, their culture, language, and customs have only slight differences. The Pomare family, the ruling chiefs on the island of Tahiti, were also the high chiefs of the Tuamotus. The history of these islands, therefore, is closely interwoven with the history of the Society Islands and the French control there.

Resources and Economy. These coral atolls have long been famous for their pearls and pearl shells. Modern methods of collection glutted the market and brought drastic French control, and the increased interest in cultured pearls has again stirred this industry. The second major product, copra, has lost its importance since 1970. Tourism has been promoted by the Tahiti Tourist Development Board in Pape'ete and now with several flights a week to Rangiroa, this island has become a vacation paradise away from the bustling city of Pape'ete. More famous than Rangiroa is the Moruroa Atoll in the southeastern end of the chain in the Gambier group. It was here that the French began their nuclear testing in 1963, an action highly criticized by islanders throughout the Pacific.

RELATED ENTRIES: French Polynesia; Moruroa Atoll; Pomare Family.

SOURCES AND READINGS: Eugène Caillot, *Histoire de la Polynésie Orientale* (Paris: Ernest Leroux, 1910); Kenneth P. Emory, *Material Culture of the Tuamotu Archipelago* (Honolulu: Bernice P. Bishop Museum, 1975).   *Robert D. Craig*

TUBA. A popular, widespread drink in the Pacific islands, tuba is made by fermenting the juice of the coconut blossom. Tuba makers become expert at their craft, and each has personalized techniques for preparation; but they generally conform to the following pattern.

A tender, green, blossom spike, about eighteen to twenty-four inches long, is left unopened and is patiently bent downward until it is level with the base of the blossom. Some makers slice the base of the blossom with a knife, making a sharp-angled, shallow cut extending almost all the way around the blossom on the underneath side to help the bending process. A piece of gunnysack or some palm fibers is then tied around the blossom to prevent budding into maturity. This binding can cover the whole length or can be intermittent from base to tip. Rope or twine is attached to the blossom from a lower stalk to insure bending, and it is shortened daily. Results are seen in three to four days. The tip is then snipped, releasing the juice, and the glass or bamboo container is filled in a day. A good tuba maker can make a bud last from six to eight weeks.

Sweet or "ladies tuba" is made by collecting juice in the morning before the sun beats on the sap and also by washing the container after each tapping. For real gusto, the maker will leave the settlings in the bottom to activate a stronger brew and will let the sap drip all day in the sun to ferment. If tuba is allowed to sit for a couple of weeks, it becomes vinegar and is thus useful in cooking.

RELATED ENTRIES: Alcohol in the Pacific.

SOURCES AND READINGS: Beth F. Avery, "Micronesia's Potent Potables," *Glimpses* 18 (1978).

Dirk Ballendorf

TUI A'ANA AND TUI ATUA. Two of the four highest-ranking political titles in Western Samoa are *Tui A'ana* and *Tui Atua*. Tradition tells that it was Pili (half-divine, half-mortal) who divided the island of Upolu between his three sons. West Upolu fell to his son Ana, hence the title *Tui A'ana* ("king of Ana") and eastern Upola fell to Atua, hence *Tui Atua*. The central part fell to *Tuamasaga*, the third major title on Upolu. Anciently, persons who held these titles were sacred and all forms of taboos surrounded their daily activities. Their persons, food, and belongings were sacred. These titles were not hereditary in the normal sense of the word, but were conferred by senior orator-chiefs in their particular districts. Candidates for these two titles, however, were chosen only from the sacred family of Tupua (with titles *Tamasese, Mata'afa*, or *Tuimaleali'ifano*) and frequently the former holder of the title "suggested" or "appointed" a successor. During the Tongan domination of Samoa (ca. 1200-1600 A.D.), these titles presumably were never bestowed, but with the expulsion of the conquerors they were reestablished and have continued into modern times. Their genealogical records tell fascinating details of the individuals who held these titles through the centuries. When a major chief gained control of the four major titles he/she was called *Tupu'o Samoa* ("king/queen of Samoa"). Frequent, almost incessant, civil wars raged in Samoa for control of this title. Especially significant were the civil wars of the nineteenth century as the Western powers of Great Britain, Germany, and the United States attempted to gain possession of the islands. Under German control from 1900 to 1914, Western Samoa's governors declared many of the titles to be defunct and several dissidents were exiled. After independence from New Zealand (1962) and the death of Tupua Tamasese Mea'ole (1963), the two titles *Tui A'ana* and *Tui Atua* were revived once again. Tupuola Efi (eldest son of Tupua Tamasese Mea'ole and present prime minister) was elected to the title *Tui A'ana* and Tupa Tamasese Lealofi IV was elected *Tui Atua*.

RELATED ENTRIES: *Malietoa*; *Tui Manu'a*; Western Samoa.

SOURCES AND READINGS: J. W. Davidson, *Samoa Mo Samoa* (New York: Oxford University Press, 1967); Augustin Krämer, *Die Samoa-Inseln*, 2 vols. (Stuttgart: E. Nägele, 1902).   *Robert D. Craig*

TU'I HA'ATAKALAUA. The Tongan title *Tu'i Ha'atakalaua* began with Mo'ungamotu'a, the son of Kau'ulufonua Fekai, the twenty-fourth reigning *Tu'i Tonga*. The *Tu'i Ha'atakalaua* was organized in order to protect the *Tu'i Tonga* in his vulnerability as the supreme seat of power and to remove some of the responsibilities of that office concerning the day-to-day business of the islands. This line of chiefs came to rival the *Tu'i Tonga* in importance and there were sixteen holders of the office before the last bearer of the title, Mulikiha'amea, was killed in battle in 1799.

RELATED ENTRIES: *Tu'i Kanokupolu*; *Tu'i Tonga*.

SOURCES AND READINGS: Noel Rutherford, ed., *The Friendly Islands, A History of Tonga* (Melbourne: Oxford University Press, 1977).   *Vernice W. Pere*

TU'I KANOKUPOLU. A Tongan title, *Tu'i Kanokupolu* began with Ngata, which consisted of a line of chiefs of highest rank and which controlled the area of Hihifo. The title grew in both prestige and power. It could be held by man or woman, and much intrigue surrounded the bestowal of the title through generations of Tongan rule. Several holders of the title were murdered, and a two-generation period of civil war erupted at the close of the sixteenth century. In 1845 Taufa'ahau, the nineteenth holder of the title, invested it with more authority and prestige than it had ever possessed. Since his time, every holder of the title has been his direct descendant and has held the throne of Tonga as well as the *Tu'i Kanokupolu* title. To date there have been twenty-two *Tu'i Kanokupolu*, with King Taufa'ahau Tupou IV the present holder.

RELATED ENTRIES: Taufa'ahau; *Tu'i Ha'atakalaua*; *Tu'i Tonga*.

SOURCES AND READINGS: Noel Rutherford, ed., *The Friendly Islands, A History of Tonga* (Melbourne: Oxford University Press, 1977).   *Vernice W. Pere*

TUI MANU'A. Anciently, *Tui Manu'a* was the highest-ranking chiefly title in all of Samoa. Its distinction lay in the fact that it was traditionally the first established by the god Tagaloa on the islet of Ta'u in the Manu'a group. His half-mortal son Pili became the first *Tui Manu'a* whose three sons Ana, Tua (twins), and Tuamasaga divided the island of Upolu and became the founders of the high-ranking titles in the Western Samoa islands. The *Tui Manu'a* title lost its political power over the islands when all but Manu'a were conquered by Tongan royalty (ca. 1200 A.D.). In the subsequent centuries and especially during the international rivalry for control of the islands in the nineteenth century, the Manu'a islands became politically and geographically isolated from the rest of the archipelago. When U.S. Commander Tilley visited Manu'a to gain U.S. cession of the islands in March 1900, he was confronted by *Tui Manu'a* Eliasara. Eliasara finally recognized U.S. sovereignty, however, and raised the U.S. flag, but he did not agree to cession of the Manu'a group. In 1901 the junior-ranking chiefly titles on Tutuila overstepped ancient bounds and boldly claimed right to the *'ava* ceremony normally reserved for the *Tui Manu'a*. After a lengthy court battle between the usurper, the *Tui Manu'a*, and U.S. justice, the U.S. courts ruled in 1902 that the highest chief in Manu'a was not higher in family rank than any other Samoans. Each of the three districts were of equal weight in the eyes of the government. Finally in 1905, the *Tui Manu'a* signed the act of cession of the lands to the U.S. government. *Tui Manu'a* Eliasara died on 2 April 1909. After fifteen years of vacancy, the title was claimed by Chris Young in July 1924. The U.S. naval administration disclaimed the act and brought Young to Tutuila where he was detained and where he became involved in the political Mau movement.

The U.S. naval administration claimed that since the title is regarded as "royal" in nature, the U.S. Constitution does not recognize it and, therefore, the title remains vacant today.

RELATED ENTRIES: American Samoa; Western Samoa.

SOURCES AND READINGS: J. A. C. Gray, *Amerika Samoa* (Annapolis, Md.: U.S. Naval Institute, 1960); Augustin Krämer, *Die Samoa-Inseln*, 2 vols. (Stuttgart: E. Nägele, 1902).   *Robert D. Craig*

TU'I TONGA. The rulers of Tonga, the *Tu'i Tonga*, were believed to descend from the god Tangaloa 'Eitumatupu'a through his son, 'Aho'eitu, born of a mortal woman. 'Aho'eitu became the first *Tu'i Tonga* (ca. 950 A.D.) and since his reign there have been between forty and fifty *Tu'i Tonga*. The person of the *Tu'i Tonga* was considered sacred and whatever he touched became *tapu*. He was borne on a litter whenever he traveled. Ordinary mortals could not use anything he had touched and were required to serve his whims in all things. All seasonal produce was *tapu* until the first fruits had been offered to the *Tu'i Tonga*. During the reign of 'Aho'eitu, the *Falefa*, or four houses, were organized to attend the *Tu'i Tonga* in various functions of protocol and service. The twenty-fourth *Tu'i Tonga* reorganized the political hierarchy throughout Tonga by appointing governors over Tongan possessions and reapportioning chiefly lands. He also inaugurated a new chiefly line intended to relieve the *Tu'i Tonga* of some duties. This new line, the *hau* (temporal ruler), came to rival the *Tu'i Tonga* but it died out when the last holder of the title died in battle in 1799. However, the sixth holder of the new title began a line of chiefs with his son. Intrigue, battle, and murder often marked the change of titles until the time of Taufa'ahau who made himself ruler over all the factions within the Tongan islands. In 1845 he took the title of king and reigned as George Tupou I until his death in 1893. The nobles and chiefs of Tonga today all descend from the three lines originating with 'Aho'eitu. These chiefly lines are the *Tu'i Tonga*, the *Tu'i Pelehake*, and the *Kauhala'uta*.

RELATED ENTRIES: Tonga; *Tu'i Ha'atakalaua*; *Tu'i Kanokupolu*.

SOURCES AND READINGS: Noel Rutherford, ed., *The Friendly Islands, A History of Tonga* (Melbourne: Oxford University Press, 1977).   *Vernice W. Pere*

TUNGI, WILLIAM TUPOULAHI (1887-1941). A Tongan ruler, Tungi was the son of Tuku'aho and the grandson of Tungi. He was born 1 November 1887 and was educated at Tupou College and Newington College, Sydney. He married Sālote Mafile'o Pilolevu, heir to the throne, on 19 September 1917. Thirteen years older than his bride, Prince Tungi was a direct descendant of the *Tu'i Ha'atakalaua*, the second royal line. In 1923 he succeeded Tui'vakano as premier of Tonga and in later years he had charge of foreign affairs, public works, education, health, and agriculture. As the largest landowner in Tonga, he was particularly interested in the latter and in 1940 put through Parliament the Agricultural Organization Act which provided for the complete organization of Tongan agriculture along modern lines. In the 1937 New Year's Honors, he was created a Commander of the British Empire. Tongans referred to him as *koe tangata alafua*—"a man of many parts." Tungi maintained close contact with the Tongan people and was a wise and unfailing support for his wife in her long reign. He died 20 July 1941.

RELATED ENTRIES: Sālote (Queen); Tonga.

SOURCES AND READINGS: Noel Rutherford, ed., *The Friendly Islands, A History of Tonga* (Melbourne: Oxford University Press, 1977); *Pacific Islands Monthly*, August 1941, p. 20.   *Vernice W. Pere*

TUPAIA (?-1770). Tupaia was a high priest from Ra'iatea (Society Islands, French Polynesia) who in 1769 was in exile on the island of Tahiti during Captain Cook's first visit to the island. When Cook left, Tupaia was chosen to accompany him on his voyage of exploration. "We found him to be a very intelligent person and knows more . . . than any one we had met," wrote Cook (Cook I:117). Tupaia acted as Cook's navigator and named over 130 islands around Ra'iatea, many of which finally found their way onto the maps of the Pacific which Cook brought back. Tupaia also acted as interpreter when they arrived in any of the other Polynesian islands. Tupaia was highly regarded among the Maoris (New Zealand) where he conversed with their religious leaders at great length. He related his legends and mythology to the Maoris whose stories were not nearly as complete as his. Tupaia became ill in June 1770 and died in November at Batavia (Jakarta) while Cook's ships were undergoing repair.

RELATED ENTRIES: Cook, (Captain) James; French Polynesia.

SOURCES AND READINGS: James Cook, *The Journals of Captain James Cook*, ed. J. C. Beaglehole, 3 vols. (Cambridge: The Hakluyt Society, 1955-67), es-

pecially volume 1; Patrick O'Reilly, *Tahitiens* (Paris: Musée de l'Homme, 1962).   *Robert D. Craig*

TUPU'O SAMOA. Meaning "king/queen of Samoa," *Tupu'o Samoa* was an ancient title accorded to a Samoan who gained rights to the four highest-ranking titles (collectively called the *Tafa'ifā*) in Samoa: the *Tui A'ana*, *Tui Atua*, *Ngatoaitele*, and *Tamasoali'i*. The first to hold this title was Queen Salamasina (ca. 1500 A.D.), but upon her death the four *Tafa'ifā* titles again were controlled by separate lines of the family. At the time of European intrusion, the title had been seized by a war-priest of Manono island named Tamafaiga. Upon his death in 1831, Malietoa Vai'inupo gained the title until his death in 1841. Division of his titles led to the incessant wars of the nineteenth century, aggravated by the foreign powers of Great Britain, Germany, and the United States who supported rival families in their struggle for the title. When Germany gained control of Western Samoa, the title was transferred to the German emperor in Berlin, and since 1900 it has never been used in Samoa.

RELATED ENTRIES: American Samoa; Malietoa; *Tui A'ana* and *Tui Atua*; *Tui Manu'a*; Western Samoa.

SOURCES AND READINGS: Augustin Krämer, *Die Samoa-Inseln*, 2 vols. (Stuttgart: E. Nägele, 1902); J. B. Stair, *Old Samoa* (London: Religious Tract Society, 1897).   *Robert D. Craig*

TUVALU. Formerly the Ellice Islands, Tuvalu has been an independent nation within the British Commonwealth since 1 October 1978. The group consists of nine small islands situated on the western margin of Polynesia between 6° and 11° south latitude and 179° and 180° east longitude. Until 1978 Tuvalu was known as the Ellice Islands and formed part of the Gilbert and Ellice Islands Colony (GEIC); but the Ellice islanders separated from their Gilbertese neighbors and resumed their traditional name Tuvalu. From north to south, the nine individual islands are Nanumea, Niutao, Nanumanga, Nui, Vaitupu, Nukufetau, Funafuti, Nukulaelae, and Niulakita. Niulakita, formerly uninhabited, was not considered part of the group in traditional times, hence the name Tuvalu which means "eight standing together." Today Niulakita is run as a copra plantation by the people of Niutao.

With a total land area of only 26 km², Tuvalu is the world's smallest country after Nauru. It also has the highest population density of any Pacific islands group with 286 persons per km². The population enumerated at the latest census held in May 1979 totalled

7,349 persons living within Tuvalu. Seventy-eight were Europeans and of the remainder nearly all were Tuvaluan or part Tuvaluan. Another 1,800 Tuvalu citizens were either studying or temporarily employed overseas. The greatest proportion in this latter category is working, or living with their families, at Nauru. The main island of the group is Funafuti, where a highly centralized administration has been established.

The climate is characterized by consistently uniform temperatures which seldom fall below 75° F, a high relative humidity, and a generally high rainfall. The rainfall tends to increase with latitude and the wettest months are from December to February. But within these parameters the rainfall is highly variable: there is neither a predictable rainy season or a dependable dry season. The total rainfall for individual islands may vary markedly from year to year, especially in the northern islands. The southeast tradewinds prevail most of the year and moderate the humidity, but strong westerly storms occur between October and March. Hurricanes are rare because of Tuvalu's proximity to the equator, but severe cyclones are occasionally experienced. The last occurred in 1972 when Funafuti was flattened by hurricane Bebe.

Compared with the large volcanic islands to the south, the tiny atoll and reef island systems of Tuvalu have quite limited potentials for supporting a varied terrestrial biota. The environmental constraints are many: the small size of the islands (none exceeds 5 km² in size); a maximum elevation of approximately six meters; soils that are on the margins of fertility; and freshwater supplies restricted to shallow subsurface lenses. As a result of a generally adequate, if somewhat inconsistent, rainfall, dense scrub grows between the coconut trees which dominate the low-lying landscape. Otherwise, the environment severely limits the range of plant life able to survive. Apart from the ubiquitous coconut palms, the other large trees are varieties of pandanus (a significant source of food when in season), and the *fetau* (*Calophyllum inophyllum*) and the *puka* (*Hernandia peltata*). Both are used for constructing the hulls of canoes. The only root crops are taro and *pulaka*, coarse tubers grown in specially constructed pits that reach down to the freshwater lenses. Breadfruit and bananas, both staples in the contemporary diet, did not reach some islands until introduced by missionaries in the 1870s. The native fauna of Tuvalu is typical of other atoll environments, being devoid of larger mammals and limited to a restricted range of sea birds, the Polynesian rat, a few lizards and geckos, and a variety of insects.

History and Legend. The origin of the Tuvaluans lies in Polynesia with the individual islands most probably being settled piecemeal by parties drifting or voyaging from the larger islands to the southwest. No archaeological work has been carried out, but legends and language indicate a predominantly Samoan heritage with significant Tongan and Gilbertese influence, especially in the northern islands, and that most of the islands were settled separately between the fourteenth and eighteenth centuries. Such dates, however, are highly speculative, especially as archaeological work elsewhere is constantly pushing back the accepted time depth on many other Polynesian islands.

The first settlers to Tuvalu must have lived a precarious existence until they came to terms with the barrenness of the islands in which they found themselves. The basic crops in many other parts of the Pacific were initally not available to the first settlers, and it is probable that pandanus assumed a fundamental dietary role while coconuts and other introduced plants were gradually becoming established.

Before European contact in the early nineteenth century, each Tuvalu island had developed a political and social system well suited to the territorial and ecological constraints of small atolls. Human survival was a function of collective effort, hence a preference for *kaitasi* (collectively-owned) type of land tenure as against *vaevae* or individual ownership and the development in some islands of *puikainga* or corporate land holding groups to exploit available resources. The typical settlement pattern which evolved was a series of hamlets on each island where extended families formed the units of production. Kinship was bilateral but a patrilineal bias obtained.

Since the eight (inhabited) islands shared the same narrow range of resources and were self-sufficient in any case, there was no scope for the complex, institutionalized trading networks found in other parts of the Pacific, though ceremonial and social visits (*malanga*) between islands took place from time to time. Poverty of resources also muted social stratification; communalism and consensus were emphasized instead. But there was nevertheless a distinction between chiefly families and commoner families and rank was normally ascribed. The government of each island varied, but typically it involved the existence of two or more chiefly families. If only for logistic reasons there seems to have been little interisland warfare in traditional times, and the most extensive polity was normally the single island. While the pre-1850 population is a matter of some speculation, it is clear that it never reached the oft-quoted figure of

20,000. Such a number is more than double the present-day population which, moreover, is heavily dependent on imported foodstuffs.

Early Spanish sightings apart, Tuvalu experienced contact with the West at a relatively late stage. With the opening of various transpacific shipping routes in the early nineteenth century, followed by the discovery of the ''On-the-Line'' whaling grounds of which Tuvalu formed part, the group began to be visited by a steady trickle of European shipping, and by 1825 the last Tuvalu island had been placed on these mariners' charts. Most of the vessels were whalers, overwhelmingly from the New England states of America. Over sixty such visits can be positively documented, but the actual number would have been several times that figure.

The contact history of Tuvalu in the first half of the nineteenth century was largely one of small-scale trade peacefully conducted between the Tuvaluans and ships that happened to pass.

During the 1860s the casual, itinerate contacts of the whaler were superseded by the more organized and durable activities of shore-based company traders and missionaries. The greatest single disaster in Tuvalu's history occurred in 1863 when the southern atolls of Funafuti and Nukulaelae were raided by Peruvian slavers, loosing two-thirds of their populations. None of those kidnapped ever returned home.

Although mission work was predated by shore-based commercial contacts, the missionary impact was far greater than the traders'. Tuvalu began its formal association with Christianity as an outpost of London Missionary Society (LMS) enterprise in Samoa, and has remained a Protestant stronghold ever since. Churches and schools were founded on each island and Tuvaluans eagerly mastered the arts of reading and writing. All aspects of traditional society associated with the old religion were either suppressed or driven underground.

The period of missionary penetration and consolidation in Tuvalu largely coincided with the expansionary era of the wider-Pacific copra trade when trading companies were rapidly extending the scope of their operations. In Tuvalu itself copra production was constrained by physical and environmental limitations that rendered the group unimportant as a trading arena. Accordingly Tuvalu only assumed significance in trading company calculations as a small and expendable segment of a wider network of trading stations extending from Tonga in the south through to the Marianas in the northwest.

At the local level the individual Tuvalu islands generally accommodated trading company influence with little disruption to the tenor of daily life. Since their tiny infertile islands offered no scope for plantation agriculture and large-scale European settlement, Tuvaluans were spared the alienation of their lands, and the only Europeans to reside in the group at any time were the dozen or so company traders whose success depended on maintaining local goodwill. Some of these traders—notably Alfred Restieaux, Jack O'Brien, Martin Kleis, and Harry Nitz—became established identities in Tuvalu and left behind large families who are prominent in present-day Tuvalu.

Apart from the Peruvian incident in 1863, labor recruiting never assumed importance during the nineteenth century. Tuvaluans were recruited in succeeding decades for places as far afield as Fiji, Samoa, Hawai'i, Queensland, and possibly also Tahiti, but in small numbers. Tuvaluan population increased steadily from approximately 3,000 in 1865 to about 3,500 in 1900, and by the turn of the century one could even speak of a ''surplus population'' in the northern islands.

Seen in the context of European expansion, Tuvalu was brought within the ambit of the two major Western influences of Christianity and capitalism during the course of the nineteenth century. Yet the overall impact of the West was slight in that, mission influences apart, demands were not made on the Tuvaluans to alter their ways—and even in the religious sphere a certain congruence between the old and the new faiths can be detected. Nor were the Tuvaluans during this period exploited by outsiders, if only because their islands contained so little of economic value to actually exploit.

In September 1892 Captain H. W. S. Gibson of H.M.S. *Curaçoa* declared a British protectorate over all nine Ellice Islands. The move was hurriedly undertaken for strategic reasons—namely to prevent the possibility of France annexing the group thereby driving a wedge between Fiji and the Gilberts, over which a protectorate had been declared the month before. Although the Gilbert Islands and the Ellice Islands were technically separate protectorates, they shared a common administration from the beginning. In 1893 C. R. Swayne commenced duties as resident commissioner of both protectorates, but it was a number of years before British rule had an appreciable effect on Ellice life and affairs. But Swayne—and also his successor, the energetic and autocratic William Telfer Campbell—visited the Ellice Islands at least once a year, so a measure of administrative control was there from the onset.

The character of the new administration was determined by local conditions working in conjunction with British colonial office parsimony and the unbending attitudes of Telfer Campbell. The colonial office's insistence that the new protectorate pay its own way, together with the fact that the group had no economic resources beyond a few hundred tons of copra, meant that the Ellice Islands was run on the cheap and that the colonial administrative structure was of a most rudimentary nature. To these ends education remained a mission responsibility, and the work of local government was vested in islands councils which, in theory, the resident commissioner would advise. But this principle of indirect rule was undermined by Telfer Campbell who sought, within the limits of his mobility, to subordinate the island councils to his own will. He thus created a pattern of irregular but close and paternal oversight which persisted for the next half century.

Campbell's brand of authoritarianism clashed with representatives of the LMS, both European and Samoan, and Campbell and many of his successors did all they could to subordinate the mission to government. As a result, the LMS was forced to remove a number of its more intransigent pastors and the freedom of action previously enjoyed by the mission was somewhat curtailed.

The LMS extended its activities quite appreciably in the field of education. The Motufoua School on Vaitupu was opened in 1905 and staffed entirely by Samoans and Tuvaluans until H. Bond James was seconded from the LMS Cook Islands district to take charge of the school, where he remained until 1917. In 1912 Sarah Jolliffe arrived at Funafuti to establish a girls' school. That was the end of European resident missionaries until the Reverend Brian Ranford's posting to the group in the 1950s and the 1960s. In 1924 the administration helped fill the educational gap with the establishment of a boys' primary school named the Ellice Islands School. Under the direction of D. G. Kennedy, the school achieved remarkable results in the teaching of English and other academic subjects until it was closed down as a government economy measure. Kennedy himself is undoubtedly the most consequential figure in Ellice Islands' history. He left his mark on every area he touched—education, administration, land tenure, cooperatives, and resettlement.

The two other most significant areas in which the early colonial government intervened were labor migration and health. In 1900 labor migration from Tuvalu assumed an entirely different character with the commencement of government-sponsored recruitment to the phosphate works at Ocean Island, and

also Nauru after the World War I. The Ellice islanders concerned received the benefits of overseas contract labor without suffering the abuses normally associated with the business. In particular the rotating pattern of this migration, with returned laborers being replaced by fresh recruits, has alleviated population pressure within the group without resulting in a permanent exodus. However, there were some undesirable side-effects during the first decade of recruitment to Ocean Island when the returned laborers introduced a variety of infectious diseases which had a significant demographic effect on some islands. The government countered this new threat with an active health program by appointing trained native medical orderlies, and eventually a resident European doctor was stationed at Funafuti.

In 1909 G. B. Smith-Rewse arrived as district magistrate. He not only supervised the health policy but also inaugurated an onerous public works program at Funafuti. In these and other ways he preserved the administration's tradition of paternal control. He also attempted to reform and codify the system of land tenure which he so badly misunderstood that the whole situation had to be rectified by the Kennedy Land Commission in the 1930s and the Lake Land Commission the following decade.

In 1915-1916 the Gilbert Islands and the Ellice Islands were annexed and amalgamated to form a single administrative unit known as the Gilbert and Ellice Islands Colony (GEIC). This change in status involved no noticeable alteration in the style or content of colonial government in either group. In fact, the colonial administration became even more restricted in what it could actually accomplish. In 1918 the seat of government was moved to Ocean Island so that the government might oversee the activities of the phosphate company which provided the bulk of its revenue. Between 1909 and 1926 every resident commissioner was appointed from outside the Gilbert and Ellice Islands service. No locally stationed administrative officer had time in office to gain a detailed knowledge of Tuvalu or a proficiency in the language. As a result, the Ellice Islands became the neglected backwater of a colony, which itself was regarded as an isolated colonial outpost.

Regulations were passed which in theory gave the administration sweeping powers covering all aspects of Ellice islanders' lives and the functioning of their island councils: curfews, communal work, fishing, feasting, dancing, and games. The considerable cultural differences between Gilbert and Ellice islanders were not taken into account when colony laws were passed. In the interests of administrative conformity, uniform laws were framed for both groups, yet the laws in question were almost invariably drawn up in response to Gilbertese conditions.

World War II. Tuvalu escaped Japanese occupation during World War II, but some airborne action was seen in the group. When the Japanese overran the Gilberts in 1942, the colony's administration was transferred first to Sydney and then to Funafuti following American occupation of the group. Thousands of GIs were stationed at Funafuti, Nukufetau, and Nanumea. Large numbers of Ellice islanders worked for the Americans, gaining new skills, acquiring completely novel material possessions, and earning unprecedented amounts of money. The wartime savings accumulated by the individual Ellice islanders were often put to good use, most notably by the people of Vaitupu, who purchased and resettled the island of Kioa in Fiji.

The postwar years mark a sharp break with the past as changes in British colonial policy led to dramatic growth in and localization of the civil service based at Tarawa. For the first time large numbers of Gilbertese and Ellice islanders were brought together in a competitive situation, and Ellice islanders gained a disproportionate number of positions in the expanding administration.

Tensions were heightened in the early 1960s with the move towards self-government prompted by Great Britain, which was under United Nations pressure. Decolonization and the accompanying transfer of political responsibility proceeded at a hectic pace. Accordingly, the Gilbert and Ellice islanders were given little time or experience to adjust to the increasingly autonomous role being thrust upon them or for political institutions at the national level to develop.

It is against this wider background that the problems inherent in grouping together two culturally distinct people became apparent. With Gilbertese outnumbering the Ellice islanders by seven to one, it became clear that the latter could never hope to dominate any future national assembly. In response to these problems, Ellice islanders were, by the mid-1960s, actively seeking separation as a separate British colony rather than an independent or self-governing nation.

Britain was markedly unenthusiastic at the prospect of assuming responsibility for yet another colony at a time when she was trying to divest herself of such entanglements and made strenuous efforts to dissuade the Ellice islanders. However various local pressures, reinforced by apprehension at possible international embarrassment over the issue, finally led the British government in 1973 to appoint the Monson Commission to examine and report on the problem. In the light of Sir Leslie Monson's recommendations, it was decided to allow separation providing a referendum indicated that this indeed was the will of majority opinion in the Ellice. In August and September 1974, the referendum was held under the scrutiny of a visiting mission from the United Nation's Committee of Twenty Four, and 3,799 people (or 92 percent of the votes cast) voted in favor of separation and 293 against.

Following Monson's recommendations, the new Ellice Colony received none of the old colony's assets apart from a new buildings and a single ship. Nor was it to have any future claims on phosphate royalties from Ocean Island; and the Line and Pheonix islands, which formed part of the original Colony, were to remain with the Gilberts.

The Tuvalu Order 1975, which gave legal status to Tuvalu as a separate British colony, came into force on 1 October 1975, the same day as the first Tuvalu government was formed. Administrative separation, however was not achieved for another three months, as the old GEIC civil service continued to service jointly the new Tuvalu government in Funafuti and the Gilbertese government in Tarawa. Each government was given until 1 January 1976 to establish a civil service (as in the case of Tuvalu) or to fill the positions left vacant by departing Ellice islanders (as in the case of Gilberts). From the onset the Tuvalu civil service has been manned almost exclusively by Tuvaluans.

Following the relocation of Ellice Islands' civil servants at Funafuti, development was rapid on several fronts. A public works program was instituted to house and hold the newly created civil service, and Funafuti has been transformed from a district office of the old GEIC with a population of less than 1,000 to a national capital with a population double that figure. Constitutional change proceeded at an equally rapid pace. The Tuvalu Order 1975 gave Tuvalu a ministerial form of government with a large measure of internal self-government limited by the provision that a Queen's commissioner chaired the cabinet and held reserve powers over such matters as finance and external affairs. The unicameral legislative body, the house of assembly, was filled by the eight standing Ellice Island members of the old GEIC's legislative assembly. In the election of August 1977 the size of the house was increased to twelve with the four largest islands each returning two members; and Toalipi (now Toaripi) Lauti, Tuvalu's first chief minister, was re-elected to that position by a vote of the members. He became prime minister on independence.

Although no formal political parties exist, there is a recognized "government" side and a recognized "opposition" side to the house. Crossing the floor at divisions is a rare occurrence. The final stages of decolonization were rushed through during the course of 1978. Following a constitutional conference in London early in the year, Tuvalu was granted full internal self-government in May, only five months before independence.

The prevailing Westminster-style of parliamentary democracy was maintained by the Tuvalu Independence Order 1978. The British monarch is the head of state and is represented by a Tuvalu governor-general. The twelve-member unicameral parliament directly elected by the people has also been retained. Parliament is presided over by a speaker elected by members of parliament from among those of their members who are not members of cabinet. The normal life of the parliament is four years and the minimum voting age is eighteen. The cabinet consists of the prime minister and up to four other ministers. The prime minister is elected by member of parliament from among themselves; other ministers are appointed and removed from office by the governor-general in accordance with the advice of the prime minister. The prime minister may be removed from office by a vote of no confidence in him in parliament. Appointments to and the removal of officers from civil service posts are vested in the governor-general, who acts in accordance with the advice of the Public Service Commission. In 1980 there were 340 posts in the civil service.

The court system consists of island courts on each island, a magistrate's court, a senior magistrate's court, and a high court. The last three courts each have revisionary and appellate powers in respect of the lower courts. From the high court, appeal lies with the Fiji Court of Appeal, and the right of resort to the judicial committee of the privy council has been preserved. Land disputes are handled by a separate system of land courts and a land appeals tribunal. There are no Tuvaluans qualified in law, so the attorney-general is an expatriate. The island courts are manned by a panel of three lay justices and the magistrate's court by a lay justice. The senior magistrate's court is manned by a visiting magistrate from Fiji, and the high court by a judge who is the chief justice of the Solomon Islands.

Lacking any industry and with exports largely restricted to a small amount of copra, Tuvalu's self-sufficiency in any accepted sense of the word is impossible, and Tuvalu must in the future rely heavily on foreign aid. The only significant sources of locally generated income are philatelic sales and the imposition of high custom's duties on exports. The major source of income from overseas comes in the form of remittances from relatives working abroad, primarily from the phosphate islands and the overseas merchant marine.

For the moment overseas labor migration alleviates population pressure, which is potentially one of the most serious future problems. Unlike many of the neighboring island groups, Tuvalu has neither immigration quotas or the right of free association with a metropolitan country. Not only are population densities very high but Tuvaluans are effectively confined to their archipelago. The government-sponsored family planning program enjoys moderate success, but there still tends to be a desire for large families on the grounds that many children are a security for old age.

The opportunity for employment within Tuvalu is also limited. From the beginning the country has had a skilled manpower surplus. Accordingly the new civil service quickly filled up, and this is unfortunate for the aspirations of many educated Tuvaluans.

Given the concentration of government departments at Funafuti, virtually all development is confined to the main island where a proto-urban center is emerging replete with associated problems such as overcrowding, substandard housing, increased crime, and heavy reliance on imported foodstuffs. Decentralization and the location of some government departments on outer islands have been raised as an alternative, but this course of action would greatly impair government efficiency.

The major services offered by government are in the fields of education, health, and communications. There is a government primary school on all islands and a secondary school at Vaitupu. Dispensaries are located on all outer islands and a hospital at Funafuti. Communications take several forms. All outer islands are in daily radio-telegraph contact with Funafuti; interisland travel is either by ship or seaplane; and the Tuvalu Broadcasting Service transmits a few hours each day.

In contrast to Funafuti, the outer islands have been the scene of very little development. Apart from government employees (school teachers, radio operators, and medical staff), the local pastor, and employees of the cooperative store, outer islanders still gain their livelihood by traditional subsistence means. But cash in the form of remittances has become an indispensible adjunct to outer island life. The church remains a powerful force in outer island life, and the old precept that each island has one village and each village has one religion still holds considerable force. There are, however, small communities of people on most islands who belong to faiths other than the established congregational based Tuvalu Church, the indigenous offspring of the former LMS. The unit of local government is still the island council which is responsible for local services and affairs and which is empowered to pass by-laws consistent with statute law. Significantly the local councils sometimes feel that the national government is a remote and impersonal force much akin to the former colonial government.

Despite a century and a half of European contact, Tuvalu has been transformed from a series of petty chiefdoms to a nation-state; important features of traditional life, however, remain largely intact and outer island life has lost none of its validity. Given these qualities, Tuvalu may yet witness the triumph of its human resources over the impersonal forces of the outside world.

POSTSCRIPT: As this book was going to press, a change of government followed the Tuvalu general election of September 1981. In the subsequent vote among the newly returned members of the House of Assembly, Dr. Tomasi Puapua of Vaitupu Island was elected Prime Minister.

RELATED ENTRIES: American Board of Commissioners for Foreign Missions; American Samoa; Cook, (Captain) James; London Missionary Society; Polynesia (Settlement of); Polynesian Culture (Ancient); Tokelau Islands; Western Samoa.

SOURCES AND READINGS: Besnier, N., "The History of the Tuvaluan Language" in his *Ttou Tauloto te Ggana Tuvalu: A Course in the Tuvalu Language* (Funafuti: United States Peace Corps, 1981); Brady, I.A., "Christians, Pagans and Government Men: Culture Change in the Ellice Islands," in Brady, I. A. and Isaacs, B. L., eds., *A Reader in Culture Change: Case Studies* (New York: Schenkman, 1975); Kennedy, D. G., *Field Notes on the Material Culture of Vaitupu, Ellice Islands* (New Plymouth: Polynesian Society, 1931); Kofe, L., "The Tuvalu Church: A Socio-historical Survey of its Development Towards an Indigenous Church," (B.D. thesis, Pacific Theological College, 1976); Macdonald, Barrie, "Policy and Practice in an Atoll Territory: British Rule in the Gilbert and Ellice Islands, 1892-1970" (Ph.D. dissertation, Australian National University, 1971); Macdonald, Barrie, "Secession in Defence of Identity: the Making of Tuvalu" *Pacific Viewpoint* 16, no. 1 (1975): 26-44; Munro, Doug., "Kirisome and Tema: Samoan Pastors in the Ellice Islands," in Scarr, D., ed., *More Pacific Islands Portraits* (Canberra: Australian National University Press, 1979); Roberts, R. G., "Te Atu Tuvalu: A Short History of the Ellice Islands," *Journal of the Polynesian Society* 67, no. 3 (1958): 394-423; [Wilson, John F]., "Tuvalu Achieves Independence," *Commonwealth Law Bulletin* 4, no. 4 (1978): 1003-9.

Doug Munro
Tito Isala
Nicholas Besnier

ULUKALALA II, FINAU (?-1809). A despotic chief of Ha'apai in Tonga, Ulukalala's exploits and cunning are recorded vividly by William Mariner. Although descended from the youngest of the great modern lineages, the Ha'a Ngata Tupu, the ambitious Finau had through treachery and eloquence achieved immense power over the people of Ha'apai and Vava'u. He planned the assassination of Tuku-'aho, the *Tu'i Kanokupolu*, (1799) which precipitated a long and bloody civil conflict in Tonga. He also organized the attack on the British ship *Port-au-Prince* and massacred twenty-six sailors. Finau spared Mariner and others only that they might man the guns of the captured vessel against his enemies in Tongatapu and Vava'u. More than any other single person, he was responsible for the ravage of civil war which plagued Tonga between 1799 and 1810. However, his close friendship with Mariner provided the young seaman with opportunities to learn much about early Tongan culture which otherwise would have been unknown to the world.

RELATED ENTRIES: Mariner, William; Tonga; *Tu'i Kanokupolu*.

SOURCES AND READINGS: E. E. V. Collocott, *Ko e Ta'u e Teau* (London: William Clowes and Sons, 1926); John Martin, *An Account of the Natives of Tonga Islands in the South Pacific Ocean*, 2d ed. (London: John Murray, 1818); A. H. Wood, *History and Geography of Tonga* (1932; reprint ed., Wodonga, Victoria: Border Morning Mail, 1972).

Eric B. Shumway

UNITED STATES AND PACIFIC ISLAND BASES (1922-1942). United States-Japanese friction after 1905 presented U.S. military planners with the problem of protecting the Philippines and of supporting U.S. Far Eastern policy. The strategy developed, War Plan—Orange, emphasized the possession of a string of island bases along which U.S. power could be projected into the western Pacific. By 1922, Japan's possession of the League of Nations mandated islands left the key U.S. base, Guam, defenseless in their midst because the Washington naval treaty prohibited Guam's development as a major base. The navy's strategic thinking now centered on the Japanese islands stretching toward Guam and the Philippines, the islands which would screen Hawai'i and the Panama Canal, and the islands forming stepping-stones to Australasia.

In 1923 a naval vessel was sent on an intelligence cruise through the Japanese islands. Another cruise, jointly sponsored by the Departments of Navy and Agriculture, examined Nihoa, Ocean, Johnston, and Wake. In 1924 a similar expedition visited the islands south of Hawai'i—Fanning, Christmas, Jarvis, Washington, Palmyra, Baker, and Howland. The Department of the Navy recommended that the State Department push American claims to Howland, Baker, and Christmas but the State Department refused to take any action. After 1927 Navy's interest in the islands waned.

In June 1934 the South Seas Commercial Company approached Navy regarding establishing Pacific air routes using Midway, Wake, and Guam for the central route, and Jarvis, Baker, Howland, Johnston, Kingman Reef, and American Samoa for the southwestern route. Ultimately, Navy granted Pan American Airways the permits for the central route while encouraging South Seas on the other route. By the end of 1934, Japan gave notice that it was abrogating the treaty of 1922. Navy could start preparing bases in 1937.

In 1935 naval officers accompanied Pan American's base expedition to Midway and Wake, which they surveyed and plotted for the landing fields of the future. In May 1935 patrol planes used Pan American's facilities at Midway during the navy's war games. In March 1935 the United States colonized Howland, Baker, and Jarvis to establish the United States claim. The first expedition also examined Palmyra, Swain's Island, and Pago Pago; during the second cruise, Johnston was examined; during the third, Kingman Reef was visited along with Palmyra again, due to the navy's special interest. By the end of 1936, dredging was under way at Midway, Wake, and Guam for Pan American's operations but it was of equal benefit to the navy. In

October, the navy tried to install deep-sea moorings for patrol planes at Howland. And, at the end of 1936, the naval treaty ended.

The navy started preparing Johnston at the beginning of 1937. In May, a scientific party was carried to Canton Island to observe an eclipse of the sun. The navy made a complete survey of the island and decided that Canton would be a superior base to Howland which had proved inadequate during the search for Amelia Earhart. In late July, the navy wanted to colonize Canton but the State Department held out for negotiations with England. The Department of the Navy did get approval to develop Palmyra and reconsidered trying deep-sea moorings at Howland if Canton could not be obtained. In March 1938 colonists were landed on Canton and the United States obtained joint use with Pan American which moved onto the island, allowing the navy to use their facilities. In 1939 the Department of the Navy did a complete survey of the Phoenix and Union islands.

The Hepburn report on base needs (December 1938) recommended the development of secondary bases at Midway, Wake, Johnston, Palmyra, Canton, Rose, and Guam. Appropriations were made to develop Midway, Johnston, Wake, and Palmyra. Guam was omitted for fear of upsetting Japan. In late 1939 navy planes flew to the Philippines through Pan American's central route. The navy tested Canton in March 1940 and based a flight of patrol planes on Pan American's facilities.

The Greenslade report in January 1941 called for creating main bases at Hawai'i and the Philippines to create a balance of power in the western Pacific. Midway, Wake, and Guam were to be major air bases while Samoa, Johnston, Palmyra, and Canton were to be subsidiary bases to protect Hawai'i and the Panama Canal. The Philippines had been upgraded, making it essential that a southwest route to the islands through Australia be set up. In September the army flew B-17s to the Philippines, using new landing fields at Midway and Wake and then flying to Port Moresby through the Japanese mandated islands. The Moresby leg was dangerous in event of war. The army sent a construction crew to Canton and one to Christmas late in 1941 and contracted for runways to be built at Suva and at Townsville, Australia, to create a new bomber-ferry route.

On 7 December 1941 only the base at Midway was operational, but Wake, Johnston, and Palmyra were partly operational and Canton was usable due to Pan American. Wake and Guam, which had never been developed, were taken by Japan. But Midway, Palmyra, Johnston, and Canton were completed and even Howland and Baker were used. The southwest route to Australia had been established.

RELATED ENTRIES: Canton Island Question; Earhart, Amelia; Equatorial Islands; Oceanic Nitrates Corporation; South Seas Commercial Company.

SOURCES AND READINGS: Francis X. Holbrook, "Commercial Aviation and the Colonization of the Equatorial Islands, 1934-36," *Aerospace Historian* 17, no. 4 (1970) and "The Road to Down Under," *Aerospace Historian* 22, no. 4 (1974).

Francis X. Holbrook

UNITED STATES CONGRESS AND MICRONESIA. Since its approval in 1947 of the agreement making nearly all of Micronesia a "strategic trust" of the United States, the Congress has exercised significant influence over the region by controlling U.S. expenditures for social, economic, and political development and through its power to approve or reject any agreement terminating the trusteeship. Traditionally, the Senate has allowed the House of Representatives to take the lead in matters concerning Micronesia, but individual members of both houses, from time to time, have also taken a special, if somewhat temporary, interest in the area.

When the administration of the Trust Territory of the Pacific Islands was taken over by the Department of the Interior in 1951, the House and Senate interior committees assumed control of the budgetary authorizations for the region. Throughout the 1950s these committess authorized and appropriated less than $6 million annually for administrative and development costs. Education initiatives by the administration of President John F. Kennedy and a critical report by a United Nations Visiting Mission to Micronesia pushed the budget to $16 million in 1963. Congress increased this figure gradually each year, then more dramatically, until in 1974 it reached $80 million after which real-dollar increases tapered off. During the 1960s major decisions affecting the trust territory were made by Wayne Aspinall (Democrat, Colorado), the chairman of the House Committee on Interior and Insular Affairs. Although he permitted increased budget authorizations for Micronesia, Aspinall blocked both administration and congressional initiatives to explore a new political status for the region.

In 1970 younger members of the House Interior Committee succeeded in forcing rules changes to reduce Aspinall's control over his subcommittees. As a result, the chairman of the Subcommittee on Territories, Phillip Burton of California, became the dominant congressional force in Micronesian affairs. The creation of a Subcommittee on Pacific Affairs under Antonio Won Pat of Guam did not significantly reduce the jurisdiction of Burton's committee or his control over legislation affecting Micronesia.

In 1975 Burton was instrumental in House passage of a bill approving the establishment of a U.S. commonwealth in the Northern Mariana Islands. The lack of debate in the House contrasted sharply with the Senate where a number of traditionally liberal Senators as well as some convervatives questioned the wisdom of the measure before it passed and was signed into law.

During the 1970s, Burton skillfully shepherded legislation through Congress which provided for larger budgets and expanded federal programs in Micronesia. As negotiations over a new political status for the territory progressed, Burton attempted to introduce provisions which would be required for his support of the final agreement. Yet the congressional impact on the political status negotiations, as in most issues central to the development of Micronesia, remained limited by the sporadic and poorly informed interests of a few members. In the 1970s, Micronesian leaders moved more confidently to assert their demands for greater political autonomy, and Congress found itself primarily in the role of a spectator to the negotiations.

Through its belated generosity towards Micronesia in the form of increased budgetary and programmatic assistance, Congress intended to improve social and economic conditions in the region. But its lack of sustained interest in Micronesia prevented it from providing an informed guidance for federal policy which would enhance rather than degrade Micronesian capacities for self-sufficiency.

RELATED ENTRIES: Commonwealth of the Northern Mariana Islands; Micronesia.

SOURCES AND READINGS: Donald F. McHenry, *Micronesia: Trust Betrayed* (New York: Carnegie Endowment for International Peace, 1975).

Mark Borthwick

UNITED STATES EXPLORING EXPEDITION.

The ''Wilkes Expedition'' (August 1838-June 1842), the first exploring expedition financed by the United States government, was led by Charles Wilkes and, through scientific and diplomatic activities, proved one of the nineteenth century's most productive Pacific voyages. American mercantile and whaling interests had long called for the charting of the Pacific. In 1836 Congress authorized an expedition to promote American Pacific trade and further scientific knowledge. Controversies over scope, purposes, and leadership (Wilkes was a junior officer) delayed the project until August 1838 when the

ships departed Norfolk, Virginia, for Cape Horn and the Pacific. At its maximum the squadron included six vessels.

The authoritarian Wilkes, despite shortcomings as a sailor, brought energy and scientific ability to the ambitious endeavor, which enhanced the reputations of many of the paticipating civilian scientists, including: James Dana, geologist; William Rich, botanist; William Brackenridge, horticulturalist; Titian Peale and Charles Pickering, naturalists; Horatio Hale, ethnologist and philologist; and Joseph Couthouy, conchologist.

The expedition ranged from the northwest coast of America and northern Pacific islands, to scores of islands, reefs, and atolls in the central and southwestern Pacific, to the Philippines, Australia, and Antarctica. The crew surveyed 280 islands and prepared 180 charts, many of which (especially the first global whaling chart) were of incalculable value to traders and whalers. The charts for Tahiti were used as late as World War II. By surveying 1600 miles of Antarctic coastline, the expedition revealed a continent, although its existence was not generally accepted until the 1908-1909 Shackleton expedition. The voyage also helped lay the foundation for later American Pacific expansion and suggested the strategic value of a strong American navy at such outposts as Hawai'i and Samoa.

The ships brought back thousands of species of plants and seeds (which helped to augment the United States Botanic Garden in Washington, D.C.), birds, fishes, and insects, and large quantities of minerals and artifacts. Observatories established in Tahiti and Hawai'i contributed to knowledge of terrestrial magnetism, gravity, and meteorology. It took thirty years to publish all the atlases, charts, and reports, which, although insufficiently distributed and largely descriptive, have stood the test of time. Wilkes' own five-volume narrative, printed in limited quantities, influenced the American novelist James Fenimore Cooper.

A product of America's antebellum romantic vision, the expedition marked a turning point in the government's attitudes toward scientific explorations, facilitated Pacific trade and navigation, added substantially to geographic and scientific knowledge of Oceania, and increased American prestige in the world scientific community.

RELATED ENTRIES: *Narragansett*, Cruise of; Wilkes, Charles.

SOURCES AND READINGS: William Stanton, *The Great United States Exploring Expedition of 1838-1842* (Berkeley: University of California Press,

1975); David B. Tyler, *The Wilkes Expedition: The First United States Exploring Expedition, 1838-1842* (Philadelphia: American Philosophical Society, 1968); Charles Wilkes, *Autobiography of Rear Admiral Charles Wilkes, US Navy 1798-1877*, ed. William James Morgan et al. (Washington: Naval History Division of the Department of the Navy, 1978); Charles Wilkes, *Narrative of the United States Exploring Expedition during the Years 1838, 1839, 1840, 1841, 1842*, 5 vols. (Philadelphia: C. Sherman, 1844).   *Kenneth John Blume*

UNITED STATES IN THE PACIFIC. Americans first entered the Pacific basin shortly after the Revolution in search of trade with Asia. The Pacific Ocean to them was either a highway toward their goal or a barrier in the way. In either case, it was a zone of transit and of minor interest compared to the Atlantic and Europe.

The ship *Empress of China* sailed from New York to China and back in 1784-1785; and in the following years other vessels followed, visiting nearly every part of the vast ocean in search of goods to sell in Asia. At the end of the 1780s, the *Columbia* and *Lady Washington*, ships from Boston, carried furs from the Oregon and British Columbia coasts of North America to China, visiting Hawai'i on the way. Between 1778 and the 1830s Americans came to dominate the Northwest fur trade and visited Japan, eastern Polynesia, and the South American coast in search of wood, water, fresh provisions, and occasionally supplemental trade.

Sandalwood, *bêche-de-mer*, tortoise shell, and other products were obtained from the Pacific islands for sale in the Far East, and thus Americans were introduced to the islands of Melanesia and Micronesia in the first half of the nineteenth century. The effects of their presence there were more important to the lives of the island peoples than the trade was to the economy of the United States.

Pacific whaling and sealing began for Americans in the early 1790s in the southeast waters near the coasts of Chile and Peru. Then they pursued the whale westward and northward to the central Pacific by 1820, to Hawai'i and the Japanese grounds in the 1820s and into the north Pacific and the Bering Sea in the 1830s and 1840s. Sealing was concentrated in the far southern and far northern Pacific, reaching into Antarctic and Arctic waters until the seals were nearly wiped out on many coasts.

Both traders and whalers left their marks upon the islands of the Pacific. For Americans the impact was made mostly before 1860 and chiefly in the eastern and central Pacific. After the 1840s, their contacts south of the equator were less frequent as European powers took control of islands and as whaling activity moved northward. American crews helped introduce disease germs, firearms, alcohol, and violence, as well as new materials, tools, technologies, plants, and ideas, including Christianity.

Individual Americans advanced territorial claims to islands in the Marquesas, Societies, and other places as far west as Taiwan, but the U.S. government in the Pacific repeatedly ignored or rejected claims of American sovereignty thus advanced, and it did little to support private property claims in New Zealand or Tahiti, for example, when other countries took control there. In Fiji and Hawai'i stronger support was given; and in Hawai'i, in 1842, President John Tyler claimed a paramount American interest as against other powers.

The strategic location of Hawai'i in the north Pacific made it a center of American activity from the first days of the Northwest fur trade. Not until 1819 did the first whaling ship visit that island group, but thereafter, as the fur trade declined, Hawai'i became the central entrepôt of north Pacific whaling. Catering to the whalers and their crews became the heart of the money economy there from about 1830 to the 1850s. Together with the work and influence of Protestant missionaries from New England, whaling and trade between the American and Asian coasts gave Hawai'i the largest colony of resident Americans in the Pacific by the 1830s.

American interest on the Pacific coast of North America, dating from the 1780s, expanded through trade and travel until Oregon and California became parts of the United States in 1846-1848. These acquisitions forced the government of the United States to take a keener interest in the ocean area, if only from the standpoint of national defense. South of California, early dreams of a vast trade with Spanish America failed to materialize; and with the decline of eastern Pacific whaling contact with those shores, from Chile northward, was much less frequent, except for the gold rush traffic around Cape Horn and a brief upsurge of trade at that time.

Around the middle of the nineteenth century, a search for soil-enriching fertilizers, including guano, brought a few Americans to the central Pacific. In 1856 Congress authorized citizens to register claims to islands valued for their guano deposits and not held by any foreign power. Under that act claims were registered to more than twenty islands in equatorial waters of the east-central Pacific. Most of the guano-exploiting activities were abandoned by the mid-1880s, but the claims thus registered became a matter of legal speculation which was revived, for example, in the 1930s, when bases for transpacific aviation were in demand. The question of claims under the guano act still had to be laid to rest in the 1970s, as the emergence of independent Pacific-island nations gave a new significance to these pieces of land. At that time, the United States was disposed to relinquish its claims as it had a century earlier when Japan took over the Bonin Islands.

American missionaries played a significant role in the development of national interests and policies in the Pacific islands and in Asia. Beginning in Hawai'i in 1820, the mission came to exert major influences on political and social life there. From Hawai'i, Calvinist missionaries extended their teaching to the Marquesas, Marshalls, and Carolines, leaving the South Pacific to British and French mission groups. After 1850 and extending into the twentieth century, Mormons and Adventists from the United States penetrated even the islands south of the equator. The influences of these mission groups upon the health and political and social development of the island peoples have been a subject of controversy for a century and a half.

United States naval vessels were sent to the Pacific early in the nineteenth century to protect and police the Americans pursuing their various interests there. A Pacific squadron, based on the South American coast, often sent units to the Polynesian or even Micronesian islands after 1821. Other ships from an Asiatic squadron crossed the Pacific at times, visiting the islands and carrying out missions in cooperation with consular agents. In the late 1830s Lieutenant Charles Wilkes led a Navy exploring expedition through the eastern Pacific; and in the following decade a similar expedition charted the Sea of Japan.

In the second half of the nineteenth century American private interests in most of the Pacific declined in importance. A major cause of this was the virtual disappearance of the once-great whale fishery, displaced by the use of petroleum products instead of whale oil. A second factor was the decline of the American merchant marine as shipping changed from wood and sail to steel and steam. Pacific ports which had once received more American visitors than any others came to see them seldom if at all. In these circumstances, the presence and general influence of Americans in most of the Pacific receded, except for the North American coast, Hawai'i, and, oddly, Samoa. There was, consequently, no clear or strong United States government policy for the Pacific, least of all for its island realms.

In the 1890s when private interests in the Pacific seemed at a low ebb, the United States government suddenly reached across the ocean, acquiring Hawai'i, Guam, Wake, the Philippines, and a part of Samoa. The responsibilities thus assumed had not been carefully studied or prepared for, except possibly for Hawai'i. The national interests to be served by these acquisitions were only dimly and often erroneously defined in the bitter debates in Congress and the American press in the years 1898 to 1900. As a result, no clear line of colonial policy emerged in the twentieth century. The United States, with a long history of anticolonial sentiment, had become a colonial power in the Pacific without a colonial office, trained colonial officials, or any real model for colonial administration except that provided by the history of the continental territories destined for statehood within the American union.

Because of their relationship to military security problems, the Philippines were placed under the jurisdiction of the Department of War, while Guam and American Samoa were turned over to the Department of the Navy to administer. Only Hawai'i was set, apparently, on the normal territorial path toward statehood. Even there, questions concerning the ethnic makeup and political experience of the population made a long period of territorial tutelage seem desirable and likely, so far as Washington was concerned. No overwhelming flow of American settlers of investment entered the new possessions in the first quarter of the twentieth century. Consequently, little progress seems to have been made toward developing clear plans for their future.

World War I dramatized the rise of Japan as a world power and the potential conflict of Pacific interests between that nation and the United States. It did not, however, draw American thinking away from its Atlantic preoccupation. Dreams of a vast postwar growth in American trade and investment across the Pacific were realized only in very small part. By the time of the world depression of the 1930s, it was still difficult for Americans to conceive of the Pacific as a region that held a key to their future prosperity or security. Even missionary interest seemed to have slackened and lost influence.

It was a shock, then, to have the United States' involvement in World War II begin in the Pacific. The sudden, intense interest in the island campaigns which followed concentrated public attention on those areas where Americans were fighting. Only the most limited attention seems to have been given to the long-term American interests at stake or to the relationships of United States interests to those of Pacific allies and other peoples. Postwar planning for the Pacific was conceived in Washington very largely in military-strategic terms, centered about maintaining peace in the future, with Japan figuring as the principal threat. Some members of Congress and the armed forces wanted to maintain control over Pacific bases built by Americans during the war even if they were on islands owned or controlled by United States allies.

Creation of the Trust Territory of the Pacific Islands as a United States responsibility after the war was conceived mainly in military security terms. These former Japanese mandates in Micronesia had been used by that power as offensive and defensive wartime bases. Their inhabitants could not prevent a major power from so using them. The American aim then, sanctioned by the United Nations, was to prevent Micronesia from being used again to disturb the peace of the Pacific. Policies for the future of the peoples of the islands were not seen as a major problem at first. As in the past, policy-makers in Washington appear to have assumed that American rule would be welcomed and would benefit the peoples of the trust territory. The Department of the Navy studied the islands' histories, cultures, and eco-systems but adopted a policy of limited action in trying to change things.

Made sensitive to the tides of nationalist sentiment growing in the world's political dependencies, successive Washington administrations looked for ways to reconcile American politico-strategic responsibilities with Micronesian and Polynesian hopes. In 1951 the president turned the trust territory administration over to the Department of the Interior, ending the spectacle of military government. Similar action was taken in Guam and American Samoa. The Philippines had been on the path toward independence in the 1930s, and this process was completed in 1946, though United States influence, economic and political, continued to be strong there for some years. Hawai'i became a state in the American union in 1959, a step overwhelmingly approved by the voting population of the islands. In the 1970s, Guam and American Samoa won increasing powers of self-government including the right to elect their own governors. And the trust territory islands of the Northern Marianas opted for association with the United States as a commonwealth when the trusteeship should be ended.

In the 1960s and 1970s, the pace of life and of change in the Pacific was accelerated with the arrival of jet air travel, improved telecommunications, and a growing tourist traffic. American goods, machines, techniques, and ideas were among those from outside flooding in upon island peoples who had formerly been largely isolated from such things. North of the equator the influence of the American government and its programs was of great importance in the lives of the peoples of the Pacific. South

of the equatorial line Washington was content through the 1970s to leave development policies in the hands of the former colonial powers and subsequently in those of the new Pacific island-nations.

From an economic viewpoint the Pacific, aside from Asia, still plays a minor role for Americans in the 1980s, though new interest in the resource potential of the ocean and its floor is growing. Trade with Asia continues to be important though most of American imports and exports travel in foreign vessels as they have for the past century. After three wars in the Pacific Basin between 1941 and 1970, the influence of United States policies on that part of the world was clearly a strong one, for better or for worse. Yet from a global standpoint the region still occupies a secondary position in American thinking.

RELATED ENTRIES: Hawai'i; United States Exploring Expedition; War in the Pacific Islands 1914-1945.

SOURCES AND READINGS: C. Hartley Grattan, *The Southwest Pacific Since 1900* (Ann Arbor: University of Michigan Press, 1963); Donald D. Johnson, *The United States in the Pacific, Special Interests and Public Policies* (Honolulu: University Press of Hawaii, 1976); Donald F. McHenry, *Micronesia, Trust Betrayed: Altruism vs. Self-Interest in American Foreign Policy* (New York: Carnegie Endowment for International Peace, 1975); David Nevin, *The American Touch in Micronesia* (New York: W. W. Norton & Co., 1977); Robert Trumbull, *Tin Roofs and Palm Trees: A Report on the New South Seas* (Seattle: University of Washington Press, 1977).

Donald D. Johnson

UNIVERSITY OF GUAM. The major institution of higher education in the western Pacific, the University of Guam is an accredited five-year, land-grant institution consisting of five colleges, an off-campus program, and is the sponsoring agency for the Marine Laboratory and the Micronesian Area Research Center. Enrollment in 1980 was over 2,500.

The university began in 1952, when the island government established the Territorial College of Guam as a two-year, teacher-training school, within the Department of Education. The college, which shared facilities with a high school, had an initial enrollment of 190 students and a staff of thirteen.

In 1960 the college moved to its present 100-acre campus in Mangilao where a two-story classroom building and a library had been erected. In 1963 administrative control was transferred from the Department of Education to a five-member governing board of regents and the college was accredited by the Western Association of Schools and Colleges as a four-year, degree-granting institution.

The college was renamed the University of Guam in 1968. Enrollment was 1,800 with a staff of over 130. Additions to the physical plant have included a second classroom building, a new library, the Fine Arts Building, and the Science Building. A Student Center, three dormitory units, and the Health Science Building were completed in 1970.

Administrative autonomy was granted to the university in 1976 with its establishment as a nonmembership, nonprofit corporation under the governance, control, and operation of a board of regents.

RELATED ENTRIES: Education in the Pacific, Higher; Guam; Micronesian Area Research Center.

Albert L. Williams

UNIVERSITY OF THE SOUTH PACIFIC. A four-year, bachelor-degree-granting institution, the University of the South Pacific was established in 1968 at Laucala Bay about two miles northeast of Suva, Fiji. Its student body is made up of young men and women from Fiji, American Samoa, Western Samoa, the Solomon Islands, New Hebrides, Niue, Tokelau Islands, Tonga, and the United States Trust Territory of the Pacific Islands.

In 1965 a joint committee, the Higher Education Mission to the South Pacific, was established by the governments of the United Kingdom, New Zealand, and Australia to discuss higher education in the South Pacific. In 1966 Chairman Sir Charles Morris recommended the establishment of a fully autonomous University of the South Pacific to serve the English-speaking islands of the South Pacific. Sir Norman Alexander of England was appointed as academic planner and in his report in 1967 he made detailed proposals to bring the already existing institutions into association with the university: the Derrick Technical Institute, the Fiji School of Agriculture, the Fiji School of Medicine, and the South Pacific Regional College of Tropical Agriculture in Western Samoa. In May 1968 proposals for courses at the university were further developed at a program planning seminar. The seminar recommended that the university be divided into three schools: the school of natural resources, the school of social development, and the school of education.

In May 1968 Dr. Colin C. Aikman, professor of law from Wellington, was appointed vice-chancellor designate of the newly founded university. The university opened on 5 February 1968 with 160 students. Degree courses and courses for diplomas in education began in 1969 when the student enrollment rose to 249. On 5 March 1970, Queen Elizabeth formally visited the university and presented its Royal Charter to open the university. The charter defined the objectives of the university as: "the maintenance, advancement and dissemination of knowledge by teaching, consultancy and research and otherwise and the profusion at appropriate levels of education and training responsive to the well-being and needs of the communities of the South Pacific." King Taufa'ahau Tupou IV of Tonga became the first chancellor. The first graduation ceremonies were held on 2 December 1971 when seventeen students were awarded bachelors degrees, sixteen received diplomas in education, and sixteen received vocational teachers' certificates.

The university has gradually increased in enrollment from 525 full-time students in 1970 to over 1,600 full-time and 400 part-time students in 1979.

RELATED ENTRIES: Education in the Pacific, Higher.

Michael P. Singh

UNSHELM, AUGUST (?-1864). The first director of the Hamburg-based J. C. Godeffroy trading house in Samoa, Unshelm coordinated German commercial interests in the South Pacific. Unshelm visited Samoa several times in the 1850s, finally setting up trading operations at Apia in 1857. From Apia, Unshelm laid the groundwork for what would soon become a vast German commercial network throughout the Pacific. He established substations in Tonga and Fiji and encouraged the development of the copra and coconut oil trade. In 1861 Unshelm was appointed consul for Hamburg in Apia while retaining his original post as director of the Godeffroy firm. Lacking any naval support from Germany, Unshelm sought to remain aloof from the factional and sectarian strife in the islands. A minor run-in with the local police, however, threatened to develop into a major incident, for Unshelm tried to secure a French warship in his efforts to exact retribution from the Samoan chiefs. The impending showdown never took place though, for soon after in 1864, Unshelm was lost at sea while on a trading mission to the Fiji Islands. He was succeeded in his offices as consul and director of the Godeffroy company in Samoa by his assistant, Theodor Weber.

RELATED ENTRIES: German Colonial Empire; Weber, Theodor; Western Samoa.

SOURCES AND READINGS: R. P. Gilson, *Samoa 1830 to 1900* (Melbourne: Oxford University Press, 1970); Heinrich Schnee, ed., *Deutsches Kolonial-Lexikon*, vol. 3 (Leipzig: Quelle & Meyer, 1920); Robert M. Watson, *History of Samoa* (Wellington: Whitcombe and Tombs, 1918).   *Ralph C. Canevali*

URDANETA, ANDRÉS DE (1508-1568). A Spanish mathematician, cartographer, navigator, and Augustinian priest, Urdaneta was a native of the Basque province of Guipúzcoa. Urdaneta had accompanied the ill-fated Loaysa expedition to the Moluccas in 1525 and had remained in the Far East until 1536. He then returned to Spain, sailing around the Cape of Good Hope, and after arriving in his native land he prepared a detailed account of his travels. He also had the honor of being received in audience by the emperor Charles V in Valladolid. In October 1538 Urdaneta left for New Spain in the fleet of the governor of Guatemala. After his arrival in the New World in April 1539, Urdaneta served in various important administrative capacities under the viceroy, Antonio de Mendoza. In the spring of 1552 Urdaneta turned his attention to religious matters and entered upon a novitiate in the Augustinian order. In March 1553 he took his solemn vows in Mexico City. Because of his eminence as a cosmographer, Urdaneta had an unexpected opportunity for further travel when Philip II commanded him to serve as a guide for a new Spanish expedition to the Pacific. Miguel López de Legazpi, a native of Guipúzcoa and a long-time resident in New Spain, received the honor of being named commander of this enterprise.

Legazpi's expedition consisted of two three-masted galleons (*San Pedro*, *capitana*, of over 500 tons, and *San Pablo*, over 300), two pinnaces (*San Juan* and *San Lucas*), and a small frigate attached to the flagship. Esteban de Rodríguez served as chief pilot. This expedition left from the port of La Navidad on 21 November 1564. While at sea the smallest pinnace, *San Lucas*, under the command of Arellano, parted from Legazpi's fleet and after reaching the island of Mindanao returned from there to New Spain, arriving in August 1565. Meanwhile, the rest of Legazpi's fleet reached the Philippines in February 1565. In late April the Spaniards anchored off the island of Cebú. After overcoming the initial hostility of the islanders, Legazpi established a colony on Cebú which remained the principal base for Spanish operations in the area until 1571, the date of the founding of Manila. On 1 June 1565 Legazpi sent back to New Spain his flagship, the *San Pedro*, commanded by his young grandson, Felipe de Salcedo, with the veteran pilot Urdaneta on board. Urdaneta finally succeeded in returning to the western coast of North America despite the fact that contrary winds and currents had defeated the efforts of other pilots. Proceeding in a northerly direction to 39°50' north latitude, the vessel managed to catch the westerlies which brought her homeward. In September the first landfall was made off the California coast, near the present site of Santa Barbara; and on 8 October, the voyage terminated at Acapulco. Urdaneta had succeeded in discovering the route from the Far East to New Spain that approximated the passage used by the Manila galleons for many years. Urdaneta journeyed to Spain where he reported to Philip II the story of his voyage. Thereafter he returned to New Spain and died in Mexico City in June 1568 at the age of sixty.

RELATED ENTRIES: Spain in the Pacific.

SOURCES AND READINGS: Mariano Cuevas, *Monje y marion; la vida y los tiempos de Fray Andrés de Urdaneta* (Mexico City: Editorial Layace, 1943); Mairin Mitchell, *Friar Andrés de Urdaneta, O.S.A.* (London: MacDonald and Evans, 1964); Henry R. Wagner, "Urdaneta and the Return Route from the Philippine Islands," *Pacific Historical Review* 13, no. 3 (1944): 313-16.   *Bernerd C. Weber*

V

VAHEKEHU, ELISABETH (1823?-1901). A queen of Nuku Hiva (Marquesas), Elisabeth Vahekehu's husband, Te Moana, was the chief of the Bay of Taiohae where most of the European ships dropped anchor. When Dupetit-Thouars sailed to the Marquesas to take possession of them for France, he found Te Moana at war with the Taioa tribe who had captured his wife, Vahekehu. In return for recognizing him "king" over Nuku Hiva and helping in the return of his wife, Te Moana agreed to cede the island to the French. It was done, and Vahekehu returned to her husband. She and her husband were baptized by Catholic missionaries in 1853, she taking the name Elisabeth and he Charles. When her husband died in the great epidemic in 1863, she continued to support the French and Catholic influences in the islands. Caillot, a French writer who met her in 1900, described her great dignity and exemplary life, and wrote that her public and private life was irreproachable. She was a "mother" to all the missionaries and, according to Polynesian custom, she had "adopted" several prominent ones as her "children." After French annexation of the islands, she lived at Taiohae on a government pension in a small European-built house. She was extremely influential among the islanders and when she died in 1901, every valley mourned her passing. She was buried by her husband in a small mausoleum erected by Monsignor Dordillon not far from the Catholic mission. Caillot photographed the queen in 1900 and Pierre Loti made a drawing of her that appeared in his illustrated edition of his *Marriage of Loti*.

RELATED ENTRIES: Dupetit-Thouars, Abel; French Polynesia; Marquesas Islands; Te Moana, Charles.

SOURCES AND READINGS: Eugène Caillot, *Histoire de la Polynésie Orientale* (Paris: Ernest Leroux, 1910) and *Les Polynésiens orientaux*, plates 60 and 61 (Paris: Ernest Leroux, 1909).   *Robert D. Craig*

VAITUPU "COMPANY". An ill-fated commercial venture during the 1870s and 1880s, the so-called Company formed at Vaitupu Island was one of many attempts by Pacific islanders to participate in the commercial system imposed upon them by European interests. Its formation was instigated in 1877 by T. W. Williams, an agent of Hedemann, Ruge and Company of Apia, Samoa, as a means to monopolize the Ellice Islands (now called Tuvalu) copra trade. Williams, a most persuasive man and also fluent in the Samoan language, was the son of the British consul in Samoa and grandson of the famous pioneer missionary J. C. Williams. This family background gave Williams immediate standing with the Vaitupuans and was readily used to enhance his commercial ambitions.

The formation of the company involved three distinct stages. First, Williams prevailed upon a number of Vaitupuans to become "shareholders" in a locally based trading company organized along cooperative lines. Williams then appointed a local manager from among the one hundred shareholders and, as a symbolic gesture, provided the company with its own flag. He also provided his manager with trade goods to the value of $6,000 with which to purchase copra. At Vaitupu, at any rate, Williams achieved the monopoly he sought. Although opposed by the *ulu aliki* (head chief), the company had the support of the majority of other *aliki* as well as that of the resident Samoan pastor of the London Missionary Society who expelled from church membership all those who sold copra to anyone other than the company. Among those expelled was the *ulu aliki* himself.

The immediate upshot of the company's activities was to produce chronic factionalism and a power struggle on Vaitupu which assumed serious proportions. In effect, the company had become an alternative source of authority and prestige for men without traditional legitimacy to leadership.

With control over supply assured, Williams then sought to exercise control over freighting. He, therefore, prevailed upon the shareholders to purchase their own vessel and, in late 1879, the company was in possession of the 20.5 ton schooner *Vaitupulemele*. This prompted the shareholders to carry Williams' strategy one step further and develop a coconut plantation at Niulakita, the tiny, uninhabited, southernmost island in the Ellice group.

As early as 1881, however, the company was in financial difficulties; and two years later the situation was beyond reprieve. Not only had Williams grossly overestimated the copra-producing potential of the Ellice Islands but, worse still, he was unable to interest other islands besides Vaitupu in his schemings. Another reason for the company's collapse was the marked lack of corporate loyalty from almost everyone concerned, Williams included. At Vaitupu itself, the local manager had, in Williams' absence, bartered the trade goods for a fraction of their value in copra. Moreover, the company only realized about $3,300 from the sales of its copra, leaving a debt to Ruge in excess of $13,000. When pressed for settlement, Williams passed the debt onto the company and Ruge in turn threatened the Vaitupuans with the appropriation of their island in the event of nonpayment. They took the threat seriously and patched up their differences sufficiently to work as a community to settle the debt.

The people of Vaitupu retained their island but lost Niulakita which was sold to Ruge in part payment of the debt. They also lost the *Vaitupulemele* which went down in a hurricane in 1886. It took four years of constant copra cutting to pay off the debt, during which time community life suffered serious disruption. Mothers took their babies into the bush and hung them from trees in baskets while they worked. A delegation of Vaitupuans toured the other Ellice Islands asking for material help, but only Funafuti agreed to assist. Another delegation even travelled to Samoa to ask the German consul to waive the debt, but to no avail.

These and other hardships are still well remembered in Vaitupu, as the story of the island's *kaitalafu* (debt) has become an event of note in local historical recollection. But the involvement of the church has been completely forgotten and, surprisingly, Williams is not remembered at all. Instead, his actions have been attributed to Ruge, known locally as *Misi Luki*.

In November 1887, the debt to Martin Ruge was finally paid and on 25 November every year since a series of celebrations begins on Vaitupu known as *te aso fiafia* (the joyous day).

RELATED ENTRIES: German Colonial Empire; Ruge and Company, H. M.

SOURCES AND READINGS: A. D. Couper, "Protest Movements and Proto-Cooperatives in the Pacific Islands," *Journal of the Polynesian Society* 77 (1968):

263-74; R. G. Roberts, "Te Atu Tuvalu: A Short History of the Ellice Islands," *Journal of the Polynesian Society* 67 (1958): 394-423; G. M. White, *Kioa: An Ellice Community in Fiji* (Eugene, Ore.: University of Oregon Press, 1965).

Doug Munro

VANCOUVER, GEORGE (1757-1798). A British naval explorer and navigator, Vancouver was born 22 June 1757 at King's Lynn, Norfolk, and joined the Royal Navy at age thirteen. Seaman Vancouver accompanied Captain James Cook on his second voyage round the world aboard the *Resolution*, 1772-1775. He sailed as a midshipman with Captain Cook's third voyage to the Arctic aboard the *Discovery*, 1776-1780. For the next nine years, Vancouver served in the West Indies. In 1790 Vancouver was promoted to rank of commander and assigned to the *Discovery*. On 1 April 1791 the British Admiralty sent Vancouver with his two ships, the *Discovery* and the *Chatham*, on an expedition to reclaim British rights at Nootka Sound and to find a northwest passage. Vancouver sailed to the Cape of Good Hope, Australia, New Zealand, Chatham Island, Tahiti, the Hawaiian Islands and the northwest. In 1793 Vancouver surveyed the northwest coast of the Americas. He circumnavigated Vancouver Island, already discovered by the Spanish. For the next three years, Vancouver and his ships spent the winters in the Hawaiian Islands, where he befriended King Kamehameha I and discouraged the incessant tribal wars. In 1795 Vancouver returned to England. He is considered Britain's greatest contributor to mapping of the Pacific northwest. Vancouver died in Petersham, England, 10 May 1798. His three-volume narrative, *A Voyage of Discovery to the North Pacific Ocean and Round the World . . . 1790-95* was published in 1798.

RELATED ENTRIES: Hawai'i; Kamehameha I.

SOURCES AND READINGS: H. R. Friis, *The Pacific Basin* (New York: American Geographical Society, 1967); J. S. Marshall and C. Marshall, *Vancouver's Voyage* (Vancouver: Mitchell Press, 1955).

Joseph A. Montoya

VANUATU. Formerly called the New Hebrides, Vanuatu consists of about sixty islands running from Papua New Guinea to New Caledonia across 15° south latitude, forming an irregular Y-shape 900 km (560 mi) long. The total land area is 13,000 km² (5,019 mi²). Almost half of this consists of the two northern islands of Espíritu Santo (3,947 km², 1,524 mi²) and Malekuka (2,024 km², 1,257 mi²).

Ten other islands are over 280 km² (108 mi²) in area. The highest point, Mount Tabwemsana on

Espíritu Santo, is 1,877 m (6,158 ft) above sea level.

Land and Resources. Geologically, Vanuatu belongs to the late Tertiary period. It was produced by powerful volcanic movements alternating with periods of sedimentation. Indeed, the land is still rising. Minor earth tremors are frequent, and there are three active volcanos. One of them, Mount Yasur, on the southern island of Tanna, is a notable tourist attraction. Most of the islands are high and mountainous. Coastal plains are narrow and alluvial plains are rare. There are rivers on the larger islands, but streams are mostly small and some flow only after heavy rain. The climate is hot, humid, and wet, especially between November and April. Average annual temperatures are 26° C (79° F) on Espíritu Santo, 24° C (75° F) at the capital of Vila on the central island of Efate, and 23° C (73° F) on Tanna. Rainfall ranges from over 4,000 mm (157 in) in the north to less than 2,300 mm (90 in) in the south.

From a distance, the islands resemble green pyramids. Their natural vegetation is thick rain forest, with a fringe of coconuts on the coast. Everywhere the fauna is relatively poor. It consists most conspicuously of brightly colored pigeons and parrots, but there is also a wide variety of lizards, insects, and sea life. One species the inhabitants would gladly be without is the anopheles mosquito, which carries malaria. The disease is endemic.

The People. Most of the indigenous people are of Melanesian stock. Dark brown in color and of small to medium stature, they are basically subsistence agriculturalists. They live in small kin-based communities in which rank and power are typically earned by individual effort, rather than inherited. There is also a sprinkling of Polynesians. They tend to be taller and lighter skinned than the Melanesians and to be organized in societies based on chiefly authority. Nevertheless, both groups are closely related, even in their origins. They both belong to the large and varied class of people known as Austronesian who began the human settlement of Vanuatu about 4,000 years ago. Since the nineteenth century, other people have settled there. In 1979 the total population was 112,000. Of these, 93 percent were indigenous Melanesians, Europeans comprised 2.5 percent, other Pacific islanders were 2.5 percent, and Asians were 2 percent. While Vila has a population of 20,000, most of the people are distributed among 2,000 villages of about forty people each.

European Contact. European contact began in 1606 with the visit to Espíritu Santo of the Spanish explorer Quirós. Under the impression that he had found not an island but the long-sought Southern Continent, he called his discovery *Tierra Austrialia*

del Espíritu Santo and attempted to found a colony there. Sickness and disputes with the islanders led him to abandon the scheme after three weeks. More than 160 years passed before the next European visits. In 1768 Bougainville charted the northern islands, and in 1774 Captain Cook, who named the group the New Hebrides, explored those of the south. But it was another half century before Europeans, in the form of missionaries and traders, began to make an impact.

Modern History. From 1825 to 1865 Sydney-based merchants scoured the group for fragrant sandalwood and planted in the people a desire for European material goods. The most successful of the traders was Robert Towns, who invested his profits in northern Queensland and then, from the 1860s, brought New Hebrideans there to work his plantations. This example was followed by other planters. By 1906, when Australia ended recruitment, thirty-five thousand New Hebrideans had worked for a time in Queensland. From that experience, they acquired new ideas, skills, and needs. Yet, their sense of self-worth was unimpaired. A tradition of resistance to European domination, providing precedents for modern nationalism, may be traced back to, and beyond, the labor trade.

Also in the 1860s, other Australian planters took up land in New Hebrides itself to grow cotton. Their ventures were mostly unprofitable. In 1882, therefore, all but one of them sold their holdings to the *Compagnie Calédonienne des Nouvelles Hébrides* (CCNH), a firm founded by the New Caledonia-based businessman John Higginson. English-born, Higginson was a naturalized Frenchman who aimed to secure French control of the group by placing French settlers on CCNH land to establish coconut plantations. Although other Australians entered the group later, their share of its commerce remained inferior to that of the French.

Meanwhile, missionaries were also active. The Reverend John Williams of the London Missionary Society was killed on Eromanga in 1839 but others, more prudent, made a profound mark. Polynesian teachers of the society landed on Aneityum in 1841 and in 1848 were joined by the first Presbyterian missionaries, the Reverend and Mrs. John Geddie. Working northwards, the Presbyterians at length converted almost half the population. From 1849 they were assisted by the Anglicans (Melanesian mission). In 1905 the Church of Christ mission began and in 1912 that of the Seventh-Day Adventists. The combined following of these English-speaking Protestant missions eventually amounted to 65 percent of the population. In the 1970s this became a fact of notable political significance, for the Protestants solidly supported the nationalist party. Of the remaining 35 percent, 15 percent are Catholics, and the rest are divided between heathenism and various indigenous cults. French-speaking Catholic missionaries, Marists, arrived in 1887.

As happened in many places during the nineteenth century, the growth of European activities in the New Hebrides drew the attention of metropolitan governments to the group. The question arose, "Which European power would take over?" France had an economic interest there which she was unwilling to relinquish; England found it politically inexpedient to abandon the Protestant missionaries to French rule or to further expose her Australian colonies to "foreign" neighbors (France had taken New Caledonia in 1853 and Germany part of New Guinea in 1884). As a result of this impasse, England and France agreed in 1887 that their naval commanders should cooperate in the "maintenance of order" in the area. It was a clumsy arrangement. Besides, the settlers wished to obtain legally recognized titles to the land they occupied. Accordingly, in 1906, when the "English" (who were mainly Australians) numbered 228 and the French 401, the two governments agreed to set up a joint administration. In the resulting Anglo-French Condominium of the New Hebrides, each power established its own administrative services for its own nationals, plus a joint court to decide on land matters and on offenses "committed by natives against non-natives." A revised version of the agreement was introduced in 1922 and served as the constitution until independence in 1980.

Throughout the period of joint control, the primary concern of the French authorities was to advance French "national interests" in New Hebrides. When the CCNH became bankrupt in 1894, the government provided a subsidy and relaunched it as the *Société Française des Nouvelles-Hébrides*. French planters and traders were consistently allowed greater latitude in their dealings with the islanders than were the English. Above all, from 1920 they were allowed to import plantation laborers from Indochina. The English, in contrast, were not allowed Asian labor. Finding themselves, therefore, at a disadvantage most had sold out to French companies by 1930.

While Anglo-French rivalry was of special concern to Europeans with an interest in New Hebrides, it was, for most of the islanders, irrelevant. For many this was simply because their lives centered on their villages, but for others it was because they wished to promote New Hebridean interests against those of Europeans generally. Recorded expressions of this wish were uttered by ex-laborers on Tanna in 1905,

by leaders such as Thingaroo and Ronovoro on Espíritu Santo and Tinabua on Tongoa, and by supporters of the John Frum cargo cult movement which broke out on Tanna in 1941. Common to such displays of resistance as these, and there were others, was an awareness of a New Hebrides identity which took a definite, organized political form with the formation of the New Hebrides National Party in 1971. In 1974 its president, Walter Lini, an Anglican priest, announced the party's demand for independence in 1977. Popular support for this goal was shown in 1975 when in an election for the newly instituted representative assembly the National Party obtained 60 percent of the total votes and a majority of the seats.

Nevertheless, the assembly still found itself deprived of effective political power. It became even more impatient to end colonial rule. In 1977 it began referring to New Hebrides as Vanuaaku (which means "our land"), changed its own name to Vanua-aku Pati, and set up a People's Provisional Government in opposition to the established one. Although a partial reconciliation was achieved in 1978, such firmness ensured that the transfer of power would not be delayed for much longer. The New Hebrideans became independent in May 1980 with Lini as prime minister, and officially changed the name of their state to Vanuatu ("the land remains").

The resources of the new nation are sufficient to guarantee its population a comfortable subsistence, as they have always done. But for further economic development and improved social services, Vanuatu is dependent on foreign aid and investment. Copra remains the mainstay of the cash economy, although other products are also exported: coffee, cocoa, timber, beef, and fish. Manganese has been mined in the past. Other income derives from tourism and, since 1971, from Vanuatu's role as a tax haven for overseas companies.

Among the problems facing the new government is that of providing an efficient transport and communication system to link the scattered islands. Related to that is the problem of creating a national education system in the face of extreme linguistic diversity. There are 110 indigenous languages in the group and two official ones, English and French, though *Bislama*, a form of pidgin English, is the *lingua franca*. In 1979 the school population was evenly divided between English and French schools, making it very difficult for the new government, which desires to rationalize expenditure and promote unity, to dismantle one system in favor of the other. Indeed, it may be advantageous not to, since each language offers access to a major cultural tradition. Besides,

Vanuatu has already benefitted in certain ways from the Anglo-French duality. By the 1970s, as a result of their experience under the condominium, its people had become some of the most politically aware and broadly educated of all Pacific islanders.

RELATED ENTRIES: Anglican Missions; Bougainville, Louis; Cargo Cult, John Frum; Codrington, Robert; Cook, (Captain) James; Defense Planning for Oceania between the Wars; Diaper, William; Dillon, Peter; Hamilton, William; Higginson, John; *Hopeful* Scandal; Koukare; Labor Trade; London Missionary Society; Melanesian Recruitment to Queensland, Patterns of; Melanesians and Colonial Servitude; Nambas; Patteson, John C.; Port Resolution; Sandalwood Trade; Selwyn, George; South Pacific Commission; Tanna; Western Pacific High Commission; Williams, John; Yasur Volcano.

SOURCES AND READINGS: Bernard Hermann and Joel Bonnemaison, *New Hebrides* (Pape'ete: Les Editions du Pacifique, 1975); W. P. Morrell, *Britain in the Pacific Islands* (Oxford University Press, 1960); Chris Plant, ed., *New Hebrides: The Road to Independence* (Suva: Institute of Pacific Studies, 1977); Deryck Scarr, *Fragments of Empire* (Canberra: Australian National University Press, 1967); *Vanuatu* (Suva: Institute of Pacific Studies, 1980).

Hugh Laracy

VASON, GEORGE (1772-1838). Vason, a bricklayer, was one of the artisan-missionaries sent from London by the London Missionary Society in 1796 on the *Duff*. The missionaries in Tonga dispersed in order to evangelize more widely, and Vason went to live with Mulikiha'amea who held the high office of *Tui Ha'atakalaua*. Vason soon abandoned his vocation in favor of the status, privileges, and way of life of a Tongan nobleman. He became involved in the civil war of 1799 in which Mulikiha'amea was killed. In the unsettled conditions which followed, Vason found himself owing loyalty to two patrons at enmity with each other. He narrowly escaped a violent death by boarding the missionary vessel *Royal Admiral* as it was leaving the harbor of Neiafu, Vava'u in 1801. He returned to England and to the church and eventually became governor of Nottingham Gaol. He died in 1838.

RELATED ENTRIES: Beachcombers; London Missionary Society; Mariner, William; Tonga.

SOURCES AND READINGS: James Orange, ed., *Life of the Late George Vason of Nottingham* (London: John Snow, 1840).   *Ian C. Campbell*

VERNIER, FRÉDÉRIC (1841-1915). The recognized head of the French Protestant church in Tahiti for forty years (1867-1907), Vernier was born 2 February 1841 and arrived in Tahiti from France in 1867. He thoroughly mastered the Tahitian language and became counselor and personal minister to Queen Pomare IV. Vernier did more than anyone else to bring about the reconciliation of the English and French Protestant churches in Tahiti after the assumption of French control (1842). Gradually the English Protestant ministers left, leaving fellow French ministers to replace them. Vernier reorganized the churches, instituted the study of Tahitian in his schools, and visited the outlying parishes of the church where he always found a cordial welcome. During the War of Teraupo'o (1880-1897) between the French and Ra'iateans, Vernier acted as arbitrator in reconciling and pacifying the recalcitrant islanders. After forty years in the Tahitian ministry, he returned to France in 1907 where he died in 1915.

RELATED ENTRIES: French Polynesia; Teraupo'o, War of.

SOURCES AND READINGS: *Journal des Missions Evangeliques* (Société des Missions Evangeliques de Paris), 1er Sem. (1915): 112-18; Charles Vernier, *Tahitiens d'autrefois: Tahitiens d'aujourd'hui*, 2d ed. (Paris: Société des Missions Evangeliques de Paris, 1948).

Robert D. Craig

VILLALOBOS, RUY LÓPEZ DE (d. 1546). A Spanish explorer and navigator, Villalobos was born in Málaga, Spain. A member of a distinguished family of that city, he was also related to Antonio de Mendoza, first viceroy of the Crown in New Spain. In November 1542 Villalobos left from the west Mexican port of La Navidad in command of an expedition consisting of six vessels carrying some 370 men. Proceeding in a leisurely manner across the Pacific, Villalobos discovered a number of islands missed in the earlier voyages of Magellan and Loaysa. By the beginning of February 1543 Villalobos had reached the relatively large island now known as Mindanao and gave to it the name of *Cesárea Caroli* in honor of the Emperor Charles V. To the entire archipelago, of which Mindanao is but a part, Villalobos later applied the designation of *Las Islas Filipinas* (the Philippines) in honor of the *infante* who later became Philip II. The Portuguese disputed the presence of the Spaniards in this area, and Villalobos sailed on to the Moluccas where further clashes with the Portuguese occurred.

Villalobos had instructions to send a ship for the discovery of the *vuelta* (return route) after establishing himself on the Asiatic side of the Pacific. Accordingly, in August 1543 and again in May 1545, the *San Juan de Letrán* attempted to make a return voyage to the North American coast, but in each instance the effort did not succeed. Disheartened by the failure of these endeavors, Villalobos fell ill and died in 1546 on the island of Amboina, attended at the end by the famous Jesuit missionary later canonized as Saint Francis Xavier. Survivors of the Villalobos expedi-

tion, assisted by the Portuguese, eventually managed to make their way to Lisbon. Among the survivors was Garciá de Escalante de Alvarado who subsequently wrote for the emperor an important account of the expedition.

RELATED ENTRIES: Spain in the Pacific.

SOURCES AND READINGS: Nicholas P. Cushner, *The Isles of the West: Early Spanish Voyages to the Philippines, 1521-1564* (Quezon City: Manila University Press, 1966).   *Bernerd C. Weber*

WALLIS AND FUTUNA. Two groups of islands lying west of Samoa and approximately 230 km (144 mi) northeast of Fiji, Wallis and Futuna are Overseas Territories of France. The two island groups are ruled by indigenous kings under the French high commissioner in New Caledonia. The population (1978 estimate) consists of 9,700 of which 98 percent are Polynesians. Wallis Island has a land area of 256 km² (99 mi²), while Futuna and its islet neighbor Alofi have a total land area of 425 km² (164 mi²). The capital of the Overseas Territory is Mata Utu on Wallis Island. Most of the islanders live on subsistence agriculture and on the funds that relatives in New Caledonia send to them. The entire population is Roman Catholic and all are French citizens.

History of Wallis. The Wallisians are descendants of the first settlers who came from Tonga about 1450-1550 A.D. and who brought their Polynesian culture with them. Rivalry between the various chiefs on the island was continuous. Captain Samuel Wallis was the first European to visit the island in 1767. Several beachcombers settled on the island, but little outside contact was made until the 1820s. On 1 November 1837 Marist priests on their way from Tahiti to Sydney landed on the island. Through the influence of chief Tungahala, the French bishop, Pompallier, persuaded the king to allow Father Pierre Bataillon to remain. Within a few years, Father Bataillon converted the king and all his subjects. In 1842 the king petitioned France for protection. Captain Stanislas Mallet sailed to Wallis and on 4 November 1842 signed an agreement with King Lavelua and chiefs Malahama and Maulisio for a French protectorate. Because of international rivalry with Great Britain, the French government in Paris did not ratify the treaty until 1887. In 1900 Wallis and Futuna were given an autonomous budget separate from the other French oceanic possessions. In 1913 Wallis was declared an overseas colony of France. During World War II, the Americans established a military base there and built an airstrip which is still in use. A referendum was held on 22 December 1959 and the population overwhelmingly voted to become overseas

territories, an act confirmed in the French parliament on 29 July 1961. Today, the islanders are French citizens and are represented in the French National Assembly but hold no seat on the French Economical and Social Council. France continues to rule with the cooperation and endorsement of the traditional kings of the island.

History of Futuna and Alofi. The two islands of Futuna and Alofi were settled from Samoa. The first Europeans to visit the islands were the Dutch navigators Schouten and LeMaire who stayed for several weeks (1616). The Dutch named them the Hoorn Islands after the old port of Hoorn on the Zuider Zee from whence they had sailed. Bishop Pompallier arrived on Futuna Island on 8 November 1837 and was granted permission by King Nuiriki to land missionaries. Father Pierre Chanel, one of the Marists who remained, was murdered by the islanders in 1841. Hearing the news in New Zealand, Pompallier returned to Futuna to investigate the matter. He arrived in May of 1842 and landed two additional priests. In November of that year, Captain Mallet sailed to Futuna and Wallis where he signed a protectorate treaty with the kings of both Wallis and Futuna. Since then, the two groups of islands have had pretty much the same history. Father Pierre Chanel was later canonized and in 1976 his remains were flown from France to Futuna where they are enshrined today.

RELATED ENTRIES: Chanel, Pierre; France in the Pacific; French Polynesia; Pompallier, Jean-Baptist.

SOURCES AND READINGS: Philippe Godard, *Wallis & Futuna* (Nouméa: Editions Melanesia, 1978); Léonce Jore, *L'Océan Pacifique* (Paris: Editions Besson et Chantemerle, 1959); *Journal de la Société des Océanistes* 19 (1963), entire volume; Alexandre Poncet, *Histoire de l'Ile Wallis*, 2 vols. (Paris: Musée de l'Homme, 1972).   *Robert D. Craig*

WAR IN THE PACIFIC ISLANDS 1914-1945. Within four days of the outbreak of war in 1914, the British government was urging the Australian government to take speedy action against the German colonies of New Guinea and the Bismarck Archipelago. Accordingly, a small naval and military expeditionary force was organized under Admiral Sir George Patey, commander in chief of the Royal Australian Navy, who was also responsible for all escort duties and for operations against the German Pacific fleet. He escorted the New Zealand force which occupied Samoa on 30 August, and then the Australian force which landed at Rabaul on 11 September 1914. After little resistance, terms for the capitulation of German New Guinea were agreed on 17 September. It was thought that this surrender covered the whole of the German Pacific territories, which besides the Bismarck Archipelago included the Pelew (Palau), Caroline, Mariana, and Marshall islands. However, on 23 August Japan, in keeping with her existing alliance with Britain, had declared war on Germany. She was most cooperative with Paley in escort and anti-raider duties and in attacks on German wireless stations. Japan occupied Yap, Anguar, and other islands north of the equator. In November 1914, Australia was arranging to relieve the Japanese on these islands, but after some diplomatic exchanges the British government intervened to stop the occupation of any islands north of the equator.

The Royal Australian Navy was fully occupied in escorting the Australian Imperial Force which sailed for Europe on 1 November and in dealing with Admiral Maximilian Count von Spee's German squadron in the Pacific. This included two cruisers, *Scharnhorst* and *Gneisnau*, both outgunning all Australian ships except the battle cruiser *Australia*. On 22 August 1914 von Spee dispatched the *Embden* for a memorable raiding cruise which took her first into the Indian Ocean and then back into the Pacific. She was sunk on 9 November 1914 in an action off the Cocos Islands; but by this time she had sunk fifteen ships including a Russian cruiser and a French destroyer. Von Spee with the rest of his squadron sailed east passing through the Marshall Islands to Christmas Island which he reached on 6 September 1914. The *Nurnberg* cut the British cables at Fanning Island and the squadron sailed for Samoa where they found New Zealand troops had already landed. Von Spee was then reinforced from the Atlantic and met and defeated a British force off Chile in the battle of Coronel. He then left the Pacific around Cape Horn, after which all his ships except *Dresden* were destroyed in the battle of the Falkland Islands.

At the Treaty of Versailles in 1919, the settlement gave mandates in the Pacific in accordance with the occupation that had taken place during the war; that is to say, Japan had the mandate for all the German islands north of the equator while New Zealand had the mandate for Samoa; and Australia, on behalf of the United Kingdom, controlled the whole of New Guinea except Dutch New Guinea and all the German islands south of the equator.

The Treaty of Versailles did not create the stability conducive to disarmament but left open the danger of a naval armaments race in the Pacific. Britain naturally desired to continue her traditional policy of single-power naval superiority but, in the light of the United States policy openly expressed since 1916 to build a navy second to none, it soon became obvious Britain could not compete. The position was complicated by the Anglo-Japanese alliance which would come up for renewal in 1921. Australia and New Zealand as well as the United States were against renewal, and the United States did bring political pressure on Britain. The attempt to avoid an arms race and a rebuff to Japan led to the Washington Conference of 1921 in which an agreed ratio of five capital ships each to Britain and the United States and three to Japan was agreed. Fleet carriers were capital ships, and none was to exceed 27,000 tons or carry more than eight-inch guns. The treaty gave Japan a potential supremacy in the Pacific, and it left the United States with Japan astride her communications lines with the Philippines and no naval base west of Hawai'i.

After the fall of France in 1940, Japan made a tripartite pact with Germany and Italy since it was obvious to her that war with the United States must come. Her attitude to the United States was fundamentally defensive, but she saw that her safety lay in an early offensive which would enable her to secure an outer chain of island defenses in the Pacific. From this concept came the plan to take the initiative by destroying the United States fleet in Pearl Harbor.

War in the great expanses of the Pacific with its scattered island groups was to be a new type of warfare, and it was in the interwar years that the seeds of the new technique were sown. The British had invented the aircraft carrier in World War I, and they had passed on their knowledge and given training facilities to their ally, Japan. But after the war they neglected their own naval aviation. The formation of the Royal Air Force (RAF) in 1918 put the responsibility for aircraft development and pilots onto that service. Hugh Trenchard, marshal of the Royal Air Force, put all his energies into creating a land-based force of bombers which, in his eyes, had become the war-winning factor. The Fleet Air Arm became the neglected child of the RAF, and in the Royal Navy few who were to be the senior officers of the future learned to fly or showed much interest in aviation.

The Japanese worked on what they had learned from the British and built four fleet carriers and a number of light carriers. At first the fleet continued to be organized around the battleship, and carriers were considered principally for reconnaissance and occasional raids. It was not until 1940-1941 that they developed the idea of a carrier strike force integrated with the combined fleet and island-based aircraft.

The United States looked to the western Pacific and saw that they must depend upon a fleet of carriers. Franklin D. Roosevelt had been interested in naval aviation since 1904 when, as assistant secretary of the navy, he had seen the Wright brothers fly over the fleet. Through the influence of Roosevelt and James V. Forrestal, who had been a naval aviator during World War I, the Naval Bureau of Aeronautics had direct access to the secretary of the navy, despite Admiral Ernest J. King's efforts to ensure it worked through him. But throughout the navy there was an understanding that the carrier fleet was an essential, perhaps a paramount, weapon. In 1926 a law was introduced that only an aviator could command a carrier or a naval air station. The time might come when only an aviator would be allowed to command or control a carrier task force. Officers of riper years learned to fly—for example, King at the age of forty-eight in 1927 and Admiral William F. Halsey at the age of fifty-two in 1934. King, who was chief of naval operations and commander in chief of the U.S. fleet from soon after Pearl Harbor to the end of the war, had much experience in command of carriers between the wars, but he retained a very balanced view and was impatient with crusading young aviators. Curiously enough, neither Chester W. Nimitz, commander in chief of the Pacific forces, nor Spruance who commanded the central Pacific force in most of the naval air battles were aviators. Nimitz even disliked flying as a passenger.

By the time Japan chose to strike in the Pacific in 1941, she had six heavy and four light carriers; the United States had seven fleet carriers, but only three of them were in the Pacific. Japan had control of much of the seaboard of China and had occupied French Indochina. Britain and Russia were too much concerned with the war already going on with Germany to spare forces for a conflict with Japan which they still hoped would never come. The Japanese striking force, including six carriers, 360 aircraft, and two battleships set out on 6 December 1941 and on 7 December struck a crippling blow at the U.S. naval base at Pearl Harbor. Of the eight U.S. battleships, five were sunk, one severely damaged, and the other two hit. Eighty aircraft were destroyed and 140 damaged, but happily the three carriers were at sea and

no damage was inflicted on shore installations or oil storage tanks. The Japanese then went on to sink the only two British battleships in the Far East and to gain the footing in Malaya which was to lead to their capture of Singapore. From these beginnings, Japan proceeded with the further establishment of their Greater East Asian Co-Prosperity Sphere running from the Kuriles through Manchuria, China, Malaya, North Burma, the Philippines, and the Netherlands East Indies, which they hoped would put them in a position to negotiate peace. To protect this area from the east required the establishment of an outer perimeter which from the Kuriles stretched through Wake Island, the Marianas, and the Gilbert Islands to Rabaul and the Bismarck Archipelago.

General Douglas MacArthur was in command in the Philippines where the Japanese landed on 20 December 1941. On 29 December, Winston S. Churchill at the instigation of Roosevelt agreed to the setting up of an American-British-Dutch command (ABDA) under General A. P. Wavell covering what was left of Malaya, Singapore, Java, Sumatra, and the Philippines. But it was too late and before an appreciable force had been gathered Singapore had fallen, and the greater part of Java and other Dutch islands had been overrun.

On entering the war, the Americans had confirmed their earlier understanding with Britain that Germany must be defeated first and the war against Japan conducted as vigorously as possible with what forces could be spared. Admiral Ernest J. King, the naval member of the Joint Chiefs of Staff, made sure that every possible resource he could get was developed and used for the Pacific, the sphere he saw as vital to the United States.

The obvious threat to Australia led to some acrimonious exchanges between its prime minister, John Curtin, and Churchill. Australia had loyally sent all her experienced troops overseas: three divisions were in the Middle East and one in Malaya. Curtin wanted all the divisions back from the Middle East, but he reluctantly agreed to leave one. The other two were at first intended for Java and Sumatra under ABDA, but then Churchill and Wavell wanted them diverted to Burma. This Curtin resolutely refused. With the collapse of ABDA, the two divisions went to Australia and MacArthur was ordered from the Philippines, already almost overrun, to Australia to set up a new command, the Southwest Pacific Area. The Japanese had to fight hard for the Philippines, but most of the other islands were either undefended or held by small militia garrisons so the Japanese gained their outer perimeter without undue difficulty. MacArthur arrived in Australia on 17

March 1942. By agreement of the Anglo-American Combined Chiefs of Staff (CCS), all operations in the Pacific and Australasia came under the direction of the American Joint Chiefs of Staff (JCS). The first directive to the two commanders in chief, Nimitz and MacArthur, was to protect the lines of communications to Australia, to contain the Japanese, to support the defense of North America, and to prepare for a major amphibious offensive.

The first check to Japan came in the naval battle of the Coral Sea in May 1942. The Americans got slightly the better of this, the first naval air battle in history. Both the Japanese heavy carriers were put out of action by damage and aircraft losses and their light carrier was sunk, while both the American fleet carriers were damaged and one had to be scuttled. The Japanese got a footing on Guadalcanal and Tulagi, but their expedition to Port Moresby had to turn back. The next carrier battle, Midway, on 3 June 1942, may be regarded as the turning point in the Pacific war. Admiral Isoroku Yamamoto had been unsuccessful in his advocacy of a more offensive strategy, but after the American raid on Tokyo he was allowed to seek out the American fleet to try to complete the destruction begun at Pearl Harbor. The Japanese met an inferior fleet, but they were surprised while refuelling and lost their four carriers and most of their experienced pilots. One American fleet carrier was damaged and was later sunk by a submarine.

The Americans then began a two-pronged advance. Nimitz, entrusting the task first to Admiral Robert L. Ghormley, then to William F. Halsey, was to capture Guadalcanal and Tulagi, and MacArthur was to advance along the north coast of New Guinea to Rabaul which the Japanese had organized as their principal base in the southwest Pacific. MacArthur wanted the carrier fleet to protect his northern flank, but King and Nimitz were horrified at the idea of using the carriers, which had so hardly won the defensive battle of the Pacific, within range of shore-based aircraft, and would not trust them to commanders not expert in their use. MacArthur had to be content with the U.S. Army and Royal Australian Air Forces under General George C. Kenney, the Seventh Fleet built up around two Australian and one American cruisers, and a few old destroyers, eventually commanded by Admiral Thomas Kincaid. But MacArthur got on well with the robust Halsey who was operating independently on his flank.

On 7 August 1942, units of the First and Fifth U.S. Marine Divisions landed on Guadalcanal without difficulty, but the Japanese reacted quickly with a convoy of reinforcements from Rabaul. The battle for Guadalcanal then became one of the grimmest in the war. Both sides used their navy and air force to destroy the enemy convoys and to protect their own, and there were three major naval actions. The culminating point was the naval battle of Guadalcanal, 13 to 15 November 1942, when the Japanese tried to land 12,000 reinforcements and succeeded in getting ashore only 4,000, and these without stores or ammunition. After this the Americans had virtual possession, but the Japanese hung on to part of the island until mid-January 1943. Their total casualties were more than 24,000, while the Americans had 1,600 killed and 4,250 wounded. The naval losses were so heavy that neither side was able to offer battle for a whole year. The Americans had only one carrier left in action in the Pacific, and the thrusting Halsey realized that it was folly to use fast carriers in such confined waters. In the continuous naval battles, the Americans had lost two fleet carriers, six medium and two light cruisers, and fourteen destroyers while the Japanese had lost two battleships, one light carrier, three heavy and one light cruisers, eleven destroyers, and two submarines.

The protracted battle for Guadalcanal thwarted MacArthur's ambitious offensive plans, and the Japanese took the initiative in New Guinea where they were strongly established along the north coast and from where they threatened Papua. Port Moresby had already been saved from a sea landing, but now there was an overland danger. The Japanese from Rabaul had landed around Buna and Gona on 21 August 1942, and the next day the advance on Port Moresby began. The Australians had only a few militia detachments in Papua and an inexperienced brigade each at Port Moresby and at Milne Bay where a fighter airstrip was being built. MacArthur reacted quickly to the threat, and the experienced Seventh Australian Division, home from the Middle East, was ordered to Port Moresby with one of its brigade groups to Milne Bay. This last arrived before the Japanese landing there. After a stiff fight, the Japanese called off their venture, the first time in the campaign that one of their assault landings had been frustrated.

The chief characteristic of the fight for Port Moresby was the extreme difficulty of the terrain. The only route from Buna to Port Moresby (the Kokoda Trail) crossed the main Owen Stanley Range, rising to 6,500 feet in a series of razorbacked ridges often 4,500 feet at a time. The track was normally considered passable only by islanders and experienced Europeans unencumbered by any load whatever. Across this malarial and leech-infested land, the Japanese were opposed by the inexperienced brigade, few men over eighteen, which fought bravely. But by 16 September the Japanese were within thirty miles of Port Moresby with the Australians firmly established on Imita Ridge. But the Japanese had shot their bolt; the hardships were too much even for their frugal soldiers. They were literally starving and incapable of attacking, but they handled their fighting retreat to Buna with skill. The Japanese back in Buna hoped to renew the attack when they had secured Guadalcanal, but MacArthur deployed all his forces to destroy their beachhead.

These operations show the problem of a large headquarters understanding the difficulties of small forces fighting far away. MacArthur, in Brisbane, had no idea of the conditions in Papua. He thought the reports he received were just an excuse to avoid bold action, and he longed for the time when he had American troops under his command. When they arrived they fought just as bravely, but their progress was just as slow. He did not visit Papua until mid-October, a month after the crisis was over. He did send General Sir Thomas Blamey, who was his land forces commander and also Australian commander in chief, on 17 September to take personal command at Port Moresby. Blamey took a strong line with the commanders following up the Japanese, but his stream of corrosive messages showed little understanding of the situation in the mountains, and some officers who had done sterling work were relieved of their commands.

By the time the battle of Guadalcanal was won, the Allies were approaching the beachhead covering Gona, Sanananda, and Buna. The arrival of two U.S. divisions did not give the acceleration which MacArthur had hoped, but by 2 January 1943 only a handful of Japanese was left holding out in Sanananda and two days later the Japanese imperial headquarters decided to abandon all efforts to hold Guadalcanal and Papua. Japanese records show that of the 20,000 men they landed in Papua some 13,000 died. The campaign cost the Australians 5,698 battle casualties and the Americans 2,848, but this was nothing to the toll of sickness. The Australians had 9,249 cases of malaria and 3,643 of dysentery while out of 14,648 Americans in the battle area there were 8,659 casualties from sickness. The losses and the time spent on reduction of the beachhead after action by land, sea, and air had already made the Japanese garrison impotent and had thrown doubt on the wisdom of having pressed action to the end. Halsey, in control of operations in the Solomons, had initiated the policy of bypassing strong centers of resistance where they could be neutralized. Such a policy had

the advantage that the enemy never knew where the next blow would fall.

During 1943 Roosevelt and Churchill, with their chiefs of staff, held four major conferences. The first, in January, confirmed the decision to defeat Germany first but agreed that the greatest possible pressure should be exerted on Japan so as to maintain the initiative and to be ready for a full-scale offensive when the time came. As always, command problems were uppermost in King's mind, and he was averse to MacArthur having control of naval forces. In the advance towards Rabaul, Halsey was to give the greatest possible support to MacArthur, but he was to remain independent and later revert to Nimitz. At the next conference, TRIDENT, which opened at Washington on 12 May, and again at QUADRANT in Quebec in August 1943, it was confirmed that there should be two lines of advance in the Pacific. The central Pacific under Nimitz looked successively on the Gilberts, Truk, Palau, and the Marianas while MacArthur continued his step-by-step advance along the north coast of New Guinea. The advances were to be mutually supporting and planned so that the Japanese did not know where the next blow would fall. Nimitz was to have priority.

Nimitz' task was facilitated by Japanese reactions to MacArthur's advance. In March, and again in August, all the aircraft from the carriers in the combined fleet were sent to reinforce the air forces at Rabaul. As a result, the squadrons had to be sent back to Japan to refit, and the combined fleet was in no shape to strike the blow against the American fleet which was Japan's one hope. The priority given to Nimitz and the failure to lay down objectives beyond New Guinea disappointed MacArthur, but he received reassurance from the JCS that he should continue to plan for the Philippines.

With Papua secure, his air forces under Kenney most active, and with Halsey in strong support, MacArthur was able to secure local sea and air superiority by late 1943, and he could keep the enemy guessing as to his next objectives. The two main Japanese strongholds were Rabaul and Wewak on the north coast of New Guinea. They were the next objectives, though as policy developed both were bypassed and neutralized. In succession, landings were made on the Treasury Islands and on Bougainville, and by the end of the year MacArthur had gained a footing on the west end of New Britain and had captured Salamaua. He then landed at Saidor to cut off the retreat from Finschafen. He captured Manus in the Admiralty Islands in February 1944 and then, hopping along the coast, he was at Hollandia on 11

May, at the northwest tip of New Guinea by 30 July, and on Morati on 15 September preparing to strike at the Philippines. The large garrisons on part of Bougainville, at Rabaul, and at Wewak were now useless and only required containing by a few divisions which MacArthur could easily spare.

At the same time, Nimitz had advanced through the central Pacific and made landings in the Gilbert Islands in November 1943 and the Marshalls in February 1944. Here the capture of the formidable air base at Kwajalein showed the disadvantage of those islands which the Japanese regarded as their unsinkable carriers, while the use of the capacious harbor at Majura enabled Nimitz to move his base 2,000 miles farther west from Pearl Harbor.

At this stage, Nimitz and representatives from MacArthur went to Washington to discuss future strategy with Roosevelt and the JCS. With his base in the Marshalls and with MacArthur at Manus, Nimitz was in favor of a single strike at Formosa, bypassing the Philippines. As might be expected, MacArthur was indignant at any thought of bypassing the Philippines, the liberation of which he regarded as a point of honor for himself and for the American people. It was, therefore, decided to continue the two-pronged attack. The decision meant that Nimitz' next objective was the Marianas. Truk, the Gibraltar of the Pacific, could be neutralized from the Marshalls and heavy and successful air attacks were delivered on 17 February, while at the same time Eniwetok islets were captured. At Truk this attack destroyed more than 210 aircraft and 200,000 tons of shipping at the cost of one carrier damaged and seventeen aircraft shot down.

The Marianas were the very center of Japan's network of airfields on which their outer defenses depended. Nimitz knew, and was happy to know, that the assault on them would bring out the combined fleet. Admiral Soemu Toyoda was now in command, Admiral Mineichi Koga like Yamamoto before him having been killed in an air crash in March when the Americans bombed Palau. The attack on the Marianas began with a predawn strike on 12 June 1944, and for the main landing on Saipan two marine and one army division were used. The combined fleet had time to concentrate because Toyoda had expected an attack on the Carolines. He had to intervene, and he attacked on 19 June. He had only nine carriers against the American fifteen, and his inexperienced pilots were no match for the Americans. The Japanese lost over 300 aircraft out of the 375 engaged while the Americans lost only eighteen fighters and twelve bombers. Nevertheless, this Battle of the Philippine Sea was disappointing for the Americans. Spruance, who had done so well at Midway, was cautious and gave priority to the protection of the invasion fleet so that little time before dark was left to find and destroy the enemy. Only three of their carriers were sunk, one from the air and two by submarine, so the combined fleet, though much weakened, remained in being.

There was then some havering by the JCS whether to go direct to Formosa or first to Luzon, and it was not until October 1944 that the final strategy was decided. MacArthur was to capture Leyte and then Luzon; Nimitz was to cover these operations and was then to capture one island in the Bonins and one in the Ryukus. The Japanese were now dependent on their inner line of defenses, and the loss of Luzon would cut them off from Singapore and their oil sources. Toyoda planned to protect his fleet by land-based air forces so that he could use it to destroy any invasion fleet used against the Philippines. In order to cover MacArthur's operations, Nimitz allotted his Seventh Fleet eighteen escort carriers, but he was unwilling to allow a soldier to control any of his fast carriers. All sixteen of these were in a task force in Halsey's Third Fleet in support of MacArthur but under Nimitz' direction. Halsey, who had missed the battles of the Coral Sea, Midway, and the Philippine Sea, was determined that whatever happened he would destroy the Japanese fleet.

The Japanese plans were upset first by the speed of MacArthur's attack on Leyte, and then by their dispersal of their air resources. Their land-based air force, reinforced by aircraft taken from the carriers, was used to try to destroy Halsey's carriers which on 12 October 1944 began a three-day strike against Formosa. In the fierce air battle, the Japanese only managed to damage two cruisers, and they lost 500 aircraft and most of their carrier pilots. However, over-optimistic reports of a naval victory reached imperial headquarters, and it was decided to concentrate on the defense of Leyte instead of holding their reserves for the defense of Luzon. Thus, both the army and the air forces necessary for the vital defense of Luzon were prematurely committed.

Toyoda decided on a last gamble. His carriers, now useless because they had no aircraft, would decoy Halsey away from Leyte so that his battle fleet could slip in to destroy the invasion fleet. Halsey was deceived and left the Leyte Gulf battle prematurely with all his carriers and fast battleships to engage the decoy. The Japanese battle fleet was held off by Vice Admiral Thomas Kincaid's Seventh Fleet and did not act with the suicidal determination that was its only hope of thwarting the invasion. About half the Japanese ships escaped before Halsey returned, but their total losses were all four carriers, three battleships, nine cruisers, and eight destroyers. The combined fleet did not fight again. The American losses were one carrier, four escort carriers, and thirteen destroyers.

While MacArthur was conquering the Philippines, the First Australian Corps landed in Borneo. There was some acrimonious argument between MacArthur and Blamey, who objected to Australian forces being used as a task force directly under American command. The British Chiefs of Staff thought Borneo an unnecessary diversion and wanted their fleet employed in the main effort. This led to some differences between King, who was reluctant to allow the Royal Navy to participate in American operations, and Nimitz, who wanted the British fleet involved. In the end, the Australians in their assault on Borneo were supported by American amphibious forces, and the British Pacific fleet joined Nimitz for operations against Okinawa.

The battle for Leyte was over by mid-December 1944, and it left the Japanese in no position to prevent MacArthur from capturing the greater part of Luzon. The Americans were then in a position to seize the bases from which a final assault on Japan could be delivered. Nimitz launched his attack on Iwo Jima, in the Bonins, in February 1945, and on Okinawa in the Kuriles, which was completed in June of the same year. The Japanese, with no means of bringing the American fleet to action, concentrated on kamikaze (mass-suicide) air attacks. They had little time to organize the forces for these, and by their very nature they were a wasting asset since the pilots did not return. The Americans lost many destroyers on the outer defensive fringes, but even in the three-months battle for Okinawa they lost few ships in the vital inner area. The British carriers, four of which operated with the Fifth Fleet off Okinawa, had armored decks and proved immune to kamikaze attack.

Okinawa was the end of the long drive through the Pacific. A close blockade and intense bombing made Japanese defeat inevitable. But to the military members of the Supreme Council there was no such word as "surrender." The Russian declaration of war three months after the end of the war with Germany on 7 May, and the dropping of the atomic bombs on Hiroshima and Nagasaki in early August 1945 were necessary before the emperor could get his decision to surrender accepted by the council. World War II came to an end in the Pacific on 2 September 1945.

RELATED ENTRIES: American Samoa; ANZAC; ANZUS; Bora Bora, U.S. Military Life during World War II; Guam; Kiribati; Mariana Islands; Micronesia; Nimitz, Chester W.; Oceania, Strategic Importance of; Papua New Guinea; Port Moresby; Solomon Islands; Spruance, Raymond A.; Washington Disarmament Conference; Western Samoa; World War II Battles for the Gilbert and Marshall Islands.

SOURCES AND READINGS: Basil Collier, *The Lion and the Eagle: British and Anglo-American Strategy 1900-1950* (London: Macdonald, 1972); E. G. Keagh, *The South West Pacific 1941-45* (Melbourne: Grayflower, 1965); S. Woodburn Kirby, *The War against Japan*, vol. 5 (London: Her Majesty's Stationery Office, 1969); Gavin Long, *MacArthur as Military Commander* (London: Batsford, 1969); S. S. Mackenzie, *The Australians at Rabaul: The Capture and Administration of German Possessions in the South Pacific* (Sydney: Angus and Robertson, 1927); Clark G. Reynolds, *The Fast Carriers: The Forging of an Air Navy* (New York: Krieger, 1978).

E. K. G. Sixsmith

WASHINGTON DISARMAMENT CONFERENCE

(1921-1922). The Washington Disarmament Conference, sponsored by the United States, sought to solve the problems of the naval armament race and the open-door policy toward China in the Far East. Among a number of treaties signed were three interconnected ones which temporarily eased the tensions existing between Japan and the United States. The four-power treaty, a vague consultative pact, replaced the Anglo-Japanese alliance, which could have threatened the United States with a two-front war in case of hostilities with Japan. The five-power treaty created a tonnage ratio system for the great naval powers with Japan accepting a lesser ratio (60 percent) in return for the United States accepting a prohibition on the construction of bases west of Hawai'i. This left Japan's navy dominant in the western Pacific. The nine-power treaty, which included Japan, accepted an open-door policy toward China and repudiated any aggressive intent. The result of these treaties was that United States-Japanese friction was quieted and a measure of stability was established in the Far East. All depended, however, on the goodwill of Japan because the United States, without the needed island bases across the Pacific, had surrendered the capability of counterbalancing Japan by projecting its power directly into the Far East. The United States was not able to start needed base construction until the end of the five-power treaty on 1 January 1937.

RELATED ENTRIES: War in the Pacific Islands 1914-1945.

SOURCES AND READINGS: Ruhl J. Bartlett, ed., *The Record of American Diplomacy* (New York: Alfred A. Knopf, 1954).   *Francis X. Holbrook*

WEBB, WILLIAM HENRY (1816-1899). A shipbuilder and Pacific entrepreneur, Webb was born in New York City, 10 June 1816. At age twenty, he began a long and successful career in shipbuilding. Ships built by the Webb Steamship Lines were some of the first to transport and sell guano (manure of seabirds rich in nitrogen and phosphorus found on several islands in the Pacific). The completion of the U.S. transcontinental railroad in 1869 drastically shortened travel time between New York, Auckland, and Sydney and, therefore, greatly stimulated Pacific shipping. Webb Steamship Lines needed adequate harbors and coaling stations along the way, so in 1871 Webb instructed his agent, Captain E. Wakeman, to survey the Samoan islands and to report on harbor facilities. Wakeman's report to Webb rated Samoa as one of the richest territories in the Pacific. Webb published Wakeman's report to land speculators, politicians, and government officials. Because the U.S. Navy needed harbors and coaling stations in the Pacific, Commander Meade of the *Narragansett* was sent in 1872 to investigate the future use of Samoan facilities. Without authorization, Meade negotiated a treaty with the local chiefs granting the United States a naval station. Webb, also, suggested to President Grant the need to establish diplomatic relations with Samoa and recommended Colonel A. B. Steinberger for the job. This selection was welcomed by the Central Polynesian Land and Commercial Company in which Webb held the major shares of stock. Webb's influence with the executive branch of the government was beneficial to his expansion in Samoa in spite of occasional intervention by Congress. Webb died 30 October 1899 in New York City.

RELATED ENTRIES: American Samoa; *Narragansett, Cruise of*; Steinberger, Albert B.; Western Samoa.

SOURCES AND READINGS: J. W. Davidson, *Samoa 1830-1900* (Melbourne: Oxford University Press, 1970); J. A. C. Gray, *Amerika Samoa* (Annapolis: U.S. Naval Institute, 1960); G. H. Ryden, *The Foreign Policy of the United States in Relation to Samoa* (New York: Octagon Books, 1975); G. R. Ward, *American Activities in the Central-Pacific, 1790-1870* (Ridgewood: Gregg Press, 1966).

Joseph A. Montoya

WEBER, THEODOR (1844-1889). The head of the J. C. Godeffroy company in Samoa (after 1878 the *Deutsche Handels- und Plantagen-Gesellschaft*, DHPG) and also first German consul in Apia, Weber arrived in Samoa in 1862. Despite his young age, he succeeded August Unshelm as head of the Godeffroy firm and the Hamburg general consulate in Samoa in 1864. After 1872 he became German consul for Samoa and Tonga. Shortly thereafter Weber returned to Hamburg on business, but resumed his post as consul from 1875 to 1880. Perhaps more than any other individual, Weber was responsible for the expansion of German commercial interests in Samoa and the Pacific. Under his administration, Apia became the entrepôt for a vast Godeffroy trading network stretching from China to Chile. Weber was a skillful, if rather unscrupulous administrator, and an intriguer of the first degree. Through dubious land transactions with the Samoans he amassed considerable property in the islands both for his firm's and his own enrichment. Weber expanded the copra trade and instituted large coconut plantations on Godeffroy lands run largely by imported labor from Melanesia. He constantly interfered in the affairs of the already unstable Samoan government and played an active role in fomenting civil strife by supplying his Samoan allies with firearms. Weber wanted the German government to display as much initiative in Samoa as had the German merchants and since 1870 had urged the annexation of the islands. Although he failed in this respect, Weber became more able to rely on German naval aid in order to support his increasingly ambitious designs in the 1870s and 1880s. Weber retired from the directorship of the DHPG in Samoa.

RELATED ENTRIES: German Colonial Empire; Solf, Wilhelm; Unshelm, August; Western Samoa.

SOURCES AND READINGS: Historische Kommission bei der Bayerischen Akademie der Wissenschaft, *Neue Deutsche Biographie*, vol. 6 (Berlin: Duncker & Humbolt, 1964); Paul M. Kennedy, *The Samoan Tangle* (Dublin: Irish University Press, 1974); Heinrich Schnee, ed., *Deutsches Kolonial-Lexikon*, vol. 3 (Leipzig: Quelle & Meyer, 1920).   *Ralph C. Canevali*

WESTERN PACIFIC HIGH COMMISSION (1877-1974). In 1877 the office of High Commissioner for the Western Pacific was created; Sir Arthur Gordon, currently governor of Fiji, took on the extra duties. The office arose as an attempt by the British government to afford some form of jurisdiction and authority over British subjects residing in the many islands of the southwest Pacific then outside regular colonial control. Only New Caledonia and Fiji had at that stage come under the direct Western jurisdiction of France and Britain respectively. Yet the islands of Melanesia and central Polynesia were being subjected to an ever-increasing influx of European and American residents, traders, and sojourners. Britain and the other Western powers expected, under their understanding of international law, that the local kings or chiefs should be responsible for the due performance of "civilized" justice in their respective domains. But the reality was a growing breakdown of law and order in these areas, as the two different cultures and life-styles came into an increasing contact and conflict. The local, traditional leaders frequently could not maintain peace and harmony. Furthermore, there was a marked resistance by most Westerners to submit to anything but Western law; indeed, many of them hoped that by escaping to the South Pacific they might place themselves beyond the reach of responsibility and punishment for wrongdoings.

Consequently, by the beginning of the 1870s, with lawlessness spreading widely throughout the southwest Pacific and with many British subjects committing illegal and criminal acts with impunity, the British government found itself under increasing pressure to assert a stronger presence in the area. The annexation of Fiji in 1874 was one such step; the creation of the high commission was a second. This latter step was taken particularly with problems of the labor trade in mind. It was felt desirable to create a more definite jurisdiction than currently pertained in the Vice-Admiralty Court, at the hands of naval officers, or under vague extraterritorial legislation. The existing legal remedies and procedures had proved to be inadequate for these vast oceanic expanses. At the same time, the British government did not want to annex these scattered island territories. So a more definite form of extraterritorial jurisdiction was afforded, with the aim of bringing British subjects more directly under regular British judicial control, even though they were not residing or operating in British territory.

The Western Pacific Order in Council of 1877 extended the jurisdiction of the high commissioner over New Guinea eastward of the 143d meridian, the islands off New Guinea, the Solomon Islands, Vanuatu (New Hebrides) (reconfirmed in 1907), Tonga, Samoa, and other groups. Later, these were defined more specifically: the Gilbert and Ellice Islands, the Phoenix group, Pitcairn, and the central and southern Line Islands. The high commissioner's court was the vehicle for the administration of British civil and criminal jurisdiction in these islands. The judiciary of Fiji acted as judicial commissioners, while deputy commissioners were appointed to individual island groups in the Pacific to carry out functions somewhat equivalent to those of a county court judge and a stipendiary magistrate in England. Initially, deputy commissioners were appointed for Tonga, Samoa, New Guinea, New Britain, and the New Hebrides; two naval officers from the Australian station were also appointed as roving deputy commissioners. One of the commissioner's special powers was the authority to deport a person who was endangering the peace of the area.

Difficulties were experienced by the high commissioner in making his jurisdiction effective because his powers were too limited, funds were scarce, and the area to maintain was so large. In 1893 a new order in council sought to overcome some of these problems by extending the high commissioner's jurisdiction to foreigners (that is, others than British subjects) and generally to islanders where some form of protectorate arrangement had been entered into with Britain. British authority was moving gradually towards that of a more formalized colonial structure, and the high commission was turning into a vehicle of imperial expansion and control. Increasingly, it meant that the commission took on more than judicial functions by becoming a general administrative body. In the Solomons, the New Hebrides, and the Gilberts, a resident commissioner was stationed, assisted by various administrative and district officers. One of the most important functions which developed was the provision of health services, along with the collection of taxes. In addition, wireless and postal communications, education, labor regulation, land policy and surveys, and public works were tasks added to the original judicial and police roles. In Tonga, where islander control persisted with considerable strength, the degree of British superintendence and interference was least.

British New Guinea was removed from the commission's authority upon its annexation in 1888 and likewise Samoa by the end of the century. Fiji and Pitcairn were transferred out of the commissioner's responsibility in 1952, and the following year commission headquarters were transferred from Suva, Fiji, to Honiara in the British Solomon Islands Protectorate. In the 1970s, with the biggest remaining island groups moving towards independence, the office of Western Pacific High Commission ceased in

1974, the high commissioner becoming governor of the Solomon Islands. Among the more notable earlier high commissioners were Sir Arthur Gordon (1879-1882), Sir John Thurston (1888-1897), and Sir Everard im Thurn (1904-1911).

RELATED ENTRIES: British New Guinea; Fiji; Gordon, Arthur; Kiribati; Labor Trade; Line Islands; Melanesian Recruitment to Queensland, Patterns of; Melanesians and Colonial Servitude; Papua New Guinea; Samoa; Solomon Islands; Thurston, John; Tonga; Vanuatu (New Hebrides).

SOURCES AND READINGS: Great Britain, Colonial Office, *Annual Reports* (of the various island groups), London, England; W. R. Johnston, *Sovereignty and Protection* (Durham, N.C.: Duke University Press, 1973); D. Scarr, *Fragments of Empire* (Canberra: Australian National University Press, 1967).

W. Ross Johnston

WESTERN SAMOA. An independent country, Western Samoa is a member of the British Commonwealth. It is located in the southwest Pacific Ocean between 168° to 173° west longitude and 13° to 14° south latitude and includes the islands of Savai'i, Upolu, Manono, and Apolima. The total land area is 2,934 km² (1,133 mi²). The total population of 155,000 (1980 estimate) consists primarily of Polynesian extraction (over 90 percent). Approximately 70 percent live on the island of Upolu where the capital of Apia is located.

Climate, Land, and Natural Resources. These tropical islands are warm and wet with scarcely any temperature variation from season to season. The average mean temperature is 26° C (78.8° F). Rainfall averages 254 cm (100 in) per year. The islands are mostly of the high volcanic type with rugged mountains in the interior. The tallest mountain in Western Samoa is on Savai'i and is 1,850 m (6,069 ft) high. The soil is fertile, but only 45 percent of the land area of Western Samoa is arable; the rest is rocky or steep. There are no significantly valuable mineral resources. There have been volcanic eruptions in historic times; Savai'i experienced one in 1902, and there were eruptions again between 1905 and 1911. A reef encircles much of the islands, and the enclosed lagoons are a significant source of sea food.

The majority of the people today live in coastal villages, especially in the urban area of Apia, the capital, on Upolu. It appears that early in the nineteenth century, many people left their villages in the interior of Upolu and established themselves in coastal areas, probably to be near the ports where they could benefit from contact with the Westerners who came there.

The economy of Western Samoa is largely based upon subsistence agriculture. There are only a few small-scale private plantations operated by Europeans or part-Europeans. The government controls the Western Samoa Trust Estates Corporation (WSTEC), an agricultural enterprise. It is the largest agricultural operation in the country. New Zealand seized it from the Germans during World War I, and it remained in the hands of the New Zealand administration as reparations until 1957 when it was converted into a trust for the benefit of the Samoan people. WSTEC harvests copra and cocoa from its plantations, raises herds of cattle, operates sawmills, and has also been in the dried coconut and dried banana business.

The great majority of Samoa's agricultural exports, however, are grown by the villagers. Bananas, copra, and cocoa constitute almost the entire export of the country. The dependency upon these three crops has its dangers, of course. Hurricanes have virtually wiped out the plantings on occasions, and world market fluctuations profoundly affect the prosperity of those who grow these crops for export.

By the 1970s Apia harbor had been dredged and a portion of it filled in, in a land reclamation project. This added thirty-eight acres to the land area of Apia.

Land is held in freehold by private persons (about 4 percent of the total), or by the government (about 10 percent), by the Western Samoa Trust Estates Corporation (4 percent), or by the Samoan people under a system of customary tenure. Just under 80 percent of the land is owned in this manner. Control of customary land is vested in the traditional chiefs who direct its use for the benefit of their families. Land tenure was a highly political issue in the late nineteenth century when land speculators and foreign investors claimed to have bought up huge tracts of Samoan land. A land commission was established by the Berlin Act of 1889 whereby the exaggerated claims to Samoan land by foreigners were drastically trimmed down and quieted. Land claims are still occasionally an issue between contending parties. A Land and Titles Court has jurisdiction over all controversies concerning customary land.

The People. The great majority of the residents of Western Samoa are Samoan. About 6 percent of the population is European, and there are numbers of part-Europeans also. Other Pacific islanders were brought to Samoa in the late nineteenth century to work on the plantations established by European planters, and these people have remained to add another ethnic strain to the Samoan population. During the German administration, numbers of Chinese were brought in to serve on the German-managed plantations. Many of these intermarried with the Samoan majority and produced another component in the population structure. In 1935 the New Zealand administration sent most of the Chinese back to the Republic of China.

In recent years there has been a significant out-migration from Western Samoa. Thousands of people, including some of the best-educated persons, have left their homes in Samoa for New Zealand, Hawai'i, and the mainland United States. The money they send home adds to the wealth of the country, but the talents they take with them are a loss to their homeland.

Traditional History and Way of Life. Samoan traditional history ascribes the creation of Samoa to the god Tagaloa. According to tradition the Samoans were not voyagers from some other land; rather, they had their origin in Samoa. The tradition further states that certain persons were the offspring of Tagaloa and became the chiefs of Samoa. Ordinary mortals were the descendants of worms or maggots which crawled out of a rotten vine which had taken root early in the creation of the islands. Some traditions state that Manu'a was the first place to be created, and the first settlement and the first house were built on Ta'u in Manu'a. This explains why the Tui Manu'a, the highest chief in Manu'a, has always enjoyed such ceremonial precedence. The Polynesian demigod Maui appears in Samoan creation accounts. He is credited with bringing fire from the underworld.

Samoa was never, apparently, a single political unit. The system was a feudal, aristocratic order. Prestige was awarded to and the system governed by the holders of titles, the chiefs (*matais*). There was and is a hierarchical ranking of these titles. The Manu'a title structure is separate from that of the rest of Samoa, perhaps because Manu'a was cut off from the rest of the islands during the years of Tongan occupation, but the remainder of the country is essentially divided between two great families, Tupua and Malietoa. The most important titles of the Tupua family are *Mata'afa*, *Tamasese*, and *Tuimaleali'ifano*. *Malietoa* is the great title of the Malietoa family. These four titles are collectively known as the *Tama-a-'aiga* and have been the object of political intrigue for generations. Genealogical precedence, ability, and service to the chiefs are among the standard criteria for being awarded a title.

The usual way of classifying titles is to distinguish between two general categories of chiefs, or *matais*: the chiefs, or *ali'i*, and the orators (talking chiefs), or *tula fale*. The latter are supposed to be the executives for the *ali'i*, but they have often been able to manipulate the *ali'i* and the system to their own political and status advantage. Each extended family controls one or more titles and decides who shall bear and control the family's resources. A *matai* is supposed to bring honor and credit to his family. He can be deposed. Normally, the title changes hands when a *matai* dies or becomes too old to function effectively. With a burgeoning population has come an increased demand for a share of the status and prestige that goes with holding a title. To meet this demand titles have been split on occasion. As many as twenty individuals may hold the same title. More than 15 percent of the adult population are *matais*. Women may hold titles, but it is not common.

The village has been the standard governmental unit within the Samoan system, and it is still the villages today which govern the life of those people living in them. Here the chiefs govern the families and administer the lands belonging to the families. A weekly council of the chiefs is held to discuss village affairs, to resolve disputes, and to award judgments. In all but major crimes, the village is sovereign over legal matters. The young, untitled men serve the chiefs, and the wives and women have their own organization to deal with feminine concerns.

The decentralization of the Samoan system explains its capacity to resist the shocks of cultural change that elsewhere in the Pacific have wiped out traditional culture. Each village is self-sufficient in economic, political, and social terms.

Modern History. Archaeological evidence indicates that Samoa was settled as early as 1000 B.C. As part of the western Polynesian cultural complex, it has had regular intercourse with its neighbors in Tonga, Fiji, the Tokelaus, Rotuma, and other adjacent island areas. Samoa was occupied by Tongans between the twelfth and sixteenth centuries. In 1722, the Dutch navigator, Jacob Roggeveen, became the first European to visit Samoa. Louis de Bougainville, the French explorer, was in Samoan waters in 1768. J. F. de Galaup de Lapérouse lost twelve crewmen to the Tutuila Samoans in 1787, and one of the boats of the *Pandora*, the British navy ship searching for the *Bounty* mutineers, was also attacked by Tutuila Samoans in 1791. For a time this gave the islanders a reputation for savagery.

Contacts with Europeans were very erratic until the first missionaries arrived in 1830, although there were a handful of Europeans there by 1800. Castaways, escaped convicts from New South Wales, and deserters were the sole Europeans who got ashore in Samoa before the missionary advent. Some of these first Europeans established the so-called sailor cults which taught a garbled version of Christianity, primarily to create an opportunity for their European founders to exploit the Samoans. Some sailors may have been captured to teach Christianity, so eager were some of the Samoans to learn of this novelty. Some Tongans had been exposed and converted to Wesleyanism and these made their way to Samoa before the first missionaries arrived.

John Williams, the most famous Protestant missionary of the first half of the nineteenth century, arrived at Sapapali'i, on Savai'i in mid-July 1830 to begin the first systematic effort to Christianize Samoa. He had come from the Cook Islands to Samoa upon the behest of a Samoan chief, Fauea, who had done some travelling and met Williams. Within a few years all Samoans were at least nominal Christians. The Christian pastor was given a place of eminence in the political hierarchy of the village. By adapting Christianity to the needs of the traditional system the Samoans diminished its impact upon that system.

For generations the greatest chiefs in Samoa had carried on a struggle for possession of the *Tafa'ifā*, the collective name given to four very important titles associated with particular political districts: Gatoaitele, Tui A'ana, Tui Atua, and Tamasoali'i. Warfare and intrigue were almost a constant in Samoan history. The arrival of Westerners with new technology and new institutions provided a new dimension to the continual battling and jockeying for position in Samoan politics. Guns and ammunition were purchased by the contending parties from various Western agents, sometimes through selling off Samoan lands.

While the Samoan chiefs were struggling with each other for the traditional prizes of politics, the Europeans who had been arriving in Samoa since the early years of the nineteenth century were competing with each other and the Samoans for preeminence in Samoa. Some Europeans and Americans saw Samoa as a stopping-off point for trade between Australia and the Orient, or as territory that ought to be included in some imperial power's collection of possessions. Britain, the United States, and Germany became involved in Samoan politics to a far greater extent than could possibly be justified in strategic or economic terms. The Great Powers attempted to manipulate the Samoan situation to their individual advantages, while the Samoans attempted to manipulate the powers to their advantage. The upshot was that Samoa was elevated to a place of priority in the international politics of the nineteenth century. In March 1889 German, American, and British warships were all anchored in Apia harbor, glowering at each other over their gun ports. On 16 March a disastrous hurricane struck and only one ship, the British vessel *Calliope*, was able to escape. Almost 150 sailors lost their lives, and six ships were sunk or severely damaged.

The hurricane helped to stimulate the Great Powers into reviewing their efforts to negotiate their interests in Samoa. Under the terms of the 1889 Berlin Act—to which the Samoans were not a party—a tripartite system of rule was established in Samoa; and Germany, Britain, and the United States assumed joint responsibility for governing the country. This condominium system was cumbersome and failed to accomplish its objectives, so it was agreed that in 1900 Germany and the United States would divide Samoa between them, with the eastern islands going to the United States and the western portion being given to Germany to govern. In return for her withdrawal, Britain received concessions elsewhere in the Pacific and Africa.

The Twentieth Century. Western Samoa, the portion that became a German colony, was governed efficiently and with dispatch by its colonial governors. The Germans attempted to put down some of the traditional disputes over titles by declaring them to be defunct and they exiled some dissidents who wanted to maintain their traditional places and positions.

German rule came to an end in 1914 when a New Zealand expeditionary force occupied Western Samoa at the outbreak of World War I. After the war Western Samoa was given to New Zealand to administer as a mandate under the League of Nations. New Zealand rule was often flawed by faulty judgment, although the health of the people generally improved. The New Zealand administration was blamed, however, for permitting an outbreak of influenza in 1918 which carried off 20 percent of the population.

The administration managed to alienate a significant portion of the Samoan and part-Samoan population who united in their efforts to boycott New Zealand rule. This movement, generally nonviolent, was known as the *Mau* and lasted from 1926 to 1936. The most important figure in the movement was O. F. Nelson, a wealthy part-Samoan businessman who bore a Samoan title. Along with other part-Samoans he made common cause with many ranking Samoans who objected to the racism, the insensitivity, and the policies of the New Zealand administration. The part-European businessmen objected to government regulation of their activities and various other policies of the administration. The Samoan title bearers were concerned about maintaining their place, or enhancing it, within the political system. They resented the New Zealand administration's patronizing of them and its failure to recognize their place within the traditional system. The *Mau* was not an independence movement. Although its slogan was Samoa for the Samoans, it was, for the traditional Samoan leaders within it, a demand for the recognition of their traditional prestige. In fact, the extension of democratic privileges to Samoans by the administration was an irritant to the chiefs who regarded such things as a threat to their position.

In 1929 tensions reached such a point that in an affray in Apia between some New Zealand police and members of the *Mau* group, eleven Samoans, mostly of high rank, were killed. Among these was Tamasese Lealofi III. The movement's resistance to the administration stiffened and official efforts to put it down intensified. But the boycott lasted until 1936 when the Labour party came to power in New Zealand, and delegates from the new government managed to make peace with the Samoan dissidents.

World War II delayed any further efforts to make changes in the character of New Zealand rule. In 1946 Western Samoa became a New Zealand trust territory. The New Zealand government began to extend more power and control over local affairs to the Samoans, with a view to giving them more and more control over the country.

Government. In 1962 Western Samoa became an independent state governed by a constitution written by a constitutional convention in 1960. It is now a member of the South Pacific Commission, the Commonwealth, and the United Nations. Its form of government is parliamentary. The head of state is largely a ceremonial figure and the present incumbent is Malietoa Tanumafili II. The constitution made him and Tupua Tamasese Mea'ole joint heads of state until their deaths. Tamasese died in 1963. The legislative assembly will elect Malietoa's successor. Future heads of state will serve for a five year term. There is a constitutional provision for a council of deputies to serve as an acting head of state should it become necessary to have one. It may have up to three members and is elected by the legislative assembly. The legislative assembly functions on the parliamentary model. It is a single-house body with forty-five members, two of whom are elected from the individual voters' roll. This roll consists of citizens not living in a customary context. They are mostly of European or part-European ancestry. *Matai* title holders are not permitted to vote on the individual voters' roll. The other forty-three members of the assembly are elected by *matais* in forty-one constituencies. There are no political parties.

The prime minister is appointed by the head of state and must enjoy the confidence of a majority of the members of the legislative assembly. He is the effective head of the government. He presides over the cabinet, whose eight members are chosen by the head of state upon the advice of the prime minister.

Two types of law are enforced in Western Samoa: customary law and statutory law enacted by the legislative assembly. Customary law is enforced by the chiefs in the villages and in the Land and Titles Court as it exercises jurisdiction over customary lands and disputes over titles. Statutory law is based upon the Anglo-Saxon system. In the formally organized court system, there are magistrates' courts and a supreme court, both with original and appellate jurisdiction. Another court, the court of appeals, is an appellate court.

Local government continues to be in the hands of the chiefs of the villages. Their legal authority still remains in a grey area, however, as it has not been spelled out by the constitution or by law.

Conclusion. Western Samoa remains a conservative country and society. The *matai* system, whereby chiefs control the lives and destinies of villagers, continues to exist, though modifications are occurring. There is a limited amount of democracy—as that term is understood in the West—and only the chiefs may run for public office or vote in elections. The traditional and the modern coexist in Western Samoa either side by side or intertwined with each other. In many cases this has served as a buttress and support for the system and its people against more rapid social change, the effects of which have not always been good. The reverse is also true, of course, and many people have argued that Samoan traditionalism and conservatism have made it impossible or difficult for the people to gain the benefits from Western civilization and material culture they might receive were they permitted to share more in the culture of the West.

RELATED ENTRIES: American Samoa; Anglo-German Agreement of 1899; Berlin Act of 1889; Bismarck Agreement of 1879; Central Polynesian Land and Commercial Company; Davidson, James W.; Diaper, William; Erskine, John E.; Fautua; Foreign Residents' Society; German Colonial Empire; Island Confederation Movement; Krämer, Augustin; Lackawanna Agreement; Lauaki, Namulau'ulu Mamoe; London Missionary Society; *Malietoa*; Malietoa Tanumafili II; Mata'afa, Fiame; Mau of Pule; Mead, Margaret; Nelson, Olaf; Polynesia, Settlement of; Polynesian Culture (Ancient); Poppe, Alfred; Poweles, Guy; Pritchard, George; Pritchard, William; Ruge and Company, H. M.; Selwyn, George; Solf, Wilhelm; South Pacific Commission; South Pacific Forum; Steinberger, Albert; Stevens, Charles; Stevenson, Robert L.; *Tui A'ana* and *Tui Atua*; *Tui*

Manu'a; *Tupu'o Samoa*; United States in the Pacific; Unshelm, August; Vaitupu "Company"; Webb, William; Weber, Theodor; Western Pacific High Commission; Williams, John.

SOURCES AND READINGS: J. W. Davidson, *Samoa Mo Samoa: The Emergence of the Independent State of Western Samoa* (New York: Oxford University Press, 1967).   *Jerry K. Loveland*

WESTERN SAMOA, LAND AND TITLES COURT.

Extended families in Samoa have lands and chiefly titles (*matai* titles) which are communally owned. By custom, as recognized and validated by law, these lands and titles are controlled by and disposed of by the extended family, the *'aiga potopoto*. Another type of title, known as the *ao*, is controlled by certain villages and districts, rather than by specific extended families. Titles are hierarchically arranged, with some of them being much more important than others. The awarding of a title may be the subject of much controversy, and up through the nineteenth century contending groups even went to war over the disposition of an important title. Even today the awarding of an important title may be the subject of considerable dispute within the extended family. In the normal course of events, the government is not concerned with the awarding of titles as long as they conform to the few laws concerning them. So, for example, a title must be properly registered with the Land and Titles Court, but if a title or land becomes the subject of dispute the Land and Titles Court may make a judgment about the rights of the respective parties to the title or the lands in question. The majority of cases considered by the court involve land problems. In the United States-administered American Samoa, a division of the High Court is charged with dealing with land and titles disputes. It operates under slightly different rules than the court of Western Samoa.

In 1903 when Western Samoa was administered by Germany, a land and titles commission was created with three Europeans and several Samoan advisors in order to settle disputes over customary land and titles. It was the function of this commission, and all bodies which have succeeded it, to determine in the first place what the law or custom was regarding the disposal of particular lands and titles and then, secondly, to determine how a given case should be resolved once a hearing and investigation had been held. When New Zealand assumed the administration of Western Samoa it changed the title of this institution to the Native Land and Titles Commission (1924). The commission included Samoans and Europeans,

with the Samoans acting in an advisory capacity only. In 1937 its name was changed to the Native Land and Titles Court. Under the provisions of the 1962 constitution the court became the Land and Titles Court. The native-land-and-titles-protection ordinance of 1934 is still the basic law under which the Land and Titles Court operates. Unwritten custom is the major law applied by the court, however, and the opinions of the court have become a major statement of Samoan custom, though there is no systematic record made of the decisions of the court.

In previous years, it was common for the chief justice of Western Samoa, who has always been a European, to preside over the court as its president. Today, however, the chief justice sits only occasionally with the court. He normally deals only with applications requesting a review of court decisions. He is the only person allowed to determine whether or not a rehearing of any case will be allowed. There are no appeals of decisions allowed from the decisions of the court to a court of higher jurisdiction. Currently there are eleven Samoan judges on the court which sits almost continuously in both Apia and at Tuasivi on Savai'i. Western-trained attorneys are not permitted to appear before the court although they may help the parties in litigation to prepare their case.

Most chiefly titles are transferred without dispute. Members of the involved family are reluctant to take family affairs to court and air their difficulties in public. Yet there has been an increasing use of the court in recent years and more and more controversies over title succession are being given to the court to adjudicate. Notice of a dispute over lands or titles is first taken to the registrar of the court. He attempts to bring the contending parties together and avoid a confrontation in court. The majority of cases are decided in this fashion and disputes are settled before they ever reach the court proper. If the contending parties are unable to reach an amicable agreement, notice is given in the government newspaper a few months prior to the court hearing inviting all concerned parties to appear before the court on a particular day. In the hearing itself the proceedings are generally informal. No lawyers are permitted in the court and no cross-examinations are allowed except by the judges on the bench. After each party has had a chance to respond to the answers given to questions by the other party the court recesses and deliberates before announcing its decision to the persons involved. The court does not have the power to enforce its decisions. This is left up entirely to the police and the magistrate's courts.

Today, hundreds of petitions are filed annually with the court. The majority of the disputes come from villages closer to the urban areas rather than from those located in more remote sections of the country.

Grounds for petitioning the court in a title dispute include a claim that the *'aiga potopoto* did not actually reach a consensus on a title-bearer or that certain members of the family were not consulted who had a right to be consulted. Also, some members of the family may have an objection to the decision of the family. The decision to award a title is supposed to be a unanimous one arrived at by consensus.

In arriving at its decision as to which candidate is entitled to a *matai* title, the court is guided by a few general principles and the custom of a particular village or family regarding the disposition of the title. The court considers the blood relationship of the contending parties to the family—genealogical links are very important in this connection—as well as the quality of service rendered to the family by the disputants. The history of a candidate's residency in an area where he can be of most utility to the family is a consideration, also. Finally, the overall fitness and individual qualifications of a particular person for the title are determined by the court. Individual circumstances here may vary in light of the needs of the family.

Occasionally, though not frequently, the court is asked to remove a title from a person certain members of the *'aiga potopoto* wish to have stripped of the title. The court has recognized certain grounds for this type of drastic action, including the harshness or criminal administration of the *matai* in question, his ability to keep the family united and happy, his failure to represent the family in the affairs of the village, or his outright abandonment of the family as evidenced by his physical removal to some place where he cannot serve the family. Normally, the court will merely admonish such an accused person rather than strip him of his title.

The *matai* has the *pule* over family lands, or the right to direct their use. Disputes occasionally reach the court regarding the alleged improper use of the *pule*. Untitled persons may complain to the court that a *matai* has deprived them of the produce of their labor. Such persons are required by custom to render service to their *matai* by providing him with some of the produce, but there have been problems regarding the just and proper amount such service requires. Sometimes there are other types of disputes regarding rights to occupation of the land which likewise may be heard by the court.

Among other items considered by the court in the past have been questions regarding the rights of par-

ticular persons to wear the *tuiga*, the ceremonial headdress, and the right to bear the title *sa'otamaita'i*, an honorific reserved for certain women in certain districts. The court has also been petitioned to order certain individuals to lower the foundation of their houses on the grounds that by custom the ranking *matai* in a village is entitled to the highest house foundation. House sites for chiefs are designated in each village but there have been instances where the court has had to adjudicate a dispute within the family about the possible subdivision of such a chiefly site by branches of the family.

About one in every six adults in Samoa bears a chiefly title. About 80 percent of the land is held under customary tenure. These facts explain why the court is a busy institution. Its role is an interesting one. A modern-style institution, it has become the supreme arbiter of Samoan custom regarding succession to chiefly status, which under today's political system is a prerequisite for holding public office or voting for members of the legislative assembly. It also determines the rules regarding the disposition of Samoa's most important natural resource, her customary land. It has become the institution whereby potentially explosive family and village disputes or feuds are defused. If the traditional system of bargaining and negotiation were to be used to accommodate the parties to disputes, endemic village feuding might be the result. The Land and Titles Court, a Western innovation, has been utilized to damp down these disputes by itself becoming the institution whereby customary law is applied in an impersonal, rational, secular manner.

RELATED ENTRIES: Western Samoa.

SOURCES AND READINGS: Taulapapa Anesi, "The Land and Chiefly Titles Court of Western Samoa" in *Pacific Courts and Justice* (Suva: Institute of Pacific Studies, 1977); A. P. Lutali and William J. Stewart, "A Chieftal System in Twentieth-Century America: Legal Aspects of the Matai System in the Territory of American Samoa," *Georgia Journal of International and Comparative Law* 4 (1974): 387-401; C. C. Marsack, *Notes on the Practice of the Court and the Principles Adopted in the Hearing of Cases Affecting: 1. Samoan Matai Titles; 2. Land Held According to Customs and Usages of Western Samoa*, rev. ed. (Apia: Justice Department, Land and Titles Court of Western Samoa, 1961); Sharon W. Tiffany, "The Land and Titles Court and the Regulation of Customary Title Succession and Removals in Western Samoa," *Journal of the Polynesian Society* 83 (1975): 35-37; Walter Tiffany, "High

Court Adjudication of Chiefly Title Succession Disputes in American Samoa," *Journal of the Polynesian Society* 84 (1975): 67-92.   Jerry K. Loveland

WHALING IN THE PACIFIC (UNITED STATES).

The sperm whale, whose journeys Yankee, English, and French whalers traced around Cape Horn to the south and later the north Pacific Oceans, weighs about ninety tons or the equivalent of thirty elephants. In length these creatures often exceed one hundred feet. While these leviathans generally travel the oceans at a speed of 12 mph, they are known to attain speeds of up to 25 mph when pursued. "He is," wrote Herman Melville of the sperm whale, "without doubt, the largest inhabitant of the globe; the most formidable of all whales to encounter; the most majestic in aspect; and lastly, by far the most valuable in commerce." It was this latter quality, the value of its spermaceti oil, that led whalers to risk their lives in Pacific seas in pursuit of these dangerous beasts.

The head of the sperm whale can contain as much as 5,000 gallons of sperm oil, which by 1845 sold for $1.77 a gallon, while the rest of the whale's oil sold for 79¢ a gallon and its bone for 97¢ a pound. By 1866 prices rose to $2.55, $1.45, and $1.25 respectively. In 1840 a million gallons of sperm and whale oil and two million pounds of bone were exported from the United States. By the mid-1830s the capture, manufacture, and sale of the products of whales grew to be the third most important industry in Massachusetts after shoes and cotton textiles. Spermaceti oil, a fine lubricant, proved crucial for the manufacture of both cottons and woolens. Its chief use, however, was for the production of sperm candles; and during whaling's Golden Age (1835-1860), eight New England factories turned out 380 tons annually. Whale oil, which was provided by all species of whales, lit the lamps of the world until it was replaced by cheaper kerosene in the latter nineteenth century. The physical shape of many nineteenth-century women—for better or worse—was determined by the whalebone stays that formed corsets.

While commercial whaling by Europeans can be traced back to ninth-century Norway, its North American roots formed the foundations upon which Pacific whaling was based. Puritan and Quaker New Englanders learned how to hunt whales from the local Indian tribes who chased whales in their canoes with stone-headed spears and arrows. New England whaling, which shaped and dominated the industry in both the Atlantic and the Pacific, did not begin in earnest until the early eighteenth century. In 1712 Captain Christopher Hussey of Nantucket, while pursuing whales in the usual coastwise manner, was blown out to sea and chanced upon a sperm whale which his crew harpooned. This chance encounter altered the history not only of Nantucket, but also of whaling itself. During the following seventy-five years, the pursuit of sperm whales would take Nantucket whalers around Cape Horn to the South Pacific (1791), to the Sea of Japan (1820), and then north to the Bering Sea along the coasts of Russian-America (Alaska) (1835). Nantucket's domination of whaling was soon overtaken by her neighboring port of New Bedford, which by the early 1830s boasted of a whaling fleet twice as large as Nantucket's. Virtually every other New England port sent whalers to Pacific waters including New London in Connecticut and Sag Harbor on New York's Long Island. But New Bedford, with its oil refineries, coopers' shops, tool works, and other industries subsidiary to whaling, grew to become the fifth largest shipping port in the United States by 1850.

By mid-century the whaling fleet of the United States numbered some 736 vessels totaling 237,262 tons. The value of the fleet exceeded $21 million, while the total investment connected with the industry was valued at over $70 million. American whale fishery was responsible for directly or indirectly supporting 70,000 people.

This great New England industry depended ironically upon six regions of the Pacific Ocean: the coasts along Chile; the "off-shore" grounds between 5° and 10° south latitude and 105° to 125° west longitude; the "country whaling" among the islands and reefs of the South Pacific; the Indian Ocean; the coasts of Japan; and the Kodiak Grounds along the northwest coast and Russian-America (Alaska). The southern pursuit of the sperm whale around Cape Horn eventually led north. This northern chase uncovered valuable whaling grounds for the Kodiak or coastal right whales (1835) and the even more valuable bowhead whales along the coasts of Russian Kamchatka (1843).

It was this drearier North Pacific pursuit that actually sustained whaling for most of its Golden Age. While Melville's classic account of Yankee whaling in *Moby Dick* has forever fixed the warmer southern Pacific as the main theater for hunting the leviathan, his earlier and less well known romance, *Mardi* (1849), offers a more accurate picture of the climate under which many whalers labored: "on the Nor'West Coast in chill and fogs, the sullen, inert monsters rafting around like Hartz forest logs on the Rhine and submitting to the harpoon like half-stunned bullocks to the knife." According to Melville "this horrid and indecent right whaling" resembled "the butchering of white bears upon blank Greenland icebergs."

By the 1860s whaling declined, chiefly due to the wide use of kerosene. Oil lamps quickly became antiques, sperm candles were relegated to ornamental curiosities, while the use of whalebone corsets, sensibly, declined. Yet while Pacific whaling slumbered, it did not die. All through the late nineteenth and early twentieth century a small but reliable market remained for whale products as the industry shifted from America's east coast to its western ports. The invention of the harpoon gun and the subsequent utilization of modern technology combined with a resurgent industrial demand for whale oil, meat, blubber, and bone placed Pacific whales on the endangered-species list by the 1960s. Not only has modern technology taken the romance out of whaling, it now threatens to remove the whale itself from the romance. Thus, even Melville may have been too optimistic when he assured his readers in 1851 that "the whale immortal in his species, however perishable in his individuality . . . will still survive, and rearing upon the topmost crest of the equatorial flood, spout his frothed defiance to the skies."

RELATED ENTRIES: Melville, Herman.

SOURCES AND READINGS: Howard I. Kushner, "'Hellships': Yankee Whaling along the Coasts of Russian-America, 1835-52," *New England Quarterly* 44 (1972): 81-95; Samuel Eliot Morison, *The Maritime History of Massachusetts, 1783-1860* (Boston: Houghton Mifflin Co., 1961); Edouard A. Stackpole, *Whales and Destiny: The Rivalry Between America, France, and Britain for Control of the Southern Whale Fishery, 1785-1825* (Amherst: University of Massachusetts Press, 1972); Alexander Starbuck, ed., *History of American Whale Fishery*, 2 vols. (Washington, D.C.: Government Printing Office, 1878).   *Howard I. Kushner*

WHIPPY, DAVID (1802-1871). A beachcomber in Fiji, Whippy was born in Nantucket, Massachusetts, where his family was prominent in the whaling industry. He was left in Fiji in 1825 by Peter Dillon to collect *bêche-de-mer*. Whippy lived at first at Bau under the protection of the *Vunivalu* (dominant chief), Naulivou. He soon moved to Levuka where he lived most of the rest of his life. As *mata-ki-Bau* ("ambassador") for Tui Levuka, he was the only beachcomber in Fiji to hold a politically sensitive office and to exert an influence on Fijian politics in his own right. In the 1840s and 1850s, he was involved in wars and intrigues against Cakobau, and was one of those

Americans whose claims for damages against Cakobau led ultimately to Fiji's loss of sovereignty. Whippy was known to practically every visitor to Fiji for several decades and was the principal mediator in the 1830s and the 1840s for visiting traders. He was also a help to the Wesleyan missionaries.

Whippy was the patriarch of the early European community at Levuka. As the European settlement grew, he became increasingly dissociated from the Fijian way of life, and it was probably his brand of New England puritanism which gave Levuka its early and unique reputation among beach communities for respectability. He was also actively involved in commerce, shipbuilding, land transactions, and agriculture and was one of the earliest cultivators of cotton and sugar. From 1846 to 1856 he was American vice-commercial agent, another rare distinction for a beachcomber. After 1858 he did not live in Levuka—moving first to Wakaya and in 1862 to Wainunu on Vanua Levu. He was twice married and had a large family. His children and their descendants have been prominent in many walks of life in Fiji in both the nineteenth and twentieth centuries. He died at Wainunu in 1871.

RELATED ENTRIES: Beachcombers; Dillon, Peter; Fiji; Savage, Charles.

SOURCES AND READINGS: Caroline Ralston, *Grass Huts and Warehouses* (Canberra: Australian National University Press, 1977).   *Ian C. Campbell*

WILKES, CHARLES (1798-1877). An officer in the United States Navy, Wilkes was commander of the first large-scale official U.S. scientific expedition to Oceania in 1838-1842. Later he was noted for his action (called the "Trent Affair") in removing two Confederate commissioners to Great Britain from a British vessel on the high seas, thereby precipitating a crisis in relations between Great Britain and the United States during the Civil War. Wilkes was born in New York City to an influential New York family. His father was a successful businessman who could afford to give his son a good early education in mathematics, navigation, drawing, and modern languages. In 1815, Wilkes entered the merchant marine and on 1 January 1818 was appointed to the position of midshipman in the United States Navy. Early in his career as a naval officer, he served in the Mediterranean in the U.S.S. *Guerriere* and in the Pacific in the U.S.S. *Franklin*. He also became interested in learning the techniques of scientific investigation and received training in mathematics, including the surveying method of triangulation and in the more practical facets of geomagnetism. These accomplishments were noteworthy in a naval officer of his day and set him apart from his colleagues. In the 1830s his service record included experience in surveying Georges Shoal and Bank off New England and service as officer in charge of the Depot of Charts and Instruments in Washington, D.C. Later, while he was a lieutenant in command of the U.S.S. *Porpoise* searching for pirates off the southeast coast of the United States, he was selected to lead the United States Exploring Expedition. Wilkes had a previous record of association with the planning of this venture, having been consulted about its composition as early as 1828 and having been dispatched to Europe in 1836 to purchase scientific instruments for its use, but the appointment of a junior officer of his rank to a command of this nature was unprecedented in the navy and provoked a storm of protest. To justify his appointment, the expedition was characterized as a special service of a nonmilitary type to which the usual traditions of the United States Navy did not apply. Wilkes was issued orders to investigate whether a continent or a polar sea existed in the region of the South Pole, to chart the waters around various islands in the South Pacific, to explore the Hawaiian group, and to survey the northwest coast of North America as well as the seas off Japan. This expedition departed from the United States in 1838 and returned in 1842. On its return, some officers brought charges against Wilkes which led to court-martial proceedings against him and resulted in his receiving a letter of reprimand from the secretary of the navy. Wilkes, in turn, preferred charges against some of his officers resulting in court-martial proceedings against them. Despite this display of rancor, the success of the expedition may be attributed in great part to the methodical determination and strong convictions of Wilkes. Although his strong will often brought him into conflict with his colleagues, it furnished the foundation for persistence in scientific achievement and progress in the face of adversity which characterized the expedition.

In 1843 Wilkes was promoted to the rank of commander and by January 1844 he had completed work on a five-volume narrative history of the expedition totaling some 2,500 pages. Subsequent volumes dealing with scientific subjects were prepared by others in later years. In 1855 Wilkes was promoted to captain. In 1861 he was given command of the U.S.S. *San Jacinto* with orders to capture Southern blockade runners. On 8 November 1861 he dispatched a boarding party to the British mail steamer, the *Trent*, to remove two Confederate commissioners, John Slidell and James Mason and their secretaries. This action was applauded by the public and Congress but

brought about a diplomatic crisis in relations between Great Britain and the United States. On 16 July 1862 Wilkes was promoted to the rank of commodore and ordered to command a special squadron in the West Indies. He was recalled from this duty in June 1863 and placed on the retired list. In 1864 his temperament brought him into conflict with his superiors and he was court-martialed for disobedience, disrespect, insubordination, and conduct unbecoming an officer. For these offenses he was sentenced to be reprimanded and suspended from duty for one year. In July 1866 he was commissioned rear admiral on the retired list. On 16 February 1877 he died in Washington, D.C.

RELATED ENTRIES: United States Exploring Expedition; United States in the Pacific.

SOURCES AND READINGS: William Stanton, *The Great United States Exploring Expedition* (Berkeley, Calif.: University of California Press, 1975); David B. Tyler, *The Wilkes Expedition: The First United States Exploring Expedition 1838-1842* (Philadelphia: American Philosophical Society, 1968); "Charles Wilkes" in Allen Johnson and Dumas Malone, eds., *Dictionary of American Biography*, 20 vols. (New York: Charles Scribner's Sons, 1928-36) 20: 216-17.

Vincent Ponko, Jr.

WILKES EXPEDITION. *See* United States Exploring Expedition.

WILKINSON, DAVID (1831-1910). A linguist and government official in Fiji, Wilkinson arrived with his family to become the resident manager of the Fiji Stock and Trading Company, from Adelaide, South Australia, in 1861 after having previously migrated from England. The company's collapse two years after its establishment left Wilkinson in a precarious situation. Necessity, in part, led him to accept the position of interpreter-secretary-adviser to *Tui* Bau, chief of the independent kingdom of Bau. Together they drafted a series of laws which protected the rights of both Fijian and European members of Bau society.

Out of his friendship with *Tui* Bau and continuous daily intercourse with the Fijian people, Wilkinson acquired an unsurpassed knowledge of Fijian language and culture. His deep respect and admiration for the Fijians committed him to the cause of the preservation of the Fijian people's rights to land, independent culture, political expression, and continued existence as a race when these rights were threatened by the encroachment of European planter society.

Due to Wilkinson's linguistic skills and the degree of trust the chiefs placed upon his advice and judgment, he was selected in 1874 to be the interpreter to the cession delegation led by Sir Hercules Robinson. Much impressed by his work, Robinson recommended that he be appointed chief interpreter to the colony. In effect, Wilkinson transferred his position of interpreter from the Fijian chief to the colonial governor. As an independent official not bound to any single department, his position was one of considerable influence and power.

Wilkinson was held responsible by contemporary planter society for the protectionist policies of Sir Arthur Gordon's administration, especially those concerning land and labor which they particularly abhorred. Throughout his career as chief interpreter, Wilkinson also held positions as native commissioner, native lands commissioner, member of the legislative council, and justice of the peace. He also remained a planter, producing cotton, coffee, copra, and stock breeding. His friendship and business partnership with *Tui* Bau continued; it was said by some of his contemporaries to be the source of his pro-Fijian protectionism. His private career, however, was marred with tragedy such as the collapse of the cotton market, the destruction on two occasions of his home and plantation by fire, and the loss of his prize-winning coffee crop through disease. His only son was drowned at sea during a hurricane and thus left Wilkinson in his old age, and in ill health, responsible for his orphaned grandchildren.

As a practicing Methodist, Wilkinson also worked through his church for the improvement of the health, education, and welfare of the common Fijian, paying particular attention to improving the position of women. He believed these aims could be best achieved by the maintenance, rather than the destruction, of traditional customs and culture. To improve race relations, he arranged and led a course on Fijian language and culture and was responsible for the starting of a successful education scheme.

Although in his later years his personal credibility came to be challenged by Sir E. Im Thurn's attempts to reverse the protectionist policies which he had championed, Wilkinson continued to forward his advice on Fijian affairs to both the government and the church until his death.

RELATED ENTRIES: Fiji; Gordon, Arthur.

SOURCES AND READINGS: C. E. Gordon Cumming, *At Home in Fiji*, 2 vols. (London: Blackwood, 1881); Peter France, *The Charter of the Land: Custom and Colonization in Fiji* (Melbourne: Oxford University Press, 1969).   *Johanne M. Vincent*

WILLIAMS, JOHN (1796-1839). A missionary of the London Missionary Society, John Williams helped Christianize the Society Islands, Rurutu, Rarotonga, and Samoa. He was assassinated in his attempt to bring Christianity to Vanuatu (New Hebrides). Born 29 June 1796 in London, Williams with his wife arrived in the Pacific in 1817 where he spent most of his remaining life in the Society Islands of Mo'orea and Ra'iatea. His zeal, enthusiasm, and energy knew no bounds. He supervised the construction of a sixty-foot brigantine, the *Messenger of Peace*, to aid in the proselyting work. In 1830 he sailed to Savai'i (Samoa) where he landed a Samoan named Fauea and several Tahitian "teachers." After Williams returned in 1832 and visited the work in the eastern Samoan island of Tutuila, he left for England where he supervised the printing of his translation of the New Testament in Rarotongan (1834) and the printing of his famous *Narrative of Missionary Enterprises in the South Sea Islands*. This best-selling work sold 38,000 copies in five years. His glowing descriptions of Polynesia inspired subsequent generations of missionaries who later, however, became discouraged by the realities of Pacific life. Returning to the Pacific in 1839, Williams decided to push on to the New Hebrides where on 20 November 1839 he was attacked and killed by the men of Erromango. His remains repose at Upolu (Samoa). His love of the Polynesians, his knowledge of their languages, his interest and enthusiasm—all contributed to make him one of the greatest of the first generation of Christian missionaries to the South Pacific.

RELATED ENTRIES: American Samoa; French Polynesia; London Missionary Society; Western Samoa.

SOURCES AND READINGS: Gavan Daws, *A Dream of Islands: Voyages of Self-Discovery in the South Seas* (New York: W. W. Norton & Co., 1980); John Gutch, *Beyond the Reefs: The Life of John Williams, Missionary* (London: Macdonald, 1974); Ebenezer Prout, *Memoirs of the Life of the Reverend John Williams* (London: John Snow, 1843); John Williams, *A Narrative of Missionary Enterprises in the South Sea Islands* (London: G. Baxter, 1837).
                    Robert D. Craig

WILLIAMS, JOHN BROWN (1810-1860). John Brown Williams was a seaman, trader, U.S. consul to New Zealand and Fiji, and ethnographer. Born in Salem, Massachusetts, Williams was appointed U.S. consul at Bay of Islands, New Zealand, in 1843 and held a concurrent appointment as the U.S. commercial agent for Fiji in 1844—positions he retained until 1855 when he relinquished his New Zealand appointment. He reported in detail to the U.S. Department of State on political and economic conditions and the history and customs of the people of New Zealand and Fiji. He contributed artifacts to the National Museum (Smithsonian Institution) in Washington, D.C. and to the Essex Institute in Salem, Massachusetts. As a U.S. official, Williams received complaints of murder, arson, theft, and bodily injury; he documented indemnity claims against the Fijian chiefs for himself and his countrymen. When chiefs refused to pay claims, Williams presented them for review to each U.S. naval officer who visited Fiji; some upheld his demands, some considered them exorbitant. After Williams' death at Levuka on 10 June 1860, Cakobau, King of Fiji, accepted the overtures of William Pritchard, British consul, and entrepreneurs from Australia and New Zealand who settled the American indemnity claims in exchange for 200,000 acres of land in Fiji.

RELATED ENTRIES: Fiji; Pritchard, William.

SOURCES AND READINGS: Robert W. Kenney, *The New Zealand Journal, 1842-1844, of John Brown Williams of Salem, Massachusetts* (Salem: Peabody Museum and Brown University Press, 1956); Betthold C. Seeman, *Viti* (Cambridge: Macmillan Co., 1862); U.S. Department of State, Dispatches from Consuls at Bay of Islands, Auckland, and Laucala, National Archives, Washington, D.C.   *Rhoda E. A. Hackler*

WOODS, GEORGE AUSTIN, (?-1905). A political activist and land dealer in Fiji and Samoa, Woods, after serving in the Royal Navy and later as a coastal surveyor in the Australian colonies, arrived in Fiji in 1871 to survey shipping channels at Levuka. He immediately became involved in political intrigues and joined the settler-dominated Cakobau government as cabinet minister and later as premier. After cession in 1874, he practiced as an attorney and served as a postal officer and member of the marine board. Repeated disputes with the Crown Colony administration and ill feeling about his unpaid, pre-cession government service led to his falling out with Sir Arthur Gordon (1829-1912), the governor of Fiji. He had promoted the San Francisco-based Pacific Mail Steamship Company and acted as its Fiji agent. He was also involved in an unsuccessful scheme to take advantage of the Central Polynesian Land and Commercial Company's land claims in Samoa. He finally settled in Fiji as planter, attorney, and surveyor, and later died there.

RELATED ENTRIES: Central Polynesian Land and Commercial Company; Fiji; Gordon, Arthur; Micronesia.

SOURCES AND READINGS: Deryck Scarr, *I the Very Bayonet* (Canberra: Australian National University Press, 1973); A. M. Quanchi, "This Glorious Company: The Polynesia Company in Fiji and Victoria," (Master's thesis, Monash University, 1977).
Alan Maxwell Quanchi

WORLD WAR II BATTLES FOR THE GILBERT AND MARSHALL ISLANDS. The conflict that engulfed the world also came to the isolated, but strategically located, islands of the central Pacific. The Japanese had been awarded the formerly German-controlled Marshall Islands at the end of World War I. They captured the Gilberts at the outbreak of World War II. But until 1943, the island groups had been largely spared the ravages of the Allied-Japanese struggle in the Pacific. This was to change abruptly.

After containing the Japanese expansion eastward at the Battle of Midway and southward at Coral Sea, the Allies began a counteroffensive in late 1942. Under General Douglas MacArthur, the commander in chief, southwest Pacific, United States and Australian forces launched a major campaign to reconquer New Guinea. A return to the Philippines was the ultimate goal of this drive. U.S. military planners also began to consider other ways to bring growing United States power against the Japanese maritime defense perimeter.

Prewar planning for the strategic defense or recapture of the Philippine Islands, in the "Orange" War Plans, had consistently stressed the need to control the Marshall and Caroline groups. In 1943 a similar course of action still had appeal to strategists. By mid-year, Allied leaders had agreed to simultaneous offensives in the southwest Pacific and against the Micronesian islands. The Gilbert Islands were chosen as the site of the first amphibious landing. The Gilbert Islands were believed to be less strongly defended than the Marshall or Caroline islands and were within range of Allied land-based aircraft.

On 20 July 1943 the U.S. Joint Chiefs of Staff directed Admiral Chester W. Nimitz, commander in chief, Pacific Ocean Areas and commander in chief, U.S. Pacific Fleet, to begin planning for the Gilbert operation, code-named "Galvanic," to be conducted in November. Because they possessed vital airfields, two atolls would be stormed. Makin Atoll was already recognized as the site of the 1942 raid by Lieutenant Colonel Evans Carlson's Marine Raiders. The other atoll soon would become much more widely known —Tarawa.

During the second half of 1943, the Pacific command worked at a frenetic pace to prepare for the impending operation. In August, Vice Admiral Raymond A. Spruance, who had led American forces to victory at the Battle of Midway the year before, was placed in charge of "Galvanic" as Commander, Fifth Fleet. Under his command was the Fifth Amphibious Corps of quick-tempered but able Rear Admiral Richmond Kelly Turner. The ground troops of the Fifth Amphibious Corps were led by the equally irascible and skilled Marine Major General Holland M. ("Howlin' Mad") Smith.

In late October, Fifth Fleet task forces sortied from Hawai'i and the New Hebrides for their momentous rendezvous in the Gilbert Islands. A force composed of over 100,000 soldiers, sailors, and marines and 200 ships, carrying 6,000 vehicles and 117,000 tons of cargo, stood ready to simultaneously seize the two strategic atolls by force of arms.

The bloody fight for Tarawa would sorely test the validity of the concept for conducting amphibious landings on island bastions. Betio Island, containing the atoll's airstrip, was heavily fortified and defended by over 4,500 elite and determined Japanese troops. As dawn broke over the eastern horizon, on 20 November, carrier aircraft and the guns of three battleships, five cruisers, and numerous destroyers rocked the island with their fire. However, the ship and air bombardment was too short and too inaccurate and uncoordinated with the boat waves. The dug in Japanese defenders remained a lethal force. After assembling offshore, the assault waves, carrying combat units of the veteran Second Marine Division, made for the beach. A serious situation arose when the landing vehicles attempted to cross the coral reef, which lay exposed after an unexpectedly low tide. Many of the amphibious tractors (LVTs) in the first three waves managed to reach the beach, but following landing craft were unable to navigate the coral obstacle. The Japanese defense came alive and took a terrible toll of marines caught off shore or pinned down at the edge of the beach. However, the marines had gained a tenuous lodgement.

In the next several days the landing forces weathered many crises, but marine valor and the combined weight of U.S. air and naval support eventually overcame the diminishing number of Japanese defenders. By the afternoon of 23 November 1943 the island was secured. But the cost had been high. After four days of battle, over one thousand marines and sailors were dead and over two thousand were wounded.

The landing on Makin's Butaritari Island bore little resemblance to that on Betio. Although sixty-four men were killed and 150 wounded, the U.S. ground commander was able to signal Admiral Turner at 1300 on 23 November that Makin was secured.

The American public was dismayed at the heavy casualties of the battle for Tarawa, but the soundness of the amphibious assault concept had been borne out. In addition, the ability of carrier task forces to protect landings from serious enemy air and naval interference had been reaffirmed. The Gilberts operation had been essential as the combat testing ground for these developing methods of warfare.

The lessons learned in "Galvanic" were soon applied to "Flintlock," the operation to retake the Marshall Islands in early 1944. Aerial and submarine reconnaissance of the objectives—Majuro, Kwajalein, and Eniwetok atolls—was greatly increased. Study of Japanese fortifications and gun emplacements on Betio indicated what U.S. weapons were effective against them.

The planning for "Flintlock" provided for a greater volume of more precise, phased, and coordinated naval and aerial bombardment. Unoccupied islets near the target islands would be taken prior to D-Day and artillery batteries would be emplaced to support the main landings. New and improved equipment and weapons, from amphibious command ships (AGCs) and LVTs to flamethrowers, were obtained. Landing tactics and techniques and communication procedures were refined as a result of the Tarawa experience.

At the end of January 1944, the U.S. central Pacific force of almost 300 ships and 54,000 assault troops sailed toward its next objective, the Marshall Islands. The Fast Carrier Force (TF-58), now under a long-time naval aviator, Rear Admiral Marc A. Mitscher, displayed the inherent strength of the aircraft carrier. Between 29 January and 1 February the skies over the Marshalls were cleared of enemy planes. Tactical air superiority was absolute.

On 31 January the Fifth Fleet established an advanced air and naval base off Majuro Atoll for subsequent support of "Flintlock." That same day, U.S. troops stormed islets needed to provide artillery platforms for the main landings. On 1 February, in simultaneous assaults, Rear Admiral Richard L. Connolly's Northern Attack Force landed the Fourth Marine Division on Roi-Namur Island at one end of Kwajalein Atoll while the Seventh Infantry Division of Rear Admiral Turner's Southern Attack Force hit Kwajalein Island at the other end. By 4 February both islands were in U.S. possession. American casualties were 372 dead and 1,582 wounded, in marked contrast to the Japanese loss of 8,000 men.

Although Roi-Namur and Kwajalein were defended by a larger garrison and were as heavily fortified as

Betio had been, U.S. casualties were considerably lower in the Marshall's action. U.S. commanders had learned much from Tarawa. The amphibious operations for Kwajalein Atoll, as well as the subsequent fight for Eniwetok Atoll, were carried out with an unprecedented degree of precision, coordination, and skill. "Flintlock" demonstrated that U.S. Pacific forces had mastered the art of amphibious warfare. A seaward advance on Japan had become a viable future course of action. Indeed, the capture of the Gilberts and Marshalls presaged the doom of the Japanese Pacific empire.

RELATED ENTRIES: Defense Planning for Oceania between the Wars; Kiribati; Micronesia; Nimitz, Chester; Oceania, Strategic Importance of since 1945; Spruance, Raymond; War in the Pacific Islands 1914-1945.

SOURCES AND READINGS: George C. Dyer, *The Amphibians Came to Conquer: The Story of Admiral Richmond Kelly Turner*, vol. 2 (Washington, D.C.: Government Printing Office, 1972); Jeter A. Isely and Philip A. Crowl, *The U.S. Marines and Amphibious War: Its Theory, and Its Practice in the Pacific* (Princeton: Princeton University Press, 1951); Samuel E. Morison, *Aleutians, Gilberts and Marshalls: June 1942-April 1944* (Boston: Little, Brown & Co., 1951), vol. 7, *History of United States Naval Operations in World War II*; Henry I. Shaw, Jr., Bernard C. Nalty, and Edwin T. Turnbladh, *Central Pacific Drive* (Washington, D.C.: Government Printing Office, 1966), vol. 3, *History of U.S. Marine Corps Operations in World War II*.

Edward J. Marolda

XAVIER HIGH SCHOOL. A four-year boarding school owned by the Catholic bishop of Micronesia, Xavier High School is located on Moen Island, Truk, Federated States of Micronesia, and is operated by the Society of Jesus. The school's main building was formerly a communication center built by the Japanese military during World War II on confiscated mission property. In 1952 the mission's claim to the property was recognized by U.S. administrators, and the school was opened soon after completion of renovations. Until 1976, when female students were first admitted, the school was an all-male institution. Since its inception, more than 350 graduates of Xavier have occupied prominent positions in business and government throughout the islands.

Enrollment at Xavier is usually between 110 and 120 students from all districts of Micronesia. English is the language of instruction. Male students board at the school, but female students live on Moen Island with relatives or sponsors and commute daily to the school. Tuition has been $200 per year, per student, while boarding students pay an additional $125 per year.

The curriculum at Xavier is strongly academic, aimed at developing a student's ability to think critically. The curriculum also prepares a student for studies beyond high school, and approximately 80 percent of each graduating class have traditionally gone on to postsecondary schools. Membership in the Catholic church is not a qualification for admission to Xavier. At present, about 35 percent of the student body is non-Catholic. While religious instruction is required of all students, emphasis is on human growth and development in relation to God and does not stress doctrinal differences.

RELATED ENTRIES: Education in the Pacific, Higher; Micronesia; Micronesian Seminar. *Francis X. Hezel*

YASUR VOLCANO. A cinder cone of 361 m (1,184 ft) in east Tanna, Vanuatu (New Hebrides), Yasur volcano has been observed to be in continuous Stromboli-type volcanic eruption since first being described by James Cook in 1774. A popular climb for nineteenth-century visitors, it remains one of the most popular tourist attractions in Vanuatu. It is described as the world's most accessible volcano.

RELATED ENTRIES: Tanna; Vanuatu (New Hebrides).
Lamont C. Lindstrom

YOUNG, JOHN (ca. 1742-1835). A beachcomber in Hawai'i, John Young was probably an Englishman, but both his place and date of birth are disputed. He arrived in Hawai'i in 1790 as bosun of the *Eleanora* commanded by Captain Simon Metcalfe. He was detained on shore on the orders of King Kamehameha I who wanted a white man to assist him in his relationships with foreigners. Young became a close friend and trusted advisor and aide to Kamehameha. He controlled the use of cannon in Kamehameha's battles, and was governor of O'ahu in 1796 after its conquest and of Hawai'i at various times after 1800. Young and his friend, Isaac Davis, were the most prominent of Kamehameha's white men. Their influence on Kamehameha during his long reign was greater than that of any other foreigner. Young was twice married: first to Namokuelua (died 1804) and second to Kaonaeha, a niece of Kamehameha. His children were prominent in Hawaiian society: his second son Kanehoa (James) was variously governor of Maui and Kaua'i, his third son Keoni Ana (John) was the companion of Kamehameha III and a member of the cabinet, and his granddaughter, Emma, was Kamehameha IV's queen. Young died on 17 December 1835. His funeral was that of a high chief of Hawai'i.

RELATED ENTRIES: Beachcombers; Campbell, Archibald; Davis, Isaac; Hawai'i; Kamehameha I.

SOURCES AND READINGS: R. S. Kuykendall, *The Hawaiian Kingdom, 1778-1854: Foundation and Transformation* (Honolulu: University of Hawaii Press, 1938).
Ian C. Campbell

APPENDIXES

APPENDIX 1
Summary Guide to the Pacific, 1980–1981

Territory	Capital	Population†	Predominant Languages Spoken
American Samoa	Pago Pago	30,600	Samoan*/English
Australia	Canberra	14,248,000	English
Commonwealth of the Northern Mariana Islands††	Garapan	18,349	Chamorro**/English
Cook Islands	Avarua	19,000	Cook Island Maori*/English
Easter Island (Rapanui)	Hanga Roa	2,100	Rapanui*/Spanish
Federated States of Micronesia††	Ponape	77,192	English/Dialects of Malaysian
Fiji Islands	Suva	632,000	Fiji/Hindustani/English
French Polynesia	Pape'ete	140,000	Tahitian*/French/& other Polyn. dialects
Galapagos	Puerto Baquerizo	4,058	Spanish
Guam	Agana	115,000	Chamorro**/English
Hawai'i	Honolulu	901,000	English
Kiribati	Tarawa	56,452	Gilbertese/English
Marshall Islands†	Majuro	32,427	Marshallese**/English
Nauru	. . . .	7,254	Nauruan/English
New Caledonia	Noumea	139,600	Melanesian dialect/French
New Zealand	Wellington	3,145,900	Maori*/English
Niue	Alofi	3,578	Niuean*/English
Norfolk Island	Kingston	1,825	English
Palau	Koror	14,800	Palauan**/English
Papua New Guinea	Port Moresby	2,990,757	Melanesian dialects/Pidgin/English
Pitcairn Island	Adamstown	70	Tahitian*/English
Solomon Islands	Honiara	206,000	Melanesian dialects/Pidgin/English
Tokelau	. . . .	1,687	Tokelauan*/English
Tonga	Nuku'alofa	92,360	Tongan*/English
Torres Strait	Thursday Island	6,100	Miriam/Mabuiag/English
Tuvalu (Ellice Islands)	Funafuti	7,357	Tuvaluan*/English
Vanuatu (New Hebrides)	Vila	112,596	Pidgin/French/English
Wake Island	. . . .	400	English
Wallis and Futuna	Mata Uta	9,700	Wallisian*/French
Western Samoa	Apia	155,000	Samoan*/English

SOURCES: *Pacific Islands Year Book*, 13th ed. (Sydney: Pacific Publications, 1978); *Far East and Australasia: A Survey and Directory of Asia and the Pacific* (London: Europa Publications, 1979).

†Population figures are the most recent census or from official estimates.
††U.S. Trust Territories of the Pacific Islands negotiating for new political status.
*Polynesian
**Micronesian

Type of Government	Area km²	Area sq. miles
Unincorporated U.S. territory	197	76
Independent state, member of British Commonwealth	7,686,850	2,967,896
American commonwealth	477	184
Self-governing, in free association with New Zealand	240	93
Dependency of Chile	156	60
Independent state in free association with the United States	1,195	461
Independent state, member of British Commonwealth	18,272	7,055
Autonomous overseas territory of France	4,014	1,550
Province of Equador	7,812	3,016
Unincorporated U.S. territory	554	214
State of the United States	16,770	6,475
Independent state, member of British Commonwealth	719	278
Independent state in free association with the United States	202	78
Independent state, member of British Commonwealth	22	8.5
Overseas territory of France	19,050	7,355
Independent state, member of British Commonwealth	268,704	103,747
Self-governing state in affiliation with New Zealand	258	100
Australian territory	35	13.5
Negotiating free-association status with the United States	487	188
Independent state, member of British Commonwealth	476,500	183,977
British dependency	5	2
Independent state, member of British Commonwealth	28,530	11.015
New Zealand dependency	10	3.8
Independent kingdom, member of British Commonwealth	697	269
Australian possession	650	251
Independent state, member of British Commonwealth	26	10
Independent state	14,763	5,700
U.S. possession	12	4.6
French territory	274	105
Independent state, member of British Commonwealth	2,934	1,133

	Melanesia	Micronesia
1500		
1510		
1520		Magellan lands on Guam, Marianas (1521)
	Portuguese land in Papua (1526)	Loaysa sights Marshall Islands (1526)
1530		
1540		
1550		
1560		Spain takes part of Marianas (1565)
	Mendaña sights Solomon Islands (1568)	
1570		
1580		
1590		
	Mendaña lands on Santa Cruz, Solomon Islands (1595)	
1600		

Polynesia	World Events	
	Agreement of Tordesillas (1494)	1500
	Balboa, first European to see Pacific (1513)	
		1510
	Cortés invades Mexico (1519)	1520
	Treaty of Saragossa (1529)	1530
		1540
		1550
	Portuguese trade at Macao begins (1557)	1560
Mendaña sights Nui, Tuvalu (1568)		
		1570
		1580
		1590
Mendaña visits Marquesas, sights the northern Cook Islands (1595)		
	English East India Company established (1600)	1600
	Dutch United East India Company established (1602)	

Melanesia	Micronesia
Quirós visits New Hebrides (1606)	Quirós sights Gilbert Islands (1606)
1610	
1620	
1630	
1640	
Tasman visits Fiji (1643)	
1650	
1660	
1670	Jesuit missionaries arrive in Guam and Marianas (1668) Guamanian revolt against Jesuits (1670) Spanish-Chamorros War (1672-1700)
1680	
1690	
	Northern Mariana peoples moved to Guam (1695)
1700	
1710	Spanish exploration of Carolines (1710)
1720	

Polynesia	World Events	
		1610
Schouten and LeMaire visit Futuna and Tonga (1616)	Thirty Years War (1618-1648)	
	Pilgrims arrive in Plymouth (1620)	1620
		1630
	Europeans expelled from Japan (1637)	
		1640
	Manchu Dynasty in China established (1644)	
		1650
		1660
		1670
		1680
		1690
	Bank of England established (1695)	
		1700
		1710
		1720
Roggeveen sights Samoa and Easter islands (1722)		

Melanesia	Micronesia
1730	
1740	
1750	
1760	
Carteret claims New Guinea for Britain, sights Solomon Islands (1767)	Wallis visits Marshall Islands (1767)
1770	Jesuits expelled from Guam; Spanish colonial rule begins under viceroy of New Spain (1769)
Cook visits New Caledonia, New Hebrides (1774)	
1780	
	Antelope wrecks on Palau, crew makes way to Philippines (1783)
Lapérouse lost at sea (1788)	Captain Marshall explores islands and names them (1787)
Mutiny on the *Bounty* (1789)	
1790	
Bligh visits Fiji (1792)	
1800 Sandalwood trade in Fiji (1800-1814)	
1805	
1810	
	Spanish-galleon Pacific trade via Guam ceases (1812)
1815	
	Kotzbue surveys Marshalls (1817, 1824)
1820	American whalers begin visiting Micronesia (1820)

Polynesia	World Events	
		1730
		1740
		1750
	Seven Years' War (1756-1763)	
		1760
Wallis visits Tahiti and Wallis islands (1767) Cook arrives in Tahiti (1769)		
		1770
Cook sights Hawai'i (1778) Cook is killed in Hawai'i (1779)	American Revolution (1775-83) Adam Smith's *Wealth of Nations* (1776)	
		1780
Lapérouse loses 12 crew in Samoa (1787) First convicts sent to Australia (1787) *Bounty* Mutiny (1789)		
		1790
LMS missionaries arrive in Tahiti, Tonga, and Marquesas (1797) Tahitian Civil War; Tongan Civil War (1799)	French Revolution (1789-1799)	
Pomare I dies, son in exile (1803)		1800
	Napoleon becomes emperor (1804)	1805
Kamehameha I of Hawai'i establishes personal rule over Hawai'i (1810)		1810
	War of 1812 between U.S. and England	
Pomare I accepts Christianity; Russia attempts intrusion into Hawai'i (1815)	Congress of Vienna (1814) Battle of Waterloo, Napoleon's exile (1815)	1815
	Revolution in Latin America (1817-1825)	
Kamehameha I dies and Hawaiian *kapu* abolished; De Peyster sights Tuvalu (1819) ABCFM missionaries in Hawai'i; Bellinghausen surveys Tuamotus (1820) Protestant missionaries in Cooks (1821), Tonga (1822)	 Monroe Doctrine (1823)	1820

Melanesia	Micronesia
	Duperrey's survey of Carolines (1824)
1825 Sandalwood found in New Hebrides (1825)	Administration of Guam shifts to Philippines under Spanish rule (1825)
Dutch annex western New Guinea (Irian Jaya)	
1830 Tahitian Protestant missionaries land in Fiji (1830)	
1835 LMS Protestant missionaries arrive in Fiji (1835)	
LMS missionaries to New Hebrides (1839)	
1840 Catholic missionaries arrive in New Caledonia; Samoan missionaries in New Hebrides (1840)	
Catholic missionaries arrive in Fiji (1844)	
1845 Unsuccessful Catholic mission to Solomon Islands (1845)	
First recruitment of laborers from New Hebrides to New South Wales (1847)	
Anglican missionaries in New Hebrides (1848)	
1850	U.S. Protestant missionaries in Carolines (1852)
France seizes New Caledonia (1853)	
Tui Viti Cakobau in Fiji adopts Christianity (1854)	
1855	United States establishes consulate in Guam (1855)
First British consul, W. Pritchard, arrives in Fiji (1858)	U.S. missionaries in Gilberts and Marshalls (1857)
1860	
Discovery of nickel in New Caledonia (1863)	
French convicts sent to New Caledonia (1864)	
1865 Recruitment of laborers in New Hebrides (1864)	
Recruitment of laborers in Solomons (1868)	
1870 Cakobau establishes national monarchy (1870)	Germany acquires land in Carolines (1869)
Gold rush begins in New Caledonia (1870)	
Britain passes act to stop blackbirding (1872)	
1875 Fiji ceded to Great Britain, Hercules Robinson becomes first governor (1875)	
New Caledonian uprising against the French (1878)	Germany acquires coaling station in Marshalls (1878)
Fiji sugar industry acquires 498 Indian laborers (1879)	
1880 Australia establishes sugar company in Fiji	
France controls New Hebrides (1882)	

Polynesia	World Events	
Kamehameha II visits England and dies there (1824)		
		1825
French Catholic missionaries arrive in Hawai'i (1872)		
Protestant missionaries arrive in Samoa; Malietoa Vaiinupo of Savai'i becomes king (1830)	Vatican establishes Prefecture Apostolic of South Seas islands (1830)	1830
	Charles Darwin sails on the *Beagle* (1831)	
French Catholic missionaries in Mangareva (1834)		
Catholic missionaries arrive in Tahiti, are expelled (1836); Commercial agreement, France-Hawai'i (1836)		1835
	Vicariate Apostolic of Western Oceania created (1836)	
Catholics in Wallis (1837); U.S. commercial treaty with Samoa (1839)	Opium War (1839-1842, England and China)	
D'Urville forces freedom of Catholics in Hawai'i (1839)		
In Hawai'i, Kamehameha III establishes constitutional monarchy (1840)		1840
France annexes Marquesas; protectorate over Tahiti and dependencies (1842)		
British sea captain Paulet seizes Hawai'i, but cession revoked (1843)		1845
Tongan chief Taufa'ahau becomes King George (1845)		
G. Pritchard first British consul in Samoa (1847)		
Land division (*Mahele*) in Hawai'i (1848)		
		1850
Tongan King George I supreme (1852)		
	Japan opens door to West (1854)	1855
Godeffroy & Sohn commercial agency established in Apia (1856)		
		1860
Tuvaluans carried off to work in Peru (1860)	American Civil War (1861-1865)	
LMS missionaries in Tuvalu from Cooks (1861)		
Tongan code of laws established (1862)		
First Chinese laborers arrive in Hawai'i (1865)	Austrian, Italian, Prussian war (1866)	1865
	United States occupies Midway Island; Russia sells Alaska to United States (1867)	
	Suez Canal opened; completion of U.S. transcontinental railroad (1869)	
LMS missionaries in Tuvalu (1870)	Paris Commune; German Empire (1871)	1870
United States signs treaty with Samoans (1872)		
Malietoa Laupepe becomes "king of Samoa" (1873)		
Britain annexes Fiji (1874)		
United States-Hawai'i reciprocal trade treaty; first LMS missionaries in Papua (1876)	Third French Republic; Disraeli purchases Suez shares of stock (1875)	1875
First Japanese laborers arrive in Hawai'i (1878)	Victoria named Empress of India (1876)	
Britain establishes naval station in Samoa (1879)	Congress of Berlin (1878)	
France annexes Tahiti and dependencies (1880)		1880
	Triple Alliance: Germany, Italy, Austria (1882)	

	Melanesia	**Micronesia**
	Britain takes southwest New Guinea; Germany takes northeast (1884)	
1885	German New Guinea colonizes islands in Solomons (1885)	Dispute between Spain and Germany over Carolines (1885)
	Anglo-French joint naval commission for New Hebrides; Chile annexes Easter Island (1888)	Germany takes Marshalls, Spain takes Carolines (1886)
	Gold fields open in New Guinea; British protectorate over New Guinea (1889)	Caroline islanders revolt (1887)
		Catholics in Gilbert Islands (1888)
1890		
	Britain declares protectorate over Gilbert and Ellice Islands (1892); over the Solomons (1893)	British protectorate over Gilberts (1892)
1895		
		United States seizes Guam and Philippines (1898)
		Spain sells Marshalls, Carolines, and Northern Marianas to Germany (1899)
1900		Phosphate discovered on Ocean Island, which is annexed by Great Britain (1900)
	Fijian representation allowed in legislative council (1904)	
1905	Papua Act establishes Australian control over British New Guinea (1905)	
	Anglo-French condominium in New Hebrides (1906)	
1910		
	World War I begins, Australia gains German New Guinea and Nauru (1914)	Japan gains German colonies: Marianas, Marshalls, Carolines (1914)
1915		Great Britain annexes Gilbert and Ellice Islands Colony (1915)
		Advisory council of Guamanians established (1917)
1920	League of Nations gives Australia mandate over German New Guinea (1920)	
1925		
	First Indian representative elected to Fijian legislative assembly (1929)	
1930		
		Guam gains an elected Congress (1931)
		Japan annexes Micronesian states (1932)
1935		Japan withdraws from United Nations, establishes military in Micronesia (1935)
1940	World War II begins in Europe. Gaullists take over French territories (1940)	
		Guam occupied by the Japanese (1941)

Polynesia	World Events
Kalakaua and Kapiolani of Hawai'i crowned (1883)	
	Berlin conference; Germany establishes African state (1884)
	1885
Free Church of Tonga established (1885)	
Kalakaua seeks Samoan confederation (1886)	
Wallis Islands become French protectorate (1887)	
Hurricane in Samoa; Britain, United States, Germany hold Berlin conference (1889)	Berlin conference (United States, England, Germany); Japan's new constitution (1889)
Basil Thompson becomes prime minister of Tonga (1890)	1890
Kalakaua dies, Lili'uokalani becomes queen (1891)	Women's suffrage in New Zealand (1893)
Gilbert and Ellice Islands become British protectorate (1892)	
Hawai'i revolution; George Tupou II becomes Tongan king (1893)	Sino-Japanese War (1894)
Republic established in Hawai'i (1894)	1895
United States annexes Hawai'i (1898)	Spanish-American War (1898)
Tripartite Convention; phosphate found on Ocean Island (Nauru) (1899)	Filipinos rebel against United States (1899-1902)
	Boxer Rebellion in China (1900)
New Zealand annexes Cooks; France annexes Australs (1900)	Commonwealth of Australia formed (1901)
	1900
Britain gains control over Tonga's external affairs (1901)	Britain holds Imperial Conference (1902)
	Entente Cordiale (Britain and France 1904)
	Russo-Japanese War (1904)
	Russian Revolution (1905)
	1905
	Triple Entente (France, Russia, England 1907)
Western Samoan revolt, men deported to Mariana Islands (1908)	
	Japan annexes Korea (1910)
	1910
	Chinese Revolution, end of Manchu Dynasty (1911)
	Republic of China proclaimed (1912)
Wallis Islands become French protectorate (1913)	
	Panama Canal opens; World War I begins (1914)
World War I begins: New Zealand seizes Western Samoa (1914)	
	1915
Gilbert and Ellice Islands become British colony (1916)	
	Communist Revolution in Russia (1917)
Influenza epidemic; Sālote becomes Queen of Tonga (1918)	Treaty of Versailles (1919)
League of Nations mandate given to colonial powers for control of Pacific islands (1920)	League of Nations established (1920-1946)
	1920
	Washington Conference (1921)
Union of Free Church of Tonga and Wesleyan church (1924)	Dictatorship of Stalin (1924-1953)
	1925
	Chiang Kai-shek unites China (1928)
Mau uprising in Apia (1929)	The Great Depression (1929)
	1930
	Nazi revolution in Germany; World Economic Conference; Japan walks out of League of Nations (1933)
	Commonwealth of Philippines (1935)
	1935
	Spanish Civil War (1936)
	War between Japan and China (1937)
	World War II begins in Europe (1939-1945)
	1940
Japan bombs Pearl Harbor, United States declares war (1941)	Tojo becomes premier of Japan (1941)
United States establishes bases on Funafuti (1942)	

	Melanesia	Micronesia
1945	New Guinea becomes Australian trust territory (1945) New Caledonia becomes French overseas territory; anti-colonial movements in Solomons (1946). South Pacific Commission (1947) Merger of Papua and New Guinea (1949)	U.S. awarded trust territories in Micronesia (1945) Bikini Atoll nuclear tests (1946) Eniwetok Atoll nuclear tests (1947) South Pacific Commission established (1947) Organic Act of Guam (1950) U.S. Department of the Interior administers trust territories (1951)
1950	Reform of government in New Guinea (1951)	
1955		
1960	Legislative and executive councils in Solomons (1960) Solomon Islands constitution; House of Assembly for Papua New Guinea, elections held (1964)	Guam gains first appointed Guamanian governor (1960) Mariana Islands under U.S. Department of the Interior (1962) Gilbertese gain voice in government (1963) Congress of Micronesia held (1965)
1965	Constitution adopted in Fiji; first political organization in New Hebrides (1966) Nauru becomes independent state (1968)	Gilbert and Ellice Islands gain assembly; Future Political Status Commission established in Micronesia (1967)
1970	Independence of Fiji; legislative assembly in Solomon Islands (1970) New Hebrides press for independence (1971) Papua New Guinea name change (1972) Fiji nationalizes sugar (1973)	Guam's first elected governor (1971) Marshallese and United States begin talks regarding political status (1974)
1975	Solomon Islands constitution (1974) Papua New Guinea's independence; National Party in New Hebrides wins (1975) Solomon Islands independence (1978)	Plebiscite establishes Commonwealth of the Northern Mariana Islands (1975) Ellice Islands independence (Tuvalu, 1975) Marshall Islands elect own president; Gilberts become Republic of Kiribati (1979)
1980	New Hebrides becomes independent state of Vanuatu (1980)	

Polynesia	World Events	
World War II ends (1945)	United Nations established; atom bomb dropped on Japan (1945)	1945
	Philippines independence (1946)	
Tahitians demand more say in government; Western Samoa prepares for independence (1947)	Korean Republic proclaimed (1948)	
	Korean War (1950-1953)	1950
	Korean Armistice signed (1953)	
		1955
Western Samoan Amendment Act (1957)	Egypt seizes and nationalizes Suez Canal (1956)	
Hawai'i becomes U.S. 50th state; Wallis and Futuna become French territories (1959)	European Common Market formed; Malaysia becomes independent (1957)	
Western Samoan constitution (1960)		1960
Western Samoan independence (1962)		
French nuclear tests on Moruroa (1963)		
	Vietnam War begins (1964)	
Cook Islands independence; Queen Sālote of Tonga dies (1965)		1965
		1970
Tonga becomes independent (1970)		
	Paris Accord ends Vietnam War (1973)	
Niue gains self-government (1974)		1975
Gilbert and Ellice Islands separated; Ellice Islands become Tuvalu (1975)		
Western Samoa joins United Nations (1976)	Death of Mao Tse-tung (1976)	
Internal autonomy to French Polynesia (1977)		
Tuvalu becomes independent (1978)		
		1980
U.S. trusteeship of the Pacific Islands ends (1981)		

APPENDIX 3
Prehistoric Settlements of Oceania

	Melanesia	Micronesia	Polynesia
20,000	Papua New Guinea		
2,000	New Caledonia	Northern Marianas	
1,800			
1,600		Saipan	
1,400	New Hebrides		
1,200	Fiji		Tonga
1,000	Solomons	Palau and Yap	Samoa
800			
600			
400			
200			
0			
200			Marquesas (200-300)
400			Easter Island (400) Society Islands (500-600)
600			Hawai'i (500-600)
800			Cook Islands (800)
1,000			New Zealand (1100-1350)
1,200			

Before Christ (upper section) / *After Christ* (lower section)

SOURCE: Peter Bellwood, *Man's Conquest of the Pacific* (New York: Oxford University Press, 1979).

Chronology: European Explorers of the Pacific Islands

1520	Ferdinand Magellan (1520-1522, Spain)	1767	Samuel Wallis (1767-1768, Britain)
1527	Alvaro de Saavedra Cerón (1527-1529, Spain)		Philip Carteret (1767-1768, Britain)
1542	Ruy López de Villalobos (1542-1543, Spain)	1768	James Cook (1768-1771, 1772-1775, 1776-1780, Britain)
1567	Alvaro de Mendaña (1567-1569, 1595, Spain)	1772	Domingo de Boenechea (1772-1775, Spain)
1577	Sir Francis Drake (1577-1578, Britain)	1785	Jean F. Lapérouse (1785-1788, France)
		1787	William Bligh (1787-1789, 1791-1793, Britain)
1605	Pedro Quirós (1605-1606, Spain)	1790	Alessandro Malaspina (1790-1793, Spain)
1606	Luis Váez de Torres (1606-1607, Spain)		Êtienne Marchand (1790-1792, France)
1616	Jacob Le Maire, William C. Schouten (1616, Holland)	1791	George Vancouver (1791-1795, Britain)
1639	Abel J. Tasman (1639, 1642-1644, Holland)	1798	Matthew Flinders (1798, 1801-1803, Britain)
1679	William Dampier (1679-1691, 1699-1700, Britain)		
		1803	Adam Krusenstern (1803-1806, Russia)
1722	Jacob Roggeveen (1722, Holland)	1815	Otto von Kotzbue (1815-1818, Russia)
1766	Louis Antoine de Bougainville (1766-1769, France)	1817	Louis Freycinet (1817-1820, France)

Rulers and Administrators

ADMINISTRATORS OF THE PACIFIC ISLANDS—AMERICAN SAMOA

(First administered under the U.S. Department of the Navy, then in 1950 under the U.S. Department of the Interior)

U.S. Naval Governors

Commander B. R. Tilley (1900-01)
Captain U. Sebree (1901-02)
Lieutenant Commander H. Minett (Acting 1902-04)
Commander E. B. Underwood (1904-05)
Commander C. B. T. Moors (1905-08)
Captain John F. Parker (1908-10)
Commander W. M. Gross (1910-13)
Lieutenant N. W. Post (1913-14)
Commander C. B. Stearns (1914)
Lieutenant N. W. Post (Acting 1914)
Lieutenant C. A. Woodruff (Acting 1914-15)
Commander John M. Poyer (1915-19)
Commander Warren J. Terhune (1919-20)
Captain Waldo Evans (1920-22)
Captain Edwin T. Pollock (1922-23)
Captain Edward S. Kellogg (1923-25)
Captain Henry F. Bryan (1925-27)
Captain Stephen V. Graham (1927-29)
Captain Gatewood S. Lincoln (1929-31)
Commander James S. Spore (1931)
Lieutenant Commander Arthur Emerson (Acting 1931)
Captain Gatewood S. Lincoln (1931-32)
Captain George B. Landergerber (1932-34)
Lieutenant Commander T. C. Latimore (Acting 1934)
Captain Otto Dowling (1934-36)
Lieutenant Commander T. B. Fitzpatrick (Acting 1936)
Captain MacGillvray Milne (1936-38)
Captain Edward Hanson (1938-40)
Lieutenant Commander J. R. Wallace (Acting 1940)
Captain Lawrence Wild (1940-42)
Captain John G. Moyer (1942-44)
Captain Allen Hobbs (1944-45)
Captain Ralph W. Hungerford (1945)
Commander Samuel W. Cana (Acting 1945)
Captain Harold A. Houser (1945-47)
Captain Vernon Huber (1947-49)
Captain Thomas F. Darden (1949-51)

Civil Governors

Phelps Phelps (1951-52)
John C. Elliott (1952)
James Arthur Ewing (1952-53)

Lawrence M. Judd (1953)
Richard B. Lowe (1953-56)
Peter Tali Coleman (1956-61)
H. Rex Lee (1961-67)
Owen S. Aspinall (1967-69)
John M. Haydon (1969-74)
Frank C. Mockler (Acting 1974-75)
Earl B. Ruth (1975-76)
Frank Barnett (Acting 1977-78)

Elected Governor

Peter Tali Coleman (1978-)

ADMINISTRATORS OF THE PACIFIC ISLANDS—COOK ISLANDS

(Prior to independence in 1965 the islands were administered through a resident commissioner from New Zealand)

Resident Commissioners

Colonel W. E. Gudgeon (1901-09)
Captain J. Eman Smith (1909-13)
W. H. Northcroft (1913-16)
F. W. Platts (1916-21)
J. G. L. Hewitt (1921-22)
Judge H. F. Ayson (1922-37)
S. J. Smith (1937-38)
Judge H. F. Ayson (1938-43)
W. Tailby (1943-51)
Geoffrey Nevill (1951-60)
Albert O. Dare (1961-65)
L. J. Davis (1965-73)

Premiers

Albert R. Henry (1965-78)
Dr. Tom Davis (1978-)

ADMINISTRATORS OF THE PACIFIC ISLANDS—FIJI

(Administered as a British Crown Colony until independence in 1970)

Governors

Hercules Robinson (1874-75)
Arthur H. Gordon (1875-80)
G. W. Des Voeux (1880-87)

C. B. H. Mitchell (1887-88)
John B. Thurston (1888-97)
G. T. H. O'Brien (1897-1902)
Henry M. Jackson (1902-04)
Everard im Thurn (1904-11)
Henry May (1911-12)
Ernest B. S. Escott (1912-18)
Cecil Hunter Rodwell (1918-25)
Eyre Hutson (1925-29)
A. G. Murchison Fletcher (1929-36)
Arthur F. Richards (1936-38)
Major General Philip E. Mitchell (1942-45)
Alexander W. G. H. Grantham (1945-47)
L. Brian Freeston (1947-52)
Ronald Garvey (1952-58)
Kenneth Phipson Maddocks (1958-64)
Derek Jakeway (1964-70)

Governors-General

Robert Foster (1970-73)
Ratu Sir George Cakobau (1973-)

Prime Minister

Ratu Sir Kamisese Mara (1970-)

RULERS AND ADMINISTRATORS OF THE PACIFIC ISLANDS—FRENCH POLYNESIA

Rulers

King Pomare I (c. 1743-1803)
King Pomare II (1803-21)
King Pomare III (1821-27)
Queen Pomare IV (1827-77)
King Pomare V (1877-91)

Naval Administrators

Armand Joseph Bruat (1843-46)
Charles F. Lavaud (1846-49)
Louis B. Bonard (1849-51)
Théogène F. Page (1851-54)
Joseph Du Bouzet (1854-58)
Jean-Marie Saisset (1858)
Gaultier de la Richerie (1858-64)
Emile de la Roncière (1864-69)
Michel de Jouslard (1869-71)
Hippolyte Girard (1871-?)
O. B. Gilbert-Pierre (?-1876)
Antoine Michaux (1876-77)
Joseph H. Brunet-Millet (1877)
Paul Serre (1877)
Auguste d'Oncieu de la Bathie (1877-78)
Jacques F. Planche (1878-80)
Isidore Chessé (1880-81)

Governors

Frédérick-Jean Dorlodot des Essarts (1881-83)
M. N. Morau (1883-85)
Duapin Moracchini (1885-86)
Étienne T. Lacascade (1886-89)
Maurice d'Ingremard (1889-90)
Étienne T. Lacasade (1890-93)
Adolphe Granier de Cassaignac (1893)

Lucien J. Bommier (1893)
Jean J. Ours (1893-94)
Pierre L. Papinaud (1894-96)
Gustave P. Gallet (1896-97)
Marie-Louis Gabrié (1897-98)
Gustave P. Gallet (1898-99)
Joseph M. De Pous (1899)
Victor F. Rey (1899)
Gustave P. Gallet (1899-1901)
Victor F. Rey (1901)
Edouard Petit (1901-04)
Henri Cor (1904-05)
Philippe Jullien (1905-07)
Elie A. Charlier (1907-08)
Joseph F. François (1908-10)
Adrien J. Bonhoure (1910-12)
Charles Hostein (1912)
Léon Géraud (1912-13)
William Fawtier (1913-15)
Gustave J. Julien (1915-19)
Judge Simoneau (1919)
Jocelyn Robert (1919-21)
Gabriel H. Thaly (1921)
Auguste A. Guédès (1921)
Gabriel H. Thaly (1921-22)
Louis Rivet (1922-27)
Jean B. Solari (1927-28)
Joseph L. Bouge (1928-30)
Léonce Jore (1930-32)
Alfred L. Bouchet (1932-33)
Michel L. Montagné (1933-35)
Henri C. Sautot (1935-37)
Frédéric Chastenet de Géry (1937-40)
Emile de Curton (1940-41)
Richard Burnot (1941)
Georges Orselli (1941-45)
Jean C. Haumant (1945-47)
Pierre L. Maestracci (1947-49)
Armand Anziani (1949-50)
Louis A. Girault (1950)
Réné Petitbon (1950-54)
Jean-François Toby (1954-58)
Camille V. Bailly (1958)
Pierre R. Sicaud (1958-61)
Aimé Grimald (1961-63)
Camille Biros (1963-65)
Jean Sicurani (1965-69)
Pierre Angeli (1969-73)
Daniel Videau (1973-76)
Charles Schmitt (1976-77)
Paul Cousseran (1977-)

Vice-President

Francis Sanford (1977-)

ADMINISTRATORS OF THE PACIFIC ISLANDS—GILBERT ISLANDS (KIRIBATI) AND ELLICE ISLANDS (TUVALU)

(The Gilbert and Ellice islands Crown Colony of Britain was administered by a resident commissioner under the High Commissioner for the Western Pacific at Honiara from 1892 until independence.)

Resident Commissioners

C. R. Swayne (1892-96)

W. Telfer Campbell (1896-1910)

Captain J. Quayle Dickson (1910-13)
E. C. Eliot (1913-21)
H. R. McClure (1921-26)
Arthur F. Grimble (1926-33)
J. C. Barley (1933-41)
V. Fox-Strangways (1941-46)
Henry E. Maude (1946-48)
W. J. Peel (1948-52)
Michael L. Bernacchi (1952-62)
Valdemar J. Andersen (1962-70)
John Field (1970-74)
John H. Smith (1974-77)

Tuvalu
Governor General

Penitala Fiatau Teo (1978-)

Prime Minister

Toalipi Lauti (1978-)

Kiribati
President

Ieremia Tabai (1979-)

ADMINISTRATORS OF THE PACIFIC ISLANDS—GUAM

(Until 1949 Guam was administered under the jurisdiction of the U.S. Department of the Navy, thereafter under the U.S. Department of the Interior until 1970 when the governor was elected by voters in Guam.)

Naval Governors

Don José Sisto (Acting 1898)
Don Francisco Portusach (Acting 1898)
Don José Sisto (Acting 1899)
Don Joaquín Pérez (Acting 1899)
William Coe (Acting 1899)
Captain Richard P. Leary (1899-1900)
Commander Seaton Schroeder (1900-01)
Commander W. Swift (1901)
Commander Seaton Schroeder (1901-03)
Commander W. E. Sewell (1903-04)
Lieutenant F. H. Schofield (Acting 1904)
Lieutenant Raymond Stone (Acting 1904)
Commander G. L. Dyer (1904-05)
Lieutenant Luke McNamee (Acting 1905-06)
Commander T. M. Potts (1906-07)
Lieutenant Commander Luke McNamee (1907)
Captain Edward J. Dorn (1907-10)
Lieutenant F. B. Freyer (Acting 1910-11)
Captain G. R. Salisbury (1911-12)
Captain Robert E. Coontz (1912-13)
Commander A. W. Hinds (Acting 1913-14)
Captain W. J. Maxwell (1914-16)
Lieutenant Commander W. P. Cronan (Acting 1916)

Captain Edward Simpson (Acting 1916)
Captain Roy C. Smith (1916-18)
Captain William W. Gilmer (1918-19)
Lieutenant Commander W. A. Hodgman (Acting 1919)
Captain William W. Gilmer (1919-20)
Captain Ivan C. Wettengel (1920-21)
Lieutenant Commander James S. Spore (Acting 1921)
Captain Adelbert Althouse (1922)
Commander John P. Miller (Acting 1922)
Captain Adelbert Althouse (1922-23)
Captain H. B. Price (1923-24)
Commander A. W. Brown (Acting 1924)
Captain H. B. Price (1924-26)
Captain L. S. Shapley (1926-29)
Commander Willis W. Bradley Jr. (1929-31)
Captain Edmund S. Root (1931-33)
Captain George A. Alexander (1933-36)
Commander Benjamin V. McCandlish (1936-38)
Commander James T. Alexander (1938-40)
Captain George J. McMillin (1940-46)
Rear Admiral Charles A. Pownall (1946-49)

Civil Governors

Carlton S. Skinner (1949-53)
Randall S. Herman (Acting 1953)
Ford Q. Elvidge (1953-56)
William T. Corbett (Acting 1956)
Richard Barrett Lowe (1956-59)
Joseph Flores (1960-61)
William Patlov Daniel (1961-63)
Manuel F. L. Guerrero (1963-70)

Elected Governors

Carlos G. Camacho (1970-75)
Ricardo Jerome Bordallo (1975-79)
Paul M. Calvo (1979-)

ADMINISTRATORS OF THE PACIFIC ISLANDS—HAWAI'I

(A revolution in 1893 ended the independent kingdom of Hawai'i. After a short period as a republic, the islands were annexed by the U.S. government in 1898.)

Rulers

Kamehameha I (1795-1819)
Kamehameha II (1819-24)
Kamehameha III (1824-54)
Kamehameha IV (1854-63)
Kamehameha V (1863-72)
Lunalilo (1873-74)
Kalakaua (1874-91)
Queen Lili'uokalani (1891-93)

President of the Republic

Sanford B. Dole (1893-98)

Appointed Governors

Sanford B. Dole (1898-1903)
George Robert Carter (1903-07)
Walter Francis Frear (1907-13)

Lucius Eugene Pinkham (1913-18)
Charles J. McCarthy (1918-21)
Wallace Rider Farrington (1921-29)
Lawrence M. Judd (1929-34)
Joseph Boyd Poindexter (1934-42)
Ingram Macklin Stainback (1942-51)
Oren E. Long (1951-53)
Samuel Wilder King (1953-57)
William F. Quinn (1957-59)

Elected Governors

William F. Quinn (1959-62)
John A. Burns (1962-74)
George R. Ariyoshi (1974-)

ADMINISTRATORS OF THE PACIFIC ISLANDS—NAURU ISLAND

(Administered by Australia as a League of Nations mandate in 1921 and then a United Nations trust territory from 1945 to independence in 1968)

Administrators

Brigadier General T. Griffiths (1921-27)
W. A. Newman (1927-33)
Commander R. C. Garsia (1933-38)
Lieutenant Colonel F. R. Chalmers (1938-43)
Lieutenant Colonel J. L. A. Kelly (1945)
M. Ridgway (1945-49)
R. S. Richards (1949-53)
J. K. Lawrence (Acting 1953-54)
Reginald S. Leydin (1954-58)
John Preston White (1958-62)
Reginald S. Leydin (1962-66)
Brigadier Leslie D. King (1966-68)

Presidents

Hammer De Roburt (1968-76)
Bernard Dowiyogo (1976-78)
Hammer De Roburt (1978-)

ADMINISTRATORS OF THE PACIFIC ISLANDS—PAPUA NEW GUINEA

(The Territory of Papua was administered by Australia from 1884 to 1949 and the Territory of New Guinea was administered by Australia as a League of Nations mandate from 1919-49. These two units were amalgamated into the Territories of Papua and New Guinea until independence in 1975.)

Administrators of the Territory of Papua

Major General P. Scratchley (1884-85)
H. H. Romilly (1885-86)
John Douglas (1886-88)
William MacGregor (1889-98)
Francis Winter (1898-99)

G. R. Le Hunte (1899-1903)
C. S. Robinson (1903-04)
F. R. Barton (1904-07)
J. H. P. Murray (1907-40)
H. Leonard Murray (1940-52)
(military rule 1942-45)

Administrators of the Territory of New Guinea

Brig. Gen. Thomas Griffiths (1919-21)
Brig. Gen. A. E. Wisdom (1921-32)
Brig. Gen. Thomas Griffiths (1932-34)
Brig. Gen. Walter R. McNicoll (1934-42)

Administrators of the Territories of Papua and New Guinea

Colonel J. K. Murray (1945-52)
Brigadier Donald M. Cleland (1952-67)
David O. Hay (1967-71)
Leslie W. Johnson (1971-74)

Papua New Guinea Governors-General

John Guise (1974-76)
Tore Lokoloko (1976-)

Prime Ministers

Michael T. Somare (1972-80)
Julius Chan (1980-)

ADMINISTRATORS OF THE PACIFIC ISLANDS—SOLOMON ISLANDS

(Administered as a British protectorate from 1897 until independence in 1976)

Resident Commissioners

C. M. Woodford (1897-1919)
C. Workman (1919-21)
Captain R. R. Kane (1921-29)
F. N. Ashley (1929-39)
W. S. Marchant (1939-43)
O. C. Noel (1943-50)
Major H. G. Gregory-Smith (1950-52)

High Commissioners

Robert Stanley (1952-55)
John Gutch (1955-61)
David Trench (1961-63)
Robert Sidney Foster (1964-70)
Michael Gass (1970-74)
D. C. Luddington (1974-76)

Governors-General

Collin Allan (1976-78)
Baddeley Devesi (1978-)

Prime Minister

Peter Kenilorea (1976-)

ADMINISTRATORS OF THE PACIFIC ISLANDS—TONGA

Monarchs

Taufa'ahau George Tupou I (1845-1893)
George Taufa'ahau Tupou II (1893-1918)
Queen Salote Tupou III (1918-1965)
Taufa'ahau Tupou IV (1965-)

ADMINISTRATORS OF THE PACIFIC ISLANDS—U.S. TRUST TERRITORY OF THE PACIFIC ISLANDS

(In 1947 administration of these Micronesian islands was transferred from the U.S. Department of the Navy to the U.S. Department of the Interior until 1981.)

U.S. Naval Administration 1947-51
U.S. Department of the Interior Governors

Elbert D. Thomas (1951-53)
Frank H. Midkiff (1953-56)
Delmas H. Nucker (1956-61)
M. Wilfred Goding (1961-66)
William R. Norwood (1966-69)
Edward E. Johnson (1969-76)
Peter T. Coleman (1976-77)
Adrian P. Winkel (1977-)

ADMINISTRATORS OF THE PACIFIC ISLANDS—WESTERN SAMOA

(Administered by New Zealand 1914-62)

Administrators and High Commissioners

Colonel Robert Logan (1914-19)
Colonel R. W. Tate (1920-23)
Major General G. S. Richardson (1923-28)
Colonel Stephen Allen (1928-31)
Brigadier General Herbert E. Hart (1931-35)
Alfred Turnbull (Acting 1934-43, Administrator 1943-46)
Lieutenant Colonel F. W. Voelcker (1946-49)
Guy R. Powles (1949-62)

Heads of State

Tupua Tamasese (died 1963)
Malietoa Tanumafili II (1962-)

Prime Ministers

Fiame Mata'afa (1959-69)
Tupua Tamasese (1969-72)
Fiame Mata'afa (1972-75)
Tupuola Efi (1975-)

Individuals by Occupation

RULERS AND GOVERNMENT OFFICIALS

Shirley Baker
Francis Barton
Hiram Bingham
Charles R. Bishop
Armand J. Bruat
Paul M. Calvo
George R. Carter
Chin Foo
Sanford B. Dole
Wallace R. Farrington
Paul Feillet
Walter Frear
James Gibbon
Walter M. Gibson
Arthur C. H. Gordon
George Grey
Charles Guillain
John Guise
Joseph Guyon
Adolph B. Joske
Gerrit P. Judd
Lawrence M. Judd
Kalakaua
Kamehameha I-V
Samuel W. King
R. A. S. Latianara
Lauaki N. Mamoe
Lili'uokalani
Oren E. Long
William Lunalilo
Charles J. McCarthy
William MacGregor
Petrus Mailo
Malietoa
Joanna Marau
Mata'afa
Jacques A. Moerenhout
Charles Monckton
Basil M. Morris
Frederick J. Moss
John H. P. Murray
Nambas
O. F. Nelson
A. D. Patel
Lucius E. Pinkham
Joseph B. Poindexter
Pomare Family
Pouvana'a Oopa
Guy R. Poweles
George Pritchard

William Pritchard
William F. Quinn
Charles St. Julian
Salote Tupou IV
Francis Sanford
Peter H. Scratchley
Wilhelm H. Solf
Michael T. Somare
Soumadau
Ingram M. Stainback
Albert B. Steinberger
J. L. V. Sukuna
Tati
Taufa'ahau George Tupou I
Charles Te Moana
Teri'iero'o a Teri'iero'oterai
Tevita 'Unga
Basil H. Thomson
John B. Thurston
Lorrin A. Thurston
William Tupoulahi Tungi
Finau Ulukalala II
Elisabeth Vahekehu
David Wilkinson
John Young

MISSIONARIES AND RELIGIOUS LEADERS

Richard Armstrong
Pierre Bataillon
Hiram Bingham
William E. Bromilow
Joel Bulu
John Calvert
George Q. Cannon
François Caret
Pierre Chanel
Joseph Chevron
Robert H. Codrington
Stephen M. Creagh
William P. Crook
Joseph Damien
Edward T. Doane
Guillaume Douarre
William Ellis
Sebastian Englert
Eugene Eyraud
William Henry
John Hunt
John Hutchinson
John Jones

Louis Laval
Walter Lawry
Maurice Leenhardt
Robert W. Logan
Richard B. Lyth
Samuel MacFarlane
Louis-Désire Maigret
Samuel Marsden
Xavier Montrouzier
Teikoroi Moses
Henry Newton
Henry Obookiah
John Orsmond
Papehia
John C. Patteson
J. B. F. Pompallier
George Pritchard
William Richards
George A. Selwyn
Thomas N. Staley
John L. Stevens
John Thomas
Robert Thomson
Tupaia
George Vason
Frédéric Vernier
John Williams

EXPLORERS, MILITARY LEADERS, ETC.

Jeanne Baret
William Bligh
Lee Boo
Louis Antoine de Bougainville
John M. Brooke
John Byron
James Cook
Luigi M. d'Albertis
William Dampier
Antoine d'Entrecasteaux
Peter Dillon
Francis Drake
J. S. C. Dumont d'Urville
Abel A. Dupetit-Thouars
Amelia Earhart
Earl H. Ellis
John E. Erskine
Alain Gerbault
Otto von Kotzbue
Adam von Krusenstern
Jacob Le Maire

Ferdinand Magellan
Alessandro Malaspina
Étienne Marchand
Álvaro de Mendaña de Neira
Chester William Nimitz
Omai
George Paulet
Matthew C. Perry
Pedro Quirós
Jacob Roggeveen
Alvaro de Saavedra Cerón
Pedro Sarmiento de Gamboa
William C. Schouten
Raymond A. Spruance
Abel J. Tasman
Richard Thomas
Luis Váez de Torres
Andrés de Urdaneta
George Vancouver
Ruy López de Villalobos
Charles Wilkes

SCHOLARS, WRITERS, ARTISTS

John C. Beaglehole
Luelen Bernart
Edmond de Bovis
Peter H. Buck
Robert H. Codrington
Luigi M. d'Albertis
James W. Davidson
Peter Dillon
Sebastian Englert
Johann G. Forster

Johann R. Forster
Paul Gauguin
George Grey
Beatrice Grimshaw
James N. Hall
Teuira Henry
Celsus Kelly
Augustin Krämer
Johann S. Kubary
George H. von Langsdorf
Pierre Loti
David Malo
William Mariner
Margaret Mead
Herman Melville
Alfred Métraux
Jacques-Antoine de Moerenhout
Charles Monckton
Frederick J. Moss
Charles B. Nordhoff
Geza Roheim
André Ropiteau
Katherine P. Routledge
Carl G. Semper
Robert L. Stevenson
Tupaia

ENTREPRENEURS, MERCHANTS, ETC.

J. P. Dutrou-Bornier
Harold C. Gatty
William Hamilton

John Higginson
Crayton Holcomb
Adolph B. Joske
William Lockerby
Charles Monckton
Henry Nanpei
Apolosi R. Nawai
James Paddon
Benjamin Pease
Alfred Poppe
Charles Marquis de Rays
Alexander Salmon
Claus Spreckels
William Stewart
Robert S. Swanston
William K. Thompson
August Unshelm
William Webb
Theodor Weber
George A. Woods

BEACHCOMBERS

Archibald Campbell
Captain W. Crocker
Ernest Darling
Isaac Davis
William Diaper
Peter Haggerstein
William Mariner
Edward Robarts
Charles Savage
David Whippy
John Young

Island Names with Variant and Obsolete Spellings

AGRIHAN, Agrigan, Grigan

ANGAUR, Angauru, Niaur, N'Yaur

ANT, Andena, Anto, Fraser, William the Fourth

ARNO, Arhno, Daniel, Pedder

ASUNCION, Assumption

ATAFU, Duke of York

BABELTHUAP, Arrecifos, Baberudaubu, Babeldaob

BELAU, Palau, Palaos, Pelew

BIKINI, Bigini, Eschscholtz, Udia-Milai

BONIN, Arzobispo, Ogasawara

BORABORA, Bolabola

BUKA, Bouka

CANTON, Mary, Mary Balcout, Swallow

CHOISEUL, Lauru

DUBLON, Tonoas

EASTER, Pascua, Rapa-Nui, Rapanui, Teapy, Waihu

EBON, Boston, Covell, Fourteen, Linnez

EFATE, Sandwich, Vate

ENIWETOK, Arthur, Brown

ESPIRITU SANTO, Mariana, Santo

ETAL, Mortlock

FARALLON DE MEDINILLA, Bird

FARALLON DE PAJAROS, Ana, Uracas, Urakasu To

FARALLON DE TORRES, Zealandia Rocks

FATUHIVA, Magdalena, Santa Magdalena

FATUHUKU, Fetuku, Hood

FEFAN, Aki

FONUAFO'OU, Falcon

FUNAFUTI, Ellice

FUTUNA, Hoorn, Horn

JALUIT, Bonham

KAPINGAMARANGI, Constantin, Greenwich, Greenwick

KILI, Hunter

KINGMAN, Alice Thorndike

KIRIBATI, Gilbert Islands, Kingsmill

KUSAIE, Strong, Ualan

KWAJALEIN, Catherine, Kwadelen

LIFOU, Chabrol, Lifu

LITTLE MAKIN, Makin, Pitt

LOMALOMA, Lomo-Lomo, Sir Charles Middleton

LOYALTY, Loyauté

MAIANA, Hall

MAJURO, Arrowsmith, Meduro

MAKATEA, Aurora, Maataah, Maeteea, Mataa, Matea, Mathea, Matia, Oumaitia, Recreation, Verkwikking

MALAITA, Carteret, Mala, Malanta, Malayette

MALDEN, Independence

MANIHI, Dagenraad, Prince of Wales, Waterlandt, Wilson

MARE, Britannia

MARIANA, Islas de los Latinas, Ladrone Islands, Ladrones, Los Jardines, Marianne, Mary Ann's Islands, Thieves' Islands

MARUTEA, Lord Hood

MIDWAY, Brooks

MILI, Mille, Mulgrave

MOEN, Wena

MO'OREA, Aimeo, Duke of York, Eimeo

MOPELIA, Lord Howe, Mopihaa

MOTA, Amota, Sugar-loaf

NAPUKA, Disappointment, Wytoohee

NEW BRITAIN, Neu Pommern

NEW CALEDONIA, Nouvelle Calédonie

NEW IRELAND, Neu Mecklenburg

NIUE, Nieue, Savage

NIULAKITA, Independence, Nurakita, Rocky, Solitaria, Sophia

NUKUTAVAKE, Leopold I, Queen Charlotte

OCEAN, Banaba, Paanopa

ONTONG JAVA, Lord Howe, Luaniua

OROLUK, Bordelaise, San Augustino

PAGAN, Pagon

PALAU, Belau, Palaos, Pelew

PARAOA, Duke of Gloucester, Gloucester

PELELIU, Periryu

PENRHYN, Tongareva

PENTECOST, Arragh, Pentecote, Raga, Whitsun

PINGELAP, MacAskill, Musgrave, Piagelap

PONAPE, Ascension, Puynipet, Seniavine

PULAP, Pourappu, Tamatan

PULUWAT, Endabi Shoto, Enderby, Kata, Poloat

RABIDA, Jervis

RADAK, Ratak

RAROTONGA, Armstrong, Roxburgh

REITORU, Bird

REKAREKA, Good Hope, Tehuata

RONGELAP, Bigini, Kongelab, Pescadore

RONGERIK, Radokala, Rimski-Korsakoff

ROSE, Kordiukoff, Middleton

ROTA, Bota, Ile Sainte Anne, Sarpan, Zarpan

RYUKYU, Loo-choo, Lu-chu

SAIPAN, Seypan

SAN ALESSANDRO, North

SAN CRISTOBAL, Arossi

SANTA ISABEL, Santa Ysabel, Ysabel

SATAWAL, Sasaon, Setuahal, Tucker

SOCIETY ISLANDS, Archipel de Tahiti, Isles de la Société

SONSOROL, St. Andrew, Sansoral

STARBUCK, Barren, Coral Queen, Hero, Low, Starve

SWAIN, Gente Hermosa, Olosenga, Quiros

TAHITI, Amat, King George III, Nouvelle Cythère, Otahiti

TAONGI, Gaspar Rico, Smyth

TARAWA, Cook, Knox

TAUMAKO, Disappointment

TEMATANGI, Bligh's Lagoon, Lagoon

TEPOTO, Disappointment, Otooho

TIKEHAU, Krusenstern

TIKEI, Bedrieglyke, Romanzoff, Rumanzoff

TINIAN, Buena Vista

TOAU, Count Wittgenstein, Elizabeth

TOBI, Lord North, Neville

TOGA, Buga Buga, Buka, Torga

TOKELAU, Union

TONGA, Friendly Islands

TONGATAPU, Amsterdam

TRUK, Hogoleu, Ruk, Torakku

TUAMOTU, Dangerous, Paumotu, Pomotu

TUTUILA, Masuna, Tootooilah

TUVALU, Ellice

ULITHI, Mackenzie, Urushi

UPOLU, Oahtooha, Ojalava, Opoloo

UREPARAPARA, Bligh, Norbarbar

VAITUPU, Oaitupu, Tracy

VANAVANA, Barrow

VANUATU, New Hebrides, Nouvelles Hébrides, Vanuaaku

VAVAU, Lord Howe, Martin de Mayorga

YAP, Eap, Ruul, Yappu

Select Bibliography

General

Barclay, Glen St. John. *A History of the Pacific from the Stone Age to the Present Day*. London: Sidgwick and Jackson, 1978.

Bayliss-Smith, Timothy and Feachem, Richard. *Subsistence and Survival: Rural Ecology in the Pacific*. New York: Academic Press, 1977.

Beaglehole, J. C. *The Exploration of the Pacific*. 3d ed. Stanford: Stanford University Press, 1966.

Bellwood, Peter. *Man's Conquest of the Pacific: The Prehistory of Southeast Asia and Oceania*. New York: Oxford University Press, 1979.

Davidson, Janet and Scarr, Deryck, eds. *Pacific Islands Portraits*. Wellington: A. H. and A. W. Reed, 1973.

Davies, John. *History of the Tahitian Mission*. Cambridge: At the University Press, 1961.

Dingman, Roger. *Power in the Pacific: The Origins of Naval Arms Limitation, 1914-1922*. Chicago: University of Chicago Press, 1976.

Ellsworth, George S. *Zion in Paradise: Early Mormons in the South Pacific*. Logan, Utah: Utah State University, 1959.

Faivre, Jean-Paul. *L'expansion française dans le Pacifique, 1800-1842*. Paris: Nouvelle Editions Latines, 1953.

Findlay, George G. and Holdsworth, W. W. *The History of the Wesleyan Methodist Missionary Society*. Vol. 3. *The Pacific*. London: Epworth Press, 1921.

Friis, Herman, R., ed. *The Pacific Basin: A History of its Geographical Exploration*. New York: American Geographical Society, 1967.

Grattan, C. Hartley. *The Southwest Pacific to 1900*. Ann Arbor: University of Michigan Press, 1963.

_____. *The Southwest Pacific since 1900*. Ann Arbor: University of Michigan Press, 1963.

Griffin, James, ed. *Papua New Guinea Portraits: The Expatriate Experience*. Canberra: Australian National University Press, 1968.

Hilliard, David. *God's Gentlemen: A History of the Melanesian Mission, 1849-1942*. St. Lucia, Queensland: University of Queensland Press, 1978.

King, Frank P., ed. *Oceania and Beyond: Essays on the Pacific since 1945*. Westport, Conn.: Greenwood Press, 1976.

Laracy, Hugh. *Marists and Melanesians: A History of the Catholic Missions in the Solomon Islands*. Canberra: Australian National University Press, 1976.

Lovett, Richard. *The History of the London Missionary Society, 1795-1895*. 2 vols. London: London Missionary Society, 1899.

Maude, H. E. *Of Islands and Men: Studies in Pacific History*. Melbourne: Oxford University Press, 1968.

Morrell, W. P. *Britain in the Pacific Islands*. Oxford: Clarendon Press, 1960.

Morrison, Samuel E. *History of United States Naval Operations in World War II*. Boston: Little, Brown & Co., 1951.

Oliver, Douglas. *The Pacific Islands*. Rev. ed. Garden City, N.Y.: Doubleday & Co., 1961.

O'Reilly, Patrick and Reitman, Edouard. *Bibliographie de Tahiti et de la Polynésie Française*. Paris: Musée de l'Homme, 1967.

Palau Community Action Agency. *A History of Palau*. Vol. 2. *Traders and Whalers—Spanish Administration—German Administration*. Guam: Navy Printing, 1977.

Phillips, Clifton J. *Protestant America and the Pagan World: The First Century of the American Board of Commissioners for Foreign Missions, 1810-1860*. Cambridge: East Asian Research Center, Harvard University, 1969.

Premdas, Ralph and Pokawin, Stephen, eds. *Decentralization in the Pacific*. Waigani: University of Papua New Guinea Press, 1979.

Scarr, Deryck. *Fragments of Empire*. Canberra: Australian National University Press, 1967.

_____. *More Pacific Islands Portraits*. Canberra: Australian National University Press, 1979.

Sharp, Andrew. *The Discovery of the Pacific Islands*. Oxford: Clarendon Press, 1960.

Snow, Philip A. *Bibliography of Fiji, Tonga, and Rotuma*. Canberra: Australian National University Press, 1969.

Spate, Oskar H. K. *The Pacific Since Magellan*. Vol. 1. *The Spanish Lake*. Canberra: Australian National University Press, 1979.

Streit, P. Robert. *Bibliotheca Missionum*. Vol. 21. *Australien und Ozeanien, 1525-1950*. Freiburg: Verlag Herder, 1955.

Taylor, C. R. H. *A Pacific Bibliography: Printed Matter Relating to the Native Peoples of Polynesia, Melanesia, and Micronesia*. Oxford: Clarendon Press, 1965.

Ward, G. R. *American Activities in the Central Pacific, 1790-1870*. 3 vols. Ridgewood: Gregg Press, 1966.

West, Francis J. *Political Advancement in the South Pacific*.

Melbourne: Oxford University Press, 1961.

Wiltgen, R. *The Founding of the Roman Catholic Church in Oceania, 1825-1850*. Canberra: Australian National University Press, 1979.

Melanesia

Brookfield, H. C. *Colonialism, Development, and Independence: The Case of the Melanesian Islands in the South Pacific*. Cambridge: At the University Press, 1972.

Brown, Stanley. *Men from under the Sky: The Arrival of the Westerners in Fiji*. Rutland, Vt.: Charles E. Tuttle Co., 1973.

Burns, Sir Alan. *Fiji*. London: Her Majesty's Stationery Office, 1963.

Corris, Peter. *Passage, Port, and Plantation: A History of the Solomon Islands*. Melbourne: Melbourne University Press, 1973.

Derrick, R. A. *The Fiji Islands: A Geographical Handbook*. Suva: Government Press, 1965.

————. *A History of Fiji*. Suva: Government Press, 1957.

Griffin, James, ed. *Papua New Guinea Portraits: The Expatriate Experience*. Canberra: Australian National University Press, 1978.

Hasluck, Paul. *A Time for Building: Australian Administration in Papua and New Guinea, 1951-1963*. Melbourne: Melbourne University Press, 1976.

Hastings, Peter. *New Guinea: Problems and Prospects*. 2d ed. Melbourne: Cheshire, 1973.

Hilliard, David. *God's Gentlemen: A History of the Melanesian Mission, 1849-1942*. St. Lucia, Queensland: University of Queensland Press, 1978.

Howe, Kerry R. *The Loyalty Islands: A History of Culture Contacts, 1840-1900*. Honolulu: University Press of Hawaii, 1977.

Howlett, Diana R. *A Geography of Papua and New Guinea*. Melbourne: Thomas Nelson, 1967.

Humphrey, Charles. *The Southern New Hebrides: An Ethnological Record*. Cambridge: At the University Press, 1926.

Jack-Hinton, Colin. *The Search for the Islands of Solomon, 1567-1838*. Oxford: Clarendon Press, 1969.

Laracy, Hugh. *Marists and Melanesians: A History of Catholic Missions in the Solomon Islands*. Canberra: Australian National University Press, 1976.

Legge, J. D. *Britain in Fiji, 1858-1880*. London: Macmillan & Co., 1958.

Norton, Robert, *Race and Politics in Fiji*. New York: St Martin's Press, 1978.

O'Reilly, Patrick. *Bibliographie Méthodique, Analytique et Critique de la Nouvelle-Calédonie*. Paris: Musée de l'Homme, 1955.

————. *Calédoniens*. Paris: Musée de l'Homme, 1953.

Plant, Chris, ed. *New Hebrides: The Road to Independence*. Suva: Institute of Pacific Studies, 1977.

Ryan, P. A., ed. *Encyclopaedia of Papua and New Guinea*. 3 vols. Melbourne: Melbourne University Press, 1972.

Souter, Gavin. *New Guinea: The Last Unknown*. Sydney: Argus and Robertson, 1963.

Stephen, David. *A History of Political Parties in Papua New Guinea*. Melbourne: Lansdowne, 1972.

Viviani, Nancy. *Nauru: Phosphate and Political Progress*. Canberra: Australian National University Press, 1970.

Micronesia

Bascomb, William. *Ponape: A Pacific Island Economy in Transition*. Berkeley: University of California Press, 1965.

Bast, Benjamin F., ed. *The Political Future of Guam and Micronesia*. Agana: University of Guam Press, 1974.

Bryan, Edwin H., Jr. *Guide to Place Names in the Trust Territory of the Pacific Islands*. Honolulu: Bernice P. Bishop Museum, 1971.

Carano, Paul and Sanchez, Pedro. *A Complete History of Guam*. Tokyo: Charles E. Tuttle Co., 1964.

Christian, F. W. *The Caroline Islands*. London: Frank Cass and Co., 1899.

Fischer, John L. and Ann M. *The Eastern Carolines*. New Haven: Human Relations Area Files Press, 1957.

Gladwin, Thomas. *East is a Big Bird: Navigation and Logic on Puluwat Atoll*. Cambridge: Harvard University Press, 1970.

Heine, Carl. *Micronesia at the Crossroads: A Reappraisal of the Micronesian Political Dilemma*. Honolulu: University Press of Hawaii, 1974.

Hughes, Daniel and Lingenfelter, Sherwood G., eds. *Political Development in Micronesia*. Columbus: Ohio State University Press, 1974.

McHenry, Donald F. *Micronesia: Trust Betrayed. Altruism vs. Self-Interest in American Foreign Policy*. New York: Carnegie Endowment for International Peace, 1975.

Nufer, Harold F. *Micronesia under American Rule: An Evaluation of the Strategic Trusteeship, 1947-1977*. Hicksville, N.Y.: Exposition Press, 1978.

Palau Community Action Agency. *A History of Palau*. 3 vols. Guam: Navy Printing, 1977-78.

Richard, Dorothy. *History of U.S. Naval Administration of the Trust Territory of the Pacific Islands*. 3 vols. Washington, D.C.: Office of Naval Operations, 1957.

Talu, Sister Alaima and others. *Kiribati: Aspects of History*. Suva: University of the South Pacific, 1979.

Polynesia

Bellwood, Peter. *The Polynesians: Prehistory of an Island People*. London: Thames and Hudson, 1978.

Caillot, A. C. Eugène. *Histoire de la Polynésie Orientale*. Paris: Ernest Leroux, 1910.

Craig, Robert D., ed. *The Marquesas Islands: Their Description and Early History*, by the Reverend Robert Thomson. 2d ed. Laie, Hawaii: Institute for Polynesian Studies, 1980.

————, ed. *Tahitian Society before the Arrival of the Europeans*, by Edmond de Bovis. 2d ed. Laie, Hawaii: Institute for Polynesian Studies, 1980.

Crocombe, Ron, ed. *Cook Islands Politics: The Inside Story*. Auckland: Polynesian Press, n.d. [1978].

Danielsson, Bengt. *Forgotten Islands of the South Seas.* London: G. Allen & Unwin, 1957.

Davidson, J. W. *Samoa Mo Samoa: The Emergence of the Independent State of Western Samoa.* New York: Oxford University Press, 1967.

Davies, John. *History of the Tahitian Mission.* Cambridge: At the University Press, 1961.

Daws, Gavan. *A Shoal of Time: A History of the Hawaiian Islands.* New York: Macmillan Co., 1968.

Day, A. Grove. *Hawaii and its People.* New York: Meredith Press, 1968.

Dening, Greg, ed. *The Marquesan Journal of Edward Robarts.* Canberra: Australian National University Press, 1974.

Eason, William. *A Short History of Rotuma.* Suva: Government Printer, 1951.

Englert, P. S. *Island at the Center of the World: New Light on Easter Island.* Translated by William Mulloy. New York: Charles Scribner's Sons, 1970.

Gilson, R. P. *Samoa, 1830-1900: The Politics of a Multi-Cultural Community.* New York: Oxford University Press, 1970.

Goldman, Irving. *Ancient Polynesian Society.* Chicago: University of Chicago Press, 1970.

Gray, J. A. C. *Amerika Samoa.* Annapolis, Md.: U.S. Naval Institute, 1960.

Hempenstall, Peter J. *Pacific Islanders under German Rule: A Study in the Meaning of Colonial Resistance.* Canberra: Australian National University Press, 1978.

Howard, Alan. *Learning to be Rotuman.* New York: Columbia Teachers' College Press, 1970.

Jennings, Jesse D., ed. *The Prehistory of Polynesia.* Cambridge: Harvard University Press, 1979.

Kennedy, Paul M. *The Samoan Tangle: A Study in Anglo-German-American Relations, 1878-1900.* New York: Barnes & Noble, 1974.

Krämer, Augustin F. *Die Samoa-Inseln.* 2 vols. Stuttgart: E. Nägele, 1902.

Kuykendall, R. S. *The Hawaiian Kingdom.* 3 vols. Honolulu: University of Hawaii Press, 1967.

Lātūkefu, Sione. *Church and State in Tonga.* Canberra: Australian National University Press, 1974.

Loeb, Edwin M. *History and Traditions of Niue.* Honolulu: Bernice P. Bishop Museum, 1926.

Masterman, Sylvia. *The Origins of International Rivalry in Samoa, 1845-1884.* London: G. Allen & Unwin, 1934.

Mazellier, Philippe, ed. *Le Mémorial Polynésien.* 6 vols. Pape'ete: Hibiscus Editions, 1977-.

Metraux, Alfred. *Easter Island: A Stone Age Civilization of the Pacific.* London: Oxford University Press, 1957.

Newbury, Colin. *Tahiti Nui: Change and Survival in French Polynesia, 1767-1945.* Honolulu: University Press of Hawaii, 1980.

Oliver, Douglas L. *Ancient Tahitian Society.* 3 vols. Honolulu: University Press of Hawaii, 1974.

O'Reilly, Patrick and Reitman, Edouard. *Bibliographie de Tahiti et de la Polynésie Française.* Paris: Musée de l'Homme, 1967.

O'Reilly, Patrick and Teissier, Raoul. *Tahitiens. Répertoire bio-bibliographique de la Polynésie Française.* 2 vols. Paris: Musée de l'Homme, 1962, 1966.

Poncet, Alexandre. *Histoire de l'Ile Wallis.* 2 vols. Paris: Musée de l'Homme, 1972.

Rutherford, Noel, ed. *Friendly Islands: A History of Tonga.* Melbourne: Oxford University Press, 1977.

Tagupa, William. *Politics in French Polynesia, 1945-1975.* Wellington: Institute of International Affairs, 1976.

Thompson, Virginia and Adloff, Richard. *The French Pacific Islands: French Polynesia and New Caledonia.* Berkeley: University of California Press, 1971.

Wood, A. H. *History and Geography of Tonga.* Nuku-'alofa, Tonga: Government Printing Office, 1932.

Name Index

Page numbers in **boldface** indicate a major entry.

Subject Index

Page numbers in **boldface** indicate a major entry.

Contributors

RODERICK M. ALLEY is a Senior Lecturer in the School of Political Science and Public Administration at Victoria University of Wellington, New Zealand.

DAN W. ANDERSEN is President of the Brigham Young University—Hawai'i Campus, Laie, Hawai'i. His experience in education has taken him to Ethiopia, Nigeria, and Indonesia.

RUSSELL A. APPLE is a career historian with the U.S. National Park Service in Hawai'i and an associate in Hawaiian culture at the Bernice Pauahi Bishop Museum in Honolulu.

KENNETH W. BALDRIDGE received his Ph.D. from the Brigham Young University, Provo Campus, and is currently Professor of History at the Hawai'i campus. He is in charge of the oral history program of the Institute for Polynesian Studies.

DIRK ANTHONY BALLENDORF received his B.A. degree from West Chester State College, his M.A. from Howard University, and his Ph.D. from Harvard University. He served the Peace Corps both in Micronesia and in Washington, D.C. After serving as Director of Planning in the Department of Higher Education in Pennsylvania, he was President of the Community College of Micronesia. Currently he is Director of the Micronesian Area Research Center at the University of Guam.

GLEN ST. J. BARCLAY is a Reader in International Relations at the University of Queensland. He has written *Commonwealth or Europe?* (Brisbane: University of Queensland Press, 1970), *The Empire Is Marching* (London: Weidenfeld and Nicolson, 1976), *A History of the Pacific* (London: Sidgwick and Jackson, 1978), and, with John E. Edwards, *World War II in the Pacific* (Sydney: Holt-Saunders, 1980).

MARK L. BERG graduated from Yale College with a degree in English literature. After serving in the Peace Corps on Palau, he wrote and edited a three-volume history reader, *A History of Palau* (Guam: Navy Printing, 1977-1979).

NICHOLAS BESNIER, graduate student in linguistics at the University of Southern California, Los Angeles, has spent considerable time in Tuvalu where he has just completed several books relating to the Tuvalu language.

JAMES KEOUGH BISHOP, member of the United States Foreign Service, member of the executive seminar in National and International Affairs (1976), later director of North African Affairs, Department of State (1977-79), and Ambassador to the Republic of Niger (1979-81), is currently Deputy Assistant Secretary of State for African Affairs.

KENNETH JOHN BLUME is a doctoral candidate at the State University of New York at Binghamton.

MARK BORTHWICK works on the staff of the Committee on Foreign Affairs, U.S. House of Representatives.

GEORGE J. BOUGHTON teaches in and has chaired the History Department at the University of Guam. He was educated at Michigan State University (B.A., M.A., Ph.D.).

JAMES A. BOUTILIER is Associate Professor at the Royal Roads Military College, Victoria, B.C. He has edited a book about the achievements of Captain James Cook.

DAVID WARREN BOWEN is Assistant Professor at the University of Alabama.

MARY BROWNING is a free-lance writer and editor in Jamestown, North Carolina.

BURTON G. BURTON-BRADLEY, M.D., University of London, is a moving force at the Mental Health Services, Boroko, Papua New Guinea.

JEFFREY J. BUTLER is Assistant Professor of English at the Brigham Young University—Hawai'i Campus. He received his B.A. in Political Science from the University of Utah (1971) and completed a Masters in Education from the same institution (1972). In 1976 he received a Doctor of Arts in English from the University of Michigan.

IAN C. CAMPBELL, a Tutor in History at the University of Adelaide where he also took his Ph.D., started his academic career at the University of New England in Australia.

RALPH C. CANEVALI received his B.A. from the University of Hawai'i and his M.A. and Ph.D. from Harvard University, majoring in German history.

RUSSELL T. CLEMENT is currently a librarian at the Brigham Young University—Hawai'i Campus and is involved in bibliographical work on the Pacific Basin.

CHRISTIAN C. CLERK is a doctoral student in the Department of Anthropology, University College, University of London.

THOMAS R. COX, educated at the University of Hawai'i and the University of Oregon where he received his Ph.D. (1969), is currently Professor of History at San Diego State University and has published numerous articles on Pacific trade and environmental topics.

ROBERT D. CRAIG holds degrees from the universities of Cincinnati and Utah (Ph.D.) as well as certificates from European universities. He founded and edited the journal *Pacific Studies* for several years and served as publications director for the Institute for Polynesian Studies (Brigham Young University, Laie, Hawai'i). He currently is a member of the faculty at the University of Guam and editor for the Micronesian Area Research Center.

MARION DIAMOND is a Senior Tutor in the History Department at the University of Queensland.

PHIL DIAMOND is a Senior Lecturer in Mathematics at the University of Queensland.

JEROME EVANS received his B.A. degree from Dartmouth College and M.P.A. from Princeton University. He is a free-lance writer and editor.

J. L. FISCHER is Professor of Anthropology at Tulane University in New Orleans, Louisiana.

GARY L. FITZPATRICK is a reference librarian in the Geography and Map Division at the Library of Congress in Washington, D.C.

'INOKE F. FUNAKI graduated from the Liahona High School in Tonga (1963) and went on to receive his Ph.D. (1975) from the Brigham Young University, Provo Campus. He currently is Assistant Professor in Education at the Brigham Young University —Hawai'i Campus.

H. J. GIBBNEY is Research Officer for the Australian Dictionary of Biography project at the Australian National University.

ROBERT GRAHAM holds a M.A. degree in Pacific Island Studies from the University of Hawai'i. He has served in the Peace Corps in the Marshall Islands and now teaches at St. Ann School in Kaneohe, Hawai'i.

C. HARTLEY GRATTAN, a foremost authority on Southwest Pacific affairs, was Professor of History at the University of Texas. He was the author of *The Southwest Pacific: A Modern History*, 1963.

ANDRÉ GSCHAEDLER, now Emeritus Professor from Salem College, West Virginia, received a degree from the University of Strasbourg, France, his M.A. from the University of Melbourne (1946), and his Ph.D. from Columbia University (1954). His publications include works on Spanish and Pacific explorers.

RHODA E. A. HACKLER serves as the President of the Hawaiian Historical Society and is a member of the History Department of the University of Hawai'i.

NOELINE V. HALL (B.A., M.A., University of New Zealand) is a Senior Tutor of History at the University of Queensland. She has written a biography of Archdeacon Nesbit Brown and a number of articles.

DAVID L. HANLON, M.A., John Hopkins University, teaches at the Community College of Micronesia in Kolonia, Ponape, Eastern Caroline Islands.

ETTA HARRIS graduated from the Brigham Young University—Hawai'i Campus (B.A. History, 1979) and is now teaching in Neafu, Vava'u, Tonga.

PETER HEMPENSTALL, who teaches in the History Department at the University of Newcastle in Australia, was educated at the universities of Queensland, Hamburg, and Oxford (D. Phil.), where he was a Rhodes Scholar. He was a postdoctoral Fellow at the Australian National University (1974-75) and a Research Fellow of the Alexander von Humboldt Foundation in 1979. He has published *Pacific Islanders under German Rule: A Study in the Meaning of Colonial Resistance* (Canberra: Australian National University Press, 1978).

RICHARD HERR received his M.A. and Ph.D. from Duke University, and is now Senior Tutor in Political Science at the University of Tasmania, Australia.

FRANCIS X. HEZEL (SJ), is Director of Xavier High School as well as the Micronesian Seminar (a church-sponsored/research-pastoral institute) located in Truk, Federated States of Micronesia. His extensive publications include articles on education and history. He currently is involved in writing a two-volume history of Micronesia.

DAVID L. HILLIARD is a Senior Lecturer in History of the Social Sciences at the Flinders University of South Australia.

FRANCIS X. HOLBROOK received his M.A. and Ph.D. from Fordham University and is currently a member of the Social Studies Department of Fordham Preparatory School, Bronx, New York, having served eighteen years as Chairman of the department. His published works deal with naval and diplomatic history.

ALAN HOWARD received his graduate degrees from Stanford University (M.A. 1958, Ph.D., 1962) in Anthropology. Currently he is a member of the Anthropology Department of the University of Hawai'i and his numerous articles on the Pacific have appeared in various scholarly journals.

TITO ISALA is the Assistant Registrar (Academic) at the University of the South Pacific located in Suva, Fiji.

DONALD D. JOHNSON, Emeritus Professor of History at the University of Hawai'i, is the author of numerous articles and papers on United States foreign policy in the Pacific. His current research includes the history of the city and county of Honolulu.

WILLIAM ROSS JOHNSTON, a Senior Lecturer in History at the University of Queensland, was educated at Queensland (M.A., LL.B.) and Duke University (Ph.D.). In addition to numerous articles, he has written *Sovereignty and Protection* (Durham: Duke University Press, 1973).

BRUCE KAROLLE is a geographer at the University of Guam. He received his Ph.D. from Michigan State University.

FRANK P. KING holds degrees from the universities of Denver (B.A.), Northern Colorado (M.A.), Keele (M.A.), and Cambridge (Ph.D.). He is the author of *The New Internationalism: Allied Policy and the European Peace, 1939-1945* (Newton Abbot, England: David and Charles, 1973) and the editor of *Oceania and Beyond: Essays on the Pacific Since 1945* (Westport, Conn.: Greenwood Press, 1976).

WILL KING received his B.A. degree from Macquarie University in Sydney.

HOWARD I. KUSHNER received his M.A. and Ph.D. from Cornell University and is currently Professor of History, San Diego State University. His published works include articles on Yankee whaling and Russian fleets in the Northwest Pacific as well as the book *Conflict on the Northwest Coast: American Russian Rivalry in the Pacific Northwest, 1790-1867* (Westport, Conn.: Greenwood Press, 1975).

EUGÉNIE LARACY, with Hugh Laracy, is the author of *The Italians in New Zealand and Other Studies* (Auckland: Societa Dante Alighieri, 1973).

HUGH LARACY teaches in the History Department at the University of Auckland and has written, in addition to numerous articles, *Marists and Melanesians: A History of Catholic Missions in the Solomon Islands* (Canberra: Australian National University Press and Honolulu: University Press of Hawai'i, 1976) and, with Eugénie Laracy, *The Italians in New Zealand and Other Studies* (Auckland: Societa Dante Alighieri, 1973).

RATU PENAIA LALABALAVA LATIANARA is a retired Fijian civil servant, member of the Great Council of Chiefs (Fiji), scholar, and writer.

RUTH LIMTIACO is a free-lance writer and editor on the island of Guam.

LAMONT CARL LINDSTROM is a doctoral student in anthropology at the University of California at Berkeley, where he received his M.A. degree.

JERRY K. LOVELAND, Director of the Institute for Polynesian Studies and Professor of Political Science at the Brigham Young University—Hawai'i Campus, received his Ph.D. (1967) from The American University. His research includes Samoan political systems, Polynesian buildings and house forms, and other topics of Polynesian culture.

PATRICK C. McCOY, anthropologist with the Bernice P. Bishop Museum in Honolulu, received his Ph.D. from Washington State University (1973) after spending some time in the Pacific, specifically Easter Island, doing research for his degree with the museum.

TIMOTHY J. MacNAUGHT received his graduate training at the Australian National University and is currently Assistant Professor of Pacific History at the University of Hawai'i. He has contributed numerous articles primarily relating to Fijian history to journals and publications.

SAM McPHETRES works in the Office of the High Commissioner, Trust Territory of the Pacific Islands, Saipan, Mariana Islands.

EDWARD J. MAROLDA works as a researcher at the Operational Archives Branch, Naval History Division, at the Washington Navy Yard in Washington, D.C.

MAC MARSHALL received his graduate degrees from the University of Washington (M.A. 1967, Ph.D. 1972) and was Acting Chairman of the Department of Anthropology at the University of Iowa before his current appointment as Visiting Senior Research Fellow at the Institute of Applied Social and Economic Research Center, Papua New Guinea. His most recent book, *Weekend Warriors* (Palo Alto: Mayfield Publishing Co., 1979) deals with alcohol in a Micronesian culture.

GEOFFREY F. MATTHEWS was educated at Oxford (B.A., M.A.) and Loughborough (Ph.D.), where he is now Lecturer in History. His publications include *The Reconquest of Burma, 1943-45* (Aldershot: Gale and Polden, 1966) and, with L. M. Cantor, *Loughborough: From College to University* (Loughborough: University Press, 1977).

FRANK L. ("CHAR") MILLER is currently a doctoral student in History at Johns Hopkins University (M.A. 1977) and his research includes the history of the Bingham family in Hawai'i.

JOSEPH A. MONTOYA received his B.A. in History from the Brigham Young University—Hawai'i Campus and is currently associated with the BYU, Provo Campus.

DOUG MUNRO, B.A. (Flinders), is Assistant Lecturer in History and Politics at the University of the South Pacific, Suva. He has published several articles on Pacific history and conducted fieldwork in Tuvalu in 1977-1978 and again in 1979. He is currently completing his Ph.D. dissertation on the history of Tuvalu, 1860-1910.

HANK NELSON teaches in the Department of Pacific and Southeast Asian History at the Australian National University in Canberra.

ROBERT NORTON, anthropologist, received his Ph.D. from the University of Sydney (1972), now is Senior Tutor in Anthropology at the Macquarie University of Sydney. He has published extensively on Fijian politics and race relations.

CAROLYN O'BRIEN took her Ph.D. at the University of Queensland and teaches at the University of New South Wales in Australia.

NIGEL D. ORAN, a senior lecturer in the Division of Prehistory at La Trobe University in Melbourne, was educated at Oxford University (B.A., M.A.). Among other writings, he has published *Colonial Town to Melanesian City: Port Moresby, 1884-1974* (Canberra: Australian National University Press, 1976).

RICHARD OVERY was educated at Wilson's Hospital School in Ireland and Queen's University in Belfast. He is now a librarian and archivist at Tarawa, Kiribati.

KERRY JOSEPH PATAKI-SCHWEIZER received his Ph.D. in anthropology from the University of Washington in Seattle. He is head of the Department of Community Medicine at the University of Papua New Guinea and has written *A New Guinea Landscape* (Seattle: University of Washington Press, 1979).

ANDREW KENNETH PAWLEY studied at the University of Auckland (M.A. 1963, Ph.D. 1967) and the University of Hawai'i, East-West Center. He is the author of numerous scholarly articles on Austronesian linguistics, Papuan linguistics, and the Kalam language.

VERNICE WINEERA PERE, a New Zealander who studied both in New Zealand and Hawai'i, is currently Public Relations Manager for the Polynesian Cultural Center, Laie, Hawai'i. She is an accomplished poet as well as a recognized artist.

YVES R. PERRIN, born in France, received his doctorate from Columbia University (New York) and now is superintendent of the Latter-Day Saints school system in French Polynesia.

VICENTE PONKO, JR. received his Ph.D. from Loyola University (1959). Currently he is the Academic Vice-President and Dean of the Faculty at the University of Scranton (Pennsylvania), and the author of numerous articles on exploration and discovery including the book *Ships, Seas, and Scientists: US Naval Exploration and Discovery in the Nineteenth Century* (Annapolis, Maryland: US Naval Institute Press, 1974).

RALPH R. PREMDAS (Ph.D. University of Illinois) has taught and was Chairman of the Department of Political and Administrative Studies at the University of Papua New Guinea until 1979. Currently he is a Research Professor at the University of Alberta, Canada, and a Senior Research Fellow at the University of California at Berkeley. He has written numerous books and articles about Papua New Guinea, Fiji, and Guyana.

ALAN MAXWELL QUANCHI was educated at Monash University (B.A. and M.A.) and is currently a Lecturer in Pacific History at the State College of Victoria, Frankston, Australia.

FRANK J. RADOVSKY, acarologist and parasitologist (Ph.D. Berkeley, 1964), has been at the Bernice

B. Bishop Museum since 1969 as Assistant Director and Head of the Department of Entomology. His research has resulted in more than sixty scientific publications on the evolution and ecology of ectoparasites and their role in disease transmission. He is Executive Editor of the *Journal of Medical Entomology* as well as Associate Editor of the *Annual Review of Entomology*.

CAROLINE RALSTON received her doctorate (1970) from the Australian National University and is currently Lecturer and Senior Lecturer at MacQuarie University in Sydney. Her research on beach communities in the Pacific was published in *Grass Huts and Warehouses: Pacific Beach Communities of the Nineteenth Century* (Canberra: Australian National University Press, 1977).

BRENNA J. RASH, formerly a student in the History Department of the Brigham Young University—Hawai'i Campus, is currently completing her degree at the Provo Campus.

CHARLES REAFSNYDER is a doctoral candidate in Anthropology currently doing field research on Truk among a group of Mortlockese under a grant from the National Institute of Mental Health.

DALE B. ROBERTSON received his doctorate from the American University and currently is Assistant Professor of Political Science at the Brigham Young University—Hawai'i Campus.

KAY E. SAUNDERS teaches in the History Department at the University of Queensland.

DERYCK SCARR, author of numerous volumes of Pacific history, currently edits the *Journal of Pacific History* at the Australian National University in Canberra.

HARVEY G. SEGAL was educated at the universities of Massachusetts (B.A.) and New York (M.A.) and now teaches in the Education Department of the Community College of Micronesia.

CRAIG JON SEVERANCE received his B.A. from Yale University (1966) and his doctorate from the University of Oregon (1976). Currently he is Assistant Professor, Department of Anthropology, University of Hawai'i at Hilo.

RONALD SHOOK, member of the English Department at the Brigham Young University—Hawai'i Campus, was educated at the University of Southern California and Indiana University of Pennsylvania.

ERIC B. SHUMWAY, author of numerous articles and books on Tongan poetry, spent some time as Instructor in Tongan Language and Culture and as the Tongan Language Coordinator for the Peace Corps. He has recently been appointed Academic Dean at the Brigham Young University—Hawai'i Campus.

MICHAEL SINGH, senior History student from Fiji at the Brigham Young University—Hawai'i Campus (B.A. 1981).

E. K. G. SIXSMITH was educated at Harrow School and the Royal Military College at Sandhurst. He was commissioned in the Cameronians (Scottish Rifles), wounded at Anzio in 1944, and retired as a major general. He has written *British Generalship in the Twentieth Century* (London: Arms and Armour, 1970), *Eisenhower as Military Commander* (London: Batsford, 1973), and *Douglas Haig* (London: Weidenfeld, 1976).

WILLIAM R. SMITH, born in Lexington, Kentucky, received his M.A. from the University of Guam in 1978, currently teaches History and Political Science at the John F. Kennedy High School in Guam.

JOSEPH H. SPURRIER, Professor of History and Hawaiian Studies at the Brigham Young University—Hawai'i Campus, currently is completing research for a publication entitled *Sandwich Island Saints*.

MAX E. STANTON received his doctorate in Anthropology at the University of Oregon. He currently is Associate Professor of Anthropology and Sociology at the Brigham Young University—Hawai'i Campus.

JEFFREY S. STEEVES (Ph.D., University of Toronto) teaches at the University of Saskatchewan; he specializes in the politics and administration of development in Oceania and East Africa. With Ralph Premdas, he has co-authored *Elections in a Third World City: Port Moresby* (Port Moresby: University of Papua New Guinea Press, 1979).

WILLIAM TAGUPA, doctoral candidate at the University of Hawai'i in History, has published numerous scholarly articles and book reviews including the monograph *Politics in French Polynesia, 1945-75* (Wellington: New Zealand Institute of International Affairs, 1976). He is currently teaching in the Department of History, Kaua'i Community College, Hawai'i.

ALAN TAYLOR, a free-lance writer in Auckland, has published numerous articles on Polynesian culture and more especially on Maori folk art in New Zealand and abroad.

ANNE-GABRIELLE THOMPSON did her undergraduate work at the University of Queensland, where she also served as a Tutor in History.

ELIZABETH S. UDUI, an economist with the Bureau of Resources of the government of the Trust Territory of the Pacific Islands, holds degrees from The American University (B.A. and M.I.S.) in Washington, D.C. She has held a number of different governmental positions in Micronesia since 1964.

JOHANNE M. VINCENT took her B.A. and did an honors thesis on David Wilkinson at the University of Adelaide.

BERNERD C. WEBER, Professor of History at the University of Alabama, has numerous publications on exploration to his credit including the recently published *The Discoverers: An Encyclopedia of Explorers and Exploration*, ed. Helen Delpar (New York: McGraw-Hill, 1980).

DAVID WELCH is a history student who graduated from the Brigham Young University—Hawai'i Campus (1979).

DAVID WETHERELL teaches in the School of Social Sciences at Deakin University in Victoria, Australia.

J. D. G. WHITMORE is a postgraduate student in the School of Social Sciences at Deakin University, Victoria, Australia.

ALBERT L. WILLIAMS, Associate Curator at the Micronesian Area Research Center and Librarian of the University of Guam Archives, was educated at the State University of New York, Geneseo (B.S.) and Indiana University (M.S.).

NED B. WILLIAMS, currently working on a doctorate at the University of Wisconsin, was formerly a member of the faculty of the Brigham Young University—Hawai'i Campus. He is the author of several critical articles, plays, and short stories, many dealing with Hawai'i.

A. T. YARWOOD is Associate Professor of History at the University of New England in Armidale, New South Wales, Australia.

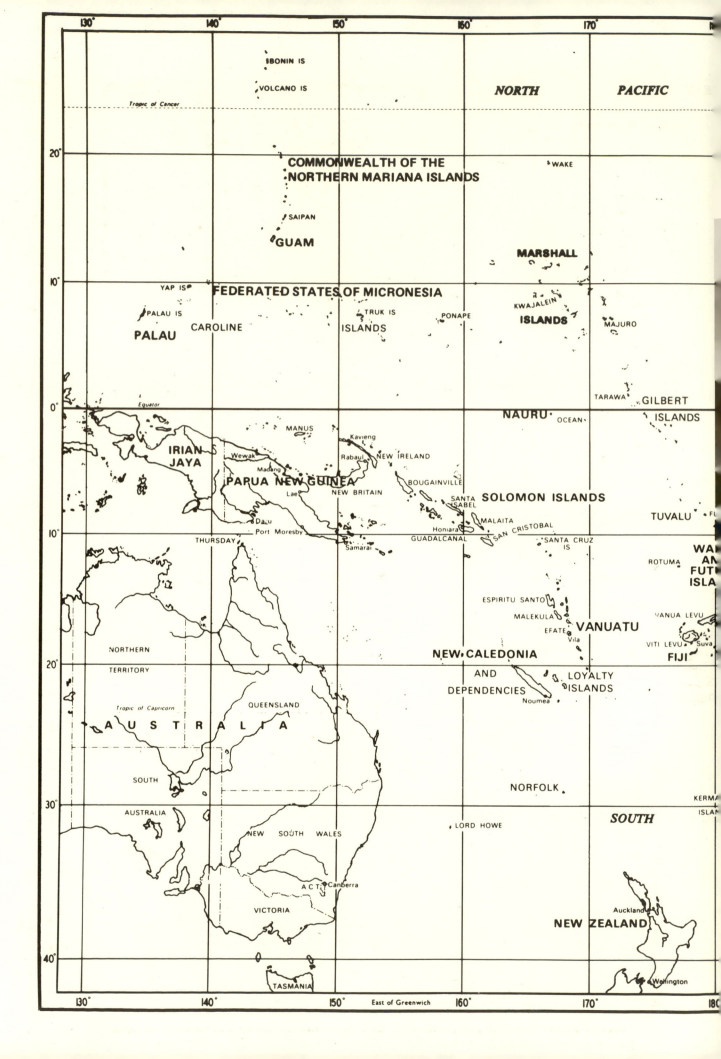